LONG WAY HOME

Long Way Home

By Clark Harrison

Barefoot Press/Copple House Books, Inc./Decatur, GA 30030

Library of Congress Cataloging in Publication Data
Harrison, Clark, 1924—
  Long Way Home
  1. Harrison, Clark, 1924— —Health
  2. Paraplegics— Georgia —Biography. I. Title.
RC406.P3H37   1985   362.4'3'0924 [B]   85-22981
ISBN 0-932298-42-7

Published by
Barefoot Press
Fidelity National Bank Building, Suite 102
160 Clairmont Avenue
Decatur, Georgia 30030

Manufactured in the United States of America

Copple House Books, Inc.
Lakemont, Georgia 30552

For Frances

CHAPTER I

The Cherokee 140 is the workhorse plane built by the Piper Aircraft Company between the years 1965 to 1973. After 1973, they made the wings longer, added twenty more horsepower and created a plane called the Warrior that carries four passengers to the 140's two person load, that is not approved for spins, as the 140 is, and that floats down the runway at idle speed where the 140 drops, clunk, once air speed is below 62 knots. The Warrior is a safe, practical and sedate machine built for the business man flyer. The 140 is fun to fly.

My 140 was built in 1969. Then, in 1979, the owner, an Augusta, Georgia attorney, took the old plane to Waco, Texas where they replaced the engine with a new Lycoming — a 160 RAM. Then the attorney added two rear seats, had the interior restyled in upholstered leatherette, painted the outside, added a couple of VORs and an auto pilot that levels the wings and had a hot little machine still with short wings and a tendency to land clunk on the runway but that can climb like the proverbial homesick angel and spin like a top once you stand it on its tail at 4,000 feet, and yank it over with opposite aileron and rudder.

That is fun, and, as long as you don't become mesmerized by the spinning, green, Georgia carpet and thoughts of the eternity that lies concealed just beyond that curtain you're all right. Just don't wait too long to pull it gently out of the dive after stopping the spin with full opposite rudder. If you do all this carefully and precisely, you won't pull the stubby wings off and you can climb back up and do as many spins as you want.

On this particular September morning I was about to start my return to Georgia after a barnstorming solo across the deserts and mountains of the U.S. to Escondido, California, just north of the Terminal Control Area surrounding San Diego.

1

"Palomar Tower" I spoke into the aging but still reliable Mark 12B radio microphone. "This is Cherokee eight seven five five November. Ready to taxi. Can you give me the information."

"Eight seven five five November," the ground controller repeated, "the altimeter is three zero one two. You are clear to taxi to runway two seven. Five five November what will your heading be?"

"This is five five November. Heading will be zero niner zero."

"Roger five five November. Contact the tower at one two zero niner when you are ready to take off. Have a good day."

California in September is often cloudy until about noon. The prevailing westerlies bring in air over the land that has cooled below the ocean temperature during the night and it is loaded with moisture rising off the warm Pacific. The clouds form at below 1,000 feet and don't burn off until the land warms up around noon. It doesn't rain but the clouds are too low for safe VFR flight over the nearby California mountains.

As I gunned the throttle full open and began the takeoff roll, the little plane vibrated satisfactorily and the 160 engine created a roaring blast of sound that was deafening to the ear drums but soul satisfying to the inner man. The air speed indicator reached sixty two knots and the little plane jumped off the runway. I gave a strong upward tug on the rudder to counter-act the torque of the propeller trying to turn us to the left as the wheels left earth and used my left hand to hold the ailerons in position to counteract any sudden gusts of surface winds as we left ground effect and lept into the westerlies.

Heading toward the waters of the blue Pacific, I watched the altimeter and the vertical speed indicator. At 79 knots, the best rate of climb for this aging workhorse, I was climbing at 500 feet per minute. Just short of sixty seconds after liftoff, I banked the short wings right, applied more right rudder to avoid slipping and glanced at the black ball suspended in its kerosene bath in the turn coordinator to be sure it remained centered.

Leveling the wings momentarily half way through the turn, I banked again to the right to enter a downwind route now parallel to the runway below. The hills around Carlsbad, brown where they were not greened by the avocado trees, rapidly became foothills of the California range that follows just inside the coast line for the length of the state. I continued to climb toward the ninety five hundred altitude I had filed for my Visual Flight Rules trip east. Georgia and home were some seventeen hundred miles away and the trip had a symbolism for me.

I couldn't say this trip across the U.S. in my own plane represented the culmination of a life-time dream. As a matter of fact, the idea that I might ever be able to fly had not occurred to me since that afternoon in Germany when I took my last step. That was thirty-six years ago and for at least thirty of those years the thought of flying never entered my mind.

Looking down at my shoeless feet, I think back now to the bright, sunny afternoon in November of 1944. Running toward the safety of the two story house, I knew the sniper was across the street looking down at me — the richocet of his bullet just above the head of our number three man had sent us all charging for safety. I was in his sights and this time he didn't miss. One half inch to either side, I would have been back on the front within a month. Six inches higher and three inches to the right and I would have been dead.

But my walking days were over and the belief I'd ever be able to do anything of significance with my life was gone as well. A few days before I was hit, I had told God, out of the dead tiredness of the filthy dirty infantry private, "Dear God, if you'll just let me sit down, I'll never complain again."

Well, He let me sit down.

And I thought now of the long, grey corridors of Lawson General Hospital outside Atlanta, Georgia where I spent a year of my life waiting for a return of use to my legs until I finally faced one day the fact I'd never walk again. On that day, I rolled my chair out into that long corridor, stretching into an infinity of grey sameness which, at that moment of despair, represented what I expected the rest of my life to be.

One long unending stretch of nothing but the wheelchair and dependency.

It didn't turn out that way, of course.

And the memories came flooding back. The bright colors, laughing faces, dancing feet of the Army hospital where youthful exuberance would not be downed and the breaking out of joy, when it came, was directly proportional to the plunging depths of midnight despondency.

Then, the day came when we were packed on a train, sent to be discharged into a Veterans Hospital. As Marcus said, "you ain't heroes no more. You're just poor crippled sons of bitches."

The parade had dispersed and we were left sitting and waiting, wondering what to do next. My Dad had said, "When life hands you a lemon, make a lemonade." But even he was stunned by the monumental hopelessness.

A return to college gave me something to do and thrust me back into the midst of my own generation, veterans who shared the experience of war's hardship and despair and now, in utter seriousness, attacked the citadels of learning in a search for meaning to it all, and more important-ly, a way to earn a living after years of absence.

With an outlet for my pent-up energy and desire, I overdid it, nearly ruined my health and made Phi Beta Kappa. And found out some an-swers aren't found in books.

Flying toward the California mountains, I think now of Frances who married me two years after I was shot. And of what Grandpa, the old German, said when we visited him on our honeymoon. "Why would a pretty young girl like you marry a fellow in his condition."

Well, in the blind way women will, Frances did. And we raised two sons to manhood, and have grandchildren to boot.

Convinced no one would hire a "man in my condition", I started my own company — the one that owns the airplane I fly today. I was the salesman and, with a pack strapped to the back of the wheelchair, at least I was out in the sunshine and talking to people.

Making my round of stores, I found the really educated people were out on the streets — the ones who did things because they hadn't been taught how difficult and complicated everything is.

The one thing I didn't do was make much money. Nor did I during my first turn at politics. After working as a public servant for four years, I suffered the agony of defeat.

And found out the only sure base or foundation for success is a first class, rip roaring, heart tearing, financially devastating defeat.

Having been involuntarily separated from the political world and burning to recapture the thousands of dollars in debt defeat at the polls had brought me, I finally hit on a way to make money.

Without any training, I found out I could sell real estate and lease office space. Without formal training, that is. I had learned to get my answers from the street.

Before I cooled off, I had sold a considerable amount of land and com-mercial property and leased an eleven story building, one hundred and forty seven small tenants — and then I was asked to get back into politics.

This time I won — in the bloodiest, knock down, drag out, stomp down political battle of the century — the results were awaited in the financial ways of London.

After the dust had settled and the blood had dried, the group of experts I brought in re-did the richest county in the southeast — and most of the changes stuck. The fact we were doing something was attested by twenty thousand citizens signing a petition to get us out of office, but that failed.

The Russian Jew, whose store I'd call on when I was a peddler, had given me the answer to running a big metropolitan county when I asked him how, as a new immigrant who scarcely spoke the language, he had been able to start his own store.

"I tell the salesmen," he said, "you are going to do the ordering for my store. All I require is two things: first, I don't want anything put on my shelves that won't sell. Second, I want your lowest price and I want it every time on every item. As long as you do those two things, you will write my orders. Cross me one time and you are through."

And that was the way I went about running DeKalb County. That included hiring the toughest and smartest managers I could find, telling them about the Russian Jew, and turning them loose.

I survived the four years, and it was even said I could have been re-elected. A month later I was in the hospital. Instead of losing my leg, for the first time in twenty eight years I was in a hospital, in Denver, Colorado, that understood and could cope with the unique problems of the spinal cord injured.

We duplicated that hospital in Atlanta, Georgia two years later.

And we organized a bank that grew to a 100 million dollar institution and that survives in the tough Atlanta market to this day.

Through it all, I was still paralyzed. In my case, from the middle of my chest down — no feelings, no movement — not even stomach muscles for balance. Nothing had changed physically since the sniper's bullet first did its work.

Then Frances and I, with the boys growing up, built the place on the Georgia coast and my two friends got me in a canoe and I found I could balance, and I could get out in the wilderness and move around.

It wasn't as exciting as politics, but it did free the spirit.

The only problem, I needed help to get in the boat and to get out at the end of the run.

It was only then it occurred to me, if I could balance in a canoe, why not in an airplane?

And now I had found something that really was as exciting as being chairman, where the risk was ultimate and the limits of knowledge to be mastered can occupy a life time.

Being on short final for landing is the critical time and in a strong cross wind gusting to twenty-five, can certainly clear the carotid arteries and flush the brain with a renewing rush of oxygen rich blood.

The above is what this book is all about.

And my devout hope is, next time a wheelchair rolls by, you may take a second look, and perhaps ask a question or two.

You might be surprised what you will find.

There are one hundred thousand active pilots who fly their own planes in the United States.

I am one of them.

I can't walk. On the other hand, I can fly.

As an old infantry man, let me tell you, when it comes to crossing the California mountains, it beats the hell out of walking.

CHAPTER II

Watching the foothills of the California mountains slide beneath the wings of my Cherokee 140, I thought about flying in general and flying the small airplane in particular.

Flying a small plane is in some respects more difficult, and it is certainly more hazardous, than piloting the big air liners. Just check the statistics. Flying a much more complex machine, the airliner pilot carries a heavy responsibility and follows a correspondingly long, slow training process. But, once qualified and aloft he is for the most part above the weather and his flight is controlled by the latest instrumentation and constant monitoring from the ground. When he gets ready to land, he can do so knowing that cross winds and lack of visibility are not going to have much effect on his ability to bring his many tons of airplane into a smooth, safe landing.

The small plane pilot, on the other hand, is constantly at the mercy of the elements and his instrumentation is usually limited and basic. Unless he has some understanding of weather and his own limitations as a pilot, he is quite easily thrown into a life-threatening situation with the outcome more a matter of luck than of control of the situation.

Having decided at age 55 to tackle the dangerous art of private flying, I had two major concerns — getting down and getting lost. I abhor the idea of being in the air and not knowing where I am or where I am going to land.

As far as landing is concerned, I finally decided the only way was to teach my reflexes to perform automatically by making, literally, hundreds of landings in every cross wind situation. I made a lot of bad landings, but, finally, I found that without conscious thought I could wrestle the little plane to the ground in just about any wind situation.

Unless the wind is blowing right at you down the runway, you do it by crabbing the plane into the wind — angling the nose in the direction from which the wind is blowing, thus assuring a straight track along the ground as you approach the runway. Then, just before the wheels touch down you lower the wing on the windward side and align the nose with the runway by applying rudder pressure with your feet. Properly done, the wheel on the windward side will touch down first, then the wheel on the leeward side and lastly the nose wheel. Done improperly, there is a good chance the plane will end up in the grass beside the runway. I know. I've done it both ways.

If you're like me and you can't move your feet, this means the last moments before touching down can become busy and somewhat dicey for the novice flyer. I control the rudder, which moves the nose of the airplane to the right or left, by means of a lever that I grasp with my right hand. When I pull the lever up, the nose goes right. When I push the lever down, the nose goes left.

This same lever turns the airplane on the ground when I'm taxing to or from the runway.

In landing, with my left hand on the wheel that controls the ailerons and thus the banking of the plane, and my right hand on the rudder bar, I anxiously watch my airspeed as the plane begins its descent toward the runway. The left hand banks the wing into the wind, while two fingers of the right hand control the rudder, leaving the thumb free to make last minute adjustments of the throttle to maintain proper air speed right down to touch down. It can be done, but it takes practice and a relaxed attitude, in the early days, toward impending disaster.

They say the only difference between men and boys is the price of their toys. In a way I believe I enjoy playing with my airplane more than I enjoyed my early years. Maybe it's taken me all the years to learn how to have fun with gadgets and games.

Personally, I have never understood why people talk down to children. As I remember my own childhood, I was the same individual then that I am today, and I took myself even more seriously. From my view point, my problems were just as overwhelming at times and I could get just as discouraged and also just as happy.

I was born in a small, two-bedroom stuccoed house built on a 50-foot lot on a pleasant shady street in Decatur, Georgia. My Dad was a salesman and the teacher of salesmen in the business school he and his partner operated for thirty-five years in downtown Atlanta.

Our town of some 13,000 souls was progressive — the home of managers for the adjoining city of Atlanta. A city of homes and churches. Blacks were crowded into shacks and hovels near the courthouse center of town, invisible in that segregated era, except for the maid who worked five days a week for a few dollars, and who fed her family by "toting" privileges, carrying the leftovers home each evening, along with discarded clothes and receiving free medical attention from private physicians who always knew a certain part of their practice would be without charge.

The schools were good with a narrow focus in the early grades on pounding the basics of reading, writing and arithmetic. The teachers were dedicated for the most part — usually unmarried women or men who saw their efforts as a calling, a profession, the backbone of southern society that made education the golden key that would unlock the future, save the country, and lead us all into better days.

The depression was still with us, although Franklin Roosevelt had given the people new hope and there was a stirring toward better days.

People did not have much, but the vast majority were honest and they cared about their neighbors.

There weren't any social programs paid for by the Federal government, so, when somebody got in trouble it was up to the neighbors to help. And they did, with a compassion kept fresh by the knowledge that all of us were skating on thin ice.

People left their keys in the ignition when they parked their cars and most families never bothered to lock their doors at night. When they did, most used such a simple lock that one "skeleton" key would unlock most of the back doors in town.

Decatur in the 1930's was an oasis of relative financial security when compared to the rest of Georgia and the South.

The War to end wars was still fresh in everyone's memory. It was felt generally, by the time I was taking history courses, that the U.S. had been coaxed into the war primarily to help the British Empire and the armament manufacturers. Britain reigned supreme in the world — the sun never set on on the Empire — and seemed to control most of the world's money. There was much talk about American boys being used for cannon fodder and a song proclaiming "I Didn't Raise My Boy To Be A Soldier " was popular.

On the other hand there was, particularly in the South, a proud heritage of patriotism and an intense and unforgiving spirit among the losers of the War Between the States. Decatur, the place where I grew up, was a part of the deep South, and immersed in the War and its after-math. One of the great battles was fought between Decatur and what is now downtown Atlanta, some six miles to the west.

Georgia had suffered in the War and the ravages were still felt some seventy years after Sherman marched from a burning Atlanta to the sea. Sherman's intent was to destroy the bread basket and manufacturing heartland of the Confederacy in order to end the war and he succeeded.

What he didn't succeed in doing was breaking the spirit of the people.

To the rest of the nation, the Civil War may have been fought to get rid of slavery.

In the South, it was a fight for the right of individual citizens to decide on who was to govern them — after all, that was what the American Revolution was all about. After the South was invaded and the homes of women and children were burned, their crops destroyed and their means of livelihood decimated, the struggle became imbedded in the consciousness of the region, not to be forgotten or forgiven during the lifetime of the survivors.

After the war, the women of the South were the ones who carried the brightest flame of rememberance and determination to defend what they saw as a cause that, although lost, remained just and noble.

As grammar school children, each year we participated in the United Daughters of the Confederacy literary contest. It was not optional — every student participated. We had to choose one of the great men of the Confederacy and write an essay on his life.

We came to learn that Robert E. Lee was the greatest American soldier — that he was offered command of the Union Armies before declaring for his native Virginia. We learned about Alexander Stephens, a near invalid and one of the greatest authorities on the U.S. Constitution to ever live. In spite of blockade, starvation and deprivation, a proud people held off superior forces for four long bitter years. The women were the ones who bore the brunt of the war, who lost the husbands who had worked the land for them and who were determined that the new generation would never forget.

As a child, I saw the results of the Civil War around me in my daily life. Tenant farmers, black and white, eking out an existence on poor unfertilized soil, lived in unpainted shacks that dotted the roadside in every direction just out of the city limits. Children were malnourished, and clad in ragged clothes. Farm machinery that had taken a place in other parts of the U.S. was non-existent in the South of the thirties.

Ragged farmers planted cotton — then corn — then cotton on poor red soil that got poorer every year, plowing mules whose ribs showed through their thin sides. The people had the energy and the native intelligence — they just didn't have the capital or the education. Looking back, I realize the significance of what my Dad did for himself and what he did for hundreds of young people from this impoverished region. He not only gave them useful training for breaking out of the poverty, he gave them confidence in themselves.

A strong Christian, although not much of a church goer, Dad had a clear mission in life — to help young people coming as he did from a rural background, to equip themselves to earn a living in the city and, even more importantly, to have confidence in themselves and faith in the future.

Left an orphan at age 11, Dad worked on the farm, living with a good family, until age 21. Then he worked his way through Business University in Bowling Green, Kentucky and began to teach.

Mother, who is 87 as I write this, remembers their courtship.

"I was living in Bowling Green with my brother while I went to school," she recalls. "Every afternoon I would borrow the pony cart and drive over to Clark's school. I would drive around past the window of the classroom where he had just finished teaching. Then, I'd drive around to the other side and Clark would jump out the low window and we'd take a ride together."

Mother was the sensible member of the team. The daughter of a German farmer, blacksmith and store owner, she had had to work hard all her life. Grandpa believed in hard work — he had shingled a roof when he was 14 years old — and he didn't have much patience with those who didn't work. He raised seven children, and although he himself had only three months of formal schooling, he saw to it they all went to college.

Dad's philosophy could best be summarized by the saying, "If the world hands you a lemon, make a lemonade." And Dad believed in finishing anything you started. As a child, I never was very smart but I was earnest and I was constantly being admonished by the two school teachers who raised me.

I wasn't naturally talented at games but I did take them very seriously. I remember playing hide and seek when I was small.

We had a agitator type washing machine with a removable agitator post and a crank type wringer on the side of the tub. The agitator was re-

When she was in her eighties Mother told me, "I used to borrow the pony cart and drive by the school where Clark was teaching. He'd jump out the low window and we'd go for a drive."

moved that day, and I remember vividly crawling into the tub and pulling the lid over the top.

It was probably the best hiding place in the neighborhood. In fact, it was so good that nobody ever found me. I must have stayed hidden a long time when it finally dawned on me that I might not be found. I finally emerged. To my amazement, the crowd of children were playing an entirely new game and apparently had not missed me.

I discovered then that I have a tendency, that remains with me today, to keep working at a thing after everybody else loses interest.

Part of this was drummed into me by my school teacher parents. I remember one of Dad's ambitions for me was that I learn to play a musical instrument. He never had tried, but he was convinced I could do it. He saw his chance when a salesman came through town offering a free guitar to anyone who would complete a course consisting of 60 lessons.

The lessons were one dollar each and were given one lesson a week. I am sure that the same guitars were used over and over. Otherwise the scheme would have not been profitable.

It was apparent to me after the second lesson that I would never learn to play. It was equally apparent to everybody else in the house, house, including Annie Grace, our maid.

"There goes Mr. Clark on that guitar," she would moan. "Plunk, plunk, plunk."

But Dad had his principles and I was destined to finish 60 lessons.

Gradually, the other students began to fall by the way side and our classes became smaller each week.

Finally, myself and a girl were the only survivors.

"Don't worry," Dad told me with a smile, "I've arranged for you to continue your lessons at the Griffith School of Music downtown. Your classmate will drive both of you each week."

Week after week, I made the tiresome trip, my skill with the guitar deteriorating from the low level at which I had peaked early in the lesson series.

Finally, the proud day came, I completed my last lesson and was awarded the guitar and the record slip that showed each lesson as it was paid for and checked off.

I still had the guitar when our oldest son was grown, and he taught himself to play it.

For myself, I learned a great lesson.

Probably not the one about finishing anything you start — which was Dad's intention.

I decided then, that if you're no good at a thing, quit.

But, to be honest, I suppose Dad prevailed after all. I seem to remain stuck with this thing of finishing what I start — even when the cost gets all out of line with the possible benefits.

Sometimes I don't like it — but I'm stuck with the way I am.

As the years have gone by, I have come to appreciate the town I grew up in, the people and their hard earned character, and having learned at an early age that it is possible to live, to be happy and to be proud without the material possessions we count so important today.

Decatur, in the 1930's, was a unique place.

It was not a society based on money — most of us just didn't have much. The kids used second-hand books that were bought each year from the more fortunate and then sold at the end of the year to help pay for a new set. If you were careful and never made a mark in your book you might even buy your books for the new year with the proceeds of the sale of your old ones — but generally a few dollars extra were needed.

Doctors made house calls, then, staying the night for a difficult birth or a crisis with pneumonia. A bed side manner was necessary if the doctor was to succeed, and that meant listening carefully to the patient's recital of his problems and answering, judiciously and with proper gravity. No one would think of leaving home to visit a doctor's office when sick; how could you. So the doctor came to the house and often had the medicine for the first treatment.

The medicine was not much. "We used to give calomel," Dr. McGeachy told me once, "That way we knew something would happen after we left, at least to the patient's innards."

What was lacking in medicine was made up by our faith in the doctor's ability to see us through.

The local banker held the power of granting or withholding the means by which a family would advance or wait for things needed or desired. When times went bad, as they did in the early thirties, the banker became the enemy who could wreck a family's day to day life.

I learned and never forgot how much difference the people in charge of such things as bank loans can make in the lives of ordinary people; and how important it is to put limits on those who control the nation's money if our freedom is to be preserved.

The lesson was direct, personal, and unforgettable. Through no fault of his, Dad lost the house I was born in on Wilton Drive.

We had to move to the south side of the railroad tracks. We became renters.

It shouldn't have happened. But as Dad would have said, "all things work for good for those who love the Lord".

The house on south McDonough had its charms. It was on a large lot, shaded by old oak trees and just a block below the campus of Agnes Scott College. Later, it was torn down to make room for one of the new buildings added to the campus.

There was a furnace, but it no longer worked and we received our heat from coal grates and gas radiant heaters in the various rooms. I had been sickly as a child — my chest caved partially in as an infant from diptheria. Later I suffered asthma that plagued me particularly in the fall. As a child, I would walk the floor at night gasping for breath.

The cold rooms with wind whistling against and through cracks around the large single pane windows kept us moving on winter nights, and probably built up my strength through the involuntary exercise. We would heat a pillow before the tiny bedroom grate, then run and dive into an icy cold bed. The hot pillow would keep us warm until our body heat got the tightly held covers warm about us. The air that we would breathe through an opening in the blanket above our head was icy cold and fresh.

At age 12, I got in a pillow fight at boy scout camp and found to my wonder that the asthma was gone.

There was another compensation to our move south of the tracks — I came under the influence of Miss Fidelle Miller, teacher at Winnona Park School. Until that time, perhaps because of the poor health and the change of schools I had slid through school, making passing grades but without learning much that stayed with me.

About the only subject I was strong in was reading. My mother read to me when I was sick and encouraged me to read.

Miss Miller changed all that and in the process changed my life. She made me learn, by rote, the multiplication tables, spelling and, most importantly, English grammar. She would stand me up in class, slapping her hands at me when I made mistakes, and forcing me to learn or be embarassed. I responded and Miss Miller began to take great pride in her new protege.

On one occasion, I let her down. I had been out of class for several days due to illness. We were to receive a visit from the wife of then Governor Ed Rivers, and various members of the class had memorized parts of a speech, to be jointly given in segments, for the benefit of our visitor.

When I got back to class, there were only a couple of days until the great lady was to arrive.

"I wouldn't trust anybody but Clark to learn a part in this short time", Miss Miller, who was now high in her esteem for my talents, announced to the class.

I agreed fully that I could handle the assignment and went about repeating the short speech over and over.

When the fateful day arrived, we all packed into the school auditorium literally filling it from wall to wall with bright, shining and expectant faces. The great lady arrived and the salute by my classmates began. I was third to speak. Each of the preceding speakers had dealt with the governor's early life. It was my job to get him through college.

I stood up before the hushed and expectant multitude. At that moment, all of my vast powers deserted me and I was left, knees shaking, palms sweating, speechless. I couldn't remember anything.

I had said the speech so many times, one of my fellow students remembered and gave me the first line.

Still nothing.

Finally, I sat down — mortified, humiliated and shaken to my core. I don't know how long Mrs. Rivers and the assembled students remembered the debacle, but it is still fresh and burning in my memory some decades later.

When I sat down, I resolved never to speak from memory again. And I didn't until high school graduation when a sadistic teacher made me do it one more time. Although I made it through that ordeal — with the same hot, sweating, panicky feeling — that was it.

Through years of public speaking, that at times reached thousands of listeners, I never again spoke from memory. I would read a speech but not speak from memory.

So, if I gained any facility in speaking ex tempore, I owe it to Mrs. Rivers and her husband's stint as a student at Young Harris College.

South McDonough saw the budding and quick annihiliation of my early interest in girls. I was about 12, at the time and our next door neighbor was a member of my grammar school class, who was just beginning to practice her feminine wiles and who had gotten me kept after school in the sixth grade. She sat in front of me and would half turn and murmur something when the teacher was busy elsewhere.

I'd answer and the first thing I knew I was staying after school — for talking — but not my attractive neighbor.

Then I would have to run to carry my paper route.

With four sisters, I should have known all about girls, but with me, familiarity just created confusion.

Finally, I decided to ask Miriam out on a date — rollerskating to the drugstore for a coke. We started out with me in high spirits. I had 15 cents which would buy us each a coke and leave me a nickle to spend later.

We arrived and were seated in the booth when disillusion struck. My date said she wanted an ice cream soda — which cost 15 cents. I said I thought I'd just have a glass of water. I have never forgotten the experience. For at least three more years I stayed away from such serious relations with girls.

The years south of the railroad taught other lessons I have never forgotten. There just wasn't much money — fortunately, nobody that we knew had much money; and things were cheap and many things were free.

My Dad was a free spirit; with five children and a wife in the middle of a deep depression, he never let us know we were poor.

He was at heart a salesman, proud of it, good at it, and believing anything was possible to the man who worked hard and feared the Lord, and used his wits. He was a Bible student from age 12, when he accepted Christ as his Saviour, and he quoted the Bible and applied it to the problems he met every day. He knew he was going to come through because he knew God loved him and was going to take care of him. And he was sure of that because his every day experiences proved it.

Dad had missed World War I — he was in his thirties and had two daughters so he was exempt from service, and was advised, on seeking to volunteer, that he could better serve his country by continuing to educate the young people.

Dad read his Bible every day, marked passages and wrote comments in the margin. And he read the whole Bible, studying the stories of the Old as well as the New Testament and applying them to his daily life. He believed that you were supposed to live the words you read in the Bible or they didn't mean anything for you.

At the same time, he didn't have a lot of patience for organized religion, although he admired individual religious leaders. He definitely did not believe that church attendance carried any guarantee of reward in the after life.

He loved the out of doors, having been a farmer as a young man, and during the late thirties he bought fifty acres of land a few miles north of Decatur, paying fifty dollars an acre. After he got the farm, he would go out on Sunday mornings and walk his land and commune with God. I feel sure that Dad carried on direct conversations with his Maker and received his instructions for the coming week during the Sunday visits.

He believed God could help him, not just because of the promises in the Bible, but because God was doing things for him every day. And he took literally the injunction not to accumulate earthly wealth but to store up riches in heaven to be available as needed.

I'm sure he didn't think this scripture meant a reward only to be received after death — to him it was a bank account to be drawn on when it was really needed — on this side of the grave. After all, who would need help in the promised land?

Because Dad was so deeply committed to his Lord, I was very surprised as a teenager at the answer he gave to a magazine quiz the family was discussing and answering. One question was, "If you were in serious trouble whom would you consult? A. Preacher, B. Banker, C. Lawyer."

Much to my surprise, Dad answered "Banker". After getting a little older and wiser, I realized that that was who Dad went to see when he was in a jam — and that was on a regular basis. Outside of money, he just didn't seem to have many problems he couldn't solve by using his wits, as he did in getting the high school teaching job, or by his good humor and friendly approach to people.

Dad had a great zest for life; he was short, about 5'8" but compactly built, quick moving and a handsome man, with a ready smile and a manner that established instant rapport with people in any and all walks of life.

He always dressed nicely and drove a good car once the worst of the depression was over. There was never any excess of money, but what was needed always came along just like the Bible had told him it would.

"These school teachers all think I'm rich", Dad would say with a smile. And, of course, he was — as rich as you can be with treasures in heaven waiting to come down on call.

Dad's free and easy attitude toward the more organized aspects of religion did get him in hot water at one time.

The minister of the Baptist church the rest of us attended got after Dad about not attending church more often.

"I told him what I was doing was just as important as what he was doing", Dad said. Dad felt he was doing the Lord's work helping young people get a start in an impoverished world, and if he wanted to rest on Sunday, then he could do that on the farm as well as sitting in church. The main thing was to obey what the Bible said about daily activities.

His children, and the people who got to know him, read Dad's actions as well as his words and found his influence to be a lasting and substantial contribution to their own lives.

Most literal in her interpretation of the Bible was my sister Julia. She recovered from polio as a child, became an excellent swimmer and physically active and adept young woman. The legacy of the illness was convulsions suffered periodically at night, but otherwise she glowed with strength, intelligence and activity.

When I was a small boy, Julia was my idol. She was a good dancer, a beautiful girl and she could saw wood or hammer nails as well as a man.

Julia read the Bible as constantly as Dad and believed as he did, the only thing that mattered was putting words into action.

After high school, and in the worst depths of the depression, Julia attended a free vocational school in downtown known as the Opportunity School. My folks had managed to buy Julia a new coat to wear to school during the winter months and they were very upset when she returned home one evening without the coat. One of the other students didn't have a coat, so Julia had given the girl her new coat. She was very content to wear her old coat to school.

After Novena raised her family and her husband died, Novena taught inmates in the state prison for several years, giving them the same quality of instruction that Dad had given his students.

Her son became a successful G.E. official, and her daughter a nurse who works with retarded and mentally disturbed adults in a self help program.

Bettie raised a family that includes a teacher, a nurse, a doctor and the wife of an F-16 fighter pilot.

After the children were grown, Bettie had an experience with Christ that made her the St. Paul of our family. She literally glows as she talks about Jesus and she has insights that exceed most I have seen exposed from the pulpit. Again, she follows Dad in a literal application of what she she reads. Working with people regardless of station or circumstance in life, seeing and believing miracles and with the child like faith Dad had.

Brenda has one son in college, one who spent a couple of years in India doing research to improve the crops of that country and one who is planning to give his life to Christian counseling.

As for myself, more than any other member of the family, I have drawn on the riches Dad stored in heaven. Although he died in 1958, I am still helped by him — in politics and in business. The people he helped are helping me.

Two things Dad told me have stayed with me.

"Never stand in the shadow of another man." Other people helped Dad, but God was the source that met his needs.

"A man should be able to stand on his father's shoulders".

I have certainly done that through the years.

Dad's cheerful outlook on life could be irritating to Mother at times.

"You beat anything I ever saw," she would say. "If somebody says something nice about you, you know they are sincere and perceptive. If they criticize you, you know they are kidding."

The Draughon School of Commerce was the best school in Atlanta and probably in the world. Dad would tell you about it.

"In quest of quality" was their motto and they practiced what Dad preached.

During the depression, the big thing was to have a job. The bigger thing was to have a job that involved wearing a coat and tie, or silk stockings in the case of the girls. Competition was fierce and the people who wanted to work in an office had to be good at their trade.

The Draughon graduates all were. I have attended four universities over the years, including the Yale Law School, and I never found one better at their assigned task than Draughon, and none that made as much sense in their approach to getting the job done.

It always seemed strange to me that it took eleven years to get through public school and four years to get through college.

At Draughon, they did it differently.

There was an assigned amount of work to do and each student proceeded at his own pace. Once he passed the tests and met the standards, he was through. Some did it in six months, some took two years. But they all graduated with grades over 90, they performed and practically all landed jobs, which was quite an accomplishment during the Great Depression.

Dad's place in the scheme of things was to sell students on coming to the school and then to teach them to sell — first themselves and then what ever products or services the company that hired them sold.

Dad was quite a talker and had to be one of the world's great salesmen.

I know that last statement is true. Dad died twenty-five years ago, and people still come and tell me how he changed their lives. And over the years, many became prominent and productive people.

Our county attorney told me "I was ploughing a mule when your Dad walked out in the field and told me 'Boy, you can do better than this.'"

"During the depression," one very successful businessman told me, "I was selling from a bread truck."

Dad told him to quit work and come to Draughon's.

"Mr. Harrison," he said, "I'm lucky to have any job at all."

"Yes," he replied, "but you'll have a real job and a future after you go to our school."

Dad traveled the state, speaking to high schools, spreading the good news about Draughon.

He was proud of the fact that he was the only representative of a business school allowed to address high school students in assembly.

Draughon required high school graduation and the principals found students worked harder to finish school after Dad talked to them.

Dad, right, traveled the state signing students for the Draughon School of Commerce.

Dad had a strategy for winning over the school principals around the state.

"First thing I always do," he would tell me, "is go by and visit the police chief — a good man to know — you never know when you might need him."

Then he would get to know the text book salesmen who called on the principals and they would discuss each man's likes, dislikes and idiosyncrasies.

And then he'd get to know everybody who worked at the school. "Don't ever forget the janitor," he'd say, "you never know when you might learn something."

Left an orphan, working on the farm until he was 21, Dad knew where of he spoke. He studied people and he studied ways to make them move in the direction he thought would be helpful.

When he and Mother married they decided to leave Kentucky. Dad said it was to get away from the cold winters, but I always suspected it was to get away from Pa Roemer, the German blacksmith, farmer, store keeper. I suspect Pa thought Dad's methods were designed more to get away from the backbreaking labor on the farm than the nobler purposes Dad avowed.

My father had an exasperating way of always taking the positive approach and seeming to shoot from the hip when making important decisions.

"When we decided to leave Bowling Green," he told me "we got a map and put it on the table. I shut my eyes and stuck my finger on the map. It landed on Atlanta."

When Dad applied for a job at Fulton High School, after arriving in Atlanta, he was told that they were looking for a man who could play a musical instrument and double as band director.

"I can play an instrument," Dad said with a smile.

After he had gone to work, the principal asked him what instrument he played.

"I play the victrola," Dad responded with a smile. The fact he wasn't fired immediately is further testimony to his sales ability. I never was told what the principal said or who led the band.

While teaching college in Kentucky, he had been asked by the president to conduct a seminar on shorthand teaching one summer. He agreed immediately to take on the task.

When the president wanted to give him a certificate of appreciation for conducting the course, my father said "Mr. Ashcraft, I really appreciate that, but before you make out the certificate there is one thing I better tell you. I never have had a course in shorthand."

The president was flabbergasted. The teachers from all over the southeast had called it the best seminar they had ever attended. He wanted to know how all these educated people had been fooled.

"It was simple," Dad replied. "I'd just say 'Now, Miss Bailey, come up to the blackboard and show us how you do it in Mississippi', That way we got the best methods from all around the south."

Dad had great respect for people, regardless of their background or present condition. He always wanted to help them improve themselves and he got excited when he would think of all the possibilities offered by life. After his mother died when Dad was two, the family of three girls and two boys was held together by a loving father through a self-help mutual effort. The girls helped in the house and the boys helped around the farm. His father was a stone mason as well.

When his father died from typhoid fever at an early age, Dad was only eleven. He was taken in by a kind family and treated fairly and with respect.

He accepted Christ when he was twelve and his simple faith never varied. He read the Bible and he believed what it said.

"Always respect the other man's religion," he told us. "He may be wrong, but if he sincerely believes, his ways must be honored."

The Great Depression was a national tragedy of immense proportion and strange in the breakdown of the morale of the people of an entire nation. As a child, I remember the news reel at our local movie house showing hundreds of young men boarding freight trains to travel from city to city to look for work.

There was no capital and no one seemed to know how to break the chain of events that had derailed the nation.

My Dad lost our house through no fault of his own. The same thing would happen in a recession of today, given the system homeowners faced then.

There was no monthly amortization of loans. To buy the house, a demand note for the principal amount was signed at the bank. Then interest was paid annually and any reduction of principal the debtor might manage.

When money became tight because of the collapse of the inflated stock market and the general slow down of the economy, the banks wanted these home loans paid off.

But the debtor could not come up with several thousand dollars at one time.

All over the country, these notes were foreclosed on. At the foreclosure sale, there were no buyers. The debtor not only lost his home, he still owed the bank.

Dad had friends throughout the Atlanta business community — he sent them the accountants and secretaries who ran their businesses.

I was a young child at the time, but I remember him telling me about calling on a wealthy friend when his home was being taken away.

"It looks like we'll lose the house and still owe on the mortgage," Dad told him.

"Clark," the friend replied, "it just happens that fellow is trying to get me to release him from a bind he is in — let me see what I can do."

Dad's treasures in heaven were about to rain down.

There was no deficiency judgment and we moved to the big, old, rented house south of the railroad. The irony was, the rent Dad had to pay would have bought a house under today's monthly mortgage payment plan.

Dad's school was busy but there wasn't much money available from the students.

"Every week, I would go out and try to sell scholarships," Dad told me. "Then, at the end of the week, when things were really bad, we'd meet with the teachers on Friday afternoon. We would go around the circle and ask each one what he or she needed that week. If somebody's rent was due, we'd take care of that and so forth. We weren't paying the regualar salaries, but we all managed to survive and eat regularly until things got better."

When money was not available, Dad would trade a scholarship for cotton, allowing the farmer ten cents a pound and then selling it for five cents a pound to raise some cash.

As young as I was, I remember Dad talking to Mother about the possibility of his having to take bankruptcy. Nobody ever explained what that was, but I knew from Dad's tone it was something very bad.

My Mother had learned how to work and how to stretch money from the old German. Grandpa had started helping his mother by delivering laundry she did for neighbors when he was nine. He gathered driftwood along the river for firewood because his father, who had come from a well to do family in Germany, was a drunkard. He was trained to make barrel staves, which paid well in those days, but he was not supporting the family.

If it didn't work, Gramdpa didn't want it around. That went for people as well as animals. Aunt Bee was in her eighties when she took her first flight with me.

Grandpa had to go to work as a nine year old child — and he learned to be tough. Once Grandpa was grown and had his own place, he applied the lessons he had learned.

If it didn't work, Grandpa didn't want it around. That went for people as well as animals. The animals were farm animals and a cat that lived in the barn to catch rats.

And no kind of game was played around Grandpa. The idea of grown men asking time off from farm work to play with a ball was incomprehensible to Grandpa.

My Uncle Ed, who was a traveling salesman, was in his eighties when he told me about Grandpa.

"Every time you went around him," Uncle Ed snorted, "he wanted you to grab a pick axe and start digging. Even if there wasn't anything that needed doing."

Uncle Ed's family owned a large dry goods store and one look at his soft white hands told the story.

"How many times did you grab the pick axe," I asked Uncle Ed.

He looked at me like I'd taken leave of my senses.

"I never did," he exclaimed.

Mother, on the other hand, was used to hard work.

"I used to get mad at Pa," she told me. "I had to help mother in the kitchen and she was the worst piddler in the world. After I got through doing my work I'd try to leave."

"No," Grandpa would tell the young girl, "you stay in there. She may think of something for you to do."

As a result, Mother spoiled her five children. It was her way of getting back at Grandpa.

"Miss Sally (mother's mother) was very tiny, Mother told us, "Pa was a big man and he thought she was the most beautiful thing in the world."

He told his daughters, who were all good sized women, that it seemed to him one of them could have taken after Miss Sally.

"We didn't let him get us down though," Mother told us. "We said, 'Well, she didn't have to marry the biggest lummox in the county.'"

Grandpa had a philosophy that was built on a rock solid base of hard times answered by hard work and he was never in doubt as to the soundess of his reasoning.

"The boss," Grandpa said, "is the one whose feet hit the floor first in the morning."

My sister, Novena, as a fun loving teenager who liked to dance the night away, learned from Grandpa.

I was visiting Pa and Miss Sally. We were having a real good time one night — the hours slipped by — and it was almost daylight before I got back to the house. "Well, Grandpa didn't say a word by way of rebuke. Just about the time I had gotten undressed and in bed, he came in to my room. 'Time to get up, Novena, let's go.' He kept me with him all day. Wouldn't even let me sit down. Believe me, I went to bed early that night and I never stayed up late on Grandpa again."

Grandpa was a man of action, not much given to handwringing, remorse or uncertainty.

"Why worry," he said, "if you can do something about a thing, do it. If you can't do anything about it, why worry?"

With time for only a few months of formal education during his childhood, Grandpa taught himself to read and write. He spelled phonetically according to his own system. I read one of his letters one time and found it easy to decipher even though the spelling was very strange.

When Grandpa was 65, he planted a peach orchard, much to the amusement of his neighbors who figured he'd never live to use the fruit. Grandpa tended the trees over the following years, consumed the fruit, and finally cut the trees down after their fruitful days were over.

So the depression and its hardships were no big shock to my Mother.

"Back then," Mother told us, "the butcher would give us a bone to make soup with. At Shield's Market, they would take the outer leaves off the vegetables before putting them out for sale. Then Mr. Shields would take little baskets and fill them up with the gleanings off the vegetables. He called them soup baskets and sold them for fifteen cents each. I made many a pot of soup with a free bone and fifteen cents worth of soup basket mix."

Our next door neighbor had two daughters, and I remember Mother setting up a big frame in our dining room and having the Morgans come over for a joint quilting bee. All the women made up their individual patches for the colorful quilts and then brought them over to assemble them into quilts.

One story Mother told all her life was the day she lost her grocery money. Dad provided $10 a week for groceries.

"I don't know how it happened," Mother would say, "I always thought I gave it to the milkman thinking it was a one. Anyway it disappeared."

Then she would tell how all the women in the neighborhood came in to help her search.

"We even turned over the leaves in the yard," she would say, "But we never found it."

My two older sisters were dating at the time. Novena had one quarter at Agnes Scott, the girls college that now enjoys a national reputation. Then the money ran out and Novena had to go to work. Our house was on the edge of the campus and, while the school was very strict on the girls, Novena's closest friends could check out to spend the weekend at our house.

I was about twelve at the time and recall vividly the crowds of Agnes Scott girls and Georgia Tech boys who would congregate at our place.

We had an old upright piano and Julia was dating Hank Simmons, who she later married. Hank was working his way through school and managed a dance band as one source of income.

He would sit at the upright banging out "On the Road to Mandalay" and singing full steam in a rich, bass voice. The old house, which was a little shaky anyway, would tremble on its foundations.

When I was old enough, I began to go once a week to Mrs. Rose's. Mrs. Rose was our down the street neighbor and she offered dancing lessons several nights a week to the high school kids.

Her house was small and the whole place was crowded, with more spilling out into the yard. The music was always full blast and in today's society would have been allowed to play maybe one night before the police, city zoning commission and recorder's court put Mrs. Rose out of business. In those gentle times, it never occurred to anyone to object and Mrs. Rose rocked along for years.

She had a clever system. She charged the girls fifty cents an evening and let the boys in free. Thus the crowds.

Toward the end of the thirties, the country began to struggle to its feet, and Dad's business entered its most productive era. When the war started, he would lose most of his students, but until that time his hard work and the quality of the effort was filling the school to overflowing.

By the time I was entering high school, the fortunes of the country, generally, and of our family in particular, had begun to brighten. Dad's school was just what young people trying to make a start in the world needed. The tuition was low, was payable by the month, or, in cases of special need, could be paid after graduation. Students got excellent training in skills such as typing, shorthand, and accounting for which there was an immediate demand in the marketplace. The school secured jobs for the students without charge and succeeded to the extent that with Dad's hard work and sales ability, the school was filled to capacity. It was the "hey day" for such schools and Dad's was the best in the city. He had over 300 students and fielded a winning basketball team.

As a partner, Dad owned two-fifths of the business. Now he began to come home and announce with increasing regularity that he and his partner had 'declared another dividend.' I remember one was for $1500, a princely sum in the late thirties. Novena was able to return as a full-time student at West Georgia and, later, to graduate from the University at Athens, Georgia.

For us it meant moving back north of the railroad to a new subdivision just started under a new government financing program called FHA. Under the program, once a lot was bought — in this case for $600 — the balance could be borrowed with repayment guaranteed the lending institution by the Federal government and with the loan to be repaid by the borrower over a long term of years at a low interest rate and on a monthly basis. No one could take the house away as long as those monthly payments were made.

I can remember a small savings account I started at the bank with money earned from my paper route and ushering at the local theatre. I was paid 1 ½ per cent. Dad probably paid 3 per cent on his house loan.

Jobs were created for those building the house and we had a place of our own.

Still, it was not easy. Even with the low rate of interest, I learned later the developer of the two streets went into bankruptcy. People had been burned so badly in the depression that many who could have owned these homes were afraid to assume even this kind of debt.

It was a golden age for me. We moved into the brand new two story brick and, since I was the only male heir, I had a large room upstairs with one window to the east overlooking a huge magnolia tree (the subdivision was sold off a large estate at the edge of town) and two dormer windows that faced south and allowed a delicious breeze to circulate through the room.

With our new affluence, and an end to the asthma that plagued me as a young child, I gained health rapidly and did well in school, building on the solid foundation Miss Miller had given me.

I began dating on a regular basis and attended Mrs. Rose's dancing classes every week with a school dance most weekends. The classes featured some instruction at the beginning of the hour and then dancing until a ten o'clock closing time. The dancing was fast and enthusiastic for the most part. The new jitter bug and gyrating tunes made for a lively evening. Between dances, couples would slip out for a walk and romantic experimentation. It was an exciting time.

When I reached 16, Dad bought the most beautiful car I had ever seen — a 1939 Pontiac Silver Streak. With eight cylinders, arranged in the 'straight' configuration, the powerful motor drove a car that could do 70 in second, 95 in high gear. That was as fast as I ever took it on the narrow, hilly highway — in those days, the two lane highways followed the contours of the surrounding countryside, creating a continuing series of blind curves and hills. At top speed, the Pontiac seemed to skip along, and, as much as I wanted to impress the girlfriend, I didn't go that fast again.

1939 through 1941 were golden years for me. Dad had me read his salesman books and I became adept at winning friends and influencing people. I had become involved in leadership roles my junior year in high school and the following September I was elected class president, a lieutenant and platoon leader in our high school ROTC, and was helping write and publish the school newspaper.

I was dating regularly, my 'steady,' an attractive red head. Most Fridays, we were at the school dance in the new gymnasium. As class president, I signed all the identification cards that admitted students to the dances, so I felt a proprietary interest in what went on inside.

I attended one fall evening in 1940 and it is etched in my mind. I had worn a shirt that was blue with a stiff detachable white collar, white detachable cuffs, and a beige sports coat. The new Pontiac was out side waiting for the drive home and the magic moments parked in a lone spot — parking and petting were perfectly safe in those innocent years and was standard for any couple lucky enough to have a car.

The gym was crowded with couples jitterbugging at a fast and furious pace. Most of us took a girl to the dances, but then we would dance with a number of different girls. Anyone could 'break' by putting his hand on the arm of the boy who was dancing, then take over, while the one replaced went to look for another couple to break on.

The worst thing that could happen was to get 'stuck' all evening with the same girl. She would be mortified and the boy would feel greatly put upon and soon would run out of anything to say. Girls who were not asked to dance would sit on the side lines and were known as 'wall flowers'.

Dances were an exhilerating experience for girls who were 'rushed' — broken on by a succession of partners — but it was agony for the 'wall flowers' and the boys who got 'stuck'.

My date was a good dancer and popular so I had a few moments to contemplate the activity. The gyrations were frantic, the music loud and with a heavy beat and I was soaking wet. There was no air conditioning since it hadn't been invented and the exhaust fan at the end of the building couldn't keep up with all the heat generated by the crowd.

"You ought to remember this," I told myself, "this is a golden time."

And it was.

We ought to do for our children when we can.

I always appreciated and never forgot during the dark years that were soon to come what Dad did for me in buying that car.

When I was wounded, I'm sure Dad's faith met it's greatest test. Dad believed in miracles and he believed faith can move mountains.

Years later it occurred to me that there was the same difference between the ages of Dad and myself as there is between my age and our son Bob's.

Dad joined the State Guard.

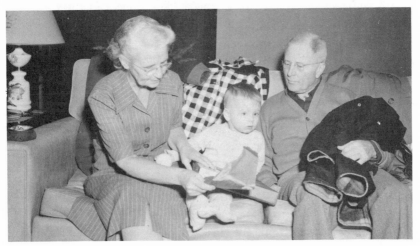

A rare photo of Mother, Dad and the new addition, Tom. This was 1951.

And I appreciate now, more than ever the ordeal he suffered when I was wounded.

Shortly after I was drafted into the Army, Dad, in his late fifties at the time, joined the State Guard, which was planned to take over duties that would relieve members of the regular armed forces. When I finally made PFC, Dad made corporal and I always felt if I'd been a colonel he would have had to have been a general.

When I left for overseas Dad's heavy hair was mostly dark brown. When I was returned to Lawson General Hospital a few months later, his hair was snow white.

"Clark," he told me, "I really believe if you will try as hard as you can, you can move that toe."

He was obsessed by the fact that my lower body, which had carried me wherever I wanted to go, was suddenly dead weight that had to be moved with great difficulty by what was left.

He said I should write a book called "The Weight of the Flesh."

My parents were told by the doctors that I could not live — that I had been brought home to die.

I asked my mother years later what she had said in reply.

"It's not true," she had replied. "I know Clark too well. If he were dying, I would know it."

When I started back to school, my parents were very proud of me. The first year, Mother would drive me to school in an old car I had bought and would help me get the wheelchair in and out. They both believed in education and although none of us knew what kind of job I'd ever be able to get, they never stopped encouraging me.

When I ran for commissioner the first time, Dad was sure I had found something I could do and he was my biggest campaigner.

The day of the election, I got a call from one of the polling places.

"Mr. Harrison," the worker said, "we've got a serious problem. There's a man over here talking to the people going in to vote and he's getting too close to the voting booth. That's a violation of the law."

I asked him then if they had warned the man and told him about the law.

"We did," the man said, "and then he wanted to go out and pace off the distance to prove he wasn't too close."

I asked if the man happened to be white haired and they replied he was.

"That's my Dad," I said. "I'll talk to him."

Before I finished my first term as a commissioner, Dad was dying of brain cancer. A part of his lower jaw had been cut out in a vain effort to stop the cancer, he was going blind in one eye and it was hard for him to speak distinctly.

"It's ironic," he told me. "All my life, I have gotten by on my looks and my ability to talk. Now I am losing both."

He had lost his business school — weakened by the loss of students to World War II and Korea. He had kept it going by a super human determination of will until he reached his 65th birthday.

It was the main stay of his life. But the day after the school closed, Dad started selling real estate — he never got his broker's license, he had had enough of running a business. He was making deals and he was enjoying himself.

He continued to try to set a good example for me and others.

In the last days of his life he talked and told me things I hadn't known about him.

Dad considered himself a tee totaler where whiskey was concerned, but he made wine with a very high alcohol content.

I finally learned from him that he would have a beer with his friends after work. I suppose he decided he didn't have to set that example to me anymore.

The only time I ever saw him cry was shortly before he died. We were talking and he began to tell me about his early days traveling to the high schools.

"After I finished my talk," he said, "I would go to the principal's office and ask him if he had a boy or girl who was doing well in school, but who would be unable to go to college because of financial reasons."

He recalled being referred to a girl who lived with her mother on a small farm. The house was a small, tenant shack, clean and as comfortable as the two could make it, but typical of those hard times.

"I explained to the mother," he said, "that her daughter could come to Atlanta and live in one of the Churches' Homes for Girls working part-time to pay the small charge for room and board. Then, our school would take the girl's personal note, which she could repay after she went to work. She wouldn't need any money from home to continue her education."

The mother looked at Dad with tears in her eyes. They signed the papers and then she said, "Mr. Harrison, I would like to give you something, but, you know, we don't have any money. All we have is some peanuts. I want you to take these peanuts with you."

Dad took the small bag of peanuts, got in his car and started the long trip back to Atlanta.

Tears began to roll down his cheeks as he told about it.

"You know," he said, "I ate those peanuts on my way back home. And that was the sweetest food I have ever eaten."

Dad died from the most frightening cancer known — cancer of the brain. Toward the end, he became blind in his left eye. Half his face became paralyzed and he gradually could not speak coherently because of the beginning paralysis of his tongue.

He didn't believe in quitting and I think to the end, he wanted to set a good example for the rest of us.

A week before he died, no longer able to drive himself, he had my mother take him on his last real estate appointment.

When he finally went to bed, our family doctor came out to see him and he talked to us.

"Clark," he said, "if we send him to the hospital, they will be obligated to use artificial means to keep him alive. That could make his death even worse because the paralysis could cause him to strangle. I wouldn't take him."

We all agreed that Dad should have the right to go home from his own home. I have always appreciated the doctor's helping us reach a decision we all felt was right.

We took turns sitting with him and reading the Bible for him.

Finally, the night before he died, he got all of us in the bedroom, had each of us put a hand on top of his, and then put his own hand on ours.

As we sat there, our hands clasped between Dad's hands, the room was suddenly filled with a clear, pure light. So clear and so pure that each of us appeared to me like cardboard cutouts against that light of the true reality.

It would be years later before I'd fully know what Dad had done for us — and what that light meant.

Dad couldn't speak, but he was giving his final instructions to his family — we were to stick together.

In all the six-month ordeal leading to the end, I never heard Dad express any fear of death and never felt any hesitancy on his part to go on to the next phase of the great mystery.

I sat with him as he drew his last breath and then looked on the still, white face in silence for several moments.

And I thought of the delegation that was meeting with their friend at that very moment.

CHAPTER III

As the rugged California mountains began to melt way beneath the 140, the flat land surrouding the Salton Sea appeared. In the far West there aren't any foothills on the eastern side of the mountain ranges. The land is flat, although the elevation is rising imperceptibly as you travel West. Then the mountains rise suddenly before you without the kind of low foot hills we have in North Georgia.

As I came over the flat land, I began to look for the expressway that marked the point for my turn back to due east. I had flown south from the Julian VOR in order to avoid the large restricted area just north of the Mexican Border known as the Air Defense Identification Zone or ADIZ. In addition to providing border security, the broad expanse of California mountain and desert is used by the Marines for range artillery firing and combat flying maneuvers. The small plane entering the ADIZ without prior approval and identification will find itself flying wing tip to an escorting jet fighter plane. It is an experience that doesn't invite repetition.

Turning east, I was soon at El Centro and the Imperial VOR. There is a large Air Force Base at El Centro. To my right was the Mexican border and a large Mexican Airport, named for a famous General and located just inside the border.

Leveling my wings, I thought back to an age that seemed eons ago on this bright and cloudless day. It was an era of innocence that would never return. Not only for me personally, but for my whole generation and for the whole nation.

"Hey, Gabby," my roommate leaned toward me so he could hear above the the sound of the wind sweeping over the open car, the roar of the model A Ford engine, and the rattle and rumble of the rocking little car. I had been staring at a small hole in the metal plate that separated us

35

from the engine compartment of the Ford. I was use to seeing the glow
of the tail pipe in our Model A when I'd been driving at a blistering 50
miles an hour, but this was different. The flickering point of light was
a bright orange.

"Gabby," I repeated, "I think your car is on fire."

Gabby looked at me intently, then slowed the rambling car and pulled
over to the curb, cutting the engine and pulling back the long hand brake
lever. He got out, went around to the open rumble seat and got the blanket
he kept there for special occasions when he and his girl made a midnight
trip down River Road.

Gabby walked around, unlatched the hood on the driver's side and
folded back the metal cover.

Flames leaped out of the engine compartment and Gabby flailed away
until the fire finally died out. He re-latched the hood, walked around and
threw the blanket back in the rumble seat, got in the car and started the
engine. He turned to me. "Yep," Gabby said, "you were right. It was on
fire."

When we got back to the fraternity house, Gabby, a man of few words,
made an exception and told several of the brothers about the experience.

"Clark didn't even get out of the car," he concluded with a grin.

In the fall of 1941, with the U.S. still at peace, I had entered the University of Georgia as a freshman.

Only a small per cent of students went beyond high school in those
tough times and the colleges had to hustle to get students.

Total enrollment at the University was about 4,000. By state law, any
one who had finished a Georgia high school had to be admitted to the
University and the requirements for entrance were otherwise non-existent.
I remember asking a boy from the northeastern U. S. why he had come
to the University and he said because it was cheap and the only school
that would accept his "D" high school avergage.

What it lacked in academic excellence was more than made up for by
the social activities available. Rush week was the big event of the freshman year. The sons and daughters of families affluent enough to pay the
cost of college attendance would, in most cases, be sure the new student
had been recommended by family friends for a fraternity or sorority.

Rush week was spent going to parties on invitation from one of the
Greek societies. When the fraternity decided it liked the freshman, a vote
would be taken at chapter meeting. A box containing white and black
marbles was passed and each member would select a marble to put into

a hole in the covered part of the box. If one black marble was found in the box when it was opened, that freshman had been "blackballed" and could not be invited to join. If all the marbles were white, the lucky rushee received a "bid" to join the fraternity. There was nothing democratic about the process. On the other hand, with money as short in supply as it was for most of us, there wasn't much snobbery either.

"Have you decided what to pledge, Fred?" Fred, who was in my dormitory and who was from south Georgia, had become a good friend in the early weeks of school. I had taken him to Decatur for a weekend and he, in turn, had helped me get on as an usher at some of the college plays and musical events. We were chatting after everyone was seated and we waited for the heavy curtains to part.

"I'll probably go KA, like my father and uncles," Fred replied, "How about you, Clark?"

"Well," I said, "My Dad wasn't in a fraternity, but he thinks I ought to join Sigma Chi because of some friends of his who have been working on on him."

The Phi Delts in front of the big old white Victorian house on Prince Ave. The Phi Delts didn't seem to care whether I joined or not, so I figured they must be a good outfit. I'm third from the right on the back row. My roommate, Gabby Montgomery is second from the right on the second row. Fall, 1941, before Pearl Harbor.

With the kind of independence Dad had drilled into me, I had already made up my mind I wouldn't join that fraternity.

"I wasn't too impressed with them or the SAE's," I continued. "Frankly, I think the SAE's try too hard, bringing in that big band and all those beautiful Atlanta pinks. I kinda liked the Phi Delts".

The Phi Delts didn't seem to care much whether anybody joined them. When I went to their house, a two-storied, white Victorian monster on Prince Avenue, the brothers seemed to be sitting on the porch drinking beer in their shirt sleeves or tending to their own affairs and pretty much indifferent as to whether I joined or not.

So, I decided they must be a pretty good outfit. The feeling was abetted by the persuasiveness of a law student named Earnest Vandiver who later became Governor of the State of Georgia.

Dad, in the meantime, with his usual positive outlook, had polled his friends and found several who were Phi Delta Thetas and who assured him that Phi Delta was the best fraternity at the University.

The University represented a new feeling of freedom for me. I had always felt free to come and go at home, but I was expected to let the family know if I was going to be out later than usual. When I checked into the freshman dormitory, a huge two story brick structure named Joe Brown with large rooms to house two students each and with a large common shower and toilet room, I found there were absolutely no rules. All the women on the campus were housed at what was called co-ordinate — dormitories grouped on a hill several miles from the main campus.

The women were strictly regulated as to hours and the theory, apparently, was that if you guard the women, you can let the men look after themselves.

Each year, a traditional "shirt tail" parade was held for all the freshmen men. They were expected to march in shirts and undershorts from main campus up Lumpkin Street, through downtown Athens, out Prince Avenue, some four or five miles, to co-ordinate. There, we serenaded the women's dorms, the girls hung out the windows yelling at us and then, we paraded back home.

Pretty mild stuff by today's standards, but group recognition of the difference between the sexes. The more intense approaches were made later on an individual basis.

Joe Brown was open all night. At three o'clock in the morning, poker games and other male diversions would be in full swing in the main lobby. Walking through the courtyard between the wings of Joe Brown, the dorm windows of the individual rooms would be open and radios blaring.

"Hey, Clark," one of my fellow freshmen yelled as I crossed the lobby, "you going to listen to the Louis fight."

"That's where I'm headed," I shouted in return as I left the rear entrance and entered the big courtyard.

The bell was just sounding for the first round and the announcer was excitingly recording the first blows.

"It's all over, folks," I was half way across the quadrangle, heading for the entrance to our wing of Joe Brown as I listened to the account coming from one of the open dormitory windows. "Louis has done it again. A knockout in the first minute and a half of round one."

Louis was one of the greatest of the fighters at that time and one of the first blacks to be admitted to professional ranks.

I enrolled in the liberal arts college, and, with my experience on the Scribbler, our high school mimeographed paper, I opted for a major in Journalism.

It was an exciting time at the University. Not only was World War II waiting in the wings, expected to involve us at any moment, but Georgia was enjoying the football team that was to become legendary in the school's history.

The powers that were in the athletic department had discovered the art of recruiting and had carried it to a fine science. With the ravages of the War Between the States having left the crop of Georgia athletes somewhat on the lean side, recruiters had discovered a rich vein of talent in the mining country of Pennsylvania and the steel mills of Ohio.

Frank Sinkwich, barrel shaped but powerful and strangely agile on the football field, was at the height of his power. Each weekend, we would watch a crowd of defenders surround Frankie, then stay glued together in a clot of humanity while Frankie emerged to run on toward the goal line. Or, we would watch in amazement as Frankie would throw a long, long pass to his former Ohio high school receiver, George Poschner.

Charlie Trippi was a freshman that year and was demonstrating his agility and the power that came from the Pennsylvania coal mines. Where Frankie looked clumsy everywhere but on the football field, Charlie was one of the most graceful athletes ever and sheer poetry in motion as the sports writers liked to say.

Polish and Italian names were still strange sounding in a south whose anscestors were for the most part Scotch, Irish, or English with an occasional French name thrown in for variety.

In Journalism classes, Dean John Drewry, a florid man with hair long for those days and a flowing, flowery line of patter in the classroom, took great delight in talking about our football team.

"We truly have an All American team," Dean Drewry would expound, "Sinkwich, Trippi, Tereshinski, all good old American names."

Nineteen forty one saw Georgia go from victory to victory thanks largely to our imported stars. But the following year, with the U.S. at war and with college boys just beginning to be drafted, was the year to remember. Two traditional rivals were Auburn in Alabama and most hated of all Georgia Tech in Atlanta. Tech had much to say about the low educational standards at the University and we called Tech a trade school which taught such ungentlemanly subjects as mathmatics and drafting. Tech said the University got most of the state money since so many of its ill-prepared graduates went into politics. We all said we were glad Tech did a good job job of training people to go to work for the University graduates who traditionally ended up as the bosses. In 1942, we were meeting Auburn at Columbus, Georgia the week before we faced our arch enemy, Georgia Tech. It was my sophmore year and we went to Columbus undefeated. Georgia Tech had already faced Auburn and was undefeated also.

Nobody was really worried about Auburn. The fall preceding we had trailed Auburn down to the last minute and a half. Sinkwich, who had been injured in a previous game, was playing with his jaws wired together and wearing a single steel "face guard" rod attached to his helmet to protect the jaw (it was the first "face guard" we had seen — up until that time, you could spot a football player in his later years by the broken and crooked nose). Then, Sinkwich threw a football half the length of the field to one of his ends to win the game.

We were trailing again that fateful year of 1942, but like I said, we weren't really worried. Sinkwich liked to get behind, then with a long run or pass snatch victory from the jaws of certain defeat, and we knew he'd do it again.

But he didn't. This time, the dramatic closing moments came and went and the Georgia fans sat in stunned silence as the realization swept over us that we were no longer undefeated and that our dreams of going to California and the Rose Bowl and becoming national champs had gone a glimmering.

The following week there was no joy in the classic city, as Athens was referred to in the press reports that crowed over the once mighty Bulldogs.

Tech was exultant. Their hero, Clint Castleberry, had carried them through an undefeated season and it was clear to all that now Tech and not Georgia would go to the West Coast and become the top team in the country.

Shocked, stunned, and dismayed, the Bulldogs licked their wounds and growled in agony and humiliation.

As the hours ticked away following the debacle at Columbus and the sores began to slowly heal, a cold resolve began to grow in the breasts of the team and of their bitterly disappointed followers.

One thing was sure. If Georgia couldn't lead the nation then, for damn sure, Tech wouldn't either. By means fair, or foul, Tech had to be stopped. The taste of humiliation was too bitter to be compounded by further crowing on the part of the cocky, prancing and hated Yellow Jackets.

That week before the game, the Georgia student body held not one, but two mammoth pep rallies. The whole student body, or at least that part that could see, hear, and locomote, turned out and the largest bon fire in the history of the school burned. Piles of boxes, trash, limbs, and paper towering two stories high blazed far into the night.

The unprecedented Monday night rally stirred such frenzy that by common tribe instinct an even more fierce burning and screaming was convened on Wednesday evening.

Out of these ashes grew a cold fury on the part of our Ohio farm boys and Pennsylvania coal miners. They knew what they had to do and they did it — for the glory of ole Georgia.

Tech arrived "between the hedges" as Georgia's stadium is called by the glory writers, in high spirits, which lasted about as long as Joe Louis' opponents were at the time.

As soon as the whistle blew, Georgia's team went for and disabled Clint Castleberry. With Clint out of action and Georgia's fury for revenge rising to a crashing crescendo, Tech was literally wiped out, crushed, routed and sent reeling. The final score in what became a dull afternoon to everyone but the screaming Georgia fans, gorged as they were with the blood of their vanquished foe, was a resounding 33 to nothing, or zip as the modern-sports casters say.

Needless to say, negotiations with Georgia were renewed by the Rose Bowl Committee and the dogs went on to become national champions.

I was always glad I was part of those days just before the full brunt of World War II wiped out college in the innocence it enjoyed in those days. And it gives me a warm feeling to mention Sinkwich, Trippi, Tereshenski, Poschner to men unborn in 1942 and discover that they know those names too.

After my first freshman quarter, I moved into the fraternity house, sharing a room that was just wide enough for a double bunk bed and a table that was usually available for me to study. My roommate, Gabby, was a senior, expecting to be commissioned in June.

The food planned by our efficient and devoted house mother, Mrs. Foster, was excellent and especially appreciated by the brothers because each day had it's menu that never varied. We knew which night we would have roast beef and which night beef stew so we could plan accordingly. The black cook fixed the soul food we had eaten at home, along with hot biscuits and fresh pies.

We had great parties that lasted far into the night, very few fights and the girls who attended the parties and dated the brothers in the evening behaved with decorum and were treated with respect. Any misbehaving, and I feel sure there was the usual amount to be expected between healthy young men and women in a charged war time atmosphere, took place off the premises. We heard gloating about taking girls upstairs during the Christmas holidays when everyone else was gone, but it never took place during regular school days — or at least hardly ever. I do seem to rememeber a girl coming down the stairs at a particularly alcoholic brawl — but perhaps she had gotten lost.

Nationally, the ADPi's were the sister sorority to Phi Delta Theta, a fact we had heard but never pursued. At Georgia Alpha we preferred to seek out our women on an individual basis and were suspicious of group activities based on greek affiliations. Except that during those glorious 1942 fall days, one of the sororities, for reasons known only to themselves, decided to adopt us as their brother fraternity and sent word to us that they were going to do so.

The girls in the sorority for the most part came from Atlanta society and apparently felt that whatever they decided they wanted, they were entitled to have.

The word was sent to us that the sorority, in order to seal the new relationship, was coming to lunch with us on a certain day.

For our part, we figured they were just being wise and had to be kidding, so we ignored the notice and were assembling for lunch in our two dining rooms when in walks the entire sorority. Being southern and being gentlemen, we watched with mouths agape as the smartly, dressed young women marched into the dining rooms and sat down at our places at the table. No arrangements had been made, so we were left to watch with our open mouths watering while they ate our food.

While this was going on, some of our older brothers held a conference to decide what to do about the chirping, brashy females who were doing such damage to our vittles.

Finally, the women finished and stood up to leave. As they began to depart, they discovered that all but the front exit had been barred. Opening the front door to leave, they found a double row of the unsmiling brotherhood stretching down the front steps along the walkway to the street — and each held one of the long, wooden paddles used to such effect on Freshmen pledges.

We didn't break any paddles, as sometimes was done on the male behinds, but we did leave some rosy bottoms on the departing guests. Having abandoned the traditional southern male — female relationship of decorum and respect for the female person, they were faced with the brute strength and savagery of the unfed male.

So ended our sister sorority relationship and as far as we know, nothing was spoken of in the future as to trying to revive it.

It was a delicious time.

CHAPTER IV

As mentioned earlier, in deciding to learn to fly, I had two major fears. Getting down and getting lost.

After gaining some competence in overcoming my first fear, that of getting the airplane back on the ground, I began to spend time with Clint and my ground school instructor on fear number two. Getting lost.

Navigating in the air is somewhat similar to navigating in the ocean. In a boat, there are landmarks to help in orientation, so long as you remain in sight of land. In an airplane there are visual ground references until you get into or on top of the clouds.

Once you get out of sight of land, you have to — in both cases — depend on instruments. Early navigation by boat depended on the magnetic compass and fixes, taken by instruments in conjunction with a time piece, on the stars or on the sun.

Early flying depended on the magnetic compass, a time piece, and visual references to landmarks.

All that changed with the advent of radio and radar. Most modern pilots depend on modern methods and never master the art of pilotage. Their charts show only distances, altitudes, and radio frequencies and they do just fine until they lose electric power due to a malfunction of the alternator or battery.

With power gone, they have no more than a general idea of where they are.

Clint, although he had flown F102 interceptors for the Air Force, is old fashioned.

He wouldn't let me use the radio for navigation until I had mastered pilotage. By the time I'd finally done that, I was a little arrogant about the fact I could find my path the old fashioned way, and so, I use radio more as a check on navigating than as my main support.

I liked ground school so much, I took it twice. Or to put it another way, I was so slow learning to fly, I figured I'd better double check what I'd learned from the books.

There is a complicated way, and I learned it, to chart and follow an imaginary line from point to point on the ground.

But, as in cooking, with experience I learned to simplify the process.

What I do today is, first, draw an orange line on my chart from airport to destination. Then mark landmarks (expressways, outdoor theatres, quarries, etc.) along that route and time the distance from one landmark to the next. My airplane flys about one inch every four minutes, so I multiply inches by four then write in the answer right on the face of the chart — an orange number in an orange circle.

Then, after taking off, I fly the magnetic heading for that route, checking my time as I go along and correcting for wind as I go to one side or the other of my check point.

It actually works — with practice that is.

Not long ago, I flew to Asheville, N. C. from Atlanta. Picked up my Aunt Bee, who is in her eighties, and the two of us flew to St. Simons Island, Georgia, spent the night and then flew on to her home in Leesburg, Florida.

My only navigation instruments were the magnetic (Boy Scout) compass and my thirty-seven year old wrist watch.

Nineteen-forty-two was an eventful year not only for the nation, but for Georgia as well. The University System became the key issue in the Governor's race that year and as a sophomore and writer for the school's Red and Black newspaper, I became involved actively in that race.

The race was a classic face-off between the forces of the old Georgia and a new Georgia that was trying to emerge.

Gene Talmadge, the incumbent, had been elected governor first when I was a child. Although he vowed he would never be a candidate for elected office, my Dad was fascinated by politics and by the colorful characters who offered to lead the state in those hard time days.

Like most Georgians, he was intrigued by Gene Talmadge. Ole Gene, as he liked to be called, sported red suspenders, known then as "galluses," and he played on racial prejudices by promising to protect the poor white farmers from the black man; and, although an educated and brillant man, he assumed the role of an ignorant, ungrammatical, but cagey and cunning leader of the common man — especially the dirt farmer who controlled the state politically under the county unit voting system.

Rural counties had a disproportionate power because the smallest of Georgia's 159 counties, with just a handful of voters, cast two votes in the Governor's race, while the largest urban county, Fulton, which included the city of Atlanta, had only six votes. The blacks didn't count, of course, since they weren't allowed to register or vote, and that left the small white farmer in firm control of the Governor's seat.

Ole Gene put it succinctly. "I don't try to carry any county that has street cars."

Gene Talmadge championed the small farmer's cause. Elected commissioner of Agriculture prior to his run for Governor, Talmadge was accused of stealing money from the state. "That's right," Gene would shout when the subject came up, "I stole it for you!"

The political speaking was done from the courthouse steps and the farmers from throughout a county would converge on the courthouse lawn to hear the candidates. Gene always made it a practice to have several of his supporters in the audience, dressed in bib overalls and usually perched on a limb of the large, old shade trees that grew on all Georgia's court house squares. After Talmadge started, he would be interrupted by these allies.

"Give 'em hell, Gene," one would holler, "Tell 'em about the city slickers."

As the temperature rose and the power of the rhetoric increased, another would holler.

"Take off your coat, Gene."

Gene would strip off his black suit coat to reveal a white shirt and broad red suspenders.

The crowd would let out a roar.

"Roll up your sleeves, Gene. Give them lying Atlanta newspapers hell, Gene".

Ellis Arnall, an Atlanta attorney, had for some time waged war through the Federal Courts, challenging one of the reconstruction measures that had hobbled the South and helped assure the South staying poor and rural. The U. S. Congress had passed laws allowing the institution of railroad freight rates that varied from region to region. The result was a rate scale that made it cheap to ship raw materials, cotton, and other agricultural products to the industrial north. On the other hand, rates were prohibitively high when it came to shipping finished manufactured goods from the South to other parts of the country.

The regulations were patently in restraint of interstate commerce and unconstitutional, but they stood for generations after the Civil War when it was no novelty to discriminate against the defeated South.

Arnall recognized the significance for the economic development of the South that an overturn of these discriminatory rates would represent. He won his case in the U. S. Supreme Court and laid the legal groundwork for the industrialization and prosperity of the South that has followed.

But in 1942, the future industrialization of the South was not the big issue. The issue that elected Ellis Arnall was created by Gene Talmadge and we college students were directly involved.

For whatever reason, Talmadge decided to fire two of Georgia's college presidents. The people generally didn't know whether the presidents should have been fired, but they did know Gene had overriden the Board of Regents, a majority of which had been appointed by a preceeding Govenor, and thereby he incurred the wrath of the Southern Board of Accreditation.

No mean politicians themselves, the Accreditation Board shouted "foul" and immediately disaccredited the entire University System including Georgia, Tech and the other smaller colleges around the state.

While the people in the small counties were sensitive to the racial issue, they were even more convinced that the future of their children lay in education and they didn't want any politician messing around with that.

Since the University of Georgia was the school most of the future politicians attended, the drama of the confrontation had immediate appeal to the students.

A few of us got together and formed the Student Political League to fight Talmadge and thereby to save the accreditation of the University System. The Atlanta newspapers, traditional champions of the one man — one vote philosophy that would take power from the rural counties and concentrate it in the cities were delighted and gave our efforts broad coverage.

The Student Political League issued press releases and, lining up the co-eds in the sororities, had personal letters typed and sent to parents all over the state, pleading for their help in saving the University by voting Talmadge out of office. The Accreditation Commission, to remove all doubt from everyone's mind, announced that it would reconsider its decision disaccrediting Georgia colleges in October, right after the September Democratic Primary. Since the Republican Party was practically non-existent in the Solid South of that era, winning the Democratic Primary was, in the words of the press, "tantamount to election".

As a writer on the staff of the Red and Black, Georgia's school paper, and as a member of the Phi Kappa Debating Sosciety, I became unwittingly involved in the election at a higher level, causing the University and the Atlanta newspapers to become defendants in a law suit that dragged on for some months following the election.

The University of Georgia makes claim to being the oldest state university in the nation. Founded by a Yale graduate, the campus centers around a quadrangle patterned after the famous Yale Quadrangle. The oldest buildings facing each other across the quadrangle house the two greek debating societies. Phi Kappa on the east was made up primarily of fraternity brothers and, in the minds of the students of the time at least, the more affluent members of the student body. On the west were the Demosthenians, theoretically representing the great unwashed — students working their way through school and claiming heritage from among the small dirt farmers.

The truth, of course, was that the Demosthenians in the Talmadge years represented the powers that were and the Phi Kappas the disenfranchised from the more urban centers for the most part.

As a member of the University debate team and a fraternity man, I was naturally attracted to and active in Phi Kappa.

On the fateful evening, the Phi Kappas had trouped over to the Demosthenian hall to debate the political dynamics of the moment and the pros and cons of the disaccreditation that was adding fuel to a fire that was becoming white hot as the September Primary drew near.

Speaking for the Demosthenians was a student known as Helbin Edwards, Jr. His father, known as "Hellbent" Edwards, was a staunch Talmadge lieutenant who was known to issue statements attacking all Talmadge foes and especially the lying Atlanta Newspapers in a way even more virulent than that employed by Gene himself.

"When ole Gene comes to Athens next week," Hellbent, Jr. was expounding, "students ought to meet him with rotten eggs and throw old tomatoes at him."

Helbin went on at length describing how Gene should be pilloried by the angry students.

Following this tirade, a Phi Kappa leaped to his feet to charge "Hellbent, Jr." with trying to incite the students to do things that would discredit them and their cause in the eyes of the public and give the victory to Talmadge.

I enjoyed the debate along with the rest of the audience. Nothing could be more stirring than the nonsense that came out of such encounters and everybody was having a great, if angry, time. Leaving the meeting, I strolled at a leisurely pace down the brick sidewalk leading between the ancient oaks that lined the qaudrangle, and on down toward the office of the Red and Black. It was a warm autumn evening, the moon was full, and I felt wonderful.

As a sophomore, I didn't receive major assignments from the upper-class staff at the Red and Black, but occasionally they let me fill space by writing a letter to the editor complaining about the university laundry or the food at the school cafeteria — better known as the "beanery". I was just getting into my journalism courses and needed all the inches of published material I could get — from whatever source. So, I figured to drop by and see if a letter to the editor was needed.

"Anybody at that Demosthenian meeting?", the editor was shouting as I entered the news room. "I hear Hellbent, Jr. was on a rampage. Sounds like a good story".

I volunteered I was present, and without asking further the editor told me to write the story.

Although I had taken no notes, I figured I could remember enough of what had transpired, so I set to work, giving the who, where, what, when and how, just like I had learned in John Drewry's class, and quoting liberally from Helbin's speech in every other paragraph.

Much to my surprise and exultation the editor printed the story without change on the front page of the Red and Black.

The matter undoubtedly would have ended there, except that the Atlanta Journal, seeing one of their bitter enemies caught in an apparent attempt to derail the student cause against Talmadge, liked the story even better.

The next day my story, again verbatim, appeared on page two of the Atlanta Journal.

The rest I learned some weeks later after the campaign had ended and Ellis Arnall had been swept into the Governor's chair.

Apparently, Helbin, Sr. was infuriated by the story, jumped in his car and drove to Athens where he confronted the editor of the Red and Black.

"All we did was quote what your son said," the editor declared. "We stand behind the story."

Then Helbin roared into Atlanta to confront the editor of the lying Atlanta newspaper.

"We picked up the story from the Red and Black and quoted it verbatim", the editor replied.

A law suit was filed but never came to trial. Fortunately, Arnall won and, in politics, that is what counts. Had Gene triumphed, my story, written from memory, would have undoubtedly returned to haunt us all.

Following his election, Ellis Arnall acknowledged the part played by students in his election. After Arnall's election came Pearl Harbor, and in the next legislative session the draft age was set at eighteen. "If they're old enough to fight, they're old enough to vote"

Georgia became the first state in the nation to lower the voting age to eighteen.

The fall of 1942 was to be our last near normal school year at the University. Every day we heard of students leaving to enter service and we began to hear of casualties — most often among those who were killed in flight training.

But for the most part, it was a normal fall quarter. We had dances every week, usually at the huge gymnasium where one of the big bands would perform. Tommy Dorsey was a special favorite, and we heard Sammy Kaye, Tony Pasteur, among others. The war time atmosphere and the knowledge that most of us would be leaving for service in the near future made it a romantic time. River road was the conventional parking place but students showed the usual ingenuity in managing to find a time and place to be alone with their lover.

The standard school attire for the girls was dirty saddle oxfords (brown and white blunt-toed shoes), skirts and sweaters. The desired adornment was a fraternity pin fastened above the left breast and constituting an informal engagement or at least the preliminary step to one. Girls weren't expected to date anyone other than the boy who had "pinned" her, once that ceremony had taken place.

Intramural sports were popular with the fraternities playing each other in football and baseball. One vivid memeory is Audley Tucker's old Mercury convertible, its slick tires bulging and the seats and running board loaded with brothers so that the auto springs were pressed flat. They were off to another game.

Across Prince Avenue from our white Victorian style fraternity house was the Prince Avenue Pharmacy. The best thing about the Prince Avenue Pharmacy was the service.

There was a balcony outside our room on the second floor and one of the favorite diversions was to sit in a cane bottom chair the Saturday morning after a big Friday night party at the house. We would sit with our feet propped up on the railing watching the little colored boy who was the youngest member of the staff, as he swept the broken whiskey glasses and bottles down the walkway.

When the beer gave out, we'd holler across to the P.A. Pharmacy, holding up fingers for the number of beers we wanted delivered.

Ah, what a life.

The horse cavalry added another dimension to my college experience.

With Hitler's legions well into the modern war tactics of blitzkrieg attack by massed tanks, screaming dive bombers and motorized infantry, the University of Georgia in 1941 through 1943 responded by offering those not interested in foot soldiery, a fast moving cavalry training program. Only the Poles, shown in the news reels of the day charging against Hitler's armor were meeting the challenge in quite the same way.

Naturally, being abreast of world developments, I opted for the cavalry. In the first place, the cavalry officers got to wear shiny brown boots that covered the calf up to the knee.

In the second place, they got to ride horses.

Having been raised in the city, I hadn't spent much time around horses, much less on one. The first time I mounted up, I discovered that my legs were too short to give me a really good grip on the situation.

And, of course, the mounts provided students weren't exactly Kentucky thoroughbreds. Abused by succeeding classes of incompetent, insensitive, disinterested and ignorant neophytes, the horses over the years had become pretty cynical, sensitive and sore mouthed about the whole process.

My first appreciation of the seriousness of the situation as concerned my physical well being came at an early stage of training. We were required to ride the horse down a 30 foot embankment that descended at an angle of about 75 degrees to a flat athletic field.

About half way down, I discovered why short legs can be a disadvantage in horse riding. I began to slide forward on the horse, and, by the time we reached the bottom of the slope, I was hanging with one arm and one leg around the horse's neck. At that point, the horse did the logical thing — he broke into a full gallop.

Fortunately, I was able to retain my grip on the horse's neck and to reach the reins with my free hand. While I didn't want to hurt the poor animal's sore mouth, I did want to stop him before I fell off and I finally succeeded. Whether the spectators thought I was a trick rider or what, I never found out. Nobody asked me, so I kept quiet.

Early on, it became apparent that the military would not prove a natural environment for me. Perhaps it was Dad's admonition not to stand in the shadow of another man. In the military, you were always in the shadow of someone and I suppose I never learned how to behave properly.

For example, we were allowed to ride the horses on the weekend with one strict prohibition — we were not to gallop the horses under any circumstances.

The first weekend we decided to take a ride, several of the fraternity brothers who were members of the cavalry troop checked out four or five of the aging nags. It was a beautiful fall day and soon we were deep in the dense woods on one of the established bridle trails. Being young, full of the juices produced in youth on fine fall days, and, we thought, unobservable, we soon had quickened our pace to a steady trot, a canter, and then a full gallop. Shouting 'Hi ho, Silver' and other appropriate remarks, we were taken completely by surprise when the woods ended. We were in the open, and being new at the business, found that stopping a horse is not accomplished quite as quickly as slamming on the brakes of a car. Unless, of course, the horse wants to stop as much as you do.

These horses were caught up in the spirit of the occasion and weren't thinking about stopping. We burst out of the woods on a long downward slope that mounted next a steep hillside.

Standing on the hill, of course, was the sergeant and several of his cadre. We had ridden into the midst of their mounted party when our horses, apparently soothed by the sight of familiar horse faces, finally slowed to a walk, then stopped, right up against the sergeant's horse, for a visit.

"You men turn around and WALK those horses back to the area."

I had the feeling the sergeant was going to remember us.

The next time I attracted the sergeant's attention, I was trying to make my horse jump. All the mounts were cantankerous, but this particular horse seemed to have had an especially harsh experience with some student in the past.

Jumping can be hard on a horse when the rider is inexperienced. As the horse clears a jump, he stretches his body and his neck to its full extension. The rider is taught to leave slack in the reins. This is not easy to learn because the reins have to be held firmly going into the jump to keep the horse headed toward an obstacle he had just as soon avoid. Then, as the horse starts his jump, the rider has to give plenty of slack. A tight rein will pull the bit against the horse's mouth and can hurt him badly as the full momentum of the jump is brought to bear on this tender spot. Apparently, this had happened to this particular horse I was riding more than once in the past — and he had had enough.

The first time I tried to make him jump, we came into the jump at a full gallop, then, at the last moment, the horse veered and the sergeant yelled.

"Hold him into the jump."

Next I started in holding the reins to prevent his turning and he slowed.

"Kick the son of a bitch." The sergeant was beginning to turn red.

I held him firmly and started kicking him.

"Not like that — kick the hell out of him," the sergeant roared. This time, I brought the horse back around, held his head tight and kicked as hard as I could, both legs going out and coming in with resounding cracks of boot against horseflesh.

The horse, trying to escape jump, rider and pain, rose up on his hind legs.

"Turn loose of the reins," the sergeant yelled. "Or he'll be on top of you!"

I saw what he meant and let go of the reins.

Next, I rode the horse further back up the trail, circled and kicked him into a full gallop. One thing I knew, the horse might not like it, but I had to shut up that dumb sergeant. I felt sure if we came in hard and fast enough the horse would have no alternative but to jump.

I was wrong.

While I had experienced difficulty stopping my horse when I was hanging around his neck, I learned a horse can stop suddenly when it's the horse's idea. The full gallop lasted until about eight feet from the jump. Then the horse stopped. He didn't slow down, he just suddenly transformed the full gallop into a dead stop and he did it without any help from me. In fact, although he stopped, I kept going. I sailed over the horse, turned sideways, and landed. When I regained coherent thought, I realized to my amazement that I had landed with a foot on each side of the jump, standing up.

They can say horses are dumb, but I am convinced that particular horse knew exactly how he was going to throw me and how I'd land and he planned to fix not only me but the possibility of any heirs of mine returning to abuse future heirs of his.

Fortunately for me, he made one critical miscalculation — the jump was slightly lower than the length of my inseam. I was defeated but at least my reproductive faculties were still in order. I decided to concede that day to the horse and, even though I rode the horse back to the stable, even the sergeant didn't ask me to jump him again.

It should have been obvious to anyone, and especially to me, that there was no future for me in the horse cavalry. Not only had the horse cavalry been ruled out by world events, but it was obvious that I had no personal talent in that direction.

It must have been that old thing of not giving up just because there was no talent — after all, I had finished those sixty guitar lessons.

When the "Greetings from the President of the United States" arrived telling me to report for the draft, my mind was made up. I'd follow the upper classmen graduates of advanced ROTC to Fort Riley, Kansas. I was sure I could qualify for Officer Candidate School and, before the summer was over be a second lieutenant, a ninety day wonder as OCS graduates were called, in the U. S. Cavalry.

I didn't know it at the time, but not since Pickett's charge at Gettysburg has a southerner made a worse military decision.

Starting with the summer quarter, I had been elected assistant treasurer for the fraternity. My roommate, Gabby (because he very seldom talked), was treasurer. Gabby was entering his senior year that fall and had had a somewhat relaxed attitude toward the schooling side of college up to that point.

He was in the Business Administration school but had failed up until then to apply much thought to the courses he took. The ideal we all aimed for was to have no afternoon and no Saturday classes, thereby allowing more time to drink beer and enjoy the deeper pleasures of college life. Gabby had arranged his schedule so near the ideal that he suddenly realized he did not have enough similar courses to constitute a major within the Business Administration department.

"Clark, I'm going to have five classes this fall under Shotgun Sawyer," Gabby told me one day and lapsed back into his usual silence.

Professor Sawyer was a legend at the University. The Business Administration courses were not the most interesting intellectual endeavors to begin with and apparently, Mr. Sawyer had earned a reputation for being especially and profoundly boring.

So much so that he had, from some incident lost to memory, been dubbed 'shotgun' and a ode to his glory had been composed and was sung by students from all departments while drinking their beer.

> *"Down, down, down with Shotgun Sawyer*
> *He is made of pure manure*
> *Horse manure*
> *They forgot to pull the chain*
> *Consequently he'll remain*
> *Til they consecrate the sewers in the street"*

Gabby paid dearly for ignoring the requirements for graduation.

As the fall term began, Gabby took me aside. "Clark," he said, "I have joined the Army Air Corp reserve and I may be called at anytime. I think you had better start learning the ropes in case I have to leave suddenly".

I agreed that would be a good idea and it was further agreed that if Gabby was still around in January I'd take over as full time treasurer — a position desired because it carried free room and board.

As it turned out, of course, Gabby and I were both still about the following March when we were both called to service within a week of each other.

Most of the rest of the fraternity brothers were gone by the end of the school year, the house was turned over to the University to be used as a girls dormitory for the duration. Coordinate, the girls isolated campus, became the school for Naval Aviation cadets.

Phi Delta Theta, down to fourteen members, was meeting in a room above the Prince Avenue Pharmacy. The University would never be the same again.

CHAPTER V

Earlier, I compared navigating an airplane with navigating a boat, and there are similarities. But there is one major difference. In a boat, you are dealing with two dimensions. You can go forward and backward or to any side. In an airplane, you have three ways to go — the third being up and down.

So, if the air is an ocean, the airplane is a submarine.

The surface of the earth is the bottom of the sea. The closer to the bottom of the sea, the greater the pressure and the slower the airplane will travel. At altitude, the airplane makes much better time in relation to the ground because of this decreased pressure.

Like the ocean, there are powerful currents stirring in the air that is the airplane's natural habitat. These currents are caused and complicated by the uneven heating of various parts of the earth, as it tips towards and away from the sun, and by the rotation of the earth on its axis.

The airplane has another peculiarity. Once it is airborne, it could care less what is beneath it.

As a friend, who has many hours flying under all conditions, told me, "If I'm flying at night in the clouds over hostile territory and I get concerned, I get real quiet. Then I ask a question.

"Where are you airplane?"

"I listen. There is no reply."

"Then I remember that the airplane doesn't know where it is. The airplane isn't worried, the airplane doesn't care."

"So, I relax. My instruments tell me where I am and my radio tells me that the weather is clear where I am to land."

We gathered at the Decatur Presbyterian Church toward the end of March, 1943. All of us draftees selected to fill the March quota for our county.

From there we boarded buses to Fort McPherson, the permanent head-quarters for the Third Army that had been built in the World War I era and that was named for the Yankee general who died near the site in the Battle of Atlanta.

The permanent part of the installation is built of red brick with the homes of officers along tree-lined streets and resembling a colonial era village in the Northern U. S. Everything has been maintained and the Fort looks today exactly as it did in 1943.

We were assigned to two-story permanent wooden barracks. This was a staging area to receive draftees, test and classify them and send them within a few days to training and assignments among the three services throughout the U. S.

Having been raised as the only son with a private room from the time I was about ten years old, I was ill prepared for the shock of army living. My only previous experience with group housing had been in the dormitory where I had shared a large room and the fraternity house where Gabby and I shared a small room in a house that contained 30 or 35 fraternity brothers.

The first night, after having raised our right hands, taken the oath and been told we belonged to the Army "for the duration", I knew I was in trouble.

The barracks was lined on each side of an aisle with double bunk beds spaced about two feet apart. Every bed was occupied.

I looked down that long aisle at all that gyrating humanity and realized that my life style would never be the same. For the next three years, I would always be in a crowd, with somebody else making the decisions. I never got used to it, and after it was over I have never minded being alone. Solitude for some reason has never bothered me as it seems to bother some others. I felt, after I finally got out of the Army that I had walked enough miles and congregated with enough people to last me a lifetime.

In classification, we took a battery of tests, were interviewed and filled in a multitude of forms.

"Harrison," the corporal told me after all the tests had been taken and all the forms completed, "with your education and your test scores, you can go to the Navy, the Air Corps, the Marines, the Coast Guard and take just about any training where there is an opening."

I told him I had decided to join the Cavalry, which was, as stated above, about the worst choice I could have made. The corporal shrugged, wrote something on my paper and my fate was sealed.

In high school and college ROTC, I had been both a private and an officer and, outside the insignia and the assignments at drill, there was no material difference. As soon as I reported at Fort Mac, I found out how profound the difference between a private and an officer is in the real Army.

Right away, we were put on kitchen police — scrubbing pots and policing the area — and right away my corruption by those in authority began. I was hard at it, scrubbing the kitchen utensils, when a corporal came by and told me to go with him. For some reason, he had decided to acquaint me with the proper way to soldier.

"Take it easy, Harrison," he told me, "you're going to burn yourself out."

We got outside and he found me a rake.

"Here," he said "hold this and when somebody looks your way do a little raking."

I was a little doubtful that his methods would get me ahead in my new environment, but it was a lot cooler than the kitchen and there didn't seem to be a lot of recognition accorded the boys working there. Since I'd soon be leaving anyway, I decided to follow the corporal's orders. I didn't know I had learned the fundamental rule of surviving the tedium of army life — never volunteer and when it's "make work time" the work might as well be at a relaxed pace.

That afternoon I had another shock. In high school ROTC we had a regular Army sergeant who, along with our regular Army major, constituted the total pay roll of the unit. We always poked fun at the sergeant. He was obviously a good-hearted man but not, in the opinion of high school juniors and seniors, heavily endowed from the shoulders up. As a matter of fact, we poked fun and made up limericks about him, behind his back, of course.

Well, I was occupied in one of those activities that may have added to the sergeant's lack of social grace after twenty years in the army — we were picking up cigarette butts on the hard packed clay of the compound when I glanced up. Coming down the wooden stairway of an adjoining building was our old friend the sergeant — looking his same dumb self. Only he was now wearing a captain's uniform and insignia.

Suddenly, our roles were reversed and I was the dumb private while he was obviously on some important military errand. I doubled over and turned so he couldn't see my face. Undoubtedly, our old sergeant would have been glad to see one of his former charges but I was determined he would not be allowed to see my fallen state.

One thing for sure, the Army wasn't bringing out the best in me.

After completing our tests and our assignments having been determined, we were each given a seven day furlough — to get our civilian affairs settled before being sent to our training stations.

I didn't have any affairs to get in order, but I did do some heavy thinking.

That night, I was back in my private room at home with the tile bath, the hardwood floors, the spacious twin beds, the window that looked out through the magnolia tree and, most of all, the blessed solitude.

I looked out the window and I thought "Boy, you have got yourself in a mess." I was right about that one.

When we reported back to Fort Mac, we were quickly put through final preparations for leaving, and within a couple of days were on a civilian train loaded with other new soldiers with papers that included our orders and a sergeant to see that we arrived at our destination.

The train was loaded with young soldiers from Georgia and Alabama. It was my first experince with a cross section of country boys and I was intrigued by their outlook on life, their way of talking and acting and their general vitality. By observing their actions, it was clear that they were used to hard work and held strong convictions about those things they believed in. Over the next four weeks, I was going to learn about these attributes of Georgia and Alabama country boys in depth.

I had not been out of Georgia at the time except for family vacations in Florida and trips to visit relatives in Tennessee and Kentucky. Now, we were headed west on a railroad day coach and I was fascinated by the scenery once we left the south. In Georgia, we knew a countryside that consisted of small farms, stunted crops and unpainted tenant shacks. The shacks had a narrow porch across the front, three or four rooms and an outhouse. Low cost living and environmental protection taken to the extreme. If there was an outbuilding, it usually consisted of a small barn, also unpainted and leaning precipitously in a losing battle against the gravitation law. Most of at least one side was always missing and the wood shingle or tin roof was likely to be painted with a sign advertising "Black Draught" medicine or "See Rock City", our biggest southern tourist attraction of the time.

During planting time, the ragged and usually barefoot, farmer was to be seen wrestling an aged wooden plow tipped with iron, below ground level behind a spavined and hollow ribbed mule that was busy twitching flys off its ears while using its long black tail to swat the insects off its rump.

If there were any cattle, they were usually of a nondescript brown — blackish color with short horns, skinny legs and sides that bulged more from internal gases generated by the fresh grass they consumed than by any healthy fat.

Now, as we left the South and entered the middle West, I was amazed at the vast expanses of flat farm land, the huge red barns and tall white silos. The cattle were sleek and fat, the cows' udders swinging low and heavy. I am sure I must have seen movies of such country, but it was hard to realize that such wealth was so near our Southland. Nearly eighty years had passed since Sherman burned his way through Georgia and the carpet baggers and discriminatory freight rates completed our impoverishment. But the line of demarcation between victors and vanquished was still there to be clearly seen.

Our destination, Fort Riley, is located next to the small Kansas town of Junction City — the name coming from the fact that two rivers come together on the edge of town.

The old Fort, built on a rare Kansas hill during the indian fighting days is of grey granite construction and still housed the diminishing horse cavalry units. We were assigned to the Cavalry Replacement Training Corps where tanks and the motorized reconnaissance units were located.

Known as the CRTC or the "flats", the training area consisted of "permanent" two-story wooden barracks and "temporary" one-story barracks built out of light framing with tarpaper covered sides. The land is perfectly flat and is located at the confluence of the two rivers. To avoid flooding, the engineers had built a dirt dykework that stood about thirty feet high and tapered at about a 35 degree angle from a top which was about twenty feet wide. The dykes stood some 500 yards back from the rivers to allow plenty of room for flood waters to spread.

Arriving in April gave us some time to adjust to the temperature during the short, moderate time of the year. The winters were brutally cold with blizzards and other assorted storms. The summers, as we came to know, were mercilessly hot with a high humidity that made clothes stick to the body. It was tornado country, as we also learned first hand during my four months there.

Looking at those desolate flats today, it is hard to recreate in the imagination the teeming humanity that occupied these acres during the war years.

Men in olive drab fatigues and steel combat helmets were swarming everywhere, six-by-six trucks, tanks, jeeps — even motorcycles gunning over the fields. Security was tight at the entrance located just inside the dyke with MP's checking the passes of all men entering or leaving. On the parade grounds, large and small units of men drilled and in the plains surrounding, the CRTC units practiced creeping and crawling in the attack, patrol in jeeps, hand grenade throwing, and hand-to-hand combat.

Just outside the camp area on the far side of the eastern dyke were located the barbed wire, mines, and machine guns of the infiltration course. There every soldier had to crawl on his belly under live machine gun bullets fired from implacements at the far end of the course. The barbed wire had to be crawled under — the bullets whistled over a few inches above a soldier on his belly. Intermittently, pre-placed explosives would go off to simulate mortar and artillery shells dropping among the advancing troops.

The rifle range, built on a huge scale to train a large number of soldiers simultaneously, was located a few miles from the camp.

We arrived around the first of April, so the weather was moderate, cooling quickly as the sun went down. I was assigned to a Mechanized Cavalry Troup, which meant my basic training would include jeep driving under all conditions.

But first, we were to be given basic infantry training. I felt right on target for officer training. All around we saw soldiers wearing a red circular patch on their left shoulder that designated them as officer candidate candidates. After four weeks of basic training they would go to the Officer Candidate School located in the old fort on the hill.

We had been issued uniforms at Ft. MacPherson. Now, we were issued additional equipment, including plastic helmet liners, steel helmets, ammunition belts, canteens, rifles, and a mattress cover.

As an enlisted man, I was not to see a sheet — we slept on narrow cots with a flat, steel webbing instead of springs, a cotton mattress three inches thick and a striped mattress cover that was replaced once a week in lieu of sheets. We slept under an olive drab, 100% wool blanket of very good and durable quality; and, we were issued a pillow, whose case was replaced each week, along with the mattress protector. We slept in our undershorts and undershirts.

At the foot of each cot was a wooden footlocker about 20 inches deep and as wide as the cot. Inside, we kept clothes in the bottom and socks, toilet articles, etc., in a wooden tray that fitted inside the locker on wooden runners so that the top could close neatly down over it. The top had a steel latch and long, steel hinges screwed to the inside of the locker and top. The latch could be locked with a simple combination lock, or, one opened by a key.

We were in two story barracks. The floors were pine and the second floor was supported by round, steel posts that lined a center aisle. Cots were spaced about three feet apart on each side of the aisle.

Outside was a paved, asphalt street and there was an open stretch of grass about 30 feet wide between us and the next building in the row.

The latrines came as a shock to one raised in such relatively private surroundings as myself. The fraternity house had prepared me for the open communal showers, but not for the double row of commodes — four on each side facing each other with no partitions, of course.

Surprisingly, after a day or two, we all adjusted to such arrangements and never gave a thought to the lack of dignity entailed.

For one thing, we were busy. For another thing, in those first four weeks, we were so tired by the time the day ended a plank bed would have presented no discomfort. We simply passed out the moment we were able to lie down. And soon our feelings became indelicate as well.

For another thing, the food was good. Under the patriotic pressures that existed throughout the country, the armed services got the best of everything. Our uniforms and shoes were of the best quality cotton or wool and leather; the rifles were new M-1's; and the food that came into the mess hall kitchen was in plentiful supply and of a quality to cause envy in the rationed civilian segment, if they could have seen it, particularly the meat — we got the best, in such quantity that there was plenty for all. Sometimes, we weren't sure the meat originated from a steer. Some of it was stringy and we suspected horseflesh; but, there was plenty.

With one exception, the food was generally well prepared. I remember especially some excellent pastry cooks and apple pie that created local legends.

The exception was the sorriest outfit I was in during my Army months — I'll tell about that later. The Army, as Napoleon noted, travels on its stomach and it was a tried and proven statement that if you had a good kitchen, you had a good outfit — or at least you did from the limited perspective of the common soldier.

Another proven truism concerned the Army's "hurry up and wait" syndrome. Great periods of feverish activity were followed by long spaces of inactivity when we began to wonder if anyone was in charge and if, in fact, we were headed in any kind of systematic fashion toward the combat we read was waging in other parts of the world.

My first four weeks at Riley stand out as among my best times in the service. For one thing, my dream of going to Officer Candidate School

was in place. With five years of ROTC behind me, good grades on my
I.Q. test, two years of college, and a bunch of former University of
Georgia graduates who had proceeded me to the CRTC, I was sure I would
soon be wearing the round red patch and on my way to becoming a second lieutenant. I didn't know plans had been already finalized to close
the Riley OCS before my first four weeks was concluded.

The other reason for a good start the first four weeks was a tall, slender
red-headed sergeant from New Jersey. Red was probably around thirty
— an old man to be engaged in the activity current at Riley. He had been
some kind of instructor in chemicals, I believe; and, he was that rare thing
— a natural born teacher.

He was dedicated — to take the raw material sent him and transpose
us us into tough — ready — soldiers. It was a pleasure to serve under
him. His intelligence assured us of spending every day in activities that
would lead to our ultimate goal. I was not to serve under an equal leader
during the time remaining before we entered combat.

We were always in a hurry those early days with a short time limit on
being ready for every activity. Reveille was early — at or before dawn to
assure full usage of the daylight.

The whistle would wake us and the sergeant would be yelling, "Fall out
in five minutes."

We'd scramble into our uniforms, fumble our way at a gallop out the
door, crashing into each other and pulling up short, dressing right in line
for the roll call.

Breakfast was filling and we soon learned why. With the pace we were
following, anything less than a heavy meal would leave us famished about
ten each morning with two more hours of strenuous work remaining before lunch.

After breakfast the first day of training, we ran to the drill area, fell
in and the lieutenant, one of those small, bouncy men, who, when in
physical shape, can run the legs off a jack rabbit.

"Run in place."

"Hit the ground."

Now up, now down, doing jumping jacks, revolving our extended arms
in small circles until the weight of our limbs made our shoulders ache.
Then we'd lie on our backs, lift our straight legs about six inches off the
ground, spread our legs, hold it, bring them together, hold it until our
stomach muscles cried with pain.

After that first day, I was all right — but, that first day, I was out of shape. Knowing that my days at the University were coming to an end, I'd spent my time relaxing, drinking beer and staying up all night.

After the exercise, in place, the lieutenant told us to follow him, and we took off at a run.

It always amazed me in service how much more we could do as a group of men than we could do individually. When we were about to give out, we'd look at those around us and we knew we had to keep going no matter how much it hurt.

Now, we were running up and down the sides of the dyke — pell mell down the side, then up and over, down, up and over. It went on for an excruciating eternity.

Finally, we were back at the parade ground doing close order drill while we cooled off. By this time, my throat and lungs were burning like somebody had pushed a red hot porker down my gullet. My vision was clouded and I was not thinking because of the numbness induced by the heat and exhaustion. At one point, I stopped and stood alone while the platoon marched away.

I caught up, but I was still semi-conscious. Finally, it was over and we had been marched to the barber shop to get our G. I. haircuts.

I finally regained my senses while waiting in the barber shop, seated at last.

One good thing, other than my physical survival of that first assault on my soft body, resulted that day. Since I had reached the age of trying to appear attractive to the girls, I had struggled to make my hair behave. Starting at about fourteen, I had tried everything, grease, wearing a sock on my head at night, brushes, combs, etc. Nothing worked. My head is big and my hair would stand up, particularly in the back around the and the crown, no matter what therapy I tried.

Then, after that first haircut at Riley, I knew I had the answer — cut the damn stuff off. I threw the comb, brush, and hair oil away and I never owned any of them again. Recently, a friend told me that I probably have the only World War II GI haircut still in existence.

After that first day of physical exhaustion, I had no more trouble keeping up and was soon in excellent shape. Standing only 5'7 ½", I weighed 145 pounds at the time, reaching a maximum of 160 before we reached combat. The hard work agreed with me, the leadership was intelligent those first weeks and I was trying hard.

Except for kitchen police, I had left Atlanta with a train load of Georgia and Alabama country boys. They knew how to work and they were enthusiastic about the army and the adventure of being away from home. Soon, they had a reputation for hard work.

The first time I was sent to report for kitchen duty the mess sergeant was ecstatic — "You're one of those Georgia boys. I sure like Georgia boys," he enthused as he handed me a mop.

Cleaning up was not my strong suit. I'd never done it as a matter of fact and had decided at Fort MacPherson that the way to avoid permanent assignment to unpleaseant tasks was not to excel at them. Being unskilled as a mopper and a pan scrubber, I was naturally slow and being unenthusiastic about the assignment, I didn't do a great deal to increase my production.

Before the day was over, the sergeant looked at me suspiciously and said, "You sure you're from Georgia, boy?"

I didn't get a lot of KP after that.

What I did enjoy was getting to know boys from all over the United States. Up until then, I had never been out of the south and the accents of Chicago, the Bronx, and Indiana sounded strange to my ears.

John Polack, of Chicago, was in the army as a volunteer officer candidate. In his late 20's and experienced in business, John had joined the army with the guarantee that he would be sent to OCS or discharged.

Ray Johnson, of Evanston, Illinois, had been in college like myself when he was drafted. The three of us became close friends in the brief time we were together.

Capturing the spirit and the humor of a draftee army serving as uniformed civilians for the duration is impossible. Attempts that I have seen on the screen fail to equate the real thing because the audience is not in the ridiculous situation that we, as GI's, were experiencing.

None of us wanted to be there, but we couldn't be anywhere else with a war going on. We were forced to do things that were ill-conceived in plan and stupid in execution and nobody took the whole game any more seriously than we were forced to at any one moment.

As an eighteen year old, I had been made an acting coporal and squad leader. Some of the soldiers under me could not read or write, while one one older man, a volunteer officer candidate like John Polack, was a Ph.D. and spoke five languages. All of which made no difference. He had to obey the silly orders I gave or I would "chew him out". He was not too adept at the creeping and crawling and the close order drill; but, he made a manly effort and, at least in my presence, showed no resentment.

After working in the fields all day, we'd be dismissed on our company street about thirty minutes before evening chow.

At that point, we would go to the post exchange where we would buy a big "belly washer" bottle of Coke or Pepsi for five cents, a pint of ice cream for fifteen cents and several big candy bars that were five cents each. Cigarettes were ten cents a pack — until we got overseas where a pack cost a nickle — and beer, which contained 3.2 per cent alcohol was a nickle a can.

Hot and sweaty, we would drink our belly washer — "Pepsi cola hits the spot — 12 full ounces that's a lot — twice as much for a nickle too — Pepsi Cola is the drink for you. Nickle, nickle, nickle, trickle, trickle" and eat our pint of ice cream while we walked back to the mess hall for the evening meal.

To eat, we'd line up outside the mess hall, picking up a big metal tray, a heavy porcelain cup and steel utensils as we entered. As we slid the tray along, the KPs would load it up. In addition, there were platters of food on the tables — we drank coffee.

Ray Johnson, John Polack and a fellow named Sam Smitthers, also from Chicago, who called himself "Sam, who don't give a damn". Sam was in his thirties. We'd all sit together.

After working all day in the hot Kansas sun, we were hungry.

We'd eat everything on our trays, clean up everything on the platters at our table, then, we'd delay leaving the mess hall until most of the soldiers had left. Then, we'd go around to the other tables and find what was left there, bring it to our table and eat that, too.

"Did you know eighty per cent of the women in Chicago don't wear pants," John might offer.

"How do you know?"

"I took a survey"

"Is it true, Clark, that all you southerners own plantations?"

"Well, all my friends do; and, of course, we have a big spread — drink mint julips; and, of course, each have at least two fine Arabian horses. Southern women all wear pantaloons, of course, under their hoop skirts."

Then, we'd go back to the barracks, get our GI blankets and go out and lie down between our barracks and the one next door. At that point, we would get out our candy bars and eat them for desert and gossip and sing old songs.

Our favorite song was "For it was Mary, Mary, plain as any name could be. But in society, in propriety, they say Marie. But, it is Mary, Mary, long before the fashion changed. For there is something there that sounds so square. It's a grand old name."

Ray had become deeply involved with his high school sweetheart, a fine girl whom he planned to marry some day. Somewhere along as their courtship evolved, they had started sleeping together and now he was tormented by the fact they couldn't be together. Nobody in either family knew what was going on and they were stuck with a miserable situation. One minute Ray would plan to go home and get married. Then, he'd decide that wouldn't be right with him liable to be killed during the war. I thanked God I had left the University without getting into a similar situation.

Ray was living until he could have his girl meet him in Kansas City for a weekend.

Sam, who don't give a damn, was divorced, older, and he planned to meet a girlfriend, also divorced, in Kansas City the first time possible. Except Sam was totally untormented by guilt or torn by indecision. He just wanted to get with this experienced woman and have some fun.

John Polack was the most pragmatic of all. Having come up the hard way in Chicago, John had learned human nature and a simple philosophy of life and a desire to get ahead by whatever rules applied in the game being played at the time. Along with it, John was a gentleman and a pleasure to be with.

"I know these sergeants say 'Don't call me, Sir!'", John would say. "But don't let them kid you. They like being called, 'sir!'" So, John always called the sergeants, "Sir!."

John wanted to go to Kansas City to visit the bars and have a good time. On privates pay, he had no delusions about acquiring a local woman and he wasn't involved with anybody who could visit him there.

Generally, I was having my eyes opened by living with men from every strata of American life. I was constantly amazed to hear about the kind of problems they had and to learn that advantages I had enjoyed were really available to only a small portion of the population.

One visible sign was what some of the men would do with the items issued to them by the government. We all received identical things; but when the lockers were left open for inspection, some were neat and orderly while others, displaying the same items, would look like a jumble of junk.

One irritant to the rest of us in those early days was a fellow named Goldstein. By some means, the rest of us could never understand, Goldstein started getting weekend passes while the rest of us were confined to the camp over the weekend.

On one Saturday when Goldstein was the only one not present, we were preparing for inspection when it became apparent that we had one too many bunks on the west side of the barracks.

I was in charge of the squad cleaning up the second floor of the barracks. I made a decision that was to stick in my mind as a lesson in human nature and how not to handle a situation between men.

"Goldstein's not here," I said, "Let's move Goldstein's cot."

Everybody thought that was a great idea since Goldstein was off having a good time while we were doing all the work. His bunk was in the middle of the west wall and soon it was neatly arranged in the same position on the east wall.

In my ignorance, I couldn't see how it could matter to anybody what part of that miserable barracks floor they occupied.

How wrong I was.

Sunday evening we were all on the second floor when Goldstein returned from his safari to the flesh pots of whatever.

Seldom have I experienced such towering rage combined with such a sense of personal and religious and racial persecution. Goldstein shouted, Goldstein implored, Goldstein cried. I could see that what we had done had aroused deep seated emotions of persecution, outrage and self pity.

We were all sort of enjoying this new Goldstein we had discovered when suddenly Mahoney decided he had had enough.

Mahoney had deep-seated emotions of his own. He was an Englishman who either was an Orangeman or hated Orangemen. I can't remember which, but somehow it was also involved with the Irish. On this particular Sunday evening, all this took an ominous anti-Semitic turn and suddenly, Mahoney was hitting Goldstein.

Although I wasn't sure Mahoney's was the best method of settling the matter, it was effective; and soon, Goldstein was no longer discussing the injustice of it all. He was picking himself up off the floor while the rest of us tried to restrain the yelling Mahoney.

I learned a valuable lesson. In the years following, no matter how trivial the change might appear, I always disscussed it ahead of time with the party involved. Particularly when territory was concerned.

Those first four weeks were drawing to a close and, although I didn't know it until they ended, so were my aspirations of going to officer training school at Riley. At the end of the four weeks no officer candidate candidates were named. Instead, it was announced that the Cavalry OCS was closing.

The weekend that ended this initial phase of training, my sergeant, Red, called me aside.

"Clark, I haven't told you this ," he said, "but I appointed you corporal because some of your officer friends told me to do it. I just want you to know that although I was opposed to your being a corporal, you have done a very fine job and I am recommending you for cadre."

I knew then I would have been an officer candidate. I appreciated the compliment because it came from a man I admired for his competence. I was to receive the second compliment that I valued as highly while in combat from my friend Frank Vacarro — and that will come later.

Red had also saved me from rejoining the horse cavalry. The army in 1943 expected Australia to be invaded at any time by the Japanese. Their exposed coastline was isolated and it was impractical to use motorized vehicles because of the difficulty of supplying gasoline in the remote "out back." So, briefly, the army found a use for the horse cavalry and my troup was selected to go up to the old fort and train as horse cavalrymen. Fortunately for the Army and myself, Red's decision left me to train and later help train as a motorized cavalryman.

That weekend, Red told me all the regular non-coms were going to take the weekend off and he assigned me to be CQ — charge of quarters — with no other rank in the troop area.

All was quiet that Saturday after chow. Nobody, with the possible exception of Goldstein, had been given a pass and most of the men were in the barracks by 10 o'clock.

I was sitting alone in the dayroom across the street from the barracks when I heard a commotion start and grow in volume until I could distinguish voices shouting. I was shining my shoes and since I was alone with no real idea of what to do if an emergency of some kind should arise, I just kept on shining.

Suddenly, I saw the face of one of the good old Georgia or Alabama boys staring at me through the day room window. The face looked pale, the whites of the eyes were enlarged and it was obvious the owner of the face was in some kind of distress.

"He's after me, Harrison," he spoke hoarsely in a loud stage whisper. "He's got a knife and he's gonna cut me."

I told him to come in the dayroom and I asked him what had happened to cause all the commotion.

"He said I cussed him," was the answer. "Then, he pulled the knife."

By that time, all of us were using profanity and I knew calling some-body a bastard or a son of a bitch could be a meaningless or even a jocu-lar way of showing friendship. The only problem was that these were Georgia and Alabama country boys and after a few beers they were liable to revert to their pre-service habits — like cutting somebody up for cuss-ing them.

"Well," I said "you stay in here with me." I kept shining the GI shoes.

Within a few minutes, a larger face was thrust against the open day room window.

"Where is the sonofabitch?" he shouted, "I'm gonna cut his throat."

I was right. The beer had been flowing freely that night and the face was flushed and the eyes slightly bleary.

"Now, Wilson," I said in what I hoped was a soothing voice, "you don't want to do that. If you do that I'll have to call the MP's and they'll call the officers and our whole troop will be in trouble."

I kept shining the brogans.

"Why don't you come in here and let's talk it over."

I kept shining and I kept talking. One thing I knew, these Georgia and Alabama boys were patriotic and they were intensely proud of their outfit.

"We've got a good outfit, Wilson," I said, "and we've got a good repu-tation. If you hurt Jones, you're going to hurt the whole troop. I know you don't want to do anything to hurt your buddies."

I could see that the talking was giving him time to cool down and the beer time to wear off.

"Why don't you come in here, Wilson, and shake hands. I know Jones didn't mean to insult you."

Jones chimed in enthusiastically that he certainly had meant no insult — that he had picked up some bad speaking habits from the Yankees who were our non-coms. Their mutual dislike of the Yankee non-coms did the trick. Wilson came in and shook Jones' hand and both were happy and relieved to have avoided shedding each others blood or bring-ing disgrace on the troop.

As for my shoes, they had never shone as brightly.

The next week, our Georgia and Alabama boys had gone to join the horse cavalry on the hill. I, along with Ray Johnson, John Polack, and Sam Smitthers and others, who had been selected as cadre, were assigned to another mechanized troop to finish the thirteen weeks of basic train-ing. From that time on I would be with soldiers from other parts of the US and would see very few of our Southern boys.

In the new outfit, we began our training in jeeps. This was the vehicle that would take the place of the horse in the cavalry's role as collector of intelligence by patrolling into the enemy's lines. The cavalry seemed determined to prove the jeep could do everything the horse could.

On my first trip into the field on the small vehicle, I had a lieutenant as a passenger. We were on a broad Kansas plain in grass that was about two feet tall.

"Catch that jeep!" the lieutenant shouted, pointing to another jeep about half a mile away.

Considering the fact I couldn't see the ground for the grass all around us, I set off at what I considered a brisk pace that perhaps would not result in our both being thrown from the open, top heavy little car if we hit a concealed hole.

"Damn it!" he shouted. "I said catch that jeep. Floor board this damn thing."

Since the order was direct, I followed it. We picked up to about fifty miles an hour, bouncing along blind with me praying to God that there would be no gullies or holes across our hidden path.

It was a foolish thing to do and we were fortunate not to be killed — no credit to my driving, but to pure fortune that that particular plain was level under the obscuring grass. Later, when I was over a major metropolitan police force, I found that we had similar problems with young policemen taking risks which were unnecessary for the job being done. In one case, a young police officer was killed and his partner permanently paralyzed while chasing a teenager playing around in a Volkswagen bug.

While we were at Riley, two young officers were killed driving a jeep at high speed around a sharp curve. After that, officers were instructed to let trained enlisted men do the driving.

We took the jeeps everywhere. Down banks as steep as the one that landed me on the horse's neck at the University, through mud, up the sides of ravines and fording rivers. We learned to disconnect the fan belt — the engine ran hot, but by driving very slowly through a stream, we could make it. By the end of our training, we could make the jeep do tricks that seemed dangerous to the untrained, but actually were conducted within safe limits.

I didn't know it, but my MOS — the number that describes your skill to those making army assignments was truck driver. The jeep performed more like our old model A Ford to me, but the army called it a quarter ton truck. The truck driver designation was to follow me through my brief army career and would appear on my discharge papers as the highest skill the army taught me.

Knowing that the OCS had closed and that I was to have no chance at a cavalry commission, my morale began to slip in the new outfit and I was to suffer a couple of mortifications that lowered my self esteem and raised my cynicism toward the whole system.

While I was in the dormitory at the University of Georgia, we had two transfer students housed in the room next to us. Unlike the other students, they stayed to themselves, participated in no all night poker games and were seldom seen by their fellow Joe Brown residents other than in the hall going to and from their room.

Their most offensive act was that they always kept their door shut. Since the rest of Joe Brown was open on a 24 hour basis, the students on our floor began to discuss what was being hidden in this room and why Frank and Milby were so unfriendly.

Different tactics were tried to bring the transfer students in line with the generally accepted student practices.

On one occasion, a panel of the door was kicked out so the door could be opened. What was found was a neatly arranged room with no openly illegal activity to be seen. The roommates didn't say a word. They simply neatly replaced the panel and closed the door.

Later in the fall we had a heavy, for Georgia, snow — about four inches. Now that the dormitory knew how to open Frank and Milby's door, the panel was kicked in again and a snow ball about two feet in diameter was rolled into the room and left to melt.

Again, Frank and Milby made the wrong move. Instead of kicking in somebody else's door or punching somebody's nose, they rolled the snowball out into the hall, repaired the panel and shut the door.

By this time, they were total outcasts.

Both were in advanced military and both were commissioned about the time I was drafted.

Now, in phase two of my basic, with all hopes of being commissioned gone aglimmering, I was engaged on a particular Saturday in getting ready for inspection. As an acting non-com, future cadre, I had the exalted job of supervising the cleaning of the latrine for inspection. Since the latrine received hard use during the week, this was a critical area and all the inhabitants of our barracks were atune to the heavy responsibility I was carrying. After that first four weeks, we were beginning to receive weekend passes. If one messed up, we were all liable to be confined for the weekend.

So, all worked hard and enthusiastically not to mess up and lose our weekend.

On this particular Saturday, we had concluded our bathroom chores and were standing rigidly at attention, breath bated, waiting the decision of the white gloved inspector.

"Harrison," the sergeant sang out. "Report outside."

A murmur went up and down the line.

"Oh, hell, Harrison's messed up."

"Boy, are you going to catch it," someone whispered sympathetically.

I went racing outside to where an officer was leaning languidly against the wall of the barracks.

I had my salute halfway up when I suddenly recognized Milby Maynard. Oh, for God's sake, I groaned, of all people and at what a time.

I finished the unenthusiastic salute and found myself trying to say "Sir" to Milby. We engaged in some small talk about the good old days at the University and I excused myself to go back and receive the verdict on whether our latrine had passed inspection.

It had, but my enthusiasm for the job was gone for that day and I realized with a sinking heart that I was now in no man's land. I wasn't an officer and I had lost rapport with my fellow privates.

"Hey, Harrison's in with the officers", one sneered.

Good old Milby Maynard.

The other incident occurred toward the end of our thirteen weeks of basic. John Polack, Earl and Sam all believed that there had to be a way for us to escape from the confines of the camp. On weekends, we had overnight passes that were good for only 50 miles from the camp. That meant we were limited to the thriving town of Junction City, located just outside the boundaries of Fort Riley. Anyone who went farther was subject to being picked up by the MP's.

My solution for the problem was to head for the nearest church. I was soon dating a very nice girl named Willa — a little on the plump side but then, I was only a private and the only difference between Fort Riley and Junction City was that the soldiers were more concentrated in town.

Willa and I had a good time, going to church suppers and walking up and down the Junction City sidewalks near Willa's house. On one occasion I got the shock of my religious life up to that point. Having been raised a Southern Baptist, I couldn't believe it when we were invited to a dance — at the church — on Sunday night. Standing in the church gym watching boys and girls holding each other and dancing on the sabbath, I expected lighting to strike at any moment and the whole Sodom to go up in a burst of fire and brimstone.

After that, I thought I'd seen and experienced everything — until I went out on the little stoop on the back of the church gymnasium and found the preacher enjoying the coolness along with several soldiers. When one of the GI's pulled out a bottle of whiskey and passed it to the preacher, he turned it up and took a long pull. It was a Methodist church.

For those who don't know — the Southern Methodist was required to take an oath not to let alcohol pass his lips — perhaps required is too harsh — say, expected. As for the Southern Baptist, everybody knew Baptists never drank in front of each other.

It was a shock. On one occasion, when Willa's sister and her husband were out of town and I had an overnight pass, Willa even had me spend the night with her — but if I tell about that, I'll get to lying and this book has been truthful so far.

Anyway, Junction City was not enough of a city to satisfy boys from Chicago and Earl, John and Sam were excited when they told me that the Jewish Progressive Club, in Kansas City was having a special entertainment for Fort Riley soldiers and that they had signed up for the four of us.

"We can go to Kansas City", Sam told me "and since we'll be guests of the Jewish Progressive Club we can leave Saturday morning." Our regular passes started Saturday afternoon, provided our troop passed inspection.

When the big weekend arrived, we were all excited and were anxious to do a good job cleaning the barracks so nothing would queer the deal for us.

I was in charge of cleaning the second floor and John had some good news for me. "One of the boys told me how we can make those floors white," John said, "you put chlorox in the water you use to scrub them and they'll turn white and beautiful." It sounded good to me. We got the bleach and put a heavy dose of it in our scrub buckets. Because we would be leaving in the morning, we decided to do the floors before we went to bed and give them overnight to bleach out.

The floors were beautiful. Not a troop in the CRTC would have floors like ours. They were bleached white like the driftwood decorators like to collect off the beach to use in the most expensive living rooms in the land.

We went to bed that night exhausted, but happy, and our heads were aglow with visions of Kansas City — the bright lights, the saloons, the beautiful girls.

In the case of Sam, he had arrangements to meet a divorcee. He knew from past experience he would not be wasting his time.

Earl planned to meet the girl he had been sleeping with and would some-day marry.

John and I planned to prowl around, enjoying vicariously the certain pleasures of Earl and Sam, and drinking what we could drink and seeing what we could see.

The thing we discovered the next morning was bad — terrible — awful — in two respects. First, it didn't have to happen. All we had to do was scrub the floors with clear water and everybody would have been happy.

Secondly, it revealed a flaw in my character that I didn't know was there — my face still reddens when I think about what happened that fateful Saturday morning.

The next morning, the floors were black — and the trouble was they weren't black all over — they were black in weird shapes with some of the white bleach areas surrounding the black.

And, it wasn't beautiful black — it was ugly, dirty-looking black.

We surveyed the damage with sinking hearts and rising disgust.

"Well," John said, "we've got our passes and nobody knows about this. I don't know about you, but this may be my last chance to go to Kansas City — I'm for leaving right now."

There was no question about Earl and Sam — they had dates — important once in a lifetime dates — not even a direct order from Roosevelt could have stopped them unless enforced by physical restraint.

And that's when I learned about the flaw in my character. I didn't have to go to Kansas City, I had a duty to my country, my troop and my own sense of responsibility to stay — face the music and help the other boys clean up the mess I had caused.

I failed that test of character. It is no excuse, but I thought about join-ing the cavalry in the first place, the closing of the OCS and, perhaps, most of all, the visit from Milby Maynard.

"To hell with it," I said, "let's get out of here before the inspectors ar-rive." And we walked away from the troop area knowing there would be hell to pay on our return.

Occasionally, crime does pay handsomely; and, that weekend, stolen by walking away from responsibility, was memorable. Certainly, it enriched my early Army experience, taught me something about my buddies, and relieved the tedium of drill, sweat and exhaustion.

In the end, the sergeant gave me the opportunity to make full restitution for my lapse, so even my conscience is clear today.

We were on the train by 11 a. m. and had soon forgotten the existence of Fort Riley, the CRTC and our buddies who were about to catch hell for what we (really I — I was the one who got the bleach and added it to the scrub water) had done.

With their big city experience and businesslike approach, John and Sam had reserved us a room in one of the largest and finest of the KC hotels. Divided four ways, the cost of the first class accommodations was well within our GI budget. The government was paying each of us $50 a month and the room — rented as a double — probably cost less than $10.

There were twin beds which we promptly stripped of coverings so that the hotel would look like the barracks and we would feel at home.

Sam and Earl planned to meet their girls elsewhere later in the evening and would use the room to change and for headquarters until that event occurred.

On the train, we had decided that the Jewish Progressive Club would have all they could handle for the weekend, that by not going to the party we would be providing more for our fellow GI's who were entertained by that worthy organization — and besides — we doubted anybody would check.

Immediately after cleaning up from the train ride, having a fresh shave, shower and cologne, Sam, who no longer didn't give a damn, set out with spirits high and the joy of anticipation in his bouncy step to find his divorcee. Ray, with a quieter joy not unmixed with reservations brought about by his knowledge no decision about the future had been reached, left to find his girl.

I felt sorry for Earl. He obviously loved the girl, felt guilty because he had not married her, but also felt he shouldn't do so because he might be killed or maimed in the coming months. The wages of sin is death and Earl was paying those wages in overtime.

All of us had a couple of drinks, ordered through room service, before we split up and after a great deal of hilarity over the long hours of freedom stretching ahead of us, we finally parted. Our train back to camp did not leave until 3:30 p.m. the following Sunday afternoon and we planned to utilize the time to its fullest.

John and I went to the first of several bars, had a few drinks, then a steak supper at a fine restaurant. We might not have rank or decoration, but we both knew how to talk. With the war in full swing, we were soon impressing the bar flies, as we GI's called the girls who came, usually in pairs, to the KC saloons. Actually, we told one pair we were high ranking officers disguised in the uniforms of privates and on a secret mission to ferret out secret agents, also disguised as American GI's in the KC area. We had plenty of decorations for valor, but had left them back at headquarters because of the assignment, etc.

Or, we were the sons of wealthy families who had joined the service as privates to learn how the common soldiers lived, etc.

About 10 p.m. we checked by the hotel lobby to see if there was any word from Sam and Earl. Nothing from Earl, so we assumed he was with his girl as planned. John had a note from Sam to call him at a certain number.

By some strange quirk of fate, Sam, who was giving a bigger damn by the minute, had failed to make contact with his divorcee. He wanted to know if there was any message at our hotel. He was waiting at the hotel where he was to meet her, but there was no sign of her. There was desperation in his voice, John said, and he was about to start making a round of the bars to see if he could find her. He said he would call us at our hotel every two hours and John agreed we'd be at the lobby pay phone at the agreed time.

John and I set out again, seeking new bar flies to impress and enlarging on our stories as the evening progressed and the alcoholic fog grew more and more dense.

Each two hours, we were back at the pay phone. John's voice was beginning to slur badly, but each time he reported that Sam sounded cold sober, that his fury against the fates was waxing and that he was giving such a big damn his middle name was about to lose its validity.

This went on all night and into the morning. When Sam called about 10 a.m. Sunday, we were back in the room grabbing some sleep. John said he was really worried about Sam. He thought Sam was cracking and he was becoming incoherent.

There was also word from Ray — I answered that one and the bliss in his voice assured me that in at least one small corner in KC all was right with the world. Ray may have spent the night in sin, but for the moment no wages were due and his joy came through the hotel phone as total.

So it went. About 2 p.m. Ray reported back to the room, a silly grin dominating his face. It was obvious that after a little rest, Ray would be ready to take on Hirohito and Hitler simultaneously.

There had been no word from Sam since the 10 a. m. conversation. The phone rang.

It was Sam.

"I found her," Sam was speaking rapidly, "She checked in the wrong hotel."

Sam sounded like he was about to hang up.

"Sam," I shouted, "our train leaves in an hour and a half."

"Clark," Sam said in his best don't give a damn voice, "Your train is leaving in an hour and a half — my train is leaving in the morning."

Every man has his price. There is a point at which even the most righteous will show a moment of weakness. I had discovered my breaking point the day before when I walked away from my buddies, innocent as they were, guilty as I was, leaving them to face the wrath of the sergeant over the blackened floors.

Now, I knew that Sam was human as well. There were things, or at least one thing — for which Sam fervently did give a damn and for which he was prepared, without hesitation — to throw aside honor, duty and devotion to comrades.

"We'll see you tomorrow, Sam," I said into the dead phone.

It was a memorable weekend. And, after all these years, I find the flaw in my character still remains. I wouldn't go back now and change a thing.

When we got back to the barracks late that Sunday evening, my worst fears had become reality. The Army, inconsistent in many things, had come through with a vengeance in a matter with which it understood so well how to deal. In these basic training days, the guilt of one imputed to the entire troop. And the sin of blackened floors was cardinal and recompense cried out to be made at once and immediately, if not sooner.

Not being able to get their hands on the acting non-com in charge and chief culprit — me — the Army made do with the souls that were available — my erstwhile buddies.

Immediately on discovering the blackened floors, the troop was issued brushes and all leaves for the troop were canceled for the weekend. In waves, the cavalrymen were sent against the blackened floors — the water flowed, the brushes waxed hot from the friction, as this went on far into Saturday night. While we reveled in the fleshpots of KC, the loyal stay at homes labored in the heat and humidity of the ruined Saturday Fort Riley evening to return the ruined floors to their government issue uniformity. As the sun was rising Sunday morning and we were stumbling back toward our luxurious hotel room, these comrades were finally allowed to cease their labor and the result of my errant leadership was declared corrected.

Now, it was my turn to face the hostile troops. Already, suspicious of me as "friendly with the officers" thanks to my visit from Milby Maynard, I was now persona non grata and sullen faces turned the other way as I walked into the barracks effecting a slight limp in a forlorn attempt to gain sympathy and understanding.

After being informed of what had happened during my absence, I was told "The sergeant wants to see you."

Only then were a few sly looks directed my way to see how I would react.

I was in enough trouble having caused the problem in the first place and my coming disaster was to be enhanced by the fact I was in far away KC enjoying myself during their punishment.

There obviously wasn't much I could say at that point that would help either their situation or mine. So, with a heavy, if satiated heart, I knocked lightly on the door to the sergeant's private room at the end of the barracks.

He was a good sergeant. In my mind not on a par with Red, but definitely a good sergeant, wise for his years in dealing with raw recruits and turning them into soldiers. He was a small, dark man named Sergeant Dracolean.

"Harrison," he said as I entered the room, "we have had a problem in your absence and we cannot help but feel that you are responsible."

As a result of my actions, he explained quietly, and somewhat sadly, the whole troop had had to suffer. They were not allowed to go to Junction City Saturday night but, instead, had to spend the night scrubbing away my mistake.

"We cannot help but feel," Sergeant Dracolean continued, "that you have let us down, Harrison."

I couldn't have agreed with him more.

"Now," he continued, "I like you, Harrison. I really do. And I believe you have the makings of a good acting corporal — even, who knows, someday, a full corporal. But right now you have a problem and, since I am your sergeant, it is my duty to point out what that problem is and to try to help you correct that problem."

I was enjoying the friendly, helpful chat with the sergeant, but I was also looking forward to its conclusion at the earliest possible time.

"Harrison," the sergeant concluded, "sometimes words will do the job in a situation like this, but in this particular case, I believe more than words are called for. Next weekend, we have our biggest inspection of basic training. Harrison, this time I want you to remain on the premises of the Fort for the weekend and I want you to be an important part of that inspection. Harrison, Friday evening after you get in from the field, I would like for you to report to the kitchen."

The week's training seemed especially strenuous. For one thing, the heat was increasing as we moved into June in the Kansas flats. We would sweat all day in the broiling sun, taking salt pills with our breakfast each morning.

I remember one morning in particular.

That hot summer morning, I decided to wash my salt pill down with the cup of hot coffee we had been served. Instead of washing down it melted in the part of the esophagus that has feeling. I still remember the gagging, hurting, nauseous feeling.

Each evening, we'd hang up our khaki coveralls, wet with sweat, to let them dry before stuffing them into our barracks bags to be sent to the laundry.

That June, in Kansas, the coveralls would dry and show white salt that had poured out of our sweat glands during the day. I did a lot of sweating after leaving Kansas, but never again in my army career would I see that white salt making outlines on my combat fatigues.

Friday evening after a full workout in the Kansas sun, I reported to the kitchen immediately after chow as the sergeant had requested.

It was soon apparent that the sergeant had given special instructions to the mess sergeant concerning me.

"Tomorrow is a really big inspection," the mess sergeant told me. "We have never failed this particular inspection and we will not fail tomorrow. Of utmost importance is that our pots and pans shine — and shine all over. It will be your responsibility that they so shine, and, in the interest of time, I suggest you start now. The inspection is at 1000 hours in the morning."

At that point, I was directed to the largest pots the Army possessed as standard equipment. Standing some four feet high and nearly three feet in diameter, it was literally necessary to crawl inside them to accomplish my assignment.

The blush of shame I had felt toward my beloved comrades the Sunday before was soon replaced by a sweaty blush of exertion as I boiled, then washed, then steel wooled every inch of the huge pots. Spurred on by the opportunity to exonerate myself from the guilt I felt toward the troop, I began to perform like my earlier friends, the good old Georgia and Alabama country boys. As I sweated and strained my soul strained for release from the load of guilt that had weighed on me from the weekend before.

At 12 p.m., or 2400 hours as the Army so quaintly designated time, the mess sergeant spoke to me.

"Harrison," he said, "you had better get some rest so you'll be fresh to put on the finishing touches before the inspection in the morning."

Gratefully, I fell into my bunk, blissful as the Elysian Fields in my state of total exhaustion. I was asleep instantly.

It seemed like no time at all, in fact, it was no time at all when a rough hand shook my shoulder.

"Let's go, Harrison," the hoarse whisper said, "be quiest, so you won't wake up any of these hard working boys."

It was now 0400 hours and I had had all of three and a half hours sleep.

Back into my pots I climbed, mindless, using a desperation stroke on the shining and huge pots.

At 1000 hours on the dot, they dragged my body out of the last pot, stood me up and pointed to a rear door as the inspecting officers were heard coming in the front of the mess hall.

"You can't go back to the barracks because they're being inspected," the mess sergeant whispered, "and you're dirty and smelly — go hide somewhere."

Once again God was in His heaven and all was right in the world. Restitution had been made and my buddies began to include me in their conversations once again.

Best of all, I knew in my heart there was a glimmer of justice in this strange Army world. Sam, giving the biggest kind of damn, had made it back to camp in the early hours of that Monday morning, late but unreported and unpunished.

John Polack had explained the situation to the sergeant — the one he called "Sir."

CHAPTER VI

Clint, the man who taught me to fly, is a perfectionist. His eight years in the Air Force included flying the hottest intercepter we had at the time, the F-102.

Clint flew the west coast, guarding the ADIZ I had to cross just after I took off on this trip from Escondido.

He left the service only because they had found out he was good at other things and he was spending too much time behind a desk.

Now, he flies every day as an instructor and with Clint it doesn't much matter what it is — just so it will fly.

He especially enjoyed trying to teach a 55 year old high level paraplegic.

"You must strive for perfection, Clark," he would tell me, "you won't make it but you won't ever be good if you don't try to be perfect."

"What you must realize, Clint," I would counter, "not only am I a 55 year old high-level paraplegic, I am also an ex-politician.

"You are asking me to be precise," I continued. "For eight years, ten years counting the time I spent running, I was in a business where if you got precise you were dead. Precision comes back to haunt the politician. Generalities and a certain vagueness are the thing. I am a big picture man."

"You may be a big picture man," Clint would retort, "but right now you'd better think small — little things like keeping your air speed up and your nose down. You start looking at the big picture and let your nose creep up and your air speed drop and this airplane will fall out of the sky. Then, you'll really be dead."

Day after day, we would fly out to the practice area, climb to 4000 feet and do the same exercises over and over again. We would do approach to landing stalls, power on stalls, slow flight, and acceleration stalls.

The problem is that if the nose is raised too high for the speed of the airplane the wind over the wing that creates lift will break up into eddies and the wing will drop.

If the pilot knows what to do when his nose starts falling after the stall, it's no problem. Just push the yoke forward and apply power and the wing will start to fly again. Of course, if the plane is too close to the ground when the stall occurs, the ground may be struck thereby ending the recovery. So, it is critical not to stall out too near the ground.

The natural reaction of the untrained novice is to pull back on the yoke once the nose starts to fall following the stall. When he does that, without the wings exerting lift, the plane will fall off into a spin.

The Wright brothers survived long enough to learn to control their first powered airplane because they had providentially placed the elevator in front of the airplane instead of in the more efficient rear position that later became standard. Because the elevator, which acted as a small wing, was in the front, it kept the plane from nosing in while they worked to regain control following the stall.

"I can't teach you to fly," Clint would say. "All I can hope to do is keep you alive long enough for you to teach yourself to fly."

I was to learn the value of the training regarding stalls that Clint pounded into me. It would happen on a return trip from Lynchburg, Virginia — completed on the leading edge of a thunderstorm.

In the summer of 1943, I was learning other lessons on the flat, hot plains around Junction City, Kansas.

The "All American" football team I had left at the University would have felt right at home with the troop I was now in. Polish, Italian and Jewish names predominated with not one Smith, Jones or Brown in the lot.

It was an education for me. In those days before television, the accents were heavy and the behavior strange to a boy from Georgia. Once I got to know these Yankees on a personal level, I found much to admire.

A couple of New Yorkers — from Manhatten — made a strong impression.

One was a very short, compactly built man — he must not have been much over 5 feet — I can't remember his name.

His knowledge had come from the streets of New York. He must have been older than the rest of us — perhaps near 30. He had a constant line of chatter, stories to tell, and a philosophy — he was street wise.

His specialty was playing spoons — with three or four spoons grasped between the fingers of his hand and using his other hand and his thigh, he could produce an impressive volume of perfect rhythm.

He was aggressive and never stood back when there was an argument or a foe to confront. Once, a group of soldiers were in the rec hall just gassing away on a Saturday after inspection and before the passes were to be issued for the weekend. For some unknown reason, a soldier walked in and mounted the stage at the end of the hall. He had been drinking and he was waving his arms and shouting.

"Gimme a rock, I gotta have a rock."

I was outside the rec hall when Whitey, one of the few southern country boys in the outfit came charging out of the side door.

He picked up a stone about the size of a grapefruit that was used to line the walkway to the building. Shouting murder and waving his long arms he ran back into the hall.

Lined up in front of the stage facing the drunken soldier were a dozen GI's, including our small friend, the spoon player. Together with Whitey and his rock, the small New Yorker, waving a wooden straight-backed chair above his head, charged the stage just as an officer coming to investigate the noise, came from the building and entered the front door.

Unable to make himself heard, the officer drew his pistol and fired into the ceiling. By this time the spoon player had knocked the drunk soldier to the floor with his chair and Whitey was standing over him, the big rock suspended high above his head by a long, rugged arm ready to smash the skull of the culprit.

Of course, no passes were issued that weekend.

But the thing that impressed me most about this man, the spoon player, and the other New Yorkers was their self discipline and the way they looked for and lived by rules. Where I came from, we had a code based on telling the truth, honoring and protecting women, paying your debts, etc.

But this was different. The New Yorker was aggressive but he was also very conscious of the rights of others and he would go so far and then hold off. He could fight but he didn't do so unless attacked or without good reason. He recognized the rights of others and confined his own activities to allow room for others to act.

I thought about this a great deal and concluded that the crowded conditions in the huge metropolis made such a code of conduct mandatory. I came to admire it, to try to emulate it — and it served me well in the remaining days in the Army and since. Respect the other man — don't drive him into a corner where he has to fight.

Then there was Frizzola — a short stocky Italian, he was always in a good humor — always friendly and he spoke with a heavy accent.

In the South, every boy started driving when he was sixteen. Your main aim in life was to acquire an automobile and to drive it everywhere. True, my use of a car had been limited at the University, but certainly that would be my first acquisition when I left the service.

It came as a shock to realize that most people in New York didn't own a car and probably never would. In fact, they didn't know how to drive.

Frizzola was beaming all over when he said, "I didn't know how to drive — and they have made me a chauffeur!"

There was Banana Nose — he brought the name with him from Italian Brooklyn and wore it proudly. "I know my enemies, but God save me from my friends," Banana Nose would proclaim loudly.

As I came to know these young men from the middle west and the northeast, I began to like, to trust, and to admire them. The differences began to fade and we all became soldiers together.

And I began to have more confidence in myself and in my ability to cope with new and strange experiences.

The rifle range showed me that I could fire a rifle with reasonable accuracy. Except for one dumb error, I would have made sharpshooter — not as good as expert, but better than the qualifying marksman.

When we moved back to 200 yards for rapid fire, we were to add clicks of elevation to our sight. I counted my clicks carefully and fired the sixteen rounds at the distant target. A range officer came running over shouting, "Who is the dummy who didn't run his sight down — you just fired sixteen rounds over the target — you put your clicks on top of what you already had on the sight."

There was no second chance since so many men were being run through the range and time and ammunition were limited. Even with those sixteen shots wasted, I qualified.

I found out that rage would help me when I reached a life threatening situation. I had learned to curb my temper in the crowded army conditions but I let it go on the pistol range.

One smart-talking GI, standing beside me on the short pistol range, started swinging his 45 from side to side while jabbering a lot of foolish talk.

"You point that thing down the range," I yelled, "and you keep it pointed down the range or I'll kick your butt."

He quieted down and began to treat the weapon with the respect it deserved.

The infiltration course taught me how rage can build when life is threatened.

Designed to simulate actual battle field conditions, the infiltration course measured probably one hundred yards in length from the point where we lined up in a standing trench, then crawled over the top to start creeping and crawling through mud and under barbed wire toward the distant machine guns that were firing live ammunition just above our heads.

As we snaked along, cussing as our jackets or pants snagged on the barbed wire, explosive charges were set off in our near vicinity.

Finally, bathed in dirty sweat from the 100 degree Kansas weather, we reached a point right in front of the machine guns that were providing our incentive for staying low and dirty. They stopped to let us up.

I found myself charging with fixed bayonet and the intent to kill that cool son of a bitch behind the 30 calibre, water cooled, World War I machine gun.

I noticed with some small satisfaction that he flinched slightly as the bayonet whistled past him.

There were deaths. The officers who turned over the jeep driving it like a Porsche around a sharp curve have been mentioned. Then one afternoon we heard sirens going out and around the dyke to the infiltration course. We heard that one of the explosive charges had been set off when a GI was lying on top of it.

As the summer grew hotter and more humid, we heard that two Puerto Ricans had died of heat exhaustion.

The big tragedy for Fort Riley that year was to come toward the end of our thirteen weeks of basic and was to teach me that my instinct for survival was intact.

It was a Saturday, after inspection and while we were waiting for our passes. Most of us were in the barracks, milling around, swapping stories and generally soldiering in the time honored way.

I went outside when somebody yelled the sky was looking funny. I looked toward the west across the flat land.

I had never seen a tornado — I don't believe I'd ever even seen a picture. But looking there at the black cloud with its descending funnel, there was no doubt — and instant recognition — that a tornado was headed our way.

We had had a tornado when I was in grammar school in Gainesville, Georgia, some fifty miles from where we were. I remember the strange yellowish cast to the sky. We learned later that downtown Gainesville had been obliterated. I knew the devastation that could occur.

I took one long look at the black funnel and decided it was headed our way. I also decided that around the massed wooden barracks was one place I didn't want to be.

With the raising I had had and with Dad's admonitions, I never found it necessary to be in the middle of a crowd in order to feel secure.

The black funnel was getting more broad as I began to run toward the dyke — some three hundred yards away. As I ran, I passed several soldiers who were wisely lying in slit trenches that had been dug between the barracks and the dyke as a part of training.

Before I got to the dyke, it started to rain — huge drops such as I had not seen before. I picked up speed and raced up the steep slope of the dyke. Crossing over the top, I threw myself in a prone position just below the crest. I figured I'd be safe here . There were no buildings or machines between the dyke and the river. Once safe, I sure wanted to see that tornado and what it would do.

Looking back, I had a good view of the barracks. I was intrigued by what I saw. With little knowledge of nature and none of tornados, my barracks buddies were reacting with herd instinct. First, as a group, they would run into the yard — look up — then, as a mob rush back into the barracks. In a few seconds, they would emerge and repeat the same pattern. This happened several times. Finally, they ran back into the building and stayed.

About this time, I heard a sound like the splitting of tons of kindling wood in the near distance. Then the funnel apparently lifted. As I watched, it passed directly over our barracks with the only disturbance a swirling of air in a gentle funnel that tipped over garbage cans, and ripped a few shingles off the roof, and swirled newspapers to mark the vortex of the funnel. Its force dissipated for the moment as it rose and passed over.

That evening the single telegraph office on the base was jammed with soldiers trying to let their families know how they had survived the tornado. The tornado had made the national news.

Next day, I walked over to the part of the camp that had been struck by the tornado and from which the splintering wood sound had come.

About two hundred soldiers, in the area waiting for the Saturday inspection, had been injured and it was apparent why the toll was so high. The full force of the rampaging tornado had struck in the area of temporary, tar paper barracks and smashed, torn and heaved them into ten blocks of devastation. The bunks, stoves, bedding and general Army paraphernalia were exposed to the full view of the curious in the bright morning sun.

Our troop had been spared, huddling in our permanent barracks be-cause the storm decided to lift a few blocks from our street.

Right after the storm, our thirteen week basic ended and most of the trainees were sent to assignments in one of the cavalry units being formed across the country.

To my dismay, I was left at the CRTC. I was assured by the sergeant that I was cadre, would be made a non-com and would be training troops. It was not so.

The next two or three weeks would be among the most disillusioning I was to spend in the Army.

When we fell out the first morning in the new troop, I knew I was in trouble.

For one thing, nobody said anything about me being cadre or a non-com. In fact, as far as I could see, I was just another trainee about to go through basic again — so much for my five years of ROTC and my influential officer friends.

For another, this was probably the worst led and the worst loused up troop in the continental United States. The top sergeant was a left over from the old army where he was probably all of a Pfc during his prior fifteen years of soldiering. His address to the troops was spent in extolling the virtues of the old Army, how tough it was, how many men he had run over the hill for insubordination. It wasn't that he was tough, it was more that he was stupid and apparently proud of it.

The mess sergeant was equally talented and had succeeded in taking the good, wholesome food taken away from the suffering civilians and making it taste so bad it was even hard for a bitter and experienced soldi-er to describe it.

But these two were not adequate preparation for what came next. Ap-parently, the powers that be had decided to upgrade the CRTC by send-ing every goofed up non-com and officer to this woe begone outfit.

The crowning glory on top of this weird concoction of misfits was the commanding officer.

He looked like an officer, had the bars of a captain and dark swarthy looks of a he man. The only problem was the captain was a drunk. And, apparently, he didn't bother to limit his drunkeness to off duty hours. In fact, he reported drunk and stayed in that happy condition until time came to leave the troops and go to the officer's club to get drunker.

The first time we went into the field to prepare ourselves for the rigors of combat, he sauntered out and announced:

"Well, boys," he hiccuped loudly, "we're out here to practice creeping and crawling. I want you men to creep and crawl vigorously for ten minutes — then take a fifty minute break. Hick!"

Lord, God, I thought. So this is the culmination of my dreams of serving the country.

It didn't take me long to make up my mind.

As soon as we were dismissed I struck out for Classification.

Classification was a power center in the Army. They decided where we peons were sent once our training was concluded.

Located in a single-story office building a few blocks from our training area, Classification was occupied for the most part by clerks who ran steel rods through the holes on top of file folders in cabinets that held the records of the trainees. If they needed cooks, they ran the rod through the holes on top of the file folders that contained cooks. If they needed mechanics, ditto for mechanics.

I went up to one of the clerks busily deciding the fate of hundreds of soldiers training at the base.

"Hello," I said "I've got to get out of here."

"What did you say?" The GI looked over his shoulder at me with a puzzled expression.

"If I don't get out of this fouled up outfit I'm in, I'm going to go crazy," I said with emphasis.

He explained he was sympathetic but really he was only a clerk who ran the steel probes through the folders in accordance with instructions.

"I know that," I said "All I want you to do is stick my folder in the next batch that leaves this hell hole."

He remonstrated again as to why that was impossible. Finally, after using every argument from my desire to enter combat to a plea to save my sanity I left, talking to myself.

The next day was a carbon of the day before, with one exception. Word had gotten to the sergeant that one of the men had gone to Classification.

"By God," he shouted "I better not ever hear of one of my men going to Classification or by God, he'll be sorry. I'll run his ass over the hill when I catch him. In the old Army, by God, etc., etc."

As soon as we were dismissed at the end of the day, I set out at a brisk walk, past the sergeant, headed for Classification.

I had decided that my ass, given a choice, would definitely prefer going over the hill, whatever that meant, to spending any more time with this bunch of turkeys.

"Sir," I said to the private clerk, "in the name of God and humanity, run that probe through my file and send me somewhere, anywhere. I have only one request, do it now before I start pounding my head against your filing cabinet."

The clerk looked at me with a quizzical look — apparently he had never seen a case exactly like mine and he decided to break the tedium of the day.

"You know they know you are over here."

I nodded my head vigorously.

"What did you say your name and number are?" I gave him that and the fact I was through basic and qualified as a jeep driver.

"Harrison," he said with a glitter in his eye, "you are probably giving up a great career here at CRTC, but I'll see what I can do."

A couple of days later, I was on a train headed for Washington State, praising the clerk whose obvious intelligence and humanity and sense of humor I had apparently touched in my desperate plea.

It was July and every click of the wheels was like a song taking me away from those hot, humid flats and that mentor of the old army.

CHAPTER VII

Stalls in an airplane at any altitude can lead to a spin. When this occurs while close to the ground, and especially while preparing to land, there is no time to recover and a fatal accident is the result.

So, it is critical when in the traffic pattern preparing to land to keep the nose down and the air speed fast enough to avoid stalling.

"Fly the airplane," Clint would admonish, "and then talk on the radio. A lot of accidents occur because the pilot is distracted and trying to follow radio instructions. Follow the instructions, but first be sure the airplane is under control."

So, we practiced, practiced, and practiced until pushing the nose down, and applying the power, became a reflex on the first sign of an impending stall.

The particular day when I was to learn first hand, the hard way, about avoiding stalls, and about flying the plane without being rattled by radio instruction, started in peace and beauty.

The flight back to DeKalb-Peachtree promised to be uneventful in the early stages all the way to the mountain range just north of Gainesville, Georgia. There was mention by the flight service man, who gave me a weather briefing prior to departure, that clouds and possibly rain would move into the Atlanta area sometime late in the day.

I was off the ground by 1:37 p. m. into a sparkling blue sky. It's known as CAVU — ceiling and visibility unlimited. I had filed for 6500 and was climbing at better than 500 feet per minute as I headed southwest toward Georgia. The beautiful lake at Lynchburg, Virginia, where my nephew was to sail his new boat later in the day, slid under my plane.

I had delivered my sister, Novena, to Lynchburg the previous day for a visit with her son, Clark, and his wife, Carol.

93

Flying along the eastern foothills of the Blue Ridge Mountains, I was looking down at farms in the flat lands below and checking my navigation both by radio and by the expressways, railroads, and lakes below.

The Smoky Mountains of North Carolina earned their name because of the blue clouds that surround their peaks most days out of the year. As they came in sight, I saw the smoke of those clouds and, checking my charts, saw the ridge north of Gainesville that I would cross. The highest elevation was 5700 feet and with skies beginning to darken more as I flew farther south, I increased my altitude to 8500. In case I was in those clouds when I crossed the ridge, I wanted as much distance as possible between my Cherokee and those heavily forested peaks.

Coming across the ridge, I found the skies darker and the clouds lower as I neared the Georgia line. I turned my radio to Peachtree's automatic terminal information service to check on conditions there.

The recording reported a 7000 foot ceiling, visibility five miles with light rain.

So, I was going to land in light rain, a new experience.

In the summer of 1944, I was inundated with new experiences.

Washington State is cool all the time and foggy on most mornings. After the oppressive heat and the sterile flats, it was also beautiful to see. I had been sent, all alone through the benevolence of the unknown clerk just as far as I could be sent from the CRTC. Perhaps he was fulfilling a fantasy of his own in giving me the break — offering this service to a stranger with the hope that a benign fate would someday send him winging westward as well.

Fort Lewis was the name of the main post. Again, I was assigned to a newly built Camp Whiteside consisting of the same two story barracks. But instead of the torrid Fort Riley flats, this camp was located in a beautiful forest. The nearest thing to it I have seen was in the Walt Disney cartoon movie "Snow White." The trees were huge and the sun shafted down through the heavy foliage in occaional broad and beautiful beams that lit the ferns and moss covered rocks that made up the forest floor. In the distance was snow capped Mount Rainier, a huge white cone, standing alone , and, on foggy days, seeming to float above the clouds that hugged the earth all around.

It never got warm. Here, in July and August, we wore wool uniforms. Every morning there was fog, and at times, it was so thick it was impossible to see the adjoining barracks a few feet away.

During my days in the army prior to combat, it always intrigued me that the army traveled at two paces. On the one hand, there was feverish activity with man-killing physical work and danger. On the other, there were jobs that involved absolutely no work, no strain, and no tension; and, in fact, very little activity of any kind.

Suddenly, I found myself, through the vagaries of fate and the clerk's steel probe, involved in the latter category of army employment.

With my five years of ROTC, two years of college, it was decided by someone to give me an executive type position that should have led rather quickly to a promotion to corporal. I should have been ecstatic.

In the first place, I really didn't have much in the way of a boss. My position, it couldn't really be called anything as mundane as a job, was to be in charge of the motor pool. With the thousands of dollars in six-by-six trucks, half tracks and jeeps, it obviously entailed a great deal of responsibility; but, at the same time, unless somebody made off with a major portion of the equipment, there wasn't much to do in the way of reporting to a superior. My platoon sergeant was a good-hearted man who had secured his position by getting to the new outfit a few weeks ahead of the rest of the men. He apparently wasn't sure what my duties were, but since I had responsiblity for all that equipment, it was obvious I couldn't participate in drilling maneuvers and the things the other men were doing.

The truth of the matter is I didn't know what they were doing. As soon as I got to the camp, I was made motor pool supervisor, and so, I never got to find out.

My duties, important as they were, did not put a great deal of strain on me. To give you a rundown, gentle reader, I will outline a typical day.

In the morning I would go to the mess hall. Since I had my own assignment for the day, I didn't have to fall out or line up. I had to get right on the job.

After a leisurely breakfast of grapefruit, a couple of eggs cooked to order, some hash browns and a big mug of coffee, I would saunter out of the mess hall, pick up the morning paper from the vending machine and amble toward the motor pool.

Now, the real work began. I would go into the office, get a supply of forms, and stand behind the counter.

Since I was dealing with truck drivers, the rush that followed was not really all that hectic and certainly something that I, with my solid military and college background, could handle.

After a while a truck driver would wander in.

"Where you going today?" I would ask.

"Today, I'm picking up garbage," he would say in a casual, off hand manner.

"Okay," I would say "you can take truck no. 17394. Sign here."

Recognizing the tone of authority in my voice he would straighten slightly, step one half pace forward, take the pencil and either sign his name or make a big "X" — in which case I would print his name under the "X."

And so it went. Obviously, at this pace we would soon have the Japs and the Germans on the run. Then, we could all go home and celebrate.

After I had issued ten or so trip tickets, the pace let up. In fact, other than watching to be sure none of the trucks or half tracks rolled off, I didn't have anything to do — not until about 1700 hours (5 p.m.) when the trip tickets would be returned and I was free to amble over to the mess hall and have a leisurely dinner before retiring for the evening.

No drilling, no falling out, no training, no nothing.

I was about to go berserk.

The only consolation — I was not alone.

Gregory had been drafted from Stanford University after his second year. An Armenian, he was probably the best soldier I met during my time in the army — including even Sergeant Red.

Gregory had tried to join the Marine Corp but had been turned down because of a large burn scar on his abdomen — a result of a childhood accident. He loved the military, had gone through ROTC and knew every major battle the US had ever engaged in, understood every concept of strategy and was totally dedicated to fighting — intelligently — for his country.

So, Gregory was assigned to drive a jeep for a captain who had been a couple of years ahead of him at Stanford. This made Gregory a little bitter. I was convinced if by some miracle the army would suddenly become intelligent enough to make Gregory a general and put him in charge of the Army, we would shorten the war.

It was a pleasure to listen to Gregory. He even made me believe that by changing some things the army could begin to make sense.

I learned after the war that, although Gregory never made general, he did make sergeant and he did get into combat, which was what he was living for. The Fourteenth Cavalry Group ended up in Europe. Gregory was driving a half track and, in one action, drove repeatedly into an area of heavy fire, dismounted, loaded, and evacuated wounded.

He was recommended for the Congressional Medal of Honor and received the next highest award.

Gregory and I whiled away many tedious hours in the motor pool devising ways to improve the Army and win the war.

Willie was the one friend I made in the Army whom I still see and enjoy today. We lost contact for about twenty years or so, but Willie lives near me now and we get together regularly.

Today, Willie is one of the top agronomists in the Federal government, being responsible for the management of vast governmental holdings from Georgia to Alaska and Hawaii. It is a dream of a job, and now that Willie and Jo's seven children are grown, they travel extensively as he discharges his responsibilities.

Willie's wife and children didn't know it until I told them (at first, Willie, himself, acted like he didn't know what I was talking about), but in 1943, in Washington State, Willie was a dog robber.

Willie was in the same boat with Gregory and myself. He had been in the horse cavalry at Texas A&M, had been drafted just before he started advanced ROTC, and had ended up, courtesy of the Fort Riley clerk's steel probe, in Washington State. The problem was Willie didn't have the good fortune to end up in an executive position like myself, or even the gentility of chauffeuring a former schoolmate in a jeep. Fate, by some cruel twist, had assigned Willie as an orderly in the officers' barracks. Try to imagine a Texas Aggie, just one quarter away from doning the shiny cavalry boots, ending up as house boy to officers a few months ahead of himself at A&M.

Willie was more bitter than Gregory and me put together.

"The only way I could get even," Willie cracked years later, "was to drink their whiskey."

Well, Willie and I got to be fast friends. After chow, we'd talk for hours about home and about the rotten luck we'd had and how we were going to get even with the bastards.

"Clark," Willie exclaimed one evening, "Let's apply for the air corps. I bet we can both get in."

I agreed that anything that would get us to doing something more profitable than motor pooling and dog robbing would have to be an improvement. Next day we went over and filled out the papers.

My time at Camp Whiteside was relatively brief — about two months — but because at age eighteen I thought I had reached a bitter dead end, it seemed like an eternity at the time. It taught me some valuable lessons that have served me well in the years following. A few years ago my wife and I were to go into a rural community for an important family event. I overheard her talking to a recent acquaintance.

"My husband," she said, "is the kind of person who can meet anyone and feel at ease."

That would not have been so without those months in the Army.

There was one incident that occurred at Camp Whiteside that made me ashamed of myself and that still brings a blush when I think about it today.

Our platoon sergeant was a slow moving, stumbling sort of man who had entered the army a couple of months before I did. Since the Fourteenth was a new activation of an old outfit, he had lucked into an early promotion. Willie and I took great delight in talking about him, laughing at his ignorance of military matters and inept efforts to control the newly organized troop. Finally, one day I said or did something that went too far. The sergeant had always been good to us and had made the mistake of showing respect for the fact we were educated and had some ROTC background. Instead of appreciating his efforts to help us, we poked fun at him and made his job harder.

"Harrison," he finally said. "I want to talk to you. I know you've been to college and have had some opportunities most people don't have. But that's no reason for you to shirk your duties. Why don't you get yourself straightened out."

He was right. I had grown lazy and in concentrating on what had happened to me, I had forgotten that other people had their problems too.

He shamed me and I never poked fun at him again. Other things that were to happen during my army experience taught me to have respect for all people regardless of their background.

Later, my life was saved by a boy with no background at all.

With my pay at $50 a month, I was putting $18.75 into a savings bond and with insurance and other deductions, I had about $22 to spend each month. Generally, that meant two weekends in town before the money ran out and I was reduced to borrowing 15 cents to go to a movie on the base.

Willie and I started going to town together where we would have a beer or two and, if lucky, find a girl who would talk with us. I remember one girl in particular. She was a co-ed at one of the nearby colleges and she reminded us of girls we had known at the University and A&M.

"I have to be very careful who I am seen with," she told us, sitting in a drug store where we were having a coke. "With the war on, this is a serviceman's town — lots of sailors as well as soldiers. If I were seen dating an enlisted man, my reputation would be ruined."

Willie looked at me and I looked at him — actually, we agreed with her and decided we might as well quit thinking about college girls until our fortunes changed. It was a strange feeling to think that there were people who thought of us, because we were army privates, as being less than desireable as social peers. I began to understand how someone could begin to feel inferior if marked by a uniform — or color.

It wasn't a bad thing to learn.

About this time, Willie and I discovered the USO. They had an active organization in Seattle to help sevicemen by providing entertainment and an opportunity for them to get to know the local people. Through the USO, we got an invitation to go on a yacht trip on Puget Sound.

Mr. Smith was a grey haired, slender gentleman, probably in his fifties, who was an engineer of some sort and who apparently spent most of his working day at a desk.

His home, which we visited, and his auto indicated that the family was of modest means. His yacht, which he based at a marina on Puget Sound, was his one indulgence.

He had asked the USO to send him four servicemen and he and his wife had invited an equal number of attractive young girls to make the trip with us.

We rode the bus to his house and found it a pleasant suburban home on a tree shaded lot. We found Mr. Smith busy in last minute preparations for our trip later that Sunday afternoon.

What we were to witness was to be a navigation competition among a number of small yacht owners like Mr. Smith to determine which one was most skillful in predicting the performance of his craft.

The object was to set the throttle at a steady speed, then cross the starting line at a precise moment so that the finish line would be crossed as close as possible to a pre-designated time. The yacht was to touch at two or three points on the sound as part of the problem.

The skill of the navigator consisted in his predicting as accurately as possible the effects of wind and tide on his craft. He had to navigate a direct line to each objective on the sound.

An officer of the yachting club was assigned to each boat to be sure the speed was constant and that a straight course was steered to each objective.

When we got to Mr. Smith's house he had all his charts out and spent some time explaining the project. He had spent his leisure time for a year checking and rechecking tides and probable winds for that season in Puget

Sound and had the latest weather report so he could predict surface wind for that afternoon. It was obviously an excercise that intrigued and excited him and the final payoff would be to beat the competition in his prediction as to the time of crossing the finish line.

It was an overcast, misty day when we all walked down the dock at the marina. The yacht was probably twenty years old and showed the effects of the salt air and ocean pounding. It was small, but provided room for us to stand on the covered deck.

Puget Sound is a beautiful tree locked and foggy place and today was a typical misty grey. The observer from the yacht club, wearing a black uniform, was already on board, checking the big diesel engine, the navigation instruments, the steering mechanism, etc. He had a notebook in which he made periodic entries.

Mr. Smith had donned his yachting cap and was visibly excited as he made his inspections of the craft and completed last minute calculations to assure crossing the starting line at the exact moment to assure a finish at the time already established for his completion of the course.

Willie and I were busy talking to the girls and swapping stories with the other GI's on board. We had spotted the cooler full of beer and a galley loaded with sandwiches and snacks and were anticipating a pleasant and exhilerating afternoon.

Mr. Smith guided the yacht carefully away from the dock and into the channel leading out of the marina. The starting line was fixed at the point where we were to enter the main body of the sound. The aged engine chugged along at a steady rate.

Our observer had his watch out to note the exact moment we crossed the starting line with an eye on the tachometer that registered the set speed of the big engine.

Just as we crossed the starting line, the engine quit.

In the dead silence, we glided along — Mr. Smith and the observer looked at each other in obvious pain.

"I'm afraid that's it," the observer said. "As you know, when the engine stops that way, you are disqualified."

Mr. Smith shifted from one foot to the other and his chin dropped down. "That's right," he said quietly.

In less than a minute, the big engine came back to life to hold its steady throb the rest of the afternoon.

We felt Mr. Smith's hurt, knowing that whatever else happened, this was not going to be a happy afternoon. All of us had felt our host's keen anticipation for the contest and now we all felt the bitterness of his disappointment. We knew that he had invited us along so we could share the excitement of what had to be a highlight of his life each year.

Willie and I looked at each other. We had had our disappointments, and now we felt very close to Mr. Smith. We would never forget the moment.

The week after we had our trip on Puget Sound, Willie and I got word that we had been accepted by the Army Air Corps and that we would soon be going to Buckley Field, Colorado for testing. If we passed our physical and mental tests, we would become Aviation Students and, later, when we began flight training, Aviation Cadets.

Since we now belonged officially to the Air Corps, we were relieved of our previous duty — mine as chief executive of the motor pool and Willie as dog robber to the officers barracks.

This left us in limbo. The Air Corps was not there to tell us what to do and the cavalry had washed its hands of us.

Fortunately, by now Willie and I were seasoned soldiers.

"The main thing for us to do," Willie told me, "is to keep out of sight. If they see us standing around doing nothing it makes them nervous and they'll put us to raking rocks or watering the colonel's lawn."

Right next to our barracks was the beginning of another row of identical barracks slated to become the living quarters of new arrivals as the Fourteenth Cavalry Group continued to grow to its full complement of soldiers.

The barracks was empty except for a large pile of mattresses that were stacked on the concrete floor of the one story structure. Willie was the first to spot this potential hiding place and once we had inspected it together, we knew where we would spend our time while waiting for the orders to Buckley Field.

We had come a long way since leaving the campus a few months before. But, then, me and Willie wadn't dumb.

Both of us liked to read, so the next day we started reporting to the empty barracks right after morning chow. There we'd each pull us out a mattress and a paper back book, stretch out for a leisurely morning whiling away the hours waiting for lunch. After noon chow, we'd be hard at it again, reading and sleeping.

Occasionally, we'd hear what sounded like somebody headed our way. Then, we'd dive for the pile of mattresses and bury ourselves out of sight.

After a few days of this, it finally occurred to the sergeant to wonder what was happening to us during the day and he started assigning us duties.

Since I was no longer the motor pool director but was rated as a truck driver, I was used to drive a six-by-six to pick up garbage or deliver supplies. One of the regular drivers took me out and showed me how to double clutch the big truck and I soon learned the code of the truck driver.

The army truck driver considered himself a professional and tended to look down on the common soldier as a foot-slogging dog face. After the first day, I assumed the same attitude — we drove — and that was it.

No self-respecting truck driver ever loaded or unloaded. I'd drive my truck to the back of one of the big kitchens, then get out and watch the poor KP's struggle and strain to get the big garbage cans, loaded to the top, onto my truck.

"Hey," they would yell at me, "how about giving me a hand with this thing."

"I'm sorry, fellow," I'd reply cooly, "I'm a driver and we're not allowed to load and unload. If I helped you, I'd have to help everybody on the route."

Which seemed more and more fair to me as I settled into the serious business of transporting goods and garbage.

On one occasion, I backed the truck up to the loading dock to pick up several sides of beef. I was leaning against the side of the truck when I suddenly realized one of the loaders was a former classmate from the University.

We passed a few remarks about the good old days and for a moment I was sorely tempted to help load the heavy sides of meat onto my truck. Then I remembered the code and the ancient tradition I was charged to uphold. With an effort, I controlled the urge and continued to lean against the side of the truck.

I thought my former classmate showed a lot of class. He kept struggling the meat onto my truck without showing any obvious resentment. As a soldier, he was beginning to respect the other fellow's soft job and instead of railing out against the unfairness of it all, he doubled his resolve to get a soft job for himself. While I respected the truck drivers code and was meticulous in my observation of it, I never did exactly understand what we were saving ourselves for. It wasn't so we would have energy for later work — that certainly never materialized.

One thing I learned as a soldier that many people never master and that is the ability to do absolutely nothing for sustained periods of time.

Later in politics and real estate negotiating, I found this an invaluable asset. You reach a point in these endeavors, after expending enormous energy to get a campaign fight going or a real estate deal working, when the absolute best thing to do is to do nothing, to experience no strain in doing nothing and to convince your adversary by your inactivity that you are capable of doing nothing for a much longer period than he is.

I learned that trick in the Army, I learned it well and it has served me very well.

On one of my final days at Camp Whiteside, a major asked me if I could drive a half track. Never having been in one, I replied, "Yes, sir. When do you want to leave, sir?"

He was pleased to have lined up a driver so easily and said we'd leave first thing after chow in the morning.

That gave me the afternoon to perfect my half track driving skills. I got into one that was parked in the motor pool and found the directions printed on the dash.

I already knew how to double clutch and now I found that shifting gears was determined by the speed of the engine as shown on the tachometer.

Next day, I found out the reason for the tachometer — with the clanging and banging of all that pile of steel, there was no way to hear the sound of the engine. The major and I spent a delightful day chasing the troops cross-country and apparently he thought my driving was okay. I was learning that if a good assignment offered itself, be sure and say "Yes, sir, I can do that." Dad would have been proud of me.

Toward the end of summer, Willie and I got our orders. We were told to get our gear together and report to troop headquarters. We were loaded in a jeep and driven to McCord Field where Willie and I sat on our barracks bags on the edge of the landing strip waiting for the early morning fog to lift.

We were about to become gentlemen again.

The Army Air Corps was an entirely different animal from the ground forces as Willie and I discovered when we landed at Buckley Field, Colorado. Everything was new, everybody's uniform was clean and neatly pressed and the atmosphere was more akin to a college campus than to the sweaty, dirty grind at Riley or the rumpled, disorganized inactivity of the Fourteenth Cavalry Group. Everybody seemed to be in the process of being tested and evaluated before being sent to one school or another, everybody was moving about briskly and everything was neat and orderly.

The one close call I had while taking my physical examination was caused by a rapid pulse. But when the corpsman told me about it, I became so despondent about going back to the cavalry that after sitting and staring into space for half an hour, I passed on the second test. The only other thing that troubled me was a test for depth perception. It looked like a long shoe box with two cords running the length of the box and a couple of pegs that looked like the old style round clothes pins. Each peg was attached to one of the cords. We had to look through a hole in the end of the box, pull on the strings, and decide when the pegs were lined up along side each other.

To me, they looked like they were alongside for some distance as the strings were pulled. Finally, I tried to estimate the halfway along the run where they seemed to line up. Apparently, I passed, but I never did feel confident about lining them up.

Later, a pilot told me they had abandoned that particular test in evaluating a pilot's ability to find the ground.

We had a test of coordination in flipping a bunch of switches in a box. I waited while Willie took his test and it seemed to me he moved twice as fast as I did.

Within a little over a week, both of us had been accepted as aviation students. That meant we would train as either pilot, navigator, or bombadier. But first, we would be sent to something called a College Training Detachment to await an opening in the pre-flight school in California.

Naturally, we were separated and I was not to see or hear from Willie for some twenty years. It had been an unusual friendship based originally on a mutually-shared bitterness toward the system that had landed me and Willie, after years of training toward commissioned officer status, in the motor pool and the dog robbing assignment. After we got to know each other, we found deep roots in similar family backgrounds and, more importantly, commonly-held ideals. When we got together over twenty years later, we both had heavy family and financial obligations. We picked up right where we had left off when we separated at Buckley Field.

There was joy in my heart when we climbed on the train at Denver that November of 1943. I had a new patch on my sleeve — a blue oval with a set of wings in the center. I was a gentleman — an aviation student headed for college and then to officer training. My ambition was to be a pilot. But after the days in the cavalry, I would have settled for navigator or bombadier. I knew now that in life it is possible to fall through the cracks and to lose those opportunities I had always taken for granted.

For the five months I was in the Army Air Corps, I was a gentleman again.

Never again would I assume that I was in some way so superior that I would reach my goal regardless of the path I followed. I appreciated now what my parents had made available to me by their hard work and I was determined to make good on this second chance.

The moment I stepped on the train, I knew things were going to be different. It was not one of the aging day coaches that had been pressed into service by the overwhelming demand for travel during the war years which served the common soldier and lowly civilian.

I had received a two week furlough from Camp Whiteside and had traveled by day coach all the way across the United States to Georgia. It was a bitter-sweet trip, but one I will always remember for the jam-packed day coaches of every breed, age, and description. One must have survived from the previous century for it had upholstered bucket seats and a pot-bellied stove sitting in the middle of the coach to provide heat.

The trip had taken four days each way. I had only six days at home. The few days in my old room on Vidal Blvd., with the magnolia tree and the breeze wafting through, are only a blurred, somehow bitter memory. But I do remember living day and night for eight days as we trundled across America on that assortment of day coaches. Everybody was polite and considerate even though most of us were being carted around the country against our will. Since the war overshadowed personality, we submitted to the bizarre situation.

But now, on my way to aviation training, it was a new world. Re-instated to the privileges of the officer class, we aviation students found ourselves on a deluxe railway car permitting three men to a private drawing room suite and food served in the dining car on heavy linen with heavy silverware.

At St. John's University, where we would spend five months waiting for our turn at flight training, we were to receive some basic college work with emphasis on English, science and mathmatics.

St. John's was small, with a normal college enrollment of about five hundred. A Catholic institution, it was part of the Benedictine Order of monks and most of our instructors were priests.

After the misadventure of Fort Riley and the Fort Lewis motor pool, I was sure I'd died and gone to heaven.

The school was part of the monastery with a lake, beautiful, wooded grounds and its own self contained world.

Fathers and lay brothers operated the farm which was part of the complex. They provided the milk, meat and most of the other food we ate. Meals were served on white, dining room linen with two big pitchers of fresh milk on each table, and bowls of vegetables, and meat. Once a week, a steer was slaughtered and we all enjoyed steak.

I watched the slaughter one week and was fascinated by the skill of the butcher who skinned the carcass in a matter of minutes.

The priests led full and productive lives and enjoyed their leisure as well. One of the fathers fed the birds as he walked along with nuts and other food in his black hat. The priests enjoyed baseball, wrapping their long skirts up around their waists, exposing powerful bare legs when they ran the bases. We arrived in November, right after an early blizzard that was just melting off; but fall was magnificent, and for that winter, there was very little additional snow.

It was the best time of my young life. Back to church I went and soon I was dating one of the town girls in St. Cloud.

It was also one of the hottest winters I ever spent. Built to withstand long spells of below zero temperature, the steam-heated dormitory was soon so hot and arid that my nose and throat dried out.

We were busy every hour of the day. When we were not in class or studying, we were doing calisthenics, playing basketball or ice skating.

With the lake frozen over, one of the priests rigged a sail and would fly from one end of the lake to the other, skimming at high speed on his ice skates.

"You need not worry about any religious pressure being put on you," the director of the school told us, "no one will try to convert you. We're here to get you ready for flight school. What you do about your relation to God is up to you."

Unless you happened to indicate on your application that you were Catholic. The Catholic boys were quickly rounded up and put into special classes after regular school hours.

American troops were in Italy and while we were at St. John's, the decision was made to bomb Mt. Casino, home base for our Benedictine monks.

"Of course, there is no question," our math teacher, a priest, told us in class that day, "if one American life can be saved, the monastery must go."

This about an ancient work of art and tribute to man's love of God — the work of generations of priests and laymen.

The decision to bomb the magnificent structure was questioned after the war. Apparently, the Germans did not occupy the structure, which had a commanding mountain top view of the attacking Americans, until after it was bombed.

And the ruins provided as much cover for German troops as the building had. One of the tragedies of war, but accepted by the Benedictines as their gift to the defeat of Hitler.

"Harrison," the instructor was shouting over the deafening roar of the L-5's engine, "this thing requires some power if it's going to stay in the air. I was beginning to wonder if you'd notice."

With that, he thrust the throttle to full power.

My instructor, for the ten hours of flying we were to receive while at St. John's, was the kind who leaves the student to figure things out for himself — until he gets in trouble. I was learning straight and level flight and was doing a good job of keeping the wings and nose properly aligned with the horizon — but, we were descending because I had forgotten to keep my air speed up. Before he corrected me, I had noticed the barn we were flying toward was growing larger and the cow in the pasture was almost life size.

"You won't solo," the instructor told us, "we don't have time to do much and there's no use running the risk of accidents. You'll learn to do S turns along a road, turns around a pylon, that sort of thing; so, we won't be spending much time on take offs and landings."

We did some spins.

"This plane will fly out of a spin by itself," the instructor shouted. He raised the nose and kicked the small plane into a spin. Around and around we went, leaving the controls free to move as they would. After about the third spin, he shouted, "Don't look like it's going to work this time." He kicked opposite rudder and eased the stick forward and then back as we leveled off.

Leaving me to fly the plane, the instructor watched closely as I flew S's along the country road, then circled the pylon that consisted of a tall, white silo.

It was a magical time. I was doing what I wanted to be doing. I was learning. I was getting a physical workout every day and I had an objective that I felt would make a contribution to the war effort. The one thing I don't remember was having the kind of thrill flying is supposed to produce in the new pilot. That would come later, much later. Now, the idea that I might actually become a pilot seemed too improbable to excite much enthusiasm. Perhaps, I had a premonition.

"Man," the other student had come into the air corp from civilian life, "I'm sick of this place. I want to get to California and start flight training."

"Not me," I said. "I've found me a home in this place. They can leave me here for the rest of the war as far as I'm concerned."

Having fallen through the cracks in the army system one time, I could recognize a good thing when I saw it. It was Camelot — too good to be true.

It was too good to be true and it was about to end.

"Men," the commanding officer called all the students to a meeting. "I've got some bad news for some of you. The war is entering a new phase. In most theatres, we are beginning to gain control of the skies. That means our pilot casualties are down. The Germans and Japs aren't replacing their losses as fast as we are building up."

The need to replace pilots was down dramatically and the pipe line of trainees was full to overflowing.

"As you know," he continued, "we are building for an invasion of Europe. The need now is for foot soldiers. We are winning in the air, but we can't bring about the final defeat of the enemy until we invade his homeland."

The matter was to be settled with typical army simplicity. Anybody who had entered the air corps from civilian life would stay in the program. Anybody who had transferred from the ground forces would be sent to the infantry.

And it applied to everybody who had not actually received his wings. Advanced students in the final weeks of flight training were soon to be buck privates in the good old infantry — Queen of Battle.

As they say, it was hard but it was fair. I feel for you, but I can't reach you. T. S. (tough ----). Go see the chaplin and he will punch your ticket.

Oh, well, I thought, at least I got a five month reprieve. Nothing lasts forever.

We, who were about to lose our gentlemen status, were given the night off to get drunk.

A few days later, we were once again on the railroad; this time in wooden passenger cars left over from the turn of the century with the coarse, horse hair, red seats that marked their authenticity as original equipment.

We marched to the train in our freshly-pressed air corps student uniform, shiny shoes, bright eyes, and bushy tails.

The trip was a short one.

Across the state line to Camp McCoy, Wisconsin.

As we stared out the window of the train, we looked over our reception committee — vulgar, dirty men with chewing tobacco and unshavened. How could such bright-eyed young future pilot, officer-types be exposed to such crudity.

Well, it would take a little time; but, by God, in a few weeks you wouldn't be able to tell us from the rabble spread out around our aged railroad car. We'd be just as dirty, just as vulgar, just as mad, and just as mean.

The Army has a great system.

You just have to remember the Army's objective is to fight.

In order to fight, you have to be mean.

In order to become mean, you have to be mistreated.

We were about to land in the hands of experts.

CHAPTER VIII

Safely over the mountains on my return from Lynchburg, I began my descent. At 4000 feet, I could see the Chattahoochee snaking down to huge Lake Lanier just west of Gainesville. As I got closer to the lake, the rain began. I could see by looking out the side window and down at a slant toward the ground. The view straight ahead was obscured by the rain striking the windshield.

This was familiar territory. Looking straight down I could see the lake below me. I had paddled the entire fourteen miles of its length in my canoe so I knew this body of water intimately.

To the left, I could see the expressway to Atlanta and I began to veer toward it so I could follow that broad ribbon of concrete down to DeKalb-Peachtree Airport.

I tuned in Peachtree Tower now to hear what kind of activitiy was going on there. Planes were landing and taking off, visibility was still five miles and the ceiling 7000 feet.

But, a thunderstorm was reported southwest of the field.

Looking down, I saw the runways of Gainesville airport slipping under me and for a moment I considered landing while I had the runways in clear view. I was at 3500 feet now, still 2500 feet above the airport, and I figured by the time I turned and circled down I could be almost to Peachtree, only 20 minutes away. Reports of visibility were still good at Peachtree. I was familiar with all the runways and, as the second busiest airport in Georgia, the tower was manned by expert professional controllers. I decided to go on.

I didn't know it, but I was headed toward trouble.

It wasn't the first time.

In 1944, in Camp McCoy, Wisconsin, I found myself about to enter a rough and a rugged time. For the first time, I found myself in the real, honest to God, army. My eyes were about to be opened.

"Together, men," the captain, who looked like a Methodist minister concluded, "we will build the finest company in the army. Now, I believe the sergeant would like to say a few words to you."

With that, the captain departed over the hill, back toward the company office. Still aglow with the warmth of his address, we newly reassigned aviation students, shoes shining, fatigues neatly pressed, turned eager faces toward the man designated to put the captain's idealistic words into meaningful action.

The top sergeant stood about six foot two, had coarse, straw- colored hair and a perpetual snarl on his heavy face.

"All right," the sergeant snarled, "if any of you goddamn bastards think you can lick my ass you step out right now." Hands on hips, he turned slowly as his mean eyes searched for a response to this challenge.

Finding none, he outlined a program designed to march, run, and dig us into the ground, using every trick he or his staff of devotees could devise to bring out the snarling worst in the rest of us.

"By the time we get through," he concluded, "you'll be ready to go anywhere just to get the hell away from here."

The sergeant was tough, but I was to find out a few days later that, although he may have looked like an evangelist, the captain was really the man in charge.

"Harrison," the captain called me over to him. He was holding a map of the terrain the troops were moving through, "I want you to go to this hill, find the first platoon, and bring them to this point by 8:05."

I started out in the general direction of the low ridge the captain had pointed out. The rest of the outfit was moving slowly across the flat land toward the highest peak among the hills that constituted our company's objective for the exercise.

The captain was trying to make something out of me. After having the cavalry OCS close down just after I got to Fort Riley and having my aviation career end just before going into pre-flight, I was becoming less than enthusiastic about my future in the army. I was back at square one — a private after a year in uniform.

The week before, I had toted the SC300, a radio that was carried as a back pack. Now, I was the captain's personal messenger.

The first platoon was no where to be seen. After dawdling along carry-ing the light carbine by the strap over my shoulder, it suddenly occurred to me the first platoon might possibly be on the other side of the mound of earth the captain had pointed out.

I held the carbine in my right hand and began to trot around the hillock.

Sure enough, there was the first platoon just coming around to meet me.

I saluted the lieutenant and told him where the captain wanted us to meet him.

The platoon was hiking in that direction when another messenger came running toward us, pumping his right fist up and down to signal that we were to double time toward our destination.

"Harrison," the captain handed me an envelope, "I want you to carry this message to the colonel. On the double!"

The colonel was on the side of a vertical slope a mile to our rear. Climbing up the incline, I had to brace myself and pull up on the small saplings to reach the colonel's command post. He had selected it because of the good view of our troops, moving in line toward our objective several miles to the front.

The colonel took my message, opened the envelope, and read it; then, scribbled a reply, sealed it, and handed it to me.

"Take this to the captain," he said, "and make it snappy."

I saluted and went slipping and sliding down the slope, breaking into a run as I hit the level ground. The sun was beating down now and by the time I reached our line, I was sweating and breathing heavily. The rest of the company was stretched out on the ground or moving slowly forward.

The captain read my note and formed an answer.

"Take this to the colonel, Harrison," he said, "and hurry."

By the time I reached the colonel, relaxing in his aerie, I was huffing and puffing.

Again, I was sent back to the captain.

And, again, returned.

And, again.

And, again.

By the time I delivered my final message, the company had taken the objective, it was late afternoon and the captain was waiting at the top of the highest terrain in the area.

I pulled myself slowly up the perpendicular hillside — sweating from the afternoon sun — panting for breath.

The captain, looking more like a Methodist minister than ever, stood, arms hanging straight down, watching as I struggled over the lip of the overhang and slowly moved toward him with my final message.

The carbine was in my right hand.

Just as I reached the level where the captain was standing, a bee stung me. Right on the end of my nose.

The ultimate degradation.

"Goddamn" — I slung the carbine as hard as I could, hitting the tree to the captain's side.

"Harrison," the captain said calmly, "You take the jeep back to camp, and be in my office at 0800 in the morning."

Next morning, while the outfit was preparing to go out on the day's work, I was in the waiting room outside the captain's office. I could hear him talking to someone.

"Sergeant," he said, "I know you were with this outfit before any of the rest of us came, and I know that our lieutenants are very young. But, sergeant, they are officers, and you are going to have to treat them with the respect their rank deserves. Running this company is my responsibility and if you can't follow my orders, I am going to get somebody who can."

The big first sergeant, his face red under the straw colored hair marched past without seeing me on his way out.

The sergeants had been running the company. I thought now of the poor Puerto Rican private, surrounded by yelling sergeants and knew, as low-men on the totem pole, none of us liked the way they had been doing it, and would welcome a change in administration.

The captain came to the door.

"Come on in Harrison."

I saluted and stood at attention in front of his desk.

"At ease," the captain sat behind his desk.

"Harrison," he said, "I think you ought to know what that was all about yesterday."

I nodded my head slowly.

"Yesterday," he continued, "I told you to have the first platoon at the line of departure by 8:05. When they finally got on the line it was 8:15. In other words, they were ten minutes late to the line of departure."

He paused. At this point, I still did not know what the problem was.

"Now," he continued, "it is crucial that all units be on line and that they all push off at the same time. Otherwise, there is a gap in the line and in an actual battle, that can be disastrous. Yesterday, there was a gap in our line of attack because of you."

I began to understand the problem.

"Harrison," he continued, "while I was waiting for you to fill that gap, I made up my mind that for every minute you were late to the line of departure, I was going to send you on a cross-country trip to the colonel. In case you did not keep track, you made ten trips to the Colonel's command post. Each time you carried a message that said, 'Colonel, please send Harrison back to me on the double.'"

I looked at the captain, saluted, and left the office.

Next day, my respect for him was again increased.

The first sergeant had been transferred to battalion headquarters.

The improvement in morale was immediate.

With the top sergeant gone and his cadre of thugs broken up, there was no doubt we had a good outfit. Not that it got any easier. The intent and wherewithall to bring out the mean and the fighting spirit was still there. The difference was, instead of picking on the weak, everybody was treated with equal sadism so that the whole outfit would be mean.

"Okay, Harrison," the corporal who was charge of quarters was shaking me vigorously by the shoulder, "time to report to the kitchen."

I looked at him incredulously. "Hey, Garber, I'm not on KP. It's Sunday morning. This is the day we get off, you remember?"

"Sorry, Harrison," he said, "I got my orders. Anybody in the barracks after 0800 goes to the kitchen."

I looked around and realized I was the only one in the barracks. Obviously, I hadn't gotten the word about this latest move to run us all crazy. From now on, although we were confined to the post every other weekend — "we're on a war time footing — half the troops have got to be where we can get ahold of them in case of emergency" — that was the explanation — now the screw was tightened. We had to be on the post, but if we stayed in the company area, we were put to work.

It was not only hard, it was unfair. But it was infantry, and this outfit was on a one-way trip to combat. From this point forward, the screw would continue to tighten until we finally found ourselves where there were no days off; and, the only reward would be to be alive for one more day of misery.

"I never realized," I told my fox hole companion, "what an art there is to digging a hole."

"Yeah," he said, "it takes a lot of skill. A lot of people never get the chance to master such a complex operation."

About the time we got the hole deep enough to get ourselves in a sitting position below ground, it began to rain.

"These summer days are really pleasant in Wisconsin," I said, "nothing like the sweating we did in Kansas."

"Yeah," he replied, "we got it made. How bout moving your poncho a little. You're pouring rain down my boot."

In the small hours of the morning, the cold set in and the rain began to make our joints stiff. It always amazed me that it was possible to sleep sitting in a hole in the ground with the rain pouring down. By morning the rain had stopped and we were able to dry out in the sun that broke though.

"Did you ever notice," I said, "that nobody seems to get a cold out here. But once we're back in the steam-heated barracks, everybody starts hacking and coughing."

"It's invigorating," he agreed, as he hopped from one wet foot to the other. "no doubt about it, we've found a home in this Army."

Then there was the hike.

The hike started right after evening chow.

"All right, men," the captain said. "We'll be marching most of the night. I want you to stay close, especially after dark. Keep up a steady pace. Don't let the space open up between you and the man ahead. Your officers will be right there with you, so follow their example. We'll take a ten minute break every hour and we should be back here by dawn. Tomorrow's Saturday, and any man who can make it to the day-room can pick up a weekend pass. Let's go!"

We couldn't really complain. All we were carrying was the nine pound rifle and a light pack. The only problem I had were the same short legs that had sent me down the horse's neck at the University. In the infantry, the pace was set by putting the tallest men at the head of the column. That put me at the rear. As the mountaineers at the front loped along, I had one of two choices. I could walk by stretching my short legs as far as possible. When I did this, my shins hurt like sore boils and got worse with each mile. Or, I could jog, which put that jarring to work wearing me down.

But, I made it. In fact, most of us made it. A few dropped out and were picked up by the "meat wagon", the ambulance that followed to pick up stragglers. Each hour it got worse as the heavy fatigue set in and the air got colder and the muscles cried out in pain.

But, we kept going through the night, keeping the pace that was set by the long-legged country boys in front.

As dawn broke in the Wisconsin woods, we rounded a curve and saw the gates of the fort. Crossing into the camp and turning down the street that led to our company area, we heard a band strike up. By God, we'd made it — and now we were stepping along strongly, invigorated by the music and sight of our barracks.

"Men," the colonel was standing by the jeep he'd used to check our progress during the night, "I am proud of you. You not only made the twenty-five miles, but you came striding down that road, ready for combat. You're a good outfit. Now, anybody who wants one, can go pick up a pass."

By this time, my feet were blistered and I was hobbling. But, the chance to leave camp Saturday morning hadn't come before. I took one look at the barracks and gave one thought to the bunk that was waiting there for my collapse; then, I turned and walked to the dayroom.

The Hiawatha was a fast train that ran between Chicago and Minneapolis. Pat, the girl I was dating in St. Cloud during my aviation student golden days, had agreed to meet me in Minneapolis where her sister lived.

I stayed awake on the train, but as soon as I got to Pat's sister's, I took them up on the offer they made after one look at my tired face. I crawled in bed and passed out. Noon, Sunday, I came to; so, my visit with Pat was abbreviated as were all my activities away from Camp McCoy during those days.

A large billboard had been erected on the street leading to our regiment's area on the Fort. It told in bold strokes the stages of training we would be involved in and showed the date we would ship out for overseas. At that point, we didn't know whether we'd be heading to the Pacific or to Europe; but, the odds seemed to favor the latter. June 6 had marked the D-Day landing in Europe and casualties announced as our troops tried to break out of the encirclement at St.Lo indicated that's where this outfit would be headed.

Actually, we would not go as a unit. Like the troops that preceded us, we would go as casual replacements, filling in as casualties occurred among the front line troops. It was not an enviable position to be in. We wouldn't know the people we'd join on the front and probably wouldn't know the replacements we were to travel with.

But, it suited me. I was not only ready to go anywhere to get away from Camp McCoy, but, at age 19, after a year in the Army and having two programs fold up on me, I was ready to accept my position as private and get involved in the war.

It was certainly nothing to be ashamed of. When it came down to it, after all the bombing was done, somebody had to go in and actually defeat the enemy on the ground and take his territory before the war could come to an end. And that was what the infantry was all about. The war was reduced to a one man conflict and it didn't much matter when the metal started flying what kind of rank a man carried. It was what war ultimately was all about. And I was ready for it.

A revealing thing happened as the day arrived for our casual replacements to ship out for overseas. During training, our non-coms, who had trained the previous privates and sent them across to join other outfits, had talked tough about combat and how anxious they were to be involved.

As the day drew near for the troops to ship out, much was said about how much they wanted to go. Unfortunately, they would have to stay at McCoy to train the next batch of replacements.

The week before we were to ship out, they got their chance. One non-com was going to be required to accompany the casual replacements. It could be anybody, any rank.

We waited with baited breath as the hours passed following issuance of the appeal for a volunteer to fill the slot.

We thought of the rough and tough words we had heard from the rough and tough sergeants who liked to gang up on the single, weak kneed private who had goofed up.

The silence was awesome.

Finally, we heard. A volunteer had stepped forward.

The Puerto Rican cook was a T-5, a technical corporal.

Having been assigned to the kitchen because of his willingness to work hard at whatever job was thrust upon him, he had finally been promoted to T-5, and now, he saw his chance to make a choice on his own. He was grinning and laughing as he looked around at all the admirers and enjoyed the unspoken sigh of relief from the other non-coms.

I identified with the Puerto Rican cook.

I felt for him and I was ready to leave McCoy with him.

I had only one regret.

I, too, had been promoted.

After 14 months in the Army, I had been promoted, without my knowledge and consent and together with a group of old and passed over soldiers, to the exalted rank of Pfc.

I resented the loss of virginity in regard to the question of rank. If I couldn't be an officer, I sure didn't want to be anything in between. The

After fourteen months in the Army, I was promoted to private first class. I wasn't sure I could handle the responsibility but the $4 raise was nice.

non-coms did the work and missed the white table napkins and heavy silverware.

You might say I was becoming bitter again.

I didn't want a damn thing from the Army at this point and I especially didn't want anything they would think would give them a way to make me follow the dumb directions we received.

I didn't want anything the bastards could take away. But as in all things since I had left civilian life, I wasn't asked and I didn't have a choice.

"Yeah," one of my fellow privates said slyly, "Harrison's been brown nosing the captain."

"Yeah," another chimed in, "He's in with the officers all right. I told you."

"Oh, for God's sake," I said with a groan. "Even in the peace-time Army everybody makes pfc after six months. I've been in fourteen. In case you didn't know it, I am qualified to ride a horse, chauffeur a quarter ton truck and fly an L-5. You guys are just jealous because you couldn't cut it."

I wrote my sister, Novena, whose husband Windy was a Major teaching in the infantry school at Fort Benning.

"Well," I wrote, "the money's good, of course, four dollars a month raise brings me to fifty four dollars a month. But, I'm not sure I can handle the responsibility."

For everything that happened to me from that day forward, I have to take personal responsiblity. The truth is, I didn't have to go overseas, just like I didn't have to go in service when I did and I didn't have to go in the cavalry.

A week before the troops were to ship out, the sergeant called me into his office.

"Harrison," he said, "you're not going with the other men."

I looked at him with horror. "What do you mean, sergeant."

This sergeant was the one in the outfit, along with the captain, whom I liked and respected.

"I've been checking your record," he said, "and you didn't make it to the rifle range. That was the week you were in the hospital."

Alergic to poison ivy, I had covered the inside of my thigh with big blisters. When I reached the point of collapse, I was finally sent to the hospital.

"Oh, no, sarge," I said with a groan, "don't do that to me. I qualified in basic. Sarge, I've been shifted around in this Army all I can stand. You know I can handle that rifle. In the name of God, don't make me stay in this place any longer."

"To tell you the truth, Harrison," the sergeant said, "the captain wants to make you a non-com. He thinks you've got good stuff. It's an opportunity."

"Please talk to him for me, sarge," I said. "I really don't like the Army and I really would like to do something that might help my country in some small way."

"You're nuts, Harrison," he said, "but I'll see what I can do."

I left his office and walked to the back of the barracks and out the back door. I sat on the small stoop with my feet on the top step and stared into space.

I couldn't believe it was happening to me. Shortly after the pfc thing had happened, I had made one more stab at trying for OCS. By this time, I was disgusted with the Army and convinced I'd never have a chance to show what I could do. When word came for me to report to the qualifying board to discuss my chances, I was out in the field and I had to hurry in to change into my dress khaki's.

Changing my clothes, I suddenly realized that I never had sewn my pfc stripe on — and never planned to do so. But, going to the board as a pfc without a stripe would certainly indicate a certain disrespect for the Army way.

I was able to borrow the stripes, but didn't have time to sew them on properly, just tacked them at the corners, and of course that looked shoddy.

But, even more shoddy was my attitude. I felt beaten and degraded by what had happened to me. If I had ever had intelligence, I felt it had been blunted by the stupidity of the Army and I was disillusioned about merit serving a purpose in the Army maze.

To top my humiliation, the colonel who headed the board and who interviewed me was an old horse cavalry officer and was familiar with the university.

"Harrison," he said softly, "name the parts of the harness worn by the Army horse."

I looked at him incredulously. "I don't believe I can do that, sir," I said.

"Are you sure you were in the cavalry at the university," he said. "You know, Harrison, you don't seem to have much in the way of energy and drive. Now, that fellow Sinkwich who played football for Georgia, had plenty on the ball."

"He did, sir," I agreed. "I've seen him play a number of times. And I can tell you that he did have a lot of drive. But, he didn't waste it when he wasn't playing. When he was finally tackled, he would lie on the ground, resting a couple of minutes, then he would get up like he could barely move and he'd shamble back to the huddle like he was on his last legs. But, when he got hold of that ball, he went like a bullet and nothing could stop him."

"Well, Harrison," he said, "that may have been true of Sinkwich, but, I've got to tell you that I think it would be a mistake to make you an officer. Looking at your record, you seem to have all the qualifications. But, you are very young; and frankly, you don't make much of an impression. When you get out in front of troops, they can't see all your qualifications. All they can see is what they see and it had better impress them."

I saluted, turned around, and walked out. I walked back to the barracks, ripped off the single stripes and returned them to their owner.

Now, I was sitting on the back stoop of the barracks, staring into space, and thinking that now I faced three more months of this chicken outfit, these dumb non-coms, and that the whole thing didn't mean a damn thing.

Surely, by all that was holy, they could at least leave me alone now and let me go with the other boys to finally get involved in something that counted.

"Okay, Harrison," the sergeant walked around the barracks to where I was seated, "I talked to the captain and he said if that's your decision, let you go."

I looked at him. "Thank you, sergeant," I said. "And tell the captain, I thank him, too."

CHAPTER IX

The rain was coming down harder now on my little Cherokee, and I descended another 500 feet and got closer to the I-85 Expressway I was following. With visibility obscured, I didn't want to miss my turn to the airport.

Out of the corner of my eye, I saw the needle on my navigation radio move and the flag swing from TO to FROM. I had just flown over the Norcross VOR station. It was time to let Peachtree know I was coming.

The tower acknowledged my call and told me to report a left base for Runway 16. Runway 16 is one of the original runways at Peachtree - the one my ambulance plane had landed on this same time of year in 1944. It is a short runway and with the problems I was having seeing not the one I would have chosen at the moment.

I knew I was only moments away from the expressway cloverleaf that would mark the point at which I was to make a right turn to the airport. I had descended again when the tower called and asked my position.

"Five five November, just over the cloverleaf. Turning base. Runway one six."

"Roger five five, November. State your altitude."

On a clear day, the tower would have been able to see my plane at this position. The controller was searching for me through the obscuring light rain.

"Twenty-five hundred." I switched on my landing light. "Five five November."

And then, I saw the airport with runway sixteen.

I was five hundred feet too high.

I cut the power, pulled the flaps and began as rapid a descent as possible as I made a left bank onto final approach. The rain was coming down hard as I crossed the number, high and fast. I was two thirds of the way down the runway and still twenty feet above the asphalt.

"Go around five five November. Do a right hand pattern."

I thrust the throttle full open, raised the nose of the Cherokee and roared over the end of the runway rapidly gaining altitude. As I banked right, I called the tower to report I was on right downwind.

Ahead, low clouds were drifting across my flight path and as I turned, I lost sight of the field below.

Now, I could not see the grainery below, one of the checkpoints I used to determine when to turn base.

"Five five November," the tower called, "I've lost sight of you. State your position."

"Just turning base."

"Five five November, why don't you take Runway 20 left. Wind is calm." Two zero left is our longest runway.

As I broke out of the cloud, I saw one six below me.

"I have you now, five five November," the tower said. "You seem to be lined up for one six. Cleared to land one six."

Again, because I didn't have the familiar landmarks to go by, I was high. Half way down the runway the tower told me to go around.

"This time," the controller said, "make a left turn and a left downwind for two zero left."

As I banked left, I stayed close to the field so I wouldn't lose sight of it again. I had full power but was keeping the nose down so I wouldn't climb back into the clouds. I watched the air speed indicator and kept it at eighty knots to avoid a stall as I made the tight turn.

As I turned base, the controller told me to side step to two zero right, a shorter parallel runway usually used by light planes.

Again, the unusual approach and the high speed I was using to avoid a stall in the steep turns so near the ground left me too fast and too high.

As I did the third go around the experienced and patient controller said in a calm voice.

"I tell you five five November, this time take two zero left, stay as close to the field as you can and we will turn up the lights."

As I came around to the downwind side of the long runway, I heard the controller announce to another plane.

"The field is closed. We're below visual requirements. Only IFR traffic can be accepted."

I hugged the left side of the runway, made a long run past the end before making a turn and kept my altitude down to 500 feet on base.

I made a gradual turn, banking only slightly and keeping air speed at 80 knots.

As I turned on final, the bright RAIL lights that made a visual path to the threshold of the runway came up bright along with the lights lining each side of the mile long runway.

"Five five November. I've got it this time," I reported.

I came in low but with plenty of speed. The Cherokee was bouncing now and I figured the wind was no longer calm and might be coming from any direction.

The thunderstorm that had been reported southwest of the airport had finally reached us.

Holding the nose straight, I eased slowly down, flying along the runway until I felt and heard the wheels touch down.

"Five five November," the tower said, "take a right turn at the end of the runway, cross two zero right and report to ground control on one two one seven when you are clear of the active."

I had taken the entire length of the longest runway. But I was down — and I was alive.

The rain was coming in sheets now and I was taxiing slowly as I turned off the runway, peering through the darkness for the yellow taxi line.

"Five five November," I acknowledged, "clear of the active. Much thanks."

And thank you too, Clint.

My trip was over.

In the fall of 1944, the trip that was to end in disaster for me was just beginning.

The Mauretania, sister ship to the Lusitania, whose sinking had gotten the U. S. into World War I, was designed to carry 4000 passengers and crew in luxury.

In the fall of 1944, it was tied up to the dock in New York Harbor in the process of loading seven thousand GI's for the five day crossing to Liverpool, England through the sub infested waters of the North Atlantic.

Passengers boarding the luxury liner had used the ascending gang plank to the upper decks. On September 21, 1944, we dog face infantry replacements, had an easier boarding — our short ramp went straight and level into the lower decks where we would be packed like cattle. As we waddled across the short ramp, each of us was carrying a sixty-pound pack — really an olive, drab barrack's bag with straps that held two of everything the private soldier is issued.

On our heads were the heavy steel helmets — straps never fastened on the infantry soldier. Experience had taught that concussion from an exploding shell can snap the soldier's neck if the strap is fastened under the chin.

"Look at the size of this monster!" I was looking up in amazement.

"Oh, my God," Bob Simpson groaned as he threw back his head to take in the towering wall of steel that was the ship's side. The back of his helmet had caught in the top of his pack. It rolled off his head, hit his shoulder, bounced on the ramp and splashed into the dark, quayside water below.

"Bob," I said, "here we are getting ready to be shot at and you go and lose your steel helmet. You're out of luck, buddy. Once you get on this ship, they don't replace anything. That's why they've got us loaded like pack mules."

"Oh, well," Bob sighed. "When one of you guys get shot, I'll use yours."

Once we left Camp McCoy, Wisconsin, our mass of casual replacements were put on sealed railroad passenger cars with a guard at each end of each car to be sure we arrived at our destination with no additions or subtractions from our number and in war time secrecy. Bob and I had met on the train and passed the time telling stories and comparing past histories.

"Bob," I asked him, "if you were studying to be an English teacher, what are you doing in the dog face infantry. Looks like they'd have had you writing a history of the war."

"Actually," Simpson replied, his large adams apple bobbing in his scrawny neck, "that's exactly what I am doing. My editor wanted me to get a little first-hand color on the life of you dirt eating, mud sloggers, then he'll whisk me back to New York. Bill Mauldin will do the illustrations and Ernie Pyle will write an introduction for my book."

Bob Simpson was one of the poorest physical specimens I had met in the army — and with the kind of citizen army we were in that was saying a mouthful. In this stage of the war, with the invasion of Europe multiplying casualties, the bottom of the barrel was being emptied.

Bob looked like he wouldn't weigh over a hundred pounds soaking wet, he had a receding Caspar Milquetoast chin, and an incongrous heavy stubble of red beard.

Left to help his widowed mother after his father's early death in a Pennsylvania coal mining accident, Simpson had worked hard at menial jobs since he was a kid.

"The worst job was in the ice house," Simpson said, his narrow shoulders hunched as if feeling the cold again. "That ice is heavy — I was freezing all the time."

He had fared no better in the Army. Because of his size, he attracted more than his share of kitchen police and other undesireable chores.

"I was always on the list for KP," Simpson said, "and when I reported, I always wound up among the pots and pans."

In spite, or perhaps because of, his miserable childhood, Bob maintained a jaundiced eye and an off balance sense of humor toward the more bizarre circumstances of daily Army life.

After a couple of days in a staging area near Washington, D. C., we were loaded back on the train, and made our final trip to the camp near New York Harbor. During the war years, New York was the heart-beat of America. The City saw the young Americans off to war and welcomed them home. I had come to know some of the boys from Manhattan Island and found them to be good soldiers and interesting in their unusual background that was so strange to me at the time.

Used to living crowded together with a necessity to live by the rules, I found them law abiding and obliging — just the opposite to the image sometimes cast of the big city.

I had been prejudiced in their favor by my experience as a child with my brother-in-law, Hank, Julia's husband. I was twelve at the time of Julia's death. Hank, who had worked for the telephone company in and under the streets of New York City, had spent a lot of time with me and taught me to appreciate his innovative, hard-working Yankee ways.

Simpson and I went to New York together.

The USO on the island was jammed with every branch of the service, but highly and efficiently organized, and the private soldier was treated like a celebrity.

"Two tickets for 'Life with Father'," the attractive brunette sang out, "coming up for the men in olive drab."

The seats were seventh row, center for the most popular show on Broadway,"Life With Father."

After the show, Bob and I decided to take in a night club. We had heard of the Latin Quarter.

The huge night club was packed. When the maitre d' saw our olive drab, unadorned by rank or metal or insignia, he waved us forward.

"Right this way gentlemen". Bob and I looked around to see if he was talking to somebody behind us.

In the center was a large stage with tiers of tables and chairs for the patrons rising several levels on all sides. The small tables were jammed and we couldn't see an empty seat.

Except for two — on the first level above the floor — in the center.

By this time, Bob and I were feeling pretty good. The main attraction was a wild apache' dance — in the finale, the male star ran up a long wooden ramp, flung himself into space and landed, spread eagle, on a big barrel that smashed into bits.

We were feeling no pain when we left the night club. We decided to see what Times Square looked like at 2 a. m.

"Hey," Bob said, "I thought this place would be crowded." A few drifters wandered around the periphery of the big, asphalt junction. We went down into the subway and watched an empty train rumble past the deserted loading platform.

"Well," Bob sighed. "Apparently people go home at night in New York just like they do in Reading."

"Can you believe the way they treated us,", I said.

"Yes," he replied, "almost like we were human. Sometimes in this Army you feel like the only entrance is through the back door with your hat in you hand pulling at your forelock."

"The uniform helps maintain the aura of inferiority," I agreed, "At least we know what it feels like to be a third-class citizen."

"Everywhere, but New York," Bob said with a crooked smile.

After the royal treatment we had received, we felt like New York knew what the war was about — and who was fighting it.

Six months later, the first civilians I saw after I returned to the U. S. were the New York women who came to Mitchell Field hospital to bring food to the wounded soldiers. It was magnificent. Half starved after the war zone dehydrated, canned and ersatz food, we were fed steak — and brought cake and ice cream — and anything we could think of to ask for.

To those of us who knew New York during the war, it will never be the dirty, crime-ridden deteriorating sink hole depicted by the press in recent years. To me, it remains America's heart beat.

The Mauretania crossed unescorted. Because of her superior speed she was able to zig zag every seven minutes so that the German wolf pack, traveling slowly under the ocean surface, did not have time to draw a bead on the huge vessel.

When we had entered the ship, Bob and I, with a couple hundred other GI's, were herded into what looked like a mess hall several decks below the water level.

"Hey, sarge," one of the GI's yelled. "Where we going to sleep?"

"This is it," was the reply. "You can sleep on the tables, on the benches, or on the floor. Make yourself at home."

"Well," Bob said, "At least we won't have far to go for dinner. I wonder if we should dress."

Meals were served from buckets at the end of the room and consisted mainly of varying types of stew.

We were free to roam at will and soon Bob and I were on the open deck, walking in a dense stream of GI's.

"Hey," Bob grabbed me by the arm, "Look through this window."

The blinds were tightly drawn, but through a crack we could see white linen, a platter of fresh biscuits and gleaming silver.

"Those bastards," I said, "look at that".

"Rank has its privilege, Clark," Bob said philosophically. "At least they're keeping it hid from the peons."

"They're scared we'd throw 'em overboard if this crowd of rabble saw that luxury," I said.

The huge ship plowed along sedately through the dark and forbidding North Atlantic.

Only as we neared the British coast did we appreciate the turbulence of that icy ocean. Our ship was so large it was little effected by the waves. Then we were met by a destroyer, the first of a convoy of warships and planes that were to guard us as the ship slowed near land.

Now, we watched as the destroyer, small as a wood chip compared to the Mauretania, rose and fell, swayed and rolled as it plowed through the massive waves.

Nearer shore, barrage balloons trailing long steel cables that would snare an attacking German plane, guarded the harbor as we unloaded at Liverpool.

The big camp near Manchester was for staging only — we would spend three weeks in England and then be shipped across the channel to France.

In the barracks, Bob Simpson and I joined the crowd to hear an announcement.

"Men," the lieutenant had been to France, been wounded, and now was sending replacements through the staging process, "we can't give you a pass but every other night. Those are the regulations. You are on your way to France, though, and I would like to point out that there are some rather large holes in the fence down that way." He pointed through the open door.

Every evening a line would form at one of the holes. Later as the night progressed, the soldiers would line up outside to crawl back in. Periodically, there was a crack down and a few soldiers were arrested. Since we were on our way to the front any detention ended with the next shipment to France.

"Men," the sergeant was standing in the center of the tar paper barracks, "I've got five passes to the Red Cross dance. Anybody interested come draw a number from the hat."

I was not one of the fortunate five, and, under the duress of our soon departure from civilization in general and girls in particular, I fell in with a bad crowd.

"Don't worry about it, Harrison," the speaker was of the guardhouse lawyer type, "I know how we can get in the Red Cross dance."

With thousands of men about to leave for France surrounding the building, a galvanized iron fence had been constructed surrounding the recreation center. Every entrance was guarded by two soldiers from the cadre that ran the base.

The three of us gathered at the rear of the compound fartherest removed from the guard posts. It was dark in this corner, and one after another we leapt for the top of the galvanized iron fence, pulled ourselves up and carefully over.

The last man over the galvanized wall hit the metal with a loud gong. In a flash, we were surrounded by guards. Their M-1 rifles pointed at our middles, we were herded into the presence of a fierce-looking major with a large red handle bar mustache.

"Do you know what I'd do to you if this was my property," the red-headed major was standing with his hands on his hips glaring at the three of us. "I'd take my 45 and put a bullet right between your eyes."

As soon as our interview with the major was concluded, we found ourselves standing outside the compound. We had about given up on the chance of meeting any girls that evening when our guardhouse lawyer rejoined us. The persistent type, he had been conducting a survey of the situation.

"Hey," he whispered, "I found a better way to get in."

We followed him into the canteen that was open to all and where those denied entrance to the dance were served doughnuts and coffee as a kind of consolation prize. The doughnut shop was connected to the dance hall. Giving a signal, our guardhouse barrister slipped behind the counter. Following him, we found ourselves being led by one of the girls through the kitchen. Now, we were inside the dance hall again.

Our only anxious moment came when we spotted the red headed major, but we were more criminally adept now and we managed to slip from whatever room he was occupying in time and to elude his glance for the rest of the evening.

I was destined to see the fierce looking major two more times — an Episcopal minister, he preached the sermon on Sunday. I didn't enjoy the sermon much and with head lowered, I slipped out as quickly as possible after shaking hands with the major on the way out.

Just before we left the camp, the same red-headed major conducted the final inspection of our replacements. We were standing in formation, chafing under the weight of our sixty pound packs as he made his rounds.

I don't know if he recognized me, but he stopped in front of me. He stood there a few moments, looking me up and down.

"Soldier," I was standing at attention, eyes straight ahead, "Do you like that pack?"

"No, Sir," I snapped.

"Do you like that rifle?"

"No, Sir," I sang out.

"Do you think it will do a job for you?"

"Yes, Sir."

"Soldier," he said, "do you like the Army?"

"No, Sir!" I shouted.

"Good soldier," and he moved on down the line.

Never underestimate the power of the young to find fun, frivolity and the opposite sex under the most dire circumstances.

We were only in England three weeks, but, thanks to my illegal entry into the Red Cross dance and use of the hole through the fence, I met and dated a small and very pretty girl named Pat several times.

The first time was at the dance.

Pat and I hit it off right away. She was a good dancer and after a number of energetic rounds, we had some punch and decided to take a little air in the yard that was enclosed by the galvanized iron fence.

There were several large trees and we went around to the far side of one. After the closeness of the dance, I found myself holding Pat again and emboldened by the wartime contraction of time in such matters, we found ourselves embracing.

After all, I was going to France in a couple of weeks.

The door to the dance hall opened and we heard someone stumble down the steps.

The other drink being served was the famous 3.2 beer. It might not be as intoxicating as Mexican beer, but it certainly had maintained a diuretic potency.

I held Pat tighter and we began to kiss.

Then, we heard a stream hit against the other side of the tree.

We held each other tighter.

As they say, love will find a way, even under the most stressful circumstances.

After the dance, Pat invited me to visit her home at 24 Winnington Lane, Winnington, Cheshire.

Pat's home was one of a large development of row houses that were built for the working men of the nearby factory. Sitting probably ten feet from the street behind a tiny yard, it was minute in every way. The small living room was heated by a miniature fireplace with an open grate.

"The worst thing about the war," Mrs. Hughes put a single lump of coal on the fire, "is that we can't get the scissors, kitchen utensils and things that used to come from Germany. They were cheaper and they were better than what we can get now."

For tea, Mrs. Hughes served scones and generous slices of cold lamb. I didn't want to eat their food — we had so much more than the English — but she insisted.

I was in their home several times before we shipped out and was always treated graciously. The only exception was one evening when Mr. Hughes was present. I could feel his resentment toward me and the American Army in general. It was understandable. They had been suffering with the war for five years, rationing kept them just above the starvation level and their pay was a fraction of that received by the young Americans. Most of their young men were serving far from home and there was no end in sight.

Conservation was practiced by everyone on the island by necessity, soldiers as well as civilians. When Mrs. Hughes wanted to heat water for tea, she would put a small coin in the end of the hot plate. The gas would come on just long enough to heat the water then shut off again.

In the brick, single-story English barracks where we were quartered, the most irritating feature was taking a bath. The concrete slab floor was always cold to the feet, and the shower was rigged so it was necessary to pull a chain and hold it to get the shower to run. Release the chain, and a spring shut off the water. It was a skill I didn't master in the brief time we were there — to get a good shower trying to soap with one hand while holding the chain with the other.

But most touching to me during my visits with Pat was watching Mrs. Hughes carefully pick up one lump of coal with her tongs and place it carefully in the small grate. I began to understand why the British wore such heavy woolen clothes.

By their standards, all Americans were rich.

When we crossed the channel, we got a taste of what the common British soldier and sailor endured. We had our only meal served by the British to British war-time standards.

It was breakfast. The eggs were powdered and the sausage apparently made from sawdust. We gained a new appreciation for the men who had survived such food along with the hazards of war. England was a nation of heroes.

When our staging was complete, we were transported by train to South-hampton, the port of embarkation across the channel to France.

Standing in the huge sheds that adjoined the shiploading dock, Bob Simpson and I looked with interest at the men who filled the shed next to ours.

As replacements, we had no shoulder patch or other identification. These men wore an assortment of patches from a broad spectrum of outfits. "Yeh, I was hit at St. Lo," the soldier's mouth had a nervous twitch. "All of us are retreads. We've been in the hospital and are on our way back up."

"They say they're sending us back as military police," one of the men was saying. "But, I don't trust them. We'll end up right back on the front."

Crossing the channel into France was an adventure for those of us who had not been there — but for these men there was no romance left. It was as if they were from another time — an older, wiser generation.

The day was overcast as we lined the ship's deck looking out toward the French coast. It had been three months since American kids had died on the beach, known as Omaha, but the wreckage of war was apparent everywhere.

A long line of freighters, run into the shore and sunk to make a break-water, had created a harbor for the flat-bottomed landing craft. Once inside, the water leading up to the beach was relatively calm as our ship slowed to a stop, lowering massive anchors to secure our large vessel.

Heavy rope made a net of squares to give the men a hand and foot hold to descend to the landing craft.

It was a hazardous descent, even in the relatively regular swells inside the breakwater. We were loaded down with the sixty-pound packs that tried to pull us away from the ship as we made the long climb down.

Far below, the flat deck of the landing craft, like a wood chip on the water, would rise and then fall in a regular cadence. There were about ten feet between the high and low elevations of the bobbing craft.

"Watch it carefully, men," the sergeant was stationed at the rail as we each took our turn over the side, moving in groups of five. "Watch the rise and fall of the deck and jump just before it reaches the top of the wave."

If the jump was made after the descent began, a disastrously long fall could result. If at the beginning of the rise, the rising deck would multiply the force of impact.

The Navy quartermaster eased us away from the ship and turned the heavily laden landing craft toward the beach. The sides were high enough to crouch below, but once the craft ground up on the beach and the massive tail gate swung down to make the ramp, the soldiers who preceded us that June day had been exposed to German fire.

Scattered up and down the beach were abandoned tanks, artillery pieces, jeeps that had not survived the D-day landing and had yet to show the rust that would devour them.

"You mean those guys climbed that," I was talking to Simpson.

"And with the German Army pouring mortar, artillery and small arms fire at them," Simpson agreed with a low whistle.

The walls of the cliff that sat far back from the beach were virtually perpendicular and seemed a least a hundred feet high. The massive German concrete pill boxes loomed far above the beach along the rim of the towering cliff.

Now, a steady stream of the young soldiers from our ship were struggling up the paths worn to the summit by the thousands who had landed since D-day. The heavy packs made it slow going, but the vision in our minds of those who had inched up these trails, under fire, on D-day assured our steady progress.

Wars are fought by kids — and God have mercy on the politicians who forget that truth and betray that trust.

St. Lo, just off the Omaha Beach, had been battered to the ground in the time that the Allies had struggled to break out of the perimeter forged to contain the landing hordes.

"The Germans didn't do any damage to us," the citizen of St. Lo was speaking clearly and distinctly and looking me straight in the eye. "You Americans came in and destroyed everything we had."

And, it was true. When the Germans attacked France in 1940, the rapid crumbling of resistance, had left the towns and countryside virtually untouched at the beginning of the war.

The stubborn resistance of the Germans when the Allies hit the beaches on D-Day in that summer of 1944 was in sharp contrast up until the breakout at St. Lo. We could understand the hostility of the Norman. The United States of America, finally roused to a frenzy of revenge, was cutting a swarth of destruction across Europe that dwarfed earlier efforts of Hitler. We would run into more bewilderment and hostility among the refugee population as we came closer to the front.

"Look at that," Simpson said pointing toward a large opening in the earthen hedgerow. The farms in this part of France were divided into small fields separated by dykes of dirt mounded several feet high and topped by heavy growths of close-packed hedges. They were there simply to divide one field from its neighbors, but every hedgerow was a natural earthwork for the defending Germans.

"Those hedgerows are why they held us so long," Simpson said, "cross one and another was waiting a hundred yards away. Those guys really caught hell."

The American tanks were useless in the beginning. They could plow up over the hedgerow but when the tank was going over, the thin underbelly was exposed and the Germans were waiting to fire an anti- tank shell into it.

"They finally broke out when some genius welded a big plow across the front of the tank and they holed straight through," Simpson pointed to the wide opening leveled through the hedgerow.

"American ingenuity," I agreed.

Without anybody to tell us what to do, we replacements were already dirty, disheveled and unshaven. Simpson and I looked like Willie and Joe in the Mauldin cartoons of life at the front. We were standing on the curb, coats hanging open and rifle slung upside down from our shoulders. We looked like we had been through a hard campaign.

"Well, what do you know, Simpson," I pointed down the street at a procession of freshly washed, sparkling vehicles. As they drove smartly by, the drivers and troops were neatly dressed and seemed to be sitting at attention — the only thing lacking were neck ties and pressed trousers.

"Yea," Simpson said, "reminds me of our Infantry Day parade."

We didn't know it, but we were looking at the outfit we would shortly join — the 104th Timberwolf Division, under General Terry Allen. By the time we crossed France, they would have been bloodied and we were to be their first replacements. For the moment, we felt like we were the veterans and they were the Boy Scouts.

From St. Lo, we were packed on to the big six-by-six Army trucks and rode with the canvas top removed across the flat French countryside. The rumor was we were going to Paris — but the closest we came to urban life was a town with a banner stretched across the road proclaiming, "Welcome to our glorious liberators."

We made a left turn there. We never made it to Paris.

After a day on the trucks, we reached a railhead, unloaded, and were filed into a line of small French freight cars made famous by Americans in World War I as the "40 or 8" — they carried forty men or eight horses. Simpson and I counted, and our car had only 39, including one second lieutenant who was nominally in charge, but who, in practice, showed the good sense of keeping a low profile among our rabble.

"You know, Simpson," I said as we clacked along the narrow guage rails at an agonizingly slow rate, "I used to really like chocolate."

It was to be a three day trip by rail and for those three days all we had to eat were the hard chocolate bars that provided a maximum of nutrition in a minimum of cargo space. For years after, I couldn't eat chocolate and, even today, I imbibe very seldom.

"Yea," Simpson agreed, "and I used to like to lie down. Whoever devised this space allocation knew what he was doing. We can sit and we can stand, but if anybody lies down somebody's got to leave."

A few tried to ride on top, but the low and narrow French bridges and tunnels soon stopped that. Needless to say, tempers became somewhat frayed as the hours drug on.

"If we couldn't step on the lieutenant's luggage, I couldn't take this," Simpson said. As ranking officer, the lieutenant had placed himself and his expensive officer's baggage by the open door of the car. Each of us made it a part of ritual to step on the lieutenant's baggage anytime the train stopped and we were able to dismount.

Other breaks came as we passed through the orchard country. It was harvest time and smiling farm workers threw apples through the open door as we moved slowly past.

Every hour or so the freight train would screech to a stop. We never knew whether it would be stationary five minutes or three hours. But, it was the third day and I had made up my mind I was going to get me something to eat.

"Hey, Clark," Simpson hollered, "you better get back here. This train's liable to pull out any minute."

"If it does, I'll catch the next one," I shouted as I trotted across the tracks toward the small French village.

"Hello, young man," the Frenchman spoke perfect English, "what are you looking for?"

I explained my situation.

"Come with me," he said, and we set off down the village street. I was listening for the long blast on the whistle that would tell me the train was about to pull out.

"You sure speak good English," I said as we walked quickly along.

"Well, I should," he said, "I'm British. Came over in 1917, liked it, married a French girl and stayed."

He turned down a path and disappeared behind a house. When he reappeared, he was carrying a small bottle and a half loaf of the hard, twisted French bread.

"I'd give you more," he said, "but our town's been cleaned out. Germans were here one morning and by 10 a.m. they were gone and the Americans came driving through in their tanks and trucks."

The place had gone wild. Home-made American and French flags appeared at every window, and the streets were filled with people hugging and kissing the young American soldiers.

"We gave them everything we had," he said, "All our food and all our wine. It was wonderful."

The long blast on the train whistle came just then. Thanking him profusely for something other than chocolate to eat, I ran across the tracks toward the freight train.

We didn't leave right away, so I pulled the cork out of what I thought was a wine bottle and took a big swig.

"Phew" — I spit the liquid out, gagging and coughing. One of the older men was standing nearby and I handed the small bottle to him.

"I don't know what it is," I said, "but it's too hairy for me."

He took a sip of the fiery liquid, rolled it around in his mouth and gazed skyward in rapt bemusement.

"Why, son," he said in a soft southern accent, "that's cognac and I am most obliged to you."

I was more of a beer drinker at the time.

But, my! Did that bread taste good after three days of chocolate bars. The countryside was unscarred for most of our trip. The Germans pursued by Patton had been going hell for leather back to the Fatherland at this stage and had put up little or no resistance.

The exception was the railhead where the allied air power had concentrated to break up their re-supply efforts during the battle of St. Lo.

As we pulled slowly through the intersection, we were awed by the power of bomb and strafing cannon. Railroad cars lay twisted and riddled like toy trains smashed by a giant hand.

We left the train when we neared Belgium and transfered to six-by-six trucks that carried us to a large, open field, covered with thick, green grass. Simpson and I put our shelter halves together to make a tent and were soon part of a large tent city filling the field.

"Have you ever seen anything like this mud?" I asked Simpson. "They must have gotten every rock out of this field generations ago. Let's go get some of that straw."

The mud was black and apparently bottomless. Soon the troops had beaten any traveled spots to a quagmire and were going to nearby hay racks to layer over the thick mud for sleeping that night.

We were getting more nervous now, as we knew we could not be many miles from the front.

I decided to get all my equipment in first class shape. I stripped the rifle down, oiled it thoroughly and then started working on the bolt.

Inside the bolt was a tiny spring, about one inch long and one eighth inch in diameter. We had been taught to take it out but never did so in a normal cleaning of the rifle. It was called the ejector spring and the rifle would not fire automatically without it.

"Oh, my God," I groaned. I was sitting on a pile of straw and as I twisted the spring it popped and disappeared into the straw. I knew I would never see it again — which was probably what I deserved after kidding Bob about dropping his steel helmet into New York Harbor.

Bob had gotten another helmet, but the chances of somebody replacing my ejector spring at this stage of our trip toward combat were nonexistent. My rifle had just lost its semi-automatic capability.

I was sitting staring down at the straw between my stretched out legs when Simpson walked over. He reached down.

"Hey, Clark," he said, "you better put this back in your bolt." He handed the tiny spring to me.

That night, small fires were lit in scattered spots around the tent city revealing the large body of men camped there.

Then we heard the sound of a small plane slowly circling in the darkness overhead.

"What's that?" I said in alarm. I knew we could be seen and I had visions of bombs bursting, strafing and shelling.

"Oh, I wouldn't worry about that," Simpson was talking like a seasoned veteran. "The Germans wouldn't be sending a little plane this far behind our lines in the middle of the night. Even if they did, he wouldn't be able to tell his artillery where we are in the dark. It's got to be one of ours."

I had found Simpson to be a cool customer in the strange situation we found ourselves in. All that work in the ice house and the army kitchens had conditioned him. He didn't necessarily want to die, but life had given him so much misery the present conditions must have seemed like a vacation.

The next morning, standing in the open field we watched as wave after wave of allied bombers passed over on their way to Germany. The sky was literally filled from one horizon to the other.

"Must be one of those thousand plane raids," Simpson said.

"Well," I said "if I'd gone in the Army Air Corps when I was first drafted, I might be up there flying one of those beauties."

"Well, Simpson philosophized, "right at the moment they're a helluva lot more nervous than we are. Can you imagine sitting in the green house on the nose of one of those slow moving monsters watching the ack ack burst all around you. Personally, I believe I'd rather be where I can dig a hole in the ground."

"Simpson," I said, looking at his scrawny body, receding chin and thin, mishapen fingers, "What are you going to do when this is all over?"

"Well," he said, "with me working and mother sewing, I had finished two years in a little liberal arts college at home. I like working with books a lot better than the ice house and I'd never make it in the coal mine. What I want to do is teach English. Maybe in our neighborhood high school."

"You don't seem to be scared," I said looking at him quizzically.

"Oh," he replied, "I'm scared all right. But you know, in spite of all the things my mother and I went through when Dad was killed, we still made it. Somehow we were always taken care of. After going through so much, you begin to develop a confidence that God will see you through everything — if you'll try to do what he says and believe he's looking out for you."

"Well," I said, looking up at the armada of B-17's filling the skies, "I know one thing. I wouldn't want to be in Germany today."

Loaded back on the trucks, we were soon across the Belgian frontier, rolling along the flat, lowland countryside. The road was lined now with tall trees, trunks straight and foliage high above our heads. We passed one section where the trees had been cut halfway through with a charge of dynamite strapped to the other side. Apparently, the Germans had been retreating too rapidly to set off the charges that would have blocked the road.

"Look at this." Simpson and I had gotten down from the truck and were standing by a row of eight graves, with simple crosses marking seven, and flowers piled over the head of each of them. The marker on the eighth grave was at the opposite end; there were no flowers. "That must have been the German." Jenkins pointed at the flowerless grave.

"These people are really bitter," I said.

"Before this is over," Simpson added, "they'll be bitter at us too."

Word was passed via the grapevine that we were on our way to Antwerp. A large force of Germans was trapped on the estuary there and were being pounded by the First Canadian Army with the 104th Timberwolf American Division attached. That was the shiny new outfit that had rolled past us at St. Lo.

"They must be taking losses," Simpson said, "and that's the reason we're being sent up as replacements."

"I heard there are some S.S. trapped in there with them," I added. "It's been mostly second and third grade troops they've run into so far, but now they are coming up against Hitler's elite."

The trucks were slowing now and we could hear artillery in the distance. Along each side of the road were the bloated carcasses of cows and horses killed in recent fighting in this farm area.

One of the GI's jumped off his truck and went running across the field.

"Look at this," he said, waving a rifle above his head, "it's a German rifle."

"Yeh," Simpson grunted, "he's lucky it wasn't booby trapped."

The trucks pulled off the road and we all unloaded.

"Throw all your equipment in a pile here," the sergeant was saying. "Everything but your rifle, your shovel and a light pack. You're going to have to travel light from here on."

Dusk was coming on as we lined up for our new assignments.

Six names were called out. Simpson was one of them. They were lining up to leave when somebody addressed the captain who had come to pick up his replacements.

"Hey, captain," the GI said, "what is the uniform of the day?"

"Son," the captain was visibly tired and showed the signs of fatigue brought on by the recent combat, "it's your life and there's not much we can do to help you from here on out. It's rough up there. You take anything you think will help you stay alive. Your rifle, but even more important, your shovel — get down below the ground as fast as you can — the bigger the shovel the better. And be sure you have your tooth-brush. That rifle you're carrying won't fire automatically once you get a grain of this sand in that little hole in the gas chamber."

I looked at Simpson, standing forlornly in the gathering dusk. He was loaded with two belts of ammunition, had his pockets and lapels loaded with hand grenades, and his rifle slung by its strap from his thin shoulder.

That guy, I thought, has got guts. He'll go all the way through this war and after it's over nobody will ever believe he was a combat infantryman.

Several years after the war, I heard from another GI who had been with us in Europe. He told me about Simpson.

"Bob went through nine months of combat," he said. "He carried the heaviest weapon a single soldier handles — the Browning Automatic Rifle — the BAR. He was never wounded."

"Well, I asked, "what's he doing now?"

"What he always said he'd do," was the reply. "He's teaching high school English in a small town in Pennsylvania."

I was in the next group called out — eighteen of us. We loaded onto a mess truck and rumbled away into the night.

As we came closer, the sound of artillery fire became more intense and on the far horizon we could see the blue dots of flame made by tracer bullets arching across the dark sky. From time to time, a flare would explode and slowly descend on its small parachute, providing several seconds of bright red light.

We passed a line of 155 artillery pieces, muzzles pointed toward the distant and fiery horizon. The truck driver swung his vehicle to the left into an open field.

Just as the truck came to a stop, a GI came running toward us across the open field. As he got closer, we could see he was soaking wet.

"We're trapped," he yelled. "the whole outfit is trapped across the river. I got out by swimming back."

The story came out over the next several days, as the handful of survivors drifted back to our assembly area.

The 104th had met only token resistance as it moved from the spot we had seen them in St. Lo across France and into Belgium — second and third grade troops, the young teenage boys and old men Germany had put into uniform in their last desperate callup.

"Terry Allen was going to win the war before Christmas," as one of the men put it. General Allen had earned a reputation in North Africa for aggressive action and high casualties.

"When we got to the river," one of the men said, "we should have stopped and waited to be resupplied and get ourselves together. We were out of bazooka ammunition, the machine gun belts weren't loaded, and there was no artillery support zeroed in."

The green troops pushed across the river, their officers thinking the Germans were on the run and it was not a time to slow down.

"We should have done like the British," one GI said. "They pulverize the earth with heavy artillery for three days then advance five hundred yards."

The Germans waited patiently while the entire first battalion crossed the river and began to dig foxholes. And the Germans were not tired, old men and green young teenagers — they were the dreaded SS— fanatical and hardened by five years of war. It was a trap, carefully laid, baited and impregnable.

"The 88's were lined up hub-to-hub in a big semi-circle around our beachhead," the GI continued. "When they opened up they had us at point blank range and the shallow holes we were in were no protection."

In Holland, the water table of the filled-in land is so close to the surface that it was impossible to dig a deep foxhole. Four feet down, the hole began to fill with water and the sides would crumble.

"When it got dark," he continued, "the bastards set fire to two big barns in the perimeter. That lighted up the whole area. Then they drove in two Panza tanks, lowered their big 88s and fired direct into our holes. It was horrible."

Once headquarters realized what was happening, an attempt to organize a relief was made, but it was as if the gods of war had ruled that the battalion was to die before the first rays of morning light.

"They sent up a major of artillery," another survivor related, "and tried to set up what should have been done before we ever started across. The major was going to spot and call in artillery fire to hold the Germans while we pulled back across the river."

With the major was a private carrying a rifle grenade — an attachment on the end of the standard M-1 rifle that turned it into a grenade launcher. A dummy round fired in the chamber created pressure to lob the grenade several hundred feet.

"On the way up" the soldier continued, "they ran into a machine gun nest. The GI fired his gun — but he had left a live round in the chamber. The grenade exploded on the end of the rifle, killing the major and ending any chance we had of help from the artillery.

The private survived and we all heard he had gone berserk when he learned what his mistake had cost.

One thing was sure that dark and explosive night the mess truck brought us up — we were not going to be able to join our unit until the survivors made it back across the river.

From this point forward, I would be living and fighting with strangers. Bob Simpson was the last GI I would remember by name with the exception of the Italian, Frank Vacarro.

One of the GI's and I now joined forces and began to scoop out a foxhole in the soft sand. We were below the water table before we felt we had enough of the ground above us to protect us.

"Hey, look at that." I pointed to a big number 10 can that the mess sergeant had left on the ground near where we had eaten. I tasted the liquid in it. "This is good — peach juice."

My partner was not interested so I downed most of the juice before joining him in our fox hole.

The American 155's were in the field adjoining us — a couple hundred feet away. Now they opened up in earnest, pouring heavy shells that filled the air with a massive assault of sound as the large steel cylinders screamed fifty feet overhead.

We were sitting on our helmets, our heads down , our feet in the water.

My God, I thought — I'll never leave this hole. I grabbed my knees and held on.

The peach juice began to work. Suddenly, I was faced with a dilemma. My stomach was growling.

I jumped out of the hole.

Some fates are worse than death, I thought as I crouched over, shivering, unbuttoning my fatigues.

When morning came, we moved closer to the front to await the return of any survivors from the disaster of the night before.

In twos and threes the pitiful survivors limped back into the open field where we waited.

All officers had been killed or captured with the exception of one lieutenant who had been slightly wounded, and who rejoined us after he returned from the aid station.

Two sergeants who had demostrated leadership during the disaster were promoted to lieutenant.

I had heard of combat fatigue and now I witnessed it. The near death of total mental and physical exhaustion that can come only under prolonged stretches of adrenalin — saturated frantic activity under the stress of fear of imminent death or disfigurement.

The men who made it back were more like lifeless bundles of dirty clothes than human beings. They didn't even seem to breathe, or to turn, or to twitch any muscle. They were inanimate objects — and they stayed that way all day and all the next night. Some in a small barn in the assembly area. Some lying in the open field, oblivious to the bright sun of mid-day.

When they finally began to stir, it was obvious their nerves had been torn and left raw and exposed.

There were thirty-three of them out of a company of over two hundred.

"The colonel cracked up," one of the men said. "When he heard about all those boys dying, he just went to pieces and they had to pull him out and send a replacement."

He was a reserve officer — a nice old guy as they put it, but too sensitive to the human reality of war and young men.

Our battalion had been shattered, and now it was decided to pull the 104th out of the Canadian First Army and transfer it south to join the American First under Luther Hodges. This would give some time to fill up the ranks and try to make an outfit out of our battalion before the next action.

Before we left Holland, we were carried by truck to a bath and de-lousing station to get us cleaned up.

The station was set up in a huge, olive-drab tent. There was a room to undress in and a room filled with pipes, and a couple of hundred shower heads.

We had had one other bath since leaving France — in a creek near where we camped. While we were sloshing around in the cold water, several French girls strolled by on the road that paralleled the creek causing much waving, shouting and gesturing.

On the way to battle, the Army's sensitivities were not up to peace time standards to say the least. I remember a portable johnny that consisted of an open, flat bed truck with two long, parallel boxes that contained rows of spaced holes — a kind of super outhouse without the exterior walls. It was an efficient arrangement and apparently enjoyed by men who had had to dig their own hole in the ground for the purpose. The open latrine was fully occupied when a truckload of nurses rounded the bend, adding to the general merriment of the informal occasion.

"You have two minutes to undress," the captain was shouting, "two minutes under the shower and then back out here to dress."

The water was hot, plentiful — a luxury of fantasy proportions after the weeks of filth. Apparently, there was only one valve that turned the whole thing on and off.

"Everybody out," the captain shouted. And everybody went pushing and shoving out the exit.

Everybody but me. The water was still pouring out, it was piping hot and it was going to be a long time before such an opportunity was likely to recur.

The captain came back into the shower room and took a look at me — the sole occupant.

"Hell, son," he said, "I don't blame you. I'd do the same. You take your time."

One of the survivors of the river crossing was Frank Vaccaro. Frank was a tall, large boned Italian who had come through the ordeal in better shape than most of the GI's.

Frank was a pfc. He had had his rank restored after the outfit reached combat. From Brooklyn, Frank had gone AWOL shortly before the 104th shipped out so that he could visit his girlfriend one last time. When he returned, he was put under arrest until the outfit shipped out.

As one of the thirty-three survivors of the river crossing, Frank was now made squad leader and promoted to sergeant; and I was chosen as his assistant because I was one of the handful of replacements waiting in the assembly area for their return.

Frank was cool and his nerves seemed unaffected by the ordeal with the SS. After seeing the news reels of masses of Italians surrendering on every front in the war, it was easy to believe that Italians, as a people, were cowardly.

I was about to find out there was at least one exception.

The Italians had the same problem American GI's were to have in Vietnam. Young men need to believe in what they are fighting for.

"Men," the lieutenant had halted us in a open field near a small town.
"We are going to be here for several days. Maybe a week. So, you might
as well dig in good."

Frank and I selected a spot in the open field. There were civilian refugees coming and going as we began to dig a large square hole — big enough
for the two of us to stretch out side by side. Knowing we'd be settled
for a few days, we were going to have something nice.

A young Belgian came by and watched as we continued digging.
"Cigarettes," he said.

"Sure," Frank answered, "get us some straw."

"Straw," apparently the word was similar in his language. He set off
at a trot.

Half-hour later, he was back with straw — a big bale — he was carrying
it on his back. Frank gave him two packs of cigarettes. They were Chelseas — a war-time brand smoked by civilians and troops on the front.
We got the popular Lucky Strikes, Chesterfields, and Camels from the
PX back in the States. Once we got overseas, the closer we got to the
front, the poorer the quality of cigarettes. They passed through too many
hands on the way up and the good stuff was absorbed by the supply troops
and those in the rear echelon. We got Chelseas and something called Home
Runs. At least it was one thing we had in common with the civilians
back home.

The Belgian to whom American cigarettes were a medium of exchange
in a market that didn't know the difference between brands, was delighted. He began to make motions with his hands indicating that he could
provide a cover for our growing super hole.

Frank held up four fingers for four packs and the Belgian set off again.

This time he was gone longer. When he returned he was carrying a
large panel of new siding, big enough to cover the hole we had just finished
digging.

It was a perfect fit. Frank handed over the Chelseas and we began to
shovel dirt over the siding, making us a snug, enclosed shelter.

No sooner had we gotten our hole covered than two civilians wearing
the arm band colors of the Belgian Freedom Fighters and carrying sub
machine guns came up.

Through their gestures and broken English, we finally understood that
someone had stolen siding that was to be used to build a temporary building
for refugees.

Frank and I looked at each other, then glanced at the covered dug out that would represent our first good night's sleep in days — and perhaps our last. We decided the fortunes of war had dictated that the Belgians were going to have to wait a few days for their siding.

Frank and I even acquired a piece of candle. That night we were stretched out in the dugout comparing family photos by candlelight.

"You've got a pretty girl, Frank," I said. "Do you think you'll marry her when you get home?"

"Oh, sure," Frank said. "We grew up in the same neighborhood in Brooklyn. Our families are close friends — our parents are from the old country and knew each other back there."

"The Italians don't think much of this war, do they Frank?" I asked.

"Mussolini is a clown," he replied. "People aren't going to fight for somebody like that. If the Germans had been treated better after World War I, they wouldn't be fighting for Hitler either. Americans believe in what we're fighting for."

"Yea," I said. "I wonder if we would be fighting like we are if it hadn't been for Pearl Harbor."

"Americans are no different from anybody else," Frank said. "Someday we'll be in a war nobody believes in and you'll see."

"The French and Belgians we've seen don't seem too enthusiastic about the war, do they," I said.

"Well," Frank said, "they got bled white during World War I, especially the French. So many of their men were killed in the trenches and nothing seemed to be gained. The Germans wanted revenge, but all most French wanted was peace. When this war is over, it will be different. The French are the ones who have been humiliated this time and you are going to see them looking out for themselves after this."

"I hope we have learned something," I said, "and we won't grind Germany into the dirt again after this is over. I was raised in the South and our part of the U. S. is still in poverty because of policies followed by the North after the Civil War."

"I don't know," Frank said, "Secretary Morganthau is talking about turning industrial Germany into a pastoral colony."

"What I don't like," I said, "is this unconditional surrender Roosevelt and Churchill are calling for. That's just what Hitler wants and it will cost a lot of lives. Hitler is a madman. He doesn't care about the German people. If he can't win, he'll try to take the German people down with him. What he wants is a fight to the death. Roosevelt and Churchill's edict will cost a lot of GI lives."

Early next morning we moved out — our week of rest had lasted one night.

Our six by six had a black driver and we had been rolling for over an hour when we entered the outskirts of a large city — much like Atlanta, Georgia at that time.

Except this was Aachen, the first German town we would enter, just inside the border with France; and it had been devastated.

Parts of the steel and concrete multi-storied buildings and the large churches still stood, but the less substantial structures had been leveled and the streets were littered with debris.

"The Germans still hold half this town," shouted one of the GIs standing by the road as we passed.

Our truck was leading the column when there was a loud whistling, followed by an explosion in our near vicinity.

The black driver turned sharply left, slammed on the brakes and ground the heavy gears into reverse.

"Oh, Lordy," he yelled, "they're shooting at us."

We made our escape before the gunner could bracket his shot and soon had left the downtown behind us as the column was redirected.

We spent the night in a two story German house.

"Men," our sergeant told us, "if you see something you can use to survive, take it. Otherwise, let's leave these people's stuff alone."

And, for the most part, that was the way the Americans handled themselves. There were exceptions.

"What in the sam hill are you going to do with that?" I yelled at a GI. He had a heavy silver candlestick stuck under his belt and was taking the awkward burden from the house he was leaving.

"I thought I'd give it to the captain," he said.

Well, I thought, I hope you get a weekend pass for your trouble.

I did take advantage of the one opportunity I had to spend the night on a German bed — lying on top of the bare mattress, in my filthy combat jacket, wool trousers, and G. I. shoes, was luxurious after the nights in and on the ground.

Next morning, we went on a scouting patrol through the smashed town. Walking along the littered village street, I looked in a low window and saw a British soldier sitting in an easy chair holding a cat in his lap. A pot of tea was boiling on a small stove on the floor.

The British had been at war a lot longer than we had and had a more balanced viewpoint toward the whole procedure.

We were all mixed in with the British at this particular sector of the front. At one point we overtook a group of light British tanks.

"Hey," one of the GI's yelled, "why don't you take those things up where the fighting's going on."

"What," responded the limey, "and get me bloody tank blowed up!"

I had always thought that American troops did a lot of dumb things in training — after all, we were a citizen army. But, somehow, I felt that once we crossed the ocean and became combat troops we would be sharp. If anything, however, the herd instinct seemed worse now that we were in artillery range of the Germans.

The next evening, moving out of the village toward the front, we had marched until it was pitch dark. We were on the outskirts, with only an occasional house, when the column stopped.

Oh, me, I thought. Here it come!

We had bunched up, each GI banging into the man ahead. Almost immediately, we could hear muttering and cursing up and down the line.

I thought, as far as we know the Germans are in the field, right along side us.

Then it happened. "Hey," a GI shouted, "what the hell's going on up there?"

As if that did not sufficiently give our position away, the door of a house on the curbside opened, flooding the street with light. A man came out carrying a lantern and walked the length of our line of GIs, lighting each as he passed.

"Well," one of the GIs said, "at least we found out there are no hostiles around the immediate area."

It was the last light we would see that night. We stumbled along, holding the pack of the man in front, stopping from time to time as the various units were split off and led to their positions.

"You will be replacing the First Division," the lieutenant had told us that afternoon before we left. "They are in a defensive position and will orient you before leaving."

From past orientations, we had a mental picture of a lengthy explanation of conditions on the front line, complete with maps and a blackboard.

I have never experienced such blackness as we entered those German woods. The trees were planted in rows, jammed against others in the row, and the dense growth completely obliterated light.

The front was relatively quiet as we stumbled along, falling in old shell holes, slipping and sliding as we advanced in the pulverized earth. Now we were holding tight — completely blind except when a flare would pop overhead and bathe all of us in its red light. When that happened, we would freeze in whatever position we were in.

Then we stopped and stood in the blackness for an interminable time. Finally, I decided to go forward to try to find out what was happening. I felt my way from one GI to the next until there was no one ahead.

"Where's Frank?" Frank Vacarro was the squad leader — I was bringing up the rear as second in command.

"I don't know," the GI whispered. "They left me standing here."

About that time, Frank came to get the next man. We were just behind the line of fox holes and the First Division sergeant was leading our men into position. We were out of the densest part of the forest now and could make out enough to move with caution.

When Frank and I came to our fox hole, the First Division GI was ready.

"The field of fire is that way." He waved his arm in a forty-five degree arc to our front. "And there are some C rations in that box. I'll see you." He was out of the hole and moving into the night.

So much for orientation, I thought. Too bad the rest of the Army hadn't learned to be as brief.

There were three of us in the hole, the third being an eighteen year old boy named Johnson.

"You take the first watch, Clark," Frank said, "then call Johnson. I'll take the last shift."

Frank knew the early morning shift was the toughest and he was giving us a break. Johnson was new, an eighteen year old in the army just long enough to have finished his thirteen weeks of basic.

The First Division dugout we were feeling our way into had been well constructed of felled trees, covered with a thick layer of dirt. It was big enough for two men to stretch out and sleep. A shallow trench deep enough to crawl in led some ten feet forward from the entrance to the dugout and there was a T crossing for that ditch, about eight feet long and deep enough to stand in.

Standing alone in the trench, I could make out faint outlines of trees ahead but nothing to either side. This was the front and, presumably, our German opposites were standing across the way with their guns pointed at us.

"For God's sake don't start shooting," one of the veterans advised us just before we came up. "As long as they're quiet, don't stir them up."

It was quiet now.

No flares were bursting — not a sound was to be discerned.

And then I heard it.

Steady, deep breathing — over to the left. I visualized a German crawling toward me.

I turned slowly, pushed the safety in my trigger guard forward — ready to fire.

Hold it, Clark! I eased the safety back on. Don't forget you are in a line. That may be the GI in the next hole. I stood listening intently. The breathing continued methodically. There was no sound of movement. Gradually, I relaxed.

The next morning I would see the GI standing in his hole, not ten feet to my left. I had come close to killing one of my squad.

I could not see the dial on my watch, so I waited — and waited — and waited. Until I felt most of the night must have passed. I had learned from past night guard duty how the minutes drag.

I woke Johnson and crawled in beside Frank.

Within five minutes — Johnson was back in the dugout waking Frank up.

"Johnson," I whispered, "get back out there — you've just gotten started."

That night remained quiet, except for occasional gunfire. And then a half dozen shells exploded in our area. One a near miss.

"Clark," Frank was in the crawl trench at the opening of the dugout, "there's something out here."

I was instantly awake and crawling out into the trench.

"Here, Frank," I handed Frank one of my hand grenades and lay stretched out in the trench behind him.

Next morning Frank told me, "You're a good man to have in a foxhole, Clark. You know how long it takes to stand a watch — and I know I can count on you when I need you."

"Well," one of the survivors of the river crossing told me the next morning, "you're a veteran now. That was quite a shelling we had last night."

I had been back in the dugout when the shells hit so I didn't feel much like a veteran. I was tired and dirty from the intermittent sleep in the hole.

The next afternoon, Frank and I left Johnson and walked through the woods toward the German pill box that had become platoon headquarters. As we walked along the path it took an abrupt 90 degree turn. In the angle of the turn the exposed butt of a large artillery shell protruded from the dirt and leaves.

"If you come back through here tonight remember that turn," Frank said.

I would remember it all right — I can still see it today.

I was left in the pill box and Frank continued on to company headquarters for instructions.

"I think we'll be pulling out tonight," Frank said before he left. "If we
do, you'll have to go back in behind the squad and pull them out."

I thought about that unexploded shell at the turn in the path.

As dark approached, noise outside the pill box increased. An occasional shell would explode nearby, rifle fire and the distinctive stacatto of the
German burp gun — an automatic weapon so called because of the rapid
rate of fire and the short bursts the Germans used. Men wounded by
a burp gun had a common pattern — one shot in the lower left abdomen, one in the center of the gut, and one in the upper right chest —
caused by the recoil of the rapid fire weapon rising to the right as it fired.

The concrete pill box was a black hole, lit by a couple of sputtering
candles. There were a few bunk beds with hard straw mattresses, and I
tried to stretch out for a while.

When sleep wouldn't come, I joined the two men loading machine gun
belts. It was slow work. Our fingers moved awkwardly as we listened to
the sounds of combat just outside the walls.

This was the headquarters for "D" company — the machine gun company that had men scattered up and down the line in their own "nests".
The radio man was in contact with the scout who had been sent to check
on each position in order.

"These crazy fools are shooting at me!" The voice coming in over the
signal corp radio sounded desperate. "Every time I try to move behind
the lines somebody shoots or throws a hand grenade."

The operator in the pill box tried to settle him down. Then, he would
call from the next position reporting the same action by the GIs. The
combination of green troops with the combat fatigued survivors of the
river crossing was creating havoc in the dark behind the line of dugouts.

I was thinking of the part I had to play when Frank returned. How
was I going to find our men in the dark — let them know it was me —
avoid the unexploded shell and the firing and grenades of the green troops?

"This is a great life," one of the GIs said, "try to stay alive today so
you can get shot tomorrow."

At that moment, a German burp gun exploded into action just outside
the concrete bunker.

"Oh, God," the D company man stumbled into the pill box, "it's un-
believable out there. You can't move without somebody taking a shot
at you."

His voice was shaking and his body was trembling. We all hunkered down around him, listening as he poured out his story.

The night passed and I was never called — it was after dawn when Frank came into the pill box and we went out to gather in our squad for the withdrawal.

Later, we learned what had happened that night to save me from the trip behind the rattled troops.

It involved a young, red headed soldier Bob Simpson and I had come to know during our trip across in the Mauretania.

He was slight of build, eighteen years old, and had a light-hearted way on looking at army life and laughing at its absurdities.

When I saw him a couple of days after our withdrawal from the front, he was a different man.

The most noticeable thing, next to his restless, darting eyes, was the twitch in his lips as he talked.

"They sent me in to get one of our boys who had gone off the deep end", he told me.

It was one of the survivors of the river crossing. When the battalion was trapped by the SS, he was with a friend he had had since basic training in the new division. That night, they were able to make it back to the river, swim across and stumble, leading one another, back to safety.

"Two days ago," Red told me, "his buddy was hit by an artillery tree burst. He died in his friend's arms."

After much persuasion, the medic was able to get the body of the dead soldier away from his friend and it was evacuated to the rear.

When the troops were preparing to withdraw from the front, late that afternoon, the friend of the dead soldier was nowhere to be seen.

"Finally," Red said, his mouth twitching, "they found him hunkered in the back of the dugout he and his friend had shared. He wouldn't come out no matter how they tried to reason with him."

Word got back to the battalion commander of the situation, and he made the decision to delay the withdrawal until the mentally disturbed soldier could be brought out.

"Since he was in my squad," Red told me, "they sent me in to bring him out. It was pitch black by that time."

Red had the same experience the D company messenger encountered.

"It was horrible," Red continued, "every time I'd make a move or a noise, somebody would fire his rifle or throw a hand grenade. It would have been suicide to have continued."

Finally, in desperation, Red got one of his buddies to go with him.

"We didn't know what else to do," he said, "so we went in singing 'The Old Grey Mare' and a couple of other songs we used to sing in training. Then, we talked at the top of our voices, telling them we were Americans and to let us through."

Finally, the nerve shattered GIs comprehended what Red and his friend were trying to do and they let them through.

By that time, Red's nerves were shattered.

And I was saved from a similar experience.

With the dawn, it was a simple matter to pull our squad out.

Withdrawing from the line, we had been pulled back into the village and had slept most of the day after safety was reached and we waited to be moved back up. Apparently, supplies were beginning to catch up with the troops along the German border and this time we were to move into an attack.

The destruction that was being brought to bear against the Germans was massive, and awesome to behold.

From our position, once again just behind the front lines, we would listen all day to the rumble of artillery — all up and down the American lines it was a continuous roar with the answering fire of the German 88's being heard as individual shots — a long whistle followed by an explosion that varied in proportion to the nearness of the miss.

We were all progammed to hit the ground at the first sound of that whistle.

Actually, we were told, we'd never hear the one that hit us — the shell traveled faster than the sound. But, regardless of the scientific facts, our bodies seemed to want to get horizontal.

Then we'd jump up and continue what we were doing once the explosion came.

The Germans were beginning to surrender in larger numbers. For the most part they were grey haired men and young teenagers who were obviously relieved to be out of range of the American bombs and guns.

I can remember being especially touched by one platoon of Germans who passed us in the village. At the rear, two soldiers were dragging a man who appeared to be my Dad's age. The Germans were paying an awesome price for Hitler's madness and the cruelest burdens seemed to be falling on those least able to bear them.

That night we pushed off again in a forced march that was to bring us the nine miles to Stolberg, one of the suburbs of Aachen.

Again, it was dark, but on the open road not as pitch black as it had been in the forest. We were still exhausted from the sleepless nights on the front and twice I saw a GI walk off the road and stumble into the ditch.

Several times, I awoke to discover I had been marching along the edge of the road asleep.

It was still dark when we reached the school building in Stolberg that was to provide us shelter for the next five days.

When the sun came up, we went about exploring the school — a large, one-story modern building, it reminded us of home — particularly the bathrooms. The gleaming chrome and porcelain made us conscious of the German influence on American life.

"We're more like the Germans than we're like the English or French," I told Frank, "on the outside, anyway."

"It does look familiar," he said. "Look at this magazine."

Apparently, this had been a girls' school. We found several magazines, again like the slick photograph filled U. S. magazines. One featured healthy, blonde young women in shorts and T-shirts exercising in formation. "Hitler wasn't all bad," I said, "look at the way he developed the German youth." Bringing Germany out of the doldrums of depression had been a major Nazi accomplishment. "Too bad he's sick in the head."

"Yea," Frank said, "these kids look good, but he had them turning in their own parents when the old folks protested against the Nazi."

"If Hitler had been assassinated before September, 1939, he would have gone down as a national hero, " I said, "the autobahns, public buildings, work projects, and rebuilding the armed forces put people back to work in a country that idolizes work. But he built on hate — and hate goes so far before it meets its own creation — the hate that comes in reply."

A middle aged German couple were in the building. Apparently, they had something to do with the school and had elected to stay when the rest of the Germans pulled out. They could not speak our language, but by their actions, showed that they wanted to reassure us as to their friendly intentions. They could have been Americans by their dress and manner and they were constantly smiling.

Shells were beginning to fall in the area and we beat a hasty retreat to the basement under the school.

It was unlighted but with enough height for us to stand and move about comfortably. For light, a cache of torches that must have been used in ceremonial parades were found. They were tapered, about three feet in length and burned with a yellow flame and black smoke. Four or five were kept burning to provide light for the large basement that housed our company.

"Men," Lt. Fox had gathered us around him in the flickering light, "we are going to push off in the morning in the biggest attack since the break-out at St. Lo.

"Since we hit the German border, we have been stopped. As much by a lack of supplies as by the stiffening resistence of the Germans. The Germans are fighting for their own soil now and their supply lines are getting shorter every day while ours are getting longer.

"That's the reason they were fighting so viciously at Antwerp. Once we secure the port there, our supplies can be docked just a few miles from the front. Right now, they have to come all the way from Cherbourg, France.

"We felt it when we ran out of ammunition before we made the river crossing. And that is why you were issued loose ammunition and had to reload your single rifle clip.

"The supplies have been building over the last couple months, and we are ready now for a major assault against the Fatherland."

"Our attack will be preceded by the heaviest tactical air assault against the Germans since the war began. We're in this basement because those bombs are going to be dropped right in our front. Starting tomorrow, don't be surprised when this building starts to shake to its foundation. Right after the bombing stops we will leave here and push off.

"There is one thing I want to warn you about. We got clobbered when we crossed the Maas because we got out ahead of the rest of the line. We were over on the German side of the river by ourselves and we didn't have a chance.

"Tomorrow, when we push off, I want each of you to look to his left and to his right. If there's nobody coming along with you — stop. This outfit is not going to be the point any more."

Frank and I had been with our squad for only a week now and not only were they unknown to us, they didn't know each other. We gathered in a corner of the basement trying to get acquainted so that, when we pushed off tomorrow, we would at least recognize each other.

"Clark," Frank had called me to one side, "I want to talk to you about the men. They are casual replacements and neither of us know them, but I do have some impressions."

We talked about one GI who was past 40. Since he had joined us, he had developed a racking cough and it was obvious he was terrified beyond having conscious control of himself.

"We're sending him back tonight," Frank said. "I don't want anybody here who's not ready and willing to stay. And that cough will get the whole squad killed."

Then we talked about another man, thirty-two, married, with three children.

"He's scared," Frank said, "but not any more than anybody his age with a family would be. I think he'll be okay."

There was one other GI, a young boy, thin blond hair, and a washed-out expression in his face. When I had shaken hands with him, his hand felt like a dead fish. He didn't act as if he were afraid, but he seemed to be totally lacking in vigor and drive.

"I don't know about him," Frank said. "I just don't think he will come through when we need him. He looks all washed out."

The old man was sent back, but Frank never did get around to replacing the washed out young boy.

I was to be glad a few days later that he wasn't. Of our squad, he and Frank were the two I would remember.

As often happens, after psyching up for a dreaded experience, the next few days were anti-climactic. The weather turned foul, the Air Corps was unable to fly its bombing sorties, and we spent the next three days and nights holed up in the dark basement.

When we finally emerged, the day was beautiful — a cloudless, blue sky, mild autumn temperature, and an apparent removal of the war from our area.

No artillery of any dimension was using us for a target, and, apparently, the bombing airplanes had moved to another sector. It was a big push, all up and down the allied line that November 17th, but, as it will, the heavy action was obviously taking place elsewhere.

Coming out of the school building, we were split into units and began to pick our way, single file, through the village of Stolberg, toward the outskirts of that small town. The German houses we passed reminded me of Decatur, my home town, and the streets were paved and lined with brick houses, just like our streets.

Now our squad was alone, picking its way forward. When we began to hear machine gun fire, we dropped to the ground and began to crawl along the edges of the narrow curving road.

Others had been there ahead of us. In the ditch by the road, I found a U. S. helmet. The small captain bars on the front of the steel helmet revealed the rank of the officer; and the neat round hole between the silver bars told the fate of the wearer. It looked like a fresh, new helmet. I tossed it back into the ditch.

There was a stone wall here and I was lying against it when I heard the tank. I looked back over my shoulder, then moved closer against the wall as the tracks clanked toward me, passing with a couple of feet to spare.

There was a bend in the road ahead, and the tank stopped to let the infantry go ahead to explore what was waiting beyond our line of sight.

I got up slowly, eased around the side of the tank, and followed the GI ahead. As assistant squad leader, I was bringing up the rear.

The GI just ahead of me was carrying a rifle grenade launcher on the end of his weapon. "Hey, Smith," I called softly, "you got a dummy round in your rifle?"

"Yea, Harrison," he replied, "it's okay."

As we rounded the bend, we saw the backs of two two-story houses, the one on the right a red brick with a small, stuccoed out- building to the rear, and a door opening at the back to the terrace level of the house. There was a low wire fence around the yard and a mound that was over the entrance to a back yard bomb shelter.

On the other side of the road, in line with the red brick, was a plain, cream brick two story with six windows, three on each floor, on our side of the house.

As we took in the scene, a pair of P-38 Lightning fighter planes passed overhead, not two hundred feet above us, their bright twin-boom fuselages gleaming in the bright sunlight.

So much for the massive aerial attack, I thought.

Then a machine gun began to chatter nearby, an American 30 caliber.

Frank had climbed the fence and was walking, crouched, toward the bomb shelter.

That thing's probably booby trapped, I thought.

Frank stepped quickly into the mouth of the dugout and quickly out. There was a muffled explosion from the hand grenade he had tossed into the bunker.

"Can't leave anything behind us," Frank called. He started running toward the house and disappeared through the rear door.

A large GI from Pennsylvania was standing beside the stuccoed out- building, when we heard a shot and saw the bullet ricochet just an inch above his head.

"Godamn," he yelled. "They're shooting at us!"

The rest of the squad hit the ground as he sprinted for the basement door.

"What do we do now?" The thirty-two year old GI called over his shoulder as he lay on the ground in front of me.

"Run for the building," I shouted and the squad sprinted toward the door Frank had entered.

Lying flat on my stomach, I took careful aim and pumped six shots, one in each window of the house to the left, the only spot the sniper could have been to fire down on the Pennsylvanian.

Lt. Fox had told us, "For God's sake, fire your weapon. That will help keep 'em down so they can't shoot us."

I jumped up and was running, crouched and zig zaging toward the house.

Then it happened.

An invisible ten-ton truck hit me — dead on.

The impact seemed to throw my body into the air. The illusion was that I was turning slowly in the air before hitting the ground. There was no pain.

Just the thudding stop and jolt of heavy impact and then I was lying flat on the gound, my rifle under me with the muzzle protruding just below my chin.

"I don't know what's wrong with me," was my first thought, "but I better not move my head. That sniper's standing in the window looking at me."

"I don't know what's wrong with me," I thought again, "but my mind is clear and I can move my hands."

From the time the tank moved up behind me, my mind had been functioning with deep clarity and lightning like response. The adrenalin that had saturated my being was making an engraved picture of every motion of that day, that I can still see clearly as I write this.

The squad was huddled in the doorway of the house. They knew now that death was in the yard where I lay.

"It's Harrison," one of them was saying, "he's been hit and he's bleeding bad."

They knew too, the sniper was still there and whoever came for me was going to be totally exposed.

Then one of the GIs was crawling toward me. As he came closer, I saw the non-descript features of the washed out kid Frank and I had talked about sending back.

"Grab my hands, Harrison," the young boy was saying. Then he was pulling me, awkwardly, a step at a time, back toward the protection of the building.

At any moment, I expected to hear a shot and feel him sag toward the ground.

As we neared the building, others in the house grabbed me and carried me inside, leaving me lying on my back on the concrete floor. To my left was an inside room. Turning my head to the right, I could see a corner of the front yard of the house, brightly bathed in the afternoon sun.

Our advance had been watched and now mortar shells began to fall in the yard outside.

"Where's Frank," I asked.

"He's gone after the sniper," one of the men said.

Lying there, I looked out the door to my right.

One of the squad was crouched just outside the door, when his helmet rose an inch above his head, then settled back down. At the same time, blood spurted from his left ear. He turned and ran into the house, stepping over me and running into the other room.

Concussion from one of the mortars exploding in the yard had raised his helmet and a small bit of shrapnel had apparently clipped the lobe of his ear.

A few moments later, Frank appeared in the door. He had dropped his rifle and was clutching his stomach. He stepped over me and disappeared into the other room.

I had lost a good bit of blood and now I lost consciousness.

When I woke, it was dark. I was still lying on my back in the doorway. The concrete floor had become cold and damp and my left arm was aching down in the bone.

The squad was still in the house, still pinned down by the fire that had started during the afternoon.

It was quiet and I could hear the squad whispering in the next room. I could hear Frank moaning.

My hands were cold and I pushed them under my belt against the flesh of my stomach.

The muscles were tight and hard as stone from the trauma of the wound. Strangest of all, I couldn't feel my hands touching my skin. It was as if I were touching someone else's flesh.

"Tell me about Frank." One of the squad members had come to me.

"One of the mortars got him in the stomach," he said. "I don't think he's going to make it."

He was a brave man. And now he was not going to marry that girl in Brooklyn or see her again.

I was alone again, staring into the blackness. I didn't know what was wrong with me. I did know I was helpless. That I couldn't move or feel the lower part of my body. I didn't know I was paralyzed because I didn't know what paralysis was. I just knew I couldn't move and, strangest of all, I couldn't feel. It was as if the lower part of my body had ceased to exist.

I had been raised by a Christian mother and father. And I believed in Christ.

I thought about Him.

A new understanding came to me.

He had suffered a humiliating death, hanging naked on a cross.

If He had died a normal death, He couldn't have helped me now.

As it was, whatever had happened to my body, He had suffered worse — and He could understand — and He could help.

I put my hand up in the blackness, and asked Him to hang on to me.

The shelling and the rifle fire had died — the front was quiet.

With my hand extended up into the darkness, I went to sleep.

CHAPTER X

"Tucson radio," I was over the mountains again and had Tucson Approach Control dialed in on the Mark 12B. "This is Cherokee eight seven five five November."

"Go ahead, Cherokee eight seven five five November. This is Tucson Approach."

"Tucson Approach this is eight seven five five November. I am approximately 30 miles west of you. Request vectoring to the Tucson Airport."

"Roger, five five November. Squawk 0134 and ident."

I twisted the dials on the transponder to 0134 and pushed the ident button. This would identify my blip on Tucson Approach's radar screen.

"Roger, five five November. Radar contact. We have you identified as 35 miles west of Tucson Airport. Fly 090 at 5500 feet."

I settled back, monitoring the guages in front of me and knowing that in a darkened room my own flight was being monitored, that I would be directed to fly at a safe altitude to clear the mountains, and that I would be turned as necessary to put me into the traffic pattern as I came to the airport.

I thought back to the night of November 17, 1944.

I thought about how I felt, lying on the basement floor of the German house.

I was 4000 miles from home, among strangers, in a hostile land where the usual German counterattack could be expected with the first light of dawn.

But the nagging, gnawing fear was gone.

I did not feel alone, and I did not feel afraid.

It was strange, but, helpless as I was, I would not feel normal fear again.

The old hymn we had sung in my Baptist childhood came back to me.

"Help of the helpless, abide with me."

When we lose our strength, God's strength shines through.

Twice in the future, I was to experience a brief panic of fear, both times based on unreasoning and unreasonable non-causes. But, I'd never know the fear I'd known in combat, even though I was to experience occasions when fear would have been a normal reaction. And I was never to feel alone again.

Or to believe in accidents.

I had passed out that night in the terrace level of the German house, listening to the squad whispering in the next room, hearing Frank Vacarro's moaning, as he slowly died from his stomach wound.

Sometime during the night the medics came for me.

I was carried from danger by those I will never know.

When I regained consciousness, it was daylight. I was lying on a stretcher suspended between 2x4 saw horses in what looked like a former school room. The room, brightly lit by sunshine streaming through the large windows, was filled with GIs on stretchers, one line against each wall of the room.

At the end of the room was a raised platform, which must have served the teacher, and standing on it, leaning over a desk, was a slender army nurse clad in olive drab shirt and slacks.

I was flat on my back, covered from the neck down by a heavy wool army blanket.

I couldn't feel anything from my chest down. But I was in no pain. In fact, I felt comfortable. The GI on the stretcher next to me was calling for water.

"Hey, buddy," I called to the ward boy a couple of stretchers away. "Can you come here when you're through?"

He finished adjusting the intravenous bottle suspended above one of the patients and then walked over.

"Yea," he said, "what can I do for you?"

"My legs," I said, "What's wrong with them?"

"Nothing, why?" he responded.

"Well," I said, "I can't feel them and I can't move them."

"Oh," he said, "I forgot. You're paralyzed."

"Are you sure my legs are all right?"

"Sure."

"How about pulling the blanket back and let me see," I said quietly.

"Sure."

He pulled the heavy blanket back. My legs were there. The left one was swollen twice normal size.

"How about that one?" I said. "Is it going to be all right?"

"Oh, sure," he replied. "It'll be okay when the swelling goes down."

"Water," the boy next to me continued to cry plaintively, "Please give me some water."

"You know," I told the ward boy, "I'm thirsty too, but I don't want anything to drink until he has some. He's been calling quite a while. Can't you get him some water."

"I'll get you some," the ward boy whispered, "but if he drinks any, it'll kill him. He was hit in the stomach."

"Oh," I said. "I don't think I'll have any right now."

I lay quietly, watching the nurses and ward men as they moved silently and efficiently, taking care of the immediate needs of the recently wounded men.

They didn't bother with me much. I didn't ask for anything — I didn't feel the need of anything. I was comfortable. I didn't cry out because I had no pain. Food and drink were brought to me before I was hungry or thirsty.

For three weeks, I lay flat on my back, on an army stretcher, without moving or being moved.

Thirty years later, I would still be paying the price of that neglect.

Allied casualties had been heavy, starting with the November 17th attack in which I was wounded. Shortly thereafter, the hospitals were flooded with GIs wounded in Hitler's desperate Battle of the Bulge that hit the Allies just before Christmas, 1944.

I was kept overseas for four months after I was wounded. My lung had been punctured by the sniper's bullet and large amounts of pus and blood had been removed. I had survived pneumonia and yellow jaundice and the bombing of my hospital in Liege, but it was thought I could not survive the long flight across the Atlantic.

The weeks in the series of hospitals, moving back from the front, were a strange time for me. I was critically ill in that the bullet had passed through the upper part of one lung before severing my spinal cord and exiting through my back.

The lung was infected and filled with pus and blood that was removed periodically with a needle and large syringe. Penicillin was given us by injection every three or four hours and the infection, which otherwise would have killed me in short order, was kept under control.

The strange thing was that I remained comfortable, lying flat on my back.

The only pain was in my left arm; the elbow in particular ached deep down in the bone. The arm was weak and I theorized that, since the bullet had entered just to the left of the junction of my neck and left shoulder, perhaps the nerve to my left arm had been temporarily effected.

My arm hurt only when I tried to move it. Now I worked continuously, moving it up and down and bending it by clasping my left hand in my right.

I knew I would lose the use of my arm if I didn't.

And it was all I could do for myself.

The one time the nurse tried to turn me on my side, about three weeks after I was wounded, the fluid in my upper lung poured over into my breathing passages and I couldn't breathe. So, back on my back I went, and for three days I had to have oxygen to breathe while the pneumonia subsided.

Other than that, I remained comfortable as I was shifted from one hospital to the next, on each move back from the front.

From the first field hospital in the school room, I was sent to an adjoining surgery tent, where I was fitted with half-a-body cast, to prevent further injury to my spine as I was moved to the next hospital.

"You've got a southern accent," the doctor was piling layers of cold plaster on my back from around my head down to my knees. "I heard a lot of southern accents D-Day. In fact, it seemed almost like a southern show."

I thought about Frank Vacarro from Brooklyn, Bob Simpson from Pennsylvania and John Polack from Chicago. I seemed to have spent my army career with Yankees.

"What's this thing supposed to do?" I asked the laboring cast builder.

"Well," he said, "you're going to be moving around a lot and this will keep your back from being injured any further."

When they carried me back out into the sunlight, the yard between the school building and the hospital tents was thronged with German prisoners. It was a strange feeling to see so many German uniforms. If they were being guarded, it was not apparent. What was apparent was the fact that these Germans were glad to be on the side of the war where no artillery shells or bombs were falling.

They passed my litter along to one of the hospital tents with great care.

In the tent was the member of our squad whom I had seen hit while I was lying on the basement floor of the house. I was relieved to know his wound was superficial — he had lost the lobe of his left ear to a tiny fragment of mortar shrapnel.

"Hey, Mike." I spotted another of the replacements from our squad. He was trying to use a bed pan and was obviously in pain. "What happened to you?"

"I got clipped in the butt," he grinned. "I was trying to get the ten-in-one rations off the top of an abandoned tank and I must have stuck it out too far."

"We got a charge out of you, Harrison," he said. "You called several times, lying out there in the hall of that German basement. Finally, you said 'What's the matter? None of you bastards got guts enough to come out here and help me?' After that, we hauled the mattress out there and got you off the floor."

"Tell me about Frank," I said.

"Frank didn't make it," he replied. "When you were hit, Frank went running out into the yard yelling he was going to get the sniper. About that time, we heard the mortars start falling and then Frank stumbled back in. He died before anybody could get up there to help."

"Frank was a brave man," I said.

The next hospital was in downtown Liege, in a multi-storied building that again resembled a school or other institution. I was put in the half cast and when we arrived, was carried upstairs to the second floor.

It was a busy place, and I found myself in a bed for the first time, in a broad hallway beneath a tall, arched, cathedral type window of clear glass.

It was a bright and cheerful place, with nurses, doctors and aides striding back and forth past my bed. A Belgian woman with a patch over one eye stopped by my bed to speak. She was a native, pleasant and friendly. She began to visit with me when she had a few moments. She agreed to teach me French, and had taught me a couple of phrases during my brief stay there.

The only distraction was the V-1 buzz bomb. One of Hitler's "secret weapons", the V-1 was introduced in the closing months of the war. It was a drone airplane loaded with a heavy bomb that exploded when the pilotless plane crashed to the ground.

Now, the V-1s were coming into Liege on a constant schedule — every five or ten minutes during the day.

There was no way to aim the V-1 other than to send them in the general direction of the city, and time the engine to quit once the small plane was over the congested area.

It was worrisome. We would hear the engine, which sounded like an old Model T Ford, in the distance and we would listen as it got closer. If the engine cut while the sound was still distant, we would relax for a few minutes until we heard the next drone.

On this particular bright, sunny day, the drone was louder than usual. Then the sound of the engine became more and more distinct until it seemed to be right in the attic of our building.

Just as the engine noise became a deafening roar, it suddenly cut off. There was a deadly silence. The seconds ticked off and then — the explosion rocked the big masonry building.

The tall cathedral window I was lying beneath collapsed in a shower of glass, wood and plaster that covered my bed and my face.

I lay perfectly still. People were running up and down the hall and the nearby stairs, most of them with blood streaming from their hands and faces.

The Belgian cleaning woman ran to me and began to pick the glass and debris from around my face. I lay still without moving. I had not been scratched.

I was hurriedly placed on a stretcher, carried down two flights of stairs to the heavily reinforced concrete basement. The plaster cast so laboriously constructed by the doctor was left leaning against the wall. My billfold with all my family pictures was forgotten in the excitement.

Later, we learned that not one patient had been injured by the bomb that exploded in the adjoining courtyard. Most of the staff — those who were standing or walking when the explosion came — had been cut or wounded by the flying debris. One patient had been naked on the operating table when the glass windows surrounding the room were blown in. Again, he escaped unscathed.

This time, I was moved to a large building removed from the center of Liege and the bombings.

One day blended into the next with me lying — comfortable — with a front row experience of the American combat hospital. I was there, but not really a participant. My dressings were changed and the penicillin shots given, but the attention went to those for whom something could be done.

At one point, I was told that I was about to be sent back to the States.

"I have had a death in my family," the attractive young nurse told me, "and I am going to take you back to the States. They are afraid for you to travel alone, but now I will be able to stay with you. I'll be back tomorrow and we'll go."

I'd be home for Christmas. But, now I realized I didn't want to go. I didn't want my family to see me helpless like this.

It had been two months since I had been wounded, and my condition had deteriorated steadily. My weight was just over 100 pounds — the dehydrated food, the grey brussel sprouts, the greasy meats, were more than I could handle.

I had large gauze and cotton bandages on both hips and on my back, held in place by a broad ace bandage.

I had a tube in my abdomen that drained my bladder.

The only medical knowledge concerning paraplegics was that they would shortly die from kidney infection and the only thing to do was try to keep them comfortable while nature worked its way. Unable to move, lying in bed day after day, I had no appetite. I looked like a survivor of the Bataan death march or a German concentration camp.

When the nurse didn't come back, I didn't say anything to anybody, so I never knew what had changed the plans.

Finally, I was told that the concern was my lungs. After the bout with pneumonia, it was feared I would not survive if the ocean spanning hospital plane should lose pressurization.

Night after night lying in the bed after lights were out, I would gaze down the darkened ward, watching the nurse work over a patient returned that afternoon from surgery, using a flashlight as she tried to adjust his body to a more comfortable position.

Since I could not be flown back to the states, after about a month, I was loaded with other patients in a C-47 and flown, at low altitude, across the channel to England.

The hospital was a single story structure consisting of a number of wards built of brick. Now, all I would see was the hospital ward, then a patch of blue sky as I was loaded into an ambulance, another patch of blue sky and the ward of the next hospital.

The hospital in England was, I was told, fifty miles from London.

The ward was heated by two space heaters, one in each end of the room.

At night, with nothing else to do, the ward boy on duty would pile coal in the space heater, making the stove so hot it would glow in the dark. I would have to throw the covers off and would lie bathed in sweat.

In the morning, the temperature would drop. Everybody was busy and the fire would go out. Then, the nurse would throw the covers off of me, put a towel over my middle and leave me lying naked while she went to get her cart.

"Harrison," the nurse was standing at the end of my cot, "you've got a visitor. Her name is Pat Hughes."

"Nurse," I said, "would you please tell her I can't see her. I don't want anybody to see me like this."

I regret it now; Pat had come a long way. But, at the time, I couldn't bring myself to see anybody who had known me before.

"I don't see why it would hurt to sit you up." The therapist, an attractive young woman, had been massaging my legs and bending my knees. "Hang on to me."

I was in a sitting position. The room began to spin. She eased me back on the cot. That would be the last attempt in the four months overseas after I was shot.

The doctors and nurses didn't bother with me much during those early weeks. I didn't ask for anything — I didn't feel the need of anything. I was comfortable. I didn't cry out because I had no pain. Food and drink were brought to me before I was hungry or thirsty.

The doctors left no orders for me because there was nothing that could be done.

My spinal cord had been severed and I would die.

Because I was paralyzed from my chest down, I could not void normally. A catheter was inserted to drain my bladder, which meant infection; chronic infection that would start in the bladder and spread to the kidneys, and that would kill me.

Earlier, there was nothing that would control internal infection of that severity without also killing the patient. A sore on the exterior could be treated with harsh germicides, but the same chemicals that would kill an external infection would kill the patient if taken internally.

But just prior to World War II a dramatic change occurred.

Penicillin and sulfur drugs were discovered.

Civilians could receive the medicines only in emergency situations and under special order in the beginning because of their scarcity.

The bulk of the new drugs had been sent to the hospitals behind the front lines. All service personnel, wounded in combat, were given penicillin, the first extensive use of the new antibiotic. I was given penicillin along with all the other men with open wounds.

Apparently, it had occurred to no one that penicillin would control the kidney infection as well as the open wounds where the bullet had entered the junction of my neck and shoulder and where it had exited my back.

Nor was any thought given to the consequences of stopping the kidney infection.

Paraplegics had always died within a few months; that's what the best medical books reported and that's what the best doctors believed.

Apparently, it occurred to none of the doctors that, unlike earlier paraplegics, we would not die — we would live.

Because it occurred to no one that we would survive, it occurred to no one that care must be taken to protect our nerveless lower bodies from harm.

Without pain, we were also without the defences to protect our paralyzed limbs.

We were left alone in the early months, isolated from the normal routines of hospital care almost as if we had been lepers.

Not because we were 'unclean' but because there were those who could be saved by care, and we were not among that number — not according to the conventional wisdom of the time.

We did have something in common with lepers, however.

Lepers have the same problem as paraplegics in their lack of feeling in their extremities. And, strangely, it was only in recent years that the 'discovery' was made as to why lepers lose fingers, toes and even limbs.

It finally dawned on the doctors working with lepers that the loss of these extremities was a peculiarity of the disease only because the leper has no feeling. Without pain, he will twist a nut off a bolt with such force he will tear his skin. So, he hurts himself without knowing it and without crying out.

It was finally realized that the leper's toe in primitive countries was sometimes gone because a rat had chewed it off.

The spinal cord injured develop sores that would have a feeling person screaming with pain — simply because pressure of prolonged lying or sitting in one position has cut off the blood supply and, without blood, the flesh dies.

It has been only in recent years the medical profession has perfected ways of, not only surgically treating the more extreme pressure sores, but simple, commonplace procedures for preventing their occurrence in the first place.

Pain is a protector and a friend.

The ultimate irony is the fact that human flesh is one of the toughest substances created by God.

Cut it and watch how quickly it heals.

Bruise it with a heavy blow and see the black and blue dissolve into healthy pink skin.

Crash an airplane and, properly strapped in, see the body survive forty times the impact the metal of the airframe can endure.

But, cut off the blood supply for a few hours and it will die — never to return to its original condition.

For those first three weeks, I lay flat on my back on that stretcher. I have never been more comfortable. What I didn't know, my flesh was rotting away beneath me.

It was a couple of months before I saw a pressure sore for the first time. The patient lying next to me was having a dressing changed. The open wound was about eight inches across, a circle of black, chopped up meat at the base of his spine.

"What happened to him?' I asked the nurse in amazement. "Was his fanny grazed by an 88 shell?"

She looked at me with a start. "Why," she said, "you've got one just like it."

I looked a her.

"If I've got one of those, you turn me on my stomach, right now," I said. "That's the last time I'll lie on that."

For the next eight months, I lay on my stomach, took my meals lying on my stomach, read by raising up on my elbows while lying on my stomach.

And I drank all the fruit juice I could get.

Over the next few weeks, the doctors began to come by and remark in amazement that the huge sore was slowly healing in with scar tissue.

"Must be the vitamin C," they speculated. Every kind of salve and dressing had been tried on the sores the other patients had, including honey and vinegar. The results had been meager. So, everybody involved was interested in the comparatively rapid healing of my sore.

We were discovering the secret of pressure sores. While the vitamin C may have helped, the key ingredient was the fact I never lay on my back until the sore was completely healed.

The irony was that, once my initial wounds had healed, I was not sick, other than the kidney infections that came and went. I was more like a healthy person confined to a cell — except that my bed was more confining than a prison cell.

I have thought over the years how it was that a merciful God let people like the spinal injured survive with such limited use of ourselves. We are prisoners — prisoners of our flesh, spending an inordinate amount of time to do simple, everyday things that normal people do without thought or effort.

The Bible tells us, in a passage Christ quoted as referring to himself, "the stone that was rejected has become the head of the corner."

Lying in the hospital bed during those months, or sitting in the high back, wooden wheelchair, I felt totally rejected.

But even then, something in my spirit told me that I wouldn't always be that way. There had to be some reason to the senseless deprivation we were enduring.

For my part, I made up my mind to at least try to do something, with what I had left, that would count in a significant way. To justify what had happened to me — and happened while defending my country in a cause I knew was just — I would have to make my life count for something.

It only seemed right.

And I did , eventually, reach a position where my life did count.

The strange thing was that those months of hopeless inactivity became a deep pool of strength for me — a reservoir that made it possible for me to endure shocks and pressures that otherwise could have destroyed me.

Looking back over the years, it is hard for me to believe the bizarre turns my life took after I was paralyzed. Finally, I have come to believe that we are mistaken when we assume nothing good will come out of defeats and tough situations we face.

"Clark", I was talking many years later to a high school friend. His career in the Army had been the opposite of my disjointed, unsuccessful and finally disastrous three years. He had gone in a year earlier than I did, graduated as a multi-engine pilot, flew 58 missions over the hump, from India into China, carrying fuel to the Flying Tigers. "What I don't understand about you is why you are not bitter after all that has happened to you. I know I would be bitter, and yet you have your sense of humor, enjoy life. I don't understand how you do it."

"Well, Bob," I replied, " you and I were both raised to believe you make your choices and then you live with them. After I finally realized I was permanently paralyzed, I really had only two choices. I could kill myself or I could make the best of the fact I was never going to walk again."

Suicide was never an alternative I considered, I explained. I had been taught and still believe that taking your own life is not allowed. God puts us on this earth and promises to take care of us. Now, He may not always do that in a way that makes sense or is pleasing to our human way of doing things, but the promise still stands, and someday, I believe, we will learn the meaning of the life we have led. I believe we will discover that things we thought important will turn out not to count and things we dismissed as not being of any significance will assume great importance. Be that as it may, the decision as to when this life ends is up to the One who put us here in the first place.

On the other hand, I don't pass judgement on those who have taken their own lives. That's not up to me either.

"Once I decided to live," I continued, "it's just a question of what makes life more tolerable. For me, I found bitterness a poor comrade and bed fellow. As one of our mountaineer cartoon characters said, 'love is better than hate, because it makes you feel better.' After the years have passed, I can tell you one thing, my life has been much richer than it would have been if this thing had not happened to me. I have known more people, known them more intimately and have done more exciting things than I would if I had not been shot. And I have learned to appreciate the good things, which is just as important as having them — really more important."

After I took office as chairman of our county, we were faced with a monumental debt, a breakdown of vital county services and a population that was showing its anger by the first, and nearly successful, campaign to have me recalled from office. I may not have been responsible for the mess we were in, but since I was in charge, the public anger and frustration centered on me.

I can remember sitting in my office, shaking my head in wonder and slamming the desk with my open hand to relieve the pressure.

Then I would remember, "By God," I'd think, "I have survived worse."

Certainly, the months of helplessness I had experienced became a deep pool of strength for me when I found myself at the center of that pressure cooker as chief executive officer for our metropolitan county, with nearly half a million people to serve, under the pressures of people crowding into a melting pot from every part of the country and world.

At one time, I faced the general anger of most of the tax payers in our county, and the specific, harsh and unforgiving anger of those whose personal plans had been thwarted by rulings of our government.

"Honey," my wife Frances was crying. When I finally got her calmed down she said, "Somebody just called me and said they were going to shoot you."

"Oh, I wouldn't worry about that," I laughed, "they tried that once and it didn't work — in fact, I've been innoculated against shooting."

The danger was real. Or at least my successor thought so. He employed a full-time body guard.

For myself, I figured that if anybody wanted to shoot me, they'd shoot me. They wouldn't call my wife up and warn me.

One Friday afternoon, the police chief called me.

"You're a hard man to catch," he said.

"What do you mean?"

"Well," he continued, "Thursday we received a tip that somebody was out to kill you. We followed you around all day Thursday. This morning I had a man waiting outside your house and you never came out."

"When did he get there?" I asked.

"Eight o'clock."

"Chief," I said, "I left at seven."

The death threats never bothered me, but the daily conflict in the neighborhoods and between the politicians and the various levels of bureaucracy, could have pushed me over the brink if I had been a little younger, or if I had not had that reservoir of strength created by the months of helplessness in the hospital.

When things got really rough, I'd think about those months when I could do nothing except slowly rot away, and I'd think, "By God, I've been through worse."

I have had to face some tough situations and pay off some heavy debts, and they have been made easier by those early days of helplessness.

I don't believe I hold on as tightly to things that need to be let go, I don't believe I panic under pressure or in danger as quickly, I don't believe I try as hard to hold back others, through jealousy, who are trying to do their jobs. Perhaps, the Lord needs a few people who have lost it all to help others who fear they might lose it all.

And sometimes I think of Bob Simpson, who had been prepared for combat by the rough life he had — in the ice house — as low man on the army totem pole and high man on the kitchen police list — and the way he had settled me down as we came closer to the front.

CHAPTER XI

Old airplanes never die.

Not as long as they receive a little tender loving care and the replacement of a part now and then.

My plane was manufactured in 1969, which makes it a relatively recent model. Planes are still flying that are forty, fifty and more years old. Some on a daily basis.

The DC-3, the early twin-engine air liner is the classic. The last one was built in 1946 — and a fleet of the aging passenger and freight carriers still flies every day — in all parts of the world.

Unpressurized, the DC-3 flies low and slow — not much faster at 135 mph cruise than my little plane — and at altitudes of six or seven thousand feet. Thus, it is bumpy flying on a hot day. Since it is a tail dragger, passengers boarding have to walk up hill to get to their seats.

But, they are safe, dependable, and they keep on flying with no end in sight. Many of the packages you receive through overnight delivery have brought to your town by the aging DC-3.

During World War II, the Army version of the DC-3 was known as the C-47. In Vietnam, some thirty-odd years later, the Army was still using them as heavily armored gunships that, flying low and slow, attacked enemy ground forces.

I was flown across the English channel in a C-47 after I was wounded. And I rode a C-47 one final time in that spring of 1945.

As the weeks and months crept by, it was finally decided to send me home — at least, the doctors decided, I might live to see my family before I died.

In March of 1945, the C-47 hospital ship was calling the Atlanta Naval Air Station.

"Atlanta Navy, we have a load of wounded for Lawson General Hospital."

It was a blustery March day.

"Roger, Army C-47 4394 Whiskey. We are clearing you for a straight in approach landing runway one six. Be advised we have strong surface winds here — one one zero at eighteen gusting to thirty five."

The C-47 responded and requested that ambulances be summoned from nearby Lawson General Hospital to meet the plane.

The C-47 was flying at nine thousand feet as it cleared the North Georgia mountains and began its descent to pattern altitude. I was lying on my stomach, but by raising up, I could see out the window to the mountains below.

I didn't want to come home. In England I had refused to see Pat Hughes.

When I told the nurse not to send Pat in, apparently she agreed with my decision. At least, she didn't argue.

With sores on both hips and my back, I was wrapped all around with bandages. A tube from my bladder drained into a bottle by the bed. I was skin and bones, with a yellow cast to my skin from the bout with yellow jaundice.

My family didn't know what was wrong with me. The government had a policy against our describing our injuries in our letters home. The censors enforced it.

I was ashamed of the way I was — helpless, skin and bones, wrapped all around to cover the huge pressure sores. I would have preferred to stay in England, another year if necessary, until I could walk back home like a man.

Two things sustained me during our approach to the front, the two and a half weeks on the front and in the months after I was shot.

First, were two passages of the Bible I had learned in the Baptist Sunday School as a child: The Lord's Prayer and the Twenty Third Psalm.

I said them over and over when I was frightened, which was most of the time once we were in sound of the guns.

Especially the promise in the Twenty Third Psalm.

"Yea, though I walk through the valley of the shadow of death I shall fear no evil for thou art with me, thy rod and thy staff they comfort me."

The other thing was a dream.

In the dream, the war was over and I was going home.

My family didn't know I was coming. They didn't even know I was back in the country.

I was walking down Clairmont Avenue, under the shade of the big oak trees, along the sidewalk lined with the beautiful dogwood trees.

The dogwoods were in bloom, the white blossoms creating an avenue as I strode along.

Then I was turning into the broad entrance of Clairmont Estates, turning right into Vidal Boulevard.

There was our house.

There was the tall magnolia tree that shaded my second story room in the brick home I had left to go to war.

I walked up on the stoop and rang the bell.

And the dream ended with my family all around, hugging and kissing me and all of us crying.

It didn't turn out that way.

For one thing, I was in piteous physical condition.

In England, I had finally realized I was starving to death. If I had been up and active, I could have eaten the food. But the daily tray of greasy meat, grey, watery brussel sprouts, the powdered eggs, just wouldn't go down when I was lying in bed, not moving.

One morning I looked down. My ribs were sticking out, the bone of my hip was prominent.

"My God," I thought, "I'm starving to death."

When it comes down to it, I'm a survivor.

I made up my mind something had to be done.

First, I would get hold of the dietician. There must be some food somewhere in this hospital I could eat. If the dietician wouldn't help, I'd get hold of the commanding officer.

If I couldn't get any results from him, I'd go to Franklin Roosevelt. I knew he was paralyzed, and I was sure he'd do something.

"Harrison," the dietician needed only to be asked, "we've decided you need a special diet. Starting today, we're going to get you some special food. I believe you can eat fresh eggs, fruit juice, and we're going to get you some canned soup."

Sure enough. The eggs were wonderful, and I had no trouble eating them. And the orange juice was out of this world.

There was one problem. The canned soup didn't appear.

I decided something had gone wrong.

Where was the soup I had been promised and that I was convinced would be delicious and would be just what I needed to fill in my hollow ribs and cover my bony hips?

I became a little psychotic about the situation.

Every night when lights were out, I would hear the staff talking and laughing, somewhere down the hall.

After a few days and nights of no soup, a devilish idea took hold in my mind.

"Those bastards are in there having a party — and eating my soup. I can see them, laughing, gesturing, and slurping up my good soup. Meanwhile, I'm lying here starving to death."

After a few sessions with that devil, I had a talk with myself.

"Take it easy, Clark. They may be eating your soup, but if you don't stop thinking this way you're going off the deep end. Just like those characters you studied in psychology class at the University."

I never did get my soup, and I still suspect the ward boys and nurses, but they didn't haul me off the ward in a straight jacket either.

Once we were delivered to the care of the Army Air Corps, to be flown back to the states, our daily menu took a turn for the better. With access every day to the U.S., the Air Corps devoted a good portion of their scarce space to bringing American style food to the foreign shores our troops were occupying.

Loaded on the big four-engine C-54 that would transport us, by way of Scotland, the Azores, New Foundland and eventually to New York, our cuisine was immediately improved.

Fresh milk.

Overseas we dreamed of fresh milk, of lettuce, tomato, and mayonnaise sandwiches.

On the plane, we had fresh meat, frozen English peas, fresh orange juice.

All the things that were unobtainable to overseas GIs. Maybe the supply companies attached to the air bases were eating well but nobody else in khaki.

Now, as guests of the Air Corps, we were back among the chosen few.

Things were even better after we landed at Mitchell Field, New York.

The most gracious portion of the female population of the city seemed to be mobilized to welcome the boys home. Especially those of us who arrived on hospital litters.

Ice cream, any flavor, homemade cake, any kind, steak, any cut cooked any way we might specify. And lettuce, tomato and mayonnaise sandwiches with a big glass of cold milk.

Then, they brought a telephone to my bed.

"Time to make your call home," the pretty middle aged woman had a big smile on her face.

I gave the operator the number I remembered so well.

I was stunned when she answered a few moments later,

"That number has been disconnected."

I took the black phone down from my ear and lay looking at it in shocked silence.

I had not had any current mail from my family. During the months after I was shot, my mail made a tortuous journey. First, to the staging area near Manchester, England, then, tracing me, across the channel, through France to the post offices just behind the lines.

"A lot of those post offices were overrun during the Battle of the Bulge." The ward boy who brought the mail was trying to let me understand why he never stopped at my cot.

When I finally received mail, it was in a pack with a rubber band around it, a month's supply. My family was writing every day.

It was wonderful to have, but all the news was weeks old.

And nothing but good, hopeful, encouraging news.

Nothing about my family moving, or anything to explain why the phone had been disconnected.

"John Summerville," I had picked up the phone again and had the long distance information operator on the line. "In Decatur, Georgia. He lives on Lamont Drive."

All the time since I had left to go in the Army, John, the father of one of the girls in our neighborhood, had written me. At least twice a month, a long typewritten letter talking about what was going on around Decatur. An investigator for an insurance firm, Mr. Summerville wrote several of us as his contribution to the war effort. I had spent many enjoyable evenings in his home.

"Those people have moved," John didn't know I was listening on the phone, "it's pouring rain here, my boss from New York is here on his annual visit and we are just sitting down to dinner. Those people live on a dirt road, way out in the country."

I hung up the phone and lay staring at the ceiling, the volunteer standing by the bed with a worried expression on her face.

"What's the matter."

"My folks have moved. And there's nobody to tell them I'm trying to reach them."

An hour later, the volunteer returned, the big smile back on her face. It was my folks, each taking a turn laughing and crying.

"I'm paralyzed," I told them, "but don't worry, the doctors assure me it's temporary. I'll be good as new before long."

"When we got your letter saying you were 'still kicking'," my Dad was talking, "I decided you'd had some kind of disfiguring facial wound."

"No," I said, "I'm just as good looking as ever. Just not very good giving information in a censured letter."

"The weekend you were wounded," my sister Novena was on the line, "I was at Fort Benning with Windy. Something told me something had happened to you. The feeling was so strong, I got in the car and drove to Atlanta. Of course, nobody had heard anything, so I went back to the Fort Sunday evening."

"Don't worry about the house," my Dad was back on the line, "I had to sell it to keep the business going. We're living across the road from the farm with the Vandergriff's. I'm going to build a new house. Now that we know you're all right, everything is going to be fine."

When I got home, I talked to John Summerville, and I learned what had happened that night when I first called.

"My big boss was down from New York," John said. "He comes once a year and we spend quite a bit of time entertaining him. We were just sitting down when the phone rang."

After John hung up the phone, he returned to his guests in the dining room.

"What was that," the New Yorker asked. John explained who I was, that I had just returned from overseas and that my family now lived on a dirt road, far out in the country.

The boss stood up.

"Get your coat, John," he said, "we can eat later. Right now we are going to get that boy's folks."

The dinner was put back in the kitchen and the two men set out in the rain, driving out Lawrenceville highway to where the narrow Steel Mill dirt road cut off to the left, then slipping and sliding to the big farm house where my Mother and Dad and my younger sister, Brenda, shared a small upstairs apartment.

"John," the boss eased himself into his seat as the reheated supper was being brought from the kitchen, "I wouldn't have missed that for the world. You have made my trip."

"So much for hard-headed, hard-hearted Yankees," John concluded.

"Yeah, Mr. Summerville," I agreed, "I've learned something about Yankees myself in the last couple of years."

The C-47 was on final approach and I could see the huge hospital complex to the left of the air field.

The left wing of the air liner dropped sharply just as we reached for the safety of the ground.

"At least," the thought rushed through my mind, "I'll die at home."

Then the plane righted and we were taxiing to where the Lawson ambulance waited. The pilot walked through our part of the plane to leave.

"Hey, that was a close one," I called.

"Yeah," he grinned, "we were sweating."

There is something good and solid and wholesome about home and an atmosphere about these United States that speaks more loudly then words. I think it must have something to do with freedom and with people just going about their daily tasks, knowing that whatever they have is their own, and knowing and caring about the people around them.

I could feel it in the ambulance driver, a local fireman doing off-duty volunteer work. He knew who I was and what had happened to me, and he knew my family.

In spite of my earlier hesitancy, now that I was back on solid earth, on my home ground, I realized I was in the right place. I didn't know what the future would hold, but I did know one thing — my family would want me, regardless of my helplessness — no matter how disfigured my body might be.

That was a rock of assurance.

I thought, also, of all the strangers who had helped me from the time the bullet struck me until my stretcher was unloaded at our DeKalb airport.

CHAPTER XII

Tucson is surrounded by mountains. No problem when you are cruising a couple of thousand feet above the tallest peak.

When you get ready to come down, past the mountains, and into the flat basin that holds the air field, it's another matter.

Especially when you're used to landing in the fairly flat Piedmont area around Atlanta. Fortunately, visibility was good as I came skimming along in a rapid descent, Approach Control calling out the next safe altitude I could descend to, and my eyes confirming that the mountains below gave good reason to descend no further.

If I had been in the clouds, I'd have been especially dependent on my unknown friend in a darkened room watching the blip my small plane made on the radar scope.

As it was, I could see the mountains and the ridges, and understand the changes in altitude and direction as they were given over the radio by the unseen controller.

Life seems to have a pattern — or perhaps it's a lack of pattern. The things we dream of often come out entirely differently, the things we fear usually never materialize. Sometimes, our enemies come to our rescue and our friends desert us when the chips are down.

In that March of 1945, I had not wanted to come home. Not until my sores were healed, my strength had returned, my legs were normal and being used again.

The reception in New York had been beautiful and fantastic with the volunteers and the hospital workers all joining together to make our homecoming memorable — and to wipe away, to the extent any human could, the months of separation and the physical and emotional scars.

It was a memorable experience for us and it must have been a deeply and emotionally satisfying experience for those who came to wait on us and to serve us. I suspect most of them were treating war scars and wounds of their own by doing what they did.

Then there was a time events seemed to confirm my fear of going home.

There was the moment when I found out that my family had suffered from the war by losing our beautiful home.

And then it became almost funny.

Leaving Mitchell Field in the C-47, bumping along at low altitude, we made it as far as Richmond, Virginia. There we were unloaded and placed in a hospital near the field.

No big reception here, but the staff was ready and we were served true southern fried chicken. A unique treat to welcome us back into our region of the U. S.

Then, we were unloaded at the Atlanta Naval Air Station, just eight miles from Decatur and my home.

The ward was empty, bed frames lining each wall. The ambulance crew brought my litter in, put it on the floor and told me goodbye.

I lay there some five or ten minutes, thinking.

"Harrison, right?" the nurse was in a hurry. "Well, you missed supper, but I'll see what I can do."

She disappeared. Some twenty minutes later she returned and put a tray on the floor by my litter.

"Sorry, Harrison," she said with a grimace, "the kitchen was closed and this was the best I could do." She disappeared again.

I lay in the vacant ward, staring at the tray beside me.

Cold spaghetti and a cold hot dog. Water to drink.

"Well, Clark," I mused. "Welcome home."

Things changed rapidly after that. I was re-located in a four man ward and then my family was there and began to do all they could to ignore the way I looked, my helplessness and the pain all of us felt.

In the beginning, it was not too good.

The old bed I was placed in was swaybacked. With the big bandages wrapped all around me and the tube coming out my abdomen, I usually, because of the sagging bed, managed to wake up in the morning soaked to the chin with urine.

After that first cold hot dog and cold spaghetti supper, we were well fed. My family brought a whole dinner with chicken and bisquits and blackeyed peas and turnip greens and sweet potatoes — all the things we southerners learned to love because of the hard times following the War Between the States. All the things the experts now say are good for your body.

Mother was out every day.

"Son, is there anything at all I can bring you."

"Yeah, Mom," I said, "they give me all the milk I ask for. But I still could drink more. Do you suppose you could slip me in a little extra to drink between meals?"

You better believe from that point on, every time Mother entered the gates of Lawson General Hospital there was a quart of fresh milk in the car.

One night she was stopped by the guard at the gate.

"Lady," the guard said, "what's in that paper bag?"

She looked at him.

"Why," mother said, "it's a quart of milk."

"Well, I'm afraid I'll have to look at that."

Mother handed him the bag.

"I'll be damned. It is milk."

Mother got a large charge out of telling the story to me and others later.

In the early days after I was finally brought to the big general hospital a few miles from home, it was the same as in Europe.

Nobody knew what to do with a patient whose spinal cord was severed, so nothing much was done. We were fed, our dressings changed, our catheters irrigated. All the things you do when there is really no way to cure what's wrong — and you are waiting for the end.

Then, things began to change.

The Lawson General doctors were having a conference.

"We're going to have to start some kind of program for the paraplegics," Col. Lowery was saying. "We can't just rock along doing nothing but dressing their pressure sores."

But what could be done. Infection was bound to take them out, wasn't it?

"Well, we don't know," the surgeon continued. "With penicillin they may live quite a while yet."

What a way to live, one of the younger doctors said with a grimace. They can't control their kidneys or bowels. They have to have an enema every other day. How are we going to keep people on those wards to take care of them.

"I don't know," Col. Lowery said, "but we've got to try. It's not their fault they're in this fix. Maybe they'd be better off dead, but that's not up to us. We've got to try."

And try they did. New beds were brought in and fitted with Balkan frames — bolted to the bed, they made a wooden frame work from which a trapeze was suspended. By grasping the trapeze the patient could turn himself in bed — a major accomplishment.

There were approximately fifty paraplegics and quadraplegics at Lawson and the program there was one of the first to try to deal with the problem in a systematic way.

No expense was spared. It was decided that at least we didn't have to be human skeletons. We were assigned our own dietician who came every day to take orders for the next day's menu. The rule was that the paraplegic wards could have anything the kitchen had and patients could have it anytime they wanted it.

One of our buddies, who finally became grossly overweight, regularly had steak and chocolate milk for breakfast.

Then we were sent to the brace shop. Those of us who would go. I was suspended by the shoulders and neck like a swinging side of beef while a chest brace was built to go with my long leg braces. The whole contraption looked like something out of the middle ages' torture dungeons. I actually took a few "steps" teetering like a stick of wood, braced from shoulders to shoes.

The therapist was a short woman. I couldn't see her standing behind me, "The most important thing is to learn how to fall. Once you do that you will gain confidence."

Left: At Lawson General Hospital we loved our WAC's and nurses. We didn't know they were waiting for us to die. Right: Scott wore blisters on his feet walking in the shoulder-to-foot braces. He finally did like the rest of us and gave up.

World War II paraplegics. We survived because of penicillin.

And also break my neck, I thought. Not feeling my feet, my legs, my body beneath me, I felt like a bust sitting on a mantle — except I was swaying on the brink of disaster.

I finally decided the whole thing was too ridiculously dangerous and impractical. I did use my long leg braces to walk between the parallel bars. I wasn't going anywhere very fast or far, but the exercise did me good.

A fellow patient named Scott did spend hours every day swinging along in the whole rig, braced from foot to armpits, until he wore blisters on both feet. And of course, the surface had to be perfectly flat. Eventually he gave up,too.

They painted the wards bright colors, and removed half the beds so there was room for a large enclosure around each bed, with moveable curtains to screen off the patient while the many dressings were changed and the enemas given.

They took us to physical therapy, where the attractive therapists got down on the mats with us and taught us how to crawl, by shifting our weight with our arms and shoulders.

On a good day, I could crawl five feet in thirty minutes.

For those who wanted to work on crafts, the occupational therapist came every day with whatever the patient wanted.

There were four or five workers for every patient, and that didn't count the volunteers from the Red Cross and the various ladies' groups that served the hospital.

They were a lively group.

The word was out in the hospital, "For God's sake, don't let them put you on the paraplegic ward — you might end up giving enemas — the place stinks."

But those hardy souls who did get tabbed and were not able to wiggle out of the assignment, found we were an interesting group, somewhat cynical, but not without our lighter moments.

Since we were obviously not going anywhere, we were in no hurry and we had nothing to prove. We didn't know we were condemned to die-according to conventional medical wisdom — nobody told us that. They didn't even tell us we'd never walk again. The job was big enough without compounding it by giving stultifying news to the patients.

What we did sense was that, for some reason, we were a privileged class — we could command the kitchen staff, all the visitors seemed somewhat in awe and the staff acted like there was no tomorrow.

"Take care of the patients first," General Sheep, the commanding officer, visited our ward every day, "then you can clean the ward."

That alone was enough to let us know something was up. The Army always started cleaning the moment the immediate and imminent danger of death by shot or shell was gone.

Our staff was, to say the least, interesting.

There were a couple of GIs who were tagged to go to medical school at the expense of the government and who were putting in time until an opening was secured for them.

Pover and Munson.

Cynical as we were, we always felt they were using their superior I.Q.'s to do a little soldiering — both impressed us as being more interested in a soft job than in any long-term service to humanity.

Perhaps the hospital administration suspected the same thing and was retaliating against the two by assigning them to the paraplegic ward.

Pover, a former race car driver, apparently decided that, as the infantry is the only real Army, giving enemas to paraplegics must be the ultimate in the practice of medicine.

He became an expert, taking pride in his results, the efficiency with which he arranged his apparatus and the speed with which he completed his task.

Everybody admired Pover's professionalism and called on him as their enema giver of choice.

Munson was large, and overweight — not grossly so, but in a way that made visual his love of the good life.

He was from California, but we had the feeling he probably was not a surfer — the muscles were too well concealed under his ample flesh.

What Munson did enjoy was dancing, especially with a WAC named Rankin. Rankin was full of beans. She had a nice figure, but a little on the same wave length as Munson's — well revealing her love of good eating. She was a diamond in the rough, a free spirit who must have found the normal army routine somewhat restrictive and the paraplegic ward a welcome haven of freedom for the expression of her libido.

We all loved to see Munson and Rankin dance, particularly after they had had a swig from the bottle they occasionally brought to their on-duty hours.

Nobody seemed to object to a little fun and friviolity in this place of soon-to-be-dead young men, so the good times were allowed to roll.

Our favorite ward boy was a tall redhead named Jarbo.

Jarbo worked hard and took a leadership role on the ward. He was a sergeant and he was treated with respect because he knew what to do and when to do it.

The same was not always true of our nurses. We had one silly, little nurse we called Frizzy. She may have been a very competent professional, but the fact she was forever giggling like a school girl detracted from her Florence Nightingale image.

Jarbo was the only one who really knew how to handle Frizzy. After the first few days, he simply gave her simple but direct orders, which Frizzy would flit about trying to perform. On one occasion, Jarbo found it necessary to give Frizzy a spanking as part of his strict displinarian regime.

Frizzy responded by crawling under one of the beds, still giggling.

If Frizzy was silly, Milly was the soul of dignity and one of our very favorites. Milly was always a lady, always performed with quiet efficiency and was always sympathetically interested in our well-being.

Milly slipped one day on the highly polished floor. The image of her regaining her lost dignity, struggling to her feet in as lady like a way as possible, then patting her neatly coiffured hair back into place is a memory that is as vivid as it is cherished by me today.

Milly had an opposite and her name was Alma. Alma and Milly may have been sisters under the skin, but the part we could see belied any relationship at all.

The nurses' uniform, modest on the modest, could be provocative on Alma.

She always left the top button unbuttoned.

"I looked in there and saw they were naked," my fellow patient told me after Alma's visit behind his screening curtains, "so I reached in and gave them a squeeze. She didn't seem to mind."

"Perhaps it had happened to Alma before," I suggested.

That was a possibility, he agreed.

"Alma," he continued, "why don't we conduct a scientific experiment. I haven't used this thing of mine for a long time, and I know it's rusty, but I'm sure science would like to know if a paraplegic can still do it."

Alma had been engaged to a fellow officer recently, but the affair had ended in a dispute and a violent quarrel.

"We were in the woods back of the officers' club," she recalled, "and I told him I never wanted to see him again. Then, I pulled off my engagement ring and threw it in the bushes."

Alma had shown us the solitaire diamond — all of one eighth of a karat according to the joint estimate of the patients.

Alma grinned.

"You better believe, as soon as he left, I was on my knees scrambling around in those bushes until I found my ring."

Alma felt she was entitled — she had earned it.

Alma was open hearted, but even more universal in her love for mankind was one of the enlisted WACs.

She hugged and kissed everybody on the ward, taking the curtained off privacy surrounding each patient during treatment time as an invitation that could not be courteously declined.

If there had been a communicable germ at large in the ward, we would all have been victims. Or perhaps, we were saved by the large overdoses of penicillin injected into our blood stream every three hours.

Being handicapped, we felt we couldn't be too choosy and so took advantage of what came through the curtains. Like all good things, it would not last, of course. Somebody took advantage of the poor girl and we heard she had been shipped home in a family way.

The WACs came from every walk of life. One good ole girl had a scarred face and an easy, confident manner that invoked a feeling that she could take care of the trials and tribulations that came her way.

"I bet you've ducked many a beer bottle in a juke joint," I told her one day.

"Yea, honey, you better believe I have," she agreed, "I remember one time I was in a bar in Mexico. This little senorita started making eyes at my boy friend. Well, it didn't take much of that to get me riled up and I jumped her, threw her across the room."

When the Mexican woman came off the wall, she was holding a knife and making expert slashes as she approached our heroine.

"Didn't do her no good, though," the WAC continued. "Just as she came down on me with the knife, I ducked down like this. Knife caught me in the back of my shoulder blade. Didn't hurt nothing."

One of our WACs was a trapeze artist. The very thought of flying through the air from one skinny swing to the next sent shivers through me. I asked her why she did it.

"The only time I feel alive," she said, "is when I'm up there. I wouldn't want to live without that thrill."

Thinking back over the years, I know we really loved our WACs and our nurses. They had gone into service because they wanted to help and they stayed the course on the paraplegic wards despite tasks that had to be repellant to a young woman in the extreme. One thing was sure, we couldn't get along without them.

We did know how to get their goats.

One way was to call them angels of mercy. For some reason, the image of Florence Nightingale in her long starched uniform did not appeal to them. I think they preferred to think of themselves as femme fatales on a brief, if unpleasant, side trip.

Another way was to accuse the staff of not giving us the advantage of the latest in medical technology.

"If you people would just give us some prostigmin," I told the nurse one day, "we'd all walk out of here."

"What's prostigmin," she queried.

"It reroutes the nerve system and builds new passages," I replied, "of course, not being a doctor I can't give you all the Latin jargon, but I know it would work."

"And where in the sweet world did you learn about prostigmin, doctor," she said sarcastically.

"It's in the Readers Digest." I replied, "I thought you medical people were supposed to keep up with the latest things."

Soon the other patients took up the cry. It did seem grossly unfair that we were being held in a paralyzed state just because the staff could not take the time to keep abreast of developments. Especially when they had filtered down to the level of the average peruser of the Readers Digest.

"You characters had better shut up," the boss nurse was getting tired of our haranguing. "Or I"m going to get some of that prostigmin and you're going to have to take it."

"Now, you're talking, nurse," we replied, "we'll all be up and out of here if we can ever get some prostigmin."

For a couple of weeks, several of us got shots — of sterile water probably, but at least it shut up talk of prostigmin and the Readers Digest.

It helped to pass the time.

One of the first paraplegics to arrive at Lawson after my inauspicious first day was Dick Haltom.

The first time I saw Dick was the day after I arrived. He was being carried into the ward on a stretcher. I noticed his color first — Atabrine tablets he had taken for the past two years to ward off the malaria so common in the Pacific theatre, had turned his wrinkled face a dark yellow. Dick was only four years older than I was, but he looked like he was at least forty.

And he was in command. His feet were in half-plaster casts, with the plaster extending at least four inches above his toes. The attendants were trying hard to handle him exactly right and I was reminded of how some Eastern potentate would have looked in similar circumstances.

"Be careful of the foot." Dick was propped up on one elbow while he pointed with a shaky hand toward the foot with its extended white cast that the ward boy was lifting toward the bed.

I was to find out that Dick was in constant pain. He could move one of his legs but not enough to do him much good. His spinal cord was partially intact so that he had feeling in much of his body and his pain could be excruciating at times.

Dick squinted hard, and his mouth assumed a rigid line as he directed the anxious movements of the two ward men who were concentrationg intensely on Dick's sharply enunciated commands.

I decided I must be looking at at least a colonel. Surely they weren't putting general officers in with common soldiers.

"All right, men," Dick softened his glare somewhat. "If you will just ease me down — very slowly — I believe we'll have it made.'

It came as a shock to learn that Dick was a private first-class like myself.

Dick had been in the pacific nearly three years, participating in a number of island invasions and jungle engagements and finally being wounded by a Japanese sniper on Luzon in the Philippines. He was proud of the fact he had remained a private in the infantry through it all.

"Well, you know," he would say, "I figured if I had to go I might as well get in the real Army. Anything outside the Infantry, they're just playing games. But I didn't want any kind of promotion. I had all the responsibility I wanted just looking after myself."

Dick is a story teller and has a fine sense of the comic in every day life. The Army provided a mother lode of material for him.

Dick told about the time he missed his Atabrine tablet for five days.

"They lined us up every day and checked off our name when they handed us the Atabrine. Then they would make us take it while they watched."

Because he had worked in his father's drug store, he was for a time put in charge of the PX for his unit and had to acquire the supplies for sale. On this occasion, Dick had been out of the camp for five days on a buying trip to an adjoining island. When he went to chow the first morning after his return, the lieutenant and sergeant were passing out the Atabrine tablets as usual.

"Let's see, Haltom," the lieutenant said. "Haltom, you haven't had your Atabrine in five days. Give Haltom five Atabrine tablets."

The sergeant handed Dick five pills. Dick began to protest that taking five Atabrine at one time would make him sick. "Haltom," the lieutenant shouted, "I don't care about that. All I know is you're behind on your Atabrine and you are going to take the full amount just like everybody else."

"And you know," Dick said, "that lieutenant thought he could make me take them."

"That's a direct order, Haltom," the lieutenant yelled.

"Lieutenant," Dick looked him in the eye, "I'm not going to take those pills and any silly ass who thinks he can make me is going to wish he hadn't tried."

The matter was finally dropped when it came to the attention of the company commander who dismissed the lieutenant's charges.

Dick, who had been in and out of combat in the jungles and on the beaches of southeast Asia for some two years when he was wounded, recalled the stress of battle and the varying reactions of soldiers to that pressure.

"The Japs were right up next to us in the jungle," Dick recalled. "We could hear them and they could hear us, but we couldn't see each other. At night, we'd get to yelling at each other."

"Tojo eats ----", one of the GIs would yell. "Tojo no eat ----" would come back the Japanese defense.

"At night, they liked to infiltrate our lines," Dick said. "They would come slipping in and jump right in the fox hole with you, then jump out. You'd find yourself trying to stab your fox hole buddy. That sort of thing could be unnerving."

The Japanese liked to bark like dogs at night.

"We'd be crouched down in our holes with our vital parts twitching," Dick said. "And then they would start that barking. I always felt that if I could ever have gotten up the nerve to bark back, I would have I would have felt better. But I just never could do it."

"You know," Dick said, "the front line troops really respected the Japanese combat soldier. They were brave men and we felt like they had families and girl-friends at home and they didn't want to be there any more than we did. The men in the rear areas talked about hating the Japs, and, if we sent a prisoner back, one of us had to go along to protect him. The boys on the front respected the Japs."

Dick said you never knew who would crack under the strain of combat in the jungle, or who would come through when the chips were down. A young officer in his outfit was from a small town in Mississippi near Dick's home of Batesville.

"He was a star football player. Big strapping hulk of a man — made a fine looking lieutenant," Dick recalled. "The last time I saw him, they were carrying him out of the jungle tied up like an animal, his eyes snapping around in his head."

On the other hand, there was the company clerk.

"He was what you'd call effeminate," Dick said. "He was very neat. When he dug his foxhole he would pad it with palm fonds and underbrush. Then he'd get in the hole, lean back, put his feet up and light a cigarette, tapping the ashes off with a straight forefinger like a girl. You would have thought he was at a society tea for goodness sake."

And he lasted the whole campaign without ever changing his neat and precise ways or showing any nerves.

Once a campaign was over and the troops were returned to a condition of safety, Dick had a problem.

"I had a bad attitude," Dick recalled. "Or at least it was an attitude that some of the sergeants and officers apparently found offensive.

"In the first place, I never wanted to be anything but a private and I succeeded in that ambition for almost two years.

"Then, one day, they called us all out to the company area. There were six of us left after the company was withdrawn from the line. We knew something was up. The captain had us all stand at attention, then he started to read from a sheet of paper.

"We were all of us promoted to private first-class — all of us the oldest, in terms of service, surviving yardbirds in the outfit.

"I found it very offensive. To me, being a private carried a certain dignity not available to other ranks. It implied you had great talents yet to be discovered.

"When they made us privates first class, it sent a message that we had been noticed and evaluated and the result indicated they didn't think much of us.

"Well, my feelings in the matter became a bone of contention. I never did sew on my stripe.

"In the first place, you know, it's not easy to sew on a single stripe and get it level and make it look good. So, I never did sew mine on.

"'Haltom,' the sergeant would bark, 'where is your stripe? When are you going to sew on your stripe!' He'd get mad and one thing would lead to another.

"I think part of the problem was that the captain, the first sergeant and I were all about the same age. Frankly, I felt a certain disdain for some of their posturing and strutting and I let them know it."

"How did you avoid being promoted above pfc?" I asked Dick. "With all those casualties, you should have gotten a battlefield promotion."

"Well," Dick said, "I was able to avoid that. Now, I got a lot of assignments nobody wanted. They'd say 'take five men and do so and so' something nobody in his right mind would voluntarily do. But they didn't go so far as to promote me. They brought in replacements for the non-com and officer jobs. It was my attitude, I think."

At one point, Dick's attitude led to a not quite official court martial.

"They didn't have any charges," he said, "but they felt something had to be done.

"The first sergeant came and got me. It was the kind of thing they did when they were going to bestow a medal or a promotion, only in my case the purpose was more sinister.

"I knew something was up when I entered the room — it was the front parlor of a big plantation house we had overrun. I knew it had to be official because they had army blankets spread over the tables. Behind the tables, in full dress, was the captain, the executive officer, and the first sergeant.

"I was standing rigidly at attention, my fingers splayed out like this to show the strain I was under.

"'Haltom,' the captain barked, ' you can stand at ease.'

"So, I stood at ease.

"Then the captain launched into a dissertation about my past and present conduct. I could see right away there wasn't much meat there, but I just stood there, looking at him.

"'Well,' he summarized, 'it boils down, Haltom to your attitude. You have a bad attitude.'

"I looked at him.

"'Captain,' I said, 'I am just a simple private soldier. I find myself many miles from home and loved ones. Frankly, sir, if you take away my attitude, I won't have anything at all.'

"I would have been all right, I think, but when I said that, the executive officer, who didn't like the captain, anyway, busted out laughing. It was like an explosion. He was pounding on the table.

"The sergeant was holding a book up in front of his face — and shaking.

"And the captain was getting a violent shade of red and was having trouble breathing.

"'Dismissed, Haltom,' he finally got out, 'we will get back to you later.'

"I had to dig three garbage holes. A garbage hole is eight by eight by eight feet deep.

"But since it was not a real court martial, I did it on company time. When the troops were drilling and doing other chores, I dug the three holes. No night work, no Sundays."

I asked Dick if the captain was a good officer.

"He was a good combat officer," Dick said, "but he wasn't much good otherwise. He was wounded about the same time I was and was evacuated on the same ship. The first sergeant pulled me back from the exposed, flat Phillipine plain where I was finally wounded."

Dick's total ambition was to go back to Batesville, Mississippi, and work in his father's drug store as he was doing when he joined the army. And that's what he did. After the war, he worked for the Haltom Drug Company until his Dad sold the business to him. Then Mr. Haltom worked for Dick until he died at age 94. "All I wanted to do," Dick said, "was work in the drug store all day, then come home and sit around poking the fire after supper. Like an old man for goodness sake."

"When he passed 90 Daddy got to where he couldn't see or hear well enough to sell and make change," Dick told me recently, "so he started working in the front of the store where he could catch the shoplifters. He did a good job, too."

Dick and I were in bed next to each other for a year and the four paraplegic wards became our whole world. There was plenty to see and do to while away the hours. The place was teeming with people and some of the patients and their visitors and the various attendants became characters we would never forget.

Some of the paraplegics and the quads accepted their situation and some did not.

I remember one older man named Davis who, I feel sure, finally willed himself to death. His reaction to what had happened was to turn his face to the wall, take a minimum of nourishment and withdraw within himself.

He was older than the rest of us and, because he wouldn't eat, he remained not much more than a human skeleton. He would not talk to the rest of us or take any part in the horseplay that helped relieve the tedium of the long days. He was so thin, the doctors had him put on a Stryker frame — a narrow padded board that revolved between two end metal frameworks. By strapping another board on top, it was possible to turn the patient, and thus avoid pressure sores, without disturbing him. Davis reminded me of some kind of Hindu mystic, lying on a bed of spikes as he reclined, day after day, on the narrow Stryker frame.

He was married to an attractive woman who, in the beginning, visited him every day. When she was there, we never saw him talk to her and he would often turn toward the wall rather than toward her.

Finally, she stopped coming. None of us blamed her or thought harshly of her.

In England, I had the experience of lying next to one young soldier who gradually lost touch with reality and finally became insane.

He was the soldier who had the big pressure sore on his back — the first one I had seen.

He was a small man, almost bald — very quiet and very nice. He spoke German fluently, and the people who had worked on the ward said that he had spent a good bit of time conversing with some German prisoners who had worked as attendants, before I got to the hospital.

He was from the middle west and, apparently, his family spoke German although he had been raised as an American.

Everybody that had known him when he first had come to the hospital remarked about how friendly he had been.

When I arrived, a change was already taking place in his personality. At first, he seemed only testy. He began by complaining about the kind of service given him, and each day he seemed to become more aggressive in his complaints.

Finally, I got tired of listening to him.

"Hey, Ed," I said, "why don't you quit griping all the time. There's nothing wrong with you isn't wrong with the rest of us."

I'll never forget the level look, the cold blank stare as he replied, "There's not a damn thing wrong with you."

He had been in the bed next to me for some time and had seen the nurses — or should have seen the nurses — changing my dressings and irrigating my catheter.

I knew immediately he was losing touch with reality and I had no desire to continue the converstaion. From the way he said it, and from the little I had read in my psychology courses, I had a strong feeling he saw in me an "agent" planted to spy on him.

As the days passed, his complaints became more strident and less related to reality.

He began to talk to people who were not there.

"Sergeant Bloom," he would shout, "come over here. Quick, sergeant Bloom."

Apparently sergeant Bloom was someone he had leaned on heavily in the past.

And then, he would talk to his wife, for hours. We were in England. She was across the ocean, back in the United States.

He would lie on his back, staring at the ceiling, and describe, to no one in particular, pictures that he saw projected there.

Shortly before I was moved from the ward to be sent back to the U. S., he became more aggressive as he became convinced the staff was mistreating him. When they came to change his dressings, he became alarmed, thinking they were going to hurt him.

Every day, the G. U. man would come with a purple solution and a large syringe to irrigate the catheters that drained our bladders. Now, he became extremely excited and began to shout for sergeant Bloom, yelling that they were trying to poison him.

I was relieved to leave his side and learned later that he had become violent after I left and had to be kept in a private room under guard.

There were the good times too — even in those early months as the personnel and the patients struggled to make the best of the bad situation.

"Do you remember how the preachers used to surround Harry?" Dick recalled recently. Harry was brought up a hard shell Baptist and his widowed mother saw to it that any ministers of the denomination came by to see Harry when they were in Atlanta.

"Harry," one of the ministers was talking in a loud voice so the whole ward could hear one Sunday afternoon, while pointing a long finger at our friend, "what would you do if one of your fellow patients came to you this afternoon seeking salvation. What scripture would you quote to guide him?" Harry hemmed and hawed and obviously was rusty on his Bible verses after Georgia Tech and his Army service, so we all got a sermon on which verses would do the trick.

Being severely injured and unable to get away as easily as the ambulatory patients, we were constantly being visited by people who sincerely believed their particular brand of religion could have us up and out, or, at least, could explain why we were in such a fix.

Dick and I were sitting in our wheelchairs out in the center aisle of the ward one day, when one well-meaning lady evangelist visited us.

"Young man," she had fixed her attention on Dick. I always looked healthier than Dick and, being free of pain, didn't squint my eyes and work my face and body the way Dick did when a bad one hit him. "I want you to know one thing. You are not just suffering for your sins. You're suffering for my sins, and for his sins (she pointed at a doctor who was passing by, an obvious sinner) and for everybody's sins."

"Lady," Dick said, giving her a level look. "I sure wish you would quit sinning so much because I sure do hurt."

At the other end of the religious spectrum there were Jack and Agnes. Jack was one of the wealthier patients, being a sergeant and drawing over a hundred dollars a month. In addition, he obviously had a way with women and Agnes was crazy about him. Jack had a drinking problem — he never could get enough — and he and Agnes went everywhere together.

One night when Jack came back to the ward, he and Agnes had been to the Southeastern Fair. Apparently, they had ridden most of the rides, including the whip and one where you sit in a swing while you are spun around beneath a big wheel.

"What did you do about you feet?" I asked.

"Agnes held them up until we got started," Jack replied.

The whip was apparently too much for him and Jack was the first to get a pressure sore on his buttocks.

One weekend, Jack, flush with the big sergeant's salary, hired a taxi and took Agnes all the way to his home town of Dublin, Georgia, some 150 miles away.

On most afternoons, Agnes would come by after she got off from work in the hospital cafeteria.

She would sit by Jack's bedside in a straight chair and before long she would be tilting the chair forward on its front legs while she hugged and kissed Jack. On most afternoons when the loving became serious the chair would lose its footing on the highly polished floor.

Whomp! We'd hear a crash.

"There goes Agnes," one of the patients would yell as Jack's girl-friend disappeared under the bed. Agnes never seemed to mind the attention and hitting the floor, because the next afternoon she would be back tilting her chair as she lay on top of Jack.

Our favorite was Marcas. We first heard about Marcas from the girls who tried to wait on him. Marcas was a holy terror. He was so bad they had him in a private room where he would cuss, scream and throw things at the hapless WAC or nurse who tried to do something for him.

Marcas was from Michigan and he had come up the hard way, working on the farms or in the factories, at whatever menial job he could find to keep himself fed. Marcas had not had the benefit of much education, and while he held strong opinions, they were usually buttressed only by whatever misinformation he could pick up on the street or by personal observation and deduction.

His problem with the hospital was a misconception he had formed that hospitals are supposed to make you well. Obviously, this hospital was not making him well, so obviously, the doctors, nurses, WACs and ward boys weren't doing their jobs, and since he remained paralyzed, Marcas' only recourse was to scream at and curse them until they shaped up.

Finally, one of the doctors decided that, since isolation didn't seem to be improving Marcas' disposition, they might as well throw him out into the general ward and see if we could help him. It was a wise decision and the transformation in Marcas' conduct was almost magical.

As soon as the lights went out on our ward Marcas' first night amongst us, he began to scream and curse. The ward remained quiet until we had heard a capsule version of Marcas' screaming fit and then Andy, the patient who ate steak and chocolate milk for breakfast, raised up on one elbow.

"Shut your mouth, you dumb sonofabitch," Andy yelled. "There's not a godamn thing wrong with you that's not wrong with the rest of us, you cry baby."

Well, it didn't work. Marcas kept screaming and whining. Finally, Andy rang his bell for assistance, got into a wheelchair and took a large pitcher of ice water from his night stand. With the ward boy pushing, Andy went to Marcas' bedside and dumped the entire icy contents on top of Marcas' head.

What kindness and love had failed to do was accomplished by Andy's ice water. Now, Marcas understood that there were others in the boat with him, and he became our most cooperative patient.

Marcas' spirit was not broken, of course, and he still had his aberrations and opinions based on personal deduction. And he stood staunchly behind them, no matter the public pressure brought to bear by the rest of the ward.

"I used to pick pickles," Marcas asserted one day.

"You mean you picked cucumbers and then the factory pickled them" one of the patients called out.

"The hell I did," Marcas shouted. "I picked pickles."

"Marcas," came back the rejoinder, "pickles don't grow. Cucumbers grow and then get pickled."

"Dammit," Marcas was hopping mad now, "was you there, Charlie. I was there and I reckon I know what I was picking and what I was picking was pickles."

On another occasion, Marcas maintained for as many days as anybody would continue the argument, that President Roosevelt was not paralyzed.

"Hell" Marcas yelled, "there wasn't nothing wrong with him. I seen him walking."

Marcas displayed his deductive reasoning one day when we got in an argument about what kind of pension we'd get.

"Hell," Marcas started, "I know what I'll get. I got two legs and one arm I can't move — that's three out of four. I'm 75% disabled."

Marcas was a philosopher. One day, one of the patients called out, "I wish I was dead. Hell couldn't be as bad as this."

Marcas raised up, "Oh, yeah," he hollered from down the ward, "strike a match and hold it to your finger."

Marcas became one of the favorites of the patients and workers on the ward. Once he was accepted as one of the group, he became our most considerate and helpful member.

A tougher case was Hart, whom we came to call "Hotfoot" during our long weeks and months of endurance of his whining and yelling.

Hart was from the mountains of North Carolina and, like Marcas, had not had the benefit of much education. There is no doubt in my mind that Hart was in pain and certainly he never accepted it gracefully.

I first endured Hart in the hospital in England. His bed was several beds away and across the aisle from mine but his voice carried so well he might as well have been in the same bed with the rest of the ward.

Many of the patients at that time were fresh from the battlefield and the night was filled with the shouts coming from their nightmares.

"Sergeant Blue, bring that jeep up here" one of the patients would yell and then give instructions for the coming attack, taking us all back to the horror of the front.

Hart was different. He was completely absorbed in his current situation and the burning in his feet that gave him his name of "Hotfoot." Since he had been wounded in the spine, his nerves were giving false signals that he could not understand were phony.

In England, he was constantly yelling for an enema since he felt the signals indicating such a need. Then he would decide the catheter that drained his bladder was stopped up. When the urologist wouldn't come immediately, he would pull the rubber tube out, blow on it and swing it around his head.

It seemed to go on all the time and the greatest day of our lives was the day Hart was shipped back to the U.S. and we were left in peace back in England.

When I got to Lawson, all was relative peace and quiet for the first weeks. Then, after we moved into our shiny new ward, I was being treated behind the drawn curtains one morning when I heard a familiar whining voice.

"Oh, my God," I thought, "that's Hotfoot!"

What added to the irritation caused the rest of us was the fact that "Hotfoot" was not really a paraplegic. He could move his legs and, in fact, finally walked out of the hospital. Like I say, he undoubtedly was in pain, but he did nothing to help himself until his body finally healed of its own accord. And he included the whole ward in his sufferings in the most irritating way.

The thing that finally caused the most compassionate to get fed up with Hart was what he did about his legs. They were somewhat more comfortable when bent at the knee, so Hotfoot refused to straighten them out regardless of the pleadings and warnings of the medical staff. Finally, it was impossible for him to straighten them out. The doctors knew he could walk if he would and that the pain would lessen if Hotfoot would only move his legs. But there was no getting through his hard-headed determination.

Finally, the staff held a conference and decided to help Hart in spite of himself. They knocked him out with anesthetics, took him to the orthopedic room, straightened his legs as much as they could and put them in plaster casts.

Now the pain was really bad — so bad they put Hart on the back porch so the rest of us could get some sleep.

"I'm going to kill myself," Hart would yell. Then, he would grab one of the metal Emerson basins and start beating himself in the head. "Bring me a knife," he'd scream, "so I can kill myself."

We had a tough little nurse from Boston who finally had enough. We called her "The Wedge" because of the way her body sloped from wide hips to narrow shoulders. The Wedge marched to the kitchen, picked up the biggest knife in the place and carried it to the back porch.

"Here," she yelled at a stunned Hotfoot as she handed him the big butcher knife, "go ahead." With that she whirled around and left him, closing the porch door behind her.

Hart finally got up on crutches, and, as the doctors had predicted, his pain began to diminish.

His wife, we learned, effected his final cure.

Hart refused to try to drive the car and his wife was taking him back to their North Carolina home when they got caught in a heavy snowstorm.

Finally, she stopped the car and refused to go further in the blinding snow on the narrow and winding mountain road.

"Get out, woman," Hart yelled. While she went around to the other side, he slid under the wheel; and then drove on home.

After that, we would see Hart calmly shooting pool in the recreation room and he was finally discharged and left the hospital walking without a limp.

CHAPTER XIII

Tuscon is the desert. Surrounded by mountains, the land the city is built on is flat and eight months out of the year the weather is ideal. The average temperature is 70 degrees, the skies are sunny and the dry desert air makes the bones feel good. The rest of the year is like living in a frying pan.

The mountains that ring the city stand out in bold relief against the blue and cloudless sky. Before starting the engine of the Cherokee, I set one VOR to home in on the Cochise Station, some 60 miles east and on the Tucson side of the highest mountain range, the lower end of the Rockies, that I would have to cross. The other VOR, I set for the San Simon station, north of my route. With the OBS set for the 180 degree radial, the needle for that VOR would center as I crossed the highest point of the mountain range — shown on the chart as just over eight thousand feet.

From that point, the mountains drop precipitously to the flat desert, and the broad opening that divides the Rockies and that gave El Paso its name.

When I called the Tucson tower to let them know I was ready for takeoff, they advised me to change frequency for departure control just after liftoff.

As the 140 left the runway and soared into the crisp desert air, I twisted the dial from the tower frequency.

"Fly a heading of one zero niner degrees," departure advised.

In the CAVU (ceiling and visibility unlimited), I found myself steered south of my plotted course of zero eight two. The reason was obvious as soon as the 140 had gained altitude — the 109 heading took me along the expressway and through a pass in the mountains. Once the nearby mountain range was past, I corrected course by flying left, toward the needle, until I was back on the zero eight two radial to Cochise.

The 140 was climbing at 500 feet per minute and I soon had the altitude necessary to put a couple of thousand feet between me and the next range of mountains that lay ahead.

Half an hour later, right on schedule, my San Simon VOR centered as I cleared the mountain range. On the eastern slope, I looked down on a mine nestled in a valley that extended into the surrounding range, and was impressed again by the flatness of the terrain leading up to the base of the rugged peaks.

"Don't let that desert fool you," a pilot friend had warned me before I left Georgia. "That flat looking land is covered by hummocks that will tear your plane apart. If you can, always fly parallel to a road in case you have to land."

Those months at Lawson General had been organized to divert our minds from the reality of our injuries. The support from the skilled medical people provided by the Army and the volunteers from town could not prepare us for the hard landing we paraplegics and quadraplegics were about to make.

Within the brightly colored wards of Lawson General Hospital, we led an existence suspended and shielded from the harsh reality of our new situation, in the same way my little single engine plane was now suspended above the hostile desert.

We had suffered one of the worst injuries the soldier is subject to and we were acutely conscious of our reduced ability to care for our simple everyday needs.

At the same time, we were sustained by the totality of the situation.

We were soldiers — and we had sustained our injuries doing what a united and victorious nation expected and wanted its young men to do. Being young, we were conscious of the approval of those around us — and of the good will and sympathetic feelings of the people who joined with us to try to help us overcome the catastrophic thing that had happened to us.

We had the best of what the nation could supply. The finest doctors and nurses, unlimited attendant care, the finest food.

All of which shielded us — and helped us forget the reality of what had happened to us.

Carried forward by the daily routine, the visitors, the flow of young men and young women in and out of the ward as we were waited upon, we were sustained by the fact we were still soldiers, still part of a unit and of what the whole country was involved in.

We were supported in the same way we had been supported on long marches or in the tough obstacle courses of our days in training — then, ready to collapse, we would look at the soldier straining beside us — "if he can make it, I can make it too."

We were part of a unit.

The young person whose spine is severed in an automobile accident, a diving accident, or a freak fall, doesn't have the advantage we had of being part of something bigger than himself.

On the other hand, he benefits from the lessons learned in those early days when there was no apparent answer to the problem.

Modern treatment of the spinal injured involves an analysis of the situation made by a team of specialists in the early days after the injury. Then the patient and his family are given the facts as uncovered and the prognosis for the future.

Once it is established that an injury is such that paralysis will be permanent, the patient is told.

The difference is that today, the patient can also be told what he and the staff can do to improve his ability to meet and cope with the situation.

And there are role models that can be pointed to. Individuals with an equal degree of disability who have led full and productive lives.

In 1945, there weren't any role models, and the program started by units like Lawson General had not produced much in the way of results. The prognosis still was that the problem would be solved by the deaths of the patients.

So, they lied to us. We were told that we would recover the use of our bodies. And in the context of those times, I cannot argue with that decision.

Dick Haltom's dad summed up the feelings of most of the families when he told Dick, "Son, I don't believe one little bullet could do that much damage."

My Dad, who had inspired thousands of young people to overcome their problems by positive thinking and action said, "I believe if you concentrate hard enough, you can make that foot move."

So, as the long hours in the army hospital slowly passed, I would sit in the old fashioned, high-caned back wooden wheelchair, the leg rests extended to raise my feet. I would look at my big toe on my right foot.

"If I can put all my mental energy into one massive thought wave," I would decide, "that big toe will move."

I would sit and concentrate.

And concentrate.

Finally, the toe would move.

After another thirty minutes of sitting and concentrating, it might twitch again.

That gave me encouragement. I had plenty of time to sit and concentrate, so I believed that sooner or later I would be back in control of my body. Of course, the twitching of the toe was reflex, and I really knew that, but I'd still sit, hour after hour, and try.

The morning I faced the truth is burned into my mind so that I can see it vividly today.

And as I think of that day, I reaffirm my belief that there aren't many "accidents" in our daily live; that we are guided in the important matters that control our future.

The time had come for me to face the facts.

I don't remember ever having gone into the doctor's office on our ward. But I was there that bright sunshiny morning. And on the doctor's desk was a mimeographed paper dealing with spinal cord injury.

I remember reading only one statement.

"The ability of the individual to cope with the fact that his paralysis is permanent depends to a large extent on his intelligence and his education."

For the first time, the words "permanent paralysis" had come to my consciousness. And I knew immediately they applied to me.

After I read those words, I backed my wheelchair out of the doctor's office and rolled out into the hallway.

Lawson General occupied over fifty acres of ground, with row after row of single-story buildings, each a ward like the one we were housed in. Connecting the rows of parallel wards were long hallways that ran perpendicular to the wards and stretched, it seemed, almost into infinity.

I sat now, stunned by the words I had read, and looked down the endless, grey hall, spotted at regular intevals by doors into the succeeding wards.

All alike, all a dull grey that repeated endlessly as far as the eye could see.

"That's my life," I thought. "The future will be one long ordeal of helpless, hopelessness. I can't do anything. Not take a walk in the cool of evening, not climb a mountain, or swim a river. Not romance a girl or fight a battle — nothing but this same nothing — day after monotonous and meaningless day — no color — no action — all endlessly grey."

I left the long grey hall, rolled back into the ward and had one of the ward men help me back into bed. It was as if I had fallen into a deep, bottomless black pit. I knew my life was over — but it was not ended.

I was always going to be dependent. I was always going to need help — doing the simplest things — getting out of bed — going up a step — trying to pick up an object too high or low.

My Mother recalls. "When I came into the ward that afternoon, one of the nurses took me aside. 'We don't know what's wrong with Clark,' she said, 'he's always been our morale builder. Joking and laughing. But something has put him into a deep depression. We don't know what's happened.'"

"After the nurse talked to me," mother continued, "I started to pray and I know that God gave me the answer. I began to think about Emory University and I talked to you about going back to college."

After Mother left, I lay in my bed thinking — struggling.

My Dad's whole life had been devoted to helping young people overcome impossible financial obstacles to get their educations and to become strong, productive citizens. He had literally changed the lives of thousands of young people — many of whom have talked to me about his help over the years.

And, all my life, it had been drummed into me that you make lemonade out of lemons. You don't quit, and you can overcome anything if you make up your mind to do so.

But, this was different. This was impossible. How could I ever make a life out of this complete helplessness.

Finally, that afternoon I hit the bottom of my bottomless, pitch black pit. I lay there on my stomach and I prayed.

"Dear Lord, I've got sores on my hips, my heels, my ankles and my back. I've got a tube going into my belly to drain my bladder. I can't get out of bed without help. I can't walk and most of the time I'm fighting infection.

"There's just one thing I can do, Lord, and that's breathe. So starting now, I'm going to breathe deeply."

A peace came over me finally and I thought, "This has got to be the bottom — I can't get any lower and stay alive."

There is one thing about being on the bottom — there's only one way you can go and that is up.

That afternoon, I decided I was going to leave the hospital as soon as my sores were healed. There was no reason I couldn't go to Emory and complete my education.

As the years go by , I believe less and less in accidents. Too many times God has supplied what I have needed. He is, indeed, the help of the helpless.

When I was bleeding on the battlefield, the young soldier Frank and I thought was incompetent, crawled out to pull me to safety.

The afternoon the final truth about my paralysis came to me, Mother walked in and started talking about college.

But I needed someone to help me do it.

I didn't know it, but the Lord had already sent someone to pull me out of my bottomless pit and back into life and struggle.

The first time I saw Frances was a few days after I had been brought to Lawson. I was in the swaybacked old metal bed in a four man room when she walked in with an arm load of long stemmed red roses.

"Hello, Patsy," I called, "what are you doing here?"

She grimaced. "I'm not Patsy, I'm Frances."

All I knew about Frances was that she was Patsy's older sister. I had known Patsy in high school, but Frances had attended private school. Both were beautiful girls, with a strong family resemblance.

I had had a few dates during the summer after I got back to Lawson. One with my former high school sweetheart. Leaving the hospital was a major production. We were in the old wooden chairs and to get us into a car, the attendant had to lower the high back of the chair. Then we were pushed and pulled up the wheelchair back to the front seat of the car.

I will never forget one of those dates. I was being helped in and one of the attendants was holding the glass jar that my catheter drained into. My date, an attractive young woman I had known for years, looked at me as if a light had suddenly dawned for her.

She frowned and said, "You're going to be this way the rest of your life, aren't you?"

Dating a wounded hero carried a certain romantic aura in those closing days of the war, but it was obvious she wanted no part of anything as permanent as paraplegia.

Frances had a different attitude.

Frances is a very intelligent person of deep and strongly held convictions. Her father was a Superior Court judge for many years, a scholar and a philosophical man of insight. Frances inherited all of his best qualities. Her strong religious conviction had been buttressed by personal trials, and her will strengthened by overcoming her own personal ordeals.

When World War II started, our town became a center for the training of young men. Frances felt great empathy for the soldiers far from home and most Sundays the family entertained several GIs that Frances or Patsy had invited home from the morning church services.

"I wrote all the boys that visited us," Frances told me later. "Some of them were not very educated and not too attractive but that wasn't their fault. And they were so lonely and homesick."

One of our local ladies, who had lost her son early in the war, organized a group of girls who called themselves the S.O.S. They came to Lawson every week and visited with the patients.

At the end of summer, I had the ward boys roll my bed out into the yard one afternoon. Frances was visiting, sitting on the edge of my bed in the bright sun light.

"Well, I don't know who I'll date now that everybody is going back to college."

"How about me," Frances said.

"You're a lot older than I am," I rejoined.

"I am not!" she was incensed. "We're the same age! In fact, we went to kindergarden together."

Frances had gone to a private girls school, as I said, and had not been part of the crowd I had gone with my last two years of high school.

We started to date regularly. Frances would drive me in the car and her visits to the hospital became almost daily.

When I finally left the hospital and was living at home, we were together constantly and found more and more the hopes and fears, likes and dislikes we share in common.

Frances, as I began to know her then and have come to know her over the years, is a quiet person who feels deeply and who is constantly thinking of what she can do to help those she loves.

She is a very passionate person. I always attributed that part of her nature to her Indian heritage. When she feels, she feels strongly and it is impossible for her to forget when a slight or a wrong has been done to someone she cares for.

Frances likes to putter around doing little things that capture her interest and fancy. She is a genius in making things grow and can fill our big screened-in porch with beautiful ferns and plants that she has raised from seed or cutting.

She is an artist who paints rich and compelling things.

She designs her own needlepoint patterns and they are strikingly handsome.

Frances hates house work. And is forever at it.

She lives in a jumble of projects, plants, and paintings and seems constantly frustrated by the fact she cannot become neatly organized.

But, you had better believe she can fight like a tiger, organize like J. Paul Getty and take on and lick the world when her husband or sons are at risk.

In 1945, as my relationship with Frances deepened, of one thing I was sure — I would never marry. I was not going to marry someone who would have to take care of me rather that the other way around.

With my relationship with Frances becoming more serious, I had begun to look around the ward at the married couples.

The men I came to know in the hospital who already were married when they became paralyzed faced enormous pressure.

Fueled primarily by the man's deep fear of rejection, the knowledge that he was no longer the man she had married, the situation was volatile. The reactions of different patients were revealing.

There were a few who made it without any apparent question on either side. There was one older man who had obviously been married at least ten years, the age of their oldest of three children.

I did not know them well, but from watching during the family's visits, I had the feeling that his injury was accepted as something that had happened to them all, that they had the inner resources to handle it, that he would do what he could do, they would do what they could do, and they would all move forward together.

Then, there was Davis — the living skeleton on the Stryker frame. His solution was to turn his face to the wall when his wife visited him until, finally, she no longer came. He willed his marriage to death.

The wives, those who wanted to make a go of it, were uncertain as to how to handle the situation. On the face of it, they no longer had someone to depend on. Instead, in one respect it was as if they had a child to take care of, but a child who could not be disciplined and led in the normal way.

What made me most uncomfortable were those patients who reacted by ordering their wives around and treating them with contempt as the woman tried desperately to make up for what had been lost. Eventually, the result in such cases was bitterness on both sides and divorce.

And when divorce comes, it reveals the power of a marriage — for evil as well as for good.

The Bible tells in a few words what happens as the marriage vows are exchanged and the marriage consummated — two people become one.

And it is a profound "oneness" that goes beyond two bodies merging into a single body.

In marriage, the two souls merge and in many respects become a united identity.

"What God has joined together, let no man tear asunder."

That law is violated constantly, but always at a cost. Over the years, I have seen family, friends and acquaintances endure divorce, and it is always shocking to see the tearing, rending assault the process makes on the parties concerned. It defies understanding.

It seems to me that, when people marry, they stand naked before each other. They reveal themselves in a way that each never reveals himself to anyone else — not just in body, but more importantly in spirit. The parties see not only the strengths but the weaknesses. Only love can ignore and cover over the weaknesses and the ugliness we all are humanly subject to.

When that mutual revelation is marred by divorce, the parties reach a state of bitterness that is probably not matched in any other human relationship.

The split up of a marriage is a defiance of spiritual as well as man-made law. The intent of that law is that people support each other and together support their children so civilization itself can survive. The intent of God in creating the marriage relationship was to provide love and nurture in a harsh, unforgiving world.

When the marriage breaks up, the participants are left naked to the world, as well as to each other, and deep and profound feelings of guilt and bitterness of great power result. In order to maintain one's integrity and worth, it becomes imperative to tear down the estranged partner to show that the break was his fault — that he was bad and that she was justified in severing the marriage — and the same applies from the male point of view.

The time comes when there seems to be no doubt that divorce, with all the trauma it contains, is the only viable alternative. But the scars run deep and the healing takes years.

The raw power of marriage is revealed by estrangement and divorce. When Frances and I married, that power was the force that lifted me out of despair and helplessness.

Looking back over the years of our marriage, I realize the power that the new relationship had for me in those days when the wounds suffered on the front were still fresh and the agony still deep.

As a young man, wrenched from the full strength of that manhood by the sniper's bullet, I still possessed the normal sex drives and desires.

Because the marriage bond is so powerful, in our case it was able to begin to heal me in a way that nothing else could.

By becoming one with my wife, I was now able to do those things I could not have done before — she was always there and her physical health became my physical health.

In my mind, the trap was sprung open and a new freedom was waiting for me. Because we were one, I could ask things of my wife I could not have asked of anyone else.

As I brought her fulfillment and joy, my own confidence and strength were multiplied.

The bond was a powerful one — and the new life we found together was enjoyed, but not fully appreciated until many years had passed.

Next to regaining use of my paralyzed limbs, nothing else could have brought me the new sense of worth our marriage did.

One of the tragedies of life today are the lies people have been exposed to in recent years in the so-called "sex revolution".

Advertising, magazines and books and TV shows give young people a false idea about love and marriage. They are led to believe that promiscuity is the norm and that if they aren't involved with a number of sex partners and able to spend the night with casual acquaintances, there is something wrong with them as lovers and as people.

The delights of married love are never portrayed. Instead, marriage is most often shown as a running battle with no redeeming feature.

These lies mislead young people, breaking apart normal healthy human relationships and generally causing heart ache and tragedy.

The truth about marriage, the fact that it heals wounds, gives meaning to life and provides the nurture and love that fulfil normal human needs, is not told.

As it was, I couldn't have married anyone better able to cope with the problem.

I was always made to feel that I was the husband and it was up to me to provide and to take care of her. That is powerful medicine for a young man — especially for one who has been blown away by a catastrophic disability.

"Well," Frances would say, "you can do it if you really want to."

On the other hand, she had infinite patience while waiting for me to overcome my fears and try some new venture.

When I started writing this book, Frances told me, "Try to recall and tell about how hard it was to get started, how discouraged you became and that you were not always confident and self-assured. That way you can help other people who are new at facing a terrible and overpowering experience."

It was tough. And I would never have made it without her.

We enjoyed each other. We would sit and talk by the hour, discussing the people we had seen that day and the things we had done.

Periodically over the early years I would land back in bed because of a breakdown of one of the old pressure sores — and it would be just the two of us, there in the bedroom — for weeks or months.

"Bobbi," Frances' father, Judge Guess, had a farm and several horses. He loved to visit it with our friend Bobbi, an avid horse woman from Tennessee, "Nobody will ever know how much Frances loves Clark. We went to see them the other day and she was changing the dressing on his hip. Bobbi, the yellow pus was coming out of that place just like it comes out of one of these horses who infects a leg.

"There was my little girl, changing that dressing and cleaning that deep sore and she never faltered."

And Frances never complained about the fact most of our money seemed to go for doctors and hospitals.

Whatever life I have had was Frances' gift to me and her generosity at such a young age with so many uncertainties, as well as so many certain and real problems, amazes me to this day.

Marriage is a great mystery. It deserves the protections our people have built around it.

We tamper with it at our peril.

CHAPTER XIV

The VOR was set for 111.2, the Columbus Stockyards — and there was desert below, spotted with scattered mountains that were in stark relief against the surrounding flatness.

What looks like lakes on the sectional aeronautical chart are actually dry depressions in the barren wasteland, with the sands rippled by some past flash flood.

The Columbus Stockyards are just that and from three thousand feet the corrals stand out clearly against the tan and dusty earth. The sky is a sparkling blue and the air between the 140 and the ground is crystal clear and unblemished by the haze so often encountered in the southeastern United States.

Tracking out on the 258 radial FROM Columbus Stockyards, I was able to discern the magnificient pass that gave El Paso its name, soon after the pioneers found this route around the Rocky Mountains. Mexico is immediately to the south and it is easy to see why the victors in our war with Mexico insisted on including this piece of real estate as part of the United States. Massive mountain ranges come up to the pass from north and south, with the pass itself a flat expanse, miles across, connecting the western states with the far west.

It is an impressive sight. Coming west I had landed at El Paso.

"Five five November, get clear of the runway," the tower instructed.

I had just taxied off the runway, had turned with the taxi way and was headed toward the direction from which I had landed.

"This is Five Five November," I replied, "I am clear of the runway."

"Well, get as far from the runway as you can," the tower replied, "That's a 727 landing behind you."

As I looked up, the big airliner was coming over the numbers and settling for a landing. Fortunately, it touched down before it reached the spot where my plane was taxiing.

The danger to a small plane from a large jet airliner is something called wake turbulence. As the plane, weighing many tons, settles toward the earth, a violent vortex of swirling, turbulent air is created off the tip of each wing. The twin swirling vortexes are strong enough to turn a light plane sideways or upside down and can cause the pilot of the small plane to be thrown about with such force that he can lose control of his craft.

The vortex descends behind the airliner and it can be blown by the prevailing wind to one side or the other. The small plane pilot is taught to stay above the path of the landing jet and to land beyond the point at which the jet touches down. If the small plane follows an airliner at takeoff, it is important that the smaller plane leave the runway before it reaches the point of lift off for the larger plane. If these rules are followed, it is possible to operate into and out of large airports, sandwiched in with the airliners. But the pilot so unfortunate as to place his machine in the path of one of these monster vortexes may have taken his last airplane ride.

The controller had left his microphone open and I heard his side remark to one of his co-workers, "Well, that's enough excitement for one day."

The evening in 1945 that official word came that Japan had accepted the U. S. ultimatum that followed the obliteration of Hiroshima and Nagasaki, pandemonium broke out over the U. S. Mass celebrations occurred simultaneously everywhere — men and women hugging and kissing total strangers — sirens wailing, fireworks exploding.

On ward 2-B, Lawson General Hospital, the sixteen paraplegics were watching a movie when the door to the back porch opened behind the movie screen and knocked it to the floor.

"The war's over," the young woman, a girl I had known from our neighborhood, was breathless with excitement, "Japan surrendered!"

"Yeah, that's great," Marcas snarled, "how about puttin' the screen back so we can finish the movie."

The attractive young woman stumbled through the dark ward, past the projector and let herself out the door to the hallway, obviously bewildered and subdued by the lack of reaction.

For the patients, until then members of a team fighting for the defeat of our enemies, it was the end of everything. We knew that the kind of support we had drawn from the Army and the country would end with the end of the war, and now it was on us.

"All right, you wounded heroes," Marcas yelled through the darkened ward, "You're just crippled sons of bitches now."

Everybody laughed and called insults back at Marcas, but we knew there was truth in what he said. Our worst night every week was Saturday, because there were no visitors — everybody was out having a good time. Now, the biggest celebration of our lives was going on and we were not part of it.

I felt somewhat like I had as a child when I had emerged from the washing machine and found that the game of hide and seek was over.

I had made up my mind to one thing — I didn't know what kind of care we would get from here out but I was resolved not to stay and find out. As soon as I could, I was going to leave the hospital and go home.

But not yet. First, I had to become as independent as possible. I had heard that Col. Fred Dunlap had made a trip to the bathroom unassisted and now I went to see him.

He had a shiny new tubular steel wheelchair and had worked out a way to get from the bed into the chair and from the chair onto a commode.

"Yeah, Clark," he told me, "this is the Traveler model made by Everest and Jennings. The large wheels are in the front and I have this back that can be removed."

With the leatherette back off, it became a simple matter to get into and out of the chair. Before long, I had a chair similarly equipped and was on my way to the bathroom.

The first time I sat on a commode it was a strange sensation. I couldn't feel anything under me and I couldn't see anything under me. I felt I was suspended in mid air.

But it worked — and I knew I could take care of my body functions — all alone — by myself. It was a great feeling!

The Army eased us down gently. Lawson General would be phased out as the patients were discharged. Since we could not be dismissed as patients, we were to be sent to a big Army hospital in Memphis, Tennessee. Then, when only permanently disabled were left, the hospital would be turned into a VA facility and we would be discharged from the Army.

Very neat and bureaucratically orderly.

We were to be shipped in railroad cars that were backed into a siding at nearby Chamblee. It was a forlorn procession of ambulances carrying patients on stretchers that assembled at the small, outdoor platform next to the rail line. I had sworn when I rode a day coach across the U. S. for the last time as an Army private that I'd never ride a train again — but here was this final journey yet to be made.

In 1946 Kennedy General was a permanent installation consisting of a number of large, red brick buildings. It was still under army control and, like Lawson General, was staffed with some of the most competent medical people in the country.

I was most impressed by the work being done by the German prisoners of war. They ran the place, making braces in the brace shop, manning the mechanical equipment of the hospital, and serving in any function that required willing hands and hard work.

The transition to Veterans Administration control was made shortly after we arrived as patients. The prisoners of war were being sent home and VA workers were taking their places.

Jack, Agnes' lover, and I decided we would go exploring soon after we arrived at the new facility.

We heard that there was an enlisted men's club on the base and that they served beer. Since we were still in the Army and since we were enlisted, we decided it would be just the place for us to visit.

We were in our pajamas, of course, and we were in the old, high cane-backed wooden wheelchairs. Fortunately, we didn't know the facility we planned to visit was all the way on the far side of the big complex. Otherwise, we would not have started out and we would have missed a memorable adventure.

Pushing down the long corrridors, up and down ramps, out on the sidewalks, asking directions, we proceeded on our way.

The club was located down a long slope, so we enjoyed a little respite as we turned and wheeled toward our final destination.

Entering the club, we noticed right away we were the only ones present who were in pajamas. Everything else in the place was strictly GI olive drab.

"We better get two apiece," Jack whispered as we rolled up to the bar.

The surprised bar tender served us four beers on a tray and one of the men who had followed us to the bar volunteered to take the tray to a table.

We noticed we were receiving the covert glances of the other GIs and we began to think we might have done something wrong.

"Sorry, fellows," the sergeant had sauntered up just as we finished our first beer, "you're out of uniform. You'll have to go back and change into your O.D.'s."

"Gosh, Sarge," Jack assumed his best wounded hero smile, "we'll sure do that. But I wonder if we could finish our beer."

"Yeah," he said doubtfully, "but make it snappy."

We downed our other beer quickly and headed for the exit.

It was not to end there. We had violated the rules and we were not through with offended authority yet.

We were sitting outside contemplating the situation, when a corporal walked up.

"Boy, these guys burn me up," he offered. "These guys never heard a shot fired in anger. They been sitting back here safe and sound and they can't even let a couple of wounded soldiers have a beer."

He suggested we roll over in the bushes and he would go get us some more beer. A couple of minutes later, he was back.

"No soap, fellows," he sounded concerned. "They've sent for the officer of the day. You'd better make a run for it."

As we watched through the windows, we saw an officer and a sergeant stride into the club look quickly about and head for the door where we had exited.

"You'll have to leave the area," the officer was stern.

We looked at the long slope of the sidewalk ascending to the main road expecting at any moment to hear the officer or the sergeant offer to give us a push. We were pretty tired after our long journey coming over to the club.

They just stood glaring, hands on hips, so we started our laborious trip to the top of the rise.

By this time, a patrol car had arrived, summoned to take care of the unusual situation.

When we reached the main road, we were winded and decided to sit a few minutes to catch our breath.

"All right, men," the driver of the vehicle was hidden by the bright glare of his headlights, "move on out."

By this time we were exhausted, and we were sure someone would jump out of the vehicle and give us a shove to whatever point would ease their concern about two wheelchairs being loose in unauthorized territory.

The motor kept turning over and the headlights glaring as the detachment waited for Jack and I to make our move.

Finally, Jack and I turned in the direction from which we had come and laboriously began to roll the big, heavy wooden wheelchairs along the macadam road.

The command car fell in behind us, maintaining a ten foot interval and creeping along in low gear until the commander no longer felt threatened by our presence.

Having been an Army truck driver, I could understand the strict code that led to what may have seemed a bazaar situation to the uninitiated. The officer of the day's job was to see that everybody who entered the club was entitled and was in proper uniform. The detachment that followed us down the road were ordained to keep law and order.

It was up to a different group of soldiers to push wheelchairs.

The transition to Veterans Administration control was made shortly after we arrived as patients. The prisoners of war were being sent home and VA workers were taking their places.

We had a preview of the change from Army to VA in the serving of our meal trays each day. Under Army control, at each meal time, two Germans pushing wheeled patient litters, loaded with the still warm meals, would arrive on the ward — at the same time each day.

One would push a litter while the other would place the trays by the patients' beds.

After allowing time to finish the meal, they would return and pick up the trays in efficient, reverse order.

The meals were on time, the food was warm, and the trays were removed promptly.

Then the VA took over.

From that day forward, we were witnesses to the change in motivation and performance. Instead of being motivated by a desire to serve quickly and efficiently, apparently the new ward boys were motivated by a desire to put in the time required to be physically present from pay day to pay day.

The litter was abandoned. Each meal, one ward man with one tray would walk in, leave the tray with a patient, then leave the ward. He would make the long trip back to the kitchen, get one more tray and repeat the process. Needless to say, the food was late, cold, and stayed with the patient for an hour or so after the meal was completed.

I had already made up my mind to leave as soon as the VA took over operation of the facility.

Now, my resolve to leave the hospital intensified.

A couple of weeks after I got to Kennedy, I started asking who I could see about being discharged from the hospital. Nobody seemed to know. Finally, I stopped a major, one of the remaining Army doctors, on his rounds.

"Major," I said, "I'm leaving the hospital."

"You can't go yet," he replied, "we aren't through with your treatment."

"Major," I said, "what I've got, you can't cure. I'm going home."

"And what are you going to do there, Harrison?" he asked.

"I plan to go back to college," I replied.

"You can't go to college with that tube in your belly," he said sarcastically.

"Major," I said, "maybe not. But I'm going to be caught trying."

The next morning, I started making the rounds. I went to the supply room to find out what I was supposed to turn in (my pajamas, my urinal bottle, the combat jacket they had issued to replace the one the German made the hole in?)

Getting no satisfaction there, I went to the main office and asked for the forms to fill out to be discharged. They looked at me like I was slightly addled in the head.

Finally, I called home. My good friend L. A. Scott, Jr., who was a dive bomber pilot in the Navy prior to his discharge, had promised to come get me.

"Scotty," I told him over the phone, "apparently there's no procedure for being discharged from this hospital."

"Fine, Clark," he said, "when can we pick you up? Dot and Frances say they'd like to come with me."

After I had been home for a couple of weeks, I got a letter from the V. A.

"Your furlough is over. Report back to the hospital by July 15, 1946."

That's the first I had heard about being on furlough, so I wrote back explaining that apparently there had been a mistake. I had not applied for a furlough. I had left the hospital for good never to return.

The answer was prompt. My furlough had been extended for two weeks and I was to report back August 1.

I called my good friend, Col. Fred Dunlap, still a paraplegic patient at Kennedy.

"Colonel," I said, "I went all over the hospital trying to get a permanent discharge. Apparently, they aren't set up for such."

"OK, Clark," he said, "I'll work on it." But apparently Fred got the same run around I did.

I was about to get my first lesson in the difference between the totalitarian regimes we had fought in the war and the good old U.S. And the difference was the much maligned, much cussed and lowly politician.

The stakes were high. At that time, the government went on the theory (which seems rather logical to me, even today) that if you're in a government facility being housed, treated and fed, you are not eligible for the regular disability compensation. At the time, patients received $20 spending money a month while those paraplegics out of the hospital were paid the munificent sum of $300 a month. This was a lot of money in 1946 and included compensation for the loss of the use of two legs, kidneys, bowels and an allowance for an attendant.

After several more letters and phone calls to Kennedy General, someone suggested, "Why don't you call Scott Candler?"

From just before the beginning of World War II until 1955, Scott Candler was the commissioner of DeKalb County. During the time, Dekalb was for the most part rural, being the largest dairy producer in Georgia, but it was beginning to grow as it assumed a role as the "bedroom for Atlanta."

The suburbs were beginning to push into DeKalb and DeKalb was blessed with one man rule. Over the early post-war years, millionaires would be made among the developers who cut the streets and built and sold the houses. The biggest millionaires would be the former dairymen who were learning the value of cow pastures and the sons of the sharecropping, tenant farmers who had been toughened by the hard scrabble days of post Civil War Georgia.

They were a tough breed and Scott Candler was the boss. As commissioner, he curbed and sewered and lay water lines in the streets the developers built. The developers in turn were the largest source of political contributions, not only for local races but for the national political contests as well.

"When were you discharged, Clark?" Scott, a winner of the Silver Star while serving with the World War I Rainbow Division, shouted.

"June 6th."

"I'll call George," Scott hollered and hung up. Mr. Candler never talked. He either shouted or hollered.

"George" was Georgia's revered senior senator, a national leader in the bipartisan coalition that led the U.S. to victory in the war. He was one of the most powerful forces in the country and a call from his office was not ignored.

Within the week, I had a nice letter from Washington announcing the day of my discharge as June 6 and enclosing a check in full for my pension from that date.

I decided that being a politician, even a local one, might be the very antidote for the feeling of helplessness I had endured since being shot.

I was home and I had my pension. What I didn't know was that, although my health problems had been brought on by a combat injury, I was going to have the privilege of paying for my hospitilization over the coming years — and that would include a couple dozen operations.

Our leaders in Congress had decided that if you were hurt in service, the VA would take care of you or you would take care of yourself.

I decided to do it myself, but the Veterans Administration hospital did get one more crack at me before I gave up on them for good. I had been out of the hospital for four years but now I had a problem.

"You'd be foolish to pay for this yourself." Our family doctor was talking about an operation to correct the decubitis ulcer that forced me to drop out of Yale Law School. "Something this major could cost you $1500."

He explained that the same surgeon, a great doctor named Kanthak, would perform the operation at the VA and the government would pay for everything.

Frances didn't want me to do it, but finally I decided that it would be foolish to use our money if I didn't have to.

The Atlanta VA at the time was using the old Lawson General facility, along with the old World War I hospital on Peachtree Road. I was sent back to Lawson.

I was lying on a stretcher on the reception room floor where the ambulance attendants had left me.

"What are you here for, Harrison?" The clerk was standing over me with a clip board in his hand.

"Dr. Kanthak is going to do a skin flap on my buttocks," I replied.

"Oh, yeah," he snapped. "We'll decide what we're going to do and who's going to do it." He wrote something on his clip board and strutted off.

Oh, God, I thought. That sounds familiar.

I was put on one of the old wards. This time, there were no bright colors and there were twice as many beds jammed close together, all occupied. Most of the patients were ambulatory but on my left was a man so badly burned that most of his body was covered with bandages. I never heard him speak.

I learned soon after I got there that the bandages on my deep ulcer would not be changed. Apparently a nurse had caused a patient to get an infection by changing a bandage without proper sterile procedure — now only doctors could change bandages — and they didn't have time.

Every other day I went to the latrine, balancing on a commode too high for my feet to reach the floor and located just in front of the hot water pipes for the ward.

After two weeks, the only medical attention I had received was an x-ray of my lungs.

And they were going to operate on my fanny.

In this case, a patient had died on the operating table from some lung complication and from then on, every patient, regardless of the procedure to be done, had to have his chest x-rayed.

I was beginning to realize the implications of political medicine — the welfare of the patient played a poor second to the need for the staff to cover their own hides from the political probers.

I told one of the doctors I was going to leave and go home.

"If you leave," he threatened, "you will be going against medical advice."

"So be it," I replied.

"Harrison," he said, "if you leave against medical advice, you cannot be re-admitted in less than 90 days."

"Doc," I said seriously, "can you possibly make that permanent. I'm afraid I might get run over some day, they'll find out I'm a veteran, and they'll send me back to this damn place."

Next day, Frances had our local funeral director bring his ambulance to the back door of the ward. They came in, got me, and I left. I entered Emory Hospital a few days later, was operated on the morning after my admission and was back home within 10 days. That was in 1950 and so far, through at least two dozen operations, I've stayed out of the VA as a patient.

I did visit Kennedy General one more time. We had gone to visit Dick and Nina Haltom. Batesville, Mississippi is only 50 miles from Kennedy and we decided to go have a look.

It was about eleven in the morning and one of the first things I saw was a patient, dead drunk, sitting in the hall. He shouted and waved his whiskey bottle at me.

"Actually," the young intern told me, "we don't put any limit on the amount of liquor they can bring into the hospital. We are doing a survey on how long a paraplegic who has unlimited liquor can live."

He was being facetious — and callous. He and another doctor were dead serious when they advised me to have my legs amputated.

"Think of how much easier it would be to move you around," they said.

"Well, I don't know," I said, "I've become attached to them and they do have a certain cosmetic effect."

They actually talked a young black paraplegic into having the operation. After that, he couldn't sit up or drive a car without being strapped in.

Undoubtedly, there are dedicated people working for the VA. I find veterans and their families who praise the hospital system.

For me, the problem was having no choice as to who was to treat me or what was to be done. I had only one choice. I had to either accept what was offered or go elsewhere and pay the full cost.

And, of course, I was not eligible for individual hospitalization insurance because of my combat injury.

Paying for all those opertions kept us poor for a good many years, but I survived and remain in good health after some rather strenuous activities.

No nation on earth has been more generous to its veterans than the United States. The citizens pay for the best and the pensions are certainly the most liberal that exist anywhere.

Unfortunately, the hospital system is set up in a way that hurts the morale of staff as much as that of patients and runs counter to American principles of freedom of choice and competition between suppliers of medical service.

It seems to me the only solution that might stand a chance of implementation, if enough veterans and politicians could agree, would be a re-insurance program.

Such a program could take care of excessive losses while putting the individual veteran who is no longer insurable because of service injury, and who wants treatment outside the VA hospital system, in a position to buy insurance coverage at rates that would apply to a healthy person of the same age.

"Not everybody is as big a sorehead as you, Clark," my good friend Murphey told me one day.

Which is true. But it seems to me there should be a program even for us soreheads.

In this sweet land of liberty.

CHAPTER XV

The field elevation at El Paso is 3,956. That means that when your plane is sitting on the runway, you are 3,956 feet above sea level.

There are four ways to measure altitude when you are flying. One is measured as above mean sea level, and that is what is shown as the field elevation of the airport. That measurement is exact and means that if you bored a hole in the ground down to the level of the ocean, your measuring stick would show 3,956 feet.

That's simple. Then it gets complicated.

In the airplane, you don't have a measuring stick. You have an altimeter. The altimeter is really a device for measuring air pressure — the higher you fly, the less air pressure, and the greater number of feet above sea level will be shown.

The problem is, when air is heated or cooled, the altimeter is effected. So, when you think you're 5,000 feet above the level of the sea, you may really be at 4,000 feet, which is not too important, unless you happen to be flying at night or in the clouds. Or you happen to be flying over the mountains and discover, as you get near the next range, that you're a thousand feet lower than planned and you get caught in a downdraft — or your plane can't climb high enough quickly enough.

This is why I kept the 140 at 9,500 feet as I passed over El Paso and headed toward Guadalupe Pass. I had to be at least 3,000 feet above the ground to overfly the airport and stay out of the tower's airport traffic area. The extra footage was for my own peace of mind — and to conform to the Visual Flight Rule — going east, you must fly odd thousands plus 500 feet.

Flying comes somewhat naturally to somebody who's spent over thirty seven years in a wheelchair. In both cases, you must be very careful. And in both cases, you are constantly solving a series of small problems. Like football, being a paraplegic is a game of inches. You find that out teetering on the edge of the bathtub before making the final leap to the safety of the wheelchair and also in figuring how far you can lean over to pick something up off the floor before the chair tips and throws you on your head.

Both enterprises can be exciting and the penalties for miscalculation can be severe.

The greatest plunge I took, along with Frances, was when we decided, against all logic including my own, to get married.

Looking to football again, I will paraphrase the immortal Vince Lombardi, coach of the Green Bay Packers until his untimely death. He was talking about winning.

"To the young man, sex is not the main thing, it is the only thing."

And the fact that I had been shot and paralyzed didn't seem to affect that compulsion and obsession at all. When I went to Mayo Clinic for the operation that saved my life and restored my health, the surgeon, a man with a scientific thirst for knowledge, asked me.

"Why do you like to do it, Clark?" he asked. "You don't have any feeling from the waist down."

"You know, Doc," I replied. "I never thought about that. But I do. Maybe, I just like to inflict pleasure on women."

Which I thought was a pretty smart answer for such a probing question.

After I started to Emory University, one of my initial courses was something taught by the psychology department called Physiological Psychology, and which taught how the nerves control the body.

In the case of the sex function, the nerves of the spinal cord are not concerned, other than those transmitting feeling. Down each side of the spinal cord are chains of ganglion that control certain involuntary functions including sex.

The sniper's bullet severed my cord but left these ganglion untouched.

Each case is different. In my injury, I was left able to perform, but unable to father a child, which I suppose put me ahead of my time and the vasectomy crowd.

I know of one quadraplegic who is the father of a beautiful little girl. "We prayed about it a lot and we kept trying and trying," he told me. "I think it happened one morning about 3 a. m."

On the other hand, one of the most successful and productive marriages I know involves a friend who was a fellow patient at Lawson, who walks as well as anybody, but who, through one of those strange twists of the spinal injury, lost the sex function. Both he and his wife are professional people who live full, rich lives and make large contributions every day to their clients and their community.

At our Shepherd Spinal Center they have a course on sex, which intrigues me. I had to learn about that sort of thing the best way I could.

The other obsession of the young man is to have an automobile. Since I was going to have to have hand controls, there was only one logical choice. In 1946, there was only one automobile with automatic transmission and that was the Oldsmobile hydromatic. Without the need to shift gears, it was a simple matter to add hand brake and accelerator attachments. So all the paraplegics ordered Oldsmobiles with the government paying the cost.

Naturally, I decided to buy a Ford. I had always wanted to own a Ford and saw no reason to change because I was paralyzed. As Murphey said, it was that sore headedness showing up again.

The Ford I purchased was hard to come by. At the end of the war, any kind of car that would run would command a top price — the problem was to find an owner willing to sell. New cars sold on the black market (to avoid price control regulations) as 'used cars' at a price well above the published retail.

And, of course, it was impossible to get a new car without a long wait. Except for me.

Because I was back in my own home town of Decatur, I got one of the earliest 1946 Fords off the recently retooled assembly lines.

It was black, had a V-8 engine, and was controlled by the damnedest Rube Goldberg system of cables, switches and vacuum tanks you can imagine. Henry Ford, the old man himself, paid for the controls and paid his dealers to install them. I never saw or heard of another one like mine, or saw a paraplegic driving a Ford, so I may have owned the only hand-controlled Ford in the United States.

There was a small lever on the left side of the steering column. When it was in the neutral position, the clutch was down to the floor board. As I pulled the lever down, the clutch would slowly come up. When I turned loose of the lever, the clutch pedal would go back down to the floor.

So, I'd put the car in first gear, pull the lever down (which also caused the accelerator pedal to go down) and start moving. Then I'd release the lever, shift into second gear, etc.

To stop, I pushed the same lever up, at which point the clutch was disengaged and the brake pedal went toward the floor.

We drove the car for four years, going all over the eastern U.S., from Connecticut to Miami to New Orleans to Minnesota, putting over 60,000 miles on it. Every 1,000 miles I had the oil changed and the car greased. Every three months, I had it hand waxed. A mechanic who worked on it one time told me "That's the greasiest car I ever worked on. I was lying under it, adjusting the hand control, and a big glob of grease fell right in my eye."

The only problem I had was with the hand control. Every six months, the cable to the clutch would break. But when it happened, I would always have someone with me who could drive it home — my angel at work.

When I traded, I received $1,100 for the car — just $500 less than I had paid for it.

"Let's go to Minnesota for our honeymoon," I told Frances one evening when we were planning our wedding.

"Why do you want to go way up there?" she asked.

"Well," I replied, "People are going to be wondering if we can make it by ourselves — we might as well lay that question to rest right away."

I had spent my five happiest months of military service in Minnesota as an aviation student at St. John's University, Collegeville. I called the mother of the girl I had dated while stationed there (the girl was also married by now) and she arranged for us to stay at the Maple Hill Resort on Clearwater Lake.

After we had gotten to our room in St. Cloud's only hotel, I called Mrs. Hammond. First, I had ordered drinks and we were waiting for room service.

"Oh," she cried, "I'll be right over."

Mrs. Hammond, who was president of the local Women's Christian Temperance Union and a pillar of the Methodist Church, arrived almost simultaneously with the drinks and we just had time to put them on the shelf in the bathroom before letting her in.

"You will really love Maple Hill," she told Frances. "They've got running water in the cabins this year and they even installed flush toilets on the hill."

Frances had left Decatur for her honeymoon with an elaborate trousseau including five hat boxes. By the time Mrs. Hammond left, I could see she was upset by the preview of the luxury resort I had selected.

And I was upset because all the ice had melted in the drinks.

We spent the next day scouring that part of Minnesota for a resort cabin with an indoor bathroom. The one we found would have destroyed the honeymoon budget, so we finally gave in and went back to Maple Hill.

The cabin had only a sink and a gas hot plate and there were no interior walls — just the exposed 2x4's that held the roof up.

In other words, it was a standard Minnesota fishing camp cabin.

That night, Frances cried herself to sleep.

Two weeks later, she cried because we were having to leave.

June and Elmer Froyen, the Norwegian couple who owned the resort had taken us under their wing. We used their bathroom in the big house on the hill and ate most of our meals as their guests.

Elmer rigged up a chair in his fishing boat and took us fishing every day. And Frances found out she was a natural born fisherman — her catch always exceeded mine.

But most of all we enjoyed the Swedes and Norwegians who lived in the area or came out from Minneapolis as guests.

Frances carried five hats on her honeymoon — and ended up at a Minnesota fishing camp.

And I was beginning to understand what marriage meant — two be-coming one flesh. Now I had someone who was part of me to help solve the problems and to see to it I was involved in the action.

Frances' attitude was 'sure, let's do it.' And she could come up with a way how.

My one close call came while we were fishing in Elmer's big round bot-tom boat. We had started out with a metal chair tied to the boat with rope. Finally, after several successful trips, I was sitting in a canvas and wooden folding chair that was not fastened to the boat.

Elmer, in the far end of the boat, leaned over the side to fill the min-now pail — the boat tilted just enough for me to lose my balance.

I pitched over the side and found my head under water, in a blur of whiteness, my arms thrashing about with nothing to grab hold of, and my body still in the big boat. I know now that if I could have gotten out of the boat, I would have been able to swim, but in the fix I was in, half in and half out of the boat, I would have drowned without help. I had no stomach muscles to straighten myself back up.

Elmer jumped out of the boat, waded to my end and easily pushed me to a sitting position.

We were more careful after that.

I made it a point to go out in the boat again the next day so I wouldn't develop a fear of the water.

Elmer was the most conscientious man I have ever known, particularly where the law was concerned.

He told me when we first got to Maple Hill he was sure I wouldn't need a fishing license since the game warden never checked.

On one of our last fishing trips, we had started to go in when Elmer said.

"I believe that's the game warden."

Sure enough, he was at dock side checking licenses.

Elmer steered us back into deep water and we sat and we waited.

Finally, dark was settling and the mosquitoes were biting and we gave up and headed in.

After exchanging pleasantries, Elmer's friend, the game warden, waded out and between them they carried me back to the wheelchair.

Elmer was really bothered because the game warden had not asked for our fishing licenses.

After several days, he could stand it no longer and he looked the game warden up.

"You know," he said, "I don't know if that fellow from Georgia had a fishing license."

"Listen," the game warden said, "anybody who'd come all the way up here on his honeymoon don't need a fishing license."

Going over a thousand miles to a strange new environment as our first act after marriage proved a good thing for both of us, and set a precedent we would follow in the years ahead.

By choosing a daring and different course from the beginning, we learned that doing the bizarre is a good antidote for fear and the feeling of incapacity. Limited as I was in performing the simple acts of every day living did not mean I was equally limited in accomplishing the big things.

In fact, we learned early on that the problems and limitations also represented opportunities.

I couldn't walk, but, because of that handicap and my generous veterans pension, I had the economic freedom to make the trip to Minnesota — something the typical struggling young couple would have had neither time nor money to attempt.

And, being in the wheelchair opened all kind of doors as well. Intrigued by someone being that far from home in a wheelchair, the people we met wanted to know more about us and were anxious to add to our experience by telling about themselves and helping us accomplish our goals in the trip.

Finally, we were becoming acquainted from the beginning with the help God gives when we assert ourselves in a challenging venture. We began, even in those first days, to feel guided and protected as we faced unknown situations.

Our one close call, other than my face under water experience, came on the highway going to Minnesota.

We were on a two lane concrete highway that followed the undulations of the land with a series of hills that hid the next section of road from view. I was traveling at about sixty miles an hour, but had gotten stuck behind a large truck that was moving at about fifty.

Every time I'd try to go around, another hill would come up and I'd fall back and wait.

Finally, we topped a hill with a long descent before the next rise. I started around and was even with the truck when it became necessary to accelerate because of the down grade.

I pulled the accelerator lever all the way down, and, as we reached the bottom of the decline, I was able to pull on around. The V-8 engine was going at full throttle as we cleared the truck and started up the next hill.

As we got around the truck and started up the hill, I let up on the accelerator lever. The engine did not let up at all, but continued its full throated roar.

Cresting the hill, I realized the accelerator pedal was stuck to the floor and we were about to pick up speed into the eighties and nineties as we started down — unless something was done and done quickly.

Then, I looked up and, at the bottom of the hill was a small middle western town, at the busiest time of Saturday noon, the main street crowded with people and automobiles.

"Get your foot under the accelerator pedal," I shouted at Frances.

She reached down with her hand and started pulling.

At the same time, I cut the car ignition.

We began to slow and by applying the brakes I was able to slow down and get the car under control.

Frances had pulled so hard, she had pulled the pedal loose from the rod that extended into the floor board.

After stopping and then cranking up the engine, I found we could proceed on our trip and the accelerator did not stick again. I was careful not to pull the gas lever all the way down.

By the time we returned to Decatur, we had convinced everybody, and especially ourselves, that we were going to lead an expanded life and let the emergencies that will inevitably arise be solved as the occasion demanded.

The Bible says God directed Adam to take dominion over the earth.

Adam was not a paraplegic, but he certainly had fears and limitations on his apparent ability to face a hostile environment.

Plenty of his descendants died in the attempt to take dominion, but some also succeeded in rather astounding ways, and progress was made.

Likewise, the spinal cord injured. In the beginning the situation was obviously impossible and most accepted and conformed to the conventional wisdom.

But God's blessing began to fall on those who were willing at least to 'take dominion' on whatever reduced scale that offered a beginning.

Recently, I met a twenty-nine year old quadraplegic. We were both swimming at the YMCA.

"Where did you go to the hospital?" I asked him. He named a town in Pennsylvania.

"Did they have a good rehab program," I asked him as we clung to the side of the pool.

"Naw," he said, "they didn't have any program at all."

He had broken his neck in an automobile accident when he was seventeen. He had finished high school and college, earned a master's degree in vocational rehabilitation and had held a job in that field. He was waiting now to enter a school and learn computer programing.

"Have you been to the Shepherd Spinal Center?" I asked.

"Yeah."

"What did you think of it?"

"I think it's great," he replied. "In fact, I applied for a job as vocational counselor there but they picked somebody else."   Talking to him further, I found out he worked out regularly on the Nautilus body building machine. It was obvious the muscles he could move were in first-class condition.

The Nautilus system consists of several machines, each designed to develop a certain set of muscles and each requiring that the exerciser sit on a seat inside the machine.

"How do you get inside the machine?" I asked.

"I get one of those big guys to set me in it," he said. I thought about the weight lifters I had watched and decided that would certainly be a good place to get help.

Later, I looked on while he pulled his sweat pants laboriously up over his swimming trunks. His very limited use of his hands made it an agonizingly slow process. I rolled over to where he was seated.

"Scott," I said, "how did you learn to do all this stuff. Did you learn from other quads?"

He gave me a steady, level look.

"Naw," he said, "trial and error, I reckon."

I thought about Harry Truman, another of my heroes, the man responsible for the decision to drop the atom bomb — and to rebuild Europe through the Marshall Plan.

"We'll try this," Harry Truman once said, "if it doesn't work, we'll try something else."

CHAPTER XVI

Leaving El Paso far below, I tuned the VOR to Winkler County, Texas, known since the early days of radio navigation as WINK and used over the years by military and civilian pilots alike in tracking over the west Texas badlands.

Below are the salt flats crossed by the pioneers seeking California along the southern route. And then, far off and to the left of the line of flight, can be seen the towering, magnificent butte that constitutes the northern boundary of Guadalupe Pass. The first time I saw this monstrous butte, rising vertically from the flat mesa with the flat top about on a level with my own altitude, it sent a thrill of excitement through me — not fear exactly but more a feeling of awe that I was about to pass by the towering monument with only the small airplane and its droning engine to keep me on its level.

Fear, itself, is hard to define. It can be a nagging, gnawing feeling in the gut that is with you, constantly eating at your subconscious like a large, vicious and hungry wharf rat. That was the fear in combat. I remember sitting through the entire night in the German pill box on the Ziegfried line. Our squad dug in a few hundred yards from the pill box — my job, to go behind the nervous troops in the pitch blackness and bring the squad in for the withdrawal.

The night in the German forest was so dark that you literally could not see an object held an inch in front of your eyes.

The night outside the pill box was filled with death — the sound of exploding shells — the machine guns — the hand grenades thrown by the battle-fatigued Americans, as dangerous to someone moving in the dark as fire coming from the Germans.

In combat, the most dreaded explosion was the tree burst. Artillery shells exploding as they struck the trees and raining shrapnel down in a cone of death.

The casualties were near total. There were three options to the front line soldier — killed, wounded, or captured. Which is why the Germans who lifted me from the surgeon's tent were so happy and contented. Out of a company of over two hundred, one man might survive all three options.

Only the very young are suitable for modern combat — and their chief qualification is ignorance.

Until cold steel rips warm flesh, the fear is dormant in the young. Once wounded, age comes quickly.

Another kind of fear, the chill of cold sweat, the blood racing, the disorienting panic, I can remember having on only two occasions and both times I was in no physical danger or even about to be.

A key passage in understanding the book of Job in the Bible talks of the destructive nature of fear.

"The thing I greatly feared has come upon me."

Franklin Roosevelt, himself a paralytic, was inspired in the depths of the Great Depression to give understanding to the paralyzing nature of fear when he said, "All we have to fear is fear itself."

The first time I experienced the cold sweat of panic fear, I was safe in an army hospital, it was a bright, sunshiny day, and I was comfortable in bed. For some reason, the thought suddenly came, "I'm getting well. They're going to send me back to the front!"

And the chill and panic were on me.

The second time was the night before I started back to school as a student at Emory University. I had been in my parents' home for a couple of months since leaving Kennedy Veterans Hospital. I had purchased an old Chrysler car that my mother used to visit me while I was still at Lawson and that she would use to take me back and forth to Emory.

And lying in the bed that night, the full impact of what I was about to do hit me.

In the morning, I was going to roll my wheelchair into a college classroom full of young men my age, full of the vigor of life. And I was going to be completely different.

A tube in my belly, a glass bottle hanging in a bag from the metal arm of the chair, that the tube would be draining my urine into.

Unable to stand or move freely about.

Like most unreasoning panic, it was dissolved by action. The moment I was in that class, I knew it was going to be okay.

After I returned home, Dad had a set of parallel bars put up behind the house. That't my sister, Bettie, at the door.

Seated around me were not the college boys I had known at the University before the war. These were men who, like myself, had lost three years or more out of their lives. They had seen the world and been knocked about by the vagaries of military life, and now they were serious about getting on with their lives.

Most importantly, they recognized me as one of them and they knew I was there for the same reason they were.

One amusing thing happened that first day.

It was a cool, overcast day. I was nervous and I drank a couple of cups of coffee before leaving the house that morning.

At the end of my last class, I looked down. On the floor to my left, under the urine bottle, was a puddle.

Like a first grader, I had wet the floor.

To hell with it, I thought as I headed toward home. Next time I won't drink so much on a rainy day.

I'll let the janitor figure that one out. Unless he'd worked in a grammar school, he probably never did.

That summer, Frances and I planned to marry and I was determined that we have a place of our own in which to live before we took that step. And that represented an impossible situation — with the war just ended, people all over the country were doubling up to make use of the scant housing. Nothing had been built for civilians during the war and certainly there was nothing for newlyweds. Friends of ours were living with their parents after marriage.

Somebody told me they were building temporary quarters to house married students at the University and that I should call Mr. Candler.

"Yeah, Clark," Scott Candler was speaking at his usual megabel level. "We're putting up some temporary army barracks." (Mr. Candler could always make it sound like he was out there supervising and hammmering and sawing himself). "Fellow named Major Purvis is in charge. I'll tell him you want one."

During my three years as an army private, I had never tried to use influential friends, but I figured with the strikes already against us, Frances and I needed all the help we could get.

The apartments were tar paper covered army barracks built on the edge of the campus, along unpaved streets made barely passable by dumping loads of cinders from the school incinerator on them.

The place was approriately called "Mudville".

But for us, it was heaven on earth. The workmen built a ramp to get me into the front door. The inside walls were built of plaster board; there was no subfloor so you could see ground through the cracks in the floor and feel breezes in the winter. The shower was made of thin sheet metal.

When I told Frances about the place, she thought I was kidding.

But once we got in it, it was wonderful. We had a living room, kitchen, two bedrooms and the bath. We furnished it with an old iron bed one of our families gave us and bought double bunk beds for the other bedroom from army surplus for $4.95. Frances' family gave us an old sofa we had re-covered for the living room, and we covered the cracks in the floor with a cheap fibre rug.

The curtains were made of paper.

In the years that have followed, we have never been quite so wealthy. With my pension of $300 a month, we were the posh couple in the development. Our rent was only $32.50 a month, and we had a maid named Willie, who was one of the world's great cooks. We paid Willie $5 to work for us every Wednesday. She would cook lunch and fix something for our supper.

The apartment was so small, Willie would be through doing everything we had to do by early afternoon, so, she started taking in laundry and ironing from our neighbors.

Since our friends were all living at home with their folks, our apartment became a social center every weekend.

Watching our neighbors who had been fortunate enough to get into Mudville was an intriguing experience.

Most of them were making it on the GI Bill, something just over a hundred dollars, plus whatever the men could earn doing part-time jobs. Most of the wives had some kind of job, but in those days before the minimum wage, the pay was usually pretty meager.

Our next door neighbor, who was a submariner during the war and who is now a PHD in his field, had a lovely wife who worked during the day.

One day I saw Bill standing in the window of his apartment swaying from side to side. I couldn't figure out what he was doing until he held up one of Ruthie's dresses. He was doing the family ironing.

One beautiful fall day, I had stretched out in our double bed and had dozed off to sleep. Suddenly, the driver of the bread truck that served Mudville pulled up in front of our apartment and blew a blast on his whistle to inform the tenants of his arrival.

I woke with a start, looked up at the barracks window and started grabbing for my rifle. *Deja vu* — I was back at Camp McCoy.

Several times we heard Bill through the thin walls of our apartment. Nightmares of his submarine experiences would have him screaming out. But we were all working our way out of those past days.

Frances, as a wife, had a salutory effect on my recovery and physical progress. We had attached the balkan frame to the old iron bed, with its trapeze to help me turn over.

Before we married, mother daily banged her head into one of the spars sticking out at right angles from the frame. Being a mother, and a good one at that, she'd never say a word. Shake her head and hang on to the bedpost until her senses returned.

Frances had a healthier attitude. She hit her head a couple of times and decided she didn't like the thing. I could figure out another way to turn over.

After our next move, the balkan frame disappeared and I found out I could manage without it. In fact, I came to believe the fewer such appurtenances the better.

The whole question of how much to help the seriously disabled is an interesting one. I think a lot of disabled people make it hard on themselves and everyone else by being unduly sensitive in this regard.

As a general rule, I want all the help I can get — probably because I found out in politics you can't have too many people pulling for you. And there's no better way to get a dedicated supporter than to let him do something for you.

I wasn't always that way, of course. As a young man, it would set my teeth on edge to have an elderly and infirm lady try to help me. It hurt my male ego.

And it still irritates me when I tell somebody I'm fine and they insist on moving the chair so it is out of the position I wanted it in.

On the whole, however, I think it's better to accept help when that assistance will forward the project.

Dick Haltom's dad, with his common sense approach to doing simple things, showed a spirit that appealed to me. Dick told me about it.

"Right after I got home the first time," he recalled, "nobody knew what to do with me. One day, I had dozed off sitting in my chair and my foot had slipped off the foot pedal. I woke up and heard Margaret and Mother whispering about the situation and what to do.

"About that time, Daddy walked in, heard the conversation, saw the foot, walked over and put it back in place.

"'The foot was off the pedal, is that right?' he asked the women, 'you wanted the foot back on the pedal and that's what I did, I put it back on the pedal.'"

I was learning that if, like Mr. Haltom, you addressed the problem directly, threw yourself into the middle of a situation, and then took action, a lot of the mumbo jumbo about being different from other people disappeared.

The year after we married, the year I graduated from Emory, was a beautiful time. I had found something I could do and I was working hard.

Every morning I'd leave early for an eight o'clock class driving the Ford Coupe. Frances would put the folding wheelchair between the front and back seats. I had a parking space by the entrance to the one building at Emory that had no steps. I took all my classes in that building.

After school, I'd get one of my classmates to put the wheelchair back in the car for me.

As soon as I finished lunch, I would start studying and would study until we went to bed at 10 p.m. I wasn't trying to make high grades. After the three years' interruption, I was just determined to get a degree this time.

One evening at the end of my first quarter of my senior year the phone rang.

"Congratulations, Mr. Harrison," the professor on the other end of the line said, "you have just been elected to Phi Beta Kappa."

I couldn't believe it. The highest undergraduate honor at Emory and across the educational world generally. Jokes about a Phi Beta Kappa who had a gold chain to hold his key but who couldn't afford a watch for the other end came to mind.

I put the key in a box and never did buy myself a chain, much less a gold watch.

The wheelchair was proving to offer me some advantages over the other students.

Not able to participate in the normal activities, I was finding it easy to concentrate on my studies.

I couldn't get into all the places the other students could, but I worked out ways to compensate.

I couldn't get into the main library, or at least all of us thought in those early days of spinal cord injury, that it would be so difficult as to be impractical.

But the school did have a very excellent professional librarian, and there was a room below the main library that I could reach by a private elevator.

"Mr. North," the librarian had trained at one of the Ivy League schools, "I've got to write a paper on the Russian Government."

"Fine, Clark," he said, " when do you need it?"

"Well, it's due Friday. I thought I'd drop by Tuesday if that's okay."

Tuesday afteroon I would ride the little elevator to the private room where I would find perhaps a dozen books stacked on the table waiting for me.

I would look in the index of each book in turn, copy a quotation concerning the particular subject I was covering, and note down the page number, book title, author, etc.

Then, I'd go home, get out the typewriter, and a couple of hours later would have twenty-six pages on one aspect of the Russian government loaded with footnotes from eight or ten books.

I was continuing my major in journalism but I never let myself dwell on what would happen after graduation. Who would hire a reporter in a wheelchair? How I would get the experience to go on to less strenuous journalistic endeavors?

At least it was something I could do. I was competing successfully with other students and it beat the heck out of watch repairing, considering my lack of patience putting small things together.

The future would have to take care of itself.

Then, my professor of journalism called me into his office.

"Clark," he said, "I've just been going over your credits. Unless you want to stay here indefinitely you can graduate in March."

After the war started, I had carried extra credits at Georgia and gone to school the year round. Now, I was eligible for graduation a full quarter ahead of schedule. Since the regular graduation was in June, I learned somewhat to my surprise I'd get my diploma through the mail.

So much for pomp and ceremony. As I've told my sons since, a college diploma is the most overestimated piece of paper in the world to those who don't have one, and the most underestimated by those who do.

But the biggest shock was when we were told that after graduation we'd have to vacate our apartment.

College, for me, had been something I could do. What to do now was something I had not wanted to face. I was convinced nobody would hire a journalist in a wheelchair.

"How do you know?" Frances asked. "You haven't tried yet."

One thought, I had had was to run a weekly newspaper. We traveled to Baxley, Georgia and talked to a man who wanted to sell out. Then, we went to Cleveland, Georgia, in the mountains, and talked to an owner there. At age twenty-three, with no work other than ushering in a theatre, carrying a paper route and an army rifle, the idea of borrowing money and running a newspaper from a wheelchair boggled my mind. I know now that a way could have been found, but at the time I couldn't imagine taking step one.

So, at age twenty-three with college behind me, we were renting a house that belonged to the widow of a recently deceased minister in Clarkston, Georgia, and a little girl came to the back door.

"Why don't you go to work like my daddy does?" she asked.

It was an innocent question, but it filled me with shame and I made up my mind I was going to do something — even if it was wrong.

One of my favorite classes at Emory had been taught by a professor from Yale University on loan, to teach political science.

His specialty was local government.

"The best government for a local community is one man rule," he told our class, "whenever you have government by a group, no one has final responsibility and you can't find anyone with the power to change things that are wrong."

Having tried to deal with the Veterans Hospital bureaucracy, I knew what he was talking about. Scott Candler, the sole commissioner of our county, had solved my problem with a phone call.

Now, I got to thinking about government and who can solve problems. Frances' father was a lawyer before he became a judge and we talked about law school. Lawyers used their brains more than their feet, we reasoned.

I made application for Yale Law School, took a battery of tests, and, much to my surprise, was accepted for the fall term.

Now, I could tell the little girl, if she came around again, "I'm going to be studying to be a lawyer. I'm just waiting to enter law school next month."

CHAPTER XVII

Homing in on WINK, I was looking down on sage brush and not much else. There is a small town, the county seat of Winkler County, Texas, some oil tanks, and the sage brush.

I turn toward the Southeast, making the needle on my VOR swing left away from center and I begin to look for the airport.

Problem is, there's no airport to be seen. Now, I'm banking over the oil tanks and turning toward the town. Seems the airport should adjoin the town but again there's nothing.

I glance down and realize my left wing tank registers empty. Quickly, I switch to the right tank which is still on the one-fourth mark. I begin to think I'd better check the chart and see how far it is to the next airport.

One thing's for sure — this plane's got to have fuel to stay in the sky.

When the pressure sores I had developed during the early weeks following my combat injury finally healed, I thought I was through with the devilish things.

For some reason, it never occurred to me that I could develop a pressure sore on my buttocks. Only Jack had been so effected when Agnes took him riding on the whip at the Southeastern Fair — and I had no intention of riding the whip.

While I was at Emory, Dr. McGeachy removed what he thought was a callus from my rear, but it didn't occur to either of us it could become a cause of real concern.

School and the high grades I achieved were my downfall. My very concentration on the books concentrated the weight that cut off the blood supply to my buttocks. Even then, it was several months before I began to have a problem.

The pressure sore in the buttocks is a much more serious affair than those on other locations on the body.

The eventual damage takes place deep in the tissue creating a large cavity, in my case, large as a grapefruit, that narrows in a cone like configuration as it reaches the surface of the skin. Because of the location, there is increased danger of bone infection and it is impossible for the resulting wound to heal from the inside out. No healing air can reach the inner recess and it is a difficult wound to keep clean.

On other areas of the body, the sore will heal itself, but it is still better in most cases to operate and move whole flesh over the lesion. In the case of the buttock ulcer there is no choice. A large slab of flesh must be rearranged to fill the hole, leaving a deep scar but in an area on the leg that does not bear pressure.

It is expensive surgery and there are not many surgeons willing to attempt it. More like working in a butcher shop, the operation involves such large pieces of flesh and is so bloody. The risk of failure and of reinjury is foreboding. Unless the postoperative period is handled by experts, the result can be worse than the original pressure sore.

Most plastic surgeons prefer the delicate and lucrative face lifts and cosmetic nose restructuring. When you find a doctor who will take on the repair of pressure sores you've got yourself an old fashioned hero and you'd better stick with him.

The tragedy is that the whole expensive, time wasting project is unnecessary. Just a little timely shifting of weight will keep the tough hide in one piece. Simply pushing up on the arms of the chair for the para or leaning far out to one side and the other for the quad will do more to avoid the problem than any fancy seat cushion yet invented.

The patient has to be taught, but then it is up to him. He has to maintain the eternal if simple vigilence that is required when the nerves are no longer sending signals. Using a mirror, he has to substitute vision for feeling by making regular inspections of his skin.

Since learning, I never spend a night in uninterrupted sleep. No matter how tired I may be or how sick I may feel, an area of my brain wakes my up and makes me turn at regular intervals. Although there's no feeling, I begin to get very uncomfortable if I sit or lie in the same position for very long.

But in 1948 as Frances and I prepared to move to New Haven, I didn't know about pressure sores in the buttocks.

I was building up to a major disaster because of that ignorance.

Like I say, because of my ignorance, my very determination to succeed in college was to be my undoing.

For years, I have made it a practice to visit paralyzed people. It never ceases to amaze me how they can solve problems and accomplish feats that seem impossible under the circumstances. The average person does not realize it, but the spinal cord injured, if they make any effort to participate in life, have to be physically much more active than other people. Within their limits they have to keep in good physical shape, perform athletically, and work hard. If you don't think so, take a look at the arms on one of them.

Another thing about those who want to lead a normal life is the concentration they bring to any problem.

To me, it is like the daming of a river to create a large lake. The water builds tremendous power behind the high dam. This force is then channeled through turbines to create massive power outputs.

And this happens with some spinal injured people. Unable to dissipate their energies with the small activities most people engage in each day, they sit and they think, and they concentrate, and quite remarkable things can result.

In my case, school was the one thing I could do to release the energy boiling inside me, and I was giving it all I had.

The result was to make one of the highest grade averages conferred by the University.

Competing for Yale Law School presented an even greater challenge.

To be accepted at Yale Law School, I took a battery of tests. Yale has a policy. To broaden its influence throughout the U. S., Yale looks for students from all over the country. The Dean talked to our freshman class.

"Gentlemen," he said, "you represent the cream of thirty three top universities across America. Yale has a different policy from Harvard. Harvard accepts more students, and then lets those students compete to stay in school. When you are accepted at Yale, it is because you have the ability and the background to assure your success as a student. I know of only five students who have failed during my sixteen years as Dean. We have had some students leave because they couldn't take the stress, but very few failures."

The Law School believed in putting the work to its students, and by Christmas most of us who had gone without glasses were wearing them. The typical course involved an average of one hundred pages a night to read.

"I've dated boys from both the law and medical schools," one co-ed told me, "and I found the law school works the students harder."

Frances and I had driven to Minnesota toward the end of the summer I finished Emory. We had a two week reunion with the Froyens, fished with Elmer and visited with the Hammond family. Then we drove up into Canada and arrived at New Haven late one Saturday afternoon.

We had an apartment in an army quonset hut behind the Yale Bowl that was the equivalent of Mudville at Emory — except that in the more affluent East, the streets were paved.

While we were waiting to start school, we replaced the linoleum in the kitchen — I got down on the floor and cut to make it fit around the appliances.

Then I built a large desk for the second bedroom.

Frances made curtains, we bought a new fibre rug and soon we had a cheerful and comfortable apartment.

We made friends from every part of the country.

Our next door neighbor was the son of a famous symphony conductor from Portland, Oregon, and his wife was from Weathersfield, Connecticut. They had a model A Ford and we were amused on cold mornings to see our neighbor with a large old fashioned metal tea pot filling his radiator with boiling water.

Bill, who was in law school with me, was the son of one of the most prominent attorneys in Kansas City, Missouri, and Margie, his wife, was the daughter of a gentleman who operated a fleet of trucks and one of the largest wholesale produce companies in the mid west.

Jim was studying paleontology — working on his doctorate. He was from Texas. His wife, Dell, was from Montana.

Bill and I became good friends and were in class together every day as freshman law students. Without any ado, Bill made it a regular stop every day, once the weather turned cold, to service our space heater.

Jim and Dell had us for dinner several times. On one occasion, Dell had cooked a New England boiled dinner. Being from Montana, it was obvious that she had mislaid some ingredient that was supposed to make the meal edible. It was tasteless. But the next time we visited, she served Boston baked beans. This time she hit. I had so much to say about the beans, Frances bought some. I don't know to this day what we left out, but we were still cooking at ten o'clock that evening and the beans were hard and without flavor.

But Frances had her turn. She fixed Jim a real southern meal — fried chicken, black eyed peas, turnip greens, and I made spoon bread. Jim, after those years of New England boiled dinners thought he had died and gone to heaven.

At Yale, we lived in a converted quonset hut in Armoryville. Frances is playing with our faith-ful dog, Belle. On the right is our faithful 1946 Ford coupe with the Rube Goldberg hand-controls.

Frances, Uncle Charlie, left, and Dad visit me on one of my many returns to the hospital.

Then Frances brought out the pecan pie and Jim went into orbit. He ate his piece and what the rest of us left, and all he could talk about was that pecan pie.

After that, Jim started dropping by our apartment on the off chance Frances might have baked a pecan pie.

One evening, Frances had served our two pieces of pecan pie and was on her way to the refrigerator when the pan slipped out of her grasp, flipped over, and landed pie side down on the fibre rug.

She picked it up and put the remains on the counter with some other scraps that were to be thrown away pitched in on top of the pie.

Well, Jim came by shortly thereafter and spotted the three- quarters of the pie on the counter. Before we realized what was happening, he had cleared the scraps off and was eating a piece of the pie.

Jim was enjoying it so much we didn't have the heart to tell him it had been face down on the fibre rug.

When he found out we didn't want the rest of the pie, he sat there and finished it all.

Jim's father had a chain of automobile parts shops in Texas, but it was apparent Jim was not squandering the old man's money. Jim was more interested in the age of dinosaurs and seemed to me to be lacking somewhat in what is called common sense.

Jim and Dell's sparse quonset apartment furnishings may have seen better days, but not much better, and it had been a long time. They couldn't have cost much brand new and it was plain Jim and Dell were not old enough to have purchased them direct from the factory.

Jim was finishing up his doctorate and going back to Texas, so he started arranging to carry these less-than-priceless heirlooms back to his native land.

Apparently, it never occurred to Jim that he might come out better to sell what he had — or give it away or, failing that — burn it. It represented the accumulated wealth of their marriage to date and Jim had no intention to part with any of it.

So, he bought a small trailer, loaded everything in and took a test cruise around Armoryville (so named because our quonset village was located behind the Yale armory).

On the second turn, the whole thing swayed precariously, one of the leaf springs of the trailer gave way and the contents were deposited in the middle of the street.

This meant a delay of several days with Jim, Dell and their small son Doki (named for one of Jim's dinosaur critters) sleeping on the floor of the apartment while the leaf spring was fixed.

Jim came to see me the night before they were to leave for Texas. Perhaps you could say he was my first legal client.

"Clark," he said, "I need a little advice. We were planning to leave day after tomorrow but I'm thinking about leaving early in the morning."

It seems Jim had received a ticket for going through a stop sign. He had been summoned to be in court at 10 a. m. the following morning.

"I figure if I get up and off by daybreak, I'll be well out of Connecticut by 10 a. m. and I won't have to go to court.

I agreed that he probably would not be pursued across the state line.

"But Jim," I said, "if you ever come back to Connecticut they may nab you."

Jim left with his head bent in deep contemplation.

Next morning I went out in the village street as soon as I could get my clothes on.

So far as I know, Jim made good his escape — his trailer was no where to be seen. We never heard from Jim and Dell and Doki again. Probably Jim didn't want to risk sending a letter with his return address into Connecticut.

We found this mixture of the children of the wealthy and the over-achievers of the hinterlands interesting. Certainly, the atmosphere at Yale was different from what I had experienced in the Army and in the hospital. The students worked hard, but seemed secure and not really worried about the future. Either they had money or they had the knowledge that they would be able to get the kind of job they would want for a good life.

In the law school, we were told eighty per cent of the graduates would not practice — they would either go into government, teaching or some form of service to the community. An exception was one small Jewish student.

"I'm going to practice so I can make money — a lot of money," he said. Frances and I found that refreshing.

The students and faculty were big on cocktail parties — everybody standing around with a drink in his hand talking. I despised the cocktail parties. The talk seemed designed to impress the listener on the theory the listener was someone of importance.

Besides, I got a crick in my neck — sitting down, I was always looking up to everybody else.

The pace in the school was hectic and the pressure was real. In sharp contrast to my undergraduate work, the requirement was to think — not to memorize and ape the teacher.

"But what is the law," a student asked after a lengthy give and take between professor and students on a legal point.

The professor looked at the questioner. "You think about it."

Given a set of facts, we had to tread a legal maze of precedent and principle to try to reach an answer.

"The day you enter this class," one professor told us, "given a set of facts, you can probably reach a pretty sensible judgment. After you've studied law for a year, given the same facts, you'll come up with something stupid."

I had my problems with the law as practiced in our adversarial system and with the idea of being a lawyer.

I outraged one professor as we discussed the overturn of a decision by an appellate court.

"It seems to me, it was just a matter of opinion."

Then there was the suggestion by one professor that it was just as important to know the judge and his thinking as it was to know the law.

When I recounted that one to my father-in-law he was incensed. "The law is the law," Judge Guess said. Which told me how I'd have to practice in front of him.

What really disturbed me was the fee system. Since lawyers predominate in the state legislatures, the law makes the fee sacrosanct — paying the lawyer takes precedent over every other legal obligation. That wasn't too bad in my innocent eyes, but the thought that the lawyer in a liability case could keep from one third to one half the amount awarded an injured party — a para or quad came to mind — seemed nothing but robbery of the least fortunate. The lawyer could go out and earn another fee, but I knew the severely disabled was going to have to live off his part of the judgment for the rest of his life.

I did enjoy the mental tilting that went on in the class room and I did come to admire my fellow students.

We had one student who was severely handicapped with cerebral palsy — he and I were the only disabled students in the class of over 100.

He shook all over, all the time, and when he walked, his knees pointed in, his feet out, and his laborious, shaking, progress down the hall was a distress to watch.

His head shook from side to side constantly and without letup.

His speech was painfully slow and laboriously executed.

And he probably volunteered answers more than any other student in the large class.

"I — i — — i — i — it — sa —sa sa —sa — seems — ta —ta — ta ta — to me —

Then he would work his way through a thoughtful question or answer while the class of over 100 brilliant young men patiently waited. I have never seen a greater display of courage or a more respectful audience. There was no doubt of our admiration for his magnificent achievement.

Our professors were among the great authorities on law in the country. Our torts professor was a labor arbitrator for the Ford Motor Company, our public administration teacher had held high position in the Federal government, our professor in Federal Practice had written the book that was the standard work throughout the country.

My favorite was our contract professor. He had been a judge in Germany. Being Jewish, he had fled the country in 1936 to escape Hitler.

"The American judicial system," he told us, " was set up for the benefit of the welsher. In Germany we had a better system. Instead of being antagonists meeting on the field of battle, the lawyers were agents for the judge. He told them what to do and they went out and did it — they gathered the facts and then the judge passed judgment on the guilty party. In the United States, anybody can get off if he's got the right lawyer."

Yeah, I thought. But that German mentality allowed Hitler to take over the country and run your people out — or kill them. I believe I like our system better — even if the guilty do get away occasionally.

Our professor in property law left me stunned. He lectured as if he were a talking book — in fact, he had written our text, as had our other professors in most cases. The book was big and fat, just like the writer and I could never understand what he was getting at. He had a theory of property ownership that left me completely baffled. I knew one thing, even if I passed the course, I still wouldn't know anything about closing a sale of real estate or settling a property line dispute.

Moot court was held half-way through the freshman year. Each of us had to argue a case that had actually been decided before an appellate court. Four students and a visiting lawyer represented the judges of the appeals court, and they judged, not on what the decision should be, but on our performance as advocates.

The case I was assigned involved a man who had been injured on the job working in a railroad shop. He had ruptured himself lifting a large piece of equipment.

I was to defend the railroad against the injured man.

My heart was not really on the side of the railroad, of course, but I armed myself with precedents, spent many hours writing a detailed brief and then appeared to argue the case on the big night.

I had command of the facts, knew the law as it applied in the case and gave a hard hitting presentation.

My opponent was a young Jewish boy. The four senior law students on the bench were Jewish and the outside practicing attorney was a Jewish labor lawyer.

I felt like I was going up against God's chosen people.

No decision was made. The judges were to combine their appraisal and give us a grade later.

As we left the courtroom, the labor lawyer walked alongside me.

"I think you had the best brief and the best argument," he confided to me, "but I would have voted for the plaintiff. I hate railroads."

After our appearance we were given the briefs filed in the real case. I thought mine was better than argument presented by the attorney representing the railroad — which wasn't saying much because it didn't do much to expose law or facts.

Later, when Judge Guess told me how seldom lawyers appearing before him seemed to know the law or the facts in the case being brought, I knew what he was talking about.

After the moot trial concluded, the lawyers and students headed across the street to Mory's, the tavern immortalized in the Whiffenpoof song. I excused myself from this ancient tradition — I was running a fever and was too ill to stay up any longer.

I was trying to keep myself in condition by going to physical therapy at Grace Memorial Hospital two afternoons a week. The therapist, a small but energetic woman named Ted worked hard, getting me up on braces and exercising my legs for me. Ted became a close friend and Frances was as devoted to her as I was. The problem was, it was still too early for anybody in the medical field to know much about what to do for a paraplegic — we were writing the book.

Two things were working on me. I still had the tube going through my abdomen into my bladder. I was taking eight sulfur tablets a day plus penicillin shots about once a month to try to keep down infection.

But what finally became critical was the growing decubitis ulcer in my left buttock.

I knew I had a problem, but I had no idea of the dimensions of the problem and I was determined to stay in school and to succeed.

I didn't know of anything else I could do.

We soon had our apartment fixed nicely and I was enjoying the school. Frances kept busy with preparing meals and running the apartment. On the weekends, we would drive out into the Connecticut countryside, finding one of the unique inns for our meal and enjoying the woodlands that reminded us so much of the North Georgia forests.

We went home to Decatur for Christmas holidays.

By the time we returned to New Haven, the ulcer had become infected. The half-year exams came right after our return. By then, I was going to class in the morning, then returning to the quonset hut about noon. I would drink a shot of whiskey, crawl in bed and Frances would pile every blanket we had on top of me and turn the coal burning space heater up to its highest setting.

How she stayed in the hot apartment, I don't know. But she did, and she never complained.

I would begin to shake. Never before or since have I been so cold — and I have been in some exposed situations. I felt like I was lying naked on arctic ice.

I would pull the hot water bottle under my chest and hold on for dear life.

Then I'd take two aspirins and gradually warm up. When I broke out in a heavy sweat, the chill was over and I'd feel fine until I returned from class the next day.

At the law school, the only grade given for a semester of work is the final exam. Daily reading assignments are given, but no grades are given for daily class room recitation and there are no tests. The student is free to come to class or not. All hinges on the final exam.

By the time exams rolled around, I was in the worst of the fever and chills cycle.

The exams consisted of three to four hours of writing during which time we would fill up several of the blue exam books.

The good old Veterans Administration made its contribution to the general situation.

"I've got to see you next week," the voice was gruff.

"Next week is final exams," I said. "How about waiting until they are over?"

"Well," the counselor said, "this report has got to go in. I can't wait."

I thought about the chills and fever I'd be having in the afternoons after each exam.

"We take a break during the exam at 11 o'clock in the morning. How about Tuesday?"

"I'll be there waiting in the hall at 11 Tuesday."

The government worker was right there when I rolled out into the halls. I was in the middle of the exam on torts and had already filled up two blue books.

"How are you doing?" he asked.

"Well, I don't know," I said, "it all depends on how I do on these exams."

"You better do good," he said, "if you don't, we'll take you out of school." I looked at him.

"Well," I said, "thanks for coming by."

"Yeah." He got up and shambled out.

What would we do without our friends the bureaucrats, I thought as I watched him depart down the hallowed halls of Yale. I gave a sigh and rolled back into the exam room.

The exam that sticks in my mind was the exam on contracts, the subject taught by the German Jew.

I couldn't believe my ears when the professor told us about the unusual exam.

"Gentlemen," he said with his heavy accent, "it may surprise you to be given a true false exam in the August Yale Law School. That is what you are going to get. There is only one answer for each question. The proposition is either true or it is false. It can't be both. To arrive at an answer, you are going to have to work through a maze of legal procedures. Now, some of you may be more comfortable to write out your reasoning in a blue book, and you are free to do so. You are also free, if you so choose, to simply mark true or false. Good luck, gentlemen."

By that time, I was really sick. "To hell with it," I thought sitting in the exam room, watching the other students scratching their heads, some of them already beginning to scribble in their blue books, "He said true or false and that's what he's going to get."

I groped through the maze without writing a word of explanation and simply checked true or false.

If he was the first professor to ever give a true false exam at the Yale Law School, I feel pretty sure I was the only student to take him up on his challenge.

The day we got our grades, I was in the bathroom when Bill came by. Bill and I had studied together for the exams. Where I simply wrote down everything the teacher said on a lined, yellow pad, Bill made his notes, then took them home, organized them logically, and typed out the most beautiful set of notes I've ever seen.

I was sitting on the commode when Bill entered our apartment.

Bill was so excited, he opened the bathroom door and started talking.

"Well, I got my grades," he was trying to stifle a smile. "How did you do, Clark?"

"I did pretty good, Bill," I replied, "how did you do?"

"I did pretty good," Bill said, "What did you make?"

"I made 77.9," I replied with a big grin.

"I'll be damned," Bill exclaimed, "I made 77.9 too."

We were in the top fifteen per cent of the freshman class and qualified to compete for the staff of the Yale Law Journal.

The professor who called us together to discuss the competition told us, "We have really been surprised by these grades. The students we thought would make it didn't, and some we didn't think could do the work did."

I felt sure I was one of those surprises.

The Yale Law Journal is one of the country's leading legal publications, is read by practicing attorneys and filed for future reference. Graduates who have served on the Journal staff receive some of the most important legal opportunities with the major New York and Washington firms.

Traditionally clerks to the U.S. Supreme Court are taken from their ranks. Several of the present justices on the court are former clerks.

If I had known to shift my weight in the wheelchair, I would have been healthy. Being healthy, I would have competed and might have been selected. And today, it is conceivable I would be a justice of the U.S. Supreme Court.

So much for whatmighthavebeens. Being a U. S. Supreme Court Justice would have been interesting, but I doubt it would have been as interesting as what actually happened.

At the time, I knew there was no point in my competing for the staff. The doctor didn't know how to treat my problem, it was becoming more disabling every day and I was fighting just to stay in school.

The doctor was a very fine surgeon at Grace Memorial Hospital in New Haven. He came to take a personal interest in me. My physical therapist had put me in touch with him.

He, of course, had never seen anything like the sore that was continuing to grow in dimension inside my buttock.

"That won't kill you, Clark," he said, "your kidneys are what you have to worry about."

I decided he was convinced along with others that I wasn't long for this world.

On one occasion he brought me a bottle of wine. He would come late in the evening and spend an hour or two visiting.

"Your problem is you aren't having any fun," he told me on one occasion, "go out and get drunk. Go to New York and check in a hotel and see a few shows."

"I recommend liquor for everything," he told me, "but to be honest with you, I have a problem. Either people don't follow my advice so they aren't helped, or they go too far and become alcoholics."

He didn't know what else to do, so he said he would operate and clean the place out in hopes that would start the healing process.

All this time, Frances was in New Haven with nobody to talk with and seeing me go down hill every day.

When he finally operated on me, she sat for hours, alone, before being able to see me. The doctor never came out and talked to her. I came back to our apartment a few days after the operation. The first time I went to the bathroom, the stitches pulled out and I lost a lot of blood.

The operation accomplished one thing. There was no doubt now that I would have to leave Yale and go home.

The trip back to Decatur was a nightmare. I would drive three or four hours, then would start having severe chills. With the heater going full blast and the windows shut, my teeth would be chattering. We'd find a motel, get inside, I'd drink some whiskey, get in bed and shake until aspirin finally broke the cycle and I began to sweat.

It took five days to make what should have been a three day trip.

CHAPTER XVIII

"Good pilots are never lost," according to Clint, my instructor, "although they may become temporarily disoriented."

The sweat on my brow as I turned back toward the WINK VOR was caused by temporary disorientation.

Checking the chart, I had seen that the airport was due south of the VOR station. I decided to try one more time, fly toward the VOR until the swinging needle showed my plane directly over the station, then turn to a 180 degree heading and fly the radial to the airport.

When I finally saw the airport, it was right where the chart said it would be, and I could understand why it had been invisible on my first pass. There was only one building, far from the main runway and the main runway blended into the surrounding sage brush. When I first spotted it, I decided I was about to make my first landing on an unpaved runway. Then, as I came in to land, I realized the asphalt was simply obscured by dust that had blown over it from the surrounding wasteland.

I taxied to the end of the runway, turned left down a narrow strip of pavement and heaved a sigh of relief when I saw the Chevron truck and knew avgas was available. A book for each section of the country is issued several times a year. Called the Airport Facilities Directory, it gives the latest information as to runway length and heading, availability of fuel and services, navigation aids, radio frequencies, etc. I had checked the directory that morning before leaving Tucson, but it was comforting to see that gas truck right where it belonged to be.

"Hey," I shouted to the elderly gentleman who walked over to the plane, "I need gas and I wanted you to do me a favor. I'm in a wheelchair. Can you bring me a coke?"

I handed him the money through the small window in the left side of the plane.

"Sure," he took the money, "you use 100 low lead?"

"Right," I answered and handed him the credit card.

The interesting thing I found, but that didn't really surprise me after years of experience, was the casual way most people accepted the fact that the pilot of this plane was a man in a wheelchair.

It has been my experience that people will accept just about any novel experience. They are much too occupied with their own concerns to dwell for very long on another person's situation. As long as you act in a matter of fact way, they will respond in kind.

When I was a county commissioner, we did a great deal of business with engineers, architects and consultants of various kinds. One of the most successful and admired traffic engineers we worked with, an official of the leading national concern in the field, was a gentleman with one of the worst harelips I have ever seen. It not only looked bad, but it affected his speech in a manner that people make jokes about.

He was always neatly dressed and completely professional in his presentations. But, most importantly, it was obvious that his disfigurement and speech defect bothered him not one whit. He was there to earn a fee in a profession at which he was an established expert. As a result we never noticed or were distracted by his difference once the initial impression faded.

Many people in wheelchairs are acutely self-conscious. Maybe it was the way I was raised, but it never bothered me to be different. I do try to be better.

Soon after Frances and I returned to Decatur, we were able to find a small house, built of solid granite in the unincorporated community of Tucker, a few miles from where our families were living.

Once I got off my seat, the infection abated and I felt pretty good. I believed at first the ulcer would heal. The neighbors in what was still a small, country town were kind. They brought us fresh summer vegetables from their gardens and paid us regular visits.

We brought a bed, sofa, and table from New Haven, but were otherwise unfurnished during the first weeks in the small house.

The main thing I remember about that summer was the heat. The house faced west so that the sun baked the granite all morning and then baked the full length of the other side all afternoon. There was no insulation in the attic and, of course, air conditioning was unheard of. We roasted all day and after dark the granite radiated the heat so that we were bathed in sweat most of the night.

To get me out of the bedroom, we bought an aluminum chaise lounge and I would lie flat on my stomach on that in the living room or outside on the small stoop that served as our porch.

Since I was bedridden, we received regular visits from the two local preachers and, of course, we always were prayed over rather thoroughly.

I remember on one occasion I had turned on my back so I could visit with the preacher. When he got ready to go, he and Frances stood one on each side, and he said, "Let us have a word of prayer."

I was down low, almost on the floor and they towered above me. While the prayer was going on, I opened my eyes just enough to look up at them and thought.

"This is what it'll feel like when they're laying me away for good."

That fall, our family doctor drove out from Decatur to see me. I've always appreciated the time and effort this took and the fact he had been searching since I arrived back in Decatur for a way to help me.

Dr. McGeachy was a completely dedicated general practitioner. He had graduated at the top of his class from Emory Medical School, and, although he was a surgeon, he elected to work as a family doctor. During the war, he served as a Navy doctor and maintained a field aid station just behind the Marine lines on Iwo Jima. There he performed surgery within sound of the Japanese guns a few hundred yards away.

"Clark," he said, "I've found a doctor who can operate on you."

"You don't think I'm healing, Doc?" I asked.

"No," he said. "Dr. Kanthak says this type ulcer never will heal without surgery. The ulcer occurred over the sharp tip of bone we all sit on. He will go in, shave off the end of the bone and then pull flesh over it from the surrounding area."

The idea of shaving off part of my bone chilled me.

"Doc," I said. "I don't want anything like that done. I'm afraid I might get osteomyelitis."

"Clark," he continued, "You've got to have the operation. Otherwise, you won't be able to sit up again. I'll have to tell you like I used to tell my children about their typhoid shots. I told them they didn't have to have the shots, but unless they had them they couldn't go swimming. As for the bone infection, you probably have some already."

After the abortive and final trip to the VA Hospital, I had the surgery done at Emory Hospital and within a month I was healed. The place would not bother me again for twenty-two years.

CHAPTER XIX

Now that I am qualified to carry passengers, it never ceases to amaze me how many people are willing to go flying with an aging paraplegic in a hand controlled single engined fourteen year old airplane.

It can only be attributed to ignorance.

Or curiosity.

Or something.

I prefer to fly senior citizens. As I explained to Mama Guess, if something should happen, there's not so much to lose.

One of my most interesting passengers was an 87 year old who had been a rigger in the Army Signal Corps in World War I. He served in England and France in an observation squadron. He explained that when a plane came back from combat, it was a simple matter to glue a piece of fabric over the bullet holes.

To be honest, however, you do eventually develop a certain confidence in flying machines.

And, if you are real honest, you have to admit you have a lot less chance of tearing up you and your machine than you have on a modern expressway in a modern, built out of plastic automobile.

You just have to remember certain rules.

Like always filling up your gas tank before you take off.

And being sure your pitot tube is not plugged up so you can know what your air speed is.

And keeping your air speed above a certain minimum — particularly when you're close to mother earth.

To the novice, bouncing around in the sky when the sun is heating the earth seems a lot more dangerous than just going too slow — but the former is not dangerous at all.

It is all a matter of knowledge.

Flying is one activity when being educated and knowing what you're doing pays off — big.

It's been said that flying is ninety-six per-cent boredom and four per cent sheer terror.

Like the WAC aerialist I met in the Army hospital — to be honest, the terror part is what keeps me interested. And alive.

When I was on my way overseas, I had one central plea: that when it was all over I would be able to have children.

It wasn't easy for Frances and me, but that prayer was answered.

I knew after I faced the facts of my injury, that I would never be able to father a child. But for some reason, that really never bothered me. All I had asked was that I be able to have children.

One of the greatest days of our lives was the Christmas evening when we returned from our family visits to find a telegram.

"Your son was born this morning at 1 AM."

God had given us Tom on His Son's birthday.

It had not been easy for us to have a child. We had started inquiries soon after we were married, and had learned that the normal way was to apply to the local welfare department. Their workers would make investigations of the prospective parents and, if the investigation was positive, would arrange for the adoption to take place.

I found out later that we would never have been approved because I was in a wheelchair.

But the Lord had heard my prayer and answered it by giving me a father-in-law who was a Superior Court judge and a brother-in-law who is a doctor.

After my brother-in-law, for whom we named Tom, had made the necessary arrangements, I was concerned whether the state investigators would allow the adoption.

"I wouldn't worry about that, Clark," Judge Guess told me. "They make a recommendation. Our court makes the decision."

The day the lady came out to make her investigation, Frances and I were very nervous. We had the place shining and straight and were on our best behavior.

"Mr. Harrison," the woman said, "How are you going to be able to do all the things for your child that the normal father would do. Like going fishing?"

"Well," I said, "I don't think the average father does that much with their children. Mine never did. Most of them seem to be too busy earning a living."

"But," she argued, "who's going to teach your son how to play ball?"

"I will," I said, "and since I won't be able to do a lot of things, my child will learn to be more independent."

While we were waiting for Tom to be born, we had bought some land and were building a house. The federal government had passed a law paying half the cost, up to $20,000, for a house built to certain specifications for the seriously disabled veteran.

Our families thought we had lost our minds. We went way out in the country and bought three and two-thirds acres on Clairmont Road. There were hardly any houses between Decatur and the land.

There was method in our madness. With both our families nearby, we were not going to develop the kind of independence we both wanted.

It turned out to be a good investment. We bought the land in the month of February, when nobody was looking for a place so far from town. The lot was 150 x 1000 feet and the price was $2,750.

The year was 1949. After we built our house, a large and very exclusive subdivision was built across the road from us. Then a developer came to see us. He wanted to put in a street that would touch the rear of our property and wanted us to pay a share of the development cost. We sold two lots on that street and four more lots when a parallel street crossed the property.

Out of the proceeds, we bought one hundred seventy acres adjoining the Trappist Monastery south of Conyers, Georgia.

That first land investment would provide the base that would make it possible for me to play a leading role in the organization of the Fidelity National Bank some twenty-five years later.

The house, because of the government's involvement, had to be built with four foot halls, three foot doors, an exercise room and a ground level entrance. As things worked out, the house was completed while we were in the process of acquiring our son.

We were in the middle of the woods, with only one neighbor adjoining us.

So, we had a chance to be alone as we took our new son into our new home and started the life-time commitment that is parenthood.

And, of course, we took parenthood very seriously — like most first-time parents we overdid it, as a matter of fact.

When Tom would cry out about 2 a. m., I would wake Frances up. We kept his bed next to ours. Frances would go get the bottle and I would feed him while she changed him.

This went on for three months. Finally, to simplify things we started setting the bottle in an electric coffee pot by the bed. Then Frances could heat the bottle without getting out of bed.

All of which was fine, except one night I accidentally pushed Frances out of bed and she landed on the hot coffee pot.

"How did you burn this circle under your arm?" Dr. McGeachy asked.

"I fell out of the bed and landed on the coffee pot," Frances said.

Doctor McGeachy called his nurses in to hear the tale and see the circle.

I have other memories etched into my mind.

When I told the social worker Tom would be independent, I was right. I remember once when Frances was sick. Tom was two or three at the time and he got up to get dressed and needed some clean clothes. I'll never forget watching him come into the kitchen, open the dryer and lean in and almost crawl in to get himself some clean under shorts.

Another problem we had was trying to administer medicine to our small and active son. Not having had any medical experience, we didn't have a very good technique — and the social worker was right about one thing — I couldn't move as fast as Tom.

Lord knows, I tried.

On one occasion, Tom had a fever and the doctor told us to give him an aspirin.

I tried persuasion, but it was obvious right away that Tom was not going to take the aspirin voluntarily. I tried to hold him, but he slipped away.

The chase was on.

Down the hall, through the living room, back through the kitchen.

He was way ahead of me and gaining.

Finally, I got him in the bedroom. But he outsmarted me.

He got up on the double bed, got in the corner and braced himself against the two walls.

To hell with it, I decided. This kid ain't going to take this aspirin.

After I abandoned the chase, I came back in a few minutes.

Tom was fast asleep, his little body curled up in the corner against the wall.

But things turned out all right any way, in spite of the dire predictions of the social worker.

Tom was so tired after all the chasing that he slept for several hours. When he woke up, the fever was gone.

He was always healthy. Maybe it was because we did more chasing than medicating.

I was determined that my limitations would not handicap Tom in his development with boys his age. As soon as he was walking, I bought a football, baseball, glove and bat.

I would throw him the football and he would run by so I could tackle him.

Once when he was very small, he came tearing past me at full speed, just a little farther to the side than usual. I reached way out, grabbed him and he turned me and the chair over sideways.

I knew I had broken his little bones. Then I heard him laughing and realized that the chair and I had missed him all together.

When Tom was a baby, we were limited in our social life, since we weren't much for turning him over to baby sitters — paying for my various operations didn't leave much money for entertainment or for hiring help. So, in those pre-TV days, one of our favorite recreations was the drive-in movie.

About once a week, we'd put the baby in his car bed in the back seat and go to the drive-in movie. The noise from the film didn't seem to bother Tom and during the early part of the show, he would sleep soundly.

Then, it seemed that when the movie really got interesting and especially if the plot was complex, Tom would wake up. At the most critical time, he would start crying and we often left the drive-in wondering just exactly how everything had turned out.

With experience we learned that sometimes we could quiet Tom by rocking the car bed. In an exciting finish to a movie, the baby would experience a violent rocking session. He must have wondered why going to the movies involved so much noise and rocking.

When Tom became a little older, we would play catch with the baseball. Right away, he found out that if he didn't throw the ball where I could catch it, he'd have to run and get it for me. So he became very accurate in his throwing and later became a pitcher on his baseball team.

As soon as he was six, I started taking Tom to play Little League baseball. Like most little kids, he was pretty bored with the whole matter in the beginning. They would put him in the outfield and he'd just as likely be looking the other way when the ball was hit in his direction.

He was a natural athlete and with my devotion in seeing to it he made every game and practice, he soon became quite expert.

One of the high points of my life came the day of the All Star game toward the end of Tom's five year Little League career. He was a pitcher, but since they had several pitchers they were using him in the outfield.

The other team got a couple of runs ahead and his team had gone through several pitchers. Finally, in desperation, the coach called Tom in from the outfield to take over.

I remember watching the sweat running down as he faced the first batter and wondering if he could stand the pressure.

The next few moments were to make all our efforts worthwhile. Cooly, Tom struck out the two remaining batters. When his team came up in the last of the ninth, two of the other players managed to get on base. Then Tom stepped up and hit the double that won the game.

I thought then that whatever else happened in my life would have to be anticlimactic. It was years later before my emotions were brought to such a pitch again — then it was watching son Bob stride easily ahead of the pack to break his high school's all-time record for the mile.

"How is your son going to learn to play ball," the lady asked. Both Tom and Bob started to play at age six. Tom won the All-Star game. Bob broke his school record for the mile. Which proves even expert fears can be unfounded

Both our sons have, I believe, an extra measure of strength and self confidence because their dad wasn't able to do things for them.

Recently, I was talking to son Bob.

"You know," I said, "I never have believed much in all this talk about adoption."

We had been discussing a friend of his who had left home and was deeply alienated from his father. I was remarking on how different in nature the two were.

"I heard on TV the other day," I continued, "that there are over eight million different combinations of genes and chromosomes that can be made when a male and female cell unite."

"Well," Bob said, "John's sure different from his dad. And you and I sure have a lot in common."

"We've got everything in common," I said.

When Tom's twin sons were born, a friend told me something he heard Tom say.

"I don't care what Dad says," he was quoted. "You can love your own natural children as much as you'd love adopted ones."

CHAPTER XX

Taking off from Winkler County Airport, with the safe, secure feeling in the gut brought on by 48 useable gallons of avgas sloshing around in the wings, I'm trying to figure out why I got into flying.

Even back in 1944, when I got my 10 hours of flying in the L-5 at government expense, I failed to experience flying the way some writers tell about it.

For one thing, I never did feel like a bird. I felt more like a man cramped in a very small space in a drafty machine that was making a tremendous amount of noise.

And most days the view is not all that good. In Georgia, most days are either cloudy grey, or, on those summer days when the sky looks sparkling clear blue from the ground, you are likely to find, when looking down from above, that haze obscures the visibility.

The exceptions, of course, can take your breath away. Flying over Atlanta on a clear night in a small plane is a fairyland experience. Nothing comparable can be experienced through the small window of an airliner. The city is strung with bright jewels of every color, set against velvet blackness. And the movement of traffic creates a living stream of light that tugs at the heart as you think of all the people going toward their evening joys or sorrows.

On the first flight with Frances as my passenger, we came out of the rain above Jekyll and St. Simons islands. Suddenly, it was as if God had reached out and opened a big picture window in the clouds just for us. There were the jade green islands, the pale green marshes with their spiraling creeks, and the dark blue of the Atlantic in the bright sunshine beyond.

But those weren't the things that got me into flying. I think primarily I did it for the twenty year old boy who had been taken from the Army

Air Corps and put in the infantry. And for all the young men and women who have been wiped out by a spinal cord injury and think their lives can never have excitement and movement and drama again. I know that if, at age twenty, I had heard of a 57 year old man, paralyzed as I was and after 37 years of that paralysis, flying an airplane it would have made a difference. The only thing offered to us in 1945 was watch repairing.

And I just can't concentrate that intensely or make my fingers move as skillfully as that important work requires.

To say that I was bitter when I had to leave the Yale Law School would not be entirely accurate. I had about decided that practicing law might not be the ideal solution to my problem. Sitting and poring over books had certainly worked an unkindness on my buttocks.

A good lawyer has to be a good student.

Again, as a mature man, I know now that I could have found a specialty that would have suited my physical requirements and that eventually I could have others do most of my research. But, when you're young, you can't think that way.

Primarily, I was puzzled as to just what I could do now that school could no longer shield me.

When I finally had my operation and could sit again, my Dad offered me a job in his school.

I didn't know what else to do, so I reluctantly accepted his kind offer. I worked in his office for two years, felt that I did a good job and believe he was satisfied.

But, the school was not to me what it was to him. Each of us have our dream, and, if we are very fortunate, we have the opportunity to try to live that dream. Dad's life was successful and happy because he was doing that in which he devoutly believed. But he could not transfer that dream to me.

Times had changed. The south had risen during the war years because of the infusion of new people and new wealth as the war industries were built and the young men from the north came south to serve.

Private business schools no longer had a monopoly on business training. Most high schools were beginning to offer the courses.

But, most importantly, I would never have felt that what I did there was being done on my own. I desperately needed to find my own dream and bring it into reality.

I enjoyed working for Dad, I learned a lot, and I feel I made a contribution. But, I don't know who was more relieved, me or Dad, when I came in and told him I would be leaving. He understood I was going to have to find my own way and his reaction was, as always, positive.

Dad had told me as a child, "Never stand in the shadow of another man." So he had sowed the seed that now made me want to go out and get a job on my own. As far as I was concerned, no man in Atlanta cast a longer shadow than my Dad.

After I left Dad's office, I finally went to an employment agency.

The first interview they sent me on, I was hired. Which somewhat validated Frances' observation that I really didn't know I couldn't get a job because I never had really tried.

It was a good and progressive company that was growing rapidly. They supplied everything a general hospital needed. If they didn't have it, they got it.

My first job was bid clerk. All day, every day, I would take requests for bids sent by governments and hospitals and would look up prices in our general catalogue and a number of price lists and catalogues. In the beginning, it was interesting to find out how such business is conducted.

The main problem, I was an inside man. Management looked on office workers as part of the overhead.

The work, a necessary evil, that was to be done at a minimum of expense.

My salary was $185 a month. Even in those pre-inflation days that was small pay, just about enough to make the payment on my car and buy gas to go back and forth to work.

In the eyes of the owners of the business, the salesmen brought in the money that fueled the business — and they were treated accordingly.

When they were in town, they would saunter in, looking for somebody to help them with delivery of something they had sold, or to find out why their commission check was short or late. All other work was stopped to cater to them.

The general manager would take them to lunch — taking two hours minimum. I had visions of them having a couple of martinis in a fancy restaurant, served by a beautiful waitress, while we consumed a sandwich and coke in the employee lounge during our 45 minute break.

"Harrison," one of the bright young men from the home office was chatting with me at my desk, "how can you be happy in this job with the education you've got?"

Well, I thought, if I could do it, I'd be out there with the salesmen — a part of the income that paid the bills and made the profit instead of part of the overhead.

I didn't agree with management's view of the people doing the essential detail work, but I knew I couldn't change that attitude.

My last job at the company was balancing inventory among seven bonded warehouses around the southeast. It seemed like pretty important work to me. We handled thousands of bottles of intravenous solutions that were dated and it was necessary that they be available when needed.

It was also important to the company that the stock be rotated and that an oversupply not be ordered. While I was doing the job, I was told over $100,000 in solutions had to be thrown out the back door because others doing the work, at a minimum wage, had over-ordered and the warehouses had failed to ship the oldest solutions first.

We had a formula to go by, and I began to ship supplies from one warehouse to another rather than order from the home plant. And I let our supplies dwindle as we came near the end of the year. We were charged local ad valorem taxes according to how much was in the warehouse on January first.

As Christmas approached, the warehouse manager came to my desk.

"Hey, Harrison," he looked worried, " we're about down to the floor back there."

"Don't worry," I told him, "our stuff is in box cars headed this way."

We didn't run short and we saved a lot of money.

I thought again, the big shots may ignore the people at the low end of the scale, but they do so at their peril — just like on the front lines, everybody counts.

I was beginning to feel like a monkey in a box. I never saw the fruits of my labor or the products we were moving around the south east. Somebody would shove a paper through a crack in my box, I'd scribble on it, and pass it back through the crack.

And, like school, it was the worst possible thing for my health. I might not be equipped to travel, but I was sure going to rot if I kept sitting at a desk. My eyes looked bad, I was thin, and my kidneys were acting up — the specter of another pressure sore was always there.

CHAPTER XXI

After I started flying back and forth to St. Simons Island, where Frances and I built a second home, I took some lessons from another flying instructor.

Frank has his own distinctive method of instructing.

Frank lets you fly along, learning as you go.

He reminds me somewhat of my old roommate at the University, Gabby.

If you happen to invert the airplane, Frank might clear his throat. And, if a crash seemed imminent, he would undoubtedly apply some discreet adjusting pressures to the controls to avert disaster. But, on the whole, he lets you get in and out of trouble as a way of learning.

Of course, I knew the basics of flying before Frank got hold of me.

"I've taught fifteen hundred people to fly," Frank, who instructed for the military among others, told me, "including three hundred women."

Women make good pilots, he told me. They are methodical and careful and follow instructions well.

"You can always tell when a woman is really catching on," he continued, "they start telling the instructor what to do and correcting his mistakes."

Women have one problem when they become qualified pilots, Frank says.

"Women are used to having things done properly, according to the book," he said, "men aren't like that and the women tend to get frustrated when a controller or flight briefer gets off the straight and narrow."

I haven't taught anybody how to fly, but I know what Frank is talking about in regard to women.

One of my favorite passengers is my mother-in-law, Mama Guess.

Mama Guess has flown with me half a dozen times, back and forth to the island. She is very petite and can't see over the instrument panel when the airplane is in straight and level flight. So, if I want to show her something, I have to push the nose down.

"Don't dive, don't dive," she will exclaim.

On one occasion, after several flights, and when she was reaching the state Frank described, of comprehending what was going on, we were descending to land.

What Mama Guess didn't know yet was about traffic patterns. I was on right base about to turn right and land on the runway that was perpendicular to our line of flight.

What she did know was that we were getting closer and closer to the trees and that we were headed toward the ocean.

Finally, she could stand it no longer.

"Isn't that the runway there," she was pointing excitedly to the threshold that she saw below and to our right.

"Oh," I said, "there it is!"

Teaching methods vary. The results are what count.

I have had two excellent instructors.

I will say they have both helped keep me alive, and I am grateful for that.

In 1952, I decided if the money was going to go to the salesmen I had better become one.

So, I decided to be a salesman.

I also decided that nobody would hire a salesman in a wheelchair.

So, Frances and I formed our own company.

That way, I wouldn't have to go on any job interviews, and I could decide when to go to lunch and when to take the day off.

We had made some money selling our lots, and now we invested in our own sales and distribution business. Knowing absolutely nothing about what we were doing.

The first problem was how to carry my samples. Since I couldn't carry a sample case in my hand and still have two hands to push the wheelchair, I decided to try something different. My chair had the big wheels in front as previously described.

I went to a cabinet maker in Atlanta.

"Can you make me a case that will strap to the back of my chair," I asked, "fix it so I can hang it on the handle bars, and get it on and off while I'm sitting in the chair?"

He took out his measuring tape and went to work. What I picked up a few days later was a light weight case, made of plywood with a leatherette cover, all black. The case was about six inches thick and hung by straps from the wheelchair's handle bars. At the bottom, it had straps that snapped it securely to the uprights of the wheelchair back. I could get into the chair by sliding through the back, zip the back up, reach in the back seat of the car, get the case and strap it to the back of the chair.

It had not been long since I had learned to get the wheelchair in and out of the car by myself — another necessary skill if I was to be a traveling salesman.

I learned that from another paraplegic. He was working as an accountant and was on a vacation trip, traveling alone. When he got ready to leave our house, he rolled out into the drive, got in the car, and pulled the chair in after him.

"Did you see that?" I asked Frances.

"What?"

"He got his chair in the car by himself."

"Well, I declare."

Next morning, I went to work. I didn't know how he had done it, but I figured that if he could do it, I could do it too. With Frances anxiously watching, I pulled myself through the open back of my chair into the car. I reached out, pulled up on the leatherette seat and folded the chair together. Then, I placed the little wheels in behind the front seat. Thought a while. Then, slid over into the right hand seat, leaned the left hand seat back forward, reached down and grabbed the chair above the small wheels and gave a mighty heave.

Voila!

From then on, I knew I could go anywhere I wanted to all by myself. It had taken me seven years to make that great discovery. At the Shepherd Spinal Center, the patients learn that one inside the first sixty days.

So, I became a traveling man. I did it for three years, never made any profit, but opened a whole new vista of what could be done from the Everest and Jennings wheelchair.

It was a crazy thing to do.

But most of the things I have done that finally resulted in progress have been considered crazy.

Just about everybody I called on bought something. I suppose by the time they saw my complete dog and pony show they felt obligated. It was quite an act. I'm come squeaking in, asking for whoever did the buying, then I'd whip off my sample case and start pulling out my wares.

Without any guide lines, training or experience, we were importing gift and toy items from Germany and England. It was still early after the war, and the manufacturers were anxious to make contact with anybody who might buy their goods for dollars. The items had to be small so they could fit in my sample case — and we had a good selection of things.

We dealt with the international department of the bank to arrange for payment, and we found packages could be delivered right to the house, even though we had to use an agent in one of the ports to get them into the country.

It was a lot of fun.

"Well, honey," I was waving as I backed out of the driveway, "I'll call you Wednesday."

It was to be one of my longer trips, to Chattanooga, then Knoxville, then home by Friday. Frances had been up early packing my bag.

I had had a pretty good trip, making sales at several stores on the road to Chattanooga. When I pulled into the motel that afternoon, I told the boy to get my bags out of the trunk.

"There ain't no bags in your trunk."

I looked at him. I got out of the car, rolled around to the back and looked.

Sure enough, no bags.

I was always having things go my way on those trips. Usually the person I had to see was right there waiting for me, I had very little car trouble, and I was always amazed at how I always found a parking place. In the middle of a city, there would be a space waiting for me usually right in front of the entrance to the store.

That's why I believe in angels.

On this particular occasion, I had pulled into probably the only motel in the country that was connected by sidewalk directly to a shopping center. After I checked into the motel, I rolled around the corner, bought a toothbrush, razor, and some shirts and underwear.

Next morning, I continued on my calls.

Wednesday evening, as promised, I called Frances.

She was about crazy by now, of course. Right after I disappeared down the driveway, she saw the suitcases. Never at a loss for something to try, she went in the house and called the state patrol, gave them a description and told them to have me call home so she could tell me about the bags.

My contribution was to keep her wondering whether I'd fallen off the end of the earth — at that age, I thought it was funny.

After calling on a merchant in Alabama some weeks later I chanced to strike up a conversation with a Jewish man who ran the ten cent store next door.

He told me how he had started his store after he immigrated from Russia. Arriving in this country, unable to speak the language, somehow he had found himself in this Alabama city.

"Had you ever run a store?" I asked him.

"No," he replied in a heavy accent.

"How in the world could you, a foreigner who could barely speak the language, who didn't know the business, manage to survive?"

"Vel," he replied, "I had a system. When the salesmen would call on me I told them, 'You are going to place my order for me. I have only two rules. First, you must give me the lowest price, every time. Second, you must sell me only things that will move off my shelves. As long as you obey my rules, you will write the order. Mess me up, I will not do business with you again.'"

I never forgot that Jew, and I have used his system when faced with responsibilities of my own.

Eventually, I believe we would have learned how to make money in the wholesale business. The only problem was, our star salesman was wearing out. Getting in and out of the car, hauling the heavy case in the hot sun was working on me — on my kidneys more than anything. I still had the tube going in my belly, and the irritation was increasing the chronic infection.

After three years, we decided we had better get into something else.

We sold our stock — and I learned something from that. I found out I could get a list of stores in the Middle West. I sent them a form letter with literature about the model German car that was our most heavily stocked item, and I offered an extra ten per cent discount.

I learned then that people often have more confidence in a far away source — and that retailers really love those extra discounts.

We sold out in a few days.

By this time, we knew a lot more about sources, how to handle the paper work involved in importing and how to sell.

I had sold to seventy-two stores, and we had recouped our original investment of about two thousand dollars.

Most importantly, I suppose, we both had a lot more confidence in the fact we could operate a business — and even make it profitable.

We had not made any money, but we had invested the sweat equity that is necessary to capitalize any new business. The business was established and it would have continued to grow.

From a personal standpoint, I had learned I could talk to people from all walks of life — and sell them things.

I had also had a taste of the excitement and satisfaction of running my own business, and I suppose I decided then I didn't want to work for somebody else.

It's a good thing I feel that way. Nobody ever tried to hire me.

While we were working in our own business, I became active in the Junior Chamber of Commerce. The Jaycees specialize in leadership development — and together with the store to store peddling I was doing, I was overcoming any reticence I had experienced because of the wheelchair.

The little business we started never made any money, but it got me out into the highways and biways calling on all kinds of people. I soon lost any self-consciousness as I became interested in other people and their problems, desires and dreams.

I also learned that while other people might experience some curiosity about a man in a wheelchair peddling from a back pack, people were really more concerned about their own situation and were immediately interested when I turned the conversation in that direction.

The Jaycees helped me as well.

We were constantly setting up committees to tackle any kind of community problem anybody could dream up. The things most young people do for a living are not nearly exciting enough to satisfy youthful visions and ambitions so the committees were outlets.

Anything from organizing a beauty contest to collecting toys for distribution at Christmas made us feel important. And, we were making a contribution.

One of the interesting projects in those early days involved aviation. Radio navigation systems available to private pilots in the nineteen fifties were rather limited and it was easy for a small plane's pilot to get lost. Some Jaycee who was a pilot came up with the idea of painting the town's name on top of the local warehouse. Soon Jaycees all over the state were out with brooms and buckets of paint making their contribution to the cause of aviation safety.

Before long, I had gotten myself elected to various offices in our local club and found the activities provided a natural entrance to the professional political arena a little later.

The Jaycees met occasionally at our house. Because the government paid half the cost we had built a large house with a big living room. We had been in it for several years. Because of the money crunch, my various trips to the hospital had brought, it had never been painted. The paint was peeling from the gutters and shutters. Since we were in the woods, isolated from our neighbors, we didn't give the matter much thought — it was one of the things, like the Japanese garden I'll be telling about, that we planned to do later.

Then, much to our surprise one Saturday the whole Jaycee Club appeared at our house — loaded down with paint, brushes, ladders and several kegs of beer.

Apparently, others had noticed our peeling paint, and we had become a 'project'. Soon the house was crawling with young men — climbing up and down between trips to the keg of beer. By the time everybody left, the house was gleaming with fresh paint and the trash can was full of beer cups.

I suppose we didn't give much thought to such matters as house maintenance. The parade had passed us by for a while. Now that we were starting to join back into the routine of daily life we found we no longer worried much about the formalities.

We did enjoy traveling and were able to find money for trips to various points to visit relatives. We had a good time in Miami where one of Frances' cousins had a friend who was married to a Jewish bookie. By betting with him, we made a little money and by staying with the cousin, we kept our expenses within control.

Since I had been shot fighting Hitler and his treatment of the Jews, I have taken an intense interest in God's chosen people over the years.

The Jewish bookie was an interesting study. The couple had a little boy, probably two or three years old. His father would hand him a couple of dollar bills.

"I want him to get used to handling money," he said.

Like most Jews I have met he had definite ideas about how to handle money himself.

"Nah," he'd say when we were studying the racing form and considering a favored horse, "I wouldn't bet on that horse. He'll probably win, but the odds are so low it wouldn"t be worth your investment."

Inspired by the Jaycees re-doing the outside of our house, Frances and I decided we could repaint the inside.

It was in the early days of water-based paint and we were fascinated to find we could paint up, down and cross ways without streaking the finish. I'd paint as high up as I could reach and Frances would finish using a step ladder. Then, with a long handled roller, we'd take turns doing the ceiling.

It was a big house. We were painting the large living room and had all the furniture sitting in the middle of the floor when we got to talking.

"We ought to go to New Orleans some time," I reminisced. "When we went through there on our trip to take Novena to see Windy back in 1942, we really enjoyed the French Quarter."

"I hear the food's good," Frances commented.

"We ate at Antoine's" I said. "The restaurant must be a hundred years old. The food is great. I don't know what it is about French cooking, but it's good while you're eating it, and you feel good after you finish."

"I've heard it's because they cook it in olive oil," Frances said.

The more we thought about the beauty and charm of the French Quarter, the good French food and the adventure of the trip — and the more we looked at the huge living room with the furniture piled out in the middle of the floor and the expanse of wall space yet to be painted — the more we felt there was no use delaying our trip.

Finally, we packed a couple of bags, backed out of the cluttered and half-painted living room and took off in our Ford coupe for the land of the bayous.

Between our families, Tom was arranged for.

It was a great trip — a great adventure — and great food.

Frances and Bob try out his new bike in the backyard of our Clairmont home. The Japanese garden was still in the planning stage.

When we returned home, opened the back door and made our way forward into the house we found the living room, much to our surprise, exactly as we had left it. The paint cans and brushes sat where we had left them, the new paint was just as far up the wall, and the furniture was just as we had left it in the middle of the living room floor.

Refreshed by the trip, we finished our painting chore in short order and learned a lesson. When you get tired of a job, leave it. When you get back, it'll still be waiting patiently for your return — and you'll feel more like finishing.

Painting was not the only thing about our house we put off.

The house was built in the shape of an 'L' with a covered walkway inside the 'L' from the carport around to our big screened porch.

Some day we would have the backyard beautifully landscaped. But for now we were content. All we had in the backyard were weeds. But the house hid the weeds from the public and we spent many happy hours there, watching Tom as he played, bringing our lunch out from the house and planning for the future development of our yard.

"I think a Japanese garden would be nice," I would say.

"Yes," Frances would join in. "We could have a stream and a little bridge right over there."

Every day, the plans would change, which was the beauty of the thing. We could always change the landscaping of our garden. And without any labor and without any expense.

Disaster lay ahead for the near future and we would never recapture completely the fun and light heartedness of those early years of our marriage — months of togetherness as I tried to learn how to make a living, trips where our only concern was finding a motel within our budget, our imaginary Japanese garden, our beer drinking non-professional painters and our strung out painting of the big rooms and wide halls of that first home.

When our children marry, we worry about their early trials and tribulations. But probably most of that worry is misapplied. We forget how dreams and the adventure of early going it together paper over and dissolve the realities of those early years.

Certainly, from the outside Frances and I must have seemed caught in a hard case. But from our vantage point it was all pretty great.

We didn't worry about the money we didn't have — we just didn't do the things that cost a lot of money. And we did savor those hot dogs and pop corn our money would buy at the drive in movie. With our freezer full of vegetables, we didn't have to worry about something to eat.

The eight months I lay on my stomach after leaving Yale were softened and highlighted by the meals we shared, the solitude together, the staying up all night and sleeping all day, the long talks — and the plans and dreams.

After we got into our new home on our big wooded lot, we built around Tom. A new depth, meaning and richness came with the ball games, the trips to the mountains, playing catch and tackle in our hidden backyard.

Those years healed me in a way nothing else could — with Frances, I became part of a whole person, with Tom, we became part of a whole family.

And through it all we had our hopes, our dreams and our ever changing, always more beautiful, Japanese garden.

CHAPTER XXII

There is always somebody standing around, ready to put you down.
When you are trying to show off.

Especially when you are trying to show off in front of a girl.

We all know that, but we all forget.

My first and most painful time was when I took my lovely neighbor on a roller skate date and she wiped me out financially by ordering a fifteen cent soda.

That ended my adolescent affirmative action program as concerned girls for at least three years.

It happened again the first time I tried to impress a girl with my airplane.

Mimi, of Lyon, France, ran the restaurant of that name in our First National Bank Building. Inevitably, while eating with Mimi, the subject of flying came up and first thing I knew I had committed myself to take Mimi for a ride.

When the great day arrived, everything was just perfect. It was a sparkling, clear, spring day. Not a breath of wind. We took off. Flew over the tall buildings of Atlanta, turned east to Stone Mountain, flew up, to and over Lake Lanier, where we got down low enough to see the sail boats.

I let Mimi fly the plane.

And I made an absolutely perfect landing.

In my headlong effort to impress, I also made a mistake.

On our airport we have a pilot named John, and John is a character. He built his own airplane — a little, two-seated, red aerobatic biplane about two-thirds normal size.

His specialty is flying young women in his airplane.

John is somewhat older than I am.

As we taxied back to our tie down, I mentioned John.

"You ought to go up in John's plane sometime."

After tying my plane down, Mimi and I strolled over to where John was sitting in his folding lawn chair by his little red biplane.

As soon as I introduced Mimi to John, I knew I had made a mistake. Her eyes kept going past me to the little red biplane.

Next thing I knew, John was helping Mimi into an aviatrix jacket — right out of the roaring twenties — and showing her how to don the leather helmet and goggles.

As they taxied away, John's white silk scarf blowing in the slip stream, I knew all was lost.

"You know, Clark," Mimi's eyes were sparkling as we drove back to Decatur, "you really should get an airplane like John's."

I felt just like I had when my first date spent my fifteen cents.

In the year 1956, I was about to make another major change of course.

My decision to enter professional politics did not come about easily.

My first taste of politics came about because of my political hero, Scott Candler.

Mr. Candler, my benefactor in the matter of getting my pension started when the VA wouldn't turn me loose, and in getting our first apartment in Mudville at Emory, was gone.

Politically gone, that is. His defeat was stunning to all who had watched as he ruled with an iron hand for 16 years.

He was defeated by a fish, which should have told me something about the vagaries of the political life. Actually, it was a picture of a man, his opponent, holding up a dead fish that appeared on the front page of the weekly newspaper that had recently surfaced in DeKalb. The caption said something to the effect that Mr. Candler's supporters, the wealthy developers, were trying to buy the election by giving away free fried fish at various free events to which the public was invited.

It was true the barbecues and fish fries were being sponsored by the developers, but it hardly seemed fair to associate Mr. Candler with a dead fish.

The voting public ate it up, of course.

I was asked, as the wounded hero, along with our school superintendent, to go on TV for Mr. Candler, which I was glad to do. I not only liked Mr. Candler personally, was grateful to him for helping me at two

critical crossroads of my life, but was convinced he was doing a good job
for us taxpaying citizens.

Mr. Candler was flamboyant, but I was convinced he knew not only
every road in the county, every curb, gutter and catch basin, but also
most of the people.

Our efforts on Mr. Candler's behalf were in vain.

Mr. Candler probably did know all the dairy farmers and other long
time residents, but in his desire to see the county grow, develop and attract new industry, a number of outlanders had been allowed to not only
infiltrate, but stay in residence long enough to have the franchise.

He not only was defeated, but he was defeated soundly by a little known
real estate broker who spent a minimum of money.

After his defeat was final, recorded and acknowledged, Mr. Candler
was asked, "What happened, Mr. Candler?"

"I didn't get enough votes," was his terse reply.

And that just about sums up the political game.

Mr. Candler has devoted all his energy to serving the county and it's
people for sixteen years. He had caused progress and had worked tirelessly for the downtrodden. The first time he had opposition, he was voted
out of office.

I resolved to remember that.

In the defeat, emotions were stirred to replace our one man form of
government with a multiple commission.

Mr. Candler's enemies wanted to divide authority because they said he
had been a dictator.

Mr. Candler's friends wanted to get back at the man who defeated him.

Pat Murphey's dad, who had served as mayor of Decatur called me.

"Clark," he said, "you run for one of the district commissioner jobs.
You can get elected."

Frances and I talked it over. Running around the country, pulling the
chair and my sample case in and out of the car, was definitely doing something to my kidneys. Politics sounded interesting — ours was the fastest
growing of the state's 159 counties and a lot was going on.

On the other hand, there was a stigma in the minds of most people
involving politicians. It always seemed strange to me that the one group
of people who distinguish a democracy from a totalitarian state should
be treated with such contempt by the beneficiaries of our free society.

Then I remember that what distinguishes a free society is our right to
gripe, complain and malign the boss.

Long may that freedom reign.

Dad said that he had been asked to run for the Fulton commission in years past but felt that he had more important things to do.

Even the Bible, in the book of Judges telling the fable of the trees, personifies the ruler as a bramble tree unable to produce fruit (like the vine) and therefore relegated to a political position.

But, I had seen what Scott did for me in my battle against the bureaucrats, and, once elected, the public official certainly seemed to be an independent cuss.

Besides, I needed a job.

Frances had had some experience working in a couple of campaigns and, as the daughter of a high official, knew something of living in the general spotlight.

We went to work.

Even before the law establishing the new commission passed, we had friends typing letters for us saying I was going to run.

A friend who had served in the legislature offered to introduce me to the business people in his community.

"The first time you run," he said, "it's a lot of fun. After that it gets to be work."

In the years following, I realized how true that was.

As soon as the bill passed, I went to work campaigning full time.

I had served the previous year as president of our Jaycees. The Jaycees were committed to me — we were the same generation.

There were nine of us in the race for the first district seat.

We moved around to the meetings held over the county and soon came to know each other well. I was the only one in a wheelchair, of course, but I decided I needed to do more to distinguish myself in the crowd. We would sit on the stage at the local schoolhouse behind a long table and would speak in turn. I always tried to manuever so that I would be at the end of the table and the last one to speak.

And I wore red suspenders and took off my coat, just like ole Gene Talmadge, so I'd look different from the business suit crowd.

Of course, I made a big thing out of the fact I had been a private in the army.

The meetings were sparsely attended and consisted primarily of the relatives of the candidates.

I served eight years as a county commissioner and ran three campaigns. The thing that intrigued me was how, over the years, the same subjects were hashed and rehashed over and over. The same solutions were offered to the same old problems and each time as if a bright new day was about to dawn because of the bold and innovative program that would be brought to fruition by the brilliance of the candidate. Potholes in the roads were always very big and a sure campaign winner. One innovative candidate got his picture in the paper by planting a pine tree in one of the pot holes. And, of course, zoning was big and kept getting bigger. A master plan was needed. Build the industrial tax base. Conserve the integrity of the neighborhood. The garbage problem.

One of the candidates had his own speechwriter, a portly gentleman of mature years. I remember watching him at our historic, schoolhouse political confrontations, sitting on a front row, tears rolling down his cheeks as he tried to contain the merriment our posturing and proclaiming were bringing him.

Politics got me out among people.

What I remember most vividly was campaigning for the black vote. Nobody really knew how to get the black vote, but we had all heard stories of payoffs to certain leaders who could 'deliver' the black vote. I always enjoyed politicking for the black vote. The meetings were held in the churches, and we got to hear some really rich singing and preaching along with the politicians.

On one occasion, I felt I got close to the real thing in seeking the key to the black vote. A friend told me to call a certain captain in the Atlanta police force. I did and the captain arranged for me to meet him in the heart of the black community at a place called "Blue Heaven". I was told I would get to meet a gentleman known as "The Goat" who was the head of the "Bug" operation for that part of the City.

As everyone knew, the "Bug" was a numbers game that was played by blacks primarily and that allegedly enjoyed police protection. It was played on certain stock quotation numbers that appeared in the daily papers and could be played for one penny up. A five cent bet was common and could result in a substantial payoff.

The police captain and I pulled up outside "Blue Heaven" and in a few minutes, apparently by pre-arrangement, a young man in bermuda shorts, long socks and what we used to call in college a "pork pie" flat — rimmed hat, came out to the car. This turned out to the Goat's son who was home for the summer from Harvard University. He apologized and said that his dad was out at the moment but would join us shortly.

In a few minutes, a large new Mercury automobile parked in front of us and a neatly dressed Negro took the captain's place in my car. We had a pleasant conversation. He expressed his desire for good government and I assured him I was for the same thing. We shook hands and parted. I don't know whether the Goat delivered the Negro vote, but he must have because we won.

We had spent $1300. Three hundred was money Frances and I put up. The other thousand was contributions. It was strictly a penny-ante effort.

Our big splash was ten big banners we strung across various parts of town touting my candidacy. A friend got the cloth donated, my brother-in-law, Wales, laid out the lettering and made ten copies by punching holes with nail and hammer. Then we doled them out to friends to get them painted. One couple painted theirs on the top of their dining room table, leaving an outline on the delicate surface where the paint seeped through the nail holes.

The Jaycees hung the banners. They didn't stay up long because nobody asked permission. As Hal, the past state Jaycee president said, "We didn't know who to ask."

The night before the election, my strongest opponent bought five minutes on TV. By the time I had heard his talk I felt like withdrawing. If that fellow did all he proposed, we were headed for Beulah Land.

Later, he became a multi-millionaire. He has always given me credit for making him rich — by getting him out of politics.

When Scott Candler was defeated in 1954 after sixteen years as sole commissioner someone asked him why he lost.

It bears repeating.

"I didn't get enough votes."

Which summarizes the political way of life. I had started early, and I had gotten the votes. I had asked more people to vote for me. That's really all it takes.

I was about to learn a lot about politics and the larger world. Politics is one field where you talk to and are involved with people from every segment of the human scale — especially is this true of the local county commissioner.

Our phone started ringing in the day time. And our phone started ringing at night.

People love to engage their county commissioner in coversation. For one thing, they pay his salary. For another, you could never tell when you might get something for nothing.

When I'd visit a neighborhood that had a problem, I was taken on a tour. All the local needs were exposed. The people seemed to feel the longer I could be retained the better the chances the government money would flow.

As my friend, Ernie Vandiver, who had pledged me to my college fraternity and who became governor, told me, "Clark, I don't ever get to ride on any good roads. Everytime I visit around the state, I'm ridden around on the worst roads — the ones my host wants fixed."

I was idealistic about politics and politicians and suppose I remain so today. The politicians are the only ones who distinguish our system from that of Soviet Russia, which is, to my way of thinking, a bureaucracy run amok and uncontrollable by the people who suffer under it.

To me, politics was a way to attempt to give meaning to my life. My Dad had done it by helping young people learn to earn a living in a harsh world. Local politics was a way I could help people, and try to help make their lives better and richer.

After I was gunned down by the German sniper, my most fervent prayer was to get in a position, some day, some way, where I could make a difference. Where I wouldn't be helpless and where I could change things.

Fortunately, I also learned to have some fun out of politics.

I enjoyed the game and I learned to play it with a certain amount of skill.

For one thing, you returned calls at noon or at five o'clock. That way you could clear your stack of notes without having to talk to many people.

The best way to get away from an embarrassing situation was to keep talking. Once, when invited to North Atlanta, I was told the citizenry were really lying in wait for me.

It took me 45 minutes to answer the first question.

"Are there any more questions?" I asked brightly.

Someone moved we adjourn.

I enjoyed the other commissioners.

Claude Blount, our chairman, had run the Decatur branch of our Atlanta based bank. He had done everything from making loans to sweeping the sidewalk in the morning.

"I was out sweeping one morning," Claude said, "when an old man who banked with us walked out and got into his big Buick. 'Is there anything coming, Claude?' he hollered. I looked both ways on East Court square. There were some cars parked across the street up against the court square, but no moving traffic.

'It's all clear,' I said.

The old man put the big car in reverse, backed all the way across the street and banged into one of the parked cars.

'Damn it, Claude,' he shouted, 'I thought you said it was clear.'"

People in town loved to tell of Mr. Blount's cold banker ways.

One of the stories fancied Claude had left the banking business and gone into the service station business. He was ready when his first customer drove in, his banking experience backing him up.

"How much gas you want?" Claude asked.

"Ten gallons" was the reply.

"How far you going?" the former banker inquired.

"Macon."

Looking at the customer with a cold and appraising eye, Mr. Blount asked,

"Don't you think you could make it on five?"

Mr. Blount's humor was low key, very dry, and it carried a barb.

Julian Harris represented Stone Mountain, and Stone Mountain is famous for its characters. On one occasion, the five of us were attending a public event in the town.

One of the town characters, a woman of long life who seemed some-what addled. She was wearing white men's socks that came halfway up her calf and a funny hat, and she had Mr. Blount by the lapels when Julian walked up. Julian represented the district in which Stone Moun-tain was located.

"You know, Mrs. Smith," he said, looking at Julian out of the corner of his eye, "we had all voted to pave that street, but Mr. Harris wouldn't let us do it."

With that, he turned and walked off, leaving Julian to finish the conversation.

My turn came when we were attending a meeting with the officials of General Motors. I was puffing the project and growing expansive when our chairman leaned forward.

"You can't believe everything Clark says, you know."

In those early days, things were pretty simple and we didn't have much in the way of staff to complicate them. Mr. Blount handled the money and had an excellent philosophy regarding other matters.

When a group came to him with a project, he would ask.

"What's it going to cost?"

If they said "nothing", he said, "Well, go ahead and do it then."

Zoning was right enjoyable in those days. The county was still relative-ly sparsely settled and opposition to development was correspondingly meager. I tried to be conscientious and made it a point to visit all the proposed sites with the planning director before meeting time. Walt, who represented the south end of the county and who had come up the hard way — driving a sand truck to get started as a contractor — was a strong advocate of letting people use their property any way they wanted to.

I remember one meeting in particular. We had lunch at the country club as usual and Walt had imbibed somewhat.

As soon as the announcement was made for the first zoning, Walt said gruffly.

"I move we approve that corner for a service station."

"Wait a minute, Walt," I reminded him, "we haven't heard the argu-ments yet.

Everybody dreamed of having a corner zoned so they could sell to an oil company as a service station. The developers in those innocent days had a couple of tricks they used to cash in on what they considered their hard work, their investment, and their foresight.

For one thing, they would develop their subdivision of houses, leaving the two corners where the street joined the main road marked "Reserved" on the subdivision plat. The rest of the development was covered by covenants that assured their use for single family residences for the next twenty years. Then, when all the houses were sold, the developer would apply for commercial zoning for the corners.

Soon, the county was stepping in with requirements that made such shenanigans impossible.

We were without much staff assistance in the early days and the county was without a professional purchasing agent. A good part of each meeting was spent trying to decide which vendor's products to buy. It always amazed me the hours we would spend trying to decide which offering of tires to buy. As a friend of mine who was in the business expressed it:

"Tires can be made from anything from crocker sack and chewing gum up."

Politicians live and die by what's said about them in the newspapers and on the radio and TV — the most important thing, however, is to be sure something is said, and said as often as possible.

Charlie, our representative of the area that included a part of the City of Atlanta, was especially sensitive on this issue.

"Where are the photographers?" Charlie shouted as he arrived in a rush, a few minutes late for one public happening.

"They just left, Charlie."

"Damn!" he clinched his fist, "I might as well not come."

Charlie's district represented one of the more earthy and urban parts of our largely rural county and he had some special problems as a result.

"Some drunk is always calling me about one in the morning," he told us. "But I get even. I listen carefully to what he has to say and then I ask him to give me his name and phone number so I can report back to him.

"About four a.m., I always get up to go to the bathroom. I walk by the phone, pick it up, and dial the number of my earlier caller. By that time he is really zonked out. Hello', I say,'this is your commissioner. I need you to clarify one thing about your problem.'"

Charlie really got nailed one time, and he was completely innocent. We were in the middle of a drought and everybody in the county had been asked to conserve water. They were not to water their lawns or wash their cars in particular.

Charlie lived inside an area of the county that was served by the City of Atlanta water system. The city had plenty of water and no restrictions applied to Charlie's neighborhood.

Especially hard hit in the water scarcity on the county's system was an area that Charlie represented. They were at the end of a long main, were on high ground, and literally were without water for part of every day.

They came to see Charlie about the situation and they were mad. Since Charlie was a commissioner, their anger focused on him.

"You know," Charlie said, "I have a big yard and I have an underground sprinkler system. I had just planted some grass seed and I had all five sprinklers going full blast. I mean, you couldn't come on the property without going through a shower."

And, of course, the visitors didn't know Charlie was on the Atlanta system.

In the condition they were in, it probably wouldn't have helped if they had known.

Nobody liked the City either.

Being a politician I found was much like being a doctor. You had to tell people what they expected to hear, you had to be an expert in every regard and you must never let your sense of humor be exposed. A friend of mine who is a cancer specialist told me as we compared notes on our divergent careers, "What gets me," the specialist, who is unusually down to earth, said, "is when I tell people 'I am very sorry, but there is nothing I can do.' 'I know doc,' they will reply, 'but what are going to DO?"

People want you to be serious about their problem, no matter what your mood may be at the moment, and they want you to DO something no matter how impossible, unfair or uneconomic correcting the problem might be.

I worked hard at the job. I was out every day going to meetings, driving out to look at zoning and problems I was called about. Three or four nights a week, I'd be at a dinner meeting, and I'd get several calls, most of them angry ones after I got home.

I learned some do's and don't's about politics.

For one thing, you learn never to admit a mistake in politics. To do so is taken as a sign of weakness and immediately exploited by the opposition. Nothing puts an end to a political encounter like the words, spoken with a superior air, "He admitted it himself."

When things go afoul, never apologize. Say nothing, assuming an air that implies superior knowledge, or change the subject by asking your opponent an embarrassing question.

On the other hand, if some project turns out well, immediately take credit, preferably before as many cameras and reporters as possible. Once you have taken credit for something, it is hard for the opposition to take the credit away.

There is a rough sort of justice in the politician taking all the credit he can get. You soon learn you are blamed and held responsible for anything that goes wrong in the great broad county, no matter who sowed the seeds of any particular disaster.

I used to almost break out in a rash every time it rained hard. I knew I was going to get a call from a lady in North DeKalb. My heart bled for her. Every rain, she was the first one to have her basement flooded. The commission had taken the position that other taxpayers shouldn't have to pay for the mistake builders had made in building in a flood plain and the purchaser had made in buying a house in a low lying area.

But that didn't help the lady. She felt her government shouldn't have allowed the house to be built in that location.

She had a point — which was what made it so hard to talk to her.

Names are always a problem, of course. The people who come to see you or who meet you on the street once you've been exposed on television know you. And they expect you to know who they are — particularly if they have ever written you a letter.

A sharp staff can help. I remember visiting one of our colorful governors and seeing a letter I had written several months prior lying face up on the desk in front of him.

In fact, one of the stock statements by the more daring public figure is "I got your letter" on the assumption anybody who would take the trouble to go see the governor had probably written a letter.

A quick change of subject erased any error — and when a letter had been written, the citizen marveled at the mental power of his leader.

And, of course, you never have to worry about what was in the letter. The citizen will waste no time in telling you that.

It was also important to look the other party directly in the eye, particularly when you couldn't come up with his name. Having spent a lot of time and money acquainting people with my own name, it always puzzled me that some people want to keep their name secret. I always tell anybody I don't see every day who I am. Then, I spell it if there seems to be any doubt about their understanding just who I am.

As a member of the board of commissioners, I learned to spar with the other politicians and came to feel at ease during and after these contests.

We learned to argue forcefully with one another in our public meetings, becoming red of face, gesturing and experienceing real anger. Then, we'd all go to lunch together and have as much fun as a bunch of thieves. There were so many more of the public than there were of us that we developed a certain comradery.

It was always better to listen to all sides before making a decision. The situation was often the reverse of what was first perceived.

On the other hand, I learned to take a strong position as soon as possible on a really hot issue that was dividing the public.

As long as you were undecided, both sides would call and come to see you. Once you came down flat-footed on one side or another, the advocates would leave you in peace while they concentrated on the vote that might still be changed.

It was a game, and I came to enjoy the meetings and the back-room maneuvering to accomplish things I thought to be worthwhile.

On the other hand, some things I never did learn to enjoy.

I didn't like making promises that could not be fulfilled because of the limited resources of the county, and I didn't like defending policies that didn't make sense to me, but that I couldn't change.

I was the spokesman for the commission when we held public meetings promoting our bond issue. It was the largest one to that date and included $5 million for the roads. We re-paved two hundred miles with the money. We extended water and sewer lines. The most important issue was general obligation bonds to be matched with revenue bonds to build a county hospital. DeKalb General has since grown to over 400 beds and is the second largest hospital in the Metro are.

I enjoyed the experience, but I wasn't getting rich. The salary for the part time job, at which I was spending full time, was $250 a month.

And I was frustrated by the fact I was constantly defending county policies that I had had little to do with establishing and that, in some cases, I felt were pretty stupid.

Most importantly, we constantly heard of real problems for which we had no solution, primarily because there were insufficient funds available.

I would sit in Mr. Blount's office and imagine what it would be like to be on his side of the desk, where I could really do something. I made up my mind then that I wasn't going to serve another term as a district commissioner. I was going to be Chairman or I was going to get out.

Mr. Blount had made it clear he would not run again and I discussed my ambitions with him.

"One of these days, Clark," he told me, "they will ask you to run and you won't have any trouble. Be patient."

I didn't know who "they" were but I had no intention of waiting for "them" to make up "their" minds.

The general public probably didn't realize the accomplishments of those four years, and Claude Blount was so modest in telling his own story, that they would never learn it from him. We passed the biggest bond issue to date, brought DeKalb General Hospital into being, and the county finances were in excellent shape. I will never forget Claude Blount's answer when someone asked him what kind of commissioner he had made.

"Well," he said, a wry smile barely shaping his thin lips, a twinkle in his cold banker's eye, "I'd say I was kind of mediocre."

How could you help but love a guy like that?

CHAPTER XXIII

As in the past, it was another paraplegic who convinced me I could learn to fly.

Vince, who has my same level of paraplegia, but is ten years younger met me at the Calhoun airport.

"There's nothing to it, Clark," he said, "or at least there is nothing you can't do because you can't move your legs."

"Do you really use the plane to take trips?"

He described several recent ones.

Vince told me he flies every week, usually taking the single engine plane up for a few touch and goes, or taking a friend sight seeing. Vince runs his own jewelry store to meet his part of the plane's expenses. He has partners to help defray the cost of flying.

After I flew with Vince, I visited Epps Flight School.

I didn't know it at the time, but I had been preceded.

In politics, you get to know people in every walk of life, black, white, rich and poor. Frank Putnam is a pilot with many thousands of hours of flying time. A contractor who lays pipelines, his twin engine plane has been used to follow and check pipe line construction and to take him to bid openings all over the U. S.

"You won't have any trouble, Clark," he assured me. "All you have to do is follow that needle and it will take you anywhere you want to go."

Without my knowledge, Frank had talked to Pat Epps. Epps was the first tenant in the county airport after we received the property back from the U.S. Navy. Pat's father was one of the pioneers of aviation. Pat's father built his own plane not long after the Wright brothers made their first powered flight.

Pat has flown every kind of plane, every kind of place, and in every kind of weather.

305

Among other aerobatic stunts, Pat flies his Bonanza upside down just above the runway at the annual air show.

"You really think Clark could fly?" he asked Frank.

"I don't know why not. The only thing you use your feet for is the rudder, and you don't do much of that once you're in the air."

"What about coming in, in a strong cross wind?"

"Well," Frank said, "I didn't say it would be easy."

"We'll talk to some people."

When I visited Pat for the first time, he was ready.

Clint Rodgers and Steve Shaner of the flight school had already done some investigating and had learned that a hand control was available and that pilots were flying with the control in some numbers on the west coast.

They had obtained a rudder bar and had modified the nose wheel steering on one of the school's Warriors, so the device could be used on the late model Cherokee. Both Clint and Steve had learned to fly by hand control.

Everything was ready to go. But I had a problem. No money.

In other words, it was a time for holding on rather than for flying. It would be two years before I'd take my first lesson.

Fortunately, I had had some experience at hunkering down while the storm raged. In 1956, while running for my first term as a county commissioner, I was beginning to reap the harvest from the abuse my kidneys had suffered. Sitting at an office desk for three years had taken a toll and pushing the wheelchair up and down hot summer sidewalks as a drummer had compounded the problem.

A few weeks after I was wounded, I was taken to the operating room by a young Harvard med school graduate known affectionately to the patients as "Skin Head" — because of his GI haircut — Brown.

Since I had no feeling below my chest, Skin Head didn't bother to put me to sleep as he cut a notch in my lower abdomen. The idea was to let the catheter into my bladder that way, thereby releasing other things for other uses.

They did put a little screen up between me and the surgeons, but I could watch in the mirrorlike rim of the big surgical light. Skin Head drew a line and started cutting.

"Look at that," Skin Head said, "that's the (some big latin name)."

"Naw, it ain't," said his assistant, "that's the (another big latin word)."

"Hey, Harrison," he looked over the screen at me, "take a deep breath."

"You see," Skin Head crowed, "it is the (big word). See how it pooches out when he breathes."

The only other event I remember happening during the operation was things getting real quiet for a few minutes and then Skin Head softly muttering.

"Oh, Oh!"

Considering the area in which he was working, I never forgave him for that.

The suprapubic catheter worked pretty well and certainly allowed me to do things I couldn't have done with the alternative. There were two problems with it, however.

First, it got harder and harder to replace the catheter, a job I did myself. It was a mushroom type which meant a stiff wire probe had to be run through the catheter, and the rubber stretched tight to make the end small enough to go through the opening in my abdomen into the bladder. When the wire was removed, the mushroom end would flatten out and hold the catheter inside.

I used a straightened coat hanger. As time went on, it took more pushing to get the thing in place, and occasionally the wire would slip through the opening at the mushroom end and I would stab myself.

But the biggest problem was the fact that the bladder was constantly draining and constantly empty. And more and more scar tissue was forming from my self stabbings when I changed the catheter.

For thirteen years, the suprapubic catheter going through my abdomen wall into the bladder had drained it constantly and every day, for thirteen years, I had taken eight sulphur tablets and drank nearly a gallon of water.

Now, half-way through my first term as commissioner, the fever came and the cold chills — repeating what had happened at New Haven, but more severe — the cold sweat covering my body and making my teeth chatter.

It happened about once a month.

And then it began to happen more often.

By careful planning, I managed to make my commitments during the week so I could be sick on the weekend.

"You've got a good bit of pus, Clark. You'd better take three or four shots of combiotic."

Then it became worse, and the chills and fever came more often. Frances and I had to give up long trips. If I drove more than 100 miles, the infection would start. We began going to a nearby mountain resort rather than to Florida for our vacation.

But I didn't let up. I would go to a meeting with my head buzzing, my vision clouded by the infection. I would literally hang on as the meeting would drag on and on.

Then, the infection reached my inner ear, a strange sensation. I couldn't sit between the arms of the wheelchair without holding on. If I turned loose, I would begin to sway.

Then it became really bad. The infection — so long battled — gradually and inexorably built and spread. I became very sick, took to bed, and was on the edge of delirium. Through a red haze, I would see a grotesque dwarf perched on the end of my nose leering into my eyes. I'd close my eyes and on the inside of my eyelids see a movie newsreel, all of Hitler's SA, SS, brown shirts, hysterical followers massed and marching in a

In 1958, I was dying of kidney infection. Pictured is DeKalb County's first multiple commission. Standing from left, Julian Harris, Walt Toney, Charlie Parker, Claude Blount and Wheat Williams — the man who defeated Scott Candler.

Nuremberg rally. Open my eyes, it would go away, close my eyes, and the troops would march again.

For hours, I'd sit clasping a hot water bottle against my chest. Sedated by the fever, if I didn't move, I'd finally become warm and sleepy and comfortable.

But then would come the nausea, the swollen abdomen. The feeling now that something was wrong inside of me. I'd never felt like this, something was giving away, deteriorating inside of me. My strength ebbed and flowed, but the periods of strength were less frequent and lasted for only short periods of time.

"Dear God, I am dying. In all the years, through all the rest, I have never felt like I was dying. But that is how I feel now, that is what is happening." It was a feeling inside that something was crumbling and when it went I would go too.

Others have willed themselves to die. But I found out now I didn't want to die. I remember Curly Williams. He had to have surgery at Lawson for his kidney.

"I can feel, Clark. And I can't take an anesthetic. You find out when the time comes what you'll do to live."

The shock to act came when a young doctor, assistant to Dr. McGeachy came to see me. He was getting ready to leave private practice and go to work for the VA in Florida.

"It's a beautiful place," he told me, "great golf course, and I'll have plenty of time to look after my investments."

I'll bet you will doc. I thought bitterly of my brief exposure to the VA hospital.

Then he became philosophical.

"You know, Clark, dying's not so bad. I see people die every day and it's really not bad at all."

And suddenly I realized that not only had this casual young man given me up — so had my other doctors here.

I have always tried to maintain an optimistic attitude, but I found out then that I can really get into action when the chips are down.

Frances is the same way. We got together and decided it was time to look beyond the local medical fraternity and see if there wasn't a doctor somewhere in the U. S. who could offer a little positive hope for the situation.

I had read about a new procedure to reroute the kidney evacuation function. When I asked my urologist about the operation, he looked at me, his lips a tight line, and he frowned.

He looked like an unfriendly undertaker.

From the way he described the operation, I got the impression it was about as new to him as it was to me.

A good friend in my Civitan club is a general surgeon and he promised to look into the matter.

"Ernie," I told him, "I want somebody who's done this one not once or twice but who does five a week."

I will never forget the night we got the answer. I was too sick to go to our Civitan meeting. To my surprise, the entire club came to our house. After we met and talked, everybody left except my friend Ernie, the surgeon.

"Clark," he said, "there are two places in the country that do the operation. One is in Cleveland. The other is the Mayo Clinic.

That settled it for us. We knew about the Mayo Clinic.

I went to the door with Ernie. The rest of the club was still there, standing around in the yard, talking.

Ernie's car was blocking the drive and rather than disturb our talk, they had all waited. Tears came to my eyes as I realized their concern.

I knew Mayo's was a great place. We had had one of their doctors at Lawson. He had left a legacy.

We'd see Major Baker pass through the ward from time to time. Everybody liked him and would holler 'hey, doc' as he walked past.

One day, he was working on a patient and he knocked over a full flask of sterile water, creating a big mess of crushed glass and water.

Our nurse was enraged.

She didn't know the Major. He had on his whites and no insignia. She thought he was a ward boy.

"You get in there right now," she shouted, "you get a mop. You clean this mess up."

Major Baker looked at her, turned and walked away. A few minutes later he returned, bearing a mop and a mop bucket. He proceeded to mop, carefully squeezing the mop into the bucket. He took paper towels and gathered up the scraps of glass very carefully. Then he took everything back into the supply room and completed the clean up of his equipment.

When I went to Mayo to have my kidney surgery, I called Dr. Baker and asked him if the story we had heard all over Lawson in 1945 was true.

"Yes, it was," he told me. "It was just too good an opprortunity to miss. You know, the Mayo Clinic has its stories and its traditions.

When the Clinic was still run by the two brothers, they started taking turns about going to Europe to study with the great doctors there. After their reputations were established, the European doctors began to return the visits and spend time here.

"Rochester was just a little middle western town at the time and there were no doctors. So, the brothers built a big house so guests could stay with them.

"In Europe, on retiring for the night, hotel guests leave their shoes or boots in the hallway outside their door. The staff cleans and polishes the footwear and leaves it in place for use the next day.

"It never occurred to the Mayo visitors that the brothers didn't have a staff of servants, so they would do as they were accustomed when traveling and leave their shoes outside their bedroom door.

"The Mayos had no servants, of course, but they would never mention the fact. The doctor in residence would wait until everybody was asleep, then he'd collect the shoes, take them to the kitchen and do a good job of cleaning and shining. The guests never suspected anything, but everybody at the Clinic told the story.

"The thing that happened at Lawson was too good to pass up.

"Next day, I put on my full regalia with the Major's insignia and made my rounds. The nurse nearly disappeared through the floor."

The story told the spirit at Mayo.

Mayo was one of the few places in my medical wanderings where the professionals would listen.

I told the doctor there, "Doc," I said when I was being interviewed for the first time, "I have always told the doctors how to treat me. But I figure now that I'm at the Mayo Clinic you probably know as much about my case as I do. So, I'm going to put myself entirely in your hands." He didn't smile. He replied very seriously. "It is interesting you would say that, Mr. Harrison. We have a saying at the Mayo Clinic. 'Listen to your patient, he may be trying to tell you something'."

Mayo's was a revelation to me. Located in two huge multi-story buildings, the Clinic housed over eight hundred doctors. When I had worked for the hospital supply company, I had found about half of the surgical instruments we sold had Mayo as part of their name. Now I understood why.

Over a hundred thousand people came to the clinic each year from all over the world to be treated. Many operations done there routinely did not become part of the general medical picture until years later.

"It is strange that you were sent to me as soon as you got here," Dr. DeWeerd told me. "You would have ended up here eventually. I am the only surgeon who does the operation."

After my second day of testing, I heard two doctors, who were not aware I was listening, discussing my case.

"We don't need anything else," one was saying, "it's obviously his kidneys."

Dr. DeWeerd went into details.

"Clark," he said, "your kidneys are gradually being destroyed because they cannot be drained normally. Unless the pressure is relieved, you will die. The only thing we don't know is how long they can hold out. We don't have any records to show how fast this is progressing. You could live a year, you might live fifteen, but we know this will kill you unless something is done."

He then explained that two different surgical approaches had been tried in the past, neither of which was successful. First, the kidney tubes were tied into the colon, which produced constant diarrehea and infection. Then, they were opened directly through the back and the patient stayed wet all the time.

Finally he described the operation they would do on me.

"We will remove a short section of your small intestine from the intestinal tract," he said. "We will leave it connected to its blood supply but will sew your intestinal tract back together so the drainage will not affect that. This eight inch section will be closed at one end, the tubes from your kidneys will be tied into it and the other end will open out to the surface in your lower abdomen. We will locate it low enough not to interfere with your pocket watch in case you ever want to carry one," he said with a twinkle in his eye.

At this point, an appliance would be glued over the opening to conduct the urine into a leg bag.

For the recently injured, the whole process would sound like the end of normal life. To me it was a reprieve and a return to health and strength.

After I had talked to Dr. DeWeerd, I left and went back to our hotel room.

As I came down the hall, a man was opening the door to his room. He stopped and came over to me.

One of the interesting things at Mayo's is the way complete strangers will sit at the same table in the cafeteria, or in the lobby of a hotel and share their deepest concerns. There is something in the atmosphere that seems to invoke this freedom.

"I have just been told that my wife is dying," the man said, "she is a beautiful young woman in the prime of her life and I'm about to lose her."

He paused and then said something I have never forgotten.

"I just don't believe this world was meant to be our home."

I went into my room and closed the door. Suddenly a warm glow came over my whole body. I have never had a greater feeling of peace and complete security. I was about to have intricate surgery involving a team of five doctors working for several hours. I felt absolutely no fear and was to feel none throughout the preparatory period, the day of the operation, or during my recovery. I knew that God was with me and that I would be healed.

After the operation, I spent several days in the hospital, then was returned to the hotel room.

"Well, Clark," Dr. DeWeerd told me when I revisited his office, "You can go home Saturday." He looked at his calendar.

"Do you realize that will be exactly two weeks after your surgery. I've never seen anybody heal so fast."

When we got back to Decatur, I was well for the first time in thirteen years, and I was never again to be threatened by serious kidney infection. For the first time since I had been wounded, I was physically strong and healthy and I was through taking anti-biotics.

Not only had my life been saved, but Dr. DeWeerd's skill had given me a new active life to live.

He was not the only one who had been pulling for me.

After the operation was successfully behind us, Dr. DeWeerd told me. "Did you know your wife visited me the afternoon before I operated." Then he told me what happened.

"Why are you coming to see me, young lady?" Dr. DeWeerd, staff surgeon at one of the greatest clinics in the world, asked.

"Well, doctor," Frances replied, "you are going to operate on my husband in the morning and I wanted to be sure you are feeling all right."

"Yes, I feel just fine," he replied. "I'd also like you to know that I am not going out and get drunk tonight. I'm going to a Methodist church supper and I will be in bed by 10 p.m. Furthermore, if I don't feel absolutely tip top in the morning, I won't operate on your husband."

Dr. DeWeerd looked at me.

"I'd hang on to her, Clark."

CHAPTER XXIV

"I don't believe this!" the nurse pumped up the rubber sleeve and listened to the stethoscope held to my arm. "Your blood pressure is 104 over 68."

"What does that mean?" I asked.

She looked at me and grinned, "It means you're going to live forever."

I had finally gotten my finances in a shape where I felt I could take flying lessons without offending my creditors. The first step was to have a physical exam and secure a third class medical certificate — good for the two years I figured it would take for me to qualify as a pilot.

By the time I reported to Epps Flight School, Clint had already instructed two wheelchair aviators, one a young man who had completed over three hundred parachute jumps as a sky diver before finding that he had multiple sclerosis. The other was a young woman, paralyzed by polio, who was active in sports and worked in a government job promoting the rights of the disabled.

"I won't help you unless you ask me," Clint said, "and there won't be any lowering of standards. You will have to meet the same criteria as any of our students. My job is to teach you enough to keep you from killing yourself — then you have to teach yourself to fly."

Clint was an Air Force pilot for eight years, flying the hottest pursuit plane the service had to offer. In addition to teaching beginners, he instructs in aerobatics and flies when the weather keeps the other pilots on the ground.

"Strive for perfection," Clint said. "Don't be any less than the best."

From the beginning, both of us knew we had a problem. Being paralyzed was the least of my disabilities. There were the matters of being 55 years old and a former politician.

315

"What you don't realize, Clint, I told him, "is that I spent eight years as a politician. You want me to be precise. If a politician gets specific and precise, he's dead."

"I understand," Clint rejoined, "but in this business, if you aren't precise, you really are dead."

I explained to him that I had a balance problem. With no control of the muscles from the chest down, I had a tendency to fall over.

"Well," he said, "let's try and see how it goes. You remember that saying from the old army air corp days, 'The difficult we do at once, the impossible takes a little time'".

The first few times we turned on final and I reached down to pull the flaps, I would fall over on Clint. Unperturbed, he would wait until I righted myself, keeping the Warrior on course until I did.

"Clark," he said, "I could teach a chimpanzee to land the plane."

I started bringing a banana to my lessons.

One thing we were determined to do was to get me to the point that I could do everything without assistance.

One of the obstacles to be overcome was how to get the wheelchair up on the wing. I had discovered it was no problem getting myself on the wing. Vince had shown me the secret — a strap across the top of the bars that held the foot rests. I hooked my heels on the strap, then I pivoted onto the wing and transferred my feet into the seat of the wheelchair and pulled myself on up the sloping wing.

Then, I would pull the chair up backwards. But it took all my strength and it was apparent to me that on a bad day I wouldn't make it.

It was just one of a series of small obstacles Clint and I were to tackle and overcome in the early days.

However, this obstacle looked like one that could be fatal to my idea of being able to eventually go to the airport, do the inspections, get in and take off all without assistance. Canoeing had been a pleasure for several years, but I couldn't do that without substantial help getting into and out of the boat. I wanted to be able to go flying on my own schedule.

One day I went out to the airport to find that we weren't going to be able to fly because of the weather. That happened maybe five times during my training for my private license. Clint flew when the crows were grounded.

With nothing to do, I decided to go out and think about the situation. I rolled around a Warrior that was a duplicate of the one we flew and I thought and I prayed and I asked for wisdom.

Suddenly the answer came. Why not turn the chair over backwards! I got excited, pulled alongside the wing of the Warrior and hoisted myself up on it. I slid up on the wing, then grabbed the handle bar on the back of the chair, pushed the chair forward and pulled down. The chair teetered momentarily, then tipped backwards, the handle bars coming to rest on the tarmac with the little wheels pointing toward the sky.

I maneuvered the chair around so the big wheels were against the trailing edge of the wing. Then I grabbed the little wheel, revolved the chair foot rests downward and pulled. The chair rolled up on the wing — no lifting or tugging to it. And the last obstacle rolled aside as I sat with the chair beside me, ready to be folded and put behind the pilot's seat.

I felt the same kind of exultation I had felt when I returned home from Mayo and the successful operation. I had a new life.

In 1958 I had a new vitality and I was ready for any challenge.

I had taken eight sulphur tablets every day, day in and day out for thirteen years. The infection had been constant, held at bay by sulfur and penicillin, the only guards between the paraplegic and death. The side effects were a general weakness, a slowing down of all the body funcions. This was the ball and chain, the weight that dragged and against which I had struggled.

The greatest battles fought in this world are not on the fields of combat. The greatest battles are fought by those with no strength to fight against odds of overwhelming magnitude. Grim battles, silently fought, never relenting.

Take no credit for struggle, when you have strength and will to struggle. Such struggle is the stuff and substance of life. Your obstacle is your stimulant, your work is your rest.

For the first time, I could work hard, play hard, and rest easy, sleeping through the night. They were days of Little League with Tom. Frances and I went to every game, every practice.

That year was a year of creative days, work for new thoroughfares, sidewalks to schools, traffic signals needed in growing new suburbs, and work with the professional planners.

The county acquired a new airport, the old Naval Air Station, the field where our ambulance plane had landed when it returned me home. Private and corporate planes replaced the Navy fighters on the field.

We named the field DeKalb — Peachtree.

I never dreamed one day I would be calling Peachtree Tower as a pilot.

It was a pioneer time in the county. We made the plans that would mature in a great new metropolitan city — planned the six great industrial areas, the perimeter expressway with its extending spokes, the MARTA rapid rail lines that would become reality in the years ahead.

I watched new subdivisions grow, new homes be built — at the rate of five thousand a year — new neighborhoods become reality.

Sewer lines that reduced the danger of pollution and helped preserve stream life, water lines that were the life blood of development reached out into what had been farmland.

My vote and my work helped build a good community, a vibrant, living thing. And because I had come so near to death one more time, I felt a love for life and those things that give and promote life, joy, expansion and participation. That create jobs and recreational opportunities for people.

I thanked God for my new life, for this wonderful year. Life is for the living, for taking risks, for breathing deeply of the challenge, the good and the bad.

But, as that wonderful year of fulfillment came to a close, I made a decision — to take a risk, the largest gamble I had ever taken.

I announced I would run for the chairmanship of the DeKalb County Commission, third most potent executive job in the state.

By the fall of 1959, my mind was made up.

I was not going to be a district commissioner again. I had spent four years going to meetings, answering citizen complaints, looking at zoning. I felt that I had done a good job and that I knew more about what was going on in the county than anyone who would be running.

While there were five commissioners under the multiple commission government, the chairman did the hiring and the firing and controlled preparation of the budget that was offered for approval of the board.

It never occurred to me that the fact I was in a wheelchair and would be only 37 when I took office would pose any political problem. I had been born and raised in the county, was a veteran and knew the county's business. My year of the peace that passeth understanding that followed the successful kidney operation was over. I may not have known I was getting in over my head, but my sub-conscious knew.

And, my stomach knew. Right after I made the official announcement, my stomach started to hurt. Since I have no feeling in my stomach, that was strange! It was a small hard pain concentrated right in the middle of my gut and it persisted on a daily basis all through the campaign.

I have thought a lot about whether a person should go in over his head — try something beyond his ability and resources. And I really believe, in my case at least, it is the only way I have been able to grow.

When I was a junior in high school, a group of us decided to start a school newspaper. A few issues had been printed by an earlier class, but we wanted to put one out on a regular basis.

I'll never forget our first issue. The night we were working to get it out, the mimeograph gave us all kinds of problems. We stayed at the local chamber of commerce office — they were letting us use their machine — until 3 a. m. The paper we passed around the next day was barely legible and full of errors.

But it was out. Then we set about improving it and the paper still is issued, printed professionally now, on a regular basis.

Over the years, as I have tried new things, I have thought about that night and that poorly printed paper. Make the dim outline of what you want to accomplish — then improve on it

In 1960, I was 36 years old, a nice young veteran in a wheelchair. Apparently, I decided later, that was the public perception of me. My own viewpoint was entirely different.

After serving four years as a district commissioner, I was convinced I knew more about DeKalb County than any other potential candidate for chairman, that I had worked harder, that I was more popular with the masses and more deserving. In fact, I felt the chairmanship belonged to me and once I let the public know I was willing to serve I would be swept into office by acclaimation.

Two of my fellow commissioners had reached the same conclusion concerning themselves.

Our commission meetings during the summer of the election became a circus.

And I was about to learn that going for the chairmanship was big league.

As the race began to heat up, the press seemed interested only in those off hand remarks that sounded innocent enough in casual conversation but which became sinister, stupid, or arrogant when displayed in bold headlines on page one or two.

Most of the news coverage seemed to concern fights between the other candidates.

For my part, I captured page one on only two occasions during the long hot summer.

The first time was when, at the urging of my Jaycee photographer, I got my picture taken in the wheelchair in the bucket of a front end loader some ten feet above the ground.

After the operation at the Mayo Clinic that saved my life, I was healthy for the first time in thirteen years.

And I was exuberant. Here, I get above the opposition in the 1960 race for chairman.

About the only votes that particular insanity got for me were to have me committed.

The other time I made the front page sealed my fate as far as the election was concerned.

HARRISON PROPOSES TO LICENSE
LITTLE LEAGUE TEAMS

Whatever goose I had was undoubtedly cooked at that moment.

I was just too dense and too enamored with my own visions of victory to realize what was going on.

In 1960, I was completely naive about big league political hostilities. I was about to receive my baptism of fire.

I had never borrowed substantial money other than my house mortgage, but I now became so convinced of my invincibility and the wide financial support I would receive once the campaign started rolling, that I decided to go to the bank.

Contributions up until the final weeks of the campaign had been, to say the least, disappointing. At my age, I hadn't accumulated any money, didn't have a big salary or substantial investments. And my friends were also young, trying to raise young families on insufficient incomes and were generally a poor source for funds for a political campaign.

The one group that did support me financially was the Jewish community. While I was commissioner, the orthodox synagogue bought land and applied for a permit to build in my district. There was opposition to the building, although our ordinance allowed churches in residential zones.

The vote was three to two and the synagogue was built. I was one of the three. To me there could have been no other vote.

And my Jewish friends didn't forget.

As usual, they remained a minority.

I didn't know it, but I was about to join them.

Claude Blount had been drafted to run by the movers and shakers, for the most part real estate developers and financial interests that had gone down in Scott Candler's stunning and unexpected defeat.

"One of these days, Clark," Mr. Blount had told me, "they will come and ask you to run. Then you won't have any problem."

Well, they certainly weren't coming in this election. One developer, Wash Lively, had made me the sole contribution from what was thought of as the 'power structure' — $175 — I will never forget that single check.

I didn't solicit the power stucture.

They did contact me — twice — through a friend — but it was in a vain effort to get me out of the race.

"Clark," my life time friend, told me, "I'm just delivering a message. They say their polls indicate you can't win but they feel like you will take votes from Charlie that might throw the election to one of the others."

He went on to express their concern and interest in me. If I would withdraw, they would pay all my campaign expenses to date and would assure me one of the top administrative jobs in the new government.

"They say Charlie plans to have four superchiefs who will divide the county departments between them," he said, "Charlie wants you to take one of those slots."

The idea that I could lose had never occurred to me and was, at age 36, totally unacceptable. Looking back over the hardship that followed the defeat I was about to suffer, I still wouldn't have changed my reply.

"You know," I said, "when I took the first dollar from the first contributor that foreclosed the possibility of my withdrawing from the race. I am convinced we will win, but even if I knew today for a certainty I will lose, my answer would have to be the same. Tell them there is only one job at the county I want, and I am running for it."

The shock that awaited me in my campaign was the unanimity with which the so called power structure moved. I didn't expect heavy contributions from the group, but, after all, I reasoned, I was a local lifetime citizen, a veteran of the big war and a nice fellow as well.

Outside my $175 from Wash, the tap was shut tight.

Until now, we had limited our advertising to small newspaper ads.

"Clark," my friend the advertising man told me, "you aren't having any impact. You have got to get something on the radio and TV."

That was when I went to the banker. With only a couple thousand dollars in contributions, we were obviously going to have to do something to convince the big contributors we were serious.

Frances had been working tirelessly in the campaign and knew the situation better than I did. She said she really didn't need her car. That went for $400 and paid for filming one minute for use on black and white TV — what is known as a low budget production. The only thing I can remember is it showed me waving from our front door — I didn't realize how appropriate it was for me to wave goodbye at that time — I was surely on my way out.

"We figure it will take two thousand a week," I told our local banker, "and, of course, we expect the contributions to start coming in once we are on TV and radio."

I have often wondered what my life would have been like if I hadn't always been able to borrow money. I must have an honest face — I know Dad could always get a check cashed in a strange town. Or maybe they figure I can't get away from them in the wheelchair.

In the closing weeks, I revisited my friendly banker three times, each time more convinced than ever that I was sure to win.

And I borrowed some more money from close friends.

The week before the election, we decided to take a poll.

The pollsters were ecstatic.

"Clark," one friend told me, "I have known all the time we were going to win. Now I'm convinced we are going to win big."

Apparently, we asked the wrong question.

Making random calls, friends had asked, "What do you think of Clark Harrison for chairman?"

"They're all for you, Clark," everybody making the calls reported.

Only my secret connection with the power structure hit a sour note. A few days before the election he told me, "Clark, their poll shows you are going to come in fourth."

We should have known something was wrong the night of the election.

We had moved to a new subdivision and had arranged to have food and drinks at the small clubhouse we shared with other residents.

The crowd was sparse, to put it kindly.

But the shocking thing was how fast it happened.

There was not much said on the radio about the results until about ten o'clock. The county had voting machines that could be checked and totalled as soon as the polls were closed.

The result hit us in one cold announcement.

Charlie had won — with twice the number of votes that had brought me fourth place.

We had spent $13,000 and $10,000 of the amount was represented by my loans at the bank and from close friends.

Somebody asked me during the campaign, "Clark, what is your fall back position in case you should lose."

"No problem," I replied, "I'm going to kill myself."

Actually, I have never admired providing for such eventualities as defeat. I only plan for victory — if not the first time — then later on.

For the moment, the defeat was real and so was the debt. A couple of days after the election one of the developers came to see me with his younger brother.

"Clark," he said, "we all feel bad about your losing and about the fact we couldn't support you during the election. We feel like the money you spent is part of the cost of good government, and we would like to pay off any debts you may owe."

"Jack," I answered sincerely, "I appreciate what you are offering to do, but as far as I'm concerned the campaign and the contributions stopped the day of the election."

"Clark," he said, "we know you owe a lot of money. How are you going to pay it back?"

"I'm going to sell this house," I told him, "I've got enough equity to pay off what I owe."

We didn't sell the house, but I did refinance it and ninety days after the election everybody had been paid.

Tom was nine when I made the abortive run for chairman in 1960. He couldn't understand why his daddy lost. Neither could I.

That ten thousand was the best money I ever spent.

For my part, it lit a fire in my belly — an intense desire and intention to recover what I had lost for my family. Over the years, I earned the ten thousand back — several times.

As far as the so called 'power structure' was concerned, they had learned that I couldn't be bought and that come hell or high water, I would stay whatever course I had chosen.

When they finally fulfilled Mr. Blount's prophesy and came to see me, we all knew what the terms would be.

The night of my defeat, I had made up my mind about three things.

First, I would not run again until I had built a reputation in the business community.

Secondly, I'd never put another nickel of my family's money into a political campaign — and I wouldn't run again until I had a solid base of financial support to see the race through.

Finally, I was determined that next time, I would win.

With those decisions made, I realized my stomach, which had ached all year, no longer hurt.

CHAPTER XXV

Flying is a mental process and a natural for the spinal cord injured. It involves very little physical movement, a great deal of preplanning, and a deep understanding of the forces involved. It is a constant learning process. Every flight is a new adventure because each one is different. The winds vary, the clouds blow in, the sky clears, the haze obscures, the rain blinds.

The machine is durable but vulnerable. A few drops of water in the gas will stop the engine, the radio can cease to perform, the tiny holes in the pitot tube can be clogged and the instruments can give false readings.

An untrained pilot will quickly lose his orientation when suddenly enveloped by a cloud. Without instruments or without the ability to interpret the instruments he has, the flyer cannot sense whether he is right side up or upside down, climbing or diving. It's called vertigo, which simply put, means the brain won't function to interpret the strange movements of the instruments. With no horizon for guidance, the soft greyness quickly becomes a death shroud.

On a clear day, the simple mistake of allowing air speed to drop below certain mimimums can cause the light plane to cease to be a flying machine. Reacting in a normal way and pulling back on the yoke will throw the plane into a spin.

Landing in a crosswind can result in missing the runway altogether. Following a heavy jet without knowledge of the characteristics of the turbulence created off the wing tips, the pilot of a small plane can find himself turned upside down or violently thrown against the roof of his cockpit.

Flying has been described as ninety-six per cent boredom and four per cent sheer terror.

No other industry is so preoccupied with safety as is the aviation field. It is the primary concern of every pilot and the reason for the careful check of every component of the airplane before every flight.

It is the subject of most of the articles in the flying magazines.

A monthly newsletter analyses the records of air crashes on a monthly basis from the previous year to warn pilots of the peculiar dangers of the particular season.

Safety is the obsession of the airlines to the point that it is now safer to fly commercial airlines than to drive the family car.

Flying is not a natural process for man but a learned skill purchased with the lives of adventurers who probed the limits to their own destruction. Each death has added to a store of knowledge and an improvement of machinery. In general aviation, the machine properly maintained and fueled is safe. Ninety-four per cent of aviation accidents are due to pilot error.

"My job," Clint told me, "is to try to teach you enough to keep you alive while you teach yourself to fly."

Around and around the pattern, making countless landings.

Opposite the numbers 1800 rpms, one notch of flaps.

Turning to base, watch the airspeed, seventy knots, reduce to 1500 rpms, second notch of flaps.

Keep the nose down, hold seventy knots. Watch your airspeed. Not over thirty degrees of bank.

Turn to final. Sixty-five knots. Stabilize. Third notch of flaps. Keep the numbers on that spot on the windshield.

Crab into the wind.

Left wing down. Right rudder. Hold that centerline.

Start your flare.

Pull back, pull back, pull back.

Hold it off. Hold it off.

After politics, real estate and banking, I needed excitement. Flying satisfied that craving.

Flying is for keeps.

And once you're in the air, there is only one person, yourself, who can bring you down alive.

Very little is learned from success, unless it is pride, arrogance and a lessening of the skills that brought success in the first place.

In the fall of 1960, I became a wiser, if sadder, man.

Defeat is the great educator.

The only question is whether the defeated is willing to learn and able to realize that he is not where he was before he made the unsuccessful effort. He has learned, he is tougher, and he should be smarter.

The 1960 defeat was the worst I had suffered and it gave me a mother-lode of experience and a fire in the belly that was to carry me for years to come and to place me, finally, in the chairman's seat by right of conquest.

Finally, that experience helped sustain me through the four years of challenge as chairman.

At the time, it was devastating. After the election was over, I faced up to the fact I had another pressure sore. Not a bad one this time, but enough to put me in bed for three months, healthy but unable to sit while the aggravating thing, on the surface only, slowly healed.

I had made several resolves. For one thing I was through with politics for the time. In the final weeks of the campaign, I had run up a debt that would take years to pay off and I had received only a token salary for my four years work.

Regardless of that, down deep inside I knew some day I would run again for chairman.

Except next time I would be adequately financed and I would win. And when I made another run for the job, I would have professional help in shaping my campaign.

And, I realized that to go for a job of that dimension, I needed a record of achievement as a private businessman.

Finally, when I became chairman, I would change DeKalb County. I was not going to make the effort and pay the price without real good for our community coming from the effort.

The immediate problem was to earn back the $10,000 I had lost on the campaign. Over the next eight years, I would get the $10,000 back not once but several times, but still I was driven by the resolve to earn that $10,000 one more time.

Since I was known all over the county as a result of the race, I decided a natural step would be to get a license and sell insurance to all my former friends and supporters.

With no money for an office, I had a phone installed in the back bedroom, got my license and started making phone calls.

I found out the first day that translating political contacts into hard cash was a dream. People would talk to me, but when the subject came to their insurance it was apparent they wanted an experienced agent, not a former politician.

I did learn to sell life insurance and in that way learned the techniques for selling anything at all.

If you can sell life insurance, you can sell anything — people don't like to talk about it — they're giving up money they'd rather spend on living — so you have to learn some techniques. Nobody spends more time teaching selling than the insurance industry and nobody can do it more successfully. The principles apply to other selling as well.

A friend of mine, a general agent, came to the house a couple of times a week while I was still in bed and taught me that it is possible to influence people's actions through persuasion.

"Find out what his objections are," John told me. "Never be discouraged by objections. If he only tells you 'no' you're dead. If he says 'I can't do it because —' you've got him. Then, all you have to do is remove the objections, and he has to sign."

"Give him a choice. 'Will you take one scoop or two scoops of ice cream?'. When he says 'two', you've got a sale."

"Ask him questions. As he answers, he will sell himself."

"Listen to him. When he asks you, 'Can I pay this monthly?' he has bought a policy."

"What it really boils down to is how much can he afford to put into life insurance. Once you know that, you can write his program."

It took me some thought and experience to absorb this last gem, but in the final analysis it is critical. And the soul of practicality. Only an old experienced agent could have come up with this thing of beauty.

"Don't talk yourself out of a sale. Once he has asked the question or you've answered the objection, have the pen out. Get the check. Leave."

Motivate.

"You don't have to back the hearse up to the door," my teacher would say with a grin, "but it doesn't hurt to carry a few roses in your brief case."

I never did like selling life insurance. I always felt people hated to see me coming.

But, I did learn to sell, and the lessons were invaluable in everything I did after that.

Most of the people I finally called on bought a policy, but I never got the thrill a good insurance man must get from the business.

In those months following my defeat, I was learning.

The defeat that fall season had taught me. John had taught me. But what was about to happen to Frances and me would take us to a pinnacle, dash us to the earth, almost destroy us.

Christ says if you obey Him, "your house will stand". He doesn't say that house won't suffer the full might of the crashing, tearing, deadly storm. He just promises you will survive.

I learned as a nineteen year old that I was going overseas into combat.

I prayed one prayer — 'Dear God, no matter what happens, let me be able to have children'.

God's answer was a resounding no to my having children of my own — a delayed and more wonderful yes when our adopted son Tom was born that Christmas day.

As Tom grew, hope never diminished that there would be the opportunity for another child. In the years of sickness, this seemed a remote possibility. After the miraculous operation at Mayo and renewed health, Frances and I renewed our efforts.

While I was serving as a district commissioner, the county instituted its own child placement service. Previously all placements had been made by the adjoining county, the agency that had said no earlier because of the wheelchair.

With the establishment of our county's placement service, we made application in our home county. As a commissioner, I thought if there ever would be an exception surely one would be made now.

"I have had an operation that has corrected the thing that kills paraplegics," I told the director of the welfare department. "I'm healthy now. We have living proof in Tom that we can be good parents. I don't want any special consideration, but I do ask one thing. Please find out if the wheelchair will disqualify me first, then we will make a regular application."

Within two weeks the answer was back from the placement board. "We admire all you have done", they responded. "We will not be able to place a child with you."

That was that. While I disagreed with the decision, I appreciated the courgage they had shown in addressing the problem directly.

Then, one bright and beautiful day we got a phone call that electrified us and started a chain of events that would alter our lives.

"Clark, this is Clyde. Somebody told me you want to adopt a baby. I am an attorney and, if you're serious, I have a child that will be born within three weeks that you can adopt."

Suddenly the loss of the election, the struggle to make the first few insurance sales, the years of illness and struggle seemed unimportant.

"We sure are serious, Clyde. You tell me what to do and I'll do it."

Suddenly nothing mattered except that we were going to have another child — a brother or a sister for Tom.

Like all parents through all time, we tried to decide whether we'd rather have a boy or a girl. We knew we wanted a boy because Tom would have a brother and we knew we could handle a boy, watch him grow, watch him pass through all the stages and ages that Tom had already passed through. Watch him copy Tom and see how he differed from Tom.

But wouldn't it be strangely wonderful to have a girl. Who can describe what it would be like to have a girl, a baby, a first party dress — would she be good in school — there she is graduating from college, there she is being married and having children of her own, your grandchildren.

And now began a strange, mystic course of events that would change our lives, that would make the wound in the German backyard pale, far down the scale in significance, by comparison.

A chain of events that we will never understand — that we will spend the rest of our lives trying to understand. Events that finally left us in awe of the mystery of life, of death, of God and of man's existence.

The baby was born at Piedmont hospital on a Tuesday.

"It is a beautiful little girl, Clark."

"She is perfect, Clark."

" The doctor says her health is perfect, and she is beautiful. I wish she were my daughter."

Each day I called and the reports continued to be glowing. We were to pick her up from the hospital on Saturday. The doctor had checked her again. What a beautiful, perfect little baby girl.

She is tiny, just five pounds, nine ounces, but strong and perfect.

The legal arrangements were completed.

Friday morning was bright and sunny, everybody was excited. During the night there had been a slight freeze, frost and ice could be seen on the lawn outside. It didn't look dangerous, just beautiful like every other thing on this exciting day.

Early morning the neighbor across the street called. "Frances, I've got some news, come over and have a cup of coffee." Our house in the new subdivision sat high on a hill. When we first saw it, I told the agent as we drove up the steep, winding driveway, "Some damn fool will buy this house."

Frances left the house that beautiful, sunshiny morning to go down the steep drive, across the street to the neighbor's house.

In a few minutes, the maid came stumbling into the house crying, "Mr. Harrison, Miss Frances has fallen down and she's hurt real bad. I been trying to get to her. I fell down twice and I think my leg is broken."

Two men, passersby, brought Frances into the house. She was not cry-ing. Her ankle was twisted, swollen, obviously broken. Lying on the couch, still not crying but in obvious shock, great pain. The maid was moaning and crying.

It was an hour before the ambulance arrived. All over the city the same thing was happening over and over, people falling on the treacherous, invisible ice. By the time the ambulance arrived, the ice was gone, melt-ed, it had done its work.

Frances and Pearl were loaded into the ambulance, and still Frances did not cry. She said, "It feels like a migraine headache in my leg." And I thought, "my God, how she has suffered with those things. I couldn't imagine they were that bad."

I followed in the car, we drove to the orthopedic surgeon's downtown office where Frances was carried into an inside office.

It was the worst type of ankle break. A cast to the hip was applied and Frances was told she would be incapacitated for six weeks. The maid's ankle was badly sprained, painfully twisted, and she was given a pair of crutches.

As we left the office, Frances on the ambulance stretcher, Pearl on crutches, me in a wheelchair, the doctor leaned against the door frame and laughed, "Off hand, I'd say that bunch is in a helluva shape."

Everybody laughed. "What a time to have this happen," I said, "you know we're getting a new baby tomorrow." "I never would have guessed, looking at your wife," the doctor laughed.

With all the women in the two families, I knew taking care of the baby would be no problem. By nightfall, I had arranged to have a practical nurse come and help us.

Next day Tom and my sister in law, also a Frances, drove to the hospital.

"All these years we have told Tom that he is adopted," I told her, "We thought he ought to see how it is done."

At the hospital the baby is a bundle of blankets, a small bundle. I didn't look at the baby inside the hospital. I wanted to wait until we could be alone.

"Clark, this is the most beautiful little baby I have ever seen." I was driving. My sister in law was exultant and exclaiming, "Really, she is beau-tiful." I stopped for a red light and looked over at the tiny bundle. What I saw was beautiful, perfect, tiny nose, perfectly arched eyebrows, perfect-ly beautiful.

"And her little fingernails, look at her little fingernails," I said, "Tom, what a little lady."

At home, I held the baby for a few moments, and the sensation was strange, unbelievably wonderful. The tiny warmth, the tiny and perfect beauty, the eyes large and with a fire in them I had never seen. She was an angel, so perfect and so beautiful that I was afraid and after a few moments, I handed her to the nurse. I would never forget that feeling, that feeling that I had a living bit of heaven just moments removed from the mystery of eternity.

Later I remembered feeling "She is just too perfect." Later, I remembered the stranger in the hallway of the hotel at Mayo saying, "I know one thing, this earth was not meant to be our home."

The days of that following week were frustrating. Frances was unable to care for the baby. Surrounded by the family and with the practical nurse, with my fear of such delicacy, such tiny perfection, I didn't handle this baby as I had Tom. The practical nurse did her job with irritating efficiency, recording every sip of milk, every action and symptom to be given to the doctor.

From the beginning, I felt an uneasiness. The baby's eyes had a strange, wild glint that puzzled and worried me. Then I began to notice the little spasm, clasping of the small fists, the little eyes tightly screwed shut for just two or three seconds. At first, it didn't seem serious. Then it began to worry me. I had seen so many spasms, so many of the convulsions that come with paralysis and abnormality.

I called the young doctor who had attended Kelly at the hospital.

"I wouldn't worry about that," he said, "It's perfectly normal."

"I think you'd better come by any way and have a look," I replied.

The pediatrician came to the house on Wednesday. Using his best bedside manner, he was reassuring, talking with condescending reassurance to Frances and me.

"It is just a little mouth infection, that's why she isn't eating so well," he said. "I wouldn't worry about the spasms, all babies do this when they are drowsy, they have a feeling of lost support, that they are falling and they make that little motion."

But not with the eyes clamping shut like that, I thought. I said nothing and prayed he was right. He painted the baby's mouth with a purple solution and left.

She would not eat, the nipple being held loosely in her mouth after the first few moments. And when she cried, it was a strange high pitched note as if in pain, without the healthy demanding bellow of the normal child.

Something was wrong. I called the doctor again the next day.

"Don't worry, I'm sure she will be all right. She can't eat because her mouth is sore. That ought to clear up in a couple of days."

On Saturday morning, I had two appointments, one early to discuss hospitalization insurance with the daughter of an old friend.

After making the sale, I realized that I had an hour before the next appointment. It was a long drive back to the house, but something turned me that way. As I got closer to home, my apprehension grew. I got out of the car, went into the house and looked at the baby.

Her eyes were bad, real bad, they had a weak, watery look. She was listless, moving even less than before. I picked up the phone.

"The doctor is out, I'm not sure when I will hear from him."

"You tell him this baby is sick," I said. "If I don't hear from him in fifteen minutes, I am going to call another doctor. Something has to be done right now."

Within five minutes the phone rang. "Take her to Egleston Hospital. I'll meet you there."

At four o'clock on Saturday afternoon, the pediatrician and the brain specialist called me into a private room in the hospital. This time the truth was given quickly without adornment or preparation.

"Mr. Harrison, we do not have a final diagnosis and we do not know exactly what is wrong," he said. "We think that a virus has attacked the nervous system of this baby and has gone to the brain. We do not know exactly what is happening, but we do know that damage is being done to the brain. Frankly, we think the chances of survival are probably slim. If the baby does survive, we feel from all that experience and knowledge can teach us, she will be very seriously retarded mentally."

I left the room and went to the little crib where Kelly lay, alone.

I felt that I had been led to the edge of the Grand Canyon and, as I looked at that great yawning chasm, told, "The only way you can save your little girl is to jump across."

I will never forget those who came by during those next few hours. A couple, the man, a friend since early childhood, who Frances had sent to sit with me a few minutes. An elderly woman who came, "I just want you to know I am thinking about you, praying for you, Clark."

This wonderful woman's lovely daughter in her late teens, well adjusted and a good student, for unknown, unknowable reasons, killed herself with a pistol; and, to preserve her sanity, this remarkable woman did at least one comforting thing for someone in sorrow every day of her life.

This day, she visited me in the weekend deserted hospital. I will never forget it.

And then there was the doctor, the wonderful, God sent man who came in the night, called by Frances, an eye spedialist of remarkable talent, but this night, Christ's messenger.

And, he took Kelly, our beautiful daughter, in his arms and he looked with his instrument into her little eyes and he gave hope in that black night.

"Clark, I don't see anything in her eyes that would show brain damage and that's encouraging."

I took that small hope, all he could offer, and I clung to it and thanked God for his kindness.

But most of all, it was his treatment of this little baby, fondling her, soothing, talking to her like a normal baby, like his own baby, not like a lost baby, strange, rejected and unwanted because of the damage there.

And I knew that I would never feel such gratitude as I felt to this kindly man. I knew that he knew, and yet, he had been kind to me as he had been kind to our tiny daughter. It is an unforgettable thing.

The doctor's own retarded daughter was eighteen as we talked.

In the darkened hospital room, I sat alone by the incubator, a night light the only illumination and watched my life, my love, my future die. The baby's convulsions were constant now. A tube had been inserted in the tiny vein in the head to supply fluid to fight the dehydration caused when she couldn't eat. The little body was drawn tight, then released, then drawn tight again as the waves of convulsions came and went. There was cruelty too. It was quiet throughout the darkened hospital floor. Now, on a Saturday night, only a practical nurse was left to check and call a doctor, if needed. Finally, she comes by. "I wonder if it might help if the temperature was lowered?" I ask, "I've seen a lot of convulsions and sometimes fresh air helps."

"It wouldn't do no good," she snarled, "I don't do nothing except what they order me to do."

The hours slowly passed and I prayed. "Dear God, save Kelly. I'll do anything if you'll save her, let her live, please let our baby live."

At ten thirty that night my sister Novena, who had driven from Gainesville, arrived with mother. "What can we do, buddy. We'll do anything you say."

"I've got to go home. I won't be able to take care of her unless I can go home and rest."

"You would like for us to stay with her tonight, wouldn't you, buddy?"

"Yes"

That night I lay awake on my bed and prayed.

"Anything, dear God, that you ask I will do. Take my life and let Kelly live. Please, please let Kelly live."

This can't be happening, I thought. After all the rebuffs of the previous years, of the previous year, this little girl would make up for everything. Not this, unbelieveable that this cruel thing could happen after all that had happened.

Can you face so much disappointment, such hopelessness, fight so hard without future or light, then have this tiny, beautiful bright light shine these few days only to be crushed, extinguished.

Or, the alternative, to see beauty vacated of intelligence to live daily with the shadow of what might have been. How face either alternative. How believe in a just or a loving God in a world where such a thing could happen under such circumstances. Is God cruel, sadistic, that He would deny that prayer for children made so long ago and then by this twisted circumstance snatch away a hope renewed?

Through the black, black night Frances lay at my side suffering physical as well as mental anquish. It is still dark and the telephone rings. "Mr. Harrison, this is the hospital, you better come right away."

And now I am sitting by the tiny form as the young doctor and nurse work desperately. "She is still alive, but she can't last much longer."

The little body is quiet now, no longer jerked by the spasms. You have called your minister and he is on the way. You think that Kelly has not been baptized and you try to think of the words.

"Emily Kelly Harrison, I baptise you in the name of the Father, the Son and the Holy Ghost, amen." My hand is clasping the tiny foot.

I have baptised my daughter now and I pray, "Take Kelly dear God and I will see her when I see You."

Now, I'm sitting alone, at the window, sunlight streaming in upon me and Kelly is gone. And now I know that my heart is broken and for the first time in my life I know what that phrase means 'my heart is broken'. I am surprised because I can feel my broken heart as an actual physical pain in my chest and I think how strange, I didn't know it would hurt like this, like this physical pain, like something broken, something that will never heal.

Somebody brings breakfast to me as I sit a few feet from the empty incubator, but I can't eat. It is physicallly impossible to eat. I am filled with sudden awe now; now, before the bitterness comes and I know, without understanding, that a very great thing has happened. I have been very close to eternity and the meaning of all life. I don't understand, but I do know during these moments that life has meaning whose depth is beyond anything we can comprehend. I know that I will spend the rest of my life wondering about the meaning of these moments. One thing I have learned in these few days, that time has no relation to the effect of a life. The tiny infant, related to me not by blood but by the love of a life time, has affected me and will change my life more than all the teachers, all the books, all the people and all the experience preceding.

And, another thing I have learned is the meaning of what the stranger told me in the hotel corridor, "This world was never meant to be our home."

The months following Kelly's death were bitter. They were also months of change, of facing unpleasant realities and altering old patterns now meaningless.

So much of our life is spent doing things because those things are expected, going through motions without meaning, conviction, or commitment. Old patterns are shattered only by catastrophic events. Suddenly, the pious platitudes of lukewarm, uncommitted pastors become an offense to the ears, and my own speech and shallow thoughts an offense to me.

Suddenly, I realized through my own personal catstrophe that we are surrounded by catastrophies and pain silently borne by those all around us. And I realized that my heart and my person had been of the coldest, unfeeling steel. Centered within my own selfish concentration, I had failed to see misery and longing for understanding all around me.

At first, there was only rebellion and bitterness as this new realization dawned and my eyes were opened. Having suffered my own catastrophe, I began to see the catastrophies of others as a confirmation of the cruelty of the world and of the God who created the world.

And yet, something deep inside told me 'No, God is not cruel, God cannot be cruel. I just don't understand.'

And then I felt, 'No, I don't understand and I can't understand. I must be damned and my lack of understanding and acceptance is the mark of my damnation. Because of my lack of understanding and my lack of acceptance, I am damned, God cannot love me as I am.'

And yet, again, deep within me something says that God is good — but God does not love me. If I can't be loved and I can't accept and yet I know that God is good then I must do everything I can in spite of everything. If God will not love me, yet will I try to love God.

'Though Thou shalt slay me, yet will I love Thee.'

And if I can't be saved, and yet God is good, I will try to help other people in danger, in trouble, perhaps they may be saved, perhaps they can accept what I cannot accept.

For twelve years I taught young boys in Sunday School. Now, one day, half way through a session, I told the class, "I am not going to teach any more."

And I left the class, the boys sitting there looking as I left the room. Frances and I resigned from the church. With belief gone at least honesty can come fill this void. Honesty and bitterness, deep bitterness based on unassailable logic, based on undeniable experience.

And Frances said one day, "I want to go home. I want to move back to Decatur."

CHAPTER XXVI

I took the morning off from writing this book to go to grandparents day at Michael and Joseph's school. They are in the first grade and I was impressed by the quality of work the children are doing and the obvious intelligence and ability of their teachers.

Since they are identical twins, the school has placed them in different classrooms. Martha and Tom have done a good job in this respect. Each of the boys has his own clothes and dresses to suit himself.

I asked Martha if the boys know they are twins.

"Yes," she replied.

"When did they find out?"

"When they started school," she told me, "one day they came home and said somebody had called them twins and they wanted to know what that meant."

"What did you tell them?"

"'It means you were born on the same day', I told them."

Which is the best explanation of twins I have heard.

Michael's class sang some Thanksgiving songs for us and showed us the Indian head dress they had made.

Joseph's teacher said Joseph is very proud of my being a pilot. I told her I am very proud of Joseph.

After school, we went by Tom and Martha's log house in the country and visited with Rachael.

Rachael is four, blonde and full of bouncing energy and endowed with bright and shining eyes.

I am very proud of these three children and of the mother and father who are providing them such an exceptional home.

I predict that they will grab life by the ears and make it do what they want it to do for them.

Epps Flight School is proud now that I have my license, but in the early days the reaction to the wheelchair was mixed.

On one occasion, I was sitting on the edge of the taxiway watching the planes take off and land.

"There's a wheelchair on the runway!" the controller had just come on duty. He picked up the phone and called the fire department and the security guard.

I don't know what he expected to happen, but they say he was excited.

With age and paralysis working against me, it took a lot of drill to get me ready to pass the final check ride. Landings gave me the most trouble. First, there was the problem of cross winds. When my air speed dropped just before meeting the runway, and the wing on the windward side was allowed to come up, I would side slip across the runway and even managed to land on the grass on one occasion.

"We've got one in the grass," the controller was excited again, "do a go around," he instructed the plane following me.

I managed to knock out a landing light when I taxied back on the pavement and barely nicked the propeller, but it set back the program and Clint redoubled his efforts.

Our Grandchildren...Michael and Joseph found out they are twins when they started school. Since this early picture of Rachael, she has become a gymnast.

Clint said I was real cool, just giving the numbers of the plane in acknowledging the controller's excited instructions.

"I learned in politics, Clint," I told him, "when you're wrong, don't say anything."

What I disliked most was installing the hand control each time I flew. It took two years before I got my private license and I suffered both heat and cold.

In the winter, I would lie on the wing with the cold wind blowing on my back and with my numb fingers fumbling to start the nuts that held the rudder bar in place. I learned to work fast because my fingers rapidly became stiff and wouldn't work right and the pain became intense.

In the summer, I had to be careful not to burn myself on the hot black walkway on the wing's surface. I learned early in the game that if I got on the black strip, rough as sandpaper to keep the feet from slipping, I would ruin my trousers. The so called modern miracle fabrics are especially susceptible and would become fuzzy where I slid along the rough surface.

Finally, I got a rubber mat, such as is used under small rugs to keep them from slipping.

In the summer, I had to use two thicknesses of mat to prevent getting burned.

In the beginning, it would take me thirty minutes just to install the rudder bar. Eventually, I got this down to ten minutes.

I thought I would never solo. I kept assuring Clint that I was in no hurry, and he kept telling me I was getting closer.

"Taxi over to the big hangar and let me out," Clint said on the fateful day, "I'll be up in the tower watching. You won't have any problem. Just do it the way we've been doing it."

The good thing about flying at age 57 is the way it clears the head of all the cobwebs. There is nothing like total panic and sheer terror with the adrenalin pumping in purest form to clear the sinuses and relieve the aches and pains.

By the time I got the plane back on the ground the day of my first solo, I was in a high state of excitement melding into euphoria once I realized I was safe on mother earth.

Clint signed my solo license and cut my shirt tail off.

It had taken me 23 hours.

In the spring of 1961, following my disastrous run for chairman, I took the exam and got my real estate salesman's license. The company we formed was incorporated in my name, and a friend who was an owner that first year passed his broker's license exam at the same time and had it issued in the name of the corporation.

That made it possible for us to begin selling immediately, and to use the name my ten thousand dollar loss had helped publicize.

At a PTA meeting at Tom's school, I came to know a couple who had a tract of land they wanted to sell. They listed it with me and two weeks later I had a contract. When the sale closed, I had earned a commission of thirty eight hundred dollars — a third of my political loss.

I can stand a lot of this, I thought. I decided to concentrate on selling land to the developers I had come to know in politics.

The other hot item in these days of retail expansion by the big oil companies was service station sites. I knew the zoning process and the companies knew me, so that became the other specialty for me.

Our local savings and loan was building an eight story structure in Decatur for their headquarters. I wanted to have an office in the new building, but knew I couldn't afford the rent.

Just before it was to open, I called the leasing agent again and told him my quandry.

"You want to talk to Al," he said, "he's looking for a sub- tenant."

When the new building opened we were one of the first tenants to move in — Al opened his market research office and provided me a desk in his spare room. His girls answered my phone, all for the munificent sum of $32.50 a month.

And I was across the hall from the county's largest warehouse builder and just down from the chamber of commerce.

Then I joined the Executive Club. For the $15 a month fee, I could take any client who might want to visit my office to the Club on the top floor for a free cup of coffee.

He'd never guess I was operating out of Al's store room.

My health was good.

After we had moved to the new subdivision, I had to arrange a way to get in and out of the tub in the new house. Our government supervised house had a shower that I used from the wheelchair. Both of us liked the new house because it was not built for wheelchairs — the hallways were narrow just like a regular house and there was a tub in the bathroom.

One of the county firemen made me a rope ladder which I had suspended from the ceiling. I'd pull up on it to get in and out of my wheelchair and into and out of the tub.

The first time I got in the tub, I looked down at myself.

Hey, looka here, I thought excitedly. I'm almost floating. I bet I could swim. Next day, I was down at the community swimming pool.

Up until that time, I had thought that, being paralyzed, I would be helpless in the water. Now, I bought a water ski belt for extra floatation support and got a couple of friends to lower me into the pool.

After two days of hanging on the side of the pool wearing the ski belt, I got tired of scrapping my knees, took off the belt, and found out I not only wouldn't sink to the bottom, I could swim.

I headed for the bottom of the pool, pulling with my arms as hard as I could.

I touched the bottom, but as soon as I quit pulling, I bobbed back toward the surface.

I was unsinkable.

I started turning flips under water, swimming the length of the pool under water, twisting and turning in every direction.

I was free! In the water I could MOVE!

Hallelujah!

The deep water became my best friend — it supported me, freed me, worked not only my arms but my legs as well as they followed the motion of my upper body.

I had read about the 'drown proofing' instruction given Navy cadets at Georgia Tech during the war. After I decided I didn't need the ski belt, I began to practice the technique in our pool.

I would hang, vertically, with my head just below the surface. Then, with a slight movement of my arms, I would rise to the surface, take a breath, lower my head and sink back to a level where the water was supporting me.

Soon, I realized that I could swim as safely as I had ever been able to. From then on, I swam regularly, and, after the new 'Y' opened in Decatur, I began to swim a quarter of a mile each day, five days a week. Every once in a while, I would swim a mile — it took me an hour and forty minutes.

From that point, the water never held any fear for me. I knew I could stay in it safely all day and all night, if necessary.

And, I never hurt myself the way I had by sitting too long in the chair or lying too long in one position.

It had been fifteen years since I had been shot. I could have been swimming during those fifteen years.

At the Shepherd Spinal Center, our patients learn they can swim during their first sixty days in the hospital.

The pool was something that wouldn't have happened if we hadn't moved from our house in the woods. We moved so that Tom would have children to play with in a normal neighborhood.

We loved the house and our good friends who along with us were early arrivals in the new subdivision.

Then Kelly died.

We had a beautiful home in a beautiful new subdivision, but the memories were all bad now, the lost election, the hill where Frances broke her ankle and the room where Kelly was tended. But the very idea of moving anywhere now was preposterous. The house had been refinanced to pay off the $10,000 political loss, my income was reduced. Most of the houses in Decatur were old, very few were on the market.

But, Frances wanted to go home, so we started tooking for a house in Decatur.

Thoughts about the dream I had had overseas — of turning off Clairmont into Lamont and Vidal Boulevards never occurred to me. What happened just happened — but I knew it was no accident.

We heard a house was for sale on Lamont. We were driving down that street when we saw a real estate sign.

The old house was solidly built, shortly after Dad had built the home, he had to sell while I was overseas. It was only a block from the home I had left in 1943.

It was a big house. With a full day light basement. The owner had retired from a granite quarrying firm located near Lithonia. With a cut rate price for his material, he had built the thick and heavy foundation of granite and had used granite brick for the upstairs walls. All the rooms were big. There was a sunken living room. The yard was big for Decatur, beautifully manicured and had an abundance of flowers and shrubs going back to a creek.

There was an upstairs room for Tom with a spare room that would become Bob's.

Just like what I had left to go into the Army.

A ramp to the front stoop and another down into the sunken living room were the only changes we would have to make.

After we had looked the house over carefully, I told the agent, "we like the house, but we haven't got any money."

A trade was arranged. Our only cost was $300 to pay the mover.

It was the kind of miracle that has happened for us over the years. We were back in Decatur, in the kind of house we had always wanted, on the street I had dreamed of in those long months overseas.

Before I had time to have my rope ladder installed, I sat one afternoon looking down at the big bath tub. Frances was away somewhere.

Hell, I thought, I need a bath. I pulled up to the tub, slid my feet in and lifted myself down into the water. If worse comes to worse, I can stay in here until she gets home, I thought.

When I finished bathing, I boosted myself onto the side of the tub, teetered a moment, grabbed the chair and pulled myself into the front of it.

Another blow for liberty. All I needed now was a bar instead of the soap dish to push against.

Things were getting simpler.

The old house had a healing effect on us and the Lord was to lead us in two directions that would help in that healing.

After Kelly's death, we couldn't help ourselves.

So, the help we needed came from others.

Our family doctor, Dr. MGeachy, was one of the strongest Christians I have ever known. His father had been Frances' minister during her childhood at Decatur Presbyterian Church. Geachy never talked about religion — he lived his.

He was responsible for my finally having the operation that healed me after having to leave Yale and now he became concerned about the deep despondencey that overwhelmed me following Kelly's death.

"You need to get out and have some fun, Clark," he told me. "How about going fishing with me?"

Geachy had elaborate fishing gear and a sonar in his small boat for measuring the depth of the water. He was a serious fisherman. He also told me that he was not comfortable unless the boat was pointed so that he was facing north.

"I can tell," he said.

After our fishing trip, Geachy told me he had another man he wanted me to go fishing with.

The man was a successful manufacturer's representative. Among other possessions he owned a small lake and he invited me to meet him there to go fishing.

We never got our hooks wet, but we spent an afternoon that was to profoundly affect my future.

"Clark," he said, "I can help you get over your depression. I want you to visit a nursing home."

He explained that his father had to go to a nursing home for the last few years of his life. He would visit his father regularly and had learned to cut his dad's hair.

"Pretty soon," he said, "I was cutting hair for several of the other men there."

Over the years his father was a patient he came to know and to love the other patients and had continued to visit after his father died.

I felt extremely strange the first time I drove up in the oak shaded lawn before the big frame two story house. I got out of the car, rolled up to the front steps and waited until one of the attendants spotted me and came out.

I explained I'd come to visit and she pushed me up the ramp.

Inside there was the odor of the old and the sick. I went from bed to bed.

"I'm Clark Harrison. I came to visit you."

My going to the nursing home must have pleased God.

That night, another miracle happened.

The phone rang, it was my sister, Bettie.

"Clark," she said, a lilt in her voice, "do you and Frances still want a baby?"

Foolish, wonderful question.

"You bet!"

And that was the first word we had of our son, Bob.

For the next eleven years, when I was in town, I was at the nursing home on Thursday afternoon. I stopped when it ceased to be a nursing home.

Each time I would go through those doors, I would feel a little like Alice must have felt as she passed through the looking glass. No matter what kind of turmoil I had been involved in during the preceding week, it would vanish as I began my round of visits to each of the patients.

The people were fascinating. Most of them were from modest backgrounds but they had done interesting things and each had a story to tell.

One man had been superintendent of several county school systems in the state. His unknown story was that he was a quiet worker for the famous Senator George.

"When he was in the middle of a campaign," he told me, "my job was to travel around the state and listen. I would go to the courthouse, take a seat on a bench, and talk to the people who came by. Then I would call my report in to the Senator's office. They, in turn, would tell me where to go next and where to pick up my expense money. Usually, I would find it in an envelope waiting for me at the next hotel."

During the time I visited the nursing home, there always seemed to be one angel in residence. A beautiful old woman with snow white hair who could no longer speak and who seemed to have no consciousness of the day to day activity about her. She would be supremely happy in a quiet way, smiling and nodding to whoever was working around her at the time. The attendants would give her special care and everyone who saw her would feel her radiance and joy.

You had the feeling that she had already taken up residence in heaven.

Another lady was at the other end of the scale. She was very much involved in the day to day. She was doing Jesus work here on earth, and she became my favorite.

I called her 'mama'.

The first time I saw her was the day she arrived at the home. She had come on her own volition, was dressed in a stylish black dress and was smoking a cigarette.

"My husband told me," she said, "to go to a home if he died before I did. 'I know you', he told me, 'if you try to live with your daughter and you get crossed up with her, you'll just walk out into the night!'"

At first, Etta didn't like anything about the place, but finally she decided, evidently, to make the best of things.

She was constantly doing something for the other patients. On holidays she took on the job of decorating the house. Crepe paper, pine boughs, tinsel, anything bright and shiny was used to festoon the old house.

"I'm a bone, a rag and a hank of hair," she would say of herself. And she certainly did fit that description from a physical standpoint. But the spirit was full of the love of life. Among other things, she played the piano and sang songs that went back to World War I days. She knew and quoted fascinating old poems. I'll never forget sitting on the back porch where three old men were. One of them had been a painter and told me of painting the inside of huge tanks, the flag pole on the top of an Atlanta building, and other high risk assignments.

He specialized in hazardous jobs because the pay was better.

"I went up on the roof and looked at one flagpole," he told me. The manager of the building had called him because he handled dangerous painting assignments. "The building manager didn't know it, but there was a crank you could turn and lower the pole so it was lying flat along the roof. I went back down to his office and told him I'd do it for $100. That was a lot of money then, and the job took about fifteen minutes."

The painter had suffered a stroke while painting the exterior of a big multi-storied building. Now, he was sitting with his paralyzed left arm forcing his fist into his side.

Etta didn't know I was watching when she came in carrying a little piece of blanket. She didn't say anything to the man, but she walked over, pulled his fist away from his side and put the blanket as a cushion between his fist and his chest.

While Etta was a resident at the home, Frances and I decided to have some of the patients over for an evening meal.

That morning, Frances was up early getting things ready. She had bought some chicken that she broiled and had prepared a really fine feast.

At the home, they ate about 5 p.m., so at 4 p.m. I was there ready to pick up Etta and lead the rest of the group back to our house.

It had started raining about noon and now I was sitting in the car outside the big old house and the rain was pouring down.

From time to time, I would see one of the patients peering out of the front window.

Finally, the door opened and a gentlemanly old man, who had been a clerk in a shoe store, came out under a large umbrella.

"Mr. Harrison," he said, "I don't believe this rain is going to let us go."

"Don't worry about it," I said, "we can do it another time." I thought about Frances and all the work she had been doing all day.

Just then, the door opened and out tripped Etta.

As she came out the door, the rain stopped.

I smiled at the elderly gentleman under his umbrella.

"Well, it looks like we're going after all."

When we got to the house we were a sight. The attendants had followed in their cars and now they began to unload a real assortment of humanity.

One man had a back problem that had left him bent forward ninety degrees from the waist. The nurse with him took him in the front door and then came out to get the next patient.

The man, thinking he was being left, came running out after her.

Then, when Etta came hopping through the foyer, she failed to see the two steps that led down into the sunken living room. She fell and went sailing across the carpet and rolled up against the hearth of the fireplace.

Finally, we all got seated around the dining room table and Frances began to bring in the beautiful meal.

One of the old men looked up at me and said.

"This is like magic."

Suddenly, the room was filled with that same brilliant, white light that I had seen the night before Dad died.

I gazed in wonder as all of those in the room appeared as cut- out cardboard figures against that pure light of a greater reality.

Twice, I had seen that strange light. I thought of it many times over the years.

After my sister, Bettie, had her strong experience with Christ — and spent weeks, months and years poring over her Bible — and became the St. Paul of our family — we talked about it.

"Jesus said," Bettie told me, "blessed are the pure in heart, for they shall see God."

"Bettie," I replied, "you know I am not pure in heart — I have been a soldier, a real estate agent, a banker and a politician. I haven't exactly led a sanctified life."

"Moses was a politician," she said, "David was a soldier and an adulterer. Abraham's righteousness was imputed to him because of his faith.

"What you saw was the Shekinah light. Look it up in the dictionary. It is a manifestation of the presence of God on earth. To see it you have to have faith. When Dad died, I saw it, too. When you and Frances fed those old people, you were doing precisely what Christ said for us to do.

"And, He was there."

Years later, when I was elected chairman of our county commission, I was visiting one of my best friends at the home. He had followed my campaign with great interest.

"Well, Mr. Harrison," the old man said sadly, "Now that you're going to be running the government, I don't reckon you'll have time to visit us."

"Listen," I told him, "when I get so busy I can't visit here, I'll just hire another man."

And, that's why nobody could ever see the chairman on Thursday afternoon.

CHAPTER XXVII

In all modesty, I must admit my difficulties at age 56 in learning to control the airplane were not entirely caused by my age.

It even took Clint and Steve, expert as they are at flying all kinds of planes, flying formation aerobatics, and teaching chimpanzees, a while to learn to control with hands only.

There is a problem after landing in holding the plane on the center of the runway, and in the early days, I weaved a path all over the surface and was saved only by the fact the runways are very wide at DeKalb Peachtree. The problem was one of balance. Since I can't control my stomach muscles, I don't have any. After landing, I steer by moving the rudder bar up and down while I reach under the instrument panel and pull on the hand brake with my left. Having no balance, I used the rudder bar to balance with and would veer to the left as I did so.

Finally, Clint persuaded me to push against the bar at the same time I moved it up or down. After some practice, the pushing provided the balance and my steering became more stable.

Balance becomes critical when I am doing touch and goes — landing and then immediately taking off again.

As soon as the main landing gear touches down, I turn loose of the wheel since the ailerons are not used for control on the ground. I take the rudder with my left hand, then seize the handle of the bar that controls the flaps with my right. I push the button on the flaps control bar and ease it down to the floor.

Then, I take the rudder bar again with my right hand, reach up and push the throttle to full power with my left, then grasp the wheel once more as the plane picks up speed for takeoff.

In talking with Bill Blackwood, the California pilot who invented the hand control lever, I discovered the transition described above cannot be done.

"We use two notches of flaps to land and leave them on to take off," he told me, "we never touch the flaps on the runway. After all, these guys are paralyzed."

I accused Clint of having me do the impossible and he just grinned.

"Doing the impossible takes a little time," he said.

The impossible was something with which I was becoming familiar as the years passed for Frances and me.

And, on Friday 13, 1962, the impossible happened for us again. Just a little over a year after Kelly died, our son Bob was born.

Bob was born into a going concern with an older brother to set the pace and lead the way. Tom was eleven and was pitching for his Little League team the day Bob was born.

A week later, we took Bob to his first game. I was a little concerned that a ball might land in Bob's bassinet and I think Bob may have resented the pressure to involve him in baseball. So far as I know he never participated in anything but sandlot.

The truth of the matter, we decided we had made a mistake in pushing Tom into the Little League program. After all, six is a little young to be suited out.

So, we just kind of let Bob find his own way. He got into soccer, on his own — when he was six — played through high school until he went full time into distance running.

Bob is a natural born distance runner, has the build, the slim frame and the toughness that can carry an athlete forward when he is in pain.

From the beginning, I knew Bob was going to be a tough kid. We watched him try to stand in his playpen. He would grasp the bars and pull himself about half way up. Then, he didn't seem to have the strength to pull himself upright.

Instead of turning loose, Bob would hang on, half up and half down and after a good thirty seconds would finally pull himself upright.

"He'll never be a quitter," I told Frances.

About the time Bob was born, Frances started talking about going camping. I thought she had lost her mind and attributed her desire to get out in the woods to the fact that she has some Cherokee Indian blood. Through her father 's side, she is in a direct line from the famous Sequoyah, the half-English, half-Cherokee chieftain who died in 1843and who invented and who invented the written Cherokeee alphabet. Frances is very proud of her Indian blood and never forgave the rest of us pale faces for the way we treated her forebears.

"How can I go camping?" I exclaimed. "I can hardly get around on the pavement and I couldn't move at all in the woods."

That summer we were in the North Carolina mountains at Deep Creek, in what had been Cherokee land near Bryson City.

"Well," I said, "as long as I'm sitting here I've got to have something to do or I'll go nuts. I'll be the cook."

Bob was one year old and in his stroller. He was about in the same shape I was.

Tom and Frances set up the tent. We had bought a pyramid tent that had an exterior frame. Somebody put us onto plastic after our first trip. Tom and Frances would lay a sheet of heavy plastic on the ground, erect the tent and then cover the tent with a large sheet of clear plastic. We bought two aluminum cots with thin, foam-rubber mattresses and Bob slept in a little sleeping bag on the floor between us. Tom had his own pup tent.

I had to admit using the plastic we were as dry as in the bedroom at home and about as comfortable once we settled in for the night.

The kids loved it. There were always other children around and we didn't see Tom much except at meal time. There's always plenty for children to do in the woods.

The camps provided a table. Frances and Tom would tie a huge sheet of black plastic in the trees above the table to provide us a place to eat and to sit while it was raining. In the summer, every day in the mountains it rains.

We cut Bob's playpen in half so he could ride in the station wagon with a place to play. In the camp, we set the playpen by the table where we ate.

The Coleman stove was my province on the trips. It was kept on the big picnic table and with the plastic in place, I could cook while it was pouring rain all around us. I'd do the shopping for these trips and must say I got to be a pretty fair camp cook.

Bob got to be a veteran camper during that summer. The next year, I was involved in the negotiations that led to the construction of the First National Bank Building. All the papers had been signed and I couldn't start leasing the space until construction of the building had actually started.

"Why don't we go to California?" I asked Frances one day, "I can't do much in my real estate right now and we might never get another chance."

Shortly after Bob's second birthday, we took off. My sister, Novena, and her daughter Wendy and son Clark decided to go, and Mother, who was only seventy at the time and recovering from a broken hip, decided a camping trip would be just the thing for her too.

We had a small Comet station wagon which we loaded with the tent and other paraphernalia. There was a nice rack on top that held most of the gear and we covered the floor in the back of the wagon with our mattresses so Bob could roam about and Tom would have a place to lie down.

We were gone six weeks. It was a trip we'd never forget.

About two thirds of our nights were spent camping with breaks when we'd check into a motel and get cleaned up and get to sleep in a real bed.

Our only bad weather was at Broken Bow, Oklahoma, where Frances and Tom had to set up the tent in the pouring rain and an especially cold night atop a mountain on the Indian reservation at Window Rock, Arizona. I remember hearing Mother stumping around in the tent next door before dawn on the latter occasion. The temperature was about 32 degrees and a steady wind was blowing.

"Oh, God," I thought, "I'm going to kill my poor Mother."

This was after I had learned I could swim, and I liked to swim in the rivers along the way. The hardest swimming was in the swift mountain stream at Deep Creek. The water was extremely cold and the river so swift it was all I could do to keep from being swept down the mountain side.

The rivers we camped by in the desert and in Yosemite were pleasant to swim in by comparison.

Going to the bathroom was a challenge. Since I didn't want to attract too much attention, I would go to the various camp bathroom about 4 a.m. when I'd have it all to myself.

I remember one visit at a place called Quarry Rock. I don't remember what state it was in but it was in the desert with the only vegetation a few scraggly non-descript trees spotted among the camp sites.

I got Frances to go with me since I had to go up three shallow steps to get to the restrooms. She left me there and I concluded my business.

When I rolled out of the facility, the car was where we had parked, but there was no sign of Frances. I concluded she had gone back to the camp and I was on my own. Unless I wanted to wait for everybody else to wake up, I was going to have to figure a way to get down the three steps.

Frances and Tom became expert in putting up our tent.

Frances is proud of her Indian blood. Here she and Bob visit a chief. We were on our way to California.

Finally, I let myself down on the flagstone pavement. Then, I rolled the wheelchair around and carefully rolled it down the three steps so that the open back was facing me.

With the agility of a circus performer, I now put my bag that I carried my bathroom equipment in on the middle step. I put my feet in the chair, pulled myself forward until I was teetering on top on the bag. Then carefully and slowly I tugged and pulled myself into the chair. I was exhausted and shaking from the effort.

I picked up the bag and rolled over to the station wagon. Just below the window was Frances' head. She had been there asleep all the time.

In California we saw the magnificent granite mountains of Yosemite, visited Hollywood and camped on the beach near Monterey.

North of San Francisco, we had packed up and were preparing to leave camp when Frances told me something was wrong with Bob.

"Look at all these little whelps on his body." She pulled up his shirt. It looked as if he had been bitten all over by insects.

"We better call the doctor," I said. We stopped at a restaurant and Frances went in and got several dollars worth in change. Fortunately, our doctor in Decatur was in the office when the call from the pay station was connected. She described Bob's condition.

"He's got chickenpox," she told me when she got back to the car. "The doctor told me what medicine to get and said for us to keep him quiet for about a week."

We had split up with the rest of the family at San Francisco since they wanted to go on up into Canada and we were about ready to start home. Now, we found an isolated campsite in a large Sequoya grove. We stayed a week among the huge trees and found great peace and quiet. Bob never seemed to be particularly uncomfortable and soon he was well broken out all over his body. By the time we left to head home, the places were scabbed over.

It was amazing to me how Bob, just two years old, took to camping. As soon as the sun started down, Frances would put him in his little sleeping bag in the tent and we wouldn't hear a sound out of him until we were ready to get up the next morning. Camping is a healthy, natural environment for children and one that seems to keep them supremely happy.

Tom worked like a beaver every evening while they were setting up the tent and unpacking and setting up the gear. He never complained.

I used to think about the social workers who questioned our ability to take care of children. The truth of the matter is, I believe, that children are happiest when they are learning to take care of themselves, especially when it is obvious that they are needed to work as part of the family.

And I have thought often about what adoption has meant in our family. Tom reminds me of my Dad in his physical vitality and ability and Dad would have taken sheer delight in the positive way Tom tackles the problems he faces in business and in raising a family.

Bob, on the other hand, is more like Frances' mother than any of her children or grandchildren. He has her black eyes and dark complexion and he has her down-to-earth practical way of looking at things. Frances and I often laugh at how much alike they are.

Although they are brothers, Tom and Bob grew up in entirely different environments. I have described how we, as most young parents do, spent an inordinate amount of time trying to point Tom in the right direction. As the first born, he had to bear that burden.

Bob, on the other hand, joined a going concern. He had Tom's example to follow and he had parents experienced enough to know most of the things young parents worry about never come to pass, that children learn more by example than by words, and that the main thing kids need is a chance to grow in an atmosphere of love.

My responsibilities had increased by the time Bob came along and I didn't have the time to sit and watch him grow — or to play catch and tackle with the same amount of concentration I had devoted to Tom.

But we did have some great adventures together and we became very close. Bob is a good conversationalist — and he is full of ideas.

When Bob was about nine, his mother went to Europe with her sister, Patsy, and Mama Guess. It was a once in a life time opportunity and they enjoyed it thoroughly.

"While your mother is gone," I told Bob, "you and I will go to Washington. It's about time you learned something about our country."

A few days after Frances left we went to the airport, flew to Washington National and got busy.

For four days, we visited every monument, every unusual government office, the F. B. I., the National Geographic, Ford Theatre, and three times the Smithsonian.

The Smithsonian was Bob's favorite. I think he would have spent a week going from exhibit to exhibit, reading, looking and listening.

We rode cabs everywhere and at least twice almost got stuck for the evening. The first time was our visit to the Jefferson Memorial. It was late afternoon and it suddenly occurred to me that no cabs were cruising in the area. We hitched a ride with another tourist who had hired a cab for the afternoon.

Then we took a cab to the National Zoo. It was ideal for me. We entered at the top. There was a winding asphalt sidewalk that led from one cage to the next. I'd wait while Bob went in larger exhibits like the monkey house.

It was a long and pleasant meandering trip and everything was fine until we came out at the lower end.

Again, there were no cabs around. It was getting late, and finally we were invited to leave so the gate could be closed.

Park police cruised by. I tried to explain our dilemma — they just looked, said they'd send a cab if they saw one, then drove off.

We could see the highway, several hundred yards away and above us with cars streaming by. Now, we were alone, the gate to the zoo was closed and it was beginning to get dark.

Then, our guardian angel came on duty. A cab drove up.

I looked at the driver in amazement.

"Where did you come from?"

"Well, I was driving along the highway, I looked and saw you sitting down here and figured you needed a ride."

"We sure do," I agreed. "I was just planning to get down on the ground and stretch out once it got dark. I thought we were here for the evening."

"I'm from Virginia," he said. "I'm not supposed to drive into Washington. What the heck, get in, I'll take you to your hotel."

All healthy children are active and Bob has a double dose of that. When I planned the trip, I had visions of he and I shut up in a hotel room with Bob bouncing around the walls and me chewing my finger nails.

So, I decided I would keep him busy, morning, noon and night.

The plan worked pretty well. We'd get in a cab in the morning, return in time to rest a little while before supper, then go out for the evening.

One evening we got stuck outside the Kennedy Art Center. We had watched a large black woman conduct the symphony orchestra. Again, we came out into the night and watched the crowd disappear until we were alone on the sidewalk in front of the center.

And, again, just as we were about to give up a cab appeared.

Friday before we were to go home the next day, I was pretty fagged out. I went back to the room after breakfast to stretch out for a few minutes. I figured Bob couldn't get in much trouble roaming around in the hotel alone for a while.

After I got up and went back down to the lobby, Bob came running up.

"Hey, Dad," he said, "I've been having a great time."

"What you been doing, Bob?"

"I been helping the bell boy. I met some Chinese, and I rode up in the elevator with some Vietnamese. Boy, they sure are funny."

That evening Bob downed his supper quickly, as usual, and said he'd like to go out in the lobby while I finished mine. I sat, relaxing and enjoying an after dinner drink, feeling we had had a good time and trying to think of something to do the next morning while we waited for the plane to leave for Atlanta.

Bob came running in.

"Hey, Dad," he was excited, "I earned fifty cents!"

"How did you do that, Bob?"

"Well, I was standing outside and a car drove up. I walked over and opened the door and the man gave me a quarter. Then, I opened another door and that man gave me a quarter."

"What did the doorman say?" I asked.

"Oh, he thought it was funny."

Our plane was to leave Saturday afternoon at 2:10.

"Bob," I said, "let's go down to Annapolis. It's not very far and you can see where the Naval officers are trained."

We got our bags packed and set out early for Annapolis. It is a beautiful old campus and we enjoyed seeing the museum and where the cadets worked and played. It was so pleasant, we let the time slip away. Finally, I realized we were going to have to get a cab pretty fast or we were going to be late at the airport.

"I don't believe we'll make it," I told the cab driver. I told him when the plane was to leave and he said he'd do the best he could.

I began to think of spending a few hours with Bob running around the airport.

The cab screeched to a stop at the Delta entrance, the cab driver raced around, got the chair out of the trunk and got me in it. We went flying into the waiting room.

The place was deserted.

Behind the counter, a man in uniform was leaning up against the door jamb looking at us.

The angel was on duty.

"You trying to make the Atlanta flight?"

He picked up the phone.

"Go on down to Gate 17," he said.

When we got on the plane, the attendants helped me into a seat.

As I leaned back, the plane started to move.

They had held the flight for Bob and me.

Bob and I had another adventure that developed into a real shaggy dog story before it finally was concluded.

We had built the house on St. Simons Island. Frances and Bob were living on the island and I was coming down on the weekends. Our idea was to get Bob away from some of the problems of the city schools during those turbulent times.

The twins were just six weeks old when Martha became very ill and was taken to the hospital. The babies were brought to our house in Decatur and we sent for Frances to come look after them.

This happened on Thursday.

"Bob can spend the night with the Shelby's," Frances told me. "Then, he is going on a scout canoeing trip after school Friday. They'll be gone until Sunday. You can come down and be here when he comes home."

Friday, I picked up my sister, Novena, and we drove to St. Simons. Frances drove to Decatur.

Saturday morning I got a call.

"Martha's appendix ruptured," Frances said, "She's in surgery right now."

I got back in the car, delivered Novena back to her apartment in Milledgeville, drove the rest of the three hundred miles back to Decatur.

It was after supper when I arrived at the hospital. Martha was alone in the room, tubes in her arm, out her side, in her nostril. She was still asleep. I left and spent the night at the house with Frances and the babies. Sunday morning, I drove the three hundred miles back to St. Simons and picked up Bob, who had made a fifty mile trip down the Satilla river in his canoe, at the church.

Next morning, Bob went to school. When he returned, I heard a great ruckus from down the street. Bob and a couple of his friends came running up. Bob was twelve at the time.

"Dad," he shouted, " we got a wild animal trapped in the pipe under the street."

At the time we had two dogs, Martha and Tom's cockerpoo, and a dachshund. They were both small, one shaggy and the other with a short shiny brown coat. When they ran, they literally flew along the ground, shoulder to shoulder, banking into the curves, skidding into the distance in a blur of sight and sound.

"Merlin's at one end and Fritz is at the other. Whatever it is is growling and spitting. Merlin and Fritz are going crazy."

I called the animal control unit at the county. The north end of the island is still inhabited by a number of wild creatures, deer, possums. On one occasion, Frances and I drove over a five foot rattle snake that was crossing the road.

"It could be a bobcat," the man told me. "If it is, you better be very careful. Somebody can get hurt bad if it comes out of that culvert." He promised to come help. I promised that the dogs would try to keep the wild thing hemmed up until he got there.

"Dad, dad," Bob and his buddies were bright eyed, excited and breathing fast, "I shot it with my sling shot. I think I got it."

Like most young boys, they couldn't allow the situation to stabilize with the dogs doing the holding until the animal inspector arrived.

It turned out, of course, that the wild animal was the neighbor's cat.

But that wasn't the end of the excitement.

About an hour after the bobcat episode, I heard yelling, screaming and great commotion moving toward my post back at the house.

"It's Bob," one of the younger boys was hollering and waving. "He's been hurt. He's coming."

"Oh, me, oh, me," Bob was moaning, holding his hand against his temple, the blood was streaming down the side of his face.

I headed up the ramp into the house, got a big towel out of the bathroom.

"I been speared, dad, I been speared."

They had made some long, sharp pointed spears out of some underbrush they had found on a vacant lot nearby.

"We were very careful, Mr. Harrison," the younger boy explained. "We didn't throw at each other, we were throwing at the ground."

"Yeah, but Bob stooped down just as I threw," the other boy said.

"Put this towel against your head," I ordered Bob, "hold it just as tight as you can. You boys call the hospital and tell them we're on the way."

I got in the car, loaded the chair, Bob was moaning, rigid and trembling as he looked at the blood that had dripped on his clothes.

We headed down the street at a fast clip, turning the corners like a CanAm, wheeling along with the wind flying in the windows.

At the causeway, the draw bridge was up and a line of cars was waiting for the small yacht to pass up the intercoastal waterway.

I swung into the left lane, passed the waiting cars, drove around the striped barrier pole and pulled up a few feet from the open bridge. As

the bridge settled down into place, I gunned it across, catching a glimpse
of the bridge guard shouting and waving his arms in my rear view mirror. I had the hazard lights blinking.

We swung right on to Highway 17, ran a red light then slowed behind
the line of cars waiting at the light where we had to turn left for the hospital.

I swung into the left lane, toward the cars waiting at the red light,
whipped the car left through a service station and on into the hospital road.

When we pulled into the emergency entrance, an attendant was waiting.

"Get him in. I'll come behind you."

Bob was lying on the examining table in the emergency room.

"The doctor will be here in a minute."

Bob's friends had acted cooly — we were expected.

The wooden spear had entered Bob's right temple and had severed a
small artery — thus the abundant blood. Bob had pressed so tightly with
the towel he had not lost much blood. Fortunately no lasting damage
was done. Bob has a genuine dueling scar to show for the rest of his life.
He has been able to manufacture some pretty intriguing tales about the scar.

Martha had also survived a very narrow escape.

And I had thought my life was going to be dull.

*By the time we reached Colorado on the way home from California we had a name for the
station wagon — "The Dirty Bird."*

CHAPTER XXVIII

Flight training covers three main areas. There are the take offs and landings. That covered my concern about getting down. There is navigation which takes care of the fear of getting lost. And there are the maneuvers while in the air.

The three areas are covered in two schools. There is ground school and there is the flying itself. The ground school portion is tested by the FAA by a written exam and the flying by an oral exam and a check ride.

In my case, I finally mastered the exams and the check ride by a frontal assault of repetition — practice, practice, practice.

I passed the written exam the day after I finished ground school, but I went back several months later and took the whole course over again. There is a lot to learn and it's not like my college courses. Then, I could afford to cram for an exam then wipe the slate clean, forget most of the details and start preparing for the next course.

In flying, you are studying for your life — and you don't want to forget anything.

There is a vast array of knowledge to be mastered in flying. It is a lifetime work, actually, and the basics have to be pounded into the reflexes and through the conscious into the sub-conscious and the unconscious. Otherwise, on some dark night, or stormy day, with the radio and half the instruments on the fritz you may pay the forfeit with your life and, perhaps, the lives of others. I kept telling Clint I was in no hurry — and meaning it. I was a lot more concerned about continuing in life than I was in satisfying the requirements of the Federal Aviation Administration. So, we kept peeling that onion and somehow the money was available each month to pay the bills.

The prime thrust is to keep the fledgling aviator alive when the unexpected happens and to guard him against his own ignorance and lack of skill until he has learned to do better.

The basic aerial maneuvers are taught at altitude but are really designed to avoid catastrophe when the plane is near the ground — in the landing or taking off configurations.

Slow flight is one of the main skills and it is taught so that right after takeoff or just before landing the pilot will be able to remain in control.

"Reduce your power to 1500 rpm's," Clint begins the litany. "Now when your airspeed drops to 60 knots, pull one notch of flaps. Now add back power to hold 55 knots."

In order to remain flying at the low speed with the extra lift and drag of lowered flaps, it is necessary to increase the angle of attack of the wing. In plain English, this means raise the nose. With the nose raised more power is needed to offset the drag of the slowly moving machine.

"Now pull another notch of flaps and wait for 50 knots," Clint continues, "add power to stabilize."

The process is repeated until the full flaps are extended and air speed is stabilized at 45 knots.

"Make a slow turn to the left, very shallow bank," the instruction continues. "Notice how sloppy the controls are. How much aileron it takes to make the plane respond."

Then, we practice stalls. Slowing the plane down and pulling up the nose until the air moving over the wing begins to break up and no longer lift. As the nose drops following the stall, the natural reaction is to pull back on the wheel to raise the nose. If this is done after the wings have lost their lift, the plane will fall over into a spin and will continue to spin as long as the wheel is pulled back.

"There's the stall," the instructor continues. "Do you feel the shudder. Now, push the wheel forward. Full throttle. As soon as the plane is flying, start pulling back on the wheel. You don't want to lose too much altitude. Remember, when this happens you will be near the ground."

Then we practice approach to landing stalls. We are flying at 3500 feet, but we go through the exercise of entering the pattern on downwind, lowering the first notch of flaps, slowing, turning to base, second notch, third notch as we slow. Then, instead of keeping the nose down to maintain airspeed, we pull back on the wheel as we turn to final. Suddenly, the plane begins to shudder. And this is the last thing many novice pilots have experienced before the machine falls off in a spin that crashes them into the ground, just a few hundred yards from the safety of the runway.

So, we do the exercise over and over. When the shudder starts, we thrust the wheel forward momentarily, add power, and are safely flying again.

Then, we practice takeoff and departure stalls and acceleration stalls. All designed to keep us alive and flying when we're dangerously close to the ground.

Finally, after doing these things over and over and over the reflexes are there and when the crisis comes, often when we are distracted by last minute radio instructions from the tower or by the near miss of a plane landing on the parallel runway, the reflexes are there to protect us. Like money in the bank.

After the move to Al's store room in the new Decatur Federal Building, I was beginning to make some progress toward overcoming my disastrous defeat of 1960.

The year was 1961.

I had been enjoying some success selling land and service station sites. Since I couldn't walk the ground, I had gone to pains to get every detail on the land I had to sell. I would have a topo overlaid on the site plan of the parcel from the available Geodetic Survey, then I'd find out where the sewer and water lines were and what would be involved in getting them to the property. Then, I would lay out streets for a subdivision on the property and estimate the cost of development and the profit to be realized from the sale of the lots.

For the service station sites, I would get traffic counts from the state highway department, population figures in the immediate area and projections of future growth.

Then, I would make up a looseleaf book on the property and go see the major oil companies that were buying in the county.

By doing the work of the developer or investor, I soon knew more than anybody else about the property and the developers and oil company representatives were happy to see me coming. The property owners came to like me because I could multiply the value of their property by my research.

I became especially fond of one elderly widow lady who was a client.

She was a fascinating person. She had been the first woman to attend what had been the all male University of Georgia.

"If you think the blacks had a hard time after integration, you should have seen the way they treated me," she said. "After I graduated in home economics, I rode a horse into the north Georgia mountains, calling on the mountain women, teaching them how to can and preserve their food, teaching them sanitation and how to keep their families healthy and well fed."

Her husband, who had died several years before I met her, had been a World War I fighter pilot.

They had cut a street on the land they owned, had sold residential lots and now had a strip of land remaining that ran for a couple of thousand feet along the main highway.

I visited her on land she had inherited near Penfield, Georgia and that she now operated as a cattle farm.

I think the neighbors on adjoining farms and in the small town thought she was a little daff.

She certainly was different. She drove a pickup truck, wore a man's broad brimmed hat and a man's coat and wore boots.

It made sense. She was doing a man's work.

Actually, she was a cultured person. She subscribed to the New York Times Sunday Edition, and was well read. She had inherited the beautiful primitive furniture in her home — I remember especially a magnificent hunt board.

Her chief intellectual interest was in the Indians who had inhabited that part of Georgia and she had a number of out of print volumes about the various tribes.

She was a Southerner.

I had read a good many books about the War Between the States and happened to mention Sherman's autobiography and how fascinating it was to read the words of the man who had burned his way through Georgia.

She didn't say anything. She just looked at me.

As I was leaving, she walked over and handed me a two volume set, The War Between the States, by Alexander Stephens, the brilliant vice president of the Confederacy. The work gave the constitutional basis for the position taken by the South in the war.

"I reckon I should read this too," I said.

"Yes, you should," she said firmly.

One of her relatives had told her she should sell the strip of property for twenty thousand dollars. One of my competing agents told me we would be doing well to get that amount.

There was a part of it zoned Commercial, but there was a creek and it didn't seem likely that the plot was large enough for a service station site, my specialty.

The site was surveyed, and, with the help of one of my developer friends, was filled. It proved large enough.

One of the major oil companies signed a contract.

My client was so pleased, she gave me an extra thousand dollars in addition to my full commission.

The only time I have received a tip in the real estate business.

I had gotten my widow over four times what her relatives and an 'expert' had told her the property was worth.

I had an advantage in real estate because everybody knew me from my abortive political career. They knew me because I had spent thirteen thousand dollars telling them who I was.

For my part, I was motivated by a desire to get back the ten thousand I had lost in politics. No matter how many times I got it back, I seemed to always want to get it back one more tiem.

Up until that point, Frances and I had had a pretty tough time making ends meet. The government pension was generous and increased every year, but since I was making periodic trips to the hospital to patch up my various pressure sores and had made that big visit to Mayo's and lost the money in politics, our resources were pretty thin.

Now that I was making a good commission from time to time things were better.

When I made my last service station sale, I decided to buy Frances a nice solitary diamond, something I had not been able to afford when we got married.

The tallest building in Atlanta at the time was the National Bank of Georgia Tower. On the top, 32nd, floor there was a restaurant and a bar with an unobstructed view of the city. The friend who sold me my insurance was brought into the project because he owned a Cadillac. He also had a connection to buy diamonds wholesale to replace losses by his customers.

We went to a private office in one of the downtown buildings where I picked out the solitary. It was a big one.

A few days later he, and his wife, Frances, and I rode in the Cadillac to the downtown restaurant.

With the city spread at our feet, I presented the box to Frances.

She opened it up.

The waitress said, "Boy, look at the size of that rock!"

Frances sat, her eyes wide, looking at the stone. I will never forget her next words.

"Has anybody got a dime?"

She wanted to go call her mother.

Behind every successful man there is a surprised mother-in-law. I'm sure mine was the most surprised in history.

The event that was to set me off in a new direction came about as the result of an almost casual meeting.

The First National Bank in Decatur is a branch of the large Atlanta bank. Because of the years spent in the community by Claude Blount, we thought of the branch almost as a local instituion.

The bank had acquired three acres of land a couple of blocks from the courthouse square and was talking about moving the bank to the new location so more parking would be available. The branch, because of the banking laws, was the only one First National could have in the county and it had become their largest and strongest branch.

The downtown merchants and property owners were dismayed at the idea of the bank leaving the square. And the mayor and several other leaders had called on the bank officials and urged them not to move. Or, failing that, to build a large multi-storied building on the new site.

Without knowing what was going on behind the scenes, I went, more as a citizen than an agent, to ask why the site could not be utilized for a large office building.

The executive vice president agreed to see me.

"Mr. Harrison," he said after some discussion, "the bank is not going to build any more big buildings. We just finished the building at North Avenue and we made everybody mad. The contractors who bank with us got mad because they didn't get the job. The contractor who got the job got mad because he felt we squeezed him too much on the price. And the tenants get mad at the bank every time the elevators don't work or the building is too hot or too cold."

I pointed out how well Decatur Federal was doing since they moved into their eight story building. And I talked about how much it would mean to the city in increased job opportunities and ad valorem tax base.

"Well," he said at one point, "we're not going to own another building. We might consider leasing our land to a developer, let him build and own the building and let us be a tenant."

One thing I had learned in the life insurance sales course, once the prospect signs, pick up your hat and leave. At this point, I thanked the man and rolled out the door.

"Pat," we had met in the hall between his suite and my desk in Al's store room, "they say they might be willing to lease their land and they would be tenants in a multi-storied building."

"That's what they ought to do," Pat, his father and brother had built hundreds of plants and warehouses. They had built the Decatur Federal Building, and Pat knew a deal when he saw one. "The building will be ten stories high and will cost $2 million."

Actually, there are eleven stories. The basement was finished for office space and the bank's lunch room.

I started gathering material from every source to show the growth and power of our county and how critical it was for the bank to have an impressive headquarters for their only outlet in the booming DeKalb market. The book I prepared was an inch and a half thick and it had the executive V.P.'s name in raised letters on the cover.

When I went to see him the second time, the reception was icy cold. Apparently, he had had time to reflect on his off the cuff remark and was alarmed that I was about to try to make a real estate deal out of it. After we visited a few moments, I prepared to leave.

"Oh, by the way," I said, "I brought this for you." And I left the book with the embossed name on the edge of his desk.

When we signed the deal for the eleven story First National Bank Building, we had one tenant. Claude Blount is standing behind me second from the right. The gentleman with the worried look standing behind the picture of the proposed building is the owner, Pat Pattillo. I signed 146 other tenants to fill the building.

The next afternoon, seated at my desk in Al's store room, I got a telephone call.

"Mr. Harrison," the official said, "the bank is interested in your proposition and would like to see any figures you may want to present."

One year later the papers were signed, pretty much in the form Pat had visualized in our first conversation. The preparation of plans took months longer and the construction of the building consumed a year and a half, surviving three labor union strikes in the process. The first papers were signed in October of 1962. We moved in the first tenant in December, 1965.

My competitor who had leased the Decatur Federal Building stopped me one day in the hall.

"Clark," he said, "we are going to have to help you lease the new building. You know you can't lease office space until you can show the tenant the actual space. Let him look out the window to see his view and visualize where his desk will be placed. The elevators won't be running until the last thing, so you can't get in to show space."

I had never thought of myself as the leasing agent for the building. I owned a small share because of the year I had spent as broker between the bank and the owner and I thought I might be able to rent enough space for the commissions to pay my own rent in the new building.

But the remarks made that day made me a little sore. I had played a key role in bringing the building into being and now, because of the wheelchair, somebody else would realize the bulk of the profit.

I sat and I thought and I concentrated and I prayed.

There had to be some way office space could be shown without going inside the building. And, if I could figure out a way, it would mean I could begin leasing space before the structure itself was in existence.

I had been trying to learn about big office buildings.

When I first got my real estate license, I had asked Jack, the developer who had brought me word the 'power structure' would like to pay my political debt, how I could learn the real estate business. He told me to do two things. Read a book on appraisals he recommended and go to the national real estate convention.

"The brokers will tell their secrets there," he said. "They are proud of the tricks they've learned, but they won't tell them at home where their competitors might steal their ideas. You'll learn more in three days at the convention than you'll learn in a year at home."

That September, I was pushing my wheelchair through the acres of convention rooms known as Cobo Hall in Detroit. Jack walked up to me.

"What the hell are you doing here?" he asked in amazement.

"Well," I said, "you told me to come."

I had started the negotiations with First National, and I was looking for ideas on how to lease a big building. I arrived at the convention three days ahead of the general crowd and I began asking questions.

Who at this convention will know most about multi-storied office buildings, I asked everyone I met. I ended up with six names of experts in the field.

Then I went to the registration desk at our hotel and left a note in the box of each of the six.

"I am the man in the wheelchair. I would like to talk to you."

There were over five thousand realtors at the convention. I was the only one in a wheelchair.

All six of the men spotted me and visited with me. They were helpful, but I finally realized their experience went back to the twenties, when the last of the major buildings were constructed prior to the Great Depression. There just hadn't been much in the way of multi- storied structures built since.

I kept looking for ideas.

I took some plain white sheets of paper and I wrote out my ideas of how a building could be leased. I showed it to some smart realtors.

By the time they had pointed out all the reasons my ideas were no good, I had received quite a bit of free, unintentional advice.   The main consensus was that anybody would be crazy to build an eleven story office building in Decatur, that it wouldn't rent and that the results for the owner would be disastrous.

One of the first things I had done while the negotiations were going on was to have my accountant prepare a proforma showing expenses and income for the completed building.

The picture was not encouraging. Taking the present rent per square foot from our competitors, the building would lose money over the twenty years it took to pay the mortgage.

We raised the rate 50 cents a square foot and the building would show a small positive cash flow after the first three years.

Provided the building was full of rent paying tenants.

The main thing the projections did was to motivate me. I had greased the skids to get the owners into the deal. Now it was plain to me that unless the building was leased up, and that occurred fairly soon after the doors opened, it would be a financial disaster for those who borrowed the money to build it.

So, figuring out a way to lease without showing the space became critical. Whether I was in a wheelchair or not!

First, I thought of building a model of the building and having a typical floor with moveable partitions and office furniture so the tenant could actually see his space in miniature.

I didn't know anybody who could build such a thing and I decided the whole project would be too costly and unwieldly.

Finally, someone told me that the agent who had leased the thirty- two story National Bank of Georgia building had used quarter inch grid paper to lay out his floors. Each quarter-inch square represented a square foot and made it easy to draw in walls and furniture to scale. I went to see our architect.

"How about superimposing a quarter inch grid over our typical floor plan?" I asked. Fortunately, he was open to new ideas and soon I had a plat of a typical floor, taking two large sheets because of the large scale.

The floors were divided into bays that were marked by the interior columns and the interior hall and outside walls. Each bay was twelve feet wide and twenty-five deep.

We set the rate at $4 a square foot, which made the bays lease for $100 a month. The building is a long rectangele and the bay depth is just right for the small tenant to have a reception room for his secretary and a large office for himself.

Each little square on the plan rented for $4 a year. And it was an easy task to draw in furniture by counting off the squares.

I bought a narrow roll of red tape, about 1/8" in width, that I could stick to the plan where the partitions were to be built.

Now, the thing was simple enough even I could understand it. More importantly, I could explain it to prospective tenants in a way they could understand and give them a plan that would make visual exactly how their office, furnished, would look. From that point on, no prospective tenant would leave my office without a floor plan, prepared while he was answering my questions as to his needs, and a lease for the space with a big red 'X' where he was to sign.

Knowing how to show the space before it existed, the other ingredient I needed was something that would motivate tenants to move in. Frances' brother, John, a trust officer at the bank, gave me the answer.

"Clark," he said, "what you need is a law library. These lawyers have to spend a fortune on a library and that cost is one reason more of them don't set up their own firms out here in Decatur."

I started asking where such a thing had been done and got the name of the Marshall Field Building in Chicago. The leasing manager answered with a three page letter. They had opened the big building in the depth of the depression. It had leased up and currently had over 700 attorneys. It had stayed one hundred per cent leased up since shortly after it opened. He recommended I try the same thing in Decatur.

John put me in touch with a salesman at the law book company and soon we had a list of books that would be available without charge to tenants in our building. We expanded that list by adding a complete set of tax books that would appeal to C.P.A.'s.

As soon as we returned from our camping trip I went to the bank and arranged for a loan to cover my expenses for the next eighteen months so I could concentrate all my efforts on leasing the building. The building was coming out of the ground and we had only one tenant, the bank. That left nine and a half floors of gaping concrete to be filled and tenants weren't exactly falling all over themselves to move to Decatur.

It was overwhelming and I was spending some restless nights thinking of the expense of $400,000 a year the owners would be facing in about 18 months with very little offsetting income.

Finally, I had a talk with myself.

"Frankly, Clark," I told me, "I don't think you can rent this whole building. So, why don't you concentrate on renting one office. I believe you can rent one office."

After I rented the first office, I started working on the second.

Then, I decided that with a bank and a law library what we needed was a stockbroker. Then, instead of a building, we would have a financial center that a lot of professional people would like to be part of.

Decatur had never had a stockbroker.

It took several months of negotiating, but we got the stockbroker and had a big picture in the paper showing Decatur getting its first one.

Since we had so much space, I decided to open only three floors initially. It occurred to me that some people wanted to be as near the ground as possible, so I'd give early signers their choice of the second floor.

Other tenants wanted to be on top, so we'd give the pioneers their choice of the tenth floor.

Then, I reasoned, some might want to be near the law library. I planned it to be next to my office so we could keep an eye on it and do the necessary filing. We put the law library on the eighth floor.

Finally, there were a lot of tenants in old buildings and houses who I wanted to entice into the new structure. These people were skeptical about a long term obligation, so, on the eighth floor only, we would offer early tenants a one year lease as opposed to the three years required elsewhere in the building. Interestingly, most of the people who chose this option stayed with us for many years, their conservatism keeping them in the building once they made that initial move.

Now, the life insurance sales training my friend John had given me came to my rescue.

I didn't know anything about leasing, but I did know you had to have a check to have a deal, so we required a month's rent to reserve a space. I didn't learn until the building was full that other agents didn't require that.

It made our tenants feel they had bought something — no matter who came later, their space was reserved and would be ready for them.

"Clark," my competitor told me, "if you sign Jack, you will deserve a gold medal. We tried to sell him the old Decatur Federal building, we planned a building he'd own for himself and we drew about twenty plans in the new Decatur Federal. He will waste more of your time than anybody you ever dealt with and in the end you won't have anything."

I invited Jack, who had one of the few large law firms in town, to have lunch with me at the Executive Club. He arrived with a junior partner, walked in, pulled off his coat and hung it in the closet of the private room.

"This is the first of many lunches you will buy me as we negotiate," he bellowed.

"The hell it is," I replied, "this is the last one. And I'm not paying for your partner today."

I made five plans for Jack on my quarter inch grid before turning him over to the professional designer. It was becoming obvious that my competitor had told me right about this one.

How could I put pressure on Jack. The building was just coming out of the ground, the second floor had just been poured, the space he wanted didn't exist at the time.

I knew he thought of his as the preeminent law firm in town, that he had to have the best suite, the whole end of the building on the top floor. The idea of the library, the bank, the stockbroker, the financial center all appealed to him.

But, we only had a couple of small offices leased so far in the whole big building.

An architect came to see me. Although he could afford only a little over a bay of space, he had as big an ego problem as Jack. He wanted to be on top too.

And he was ready to sign.

And to pay his $175 month's rent in advance to save his key spot — at the elevator — on the top floor.

I signed him up.

Then I called Jack.

"Jack," I said, "I have just rented the suite adjoining the space you want on the top floor. The next space I plan to rent will be inside your selected location."

Next day the junior partner joined me for lunch.

"Jack is ready to sign," he said, "but he's concerned about tying up his money for that long. It will take at least a year to finish the building and we're talking about over eight hundred dollars. What he would like to do is put the money in an interest bearing escrow account. You will have control of the money, but Jack can draw interest."

I looked at him.

"Larry," I said, "the only thing we will accept is money."

"Well," he hesitated, "I am authorized to give you a check."

"Well!" I exclaimed, "Why in the hell are you sitting there wasting our time. Give me the damn check."

That was my toughest sale, but there were other interesting ones.

After a few minutes in my office, the prospect was bound to leave with a plan and a lease even though the space he had chosen did not yet exist. With the sales techniques I had learned, the tenant felt the urgency. He had to get his check back to me or I'd rent his space to somebody else.

For their part, the owners would do anything to satisfy the tenant. The extreme was a life insurance agent who meandered into my office one day. Knowing something about sales technique himself he was doing a pretty good job of bobbing and weaving as I tried to hem him up — then he made a fatal mistake.

He told me what his objection was.

"I caught the largest blue marlin snared on the east coast in 1963," he boasted, "it is a beauty. Twelve feet long, it weighed in at eight hundred pounds. It would really look good on my office wall."

I called Pat's dad, who was doing the finishing of the building.

"No problem." I hung up the phone and held out the pen. I think he signed in recognition of my sales technique and by way of professional courtesy.

The fish was so big, it would not fit on top of the elevator. I had rented him a spot on the seventh floor.

Mr. H. A. and his workers carried the fish up seven flights of stairs and had to reinforce the wall to hold the beautiful trophy.

The insurance man is still in the building, all these years later, of course.

By the time the building was ready to receive the first tenant, sixty per cent of the space was leased. I had designed two thirds of the offices and had negotiated all the leases.

I had been able to lease space without showing it. Once we were in the building, I found the wheelchair to be no impediment in this type selling and rolled many miles up and down the halls of our building before finally leasing the final space just eighteen months after the opening. Not only was I able to show space before it existed, but I had eliminated the time required by other agents to have the space designed. While my competitors were waiting for their designer, I was signing the tenant.

My favorite conquest was the Department of Vocational Rehabilitation. We had completed the plans to their requirements, had the lease approved by the proper budget official and I was taking the head of the department through the building to see the space.

After following my wheelchair up and down the halls, we returned to my office. I rolled behind my desk and he sat down and lit up his pipe.

"Mr. Harrison," he said, "I have failed to mention one thing that might be a problem. As you know, we deal with disabled people. From time to time, we have visitors who are confined to wheelchairs. Tell me, Mr. Harrison, is this building accessible to wheelchairs?"

I looked him square in the eye, took a deep breath and said:

"I'm sorry but as a matter of fact, you can't get a wheelchair in this building."

He sat, silent in disappointment at this unexpected problem.

And then the light suddenly shown, and he broke into a grin.

He looked at and saw the wheelchair he had been following for the past hour.

With all the positive thinking and talking Dad had pounded into me and the salesmanship technique taught me by my life insurance friend, I suddenly realized something.

It was hard to see the wheelchair with me in it.

CHAPTER XXIX

Pilots are a strange breed. For one thing there aren't many of them. About 800,000 licensed, which makes them a good bit less than one per cent of the total population. For another, they don't talk about their flying much except to other pilots.

That may be because most of us feel a little guilty about doing something that is so much fun. I know that after I got my solo license and could go out all by myself and get in the plane and fly off, I kept expecting somebody to run out in front of me on the taxiway waving their arms for me to stop.

"Stop! Stop!" they would yell in this fantasy, "you didn't think we were going to let a dummy like you who is in a wheelchair take our plane off the ground, did you?"

And it was so strange that once I got off the ground, I was free to go anywhere I wanted to. Anywhere clear of clouds and the Hartsfield Terminal Control Area, that is.

Another reason pilots don't talk is because we do such dumb things. When you're talking to another pilot it's all right because you know he's probably done the same, but it's hard for a non-flyer to understand.

Only after I got my license did my buddy at the health club tell me that he had nearly washed out of cadets in the old Army Air Corps because he pulled back on the stick and landed short of the runway. And I had some laughs with a Delta pilot about his difficulty in getting a single engine private plane on the ground.

Flight instructors will stay on your case with a constant stream of advisory verbage, but once you qualify the only way you'll get advice from a fellow pilot is to ask for it.

"Pilots are funny," one of the old timers was telling me. "They'll stand around and watch you forget to untie one of the tie down ropes. You

379

can get in the plane, start the engine and try to taxi and nobody will say a word as you spin around still tethered to the ground."

Another interesting subject is the way the Federal Air Regulations have evolved.

"When somebody gets killed," my pilot friend explained, "the FAA passes a new regulation. Now, you may get killed the same way but you can't say you got killed legally."

There are all kind of purists flying. But they are pure about different things. Some fly purely for business and some purely for pleasure. Some know every rule and fly IFR. Some scoff at the rules and have no instruments in the plane other than a magnetic compass and a turn indicator.

Some scoff at anything other than aerobatics and some think any flight that fails to carry you from point A to point B is a waste of time.

But for each variety of purist, every flight is a new adventure and a chance to pit skill and knowledge against the fickle vagaries of the elements. No matter how many men or women have faced the challenge in the past, it is always a new and an equal challenge for the next man or woman to fly.

With the First National Bank Building a reality and with its financial success assured with the leasing of the final suite of offices, my fortunes were taking a definite turn for the better.

In addition to leasing the one hundred and twenty two thousand feet of office space, I had also handled the sale of the old bank building on the square to DeKalb County. The commission repaid the money I had borrowed to survive during the eighteen months before I received the first dollar from the rental of office space.

It had never occurred to me that I would negotiate leases to fill the entire building and I had made no plans at all for managing the building.

As the day we would move the first tenants into the building came closer, Pat suggested that I'd better hire somebody to look after collecting the rent and paying the bills. Elizabeth, who took care of all his corporation accounts stopped me one day in the hall.

"You need to talk to my sister," she said, "her daughter has just gone off to college and she needs something to keep her busy."

Virginia came to see me a few days later. In her fur-trimmed jacket and diamond rings, she looked very much like what she is, the wife of one of the officials of one of our local savings and loans. "I haven't worked since Cheryl was born," she said. "I used to keep books and I can do some typing, but I don't take shorthand."

A few days later, I called her to tell her I wanted her to help me open the building.

"Who else have you talked to?" she demanded.

"Nobody," I replied, "I want you to do it. You'll enjoy it. Really, it's just a part time receptionist-librarian type job."

I didn't mention we'd be handling 147 tenants and nearly a half million in rent each year.

Virginia told me later she instantly regreted having agreed to come, but decided she would help me a few days until things got sorted out.

Things never did get sorted out. When I started running for chairman, Virginia couldn't very well leave and when I was elected she agreed to stay only on condition she could have Wednesdays off.

She likes to play golf on Wednesdays.

I had signed 147 tenants before the building was finally full and each one had his or her problems, statements had to be sent out, money collected and bills paid. The building had to be cleaned and new offices built as old tenants moved out. There was the hiring and scheduling of the security guards, the landscaping to be maintained, etc., etc. When I left to be chairman, Virginia took on the leasing as well as the other chores.

We had the best run building in the city and during the fifteen years Virginia ran things, our occupancy never dropped below ninety two per cent. "I had made up my mind," she told me years later, "that when you came back from the county and got your feet on the ground, I would leave. The trouble was, you never did take over."

I looked at her. "Virginia," I said, "I may be dumb, but I am not stupid. This place ran better while I was gone than it did while I was here. This is your building. I'll find something else to do."

After working for nothing for eighteen months and borrowing money to keep my office open, I was finally beginning to receive commissions from the leases.

We had never had a luxury car, but now Frances called and told me to come look at a car on the Lincoln Mercury lot.

I think it must have been sitting there all year. It was a huge four door Lincoln, pale yellow with a black roof. Inside was pure black leather upholstery and every device Detroit could think up in those ego boosting days. There was an autronic eye to dim the lights, stereo radio and tape player, six way power seats and a thermostat that maintained a constant temperature winter and summer.

It looked like one of the limousines Daddy Warbucks used on his infrequent visits to Little Orphan Annie. I fully expected Punjab to come around and open the door for me.

Since there aren't many river boat gamblers or foreign ambassadors in Decatur, I was able to get a real good buy on the rig. In fact, the price was less than a so called economy car today.

And I liked it. The back door was hinged at the rear and there was so much room the wheelchair practically rolled in by itself. On the highway, I could set the speedometer at 80 and the kids could lie down and read on the back seat.

The morning after I drove the car back home, I came out, got in, rolled the chair in, sank back against the soft leather seats and, as I started the car pushed the eight track tape holder into the stereo.

The tune that came blasting out was "Seventy Six Trombones!" As I rode along, I thought:

I must be a success.

Nobody but a success could ride like this.

Not bad for a retired private first class, defeated politician.

I had rented a large office for myself, had had it decorated and furnished by a professional designer and had signed a ten year lease with three five year options to renew. That'll take me to age 65, I figured, then I'll have to make other arrangements. My theory was, if I was going to fill up all that space in the building, I didn't want my prospects thinking small when they signed their lease.

The fall when I finally signed up the last bit of space in the building, I was sitting on the sofa in my office, with my feet resting in the wheelchair.

Virginia came in to tell me an old friend had come to see me. Formerly the southeastern head of public relations for a large national concern, the gentleman owned a good deal of property in the county and was active in local political affairs.

"Who are we going to get to run for chairman?" he asked me after we had exchanged a few pleasantries.

"I've got no idea," I replied.

After my bitter defeat, I had taken no interest in politics and I knew I had spent all the money I'd ever spend trying to get elected.

"Well," he said, "a lot of people say the school superintendent might want to run, but I think he's too important where he is."

I agreed. We had the fastest growing and second largest system in the state and the superintendent had gained a national reputation for the excellence of educational opportunities provided our children.

He named a couple of other people and reasons why they probably couldn't get elected. Finally, he said, "Why don't you run, Clark? You're the right age, you've got a good reputation in the business community, and you know more about the county than anybody we've got."

"Sure," I agreed. "If somebody will put up a hundred thousand dollars, I'll run."

I said it knowing that it would take that much advertising to win and knowing I wasn't going to put money into a campaign again. I figured that would end the conversation and get me back to concentrating on the real estate brokerage business.

"Would you really do that?" he sounded excited. "A hundred thousand shouldn't be any problem. We spent seventy-five getting Charlie elected."

Charlie, who had won the year I came in fourth, had been defeated by the current incumbent who was no friend of development in the county.

"Sure, I'll do it," I agreed, still feeling that that would be the end of the conversation and of that particular balloon.

The next day I started getting telephone calls from the major developers. I assured each one of them that I would run if I was assured of a hundred thousand dollars for advertising.

Finally, one of them called and asked, "Just how do you want to do this, Clark?"

"Well," I replied, "All I want is a piece of paper signed by ten men, each one of whom is capable of putting up ten thousand dollars and I want it to read 'we, the undersigned agree to underwrite any campaign loss up to the amount of one hundred thousand dollars.'"

A couple of weeks later, we had a steak and bourbon dinner at the country place of one of the lawyers, the signed paper was presented to me and then taken and locked in a bank vault until the election was over. I told the signers

"I don't want a penny out of this. I'll pay my own expenses. But, I am not going to put a penny into the campaign otherwise. I have already lost ten thousand dollars in politics and that's enough. There is not a man involved in this campaign who will have as much time, effort and money in it when it's over as I'll have in it when it starts.

I knew all the men and knew they were honorable.
And all of them knew me and knew I could not be bought.
After all, they had tried that once — eight years before.

CHAPTER XXX

The day I soloed was exciting. But it was nothing compared to the next time I went out to the airport and got in the plane to taxi by myself.

For one thing, the day of the solo, Clint had gone around the pattern with me several times before getting out of the plane with the announcement he'd be watching from the tower.

His imprint was still in the right seat, his vibes were still vibrating in the cockpit and his admonitions were still ringing in my ears. My reflexes were warmed up and my mind was tunneled into the few simple things I had to do to get the plane back on the ground.

You have to understand a couple of things. For example, while the airplane may be a graceful bird in the air, it's a waddling gooney on the ground. You're sitting down low, you can see to the front and sides but are completely blind to the rear. The runway pattern is confusing, especially to the novice, because you really can't see anything but the strip of pavement in front of you. You have to creep along straddling the yellow taxi line and know which line to follow when they diverge to the different runways for take off.

What complicates this simple chore is the high state of excitement the new flyer finds himself in. On the day of my big adventure, my ears were buzzing and my sight was blurred by the massive self inflicted dose of adrenalin.

"Turn right, turn right 883," the tower called sharply.

A moment later, a Cessna roared by right in front of me. I had been about to cross the active runway, having mistaken the yellow line to runway 34 for the one that swung out to the right for 2 left.

That shook me up some more. I did my runup at 2L, pulled the door shut and called the tower.

"This is Cherokee 883," I spoke into the mike, "number one for takeoff. Stay in the pattern for touch and goes."

"Eight eight three cleared for take off."

I taxied on the runway, thrust the throttle full forward, held the wheel with my left hand and grasped the rudder bar with my right. The engine roared, I picked up speed as I hurdled down the runway. Airspeed passed 60 knots and I pulled back on the wheel lifting the rudder bar at the same time to counteract the torque action of the propeller spinning at 2700 revolutions per minute.

As the Warrior left the ground, I became conscious of the roar and pounding of the engine. It was twice as loud as it had been on past flights with Clint.

"Oh, God," I thought in panic, "what's wrong with the engine?"

I looked around wildly and then realized that in my excitement I had failed to latch the door. Lord knows I'd tried long enough. What I had done was try to fasten it by forcing the latch handle to the left instead of to the right.

As the altimeter reached 400 feet, I made my turn to the left, holding the bank until I as at ninety degrees to the runway which was growing smaller down to my left as I climbed. Then I leveled off momentarily and made another ninety degree turn to place me parallel with the runway I had just departed.

"This is 883," I called the tower, "downwind. Full stop."

I leveled off at 2000 feet. Once around was all I could stand with the racket filling the cockpit. As I came opposite the big numbers on the runway end, I eased to 1800 rpm, pulled the first notch of flaps and began the slow descent. With the runway end making a 45 degree angle back from the junction of my left wing to the fusilage, I reduced power to 1500 rpm, banked left onto the base leg of the pattern and pulled the second notch of flaps. The third notch came on as I made the turn to final approach.

Fortunately, the wind was calm as I eased the plane down toward the numbers.

As I taxied off the runway, I called ground control.

"883, clear of the active. Taxiing to Epps."

Shaking with excitement and bathed in sweat I taxied down the yellow line, thinking how good this exercise had been to clear my sinuses and open my clogged carotid arteries.

Next time I got the door properly fastened.

Dick Haltom was the first paraplegic from our hospital to return to an active business career. The move to Kennedy General in Memphis put Dick within fifty miles of his home at Batesville, Mississippi. Soon after I checked out of Kennedy, Dick went home and went to work.

"I never had any ambition to do anything but work in the drugstore," Dick told me. "Before I went in the Army, I spent some time in college and then decided I might as well get to work. Daddy was sick at the time, needed help and neither one of my brothers were interested. The family said I acted like an old man when I was just out of college. After working in the store, I was happy most nights to come home and sit around poking the fire and dozing away."

Located at the edge of the rich Mississippi Delta country, Batesville has a heavy black population and on Saturdays the drug store is thronged with blacks of every age and description. Dick knows most of them and they all know him.

The drug store is a center of life, action and unending drama for Dick and he can make it come alive in the imagination of the uninitiated as he talks about it.

"Let's go to the back of the store," Dick said to me the first time I visited the Haltom Drug Store. "I get tired of them standing around with their mouths open gawking at me."

We retreated to the rear of the store where a huge pot bellied stove constituted a conversation center while it heated the high ceilinged old store.

Of all the people I have met, and with eight years as a local politician that covers a multitude, Dick is the best story teller.

Dick's wife, Nina, was a nurse at Kennedy and met Dick when he had to return briefly to mend a broken leg. Nina understands paraplegics, having dealt with them en masse, and she and Frances have become close buddies through their dealings with Dick and me over the years. Nina can tell a good yarn too, and when she reminisces about her years at Kennedy she can highlight the problems of idle men confined together over a period of months.

People stereotype people in wheelchairs, Nina said, but they can be as mean and ornery as the kind who walk around.

"We had one of our patients who was recovering use of his legs," Nina recalled. "He was beginning to walk and it made some of the others mad. They'd get drunk in the ward at night and sit around and cuss about this other fellow starting to walk around the hospital. One patient in particular was really burned up."

Finally, the patient who was mad got drunk, got a pistol, and swore he was going to shoot the smart ass walker.

"He loaded the pistol and started rolling over toward the other patient's bed waving the pistol and shouting," Nina continued.

The other patients thought he was bluffing. Fortunately, one of the on-lookers threw a pillow just as the pistol was fired.

"It ruined his aim," Nina said, "and the bullet hit the walking man in the leg. He had been aiming at his head."

With excitement in the hospital reaching a cresendo, the FBI was sent in and a thorough investigation made. There was no doubt about the paraplegic's guilt — the problem was what to do with the shooter.

"They didn't want to send him to jail because he would have needed a nurse to go with him," Nina concluded. "Finally, they just discharged him from the hospital. The last we heard, he went to California and checked in the VA hospital there."

Paraplegics are human. Dick told me about a problem he had had with one of the suppliers to the drug store. Dick had ended up cussing the man out.

"You know," Dick said with a grin, "that fellow hates my guts. It sure is a good feeling."

Nina is right.

Until the person in a wheelchair learns how to handle it, the people around him will put him in a stereotype box. I had a taste of it after my four years as a district county commissioner. Our telephone poll had in-dicated everybody was 'for' me. But what they really saw was a nice young man who was pleasant and likeable but who could not be seriously consi-dered for the heavy responsibility of running the county.

"Clark is a nice fellow," they would say, "but his health would not stand being chairman."

What they really meant was they didn't think I was mean enough.

The fact I had now beaten the competition in leasing the largest build-ing in town was helping, and the flashy Lincoln was evoking some jealousy that couldn't hurt. And I was going to have a hundred thousand dollars to publicize the mean side of my nature.

Sooner or later everyone reaches a point where he no longer wants to be in a stereotype box. I was at that point.

The public image of the wheelchair was about to be altered.

The county has changed so much since 1968, it is hard to recreate the atmosphere that prevailed in DeKalb in that year. As outlined earlier, there was a power structure consisting of developers, builders and financial institutions actively involved in meeting the demand for new homes and commercial structures for newcomers moving southeast from all over the U. S. For years, an average of five thousand new homes had been built annually in the county.

Following the homes came the new shopping centers, industrial developments and the first hotels and multi-storied office buildings.

The Atlanta expressway system was nearing completion with close to half the total mileage in DeKalb County. And the flight to the suburbs of homeowners trying to avoid school integration was being followed by a flight of business to suburban office parks being built along the new expressway system.

It was an explosive era with the conflict over the Vietnam war building toward a climax and the struggle of the black man for a new place in the sun bringing an old bitterness to the surface.

Martin Luther King was murdered the spring I started running.

"A bomb's been put in your building. It's going off in an hour. You better get all the people out."

That telephone call was received by our office and the office of our competitor at Decatur Federal.

The black high school in Decatur was closed over the protests of the black community and the students were integrated into one school.

In Decatur, urban renewal had bought out the old negro slum located right next to downtown, the small houses had been leveled. The occupants were as much Decaturites as their white neighbors and had used the money the government paid them to buy homes from whites on the south side of the railroad. It looked as though Decatur would go the way of East Atlanta and become one hundred per cent black.

One of our leading developers, interested in building inside the city to help stem the outflow of whites, proposed to build nine new townhouses within a few blocks of the court square on what had been a city park. The city was debating sale of the land when the announcement was made that the black high school would be closed. Most residents felt that would sound the death knell for white residency inside the city.

The former mayor moved out of Decatur to the northside of Atlanta.

"Wales," I called the developer after I heard about the townhouses, "I want to buy the first lot in Charter Square and I want you to build us the first townhouse in DeKalb County."

He decided to go ahead with the project, building the houses on a cost plus basis for individual home owners. The development, consisting of a total of one and one third acres, was at the corner of the best white development in the city but extended down the street that still held the old black community.

The houses, built with zero lot lines and right at the curb of the street were all Federal period colonial with Charleston, New England, French, and Williamsburg styles all represented.

With memories of the government requirements of four foot hallways and three foot doors, we had Wales build us a two story Williamsburg townhouse.

The same spirit that had led me to buy a Ford for my first car — when all good sense dictated an Olds with automatic gear shift — made me feel there was no reason I shouldn't have a two story house — just because I was in a wheelchair.

A small elevator takes me to the second floor and the only hint of wheelchair is the short brick ramp to the back stoop and the single side bar at the tub upstairs.

I told Wales what I wanted to spend and said,

"I want something that will go with the Lincoln. I want to make people in Decatur think, 'Hey, these guys must know something we don't. If they'll build a new house like that, darned if I'm going to give up my house in Decatur.'"

Each house in Charter Square is different, but all complement and fit together in a way that gives a European air to the compact development. People visiting Atlanta from as far away as New Orleans have made a special trip to Decatur to see Charter Square.

"It violates every code in the book," Wales told me. "We had to get variances for everything. You still couldn't build it under the new city building code."

Later, while I was chairman, we would devise a new zoning and subdivision ordinance for DeKalb County based on lessons learned in townhouse development from Charter Square. Until the development was built, quality was equated with large lots in this part of the suburban U. S. Our lot in Charter Square was just big enough for the house and a small yard with enough room for Bob to kick his soccer ball.

But, we had fee simple title.

We were not a condominium and we didn't have to go to meetings with the neighbors to decide what to do with our property.

It was a subdivision with the land removed, I used to say.

I told people we were block busters. We were the first white family on Trinity Avenue.

We had guessed right. The flight to the suburbs of whites halted in Decatur and young couples began to move back into the old subdivisions.

From my bedroom window, I could see the new First National Bank Building. The small lot had a brick wall around it, so if the lawn doesn't get cut we don't offend the neighbors.

Best of all, it is a home we can live in for the rest of our lives.

We still plan to add a Japanese garden, one of these days.

We moved into the new house in April of 1968, just before the campaign for chairman started.

And now I had the new First National Bank Building, the Lincoln and the townhouse to counter my former image as a nice young fellow in a wheelchair.

Once the agreement assuring the financial underwriting of the campaign was signed, there were two objectives that needed early action to assure success for this second effort to become chairman.

In the first place, it was my intention to win this time. I had tried losing and I didn't like it. I was determined not to go that route again.

The money for a successful campaign was assured. Now, I wanted to have the best professional guidance for the conduct of the campaign.

They say a lawyer who represents himself has a fool for a client. I had learned the hard way the same is true — in spades — for the politician who does his own speech writing and advertising.

The other thing I wanted was to be sure that I had a productive four years as chairman. Having watched previous administrations, I was convinced that an individual could sit four years as chairman without making a dent in the plodding bureaucratic procession of daily county business. For three years, I had had to do dumb things because I was low man in the Army and I had spent four years as a district commissioner trying to explain county policies that often didn't make sense to me.

By this time, nothing aggravated me like having to do something dumb simply because it had been laid down by somebody somewhere in the dim past.

I had decided that during our four years we would change DeKalb County — hopefully for the better.

Reg was suggested as the man to run the campaign. We had lunch.

Reg had had a long and successful career as a political newsman and analyst for one of the Atlanta dailies and was now working independently as a writer for Life magazine and other national publications.

"Reg," I told him, "I found out I don't know how to get good publicity. When I ran before, I was either ignored or when I did get attention it was because of some offhand remark that ended up in the headlines. For example, we built the first little league field in the county while I was in office but the headline I got was for proposing that the little league teams be licensed. I was trying to give everybody an equal shot at the use of the fields, but I might as well have come out against motherhood."

Reg agreed there was a technique for getting good press.

I promised him. "Reg, you write it down and I'll read it. Until after the election, I say nothing to the press that's not written down."

And I stuck by that promise.

There are two kinds of political jobs. One is like the district commissioner job I had held for four years. People know it is a policy making job and that final responsibility is divided among members of a board. The job is important, but the public does not become intensely interested in the race for this type job. The average voter is more likely to ask the advice of friends and not to have strongly held views about the candidates.

And, he is likely to vote for a name he has heard rather than to be well informed about the individuals running.

The main thing in such a race is to get your name before the public in any way possible and to create a favorable impression on the people you meet during the campaign.

The other type job is an executive position such as the U.S. presidency, the governorship, or the job I was interested in, chairman of our large urban county. In terms of being able to affect the lives of a large number of people, the chairmanship in DeKalb County would rank as the number three political job in Georgia. In terms of direct control, the organization of the government was such that the chairman, as the job was then constituted, was more powerful than either the governor of Georgia or the mayor of Atlanta.

In 1968, DeKalb was the fastest growing county in the state and was suffering the pressures of development. Millionaires were literally made by a majority of the commission voting to approve a re- zoning petition.

Emotions ran high as the residential neighborhoods felt threatened by the influx of commercial developments. Looking on themselves as the true owners of the county, the single family residents gazed with scorn upon apartment renters and with distrust at shopping center developers.

Their fears were not unfounded. Neighborhoods were damaged and the quality of life decimated by certain changes brought about by county action.

The other side of that coin was the fact that most of the single family home owners cost the county more in terms of services than they paid in taxes. This was especially true when there were several small children to be educated in the public schools.

Without the heavy taxes paid by the commercial and industrial users of county land, the tax rate for homeowners would have become prohibitive or the services and the quality of education would have deteriorated significantly.

So, as the single family residential areas blossomed, it became increasingly important to have a balance of other types of heavy taxpaying use.

The average voter looked to the chairman as the man most able to control the drift of government in this volatile environment. Added to the threat of undesirable development was the fact that the county government performed the housekeeping functions that were such an ever present necessity in the average citizen's life. When the voter hit a pot hole in his road, saw garbage strewn from this house to the county sanitation truck, or paid his lump sum annual county tax bill, he always thought first of the chairman.

And the news media abetted his fiercely held aversion for that scapegoat. When something went awry, it was always the chairman who was brought before the viewing public to field the tough questions.

People think of politics as being dirty and they certainly read things in their newspapers and hear reports on radio and TV that substantiate that view of things.

There is a reason politics can seem almost physical in its violence when an important issue or election is at stake.

Politics is a substitute for battle.

Just read the history of the early English monarchies to get a view of the alternative. All eyes focused on the King, or Queen, and, since there were no elections to transfer power, it became necessary to execute rivals, or, if the outers were to get in, to poison or otherwise murder the monarch.

In our democracy, once the election is over, the power that caused all the uproar in early England is still there and the pressures build until every two or four years they are allowed to boil to the surface when a new election is held. The election often makes a display that is less than poetic.

A lot of people other than the incumbent and his challengers are interested in the outcome — jobs are at stake, developments are at stake, neighborhoods are at stake — the whole future is at stake.

If you don't think it makes a difference to the total community who is in charge, you have never been on the inside.

For the challenger to succeed in unseating the incumbent, it is necessary to stir the passions latent in the populace. To create the unrest that leads to revolution and the discontent that yearns for redress.

It doesn't happen automatically. The vested interests of a lot of people are at stake. They may not like the incumbent but they know how to work with him. They are afraid of the unknown of dealing with a new man. Such people want to leave things as they are.

My problem in my first ill-fated attempt at the chairmanship was two fold.

For one thing, my youth and lack of established business reputation belied ability to wrestle with the tough problems that end up on the chairman's desk. For another, I misunderstood the nature of this kind of political contest. It was not enough to be well known and well liked. The public was looking for redress of their grievances accumulated over four years of mismanagement of their affairs that had culminated in high taxes and poor or non-existing services.

Or at least so it seemed to many voters.

They wanted a champion. One who was strong, who was angry and who would not be afraid to spill a little blood as he flailed his opponent in open combat.

My nature is to be positive but reasonable. Following that course had cost me ten thousand dollars and some public embarrassment. If I was going to win, I was going to have to make a fight out of it, and that was what I decided to do. Reg agreed to be my manager.

The other thing I had decided to do was to change DeKalb County.

I knew the changes I wanted made, but I also knew the weight and inertia of the bureaucracy was such that it would take a major infusion of new leadership to make any change in the direction the county was moving.

I had lunch with two legislators whose judgment and ideas I respected and I asked them who I could bring to DeKalb to manage the government.

"I want a professional with guts," I told them. "Somebody who understands the government and who can get down in the boiler room and make the ship go in the direction we decide to steer."

They had one recommendation. Don had managed the City of Savannah until a change in the political party running the government had led him to leave. He had written a book on local government financing and was teaching at the University of Georgia.

A few days later, Don and I were having coffee at the Center for Continuing Education, University of Georgia at Athens. We talked for over an hour and before I left, Don had agreed to come to DeKalb County as Executive Assistant.

We would use the job as originally contemplated in the law that created the multiple commission form of government. I would steer and Don, as a professional manager, would see to it the ship followed the plotted course.

It was my intention to win, and Reg with his political savvy and writing ability, would guide me through the political quagmire. Once past the elections, Don and I would reshape DeKalb County.

And my finance committee would see to it we didn't run out of steam on the way there.

That's the way we planned it and that's the way it was done.

DeKalb County would never be the same.

We even changed the image some people held of wheelchairs.

CHAPTER XXXI

After 37 years of being tied to slow moving, physically exhausting, pushing of the steel wheelchair, flying and the egomania that accompanies it comes as a healthful antidote.

Flying high above a large city, or a vast wonder like the western buttes, the pilot can suffer from the delusion that the world is his personal possession and domain. The illusion becomes a flight into fantasy on a clear night.

The passenger on a jet liner sees a small framed picture, like watching a television movie on a small screen. From a small plane, on the other hand, the world becomes real, or, more accurately, unreal in the new dimension. On a clear night the black velvet of the city is strewn with costly jewels of light in strings, in patterns, some moving, others flashing and beckoning.

It is a wonderland and it is the pilot's possession.

In a more mundane way, the politician comes to own his constituency, his particular subdivision of the earth's surface. It is not altogether illusion.

Today, I drive along highways that were widened, see buildings that were built, visit a hospital that came into existence while I was leading our county. The power to do these things came from many sources and many people, but the fact they came into existence when they did and where they did was directly influenced by actions we took and by the kind of county we helped create.

Nobody else knows it as I do, because nobody else saw what was happening, what did and what didn't happen because of things said and done at a critical point in the development of events.

At Christmas, I shop at one of the region's leading shopping malls. Millions of dollars are spent and earned every year in this place and I remember the visit from the developer.

"Clark," he said, "this gentleman represents a major department store that will be our key tenant. He wants to ask you a question."

"Mr. Harrison," the visitor says, "we are not going to commit to this center unless we know the highway network around the center will be complete and the traffic lights all in place before our opening day. I want to hear you say all of this will be accomplished on time before we sign a lease."

A major center in Atlanta was bankrupted and the tenants were wiped out because the state highway department blocked the entrance to their center for over a year.

"The work will be completed," I looked him in the eye as I said it. A year later, I watched as the last traffic lights were put into operation the week before the store's opening day.

I ran for chairman for several reasons. There was, of course, the desire to prove I could do it after the humiliating defeat in 1960. But it took a lot more than that to give me the necessary motivation.

I like to see things happen. Having been forced out of the mainstream as a young man, I felt more strongly than most in this regard.

Having grown up in a poverty stricken South, suffering from the subtle but deadly effective economic suppression of the region following defeat in the War Between the States, I knew what a job means to a family, what educational opportunities mean to young people.

It is hard to visualize the present day prosperous South as it was in the thirties. The change came about in the post-World War II era when freight rates were equalized and the returning soldiers who had served in the South returned to homes in the North and West to tell about the opportunities the area held.

In DeKalb County in 1969, we were on the cutting edge of that change and I was proud to have a hand in moving the new wealth into my home community. As one of our more colorful governors during the hard scrabble days put it, "It's easier to pick tourists than it is to pick cotton."

And it was better to see people bringing prosperity from other parts of the country than to nurse old wounds or to try to preserve narrow visions.

My experience as a private in the Army and as a patient in a VA hospital taught me to hate stupidity. When practiced at the top level it can create havoc and unnecessary misery for thousands of people.

I believe fervently that "without vision the people perish." A community needs innovative and creative leadership or opportunity is wasted and suffering results.

And I like to see people treated fairly. The main thing that motivated me against the incumbent I was to face that long summer was the effect he had on the people who worked for him and the builders and developers who need county approval for their projects to go forward.

A spirit of fear seemed to dominate the courthouse.

Employees were underpaid and policies seemed to be formulated with the single purpose of continuing the chairman in office.

When the head of our county road department was publicly criticized by the chairman, I had the personal issue I needed to justify going for the jugular.

The man criticized had won the respect of our commission during the Claude Blount era for his professionalism and the impartial way he decided priorities. This very trait brought the ire of this chairman who was trying to buy political support by manipulating the priorities. In other words, corralling the vote for the chairman's re-election was more important than spending the people's money where the greatest need lay. But the thing that riled me most was the fact that the department head could have been dismissed at any time by the chairman. He would have left without causing any controversy. Instead, the effort was made to turn public opinion against a man who was doing his job.

I knew a price was going to have to be paid to get the incumbent out of office. I was prepared to pay the price.

Once the decision was made to run, the question we faced was to find an issue that would stir the people. It was a tough problem.

The year before the race was to begin, the commission lowered the tax rate. Now the public was told that the county was in excellent financial shape and was able to lower the tax rate because of efficiencies introduced by the chairman.

His battle plan was well laid. For the first two years of the administration, economy was the watchword. Projects were turned down, the budget tightly controlled. Then, eighteen months before the race was to begin, the money tap was opened. All sorts of things yearned for by various community groups were approved by the commission and work on them started.

About the time the spending spree began, the finance director for the county resigned. A few months later the budget director, a sharp young Jewish man, was fired.

Later we learned that, after these two professionals left, a budget as such was not presented to the board of commissioners. Instead, all that was shown the board was a list of projects and expenditures to be made without any corresponding information as to where the money was coming from or even if there would be enough to cover the expenses of the county.

Safeguards used over the years to protect the taxpayers' money were manipulated

The fiscal year for the county was changed to July lst rather than at the end of December. This would cloud the picture by leaving the day of accounting to six months after a new administration took office should the incumbent be defeated.

No county audit was ordered for the year ending the July that marked the beginning of the campaign and none would be made until months after the voters had made their decision.

There was an overall strategy in the careful plans the incumbent had laid to assure his re-election.

The county had received an infusion of money when two of the major financial sources were moved forward in their due date. The automobile ad valorem tax was changed to be collected prior to April lst as tags were sold rather than being due in the fall with other ad valorem taxes. And sanitation taxes were to be paid quarterly in advance rather than at the end of the year. Finally, the ad valorem tax, major tax source of the county, was changed by state law to be payable in two installments with the first due July 1 instead of the total being due in December as previously provided. As a result of this one time early infusion of money, the chairman announced in the spring prior to the beginning of the campaign that for the first time DeKalb County was not having to borrow from the banks to finance operations until tax time. It was a tough scenario for a challenger to tackle. A heavy list of popular projects were being initiated, taxes had been cut, and the county was on a pay as you go basis. In addition, the builders and developers were being shown special attention from the one man in position to favor them with zoning and project approvals.

It was a good thing I had the piece of paper that would assure the financing of my campaign. After July, I began to hear rumblings that the chairman wasn't so bad after all. Clark's campaign seemed to be going nowhere, and maybe we should leave well enough alone.

But as the summer's campaign was about to start, the chairman made two mistakes.

First, he fired the young Jewish budget director.

Secondly, he allowed himself to become involved in a two man race.

I asked one of my supporters later how it was that the chairman had not gotten a third weak candidate into the race. This would have split his opposition and, with his strong organization of supporters, would probably have assured his re-election. "He thought you were the weak candidate," he replied. "We kept telling him that nobody was behind you and that the developers didn't have a candidate."

As we continued to look for an issue, any issue that would lead us to a crack in what seemed an impenetrable armor surrounding the astute politician, I was told on several occasions to see the former budget director.

Finally, in desperation, I arranged to have lunch with him.

"The county is in bad financial condition," he told me.

"I can't believe that," I said, "According to the newspapers, the county's not borrowing money for the first time in history."

He explained that the auto ad valorem and sanitation fees were coming in early.

"It's a one shot deal," he said, "and the revenues that would have come in at the end of the year will have already been spent."

I let out a low whistle.

"He is going to borrow six million dollars in May," he continued, "and the money's not going to be there at the end of the year to pay it back." If what he said was true, the chairman was cynically lying to the people, counting on buying the election with his spending spree, and planning to keep the matter hidden until after his re-election.

Should he be defeated, the question of who was responsible for the financial mess would be clouded by the fact that an audit would not be performed as of the takeover by the new chairman. It would come some eight months after a new administration took office and blame could be laid at the feet of the new incumbent.

If we could blow the whistle on the scheme, we had the issue that would discredit the chairman prior to the election.

The problem I had was that I did not know myself whether the budget officer's story was true.

Several years prior, a senior official of one of our major Atlanta banks gained a state wide reputation by heading a commission for governmental efficiency and economy that cleaned up a mess in the state's purchasing department. Bill's interest in politics had continued and he was often mentioned as a strong potential gubernatorial candidate. Bill decided against a political career for himself and instead sought to aid men he considered honest and capable to gain high office. He had recruited me after my defeat in the chairman's race in 1960 to head the successful campaign in DeKalb

County that played a key role in the election of Carl Sanders as governor.

Now, I decided to ask Bill for his help. I went to his office at the bank and explained the apparent situation that had been revealed by the deposed budget director.

He was impressed and immediately interested.

"My problem, Bill," I said, "is that I don't know if it's the truth. I know you can do all kinds of tricks with figures and I know the former budget director is bitter about the treatment he received."

Bill called in two younger men, financial experts employed by the bank and I went over the same ground with them.

"I tell you what, Clark," Bill said, "let us get with the man and go into details of what he is saying. If it sounds like he's got something, we'll get back with you."

That was the last I would hear about the matter until the closing days of the campaign.

In the meantime, Reg was putting together a campaign that he hoped might have some effect on the public.

"Remember, Clark," he told me, "you're in a war. This guy is out to get you and he'll do it too if you don't get him first. If you try to be Mr. Nice Guy, you're licked. You've got to attack, attack, attack!"

It was against everything in my nature, but I was beginning to believe it was important for me to win, not just for the sake of my ego, but in order that things could be set right and people both in the government and in the general population be benefited.

"You are going to have one speech," Reg said. "There will be a thirty minute version, a twenty minute version, and a five minute version, but they will all be the same speech. It will be a mean speech and you are not going to like it, but it's got to be done."

You write it, I assured him, and I'll read it.

Reg had left the Atlanta newspaper where he had earned his credentials by hard hitting political reporting. He was manager of a local magazine but his real ambition was to become 'the world's greatest photographer — writer.' He also was doing articles for several national publications, and with the income from our campaign, he left his eight to five job to become altogether free lance.

He had twin problems. First, he had to let people know there was a Clark Harrison and then he had to change the image of a nice young fellow in a wheelchair.

"I want the ugliest meanest picture of you I can get," Reg said.

"With my eagle boy scout good looks, that won't be easy," I countered.

He finally got one that looked pretty mean and by overdeveloping the print made me look like a real so and so.

Then, he came by the 'Y' and got pictures of me swimming, took me to a north Georgia lake and got me fishing from a power boat, and he got a picture of me looking up at the First National Bank Building.

In all, he must have taken a thousand pictures. I found the process soul-satisfying after being ignored for eight years. The results were printed in an eight page tabloid newspaper. The cover was a family portrait, in color, that introduced me to the voters as a combination sportsman, business-man and governmental visionary.

I began to believe I was the knight in shining armor the county needed.

It is still my favorite newspaper.

We rented a small office fronting on the sidewalk right across the street from the courthouse. The chairman could look down from his ninth floor sanctuary and see the mean picture of me enlarged to several times life size, leering up at him twenty four hours a day.

"Would you say he looks confident?" I was talking to Carl, who was helping Reg with the campaign. Carl was just out of college and was eating up the opportunity to be involved in a political race. We were attending the dinner dance given by our county Democratic party just prior to the kickoff of the summer campaign.

"Yes," Carl replied, "I believe I'd say so. Let's face it, Clark, he's got reasons. And they don't all have to do with the fact he thinks we don't know what we're doing — although I must admit that is probably a major element in his sanguine attitude."

My opponent was resplendent in a white dinner jacket and was strolling like the conquering hero he was to the local political organization, smiling, shaking hands, and conversing in a quiet authoritative tone that exuded power in control.

"Well," Carl continued, holding up his left hand and counting on the football scarred fingers, "let's name a few of his assets. First, he's got un-limited money for the campaign. In case you haven't heard, every builder and developer is asked to drop by and watch as the chairman signs their zoning order, subdivision plat or permit. They may say they're for you but right now he's the one who commands the purse strings. You better believe they are contributing to him.

Secondly, the county has never been in better shape. For the first time, the county's not borrowing money for operations.

Third, Santa Claus is in charge from now to election. Have you noticed Candler Road is finally being widened, the little leagues are having all their prayers answered, and everybody's pet project is being moved up on the front burner. Always remember. You can't beat Santa Claus.

Fourth, the garbage is being picked up. They're putting on extra crews from now until November. Remember, he helped beat Charlie by having some of his loyal troops sabotage that operation the week before the 1964 election."

I looked at Carl and together we followed my opponent's progress as he pressed the flesh of the adoring politicos.

"You sound like my election committee, Carl," I said, "Even the guy who talked me into running is saying the 'judge' don't look so bad after all now that the bandwagon is rolling. Good thing I got my finance committee signed on the dotted line or they'd be disappearing into the crowd about now."

He wanted to know why I'd gone to such lengths to assure the financing of my campaign.

"Well, you learn," I said. "The time to get people committed is when they're after you — trying to get you into the race. Once the guns start to fire, everybody begins to have second thoughts. I'm like the old man who had a reputation for good judgment. When asked about it, he said, 'well, son, good judgment is the result of experience — and experience is the result of poor judgment.' I know what happens about political finances."

"But do you really think you've got a chance?" Carl had been reading the papers and listening to the crowd at the Executive Club.

"I know I can beat him, Carl," I replied with a grin. "The first day I went to the first shopping center I knew I could take him. There are too many people too mad at him."

It went with the job. No chairman could govern for four years without building a dedicated opposition. Every time the garbage man failed to make a pickup, every time a policeman was impolite to a citizen, everytime a zoning occurred, the crowd resolve to 'get rid of that s.o.b.' grew. I made a mental note to remember that when my four years were up.

"Yeah," Carl said, "but this guy cut taxes."

"I know," I replied, "and I told him right after that 'well, you just assured your re-election'. That's what he believes."

Carl was unconvinced.

"Listen, Carl," I said, "when the qualifying deadline passed last Tuesday, I knew we had him. He couln't beat Attilla the Hun in a two man race."

"Well," Carl said, "you may believe that, but the men who asked you to run don't believe it."

"What they think doesn't matter at this stage, Carl," I said, "my campaign is finanaced — and we're in a two man race."

The day I paid my $2500 qualifying fee, I held a news conference in my office at First National. All three TV stations and several radio stations were represented. It was a good thing I had a big office.

Virginia knew, of course, that I was going to run. But she was not prepared for what now happened.

She stood silently aside as the TV and radio people filed in, carrying their lights and wires, crowding in around my large office desk. The rows of people were four deep. I could see Virginia standing outside in our reception room.

"Today," I shouted, "I have paid my qualifying fee to run for chairman of the Dekalb County government. I am making this race for one reason. To get rid of the do nothing — spend everything administration that has straddled the backs of our over burdened long suffering tax payers for too long —"

I went on to talk about garbage rotting in the streets, bridges that were about to cave in, pot holed streets, political payoffs — the whole litany of disasters our people were suffering under because of the benighted leadership that was marching us into the ditch of despair from the office on the ninth floor of the court house.

I glanced up at Virginia. She was literally standing with her mouth open. She had never heard such angry words come from my lips — and she had never heard me holler.

After I finished the thirty minute version of 'the speech', the press packed up and filed out. They had more than they could use. There were no questions.

Thanks to Reg's words and my resolve, the issue had been joined.

We began to meet each other on the stages of countless school houses and on platforms in shopping centers, as the long hot summer started to unfold. We were always the featured attraction, coming after the candidates for the legislature and the district commission posts debated or spoke.

The crowds, as usual, were dismally small and consisted of the immediate families and close friends of the candidates for the most part.

Which made it easier for me to read the speech.

Each time, I'd determine how much time was allotted and then select the five, twenty or thirty minute version of the speech.

And then I would read it, verbatim, word for word, without embellishment, addition or subtraction.

Basically, it accused the chairman of a spend-everything, do- nothing administration and talked of such unappetizing matters as holes in roads, deteriorating bridges and garbage.

Especially garbage.

Each time, my opponent would refute the charges, tell of the positive accomplishments of his administration, and patiently explain that I was obviously ignorant of government and how important affairs are conducted.

He was very gentlemanly, and I felt a little like a ruffian to be attacking such a sterling character.

At the next school house, I'd read the speech again.

One theory of the summer's results I cherish is that the stupidity of that speech and the constant repetition finally caused my opponent to crack. It was a sort of political Chinese water torture.

The first big break we got, and the crucial one, came the final day candidates for the various offices could pay their qualifying fee and officially become candidates. No one failing to register by the deadline would be able to take part in the Democratic primary.

I had already been in the shopping centers, talking to people, and I knew from the first day that a lot of people were dissatisfied, and in a number of cases, bitterly opposed to the chairman.

As stated above, the fact that he had this opposition was no reflection on him or his activities. Enemies are made in that position every day and those who are ruled against, or taxed, or rendered inadequate service, never forget and seldom forgive. Often, the better job the chairman does, the more enemies he makes.

Scott Candler, who served four four-year terms, was the last commissioner in the top job to be re-elected; and that was partly because Scott bluffed the people into thinking he was unbeatable. The first time Scott had opposition he was defeated.

After Scott, each chairman was ousted after a single term.

It seemed to me the best chance my opponent could have had would have been to encourage another candidate to enter, making it a three man race. It would have made sense for his supporters to the have paid the $2,500 fee in order to have a vote-splitting third candidate in the race.

The chairman had a hard core organization of supporters and would undoubtedly have had the most votes in the primary. In the resulting runoff, there would have been a chance the vote would be light and the organization would have won again.

So, it was a surprise when the qualifying deadline passed and we were in a two-man race. I think he was probably a victim of his own organizational ability. He attracted large crowds to his rallies, he was heavily financed, and he had convinced other hopefuls that a run against him would be a waste of the substantial entry fee. On the other hand, he must have begun to believe in his own invincibility and certainly, the dumb speech I kept making and the low profile we maintained until the fatal entry fee day had passed, probably made my candidacy seem no threat at all.

For my part, I had decided that, in addition to making the mandatory school house debates, I would concentrate on personal visits to the shopping centers. I had never mastered the art of attracting large, enthusiastic crowds to support me, and I had found that speaking to civic clubs, while a good way to meet people in the early part of the year, was not the answer as the summer heated up. For one thing, once the fireworks started, the clubs would divide loyalties among the members and so would not invite one candidate without the other. For another thing, the meetings consumed too much time for the number of people contacted.

On the other hand, the shopping centers presented a golden opportunity. Being in the wheelchair prevented my going door to door in the neighborhoods, but the shopping centers were always accessible and there were always people there with whom to talk.

The initial contact was always a little awkward for me, but once I had talked to a couple of people, I'd get into the swing of it and it became great fun.

Most people would say "hello" and take my card, but I always found a few who wanted to talk, and they provided a sounding board as to what voters generally might be thinking. They also provided a means of spreading the word — I had learned about that from a story I had heard about Gene Talmadge.

Ole Gene — our most colorful governor — built his gubernatorial career on the prejudice of the white Georgia tenant farmer toward the Negro. Reprehensible, but in that era it got votes. Gene was also shrewd when it came to understanding human nature and what builds public awareness of a candidate.

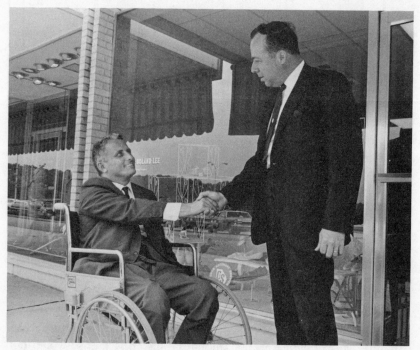

In my successful race in 1968, I politicked in one hundred shopping centers.

In the early days of his political career, Talmadge would drive his model T Ford along the country roads of the state. When he spotted a farmer plowing in the field, he would stop his car, get out, walk across the field and spend fifteen minutes chatting with the man behind the mule.

To the uninitiated, it would seem an inefficient waste of time and effort. Why didn't he go to town, where he could see ten times as many people in less time.

What Gene understood was that, after he left, that lone farmer would do his work for him. The first chance he got, he would be in town telling anybody who would listen how Ole Gene had walked out in his field and spent the time of day, just like anybody else.

He had produced a walking, talking advertisement that would continue until the election, with a message that would get through to the other farmers.

Not bad for a fifteen-minute investment.

So, I felt by my visits with individuals I was reaching a lot more people than would first appear.

For the most part, it was fun.

The only occasion that could have proven embarrassing involved a beautiful, young, red-headed woman, dressed in short shorts and carrying a baby on her hip.

"Hello," I said, sticking out my hand, "my name's Clark Harrison and I'd like to speak to you."

"Oh no you wouldn't," she pushed the door open and went hurrying into the store putting distance between us as quickly as she could.

"Oh," I said loudly, "I'm a political candidate. I just wanted to ask you to vote for me for chairman."

From across the store, she looked at me, the distance giving her courage, and, apparently seeing the wheelchair for the first time and hearing my explanation, she must have decided I wasn't a threat after all. She apologized and assured me she would consider me.

We were beginning to run ads on TV and radio. News stories of the campaign had to include me since I was the only opposing candidate for chairman. So more and more people began to recognize me and understand why I was accosting them in the aisles of the supermarkets.

About the middle of the summer, Frances became concerned.

"You're spending a lot of money advertising," she said, "but you don't have any people involved in the campaign. People are what win elections."

About this time, a friend from Jaycee days who was a public relations representative for a national retail chain, talked to me along the same lines.

"Clark," Ralph said, "what you need is a telephone committee. People to call the voters and ask for their support."

He and Frances got together and began to organize and to spot locations with a number of phones in one office from which calls could be made. One group looked up numbers while other groups met during the hours after dinner but before bed time, to make the calls.

This time, we didn't ask people who they were for. Instead the callers asked that my candidacy be considered and offered to send information or to answer questions. If the answer was not known, the voter was called later with the answer.

To their surprise, the people making the calls began to enjoy the contacts the same way I was enjoying my visits to the shopping centers. And they reported that most people seemed to appreciate receiving information about one of the contenders.

We concluded that what most people want is to feel that they know what they are doing and for whom they are voting. The candidate who can make the personal contact and give satisfactory answers is likely to receive the vote.

Frances now revealed herself as a veritable genius at campaign organization, and as a tough scrapper when the goal was defined and the motivation strong.

We both believed in what we were doing and she provided a major part of the energy, drive and hard work that resulted in final victory.

When the campaign was over, she and Ralph made some calculations.

"Clark," he told me quietly, "as well as I can figure, we have telephoned over a hundred thousand people."

For my part, I believed it. Toward the end, I had the same thing happen over and over. I would be going down the aisle of a crowded supermarket, chatting and shaking hands, when I would see a man or woman coming toward me from across the store.

"Hey," they would shout with a big grin, "your wife called me on the phone last night."

There were a hundred shopping centers in our big county in 1968. On the afternoon before the primary, I visited number one hundred.

CHAPTER XXXII

There are two kinds of learning in school — by rote, and by thinking and figuring things out.

When it came to flying, I found I needed both skills. For my exams, a certain amount of memory work and rote learning was required. But flying itself required the accumulation of just as much knowledge from every source as possible, the training of the reflexes so certain movements were made automatically, and finally, some real actual thinking, preferably done before the airplane started its takeoff roll.

I prefer to think my being a slow student was not altogether the result of age. For one thing, I do continue to be paralyzed. That meant, particularly in the early days, I could be right exhausted by the time I had hauled myself and my ever present rolling chair up on the wing and into the airplane. And it did take some right subtle moves of both hands and all ten fingers to make things happen at the right time and in the proper sequence. Finally, with a wife, two sons, a daughter-in-law, grandchildren, notes due at the bank,crises in the business, I do have a few more distractions than I had when I was twenty.

Undoubtedly the passage of fifty seven years, thirty-seven as a paraplegic, has slowed the mental and physical processes. On the other hand, experience, especially in the form of close calls, has honed the instincts as to what it takes to survive. Having had one auto catch on fire with me in it, another totalled by a cab hitting me broadside, nearly dying of exposure in the January waters of St. Simons Sound, and turning over innumerable times in the white water of the North Georgia mountains, I do tend to look both ways and expect the unexpected more than I did as a kid.

So, I kept telling Clint I was in no hurry and that I was a lot more interested in staying alive than I was in satisfying the license requirements of the Federal Aviation Administration.

My rate of progress verified the fact I was going to be more experienced than the average pilot before a license was issued. I had been through ground school twice, and had over one-hundred-fifty hours of touch and gos, slow flight, steep turns and all the other maneuvers designed to prepare the neophyte for survival in the heavier- than-air craft, when I, at last, decided it was time I got serious about passing a final checkride.

I had been flying solo since my twenty-third hour — I just couldn't carry passengers — and I had to be signed out before I could go cross-country.

What I really wanted to do was go back and forth to our place on St. Simons. I told Clint this the first day before the first lesson.

"Well," he said with a grimace, "that should be easy. Just head east. When you get to the ocean, turn right."

I was a slow learner, but after 150 hours of instruction and solo learning, I decided the time had come for me to qualify for a private license.

I have never wanted anything as badly in my life.

I finally brought matters to a head by buying my own airplane. The insurance people had quoted me a rate before they found out the fact I had 150 hours didn't mean I had a private license.

"Don't worry," I told the lady with the agency, "I'll have my license within two weeks."

Clint agreed to do his part by searching out an examiner who wouldn't fall apart laughing at the idea of a T-5, fifty-seven year old World War II paraplegic being certified to take other human beings aloft in the U. S. air space.

He located an old timer with over 6,000 hours logged for himself, who seemed to be willing to go along with the joke — at least to the point of flying with me by himself. Originally, Clint had thought he would have to go along in the right seat with the examiner in the back. But, having flown everything from helicopters to F-16's, this particular daredevil seemed prepared to try it in a handcontrolled plane.

When Clint went to talk to him, he took the plane along with the hand control rudder bar attached. "It was pretty exciting," Clint reported, "he insisted on doing some landings and we were flopping all over the place. Once we got it on the ground we did a lot of swerving around on the runway."

The day I went for the medical checkride, it was obvious the examiner was about as excited as I was. It was a hazy day, and he decided we could accomplish the first phase of my test by doing touch and goes.

"I want to see you bring it to a full stop," he said.

We did regular take offs and landings, then short field, soft field — the whole gamut.

When we finally taxied off the active, the relief on both our faces was apparent and he was enthusiastic.

"That was way above private license standards," he said, "I've tested pilots for taxi flying who didn't do as well."

At this point I need to give God a little more credit — it was one of those dead calm days — not a breath of wind.

Angels all around me.

He said he had 6000 hours logged and that flying the hand control was, to say the least, a challenge. At that point, I could have taken my final check ride at Epps, but he said he would like to give my final.

I agreed it would be better for all concerned. That way there would be no question that Epps might have favored me as a student. When I reported 20 minutes early for my appointment a few days later, the examiner was standing outside the hangar waiting for me.

"Do you want to go ahead and get started?" he asked.

I agreed and we went in to begin the oral.

Four hours and twenty minutes later, we landed and he signed my license. I was two days later than I had told the insurance company. It was a great day for me, and I felt I had opened the door a little wider for the next paraplegic who came seeking the right to fly.

Our big break in the 1968 campaign came in August before the September primary. My friend the banker called me.

"Clark," Bill said, "it looks like we may have something. Our people have checked the budget director's story thoroughly and apparently he's right about the financial condition of the county."

The first confirmation that the budget director knew what was going on had come in May. The manager of First National Bank had called me. I had asked him to let me know if the county borrowed money. "We've just gotten a request for a $3 million loan," he said.

"That's interesting," I replied. "We've just heard he is borrowing $3 million from C&S."

"He can't be," my friend replied. "We have a clear understanding that he won't borrow from anybody else without letting us know first."

I suggested he check the matter out. Later that day he called in some agitation.

"I can't believe it," he said, "C&S has just made a loan to the county for $3 million. And we had a firm understanding with the chairman this would not be done."

After this early word, we began to believe finances could develop into the key issue of the campaign. The budget director was telling us now that the county would end the year with a $7.5 million deficit. Under state law, it is illegal for a county to levy a tax rate so low as to leave a deficit at year's end.

We were not ready to close in on the issue, but we did add a new paragraph to the speech, pointing out that it had been eighteen months since an audit of the county had been made and challenging the chairman to produce such an audit before the election.

I began to charge that the chairman was trying to conceal the fact that the county was in finanacial trouble.

My opponent countered by stating that the county had never been in as good a financial position and that there was, in fact, an unexpended fund balance of $4.7 million in the county treasury.

That would probably have ended the matter and we would have gone to the polls with no more than an unconfirmed doubt in the minds of the people, and with my case appearing to be a trumped up political charge, had not a bizarre thing happened.

Apparently, my constant repetition of the speech with the charge that the lack of an audit covered a financial mess, finally got to my opponent. He decided to lay the issue at rest and, a little over a week before the election, he bought a double-truck ad in the local county paper.

It was another fatal error. It was not an audit, but it was a statement of condition certified to by the county auditors.

And it did show, in the lower right hand column, an unexpended fund balance of $4.7 million.

My opponent must have felt a moment of deep satisfaction as he looked at that 'bottom line' figure and felt that he had, at last, shut me up about the county finances.

The only problem was, the auditors, to protect their own professional reputation, had inserted a small box containing a qualification in the center of the otherwise immaculate statement. It said:

"The accompanying statement compares twenty-four months of income with eighteen months of expenses."

Don, who had been following the newspaper accounts closely, called me from Athens.

"You've got him, Clark," he said in an excited voice, "it's right on the face of the statement. The county is $7.5 million in the hole just like the former budget director has been saying."

We knew that the county was spending approximately $2 million a month, or slightly over $12 million for the six months' expenses left out of the statement. Subtracting the $4.7 million unexpended fund balance would leave the statement $7.5 million in the red by year's end.

In his effort to quell the doubt we had planted, the chairman had turned that doubt into a verified certainty.

That afternoon, I got a call from Bill. The friend whose bank had checked out the former budget director's figures.

"Clark," he said, "you've got to go on television and call this fellow a liar. That statement is the biggest fraud we've ever seen."

"Bill," I said, "let's get together and talk about it."

That Sunday afternoon — the election was to be held Tuesday — we met in my office. Several of the leaders in the campaign, as well as Reg and Bill, were present.

"Bill," I said, "I'll do it on one condition. And that is that you go on TV with me and confirm the facts."

Bill protested that he was not a resident of DeKalb and suggested that the executive vice-president of the bank, who lived in the county, would be a better choice.

"I think it's got to be you, Bill," Reg said. "Everybody knows you and associates you with honesty and efficiency in government. If Clark makes the unsubstantiated claim it will be taken as a last — minute desperation move by a politician."

"I think both you and the executive vice president should be there," I added. Champ, the V.P., was an old friend who lived near our first home on Clairmont.

Monday afternoon, we made the tape in one of the local TV studios. That evening, I was to debate the chairman in a roundup of candidates for a number of local elections.

I was in the studio waiting for the debate and was watching the studio monitor, when our advertising spot came on, the last thing viewers would see before the debates began, and the last political event before the polls opened the next morning.

"I have a brutal fact to state to the people of DeKalb County," I began, "The chairman of the DeKalb County Commission has lied to you about the financial condition of the county."

I went on to explain that the statement printed in the paper showed on its face the $7.5 million deficit we had been claiming existed.

Then the camera panned to the former chairman of the state commission for economy and efficiency in government, who called the statement a fraud on the people of the county. Then, our county citizen who was a top official of the city's most respected bank, added his own confirmation of what had been said.

The night of the primary election, Reg had me in hiding. Frances and I had dinner with the Murpheys and then sat around talking with a few close friends while we waited for Reg to call. The returns were encouraging but it obviously was to be a close election and I didn't want to be answering questions before we were sure of the outcome. Also, we had the general election and Republican opposition coming up and I had learned the hard way how an off-hand remark can spell political disaster.

Finally, Reg called and said he thought it would be all right for me to go to my office and that he would meet me there with a written statement for release.

I learned later that Reg had a victory statement in one pocket and a concession statement in the other.

A reporter from our leading radio station had established a vigil at my marked parking space at the First National Bank Building. We had planned a victory celebration in the restaurant attached to the building and he wanted to be first with a statement from me.

When I refused to say anything until Reg arrived he followed me up to the office. I was seated in a corner of our reception room. The reporter got his editor on the telephone. He then stretched the cord as far as the phone would go and held the speaker as near to me as he could with his outstretched arm. Apparently, he felt if he could get the speaker to my mouth I'd say something.

I just smiled and waited. In a while, the elevator door opened and Reg came over holding the victory statement for me to read.

Having claimed victory, we now went to the rear entrance to the restaurant where a small elevator was waiting to take me to the kitchen on the second floor.

What happened next is engraved in my memory. Coming off the elevator, we went through the darkened kitchen, opened the swinging doors and I rolled the wheelchair into a small semi-circle, the only open spot in a sea of massed humanity. The restaurant was packed. As soon as the door opened for me, the TV lights bathed me in a blinding light and everybody started cheering, clapping and shouting.

As I moved into the room, I was besieged by people shaking my hand, slapping me on the back, hollering and shouting in exultation. There were three television crews jockeying for a chance to interview me.

Sitting in my wheelchair, surrounded by the massed and cheering throng, my mind flashed back to the quiet and stunning defeat of 1960 — and to the sunny afternoon in the German backyard when I lay helpless in the sights of the enemy sniper.

Life is strange.

Experience gives us balance in success as well as defeat.

It was a great moment of victory, but it was only the beginning of what was to be one of the most bizarre and most publicized elections in the history of the state. We were front page now and we were destined to stay there through two more elections.

I had won by 1,500 votes. That night, I saw my shocked opponent make a statement that hurt him and only caused me a moment's reflection. Asked why he had lost, he said,

"Well, you can't beat a wheelchair."

I knew, of course, that you can. I had come in fourth, eight years before. I also knew that the wheelchair had been the greatest obstacle I had overcome this time.

The bitterness engendered by the campaign would last into the first year of my term as chairman and would see a last effort come close to success, when twenty thousand citizens would sign a petition for my recall from office.

One thing I could feel fairly secure in — I was no longer the nice young fellow in the rolling chair. When people thought about me the disablilty was relegated to a position of no importance.

From the endless halls of Lawson General Hospital, I had come to a position from which I could do substantial good or substantial evil that would effect a large number of people.

The night before my final election, I was told by a gentleman with wide connections, "Clark, the results of this election will be studied tomorrow by the bankers in London."

Were people surprised that I had won the victory. Months later, Reg Murphy told me that the evening before the primary he and Carl Logan, the two who were managing my campaign, agreed that they would each write down what they thought the results of the election would be and would seal the predictions in an envelope.

When they opened the envelope after the election, one had predicted I would lose by 1,500 votes; the other, that I would lose by 15,000.

CHAPTER XXXIII

If you are beginning to get the impression that I enjoy flying, you are absolutely correct.

Clint, my intrepid instructor, is the same way.

I never will forget one occasion, after we were well along in my lessons and Clint was relaxing as we cruised from the practice area back to Peachtree Airport.

"God," Clint said reverently, "I love these machines."

And you do get that way eventually. When you start to call your rattle trap old airplane a 'bird', and to pat it affectionately as you complete your walk around, you know you're hooked.

Airplanes are a little like women. They can be tempermental, and you do have to show them some attention and care.

But if you do those things, they can get you over some rough places. They can save your neck.

It is quite a love affair.

The night of the primary election, I arrived home in time to see my defeated opponent using ill-chosen words in the aftermath of his totally unexpected defeat.

Looking haggard and tired, he told the reporter, "Well, you can't beat a wheelchair."

It never bothered me — in fact I got a large charge from seeing the the smooth, organized leader, undone to the extent of making such a political blunder.

Among other things, I knew it wasn't true — the wheelchair had come in fourth in 1961.

What had changed was the occupant of the wheelchair, the times, and the circumstances.

In the next few days, the enormity of what had happened to my opponent came through to him. He could not accept the facts. How, as well organized, astute and heavily financed as he was, could he have been defeated. It had to be a fluke. Some way, he had made a mistake, and it must be corrected.

For our part, we were preparing to continue against the Republican candidate in the general election.

It didn't look like much of a job. He was a big Irishman from Boston who had been in the county only a few years and who spoke with a heavy accent. He was in the legislature and had the same name as another, very prominent state representative, George Smith.

This last seemed to be his only asset.

On the other hand, I remembered my false euphoria eight years prior when our "poll" convinced us we would win big.

And I reminded myself that my just defeated opponent had felt the same superiority over me only a few days back.

"We better buckle down and work harder", I told Reg.

"I wish I could be with you", Reg said. A few days prior to the primary election, Reg had come by the house to tell me he'd be pulling out as my speech writer. He was to become the editor of our Metropolitan morning daily.

"I'll have to take one heavy swipe at you editorially", Reg told me, "just to establish my separation from the campaign."

Reg had done well, with the dumb speech and the mean picture. Later, when he became editor of the San Francisco Examiner and then publisher of the Baltimore Sun, I was not surprised.

I always knew he had talent.

I wished Reg well and called Carl Sanders. I had managed his gubernatorial race for DeKalb County and I asked him to suggest somebody to take Reg's place.

"I'll call John," Carl said. John Harper had been Carl's press secretary while he was governor and had steered him through his campaign.

John called me and came to see me the next day. A tall, distinquished looking man, John, who was a great outdoorsman, would have looked right at home leading an English fox hunt.

John came right to the point.

"Remember, Clark," he was focusing his full attention on me, "in politics, the other guy is out to cut your throat, so you'd better cut his first."

John believed the only way to win was attack, attack, attack. "Never let him get you on the defensive," he said "or you'll spend all your time trying to convince the public you're not the incompetent crook he says you are."

John was the right one to be taking over at this juncture of the campaign. We were about to watch the battle take a bizarre turn.

"He's going to do what?" I couldn't believe what my visitor had just told me. "Didn't he take an oath to support the Democratic nominee when he qualified for the primary?"

"In so many words," Carl had picked the news up on the street. "Nevertheless, he is telling people he will run in the general election as a write-in candidate."

The news was a measure of my opponent's shock at seeing his carefully laid plans for re-election derailed by what must have seemed an inept and amateurish effort by our team. He simply could not accept his defeat as other than a soon-to-be corrected aberration on the part of the electorate.

"Well, Clark," Carl said, "you must admit we were struggling right up to the last moment."

"But we did get their attention with the news he was lying about county finances."

Reg had told me, "Just do what I say, Clark, and I'll guarantee a headline. Crumple up that so called Financial Statement he had printed in the paper and shake it at the camera."

He was right, of course. The evening paper had a front page headline "Harrison Shakes County Financial Statement At Camera."

And it must have been the right thing to do — we won the election.

But now we were about to get into the whole thing again — but with a difference. Now, my opponent would be the attacker and would be trying to throw me on the defensive.

It was apparent, as the first shots were fired, that he had decided that taking the high road, trying to stay above the smoke and fire of battle had been a mistake. It was also soon apparent that his low was as low as it goes.

No more Mr. Nice Guy.

"Who ever heard of a write in campaign succeeding?" Carl was leading a discussion as it became apparent the threat from our supposedly knocked out opponent was real.

"Well," I said, "there's always a first time. Did you happen to see the TV report on his organizational meeting."

The night before the cameras scanned a huge crowd, stamping, hollering and waving signs. All bent toward my destruction.

'The Race Is On'

"How does he do it?" I groaned. "I can't get six people to come to a rally. The only way I can see a crowd is to go to a shopping center."

"Let's face it," one of my small band of stalwarts said, "You've got about as much charisma as Claude Blount."

"I don't think you ought to talk about Mr. Blount that way — he was a mediocre chairman — I heard him say so himself."

"Also honest," someone said. "And you know how sexy that can be."

"Well," I said, "I still think we can win — if we can convince people I'm still not the chairman. The only thing we've got going for us is the burning desire of our citizens to throw the bums out. They're liable to think I'm the chairman now. If they do, we're dead."

Certainly, my fame was growing. The last few days of the campaign, we'd finally created enough fury to make the front pages of the Atlanta dailies.

Before I was finally elected, I believe many people did begin to think of me as the incumbent.

What evolved was one of the bloodiest, knock down, drag out political wars in the history of the state.

No more Mr. Nice Guy. My opponent, well acquainted with gutter tactics in the race that won his chairmanship in the first place, now reverted to type and his blood was stirred — no doubt about that.

We had spent over half our campaign fund in the primary and the publicity concerning the misleading financial statement, and the attention received in all the media following the primary victory had made me a public figure. I was recognized not only in the county, but all over north Georgia because of the broad coverage accorded the election by the three Atlanta television stations.

And I began to pick up some support from those who had been for my opponent but who felt they should now back the party nominee.

I remember one "victory celebration" in particular.

The room was crowded with people, which in itself was a new experience for me, and various members of the group were standing to give their opinions and to ask questions about our strategy for the campaign.

My good friend to be, Sidney Sisselman, whose firm sold chemicals to the county and who always took a leading role in civic and political affairs, rose to his feet and summed up the meeting.

"Well," Sidney said in his outrageous drawl — he talks like a southern darky of the old school — straight off the river showboat, "I'll tell you how I feel about it. 'The King is dead. Long live the King.'"

Sidney had been one of my opponent's hardest workers. From the night of my victory he worked just as hard for me.

Sidney understands politics.

My opponent was still chairman, he could still attract large and enthusiastic crowds to his meetings, and he could still command large political contributions.

"Clark," John said, "this guy is serious. Did you see that foot stomping, yelling, packed house of fanatics he was orating to last night?"

I asked John how he could go against his oath to support the Democratic nominee, how he could ignore the rules of fair play — and how he could expect to win when he'd just been voted out of office?

"Clark," John's shrewd eyes were peering from under arched eyebrows, appraising me as much as telling me, "when you've been King, you don't turn loose easily. Before we had elections, the only way to get rid of the top honcho was to kill him. This guy is convinced he listened to the wrong advice by taking the high road. Now, he's going to do it his way. I hope to God you can take it because you're about to have everything including the courthouse clock thrown at you."

It wasn't long in starting.

One of my opponents most vocal supporters was a minister in South DeKalb. A few days after my victory, a man called and suggested it would be good to go see him and seek his support for the General Election.

We had a nice visit.

"I just wanted you to know," I told him, "that I am just as interested in South DeKalb as in any other part of the county. I'll be glad to meet with any group down here to talk about your needs."

We parted on a friendly note and I got back in my car and drove home thinking much had been done to ease the tension, mend the fences and hopefully to pick up some support for the next election.

Next day, I got a call from the man who had suggested my visit to the preacher.

"He was real impressed with you, Clark," the caller said.

"Yeah," I replied, "he's a nice gentleman."

"You know," my new friend continued, "the thing he is really interested in is that new church he wants to build."

My caller was a member of the church.

"It will be quite a monument," he continued. "The way it's being financed is through church bonds. Most of them have been sold."

I began to wonder why he was telling me so much about the church.

"You know," he said, "if he could sell $30,000 more of the church bonds, he could start building."

I said I hoped somebody would buy them.

"Clark," he continued, "how about some of the people who are backing you. It's a good investment, pays a good rate of interest. And it sure would make the preacher happy if your folks could help him reach his goal."

I told him I didn't mind asking. After talking to one of my backers, I called him again.

"They said,'thank you'," I reported, "but they're not in any position to invest right now."

In my innocence, I thought that was the end of the matter.

"Clark," my secretary at the headquarters office was upset, "look what somebody just brought in. They're stuffing all the mail boxes in South DeKalb with this thing."

"Harrison Offers $30,000 Bribe To Preacher" the flyer said and related that I had visited the South DeKalb leader and offered the preacher $30,000 if he'd come out for me publicly.

"Well," John said, "do you think they're out to get you?"

I admitted they seemed to be and conceded I would have to be a little more careful in trusting new "friends" in the future.

"Nobody knew anything about what transpired at my meeting with the preacher," I told John, "Except me, the preacher and that son-of-a soforth who called me about the church bonds."

"It's enough to make one cynical," John said with a grin. "Now just wait until you see the afternoon papers."

There it was on page one of the Atlanta daily, "Harrison Accused Of Attempt To Bribe Preacher."

"Well," I told John, "one thing you can count on is our fearless newspapers reporting all the news. And I always thought I was a nice young fellow."

"Yep," John replied. "You'd better forget about trying to be a nice guy for the duration of this thing. This is only the beginning. It reminds me of the fellow who was running for sheriff. He came home and told his wife that he was being accused of stealing a mule. 'You don't have to worry, honey' his wife tried to reassure him, 'you know you didn't steal a mule.' ' Yeah,' he replied, 'I know I didn't, you know I didn't. The trouble is, they're about to prove it.'"

It was the time, 1968, when everybody was upset by the hippies, dope, the sex revolution. The very foundations of society were teetering under the assaults that were the legacy of the Vietnam war.

Someone in my opponent's camp hit on the idea of tying me and my campaign in with the worst aspects of the underground youth revolt.

My opponent had discovered his issue.

Peace and security would prevail if my opponent's name was written in on the ballot. If, on the other hand, we succeeded in driving him from office, the fabric of our society would rend and 'hippies will run wild in the streets.'

Improbable as it might seem in this enlighted age, the new line had a lot of appeal to a lot of people. As a matter of fact, motorcycle gangs that looked like and were criminals had taken over Piedmont Park and hippies were in charge in the Tenth street area of Peachtree Street.

Open sex was practiced in public places.

The opposition thought they saw their opportunity when it was learned that one of the local county papers, which had publicly endorsed me, had just taken on publication of "The Great Speckled Bird".

Named from a reference in the Old Testament of the Bible, "The Bird" was the official publication of the hippies in Atlanta. It's specialty was attacking known values of the establishment and attracting attention by using foul and offensive barracks -level language.

After three years as an army private, I understood what the language meant but was shocked along with everybody else to see it in print.

In order to capitalize on the situation, the opposition now decided to do something they obviously believed would tie me and my campaign to the hippies and lead to my sure downfall.

We first learned about it when people began to call the office, outraged by what had come in their mail the week before the election.

"This is the filthiest, nastiest thing I have ever seen in my life", the mother was shaking with rage, "and it came addressed to my nine year old daughter."

Again the papers were full of the account.

We learned that 5,000 copies of the four page tabloid were mailed to people all over the county. The list was a consolidation of lists of church members collected by our rival campaign office.

From the lists, it was impossible to tell the age of recipients and a number of the papers went to small children. This was what so outraged the public.

On the front of the tabloid was a picture of the editor of the local paper shaking hands with me — and the text of the first page was devoted to explaining that the paper that had endorsed me was printing the Great Speckled Bird.

Inside, were reprinted the worst excerpts of the Bird from the previous year.

The Atlanta dailies tagged the tabloid the "smut sheet" and gleefully recorded the opposition's efforts to turn me, businessman and candidate of the "power structure", into an ally of the hippie movement.

Our campaign strategists didn't know what to make of it or what kind of reaction to expect when it came time to vote. The episode was so insane it was hard to decide what people were really thinking. Obviously, different people were reacting differently to the impact of the thing.

We even heard that some were saying our organization sent out the tabloid to make the voting public mad at my opponent.

The editors of the Great Speckled Bird were delighted, of course, to see the pandemonium their paper was creating among the establishment and the state wide publicity they were receiving.

When things finally quieted down, they reprinted the 'smut sheet', titled it 'The Best of the Bird' and sold it as a collector's item to the hippies.

Through it all, Frances was the one single minded, tough minded, and unflappable driving spirit leading us to victory. Where others liked to talk and theorize, Frances was in constant motion doing anything and everything that might result in a vote for me.

She was opposed to my running, but once I had qualified she was determined the family name would not go down in defeat again. She had seen Tom's look of bewilderment and shock as a nine year old when I lost in 1961. She wasn't about to see that same look on Bob's young face. We were a team. I decided the only unique thing I could do was to go out and see people and let them see me. So I didn't give much thought to anything else.

She took over the office and the job of having friends contact voters — and was doing a masterful job.

With Ralph she organized the calling of 100,000 voters, but that was only a part of the job.

In addition to running the office and organizing the telephoning and distribution of literature, Frances was seeing that I made my appearances at shopping centers, club meetings and TV interviews and debates.

"Honey," I was excited, "I've got twenty minutes to get to a meeting in Decatur. I just sprung a leak and I don't have any clean trousers."

"You've got a pair at the cleaners," Frances said. "I'll have Patsy bring them by."

I was still a paraplegic with my kidneys draining though a hole in my side as a result of the Mayo operation. I never had infections any more but occasionally the glue that fastened my device would give way and I'd be flooded.

As they say, it was 'just another damn thing' and no reason to get off the track.

And we were certainly roaring along.

"Well, Clark," John and I were having a drink at the end of a day of campaigning, "he does play rough, doesn't he."

"I'm just glad he waited until after I beat him to start," I said. "I wonder what the voters are thinking about all this."

"Who knows," John said, "I have a feeling he may have overdone it with the 'smut sheet'. One thing about it, you've got everybody's attention now."

"What's the best thing for me to do now?" I asked.

"Lay back and watch," John replied. "We might find a way to turn this smut sheet against him. Right now, I don't think he needs any help from us to show what kind of fellow he is."

"John," I said, "Frances and I were talking about this last night. We signed up last winter for a cruise to Bermuda the Board of Realtors is having. What do you think about us disappearing for a week."

"Capital idea," John said. "Let him have the stage — he's got it right now anyway. Just don't tell anybody you're going."

So, with the north Georgia populace buzzing over the smut sheet, the hippies, the war to be King, we disappeared — for a week.

It was what the doctor ordered. Isolated from telephones, TV, radio, we plowed across the Atlantic, halfway to Africa, eating gourmet food four times a day and dozing in the salt air.

I was learning. The public, being entertained by my opponent, never knew we were missing. Apparently, it never occurred to the opposing camp we'd do such a thing and, embroiled in their own activities, they never knew we were gone.

"Mr. Harrison," we had been back from our vacation for a couple of days and I was resting after a day of shopping center campaigning, "I think I typed address labels for the smut sheet."

I had known Mary for several years and had advised her in a problem she had. It was taking a lot of courage for her to call me now.

"I didn't know what it was for, of course," she continued, "I was given a church list and asked to type the labels. The chairman's secretary brought the list down to my office."

Mary worked in one of the government offices in the court house.

"Mary," I was trying to keep the excitement out of my voice, "do you have anything that might prove the typing you did went on the smut sheet envelopes?"

"Well," she said, "I have the list I typed and I have the carbon ribbon that would still show the imprint of the typing that went on the labels."

"I'll have somebody pick those up," I said, "And, Mary, don't worry. We'll proceed quietly."

With the church mailing list, our investigator was able to recover several of the envelopes with the incriminating label and to match these against the carbon ribbon.

We had 'em. The smut sheet had been mailed from the courthouse and county employees had been used while working on county time.

John had a big grin on his face. "Well, Mr. Chairman," John was to call me Mr. Chairman from that point forward, "I do believe he's stepped into it this time."

We were proceeding quietly, as I had promised Mary, wanting to be sure we were right before the news media got hold of the story.

The date of the General Election was coming up on the next Tuesday. I got a call from a friend on Monday morning.

He worked in the crime lab of the Georgia Bureau of Investigation.

"Clark," he said, "I'm convinced that smut sheet was put together, stuffed and mailed right from the ninth floor of the court house."

It looked that way, I agreed.

"The problem is," he continued, "the public's got to know before they vote or it won't do you any good."

I asked him how he thought that could be done in the hours remaining before the election.

"Clark," he said, "you've got to get somebody in authority in that guy's office before tomorrow. We know county employees did the work, on county time, but the public doesn't know it."

"What do you suggest?"

"If you can get the sheriff to agree to go in, I believe the G.B.I. will join him. They've been following this thing in the news and helped us establish the evidence," he said.

The sheriff had his problems with the chairman, and he was ready to go. He needed someone to sign the search warrant.

"I'll sign the damn thing," Jack, the developer who had delivered the offer to pay off my campaign debt in 1960, would have plenty to lose if the write-in succeeded. But Jack was not lacking in intestinal fortitude. The son of a tenant farmer who died leaving his widow with four young sons, Jack had worked his way through college driving a taxi and selling bibles in the summer. He was tough and he was destined to become one of our wealthiest citizens.

Our campaign brought us several strong friends, people whom we got to know under stress, when the chips were down that fateful summer.

One, who remains a staunch ally to this day, was Bobbie, Judge Guess' horse loving friend.

Bobbie, who brings to mind a female General George S. Patton, had joined our organization early and she and Frances had become partners. Standing just under six feet tall, slim of waist, full busted, red headed and fierce of eye. Raised in the horse country of Tennessee, Bobbie has to be the re-incarnation of either a Roman consul or a frontier indian fighter.

Wearing slacks, her favorite move is thrusting her chest out, holding her back straight as a ramrod and hiking up her britches with thumb and fingers of each hand.

"I'll tell you one thing, baby," Bobbie had her bright eyes locked on me, "we've got the son of a bitch. We'd better move fast and lock that little bastard in a vice before he knows what hit him."

"Bobbie," I said mildly, "did you talk to the sheriff?"

"Yes," she said in stentorian tone, "and he is ready to go. He hates the bastard worse than I do."

"And Jack has signed the search warrant?" I continued.

"Signed it right there in the sheriff's office," she let out a long puff of air. "They're moving in tonight, sweetie, just as soon as that boy locks his office door."

From my bedroom window, I could just see the corner of the new courthouse and I tried to visualize how the midnight raiding party would look moving into the chairman's spacious ninth floor office.

"You know, Bobbie," I said, "the sheriff and Jack will have their necks right on the chopping block if this thing backfires."

"Well," Bobbie hesitated momentarily, "I believe they'll hang in there."

"Tell you what, Bobbie," I said, "how about you walking over to the courthouse just in case the sheriff needs a little moral support."

"I'm on my way, baby," Bobbie walked over, kissed her forefinger and marked an "X" on my forehead.

"Call me and let me know what's happening." I sat and watched as Bobbie went out the front door and crawled in her TransAm. How could I lose with troops like Bobbie.

Next day, election day, by 10:00 a.m. the story was on the news. In a raid carried out just after midnight, the G.B.I. and sheriff's office had found conclusive evidence that the "smut sheet" had been stuffed in envelopes addressed and mailed from the chairman's office on the ninth floor of the court house by county employees working on county time. Copies of the tabloid, mailing lists and other incidental evidence confirmed the facts. After the election, the chairman and several of the county employees who worked on the ninth floor were indicted. With the election over, the charges were dismissed on a technicality. Our purpose had been accomplished, so the matter was not pursued further.

The chairman had come in third and had been eliminated once and for all by the election. but he had polled enough write in votes to throw the Republican candidate and myself into a runoff.

I had polled more votes than either other candidate, but in analyzing what had happened it became apparent that the complexion of the election had changed.

In the primary, I carried the north end of the county, probably a negative vote by people mad at the chairman for zoning decisions, poor garbage service, etc.

In the general election, with a Republican candidate, the north end went to him, reflecting the leanings of this most affluent section of the county. On the other hand, I had picked up votes in the south which probably reflected suspicion in this more blue collar area of the Republicans Yankee background — he was originally from Boston.

"We can't let up now," I was talking to a member of my finance committee. They had been more surprised than anyone at my winning the first two elections. I was afraid they would now be overconfident. "We've got to keep advertising and working. With Nixon running against Humphrey, I wouldn't be surprised to see this suburban county go Republican."

There was not much issue between the Republican and myself, no debates and no feeling of conflict. He had laid low while the incumbent lambasted me during the general election. Now, I was afraid all the abuse of the accusations of bribing the minister and the smut sheet had tarnished me to the extent the next anti-vote would be against me.

The final runoff never developed into a fight and once again, I won by 58%. The strength of Nixon's election was demonstrated by his not only carrying the county but in the election of three Superior Court judges and other local officials on the Republican ticket.

"Well," my advertising agent was bragging, "we really outfoxed them." He went on to describe the advertising strategy that led to victory.

"I don't know about that," I held a pin up to his balloon. "We started running last January and we've spent $150,000. I'm a native of this county and a wounded war hero. Mr. Smith is a native of Boston, he started running about three weeks ago and he spent a grand total of $14,000, and he got 42% of the votes."

"He paid a lot less for his votes," I continued, "and if he'd had anything going for him, he would have wiped us out. I think I'll go see his advertising agency."

I was kidding, of course. The advertising had been masterfully handled. Like most elections, people were pretty evenly divided throughtout. We were feeling pretty good about winning — and the winner took all — so it was hard to believe things could have gone any other way.

I had had expert help. Most of all, I had had the unflagging and totally determined driving force that was Frances. She was not going to allow me to lose.

On one occasion, a Friday afternoon, I had been campaigning hard all week, was completely exhausted and had gone to the 'Y' for some steam and a massage. I was sitting naked in the health club when the phone call came.

"Mr. Harrison," the young girl said, "I don't know where Mrs. Harrison is and I'm worried about her. I've got to leave to pick up my little girl.

"Mrs. Harrison was sitting here making phone calls about an hour ago when she suddenly jumped up, grabbed a big stack of campaign literature. She said nobody had canvassed the project and she was going to do it. I'm real worried about her."

The project was the public housing — nearly a hundred apartments, occupied by blacks in the lowest economic scale and reputed to be the chief source of potential trouble in those strange and tense times.

It was getting dark and my wife, a young white woman was out there somewhere going door to door asking people to vote for me.

I looked at my naked body, sitting in the wheelchair, with the tube that drained my side hanging down. By the time I got dressed, in the car and out looking whatever was going to happen would be over.

"Dear God," I prayed, "please take care of Frances. I'm going to go ahead and have my massage while You do it."

She told me later with a big grin that the people, the ones who were sober, were very nice. She had made some new friends.

And had gotten me some votes.

For my part, I knew that there had been moments, perhaps five or six of those moments, when any lack of will on our part would have lost the race for us.

In the beginning, if I had compromised on the matter of financing the funds would not have been available, and we would not have been taken seriously.

If winning had not been more important than my own ego, I would not have had Reg and John's expert advise — or I wouldn't have followed it.

If we had not gone on TV and I had been unwilling to call my opponent a liar, our impact on the undecided would have withered and died.

If we had not closed in when we had the evidence of misuse of county people and funds in the smut sheet incident, we could have failed to arouse the people.

Finally, if we had let up when the runoff was between myself and the Republican, I believe we could have lost.

In the final analysis, I believe in a rip roaring, bloodletting such as that 1968 run for chairman, the people can sense the determination of the contenders. They are looking for leadership, and they are repelled by weakness.

My finance committee had raised $110,000 — and had each anted up $4,000 under the terms of our agreement. If they were mad about it, they never said anything to me. For my part, I didn't know where the money had come from other than the committee — and I had an understanding with them.

There was one exception.

A banker brought me a thick, white envelope and handed it to me personally.

It was a Friday afternoon. A couple who were life time friends had agreed to handle our finances for the campaign. As soon as I received the envelope, I called.

"Peggy," I said, "I've got a contribution to bring you."

"Oh, fine," she said, "bring it by and I'll take it to the bank on Monday."

When she came out to the car, I handed her the thick envelope.

"What is this?"

"It's $5,000 cash."

"Oh," Peggy's eyes grew large, "I'll take it to the bank right now."

Only those closely involved in the campaign ever realized the full extent to which our victory belonged to Frances.

She did receive one compliment she cherished.

Our friend Manuel, the bartender who later became chairman himself, paid Frances the ulitimate accolade.

"Frances," he said in his gruff Lebanese voice, "every political campaign needs one tough s.o.b. to see to it things get done. You are the tough s.o.b. of this campaign."

Frances smiled, but didn't say anything.

Like Dr. DeWeerd advised, I decided to hang on to her.

CHAPTER XXXIV

With my wing tanks filled once more, and a coke under my belt to replace the sweat I'd lost searching for Winkler County Airport, I taxied through the sage brush and made my radio call on 122.8 to any aircraft in the area. As the one sixty engine roared to full thrust, I held the stubby winged little plane in the center of the asphalt runway and, as the airspeed indicator reached 62 knots, left the ground and climbed steadily to 400 feet, banked right and took up my heading of 70 degrees.

The VOR was set at 114.8, Midland, Texas. Within a few minutes, I was over the large oil fields that carpet this part of Texas, watching the huge pumps as they pecked up and down like mechanical birds at the desert floor. It seemed strange that such a desolate face of the earth would conceal such vast riches.

Crossing Midland VOR and skirting the northern edge of the city, I changed heading to 65 degrees, bending course slightly northeast toward Abilene.

Shadows were lengthening as I overflew Dyess Air Force Base and followed vectors provided by approach control toward the long twin runways at Abilene.

"Five, Five November," the Abilene Tower had me in sight, "you are clear to land runway 33."

I entered a left downwind, turned to base and final over the flat, desolate Texas prairie and eased the one forty toward the long concrete runway.

As I taxied toward the tie down area, the sun was just above the horizon and darkness was falling as I finished securing the plane for the night.

When I had first conceived the idea of flying solo across the U. S. I had visions of carrying a sleeping bag and rations, landing at small remote airports and sleeping under the wing. Just like the barn stormers of old.

When the time came, however, I said 'to hell with that'. I stopped at the big airports, had the motel pick me up, had a couple of martinis, a good dinner and slept in a nice big bed with the air conditioning going.

I had enough of sleeping in the ground and eating out of a pail in the army.

Toward the end of November, 1968, I called Don at the university of Georgia at Athens. "We're ready to go, Don," I told him. We had finally defeated the Republican in the runoff election. It was our third victory and each election had been a bloody battle.

I was chairman by right of conquest.

If anybody had felt sorry for me for being in the wheelchair, they no longer did. We had spent $150,000 in the campaign and with the slugging match that finally developed, we had had news coverage all over the northern part of Georgia. My name was literally a household word, and I was recognized by people as someone they felt they knew personally.

"Don," I asked him, "can you come over to Decatur the first of December? There are a lot of changes we are going to make and I'd like to get most of them set up before we take office. As of January 2, I want to hit the ground running."

Don had already met the other two commissioners who, with myself, would constitute our majority for the first two years. They had hit it off and agreement had been reached as far as his employment was concerned. Now, he agreed to start work a month early and a few days later he was in my office in the First National Bank Building.

Together, we went over the departments and agreed that we needed to hire ten executives in order to get control of the county structure.

Don fixed up an office next to mine and got ads in the papers and telephone calls to the professional search agencies. Within a few days we had a stream of visitors coming in and out of our two offices. Each of us would interview each candidate and then we would compare notes. By the first of the year all but two of the key jobs had been filled.

I called the county personnel director.

"Bob," I said, "I want you to stay, but I don't want anybody in the commissioner's office who is there now. You can transfer them anywhere you like, but we're starting with a clean slate on the ninth floor."

As noted above, the chairman and several of the people in his office had been indicted for using county employees to address and mail the smut sheet in the general election.

The people expected changes, and they were about to get them.

It now became our job to notify the people we were replacing as department heads. We notified them through the personnel director. A couple of them wanted to see me. One was a former University of Georgia football player and he just about filled up my office door when he walked in to see me.

I have always had something of an advantage in this regard. Sitting in the wheelchair, everybody looks tall to me, from the most petite lady to Godzilla. So I can treat everyone the same.

When we had finished with the job, I told Don, "Now, we can tell everybody else that the changes have been made and we can all settle down and go to work."

We had assembled an outstanding group of executives.

Bud, a retired colonel of engineers who had been at Remagen when the bridge was captured, headed sanitation — garbage disposal would be our greatest challenge and Bud would need all his combat experience before the reorganization of the department was accomplished.

Dick, who gained a national reputation as our police chief, had been an assistant U. S. attorney. He brought us a close relationship with the FBI.

Jim came from Alabama. A former college football player, Jim built an outstanding recreation program that emphasized the inclusion of girls in the program and made our county one of the organizers of the first Special Olympics for retarded children.

Allan, with a masters in city planning from Georgia Tech and years of practical experience, rewrote DeKalb's planning and zoning ordinance to include innovative provisions for condominium and planned unit development that were to become a model for other communities across the U. S.

Bob was a tough minded professional road man who would put the selection of projects back on a 'greatest need' basis.

And so it went, all were professionals of talent and toughness.

When we had our first staff meeting, I thought back to my first meeting with our captain and the first sergeant after I was sent to the infantry.

"Gentlemen," I concluded after some rousing painting of the big picture, "now, Don will say a few words. Before I leave let me make one thing clear. When Don says something, it is me talking. You don't need to come and check with me after Don tells you something."

And then I excused myself. Don and I had a clear understanding. He would manage the county and I would take care of the politics. Because we had confidence in each other, the system worked and everybody in the county benefited.

For my part, I knew that Don's only criteria would be the greatest good for the largest number of our citizens.

Don found out that I would back him up when the going got rough. And it definitely got rough.

I also had a perfect check on how things were going. I'd tell the department heads, "I've got a computer on my desk that tells me how things are going. As long as it's quiet, I know everything is okay. When somebody falls down or starts playing games, it starts to ring."

In the management of large affairs, the chickens always come home to roost. In government, they come home more quickly than anywhere else.

I told our department heads about the Russian Jew I had met while peddling from my wheelchair pack and I used his philosophy. As long as things were properly done, they ran the county.

"I don't care how big the problem you bring in here is," I would say, "just so long as you bring the solution with you."

Our people really got to thinking about their jobs.

The summer had been spent in telling the people we had a $7.5 million deficit. Now that we were in charge, we found out that the deficit was a reality.

Not only was it real, it was also illegal. Under state law, counties had to levy enough taxes each spring to pay all obligations before the end of the year. The former chairman, wanting to keep the millage rate low so he could get re-elected, had failed to do that. Now the piper had to be paid.

I had reason to be glad Don was with me.

"Clark," he said, "we've got to have an audit as of December 31st. Otherwise, we can never establish who caused the mess the county is in and whether what we will be doing is improving the situation."

Because of the deficit my opponent in the summer battle had bequeathed us, we were going to have to reduce services — and we were going to have to increase taxes.

If you think that combination is going to be popular with your people, you just haven't experienced being King.

We took a deep breath and prepared an ordinance for the first commission meeting that reset the fiscal year to end December 31st and authorized an audit.

The immediate problem was to get some cash to operate the county on.

It looked like an impossible situation.

Don, although not a lawyer, got out the code and started reading.

"There's an old law," he told me one morning soon after we occupied the ninth floor, "that might just be the answer."

In the early days of Gerogia's counties, when the government was waiting for the tax money to come in, bills were paid and payrolls met by issuing what were called warrants. They looked like checks, but an arrangement was made with the local bank to pay them and then hold the cancelled paper until the county had money to cover. The warrants paid interest and were underwritten by the county's ability to levy taxes, so it was a good deal for the banks.

Scott Candler had been the last commissioner to pay with warrants, but now we resurrected the practice.

I was about to learn about banks.

We got the four major Atlanta banks together. Prior to that time, two of the banks had handled the county's needs. Now, I wanted to bring in the bank that had stood with me during the hard days of the summer campaign and one of our commissioners wanted to bring in the fourth bank.

I figured the shape we were in the more banks the better.

Their lawyers agreed the warrants would be legal, we agreed to an interest rate and that we would issue warrants up to $7.5 million. Don figured that would get us through April when we would be receiving enough revenue from other sources to get us up to the time we'd start receiving ad valorem — property — taxes for the year.

The banks were to each share in the major county accounts on a rotation basis.

Everything went smoothly until April rolled around. Then my old high school friend called from his bank.

"Clark, you are going to convert these warrants to notes aren't you."

"No, we are not," I said. "You have agreed to hold the warrants and we have agreed on the interest rate. We'll pay off one fourth of the warrants each December and retire the last ones just before I go out of office."

"Well," he countered, "at our last meeting you said you'd convert them to notes."

This made me mad because Don and I had talked about the matter and no such agreement was made.

"Listen," I said, "you can tell the bank that the loan they made the chairman last year was illegal. If they didn't know it, they should have, because under state law they were acting as treasurer of the county. Everybody in the county heard me saying the county had a deficit and apparently nobody with your bank bothered to check. As far as I'm concerned, you share responsibility for the county being in the shape it's in. If your people come to that meeting and say we agreed to convert to notes, I'll say so publicly."

The banks, of course, wanted renewable notes so that the rate could be increased.

When we had our meeting, all four banks were present. One of the banks raised the question of our replacing the warrants with notes.

"That was not our agreement," I said.

"Well, you said we could replace our warrants with notes," he countered.

"Listen," I replied, "do you want your money. We'll pay you your money right now."

With that, the banker became very quiet and the subject was changed.

Later, after we had gone back in the chairman's office Don said, "I was wondering just where you planned to get the money to pay him off."

"I figured one of his three competitors would be glad to get him out of the way by lending us the money to pay him off," I replied.

Don gave me a sharp look.

And so it was settled, each bank kept its share of the warrants, we paid off one fourth in December of each year and at the end of my four year term the last of the debt was retired.

The interest rate stayed at four and one fourth per cent, which represented a sizeable saving to the county. My feeling was that we were going to make the county grow, that all the banks would prosper, and that it was only fair that they see us through this difficult period.

The warrants represented a temporary solution to meeting the payroll and other immediate expenses of the county.

But there was a much bigger problem facing us.

"This government is underfinanced," Don told me. "If we're ever going to meet the legitimate needs of the people — and to pay our employees a living wage — we are going to have to increase the tax rate — and it's going to have to be a big increase."

Because of the low pay and lack of a substantial retirement program, the county had a constant problem keeping employees. The police department had a turnover rate of forty per cent. Young men who wanted to be officers would work for a year or two and then discover that they could not support a family on the pay. The fire department had a similar problem and those who stayed with the county ended up working two jobs to make ends meet.

THE DeKALB NEW ERA - Thursday, May 15, 1969

Grand Jury Confirms $7.4 Million Deficit

The present DeKalb County Grand Jury Tuesday found in a special presentment that the county had a cash deficit of $7.4 million at the close of 1968. The presentment was accompanied by three statistical tables which showed the deterioration of the operating funds in 1967 and 1968.

The Grand Jury found, however, that aside from a substantial deficit in operating funds, the county has more than $17 million of unused bond capacity without increasing the present bond levy and more than $55 million worth of available unused bond capacity.

"There is no question," the Grand Jury commented," that DeKalb County, in terms of ability to pay, is one of the soundest counties financially in the country."

PLAN BOND ISSUE

The bond funds can be used only for capital improvements and can not be used as operating funds. County officials have said they plan to hold a bond election late this year or early in 1970.

The Grand Jury said, however, that the "chief and only purpose" of its investigation was not the overall or long-range solvency of the county, nor in the total amount of its valuable capital outlay in buildings and equipment, "but whether or not there was a cash surplus or deficit at the close of the last administration on December 31, 1968.

"This Grand Jury finds, as a matter of hard financial fact, that as of the close of 1968 and the beginning of 1969, the DeKalb County General fund had a cash deficit of expenditures over all revenues totaling $7,-475,385."

The Grand Jury, which included three bankers from three different financial firms, commented that on December 31, 1968, the county had a total of $1,061,108 in available cash,

and total liabilities of $8,536,-493.

"We have determined that $8,075,724 of these liabilities were due and payable on or be-

DeKalb Starts IOUs for Debts

$3 Million in Warrants Slated; February Revenue Is Awaited

By MORRIS SHELTON

DeKalb County was to begin issuing IOUs Tuesday to cover its bills until two debts totaling $3 million can be paid off.

DeKalb Commission Chairman Clark Harrison, who was granted authority to issue the IOUs, or warrants, termed the financial task a "very unpleasant duty to perform."

Harrison said about $3.5 million in warrants must be issued while the $3 million debt is being paid off.

He said the warrants must be used for about a month and a half so other county revenue can be applied to paying off $1.2 million to Fulton National Bank and $1.8 million to First National Bank.

Until the debts are paid, Harrison said, the county can't legally borrow money.

BOTH BANKS have agreed to cash the warrants, which will later be redeemed by the coun-

ty at 4.5 per cent interest plus handling charges, Harrison said.

Harrison said he hopes use of the warrants will be discontinued by mid-February, when the county's financial picture should change as auto tag fees and other revenue begins coming in.

The commission chairman said DeKalb hasn't had to issue warrants since 1960.

Harrison's executive assistant, Don Mendonsa, estimated it will cost the county $1,500 to use the warrants rather than operate on a cash basis if the use of warrants is discontinued in mid-February.

He said about $1,000 of this would go for interest, and $500 would be for handling charges.

ONCE THE $3 million indebtedness is paid off, the county will be free to borrow money to operate on until tax revenue begins coming in later in the year.

The county will continue paying its obligations with regular pay checks during the period the warrants are in use. The

DeKalb in Red $7.47 Million, Audit Shows

An audit of DeKalb County government finances was produced Tuesday showing that the county has a deficit of $7.47 million, according to County Commission Chairman Clark Harrison.

The audit was the latest development in the county's disputed financial situation, which has been the subject of controversy since the campaign for county commission chairman in the summer and fall of 1968.

Former DeKalb Commission Chairman Brince Manning who was defeated by Clark Harrison, claimed the county had a surplus of $4.9 million when he was seeking re-election.

HARRISON, however, claimed that a near $7 million deficit would exist when he assumed office Jan. 2, 1969.

In producing the audit Tuesday, which was prepared by the auditing firm of Wolf and Co., Harrison said, "We had promised the public right after I came into office that we would show the county's position as of the end of the year."

To combat DeKalb's financial dilemma, the Harrison administration issued some $7 million IOUs, or warrants, which will probably be paid off over the next four years by a tax increase which Harrison intends to propose.

During the 1968 campaign, I had told voters the county had a $7.5 million deficit. When we took office we found out the deficit was real.

Wednesday, July 23, 1969   The Atlanta Journal   3-A

Irate DeKalb Goads Harrison on Garbage

Pick-up Cost Higher, And So Is Refuse

By MORRIS SHELTON

He added that the sanitation department has 17 supervisors in the field with radio-equipped vehicles to provide rapid service once complaints are filed.

Alarmed at the service slump, County Commissioner Bob Guhl told fellow commissioners during an informal session Tuesday that he received 32 calls concerning garbage service during a three-day period last week.

Included garbage houses as they strewn, Guhl said.

'CHARGES EMPTY PROMISES'
Legislator Blasts Harrison Concerning Road Project

A DeKalb legislator has blasted Commission Chairman Clark Harrison and charged him with making "empty promises" concerning a request for paving Maplewood Drive in South DeKalb.

Trash Pickup Lags 10 Days in DeKalb

By MORRIS SHELTON

Trash pickup in DeKalb County is approximately 1½ behind schedule as sanitation trucks and other equipment go a stepped-up "preventive maintenance" program.

Some 23 of DeKalb's 120 garbage trucks were out of service Wednesday, according to sanitation officials.

40 Garbage Trucks Idled By Breakdowns in DeKalb
County Plans in-Depth Analysis As Service Complaints Pour In

By MORRIS SHELTON

DeKalb County officials are trying to determine the cause of an abnormally high rate of breakdowns in garbage collection equipment which idled an average of 40 trucks a day during the earlier part of last week.

Maintenance problems have resulted in refuse collection during three weeks.

SUNDAY, JULY 20, 1969
The Atlanta Journal and CONSTITUTION   10-A

We had to cut services

STIFF TAX HIKE VOTED FOR DEKALB

GOP Contends It's Not Needed

DeKalb property owners will pay approximately $7 per ~0 more in taxes this year. The DeKalb Commission ~oted almost $5 per thousand more and the School ~ady upped the public ante by $2 per thousand.

by the face and

by the School board will mean the owner of a $30,000 home will pay approximately $70 in additional taxes this ~r.

~b assesses in theory at ~nt of fair market ~wner who lives ~ is given a ~mptior tax

Wednesday, March 5, 1969 The Atlanta Journal **7-A**

Property Tax Bills a Shock For Many DeKalb Owners

By MORRIS SHELTON

near 7-mill tax increase adopted this year, with 4.93 mills of it going to the county government and other 2 mills channeled into the county school system.

On paper, the tax increase would raise the total 7-mill. But many homeowners who attempted to forecast the effects of the tax increase by using standard formula found their tax increase much more than they had anticipated.

rather than the $70 used in hypothetical cases.

ADDITIONAL TAX shocks may be felt by residents who neglected to file for the $5,000 homestead exemption.

Hypothetically speaking, the owner of a $30,000 home who had his tax bill exemption of $70 increase. Without being boosted by whopping $137, amount to officials.

Meanwhile, tax officials and homeowners likely to arise later when upped mortgage companies the assessment of the tax house payments have and.

TAX OFFICIALS say the own-

Officials said the only way to increase, is to subtract last year's total tax statement from the current one, and then divide the resulting number by 12.

For example. Payments on the home increased by amount to $130, and currently payments on the home would be increased by $10 for a total monthly payment of $140.

Harrison to Seek Garbage Fee Boost

By MORRIS SHELTON

DeKalb Commission Chairman Clark Harrison says he intends to recommend hiking garbage fees for residential pickup from to $54 annually.

~n, who contends the ~epartment is losing ~r the present fee ~d he will bring the ~efore the County Com~ possibly as soon as next ~ay and that he hopes the ~ will go into effect "within ~ next 30 days."

Harrison said the garbage operations lost $1.6 million during the previous year and that his administration "is saddled ~ the very unhappy ta~ up to the tr~ pape~ ~ some ~po~

posed change would amount to increasing residential pickup and service to apartment units with individual containers from $2.50 to $4.50.

-THE COMMISSION chairman said under current planning, apartments using huge containerized pickup systems, or dumpsters as they are commonly referred to, would see no increase because complexes using this pickup system are "paying their way." ~.

He added that no increase in commercial pickup fees is planned because these firms ~aying their way.

~e fee hike for single ~esidences somewhat ~n Harrison's pro~ ~ecommended by a ~gineer's firm that ~rng the adminis~ ~ner Commission ~ce Manning to ~ scale study of ~age service.

License Fees Mailed Out, Some 10 Times Higher

DeKalb County businessmen this week were receiving their 1969 business licenses and in most cases they found the fees 50 per cent higher than last year.

The 50 per cent hike was part of the ~ administration's budget adopted by the County Commission July 1.

However, professional persons, such as doctors, lawyers, architects and others, will pay ten times as much this year as last year. Their license fee went from $15 to $150.

and Veatch of ~recommended ~thly rate be ~ for two~ ~ommercial ~ establish~ ~s would go ~ cent under the sug~ ~ed increases. Offices would pay $4 per month instead of $2.50 and small businesses would have their rates raised from $5 to $8.

Commissioners and representatives of the firm met Friday in an unannounced session to dis-

We had to raise taxes and fees.

Tuesday, September 23, 1969   The Atlanta Journal

After 3 Hot '68 Campaigns, Harrison Embroiled Again

By MORRIS SHELTON

Although DeKalb residents elected a county commission chairman in 1968, the race, in all appearances, is on again.

At a restaurant near Decatur Monday night, DeKalb Commission Chairman Clark Harrison defended his administration in a talk to a civic group.

mind when I tell them we're $7.5 million in debt and need to go $60 million more in the hole," Harrison told the Optimists.

But he contended DeKalb desperately needs more fire stations, libraries, road improvements, a new hospital, and large scale recreational im-

ence contended spending should be cut even if a reduction in services accompanied such a move.

If the average reside without a new washing or car and "can tig belts," he said, "ma: people in higher levels government will look theirs."

MEANWHILE, the r has moved to the top at most DeKalb politi sion posts.

In South DeKalb, G gist Tom Davidson ke eye on recall developr his hardware store, center in south DeKa

While the GOP say involved in the move publicans such as Da GOP chairman Home: least are fanning the

They make no b being in sympathy w call movement. An high-ranking South I publican, State Rep. lake, has been takir potshots at Harris weekly in recent new umns.

IN A COLUMN pr Wednesday, Westlak cussion about "porkb tics, charges Harrisoi ber of a political fac has used public fun sonal gain.

On the other side o the county's Democ: has moved to Harriso and recently adoptec tion urging he be give to implement his pro

From his East Atla Democratic vice chai uel Maloof, a stron; supporter, keeps his e on recall developmen been calling some of t counteract the ouster

And while the turn fling to some, other: DeKalb politics has into a seasonable thin football, simply around for four year elections.

Harrison Recall Sought in DeKalb

By MORRIS SHELTON

A petition for a recall election to dismiss DeKalb County Commission Chairman Clark Harrison is being circulated in what appears to be a broad section of the county.

Residents in north south and middle DeKalb have been mailed copies of the petition, which is sponsored by an organization calling itself the "DeKalb Recall Committee."

The petition denounced a recent 4.93-mill tax increase sponsored by Harrison and accuses him of providing "mighty poor services" despite higher taxes.

Harrison promptly signed the petition, saying: "If there is a citizen of the county who wants the opportunity to vote on the record of this administration, as far as I'm concerned, he should have that opportunity."

HIGH-RANKING Republicans, arch foes of Democrat Harrison's tax increase, said they will not actively participate in the recall effort and that they frown on such doings.

"This man was elected by the public and we are not going to get involved in any way in the recall movement," said one high-ranking Republican.

"We believe the man won and we feel it is not the American way to put him out of office before he got a toehold," the GOP source said.

The recall petition was signed by Max Davis, chairman of the dismissal movement, and T. E.

voters is filed anytime after the official has been in office nine months.

By law, the recall election must be held 30 days after the petition is filed. If the official is ousted, then a special election must be held to fill the vacancy.

Courthouse sources recalled that the only such election ever to be held in the county occurred some 35 years ago when Decatur voters went to the polls in a special election to decide whether to dismiss two newly elected commissioners.

The Decatur recall election failed by some 20 votes, but the two commissioners, who sources said were instrumental in discharging a city manager and most city employes, were defeated in the next city election.

non deficit, and uses ccount for the necessity ig taxes nearly five

think I've lost my

RRISON said, "It's unim t what happens to me per y, the thing that disturbs out it is that the people ly believe that taxes and ered and services imif they can get rid of an."

the Optimist meeting things were just begin- warm up in the county ouse nearby.

ance adjuster Max Davis uilding contractor Gene effort n, leaders of the Harri- ster movement, told some sons attending the tax- meeting that Harrison o sense of responsibility public and that recall is zen's only defense.

They claimed to have gathered some 19,000 of the 22,500 signatures necessary to force a recall election.

ATKINSON, who said he voted for Harrison but later grew "disillusioned" with him, charged Harrison has treated the public "with contempt and listened only to personal advisers who came from outside DeKalb and care little for the feelings of DeKalb citizens."

He said Harrison should have alerted DeKalb residents of his plans for a tax hike and fee increases during the campaign rather than springing such measures after the election.

An elderly man in the audi-

DeKalb Recall Effort Claims 20,000 Names

A group which is trying to oust DeKalb Commission Chairman Clark Harrison claims it has verified 20,000 signatures of the approximately 22,000 names necessary for a recall election.

The recall group plans to make a final push during the next two weeks for additional signatures then present the petition, according to Gene Atkinson, vice chairman of the recall organization.

ATKINSON SAID his organization has gathered 30,000 signatures, but he added that 10,000 had to be discounted for reasons such as illegible signatures, persons signing twice and names not being registered on the county's official voter list.

The recall movement has been under way since a few months after Harrison assumed office.

It perked considerably after the county commission approved a near five-mill tax increase requested by Harrison this past summer.

THE RECALL petition must contain the signatures of 15 per cent of the county's registered voters, or about 22,000 names, before an election is required to determine wkether Harrison remains in office.

If the vote to oust him succeeds, then another election must be held to determine who will serve as county commission chairman.

Under the DeKalb recall provision, the ousted chairman is not eligible to seek re-election.

Everybody blamed the chairman.

The problem was most acute in the sanitation department. Blacks, who did ninety-nine per cent of the work, were being stirred by the national movement for civil rights. Low pay, poor working conditions and a lack of organization had brought the system near total collapse. Absenteeism was a major problem and complaints from citizens on several occasions, particularly before and after holidays, inundated not only the department but the chairman's office as well. We counted up to 600 calls a day and felt at least that many more were unable to get through the swamped telephone lines.

One of the first things I did after taking office was to don my old combat jacket and have my picture taken riding in a garbage truck.

In going to the department to meet the men coming off duty, I felt as if I were entering a penal colony. The resentment from the black men was so strong it felt like a physical force coming toward me.

We had similar problems in the road department where overused roads in the fast growing county were coming apart or were so narrow people were having a hard time getting to and from their work.

By searching the country, we had assembled the leadership we needed to tackle the problem. Now I was determined to get the money they needed to do the job. "How much of a tax hike is it going to take," I asked Don. He gave me a hard look. "Five mills." I returned his hard look. "Well, Don," I told him. "I have decided that there is no way to get this situation straightened out without being a bastard. As long as I have to be a bastard, I might as well be a big bastard — and get the job done." We began to work on the other commissioners. Bill, the one I came to lean on the hardest during those four years, was the key. I pointed out how the county would move forward and how we would all benefit once the government could match money to words. Finally, I went to see him at his office. He came out and sat on the sofa in his reception room.

"Okay, Clark," he said with a sigh. "Just so it's less than five mills."

"Four point nine seven," I shot back.

And that's what the big black headline said.

I had established myself as a big bastard. Perhaps the biggest bastard the county had ever had.

The advice I had received that was to help me survive the white, hot fury that was to follow came from Frank. A recognized and responsible leader of the blacks in the county, Frank worked as a general utility man at the large savings and loan in Decatur.

I was feeling the pressure of all the insoluble problems and apparently it showed on my face as I rolled my chair across the banking room floor on my way to the elevator.

"Mr. Clark," Frank hollered from across the lobby, "you're taking that job all wrong. You got to be like Mr. Scott Candler. He told 'em to 'go to hell!'"

I straightened up and looked at Frank. I didn't want anybody to go to hell, but I understood what Frank was saying. There are just some things you can't do anything about and it is foolish to worry about them. As my grandpa, the old German, used to say 'There's no use to worry. If you can do something about a thing, do it. If you can't do anything, what's the use to worry.'

Well, we had done something when we raised the tax rate nearly fifty per cent.

The public response was an explosion of wrath.

The only thing that saved us was the summer I had spent talking about the deficit and the audit that confirmed the fact we had inherited a desperate situation.

That and the fact many people were so outraged they were speechless.

This latter was not true of the man I had defeated during the previous summer.

Even after I took office, he continued to make violent speeches, and now, when we raised taxes because of the mess he had left, he went too far. Finally, I had enough. The TV people called and wanted me to answer his latest blast at me.

"I'm on my way to the post office," I told the reporter. "Meet me there."

With the cameras rolling, I sat in front of the Decatur Post Office in my rolling chair. "I have been defeated in politics," I said, " and when I lost I went back to my private business and I didn't make any statements about the man who defeated me. I suggest the time has come for the former chairman to do the same."

It was the last I heard from him.

But just the beginning of a new fight with his former supporters.

With all the attention we had focused during the summer and the continuing show we were providing as we wrestled to take control of the county's problems, the press was in my office every day and I was interviewed for television three or four times a week. It always amused me when the Journal reporter would come into my office at eight thirty in the morning.

"What's going on, Mr. Harrison?" he would ask.

"Well," I told him on one occasion, "so far, I got up this morning, took a bath, brushed my teeth, dressed and ate breakfast. After that, I drove four blocks to the court house, got out and came up here, and now I am talking to you."

I must admit that I added to the show. After all the talk about the dire condition of our finances, one of the first acts I took was to buy a new Toronado for the chairman to drive. I couldn't use the former chairman's car because of the wheelchair — he had a four door and the back door opened the wrong way. So I felt it was a legitimate expenditure.

But, I could have picked a better color — politically, that is. "Harrison buys GOLD Toronado" the head line said. "Says county in bad shape financially."

That really didn't bother me since I wasn't planning to run for re-election.

But, I have to admit I added fuel to the fire storm when I asked for a raise of ten thousand a year. My heart was pure, since my main concern was to be able to pay the salaries we had agreed to for our new executives. After all, I reasoned, the chairman should make more than the men who work for him. But it did add another can of gasoline to the roaring fire — and of course I knew nobody in his right mind would vote me a raise under the conditions that existed — no elected legislator would, that is.

I told Don, "Well, Don, I tried to get my salary up. Now, we're just going to have to pay what it takes to keep our department heads."

"What we can do," Don said shrewdly, "is never quote an annual salary — just monthly — for the department heads."

By the time I left office, five of the men under me were making more than the chairman. The salaries of the executives we had brought in never became an issue and we got the job done.

The morning after the tax increase was announced, my friend, the Journal reporter was there at my office waiting for me when I rolled in.

"I hear there's a recall petition circulating," he said.

"Great," I responded, "if you can get ahold of a copy bring it up here and I'll sign it. If anybody wants to vote on getting me out of this job, I'm all for it."

Later in the day he brought me a copy and I signed it. My last week in office, the copy I had signed was returned to me and I had it framed as the prize display in the real estate office to which I returned.

The people behind the recall petition were dead serious.

WEDNESDAY, OCTOBER 22, 1969   THE DECATUR-DEKALB NEWS

DEKALB COUNTY NEEDS YOU!
RECALL HARRISON NOW
YOU can help fight Unreasonably High Taxes You can help end government-by-crony in DeKalb County
JOIN THE DEKALB RECALL MOVEMENT-RECALL CLARK HARRISON NOW!

23,000 signatures are on hand to recall Mr. Clark Harrison, the Commission Chairman. Legally this is about the number needed; however, when we finish checking these against the official voter lists, many will fail to meet legal requirements for one reason or another.

MORE SIGNATURES ARE NEEDED NOW!

If you need petitions, call 289 - 4963 (after 6 p.m. call 634-9708).

HOLDERS OF INCOMPLETE PETITIONS SHOULD RETURN THEM NOW.

We will mail your additional forms.

It is important that all signatures reach us as soon as possible.

If you are a registered voter and have not signed a recall petition, sign this one, cut it out and mail it to DEKALB RECALL COMMITTEE, P. O. Box 29552, Briarcliff Station, Atlanta, Georgia, 30329.

We Need Money!

If possible please send us a donation of $1.00 or more. Make checks payable to:
DEKALB RECALL COMMITTEE

RECALL PETITION

As provided in 1956 Georgia Laws, Volume 2, Page 3237 #361, House Bill #124 Article I, Section 6, Page 3244, DeKalb County's Commission governing authority established:

RECALL OF CHAIRMAN OR COMMISSION MEMBER

The undersigned qualified registered voters do hereby petition the Registrar of DeKalb County, Georgia, Mr. Frank Thomas, or his successor in office, if any, to certify this petition to the Ordinary of DeKalb County, Mrs. Katherine Mann or her successor in office, if any, and that Registrar verify that the registered voters signed hereunder are qualified registered voters in DeKalb County and that the names appearing hereon constitute not less than 15% of such voters, qualified and registered to vote in DeKalb County.

We the undersigned qualified registered voters of DeKalb County do hereby petition the Ordinary of DeKalb County, Mrs. Katherine Mann or her successor in office, if any, to call a Re-Call Election for Clark Harrison, Chairman of the Board of Commissioners of DeKalb County, whose term of office commenced on January 1, 1969 and expires December 31, 1972, and we the undersigned qualified registered voters of DeKalb County, Georgia do further certify that nine (9) months of Clark Harrison's term of office will have expired on October 1, 1969 prior to the official filing of this petition.

SIGNATURE OF VOTER	NAME OF VOTER (PRINTED)	ADDRESS	VOTING PLACE (School or Other)
1.			
2.			
3.			
4.			

The effort to collect the required signatures for the recall election went on for nearly a year. Tables were set up in shopping centers around the county and signatures collected on the weekends.

My favorite story coming from the effort was of a man standing in the middle of the street at a busy intersection with a petition and a pen in his hand. When cars stopped for the traffic light, he would go up and down the row of cars.

"You want your taxes lowered," he'd call into the open window of a stopped car, "sign this petition."

A supporter of mine happened to be in the line that day. The petition was thrust through the window and it had a long row of signatures representing several hours work.

"Thank you," he responded, rolled up the window and drove off carrying the long sheet of signatures with him.

Twenty two thousand signatures were required and we began to hear that the petitioners were within a couple thousand of their goal.

It didn't bother me at first, but as the months drug on the signature collecting was having an unsettling effect on the staff. Before it was over, my executive secretary had resigned to return to the city of Atlanta where she would feel more secure.

The accomplishments of our administration and of subsequent administrations dated back to the tax hike. It was a bullet that had to be bitten, and we bit it. Taking a big enough bite to do some good and to change the whole complexion and future course of the county.

And to give me undisputed title to being the biggest bastard in the county.

CHAPTER XXXV

Airplanes, young or old, do need maintenance. And regular inspections. And walk arounds.

You ignore their well being at your own risk.

And little things mean a lot.

Just a little bit of water in the fuel will stop your engine at a critical time during takeoff.

A leak in the vacuum system will blind the instrument pilot as to whether his plane is flying straight and level — or upside down — or in a death spiral.

In some models, a leak in the exhaust will cause carbon monoxide to fill the cockpit.

Recently, I noticed as I took off that my airspeed was registering zero. No big deal, until you are ready to land.

In the old biplanes, the pilot could judge landing speed by the sound of the wind whistling through the wire wing bracing. Enclosed in a modern cockpit that is no longer possible, and it is important to land fast enough to stay airborne and slow enough to stop before the runway expires.

A dirt dobber had plugged the hole of my pitot tube.

It happened the one time I failed to check that item in my walkaround.

In flying, you learn to be careful in your inspections. You also learn to improvise when your own carelessness gets you in trouble.

The instrument pilot learns partial panel flying — substituting the use of other instruments for the attitude indicator when the vacuum pump fails.

There is a simple tester for carbon monoxide that can be mounted in the cabin.

If the engine conks out on takeoff, you learn to land as straight ahead as possible — and take your chances.

In my case, the Loran C was working and gave me groundspeed to help me land.

451

People require inspections periodically, and a certain amount of maintenance. Paras and quads have some special requirements in this regard.

The key political objection I had to overcome in my run for chairman and chief executive officer of our large metropolitan county was whether, as a paraplegic, I would be physicallly able to lead the third largest government in the state.

And the key physical requirement was to avoid abusing my paralyzed parts and the kind of breakdown that had made me leave Yale and that had interrupted other pursuits since I was wounded.

I had enjoyed for years reading motivational books about how to achieve the impossible — after all, as a paraplegic, that was my specialty — and I had found one especially helpful as I assumed my four year reign as King.

It was written by a man named Peter Townsend who had headed several large corporations.

It was called "How to Earn a Living Working Four Hours a Day Without Feeling Guilty About It."

The book made several points that I found very compatable to my own way of thinking and to the physical restraints under which I was operating.

For one thing, it said that, once the experts were in place and working it was important for the boss NOT to be around all the time. After all, when you give somebody a job you've got to leave him alone long enough for him to do it.

He said to work an irregular schedule as boss. That way everybody had to work all day because they never knew when you might show up.

He pointed out that most people who say they work from eight to five really spend no more than four hours actually working. The rest of the time is spend sharpening pencils, looking out the window or at the water cooler chatting with cohorts.

He said there was nothing wrong with this — the human mechanism needs time to let the subconscious mull over the problem. As long as only four hours are going to be spent working why not, he queried, spend the other four away from the workplace.

It made sense to me.

My contention is that I spent less time on the job than any chairman we have had — and the the county got more done.

What did I do with all the time I didn't spend on the details of county government?

Well, for one thing, I visited my friends at the nursing home every Thursday afternoon.

On the ninth floor of the courthouse, we were in a superheated atmosphere of pressure, angry words, clashing interests and ideas.

When I entered the old house on Covington Road, I shed all that. I felt like Alice going through the looking glass. Suddenly, I was in a world where nothing much changed with people who had no axe to grind and who were glad to see me. A few were interested and I would tell them the latest from the county. Otherwise, we talked about their families, their memories and how they were doing physically.

With the TV people coming out several times a week, I didn't have to worry about staying in contact with the general public. Interestingly, I don't recall getting invitations to speak other than at groundbreakings and such special functions arranged by our public relations man. As a district commissioner, I was constantly speaking at civic clubs. But, after I became chairman, I was seldom asked.

I think people got the impression from seeing me on TV so much that I was extremely busy and could not have time for such engagements.

But mainly, it was because I wasn't seeking invitations — I wasn't running and didn't plan to run again. The busy round of speaking engagements followed by most politicians is self induced.

With the county humming along under the able leadership of Don, I decided there was one area where I could secure substantial benefits for the county by my personal efforts and activity.

Our state highway department was ruled by a gentleman named Jim Gillis who had been a dominant political power in Georgia for something over thirty years. In the rurally dominated legislature, the man who could decide whose road would be paved, wielded enormous power. The governor decided who would head the highway department and that director in turn could help enormously in delivering votes in the legislature for the governor's program. When we were in office, the system was beginning to change, but, as a practical matter, Mr. Jim was still the man who could provide road funds.

Our county had one of the largest delegations in the legislature but, unfortunately for the county commission, they made a practice of voting opposite to Mr. Jim.

As a fast growing county, we had staggering road needs. The engineers in the state highway department knew this and the urban areas were beginning to get more attention because that was where the people were. We were getting the expressway money but surface paving and improvements were hard to come by because of the lingering effects of the old political setup.

I decided there was no better way I could help our citizens than to get on the good side of Mr. Jim.

I decided further if I made an appointment, I'd be just another of the city politicians trying to cut into the patronage that helped move the legislature around.

So, I decided to do what the commissioners and legislators from the small counties did when they wanted a road paved.

They didn't make appointments. They just came to Atlanta and waited in Mr. Jim's ante room until he could see them.

So, that's what I did.

Monday mornings I would go to the state highway department, by myself, no staff — just me.

And I would sit and wait. Mary, the receptionist and I became close friends. She was a lovely lady from south Georgia. After we chatted, I would get on the sofa and read a magazine or just stare into space.

Something I had learned to do well when I was a private in the infantry.

Sometimes I'd wait an hour, sometimes longer while Mr. Jim dispensed with whatever business he had.

One thing I was sure of, Mr. Jim knew the chairman of Georgia's second largest county was in his reception room cooling his heels.

The longer I waited, the better I liked it because I knew there was a big gap between Mr. Jim and me that I had to close.

Finally, I would be ushered into his big paneled office.

He was a large man, in his seventies, slow and deliberate in his movements, courtly of manner with eyes made shrewd by a lifetime of dealing with the politically ambitious.

I came to like and respect him and to look forward to our visits.

In fact, I began to enjoy my Monday mornings with Mr. Jim as much as I did my Thursday afternoons at the nursing home.

In the beginning, we would go through an opening ritual. After exchanging pleasantries, Mr. Jim would slide his center desk drawer open and pull out a single sheet of paper.

I got the impression it might be the only piece of paper in the desk.

On the sheet was tallied the vote of each legislator on the last attempt to pass a cent-a-gallon increase in the gasoline tax. All the gasoline tax belonged to Mr. Jim and his roads.

Apparently, all of our legislators from DeKalb always voted against the increase. Probably because they were convinced a disproportionate share of the highway revenues were going to the rural counties.

I knew my chances of changing the votes of any of our ten prima donnas was nil, so I never answered or commented during this presentation.

I kept coming on Monday morning and gradually we started talking about other things.

Mr. Jim knew more about the inner workings of state government and politics than any man living at the time. Governors came and went but Mr. Jim continued over the years with brief, one term, interludes when he had guessed wrong on who would be governor.

He would talk about his sons, one in the House, the other in the Senate, about his hometown of Soperton, politicians from the past, hunting and fishing.

Less was said about roads than anything else.

"Clark," he told me one day, "you must be doing something. I see the newspapers are after you. I always know a man's getting things done when the papers jump on him."

Those first two years I was always on page two and sometimes page one of the Atlanta papers about some fiasco, real or imagined, we were wading through.

"Everybody's for you until time comes to pay up, then they disappear,"Mr. Jim said on one of my visits.

Then he told me about how his home county of Treutlin came into being.

"Folks around Soperton decided we ought to have our own county," he recalled. "So, the next session of the General Assembly, daddy and I came to Atlanta. He got a two room suite in the old Kimball House hotel at the corner of Five Points where the legislators all hung out. Passed the word that he wanted to see everybody about a project he was promoting."

Using one room of the suite for a waiting room, Mr. Gillis began interviewing each legislator privately.

"Every legislator had a price," Mr. Jim said, "and everybody knew what it was. For one it would be $50 and for another $500. They would wait patiently while daddy settled things with each individual."

After a while Mr. Gillis figured he had enough votes to pass the bill creating the new county of Treutlin.

"Son," he told Mr. Jim, "I've been adding up and do you know I have spent over $50,000 getting this bill ready to pass. How about you going home and see if some of the people who were so anxious for us to have our own county, won't help us out on this."

"Well," Mr. Jim said, "do you know I went all over that countryside talking to all the people who were behind us getting a county. Do you know how much I collected?"

"I can't imagine," I replied.

"I got $200," he said in a disgusted tone.

I told Mr. Jim I knew how that felt. I had found out in 1960 how hard it is to get financial help in a political matter.

When Franklin Roosevelt was President of the United States, Jim Gillis was his right hand in Georgia. I remember the incident that led to this arrangement and had heard stories about what had gone on behind the scenes. But now I got the story straight from the principal player.

"As you know, Clark," Mr. Jim told me, "Roosevelt was dead set on getting George out of the U. S. Senate. George was a conservative and was blocking a lot of the liberal legislation Roosevelt wanted passed during the 1930's"

Roosevelt was extremely popular in Georgia and the President called Warm Springs, Georgia, his Little White House, visiting on a regular basis to treat his paralysis. So, Roosevelt decided he could run a man against Senator George and defeat him.

"He got Camp to run," Mr. Jim recalled. "It was obvious to everybody that, although the people loved Roosevelt, they were not about to let him tell them who to vote for for Senator. Especially not to defeat a man as popular as Senator George."

This was the "George" Scott Candler called to get my pension straightened out. After losing the War Between the States, the South had learned the only way they could build power for the region was to elect good men to Congress and leave them there until they had built a commanding seniority.

"Well," he continued, "when I hear what Roosevelt was up to, I called Soperton and told hem, 'pass the word, vote for Camp, it will be to our advantage.'"

When the votes came in, the obvious had happened. George had carried every county in the state with the exception of Treutlin. And everybody knew Treutlin was Gillis' county.

"From that day forward," Mr. Jim continued, "Roosevelt felt he had only one friend in Georgia and his name was Jim Gillis. I was his campaign manager for Georgia in his three re-elections and no Federal appointment or other patronage was committed in Georgia without my okay."

And, I thought, the roads in and around Soperton are mostly paved, too.

"Clark," Mr. Jim told me one day when we had gotten to know each other, "that deal your predecessor made with the State is probably the worst deal a county ever made."

During my campaign for chairman, one of the big issues was widening Candler Road. It is a main artery in South DeKalb and much had been said about all the road money being spent in the north end of the county. When my opponent couldn't get a regular state contract, he told the state the county would pay 80 per cent of the cost even though it is a state highway. So, while the campaign was going on the widening was staked out and some construction work was done. And he was taking credit during the campaign for getting the project started.

When I came into office, there was no money to finish the project.

Mr. Jim Gillis and I had become good friends by the time we cut the ribbon at the completion of the perimeter expressway around Atlanta. Mr. Jim is standing behind me. Governor Maddox is to my right.

"Clark," Mr. Jim continued, "I've told our people to reverse that contract. The State will pay the 80 per cent share."

My Monday morning visits continued and became one of the bright spots of my four years as chairman.

I knew I was making progress when I was in Mr. Jim's office one day and he told me to stay while a delegation from out in the state came in. We visited a while and then Mr. Jim came around from behind his desk, put his hand on my shoulder, and told the visitors from South Georgia,

"Clark is one of us."

DeKalb County officials had tried for twelve years to get Memorial Drive from Atlanta to Stone Mountain widened.

It was finally done during our administration.

As was the long and costly Buford Highway.

In fact, more money was spent by the state on DeKalb's surface streets and highways than at any time in the past.

The times were changing. The old county unit system that had locked control of the state into the rural areas had been abolished and newly elected legislators were beginning to learn how to exert influence.

But, old ways die hard and through force of habit, and inertia politics continued, as usual for some time after the laws and apportionment changed.

I was in Mr. Jim's office when he received a call in the summer of 1970 saying all the branch managers of the C&S Bank, located all over Georgia, had been polled and all but one said Carl Sanders would make a comeback in the race for governor.

Mills Lane, president of C&S was for Carl as was Mr. Jim, but Mr. Jim was worried that Carl was not out amongst the people enough.

"What counts is stirring the people up," Mr. Jim said. "They're talking too much about Carl's gold cuff links."

His opponent was Jimmy Carter — or Jimmy Who. as he was referred to in those days.

I came to admire and respect Mr. Jim Gillis. He played the political game the way it had to be played in his day and he looked after the interests of rural Georgia because they were his people. Nobody ever questioned his honesty and integrity and there was no scandal in that regard while he was director.

My own conviction was that, while I was chairman, my job was to look after DeKalb County. Our people couldn't ride on excuses and explanations of why the state wouldn't help us — all they could ride on was asphalt and concrete.

After Jimmy Carter was elected governor, he appointed Bert Lance to take Mr. Jim's place. I waited a couple of weeks and then visited Soperton to pay my respects to a gentleman whose company I had come to enjoy and who had been DeKalb County's friend.

But, as my good friend Sidney Sisselman had so aptly stated, "The King is dead. Long live the King."

I heard that Jimmy Carter had appointed Bert Lance the new highway director on a Thursday.

Saturday morning, I was sitting in the waiting room of Mr. Lance's Calhoun Bank.

CHAPTER XXXVI

Before our Decatur-DeKalb YMCA building was built, I helped some with fund raising for the various youth programs. Once we had the building, I became one of the most faithful participants — I found that swimming and working out was what I needed to keep my paralyzed limbs limber and my mind as uncluttered as possible. No small order considering the kinds of activities I have engaged in over the years.

Eventually, I joined the exclusive health club, or healthy club as we older members like to characterize it.

"Mom," Bob told Frances, "they call it the healthy club. But I wish you could see the shape those guys are in. Little skinny legs, big fat stomachs."

Well, admittedly, some of us healthy club members have seen better days. But, we all get great mental as well as physical stimulation from our membership.

We do have some characters.

I soon will mention Leroy, the baseball umpire who made the scoreboard light up.

Another of my favorites is George Hooten.

Although you might not guess it by seeing George today, George was, until recent decades, an iron worker.

More specifically, he was one of those agile types who hang steel office building frames many stories up into the atmosphere.

After George was injured on the job some time back, he retired from heavy construction, but he is just as agile as ever when it comes to hanging words together in poetic ascension. George's verbage masterpieces are a wonder to be enjoyed.

After Roy Davis, our masseur, retired and moved back to South Carolina, Roy became ill. George and I decided to visit him and to use my airplane for transportation.

George was a belly gunner in World War II and, as in my case, became a pilot at his own expense after leaving the military service.

The flight was uneventful.

After landing at Columbia, we were guided to a parking space by a young lineman, who stood looking as George and I prepared to deplane.

George is a large man.

My airplane is a small airplane.

George has a hurt knee. At the time, he was affecting a walking stick.

George opened the door of the Cherokee 140 and tossed his walking cane out on the wing.

Then, he twisted around in his seat and, somewhat laboriously, began to extract his large frame from the small plane, choosing to back out.

George had struggled to his feet when he happened to notice the young lineman was standing, mouth agape, taking in the rather unusual spectacle.

"Listen," George said to the young man, "if you think I'm in bad shape, wait until you see the guy who is flying this thing!"

In the early days of our county administration, all was not sweetness and light.

In 1969, we were caught on the horns of a very painful dilemma. On the one hand, we had increased the tax rate by nearly fifty per cent. The other half of our attack on the overshadowing deficit was to cut spending. So, we increased taxes the same year we curtailed spending.

That was not a formula to cause peace and harmony in the community.

And our employees were suffering as well.

Soon after I took office, as an ex officio member of the pension board, I had wrestled along with other members with a perplexing case. We had a man in his late fifties who had been with the county police department thirty-seven years. He had been a high ranking officer for a number of years. At the time, the county's pension was $1 per month for each year of service plus, at age 65, social security. The man could not be declared physically disabled, he was not due social security, but he had given thirty-seven years of his life to the county and now simply did not have the physical stamina and drive to function at the salary he was being paid.

We finally found a doctor who would declare him disabled and he was able to retire at half pay.

But, it was not the way to treat a man of his statute and long years of faithful service.

We changed that.

Because of changes we made when I left office, the county had a fully-funded pension plan that allows any employee with twenty-five years service to retire on half pay at age fifty five.

And our people were underpaid.

Thanks to Don's understanding of personnel matters and the tax increase, we completely redid the pay scale for the county, placing jobs on a comparative compensation to equal private industry jobs.

But it was the way we did it that pleased me most.

The highest per cent increase went to the lowest paid employees.

"Mr. Harrison," one of the switch board operators told me, "my girl friend's husband had just been called to go to Vietnam when the pay increase came in. She got a hundred dollars a month raise and was able to keep her home."

Don had been an enlisted man in the Navy and both of us tended to identify with the low man on the totem pole.

"A flat percentage increase across the board sounds fair to most people in the public," Don told me, "but it's the most unfair thing you can do. The highly paid get too much and the people at the bottom get practically nothing."

The starting pay of our police and firemen almost doubled during our four years and the departments began to hire college graduates. Absenteeism dropped from forty per cent to about two per cent after the first year's service.

My proudest accomplishment was in the sanitation department under Bud's leadership. Starting with chaos, Bud fought as hard as the had at Remagen to bring order. It was a time of great racial unrest, Martin Luther King had just been assassinated and we expected at any time to be hit by a strike that would inundate the county with garbage.

When I went to the sanitation department and looked at the sea of angry faces, I asked, "What do they want?"

"More money," was the caustic reply.

Now, we began to pay more money, place the workers under the merit system with regular vacations and raises, we promoted blacks to supervisory positions, and upgraded the role of the drivers who were made permanent assignments of their trucks. We provided showers and uniforms and had an instructor who conducted classes for those wanting to learn reading, writing and basic skills.

The best move we made was to go to a four day week. I kept asking, since we had so much absenteeism, why not change our schedules to fit their work habits. Under the new arrangement the men had assigned routes to cover Monday and Tuesday. If they finished, they had Wednesday off. If they didn't finish their Thursday and Friday routes, they were called back on Saturday.

As an ex-private, I knew there are some jobs where time off is a lot more important than the remote possibility of promotion.

Morale picked up, absenteeism dropped and I began to get friendly waves when I passed a sanitation truck.

With money available, we improved all the services, improved the highways, acquired eight hundred acres of new park land, purchased the mansion that became the Callenwolde Art and Curtural Center, built a new jail and paid for a juvenile building, instituted the committing magistrate program and financed and planned the new emergency medical service.

With the completion of the perimeter expressway and the legalization of mixed drinks, hotels were built that in turn brought suburban office parks that added heavy revenue to the tax base.

It was a boom time. In 1971, we issued building permits in the amount of $238 million — an all-time record that was not approached until the office boom of the 1980's.

Sitting in my large, panelled office in my wheelchair, I would sometimes get to chuckling over what had happened.

The highest executive position I had held prior to becoming chairman was assistant squad leader of my infanty squad.

Now, I was the chief executive officer presiding over a fifty million plus budget, three thousand employees in twenty eight departments. We had to answer to nearly a half-million residents and practically all of them who were old enough, not only knew my name but would recognize me as someone they saw on the TV in their homes several nights a week.

When I was a private in the infantry, I don't remember ever getting close enough to a colonel to recognize what he was. Now, I had twenty-two former colonels working for me.

And they were all nice fellows, too, and much smarter than I had imagined.

One of the most ironic things that happened during my four years concerned the V. A. hospital.

The old World War I hospital, a huge rambling red brick affair, was to be closed and the patients moved to a modern multi-storied structure. The property is in our county and was to be declared surplus.

"Why don't we apply for it," I asked Don. "There are 26 acres and the MARTA rail line will have a station right across the street."

Other Federal agencies didn't need the property, the county school system didn't need it, and our crew of experts put up such a convincing case that, much to my delight, the General Services Administration announced that the property would come to DeKalb County.

As chairman, it became my job to take delivery of the deed. Since it was such a large and valuable property, the federal government decided to make a ceremony of it.

All the local dignitaries were present, our Congressman and a deputy director of the V. A., a lady, was sent down to represent the Nixon administration.

The local high school band concluded a rousing concert and the deputy director finally took her place at the podium to render the major address of the occasion. At the close of her speech, she called me forth and presented me, as chairman of the county commission, with the deed to the property.

I rolled forward in my government issue wheelchair and the opportunity was just too rich to miss. "You know," I told those assembled, "all these years I have figured that sooner or later the V. A. hospital would get me. And now, by God, I have gotten it!"

CHAPTER XXXVII

Weather, as any observer of the TV news knows, moves from west to east in the United States. The prevailing westerlies speed the return of the flyer from California toward Georgia and the difference is quite noticeable in a small plane.

When I called flight service before leaving Abilene, I was advised I would enjoy a twenty-two knot tail wind. The more I thought about that added ground speed, the more I believed I'd spend the night with Dick and Nina Haltom in Batesville, Mississippi.

I calculated I could make the 304 nautical miles to Texarkana in two hours and twenty minutes, refuel there and complete the 211 knots into Batesville in less than two hours. With the tail wind, I'd be clipping along at about 132 knots an hour.

To avoid the Dallas-Fort Worth terminal control area, I would be flying northeast until I crossed over Bridgeport VOR, then would swing due east toward Texarkana.

I would have scattered clouds at 4,000 feet, but as the land mass elevation descends, heading east I should have no trouble staying 500 feet below the clouds as required for Visual Flight Rules flying.

Texas is a big state. It would take three stops in the one forty to cross it. Texas is also composed of a lot more in the way of variety than oil wells and sage brush.

Just east of Breckenridge, I came over wooded terrain and was flying along a large lake that recalled our Lake Lanier north of Atlanta. It was spotted with homes built in the woods along the shore line, had a couple of large marinas and a private landing strip called Sportsmans World. The name of the body of water obviously dated back to earlier days in Texas — Possum Kingdom Lake.

467

Flying has turned out to be an entirely different experience from any-thing I had imagined. For one thing, it is a whole world of its own. Much more complex and difficult and with layer after layer of knowledge to be mastered. Like peeling an onion — there is always another layer beneath.

And much more soul satisfying than I had imagined.

It would have to be for flight to have progressed to become the part of our everyday lives it is now. A huge price in terms, not only of money but of human lives, has been paid at each stage of development. Recent-ly, reading the three by five cards on the Epps Flight School cork board, I saw a business jet advertised for over $4 million. Incredible that that much money could be expended to travel from point A to point B. And still we are in the infancy of this kind of travel.

Being the head of county government was also completely different from what I had imagined it would be. I knew once I was in the position, that the good Lord had been looking after me in giving me eight years to ma-ture before the load descended on me. I had taken a lot of punches dur-ing that eight years and was much better able to roll with them at age 45 that I would have been at 37.

At that, I had to remind myself when the going got rough that I really wasn't in the thing alone. There were four other commissioners, a large staff and 3,000 employees who cared about what happened and who were working to solve the problems I worried about.

We've all heard of the scapegoat. Most people don't know where the term originated. The Bible tells of a ceremony the ancient Jews performed once a year as part of their atonement. A goat was brought before the priest, hands were laid on the goat as it was held by the horns, and all the sins and misdeeds of the whole Jewish race were heaped on the poor animal. Then, bearing its miserable load, the poor scapegoat was taken far into the wilderness and released to roam and survive the best way it could, while the nation was given a fresh start.

We do the same thing to our leaders. By piling the frustrations and disappointments on the one in charge, we get a release from our own anger.

It takes a little age and experience to carry the scapegoat load.

The telephone brought the message to the chairman.

I talked to thousands of people over the four years and was always amazed at the time and detail people could expend in explaining the aggravations of dealing with the government.

There was a lot of repetition in the garbage complaints and the zoning protests, but there were interesting moments as well.

I kept a pad on my desk by the phone, and wrote down the caller's name, telephone number and address and the subject of the call. Then, I always told them to call back in a week if nothing had been done.

It was a pretty good system and I seldom received the second call. My secretary called my hand written messages 'magic notes'. The departments were good about looking into the matters complained of.

The fact that we didn't receive thank you notes was not surprising either. I had been in government as a district commissioner long enough not to expect that.

Often, the calls were abusive. I remember telling one man that if he wanted to talk like that he was going to have to do it to my face — and hung up. I forgot about the call, but when I left at noon, there he was, waiting just outside the office. This time we talked eyeball to eyeball and resolved the matter.

I never got used to people calling up, mad at me personally, about some problem I didn't know existed and really didn't feel I had caused. Finally, I told one lady,

"Lady," I said, "You don't know me and you don't know what kind of person I am. You are being very impolite."

She burst into tears when the criticism was directed toward her. Scapegoats are not supposed to talk back. It took me a while to calm her down and make her feel better.

One thing I used to enjoy doing was to pick up the phone before my secretary had time to answer. Sometimes the caller would hang up as soon as he recognized my voice, but it was fun to hear the reaction to getting to the chariman just by dialing a number.

One lady did not know who I was. She called to ask a question, which I answered. Then she asked a couple more questions and finally she said,

"You seem to know a lot. Who are you?"

"Lady, I'm the chairman," I replied, "and if it's not like I said, we'll change it."

If I had ever worried about people feeling sorry for me because of the wheelchair, I could forget it now. In fact, I was hoping somebody would feel sorry for me. The people who called me had no feeling for me one way or the other — they just wanted their problem solved — now.

There were exceptions.

The occasional friend who called on a personal matter or the even more rare occasion when I was thanked, came like the refreshing latter rain — and I remembered them with pleasure.

I took my calls and returned my calls from the office during the four years. Early in my term, I decided, however, that I was not going to survive it I had the calls coming to me at home as well. I remember one lady calling me at 8 a. m. one Saturday morning. I had been working hard all week and had been out late the night before. The phone woke me up. The caller said her husband had failed to go by and get his check on Friday, and could somebody meet him at the department that morning and give it to him. I called the department head, and gave up on sleeping any more that morning.

The most touching call came from a young woman about ten one evening.

She was crying. She had flushed her diamond ring down the toilet.

I called the head of the sewer department.

"Clark," he drawled, "there ain't no way that ring can be recovered. It's half way to the Chattahoochee river by now."

I gave him the woman's number. People might think I was tough, but there were some things I just couldn't do.

The call that decided me to take no more calls at home came about ten a. m. one Saturday.

Frances and I had finished a late breakfast and were sitting at the table talking when the phone rang.

"Is this Mr. Harrison?" The lady's voice was cultured.

"Yes, it is," I replied.

"Are you the county commissioner?" she continued.

"Yes, I am."

"You goddam lying son of a bitch."

I slowly returned the receiver to its cradle.

"Who was that?" Frances asked.

"Wrong number," I replied with a grin.

I knew one thing — there was at least one citizen out there who didn't think of me as a poor wheelchair victim.

Knowing that gave me a warm feeling.

The call also gave me an inspiration. The idea certainly saved my sanity and probably saved my life.

I had another phone installed at the house and gave the number to my secretary, the family and a few friends.

Then I turned the bell off on the listed phone.

"I tried to get you all weekend," someone would tell me on Monday morning.

"Well," I'd say, "you know how this job is — lots of running around."

As long as people could get my phone to ring, they seemed satisfied.

We had stirred deep animosities in the campaign and decisions we made angered people no matter which way they went. And, in zoning matters, millions of dollars and a man's future could be involved.

Three times my life was threatened.

I never did worry about those calls.

I always figured, if somebody was going to shoot me, they'd shoot me. They wouldn't call and give me advance notice.

With all I had been through I did not respond quite normally to the threat of danger and I never worried about something that almost happened.

I was in my office one day and the TV people were setting up to interview me. One of the men had placed a heavy light on a tall stand behind me. For some reason, it toppled over hitting the floor beside me with a crash. It just missed my shoulder as it fell.

The TV man looked at me sharply.

"You didn't even flinch," he said.

"Well," I said, "by the time I heard it, it had already missed me."

One thing that bothered me was the fact that the public would not allow the chairman to take a light hearted approach to our problems. I had always enjoyed a little humor with my misery, but the press and the people seemed deeply offended if I tried to take the light-hearted approach from the ninth floor of the courthouse.

My attempts at humor were so distorted by the media, and the facts of complex problems were so twisted in their presentation to the public that I developed a dislike for reading the newspapers. I have not yet gotten entirely over the feeling after all these years. The problem was in making an off-hand remark half in jest to a reporter, then seeing it and my name in large somber headlines in the evening paper. I got to where I could read a paper faster than anyone — skipping through rapidly. If I wasn't in it, which was rare in those early days, I'd relax and read the rest of the news.

As in the Army, the grimness of the general situation did make for some delightful humor behind the front lines.

I like to think we had a relaxed attitude so that, at least, the general turmoil was not agitated by unnecessary promulgations from the ninth floor. The tension was real because the pressures were intense. We tried not to increase them by our rules, regulations and threatenings.

One thing I came to enjoy was my birthdays.

The first year, I wrote a memorandum addressed to the staff along the following lines

"A lot of people don't like a fuss made over their birthdays, but I am different. Please feel free to make a big occasion out of my birthday. The date is September 24."

When the big day arrived, I was told to go to a certain restaurant to meet with a group about some matter I have now forgotten.

On arrival, I found our immediate ninth floor gang and a couple of close department heads in a private downstairs room to wish me a happy birthday. At great trouble, a large cake had been prepared. Embossed in the icing on top was every major mistake in statement or action that I had made that first year.

The tax raise, the garbage mess, the Decatur Power Structure were all represented.

My favorite was based on a remark I had made to a group wanting their street paved. I explained that we hadn't paved it because "it doesn't go anywhere."

That one even got an editorial in the Atlanta papers and left me appearing callous toward the poor homeowners.

The next year, I sent out another handwritten memorandum. I had decided, I said, that this year I didn't want a fuss made over my birthday.

When the big day arrived, I was pretty excited. My calendar showed a luncheon and a dinner and I was sure one of them was really a surprise birthday party.

Nobody wished me a happy birthday that morning and the luncheon passed as the routine affair it was purported to be. The evening was to be spent at a civic club in a joint appearance with Governor Lester Maddox. I thought, boy, they are really going to make a big one this year — imagine inviting the governor.

I listened to Governor Maddox speak and made a few remarks myself. Still not a word about my birthday.

As I pulled into the drive behind our townhouse, I noticed the downstairs was dark. I thought, boy, they really went to a lot of trouble. Must have walked several blocks since there were no cars around.

My heart was pounding as I opened the back door, expecting the lights to flash on and a crowd of my loyal fellow workers to mob me.

Nothing.

As I backed into the elevator, I was beginning to have doubts.

Frances was upstairs watching TV. After visiting with her a while I went to bed.

"Those sorry bastards," I muttered as I tried to get to sleep, "I took them in off the street, gave them their big chance and they couldn't even give me a birthday party."

When I got to the office next morning, I noticed several of the staff not usually there in the morning were hanging around in the reception room. The door to my office was closed.

Finally, somebody said, "Well, aren't you going in your office?"

When the door was finally opened and I rolled into the chairman's office I nearly fell out of the chair laughing.

Along the length of one wall, in crepe paper, was spelled in large letters, 'Happy Birthday'. On the tables and desk were paper plates with the remains of hors d'oeuvres, cups with melted ice and whiskey in them, cigarette butts in the ashtrays. The coat closet door was open and a woman's slip hung on the hat rack. A pair of panty hose were on the sofa.

"Well," Don said, "you said you didn't want a party, so we had to wait until you left to have it."

Then they passed me pictures of the festivity in full swing.

Out in the reception room was a fashionably dressed woman, obviously a Republican from the prosperous north end of the county. I went out and got her.

"I want you to see how your tax money is being spent," tears rolling down my face, my jaws aching from the laughter.

It was the best party I ever missed.

I like to see things happen, I like to see people employed, and I like to see competition giving people a choice of places to live and places to work.

The times were right for our county to develop and by the end of my four years we were going like a house afire.

Rezoning could make a piece of property go up ten times or more in value, and with the county filling up with people there was tremendous demand for rezoning for apartments, commercial or industrial use.

As chairman, it was my job to preside once every month over rezoning hearings. Our commission took the position that any property owner had the right to ask at any time that his property be rezoned. So, our door was open. All the property owner had to do was file a petition, put a sign on his property and we'd have a hearing and a vote. The meetings were volatile. Citizens who took no other interest or part in their government would show up en masse — mad, vocal, organized, hostile and threatening. As the meetings increased in the number of applicants, the citizens became more expert in expressing their hostility. They began to bring placards and wear buttons.

Preserving the constitutional right of the proponents to be heard called for firm action. If the chairman so much as blinked there could be riots and mayhem.

The big courtroom held about three hundred people and soon we were playing to standing-room-only crowds.

With the room overflowing with the milling and restless crowd, a side door would open promptly at 9 a. m., in would roll the chairman and the commissioners. With a commissioner pushing, we'd take a rolling run, mount the short steep ramp to the stage and wheel behind a table spotted with microphones.

First, I would explain the rules. The proponent would have five minutes to present his case, a bell would ring. Then the opposition would have five minutes and the bell would ring again. The clerk kept the alarm clock we used for a bell. The county attorney was present to give us legal advice. The planning director showed us maps and explained the recommendations of the planning commission which had met earlier and voted for or against each petition.

We voted on each petition at the end of the day after all had been heard. And we took two hours for lunch.

There was a reason for delaying the decisions. We learned early in the game that if we voted on each measure after it was heard we would never be able to get through the agenda. After the vote, everybody concerned in the case would stand up, mill around and make a general display.

There was also danger they would storm the stage and overturn our barricade of tables and microphones.

The two hour recess was so the chairman could go to the 'Y' and swim.

I had one rule. Once that bell rang, nobody said another word about his case. The reason was, as the bell rang, I would introduce the next speaker and he saw to it the previous speaker didn't use his time.

Also, we managed to leave the impression that violation of the rules would adversely effect the case.

An extreme case showed how high emotion ran. On one occasion the commission, at a regular meeting, disapproved a beauty salon that a man was operating with his wife in a residential neighborhood. He went directly home from the meeting, got a gun, walked across the street, rang his neighbor's doorbell. As the neighbor who had opposed him opened the door, he shot and killed him.

We became right expert at conducting the meetings and never had a serious rout. Toward the end of my term, we set a record. We had sixty five petitions filed for our Tuesday meeting. Starting at 9 a.m., and taking the normal two hour break for lunch, we had finished and voted on all 65 by five p.m. that evening.

After the first two years of our administration, things began to go better. We were paying our people better, the money was coming in, services were beginning to catch up with demand, and the campaign to have a recall election had petered out. A fifteen million dollar bond issue had passed assuring us of a new jail and juvenile home and money was approved to cover capital needs in the sanitation department.

I was taking a week off at St. Simons Island the fall of our third year when I got a call from Don.

"Clark," he said, "there's a move getting started in Savannah to hire me back as city manager."

After I determined he was interested in returning to his former position there, I suggested we talk about it when I got back to Decatur.

A few days later he called again.

"It's getting in the papers," he said, "and I'm going to have to give them an answer."

I knew it meant a great deal to Don to be called back. He felt vindicated by confidence that was being shown in his work and his family liked living there. The job he had done in DeKalb had doubtless played a part in making people there realize his worth.

"Don," I said, "if it's what you want to do, you go ahead and accept. We'll work out the details when I get back."

He had done a superb job and all the programs we have envisioned were in place. Don is a fighter and had enjoyed whipping things into shape. He looked forward to doing the same in Savannah.

"Clark," Don came into my office shortly after my return, "I've been going over the accounts, and, you know, I think we could pay off the rest of the deficit now."

"Oh, no you don't," I said. "You're not about to pay off those warrants, leave here a hero and leave me with people thinking we've got plenty of money. We'd be back in the hole in sixty days. The script says we're going to pay the last of that debt the day I leave office, and that's the way it's going to be."

Don was succeeded by a talented leader and administrator who consolidated the gains that had been made and came up with innovative initiatives of his own.

Curtis is a retired Marine Corps colonel who served in the top levels of that organization.

In retrospect, the two things that did most to give us a good administration and to help me survive the four years were the deficit and the recall petition.

I spent so much time advertising the deficit the summer I ran that people were convinced there was no need bringing pet projects to be funded by the county.

After we raised taxes, there was even greater consciousness and conviction about keeping expenditures down.

The recall petition helped me because some people actually began to feel a little sorry for the chairman. The wheelchair wasn't getting me any sympathy — it had really disappeared after the tax hike — so I needed all the pity I could get.

Our long summer of political warfare — resulting in defeat of the incumbent had made it easier for me to make changes — the people expected changes to be made.

As I looked back over the four years, I felt a deep sense of pride in some of the things we had accomplished. I knew from the battles we had fought and the constant criticism we had endured that the changes had not just happened. We had made them happen and we had made them happen against the inertia of bureaucracy and the violent opposition of our enemies.

I was proud that our pay increases had been done the hard way.

I thought about the young wife who was a clerk — she got a $100 a month raise — enough to save her home when her husband was sent to Vietnam.

"Yes," the head of the road department was discussing the raise with me several years after we left office, "I know about that. One of our secretaries was mad because the clerks got a bigger raise than she did. She refused her raise. We accommodated her."

We nearly doubled the starting pay of policemen and firemen. And the turnover in those departments dropped from forty to only two per cent.

We especially enjoyed increasing the pay of our sanitation workers and putting them on the same footing as other employees in regard to vacations and other benefits.

We put in the finest pension plan in the Southeast. And it was sound and fully funded and remains so today.

We had taken our lumps with the tax increase, but in the last couple of years of our administration we began to feel the pleasure of seeing some good things start to happen.

For myself, I felt my role was not only to lead but to help things happen by taking the lumps when something went wrong.

I made it my business to step between the public and the men and women who were doing their job. I always defended them in public — especially when they were in the wrong. Seeing me take the anger and frustration of the public on TV make them want to try harder to correct whatever had brought on an attack, I felt.

In my mind during those four years, I was like the Roman soldier who would gather the lances of the opposing soldiers into his arms and into his own flesh to create the opening to allow his fellow soldiers to break through.

That and make the tough decisions and then stand by them through the firestorm to follow.

Like Bob Simpson, who had crossed France with me, I had endured enough by then that a few more slings and arrows hardly mattered.

"You cost me $32,000 a year with your new tax rate," Jack my tough developer friend told me, "but it's okay. The county needed the money."

Others were beginning to feel less hostile as the money we were spending began to have an effect. They might not like us, but we were beginning to command some respect.

In my last year as chairman, I had to do something that made my friends, as well as my enemies, sure I had lost my mind.

It was 1972 and Richard Nixon was running for re-election. I had disliked Nixon since he first ran for Congress because of the smear tactics he used. I voted for him in 1968, however, for one reason. I felt the Democrats were so involved in the Vietnam thing as to be unable to change policy. Nixon, I reasoned, was a superb politician if nothing else and would see the political wisdom of disengaging from Vietnam. This was, in fact, what he said he would do.

I was convinced there was only one way to get out of Vietnam and that was to declare the war won and leave. It was the wrong war at the wrong place and we were being hurt without damaging our real foes.

The main problem was what it was doing to our young people. Tom was at West Georgia College and he was an active participant in the protest against the war.

"I'd go in a minute, Dad," he told me, "if it was like World War II. But it isn't."

As time went on, I became more convinced that the protesters were right — there was nothing noble about bombing primitive people from 50,000 feet. And the thing that tore me up was the fact that young men were being made amputees and paraplegics fighting in a war that did not have the support of the American people.

I have always been proud of the part I played in the war against Hitler. I could not imagine the bitterness I would have felt if the same thing had happened to me in Vietnam.

So, after four years, Nixon was still talking about withdrawing from Vietnam.

I had heard some strange things about positions McGovern was taking.

But at least he had played a combat role in World War II and I agreed with his position on Vietnam.

I came out for him — publicly.

So, when the picture came out in the paper, there I was in my chairman's suit surrounded by the motley crowd of long haired guitar strummers.

Everybody thought I was crazy. The only other elected official in Georgia who was publicly supporting McGovern was the mayor of one of our small towns west of Atlanta.

All of my generation may have thought I had lost my mind, but I did make some friends among the young people.

The one thing I can say to the Vietnam veteran is that we probably learned more of value to the future of this country out of Vietnam than out of any war we have ever fought. The fact that we survived and still have our freedom and are experiencing today a rebirth of patriotism is a tribute to the strength and resilence of this nation.

Our real strength is in the mass of our people and their understanding of freedom. When Nixon tried some of the tactics of the totalitarian leaders, he ended up looking silly and ineffective. To be a dictator you need people to carry out your dictates and people to obey them.

And now that our Vietnam veterans are assuming positions of increasing influence and power I feel good about the future of this country.

CHAPTER XXXVIII

Landing an airplane, large or small, represents the most critical stage of flight. All sorts of maneuvers can be safely conducted at altitude, but when the ground looms near the options become restricted and disaster is close enough to touch.

I had crash landed from politics in 1960 when I lost my first bid for chairman. So I knew something about what to expect.

The difference was, in 1960 I hadn't been flying so high.

As I reached the middle of my four year term as chairman, I was flying not only high but wide, handsome and with the throttle pushed all the way open.

As times became easier at the county, my soul began to be tested in a new way.

Even while I was being attacked by the press and the general public, there were those who were courting us.

As chairman, I had to sign the subdivision plats, the re-zoning changes, the county contracts, the pay increases and ultimately was responsible for the hirings and firings.

It was a strange feeling — being King.

Things were so because I decided they were so. Most of our visitors were reduced to stating their case in a way least apt to irritate or alienate me and most likely to gain my sympathetic assent.

No matter how dumb my decision might be, it resulted in acceptance usually without protest. The applicant wanted to be able to come and try again.

The commission could literally make — and break — millionaires — and the chairman had a great deal to do with what the commission heard and the direction of its decision.

And the chairman had everything to do with the implementation of those commission decisions.

It reminded me of my friend Leroy, the baseball umpire. Leroy said "I never argue."

"When the batter turns around and looks at me and says 'that wasn't no strike', I look him in the eye, point, and say 'look at the scoreboard.'"

The chairman decided which way the scoreboard lit up.

All the projects, large and small, ended up in that office. A lifetime in the real estate business would expose one to a fraction of the deals that were laid bare on the chairman's desk every week.

"Clark," the developers were among the most powerful in the county and they were coming to see me in the closing months of my chairmanship, "we're going to organize an REIT."

"What's that?" I asked.

"Real Estate Investment Trust," he replied. "Congress authorized them last session."

"Who's going to do it?"

"Just the three of us," he replied. "We want you to be president."

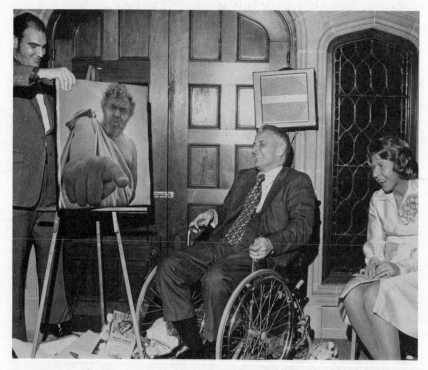

At a going away party the staff presented a portrait giving one impression of my chairmanship. John Newsome, who was Keeper of the King's image is holding the picture. Frances agreed with them on this one.

Next day, the lawyer who would handle the details came to see me.

"It's a way for the small investor to get in on the money to be made in real estate," he said. "Shares are sold and the money invested in various developments. This equity money is then leveraged by borrowing against the real estate, so the profit is multiplied. With the completion of one deal, more stock is sold and more money is borrowed."

I looked at him carefully, "That thing keeps growing, doesn't it?"

"It sure does," he said enthusiastically. "You keep adding staff, making investments, selling stock, borrowing money. There are a lot of fees and commissions to be made by the organizers."

"I can see where it would get bigger and bigger," I said. I hesitated and then asked, "What happens if it has to get smaller again?"

"There are a lot of fees and commisssions to be made by the organizers," he repeated.

That was the flaw. As heavily leveraged as the device would be, it could grow fast — like a balloon. But if anything went wrong, a project wouldn't lease up, houses in a subdivision didn't sell, a payment was missed, there was nothing in reserve to ride out the storm.

Finally, when the developers returned, I told them.

"Look," I said, "I'm not going to trade sewer taps for what I'll be doing next year. After January, we'll get together and talk about the REIT."

And that was what was really behind the visit — an effort to get preferential treatment in the assignment of sewer connections that had become short in supply and that were needed if development was to continue.

The idea behind the REIT sounded good — let the small investor participate in the impressive profits being made in real estate. Like a lot of schemes that are supposed to benefit the "little man," the REIT turned into a disaster — and, because of our bank, I would have a front row, insider seat when disaster struck.

I had guessed right about the fatal flaw in the REIT — it could grow larger, but it made no provision for weathering a storm. The other flaw was the simultaneous construction of projects stimulated by the abnormal financing and the inevitable over-building in a saturated market.

I didn't go for the REIT, but I had been thinking that DeKalb ought to have its own bank. We were no longer the bedroom county for Atlanta. We were building our own substantial commercial and office centers and it didn't seem right that the major banks were all headquartered elsewhere.

"Oscar, I think we ought to start at bank." Oscar and I had become allies when he led the drive to have liquor legalized in the county. I had favored the move as the only way to get the hotels that would bring the office parks into the county. We needed the solid commercial tax base because of our expanding population.

"You know," I continued, "the Atlanta banks charged us a quarter per cent more on our warrants that they did the city of Atlanta."

"You didn't do too bad, Clark," Oscar looked at me sideways, "You've held that rate for four years."

"Well," I said, "it wasn't because they wanted to. We need a DeKalb County bank."

"Count me in," Oscar said. "If you can get a charter, you'll make a lot of money."

We started having meetings with a few of the people who represented major interests in the county and who agreed a new bank would be a good idea in those optimistic times.

With all the new money and people in the county, I was sure such a venture would be successful. What I wanted to figure out was how to assure our having a big bank within a few years that would really be a factor in the future of the metropolitan area.

Like all Kings, I was thinking big.

Tom, director of the Independent Bankers Assosciation for the state, talked with me about the need for a bank in Atlanta to correspond with small banks around Georgia.

State law at the time prevented the larger banks from branching across county lines or from buying their smaller competitors. But every time the legislature met, the lobbyists of the big banks were busy and the feeling was the law could be changed at any time.

"Tom," I said, "why don't we organize a bank that can serve their needs and sell them stock in it?"

Tom developed the idea further and asked me to attend their next convention.

Bankers from throughout the state heard me out. The proposal was to raise five million dollars in capital stock, selling half of the stock in small amounts to residents of DeKalb, and the balance to bankers who agreed to do business with the bank.

"With this amount of capital," I told the convention, "we can participate in loans up to half a million and the deposits we carry for the correspondent banks around the state will assure our rapid growth and provide the money for staff to serve the correspondents."

The interest was genuine. The group was looking for a way to combine their strength to combat the power of the larger banks and the danger they saw of big banks gobbling up the smaller banks should the legislature pass laws making that possible.

A committee of six bankers was appointed and they began to meet with our organizational group.

From my position as chairman, I had decided two groups make a difference in the course a community follows. One is the government, which makes the rules everybody has to play by. The other is the banking fraternity which supplies the money and decides which of the players will be financed.

What I was going to find out was that each of the power groups has its own unwritten law and that the measure of success and failure is unique in each.

Without realizing it, I had positioned myself to see two sides of the movement of society from a unique vantage point during a critical period. As chairman, I had watched one of the most volatile metropolitan counties as developers shaped it for the flood tide of new citizens. Then, as our bank was organized and got under way, I watched developers and financial institutions stagger, and many disappear, under the hammer blows of a changing infrastructure. The Great Depression had demonstrated what uncontrolled money power can do to a nation — in countless incidents such as my Dad losing our home through no fault of his own — and safeguards had been installed. The right of banks to branch across state lines and into smaller communities was sharply curtailed, and the way banks handle money and the interest rates they can charge were strictly regulated.

Safeguards set up out of the wisdom gained in the Depression were swept away by men who were too young to have experienced that tragedy and dangerous concentrations were allowed, the disastrous results of which are still finally to be seen.

To the extent we could, our group tried to reverse the trend, but we were not successful.

In the last six months of my term, the spotlight shifted to the election of my successor. The county had settled into a consolidation era as the new programs were absorbed and became a part of the established order of doing things. Builders began to actually produce the townhouses, condominiums and high-density planned unit developments, the new zoning and subdivision regulations we instituted had made possible. Surrounding counties began to adopt some of the ideas, and DeKalb's new code ceased to be referred to as "those crazy regulations in DeKalb."

Because I was not a candidate, we were able to finish out the term without the pressure to spend money to attract votes.

I was involved briefly when my old enemy, the former chairman, made the primary race for his old job.

He was still the master politician and having a strong impact.

I was resolved to keep quiet, lest what I said boomerang and get votes for him; but, he finally got through to me.

The commission had passed an ordinance in an effort to reduce the litter of the elections. Under the new rule, political signs could not be put on the county right-of-way. That limited them to the yards of supporters who gave their permission. And they had to be removed shortly after the campaign ended.

In trying to enforce the ordinance, the county planning department had a truck that made daily rounds picking up signs that had been posted in the right of way. The candidates were encouraged to come by and pick up their signs and put them up again on private property.

Most of the candidates went along with the ordinance. My old opponent not only ignored the ordinance but announced he was doing so. Every day we'd truck in a load of his signs, they'd pick them up and put them out again in the right of way.

Considering the bad blood between us, I am sure it looked to my opponent that I was behind the move to get his signs off the street.

If I had thought of it, I might have done it. As a matter of fact, I had not instigated the ordinance, which was passed in response to public pressure, and I didn't know about the truck until somebody told me what was going on.

But it finally got to me and the blood started stirring.

"Be careful, Clark," John, the county public relations man was a professional who called the shots in our dealings with the press and TV, "you might just get this guy elected."

"I know it, John," I said, "I want you to write out a statement and I'll write one and have you look at it. But, damnit, a man who is seeking the job that involves passing and then enforcing county ordinances shouldn't be publicly flaunting the law."

We called a press conference — the only one I held during the campaign. The media knew that something was up since they had reported the sign controversy.

The room was packed. All three TV stations were there with blinding lights hitting me as soon as I rolled through the door of our commission meeting room.

I had my two written statements in my lap. But when the blinding lights snapped on, the whirl of the cameras started and the bank of microphones faced me, something snapped.

The memories came flooding back — the minister's "bribe", the smut sheet — the hippies — the death threats.

I dropped the written statements and started talking, hard and fast — reminding anybody who read, listened or watched TV of what it had been like during that administration and that campaign.

When I left the crowded room and rolled back into our office, I told my receptionist,

"Well, I think I just got him elected."

When the votes were counted, he had come in third. It was his final race.

One of his oldest and closest supporters came to see me in December, just before my term ended.

"You know," he said, "if you hadn't made that speech just before the primary, he would have won. We had polls showing him with thirty eight percent of the vote with the other two each getting less than that. He would have won the primary and with our organization, we'd have won the general election with Nixon heading the national ticket. You reminded a lot of people of what had happened in that other campaign."

The last week in December, we called the press in and got a picture of me tossing the last of the paid up warrants in the air. The deficit had served us well by keeping public pressure at bay while we made necessary changes in the structure and financing of our government.

After the election, I called the new chairman in.

"Bob," I said, "you might as well shape the budget from the beginning the way you want it. You go ahead and chair the budget meetings for next year. I'll be in my office if you need me."

He thanked me. "You know, Clark," he said, "I have one regret. I didn't beat the incumbent."

I knew what he meant. It was going to be harder for him to make changes since the employees had not been drawn into the election by my running.

We'd done him another disservice. We had left a surplus.

"We show $3.6 million in surplus," the finance director told me. "Actually, we've hidden money in several depreciation accounts. The real surplus is closer to $8 million."

The succeeding commission would build a parking deck and administration building out of funds we left them.

Because I was not a candidate, most of the substantive changes we made have remained in place. Most of the department heads we brought in were gradually replaced. Several remained to play an important future role.

One of my proudest achievements was to go four years without a garbage strike — four years immediately following the assasination of Martin Luther King. My door had always been open to the union organizer and we had worked hard to meet the legitimate needs of our workers and to move our blacks into supervisory positions.

In the closing days of our administration, the union organizer paid the ultimate compliment by telling me he would like to go to work for the county.

We shepherded the county through its most dynamic period of growth and change. Two years after I left office, many of the big developers who had formed the county's "power structure" would be out of business or on the ropes, victims of the REIT blowout that culminated in the bank

My reign as King lasted four years. The week after I left office, I couldn't get anybody to eat lunch with me.

crisis of 1974. As the developed parts of the county filled up and began to age, the school department would begin to close the "new" schools I had seen blossom as part of our explosive growth.

A ton of books have been written on how to make the fight to the top. I don't believe I ever read one that tells how to climb down.

Our final days on the ninth floor of the DeKalb County Courthouse reminded me, I told the staff, of what I had read about Hitler in his bunker at the close of World War II. We could hear the shells bursting all around our bunker on the ninth floor, we kept sending out orders, but not much was being done to forestall the inevitable.

I had sat with Claude Blount in his final days as chairman.

"It reminds me," Mr. Blount had said, "of the old negro who was returning from the funeral and was asked how it went. 'Well,' he said, 'de wasn't many dere and what wuz wuzn't carrying on much.'"

My last press conference concerned the final retirement of the $7.5 million deficit that had served us so well and the front page had a picture of me tossing the paid up warrants — a mail sack full — into the air.

It had been a Golden Age in suburban growth and development and, once the anger died and our new programs began to bring peace in the neighborhoods — a kind of Camelot to those of us who had been at the center of the maelstorm.

Some eight years later, when I had finally fully recaptured my private citizen status, a rather touching thing happened to me. On several occasions, when I was lying on the wing of the Warrior attaching the hand-control to the rudder, one of the county fire trucks, part of the firehouse that served the airport, would stop by my plane.

Finally, Clint asked me, "What's the fire truck doing stopping by your plane?"

I looked at him, "Well", I said, "I do have some friends in the fire department."

CHAPTER XXXIX

Coming in at 2500 feet over Texarkana, I thanked heaven again for approach control. They had me vectored and I was going to pass over the airport any minute now.

As usual, I was having trouble spotting the field and had taken bead on an industrial park and a shopping center before I finally saw the landing strip. I was right on it and had to veer to the right to avoid flying right over it. The active was 22 and after a couple of turns I was on right downwind. Turning to base and final, I had dissapated my speed down to a landing velocity and skimmed over the flat terrain to a smooth touchdown on the long concrete runway.

I taxied toward the FBO and was guided into a tie down space by the attendant.

He brought me a Coke and took my credit card into the office. The wait seemed rather long and finally he returned to tell me they were having trouble checking my credit card — computer problem, no doubt.

Even us birds have problems.

In 1972 I knew I was about to leave the center of power. But I didn't know just how chilling the coming 'cold turkey' withdrawal would be.

My plan was to leave my position of power in government, and step into a new power role as chairman of a growing and dynamic bank.

I was about to find out how some of the people our county government had turned down had felt.

Washington denied our petition for a charter for the Independent Bank of DeKalb County.

We heard via the grapevine that the Controller said it looked like a bunch of state banks was trying to get a national bank charter. Which was what it was. In our innocence, we had said so in the application.

489

It seemed like a brilliant plan to me, but the scoreboard lit up the wrong way.

Life has its ups and its downs. The rejection of our bank charter was the beginning of a toboggan slide toward the abyss for me.

Coming out of the chairman's office was somewhat akin to falling flat on my face in that German's backyard. The war was over for me and there was really nothing waiting for me to do.

Virginia was running the First National Bank Building. There was nothing for me to do there.

Not only was there nothing for me to do, but I had also forgotten how to do it.

During the four years as chairman, all I had to do was sit and let the other people do things. Then they'd bring the finished product and I'd say "yeah" or "nay" along with perhaps a profound observation or two. There was a group of people standing around waiting for me to let them know what I wanted, then they would crank up and get the project moving. It may have been soul satisfying but it was poor preparation for getting back in the real world.

I could go back into real estate brokerage, but I had a problem there also. I had made a lot of enemies by deciding this or that and I didn't know who was lying out there in the bushes waiting to pounce on my first move.

I also seemed to have picked up a tone during my four years as King that made people think I was trying to force some action rather than merely proposing it as a real estate negotiator.

Maybe it was all in my mind, but I was certainly having a struggle trying to figure out what to do with nothing to do with.

One thing I did enjoy and that was my own company. While I was with the county, I had people after me everywhere I went. And they didn't come, of course, unless they wanted the county to do something for them.

Now that I was an ex-politician, nobody was interested in being around me.

I remember sitting alone at a table for two at the Executive Club.

"What's the matter?" my friend Bill asked me with a grin. "Can't you get anybody to eat with you, Clark?"

"Bill," I replied, "I am quite content to be in the company you now see me in."

And I was.

But there was more than rejection and loneliness awaiting me.

My prayer had been I would be able to get through my four years as chairman without a recurrence of the paraplegic problems. They say ninety percent of those problems happen to ten per cent of the paraplegics.

I am definitely in the ten percent.

It was undoubtedly true that pushing the wheelchair down hot city sidewalks when I was a peddler had aggravated my kidney problem. In that case, activity was causing the problem.

But the pressure sores came from inactivity — sitting or lying too long in one position.

So, with the kidney problem solved, the more active I am the better I get along — as long as I watch myself.

About my third year as chairman, a friend called and told me about a cushion that had just been put on the market that would prevent pressure sores from sitting. Composed of a man made gel, it was formed to duplicate the density and resilence of human flesh. It even felt like flesh — like 'sitting in your mama's lap' — and the theory was that it would provide the extra cushion and prevent concentration of weight that caused the pressure sores.

The problem was it protected the skin, but didn't prevent the blood supply deep below the surface from being cut off.

In my last couple of years in office, I had developed the habit of backing my chair up to the sofa, pulling myself back on it and sitting with my feet and legs in the chair while I had a drink or two after five o'clock. It was a lot of fun sitting there sipping the whiskey and swapping war stories with my cronies, but it was playing havoc where the weight concentrated in my unfeeling buttocks.

By the time I discovered a lesion on the surface of my skin, I had a deep cavern inside the buttock where the original ulcer that caused me to have to leave Yale had been.

Then, one morning shortly after I had left office, I looked in the bathroom mirror and couldn't believe what I saw.

My face was grey, drawn — I looked like a cadaver.

What had happened was that I was losing the protein out of my body now that the deep ulcer had finally opened to the surface.

The surgeon who had operated on me twenty-two years earlier had died. Now, I went to a very fine plastic surgeon in Atlanta.

He had never seen anything like it — his specialty was cosmetic surgery — he told me to go to bed and the place would heal.

"That kind will never heal without surgery," the young doctor who was his associate, had been passing and came into the room where I lay on the examining table.

I knew that was so — after all, I had spent eight months after Yale lying on my stomach to no avail.

But I wanted so bad to believe it would go away that I went home and went to bed.

The older doctor tried to reassure me. When it didn't heal after six weeks, he suggested I stuff the place with guaze and go back to work. Even I knew better than that. And I finally faced the fact this was the same type sore eight months lying on my stomach had failed to heal.

Besides making me heartsick, my strength was being sapped. I knew that the doctor had decided nothing could be done because the place was so large. One of my friends had lost his leg because of a similar problem.

In my desperation, I remembered a young friend who had gone to a place out west after he was paralyzed in a construction accident. I made it a practice to visit other quads and paraplegics over the years and I had visited him just before he left to go there. His father was in my Sunday School class and now I called and talked to his mother. I described the problem.

"Yes," she replied, "I'm sure they treated things like that."

Once again, I was to have something happen to me that convinced me that our lives do have purpose and that we are looked after. The pressure sore was going to change my life and be a link in a chain that would benefit a large number of paralyzed people over the years.

The night I arrived at Craig Hospital near Denver, I knew that I was in a place unlike any hospital I had ever known. I had avoided the VA spinal cord centers, and the general hospitals I had been in were worse for me than being at home.

Catching a cab from the airport, I arrived at the hospital after the evening meal.

Pandemonium reigned. Stereos and TV's were blasting, patients, most of them teenagers or in their early twenties, were rolling up and down the broad hall, doing wheelies, talking loud and gesturing.

My room was a four patient ward. The three occupants each had his color TV going on a different station.

The nurse who came in after I had undressed was obviously competent. She examined the ulcer carefully, cleaned it out and stood by my bed looking down at me. "Yes," she said, "it's a bad one. But, we can help you. I've seen worse."

Craig, which had been a TB sanitarium before that disease was conquered by the new antibiotics, had specialized in spinal injuries for about 20 years, and they had discovered some basic truths about the problem.

After the acute state, it really ceases to be a medical problem. A spinal injury cannot be 'cured'. Instead, an inordinate amount of care must be taken in turning the bed patient to avoid sores and arrangements must be made to handle loss of control of kidney and bowels.

But the big battle is the deep despondency that follows when the patient learns that he is permanently paralyzed and can expect to be helpless the rest of his life.

Hospitals are set up to cure people and send them home — not to deal with depressed, helpless young people. The problem seems so hopeless, traditional medicine wants to throw up its hands and go on to something it can do something about.

Craig had discovered nothing is really impossible, until you decide it is.

Most spinal cord injury happens to young people and, properly led, young people will tackle the impossible.

The first thing, once the injury has been stabilized, is to fight the depression. Craig doesn't look or act like a hospital.

None of the staff wear uniforms and the place jumps with music, noise and activity all day and well into the evening.

Where I was left flat in the bed for four months, the Craig patient is turned regularly on a set schedule. He is moved into the big therapy room every day. As soon as able, he is required to dress, go to breakfast and be in therapy by 9 a.m. Nobody stays alone in his room during the day unless he is critically ill. If a patient has to stay in bed, his bed is rolled into the therapy room. If he has to lie flat but can get out of bed, he is strapped to a tilt table — in the therapy room he is tilted as close to a standing position as possible. If he has to lie flat on his stomach because of an ulcer, he is put on a litter that has big wheels in front and is able to push himself all over the hospital.

And, he has to work. Weight lifting, working on the mat, wheelchair classes, transfers from bed to chair to auto, in and out of the bathtub. There is occupational therapy, physical therapy and classes on sex.

Of all things.

Basically, the place is a domitory and gymnasium attached to a hospital. The antidote for pain and depression is hard work. On the weekend, there are beer parties and trips to various town activities. There is a swimming pool where patients learn — while they are still patients — that they can move more easily in water.

Something I learned by chance ten years after being paralyzed.

In two to three months, the patient learns to do things it had taken me twenty-eight years to learn — and some things I was only now learning. I had been active, but now I began to believe I could do much more.

Correcting my pressure sore required major surgery — the moving of a large slab of flesh from the back of my leg to fill the void inside my buttocks. Again, I recovered rapidly and the doctors learned something from me.

"Mr. Harrison," the doctor said, "you certainly are limber. Most paraplegics have frozen joints by the time they've been paralyzed as long as you have."

I told them about my swimming five days a week. "I can swim a mile without stopping," I said.

After surgery, I had to lie on a Stryker frame — like an ironing board with wheels, the apparatus Davis had used so many years before, when I was a twenty year old, to will himself to death. This time, they gave me two short sticks with rubber tipped ends and told me to propel myself around the hospital. I was soon going down the hall, into the elevator and down to the cafeteria. My only problem was attracting attention so somebody would bring me a tray — I ate my meals lying face down, my head supported by a padded oval that surrounded my face.

Before they would turn me loose, they said I would have to learn to use a wheelchair like everybody else in the country was using — one with the big wheels in the back.

I refused.

I may have been King, but I was no longer enthroned.

They took my strange wheelchair and hid it. I never saw it again.

I had to learn to get in and out of the bathtub without using a grab bar.

"Why do I have to do that?" I complained. "I have a grab bar at home."

I was sitting fully dressed with my shoes on and with my feet protruding down into the tub. It looked dangerous to me — there was no water in the event I slipped and fell. I couldn't visualize myself being able to get back up on the side of the tub and back into the chair once I was down in the depths of the tub.

The athletic young lady was adamant — "You'll find yourself in a motel one of these days and want to take a bath. Get in there."

Frances and Bob had come out to be with me. The first time Frances and I came to a sidewalk curb in the new chair, she pushed me over the edge, just like we did in my old chair — and deposited me in the middle of the street. It was going to take years to get used to the new way of doing things — and I stubbornly maintained to the end that my old way of doing was better. But I had been converted.

There was a paraplegic with the same level paralysis that I had — and he could walk. In fact, he could go up and down stairs. In fact, he would race Bob down the hall.

He had been paralyzed as a child and now, at age 9, had finally come to Craig and convinced the doctors to try him in braces. He was so agile and so close to the ground that he could swing and twist along on the long braces, fastened a foot apart at his ankles, and crutches. I would have killed myself.

Like the old man said, "About the time you say something can't be done, some young whippersnapper comes along and does it."

I healed quickly after the surgery and the time came for us to head home. The weekend after my discharge, we checked in a hotel and I rented an automobile equipped to be driven by hand.

We spent the weekend driving through the mountains, visiting Cripple Creek, the old mining town, and the North Pole where Santa Claus has a year around place for animals and children.

When we boarded the plane to return to Decatur, I knew that once again I had a new lease on life.

The most important thing I had learned was that I could lead an active life without having pressure sores.

The answer was not a fancy seat cushion.

It was so simple I found it hard to understand why I hadn't figured it out for myself.

Simply relieve the pressure every few minutes by raising up off the seat of the chair.

If I had known that in 1949, I would have graduated a lawyer from Yale. And I wouldn't have wasted all those months lying in bed.

I wanted to bring Craig to Atlanta, where young men and women were still suffering from ignorance about spinal cord injury and complications.

While I was waiting for my operation, I had gotten a call from our lawyer in Decatur.

Without my knowledge, our attorney had reapplied for a bank charter, changing the features the Comptroller had objected to, and it had been approved. The board had elected me chairman. My life wasn't over. I had something to do — a new challenge.

And, although I didn't know it, I would be doing things I had always thought impossible for me.

One thing I did know, we had to have a Craig in Atlanta that would serve the southeast. I didn't know how, but I knew it had to be done.

CHAPTER XL

Having finally gotten approval of my credit card, I finished my Coke while the attendant gassed the plane. Taxiing out I realized the afternoon was progressing and I still had a couple of hours of flying ahead of me.

The next stop and the last one before DeKalb-Peachtree, would be Panola County, Mississippi. I had stopped with Dick and Nina on the way out and was looking forward to seeing them again.

Like they say, ninety per cent of the problems happen to ten per cent of the paraplegics and in spite of all I'd learned at Craig, I could still manage to come up with a paraplegic problem.

Going out to California, I had been taxiing out toward the runway at Abilene when I realized my right shoe was hung under the rudder pedal. I had to call the tower and tell them I was having a little problem and would be delayed momentarily before I could take off.

I finally yanked my foot loose.

I decided then to fly barefooted to avoid a repetition of the problem.

Which was fine until the next day when I took off from El Paso. As I gained altitude, I began to get cold. Since I was going to 12,500 feet to get over the Rockies, I decided to turn on the heat.

The cabin heat for my old Cherokee comes right off the manifold shroud through a square tube lying along the floor in front of the pilot's seat — right where my foot rests against it.

Having no feeling, I managed to blister my right foot. No big problem, but I was looking forward to having Nina, the former nurse with so much experience with paraplegics, take a look. It wasn't infected but it did look a little mean.

I didn't exactly relish getting back into the southeast. It was already turning hazy and there were scattered clouds at about 4,000 feet. I had planned my flight for 5,500 altitude, but now I dropped down to 3,500

— proper and acceptable for an eastbound VFR flight but still a little worrisome. I would be glad to see Batesville before the sun got much lower or the haze much thicker.

Thinking back to the early days of struggle as we fought to create a new bank in the fiercely competitive Atlanta market, I remember days when our vision was just as restricted.

Nineteen seventy-four was a watershed year — the end of an era — the year the REIT real estate bubble burst — the worst washout for the banks since the Great Depression.

Fidelity National Bank opened its doors February, 1974. Within sixty days after receiving our charter from the national banking authorities in the fall of 1973, we had sold two and a half million dollars worth of bank stock.

A year later, it would have been hard to sell two and a half hundred dollars worth of new bank stock.

I have done a lot of hunkering down in my life, but I was going to set a new record in that department before our bank finally stabilized and began a rise to any kind of prominence.

My plan was to be a millionaire by 1977. Instead, ten years later, I was still hanging on, paying debts, and praying.

The Atlanta banks lost millions in real estate loans in the months that remained in the year we opened. In the six months after the temporary trailer we called Fidelity National made its debut before a waiting world, our bank managed to make real estate loans that would result in over $600,000 in losses — and every dollar came out of the pockets of our valiant band of stockholders.

In the beginning, it was exciting.

"I never thought we could do it." George and I were feeling good after the bank finally opened. "I talked the Comptroller into giving us a charter, but I never thought we'd sell $2.5 million worth of stock."

"No problem, George," I replied. "I had over seventy names of people who had called me. I never tried to talk anybody into buying and I didn't ask anybody outside those who had called me first."

Each director had agreed to be responsible for ten per cent of the stock — to keep five and to sell five. We wanted the stock to be widely held. We figured those who had stock would put money in the bank.

"I want us to be a big bank," I said. "With the stock we've sold we can start out making quarter of a million dollar loans."

If the way to learn how to do something is to start by doing everything wrong, we were about to become experts. Before it was over, we'd KNOW why a new bank shouldn't lend outside its own territory, why a banker with years experience in a large bank is not prepared to run a small, new bank.

Not in the swift and deep waters of a large Metro center.

I didn't make the loans that went sour, but looking back I have to take a lions share of the credit for the chain of disasters that were about to befall us.

"We want to take the Atlanta banks on," I was expostulating to the advertising agency that would design our very effective ad campaign.

"We are courageous to start a new bank in the Metro area," I said. "We aren't going to be timid and pussy foot around about loaning money to good people."

The ad campaign was impressive. We started off by saying we were a bank, while the other banks in Decatur were mere branches. We said you didn't have to go through a lot of red tape and you didn't have to wait on a committee — at our bank we had one man who could make you a loan on the spot.

For a symbol, we had an artist draw a stylized lion's head to let everybody know how courageous we were. It would have made a great political campaign and we would probably have gotten elected. The problem was, we weren't running for office, we were in the banking business. And the banking business is different from politics.

For one thing, in politics your enemies have to wait until the next election to get even — assuming somebody doesn't shoot you.

In the banking business, opportunities are presenting themselves every day when somebody can do you in.

And we succeeded from day one in making all the other banks mad at us with the insinuations of the campaign.

We were a sitting duck — we didn't need any enemies. What we needed was a little sympathetic toleration as we stumbled along.

By the time we learned a few lessons, we were dangling on the ropes, stunned and hoping only to survive.

For one thing, we learned that banks are very protective toward their business and their customers. They don't knowingly give away either. Bankers are very gentlemanly, soft spoken, keeping their knives and razors carefully concealed. You don't know your throat has been cut until you try to move your head.

One rule, learned the hard way, was never bother to ask your competitor about a former employee. You can believe he will praise the former to the skies and assure you he left under the best of conditions.

There's nothing your competitor would rather do than saddle you with the crook or incompetent he just fired.

The same goes for customers. When a customer is sent by another bank you can believe he is bringing trouble.

Every con man in the city had our number in those early days and gave us a try. Maturity finally revealed to us how dumb our campaign had been. Everybody with a scheme was looking for a new bank, especially one that held itself out as we did — as being courageous about lending money.

At the same time the new bank is being tried by the promoters, it is most vulnerable. The big bank has backup in staff and in experience with the customer built over a period of years. We had in mind making large loans to new customers. Later, I decided people don't have the same compulsive urge to repay a small new bank as they do the large bank. The established bank has helped the customer slowly build his credit, starting with small, short-term loans. They know his strength and weakness, whether he can meet the repayments required by the loans. They know how far to go with the customer.

The new bank is trying to take customers from old banks and in the process will often exceed the bounds of prudence. For his part, the customer knows the small new bank won't have the resources to pursue him in the relentless way of the older institution.

Adding to this general situation was the climate of the times. Through the REIT's, the banks had been shoving money at the developers, often lending more for a project than the project would cost, and thus giving the developer a tax free windfall.

The established developers were so covered up with money that they began to let the details slide and to start projects prudence would have vetoed when the bankers were more austere.

It was becoming apparent to the sophisticated investor, just about the time our bank opened, that there were too many projects being finished for the market to absorb.

We should have suspected something when developers with well established banking relations started coming to see us. With the older banks beginning to see the storm signs, credit began to tighten and the developers started showing up in our office.

"John Street was in to see me today," the president was elated as he talked to the board, "You know, he's doing the Meadow Lark development up in Cobb County."

"Do you think he'll bring his accounts to us?" one of the members asked.

"Well," the president continued, "he'll bring the account for the subdivision and his personal account. But since he owes $5 million to his bank he can't bring his operating accounts right now. When we get big enough to take over his big loans he'll bring it all."

"What does he want the money for?" the member continued.

"Well," the President said, "he needs $25,000 to meet interest payments for the quarter, the other $25,000 is for personal expenses."

"Why doesn't he get the money from his bank?" one of the directors asked.

"He's got his major financing in place, and he doesn't want to disturb that," the president continued, "I think it will help us get our foot in the door and later we can get his major accounts. He's solid as a stone, has been building and developing since 1950 and shows a net worth of $3 million."

What we didn't know, but would later, with our hard earned experience immediately suspect, was that the big bank had cut off his credit the day before.

He was scrambling to buy time by borrowing his interest payment. When the next payment was due, he'd file for bankruptcy.

We learned another bitter lesson during those early days — stay on your own territory — where your lawyer knows the judge. Most of the money we lost went to strengthen the economy of Cobb County.

"What in the world is 'Auntie's Bottle Shop'?" We were going over the doubtful loans. "Do they sell baby supplies?"

"It's a liquor store in Marietta," the officer reported, "we have a lien on all the stock."

We never got a dollar, or a bottle, from the collapse of 'Auntie's'.

"Consecrated Life Center," the director snorted, "where is that?"

The lending officer explained it was also in Cobb County.

"How can we lend money to a church in Cobb County?" Our director was beginning to wise up. "I thought the only reason banks loaned money to a church was because local stockholders were involved."

It was the first time in memory that a church took bankruptcy — our money was retained as an unplanned contribution.

"You know," one of the board was philosophizing, "I've heard that you can loan money to some churches but not to others. If you loan to one

church, you always get your money. Made up of hard working literal minded people, they believe if the church misses a payment the doors will be
padlocked. On the other hand, there are other churches, being part of
the establishment, that don't worry about borrowing money. They know
that the bank can't do anything if they don't pay, so they don't worry
at all and borrow all the money you'll lend them."

Toward the end of our first year, the bank's accountant came to see me.

"Clark," he said, "you've got a serious problem at the bank. In making
the audit, we've uncovered several large loans that are in trouble. To give
a true picture, I am going to have to classify about $165,000 as doubtful
loans, and I really think you'd better write them off."

When I asked him what that meant, he explained that since we did
not have enough in the loan loss reserve, our capital — the value of the
stockholders' ownership — would be reduced. "You've got other loans
that look like they may go bad," he explained, "and it will look better
if you go ahead and write these off now rather than have a much larger
write off next year."

We were stunned. Most of the loans had been made by our 'one man
who can make an immediate decision' and the board didn't know of their
existence.

Thinking back over our 'aggressive' advertising campaign, I knew I had
to take a major share of the blame. If you were going to make that kind
of approach, everybody who made loans had to be forewarned that we
didn't really mean what the ads said. I began to appreciate the glass eye
banker approach personified by Claude Blount. We could do the agges-
sive ads, but we better be sure we had a steely eyed Claude Blount type
to actually pass out the money.

Before it was over, we had lost $600,000 and the value of our stock
had dropped from $20 to $15 a share. It was a bitter pill and it would
be some bitter years later before our stock would be worth what we paid
for it.

The only thing that kept us from being wiped out and the bank merged
into one of our large competitors, was the fact that we were overcapitalized.

Ordinarily, a bank like ours would have been started with a half to
a million dollars capital. Because we wanted to be a big bank, we had
started up with $2.5 million.

We did it for the wrong reason — we wanted to get big customers by
being able to make big loans — but it saved us.

Comptroller of the Currency

OF THE UNITED STATES

TREASURY DEPARTMENT

Washington, D. C.,

Whereas, satisfactory evidence has been presented to the Comptroller of the Currency that

located in   DECATUR,   State of   GEORGIA,   has complied with all provisions of the Statutes of the United States required to be complied with before being authorized to commence the business of banking as a National Banking Association;

"FIDELITY NATIONAL BANK",

Now, therefore, I hereby certify that the above-named association is authorized to commence the business of banking as a National Banking Association.

In testimony whereof, witness my signature and seal of office this   8TH   day of   FEBRUARY, 1974.

James E. Smith

Even with our losses, at the end of our first year we were still the soundest bank in Atlanta — from the very high per centage of stockholder's equity to our total assets.

One of our small competitors had one million dollars in capital and got caught in the same trap because of real estate loans. The majority stockholder got a call one Friday afternoon.

"Mr. Brown," the staff person from the comptroller's office said, "either you get up another $1 million capital, or merge with (he named an Atlanta bank), or you don't open Monday morning."

The merger was their option and the stockholders lost most of their invested money and their ownership of the bank.

We were learning that bankers play with the stockholders' money — when a loan goes bad and the loan loss reserve is used up, there is only one other available pocket to reach into.

Our board meetings lost their exuberance. The ad campaign had been successful in bringing in deposits but every meeting was marred by bad news from the loan committee. Our hold on the bank seemed as fragile as the small building — really, three trailers joined together — from which we operated.

"Gentlemen," the bank examiner was grim, "this report is bad. The rule is that when forty per cent of the bank's loans are classified, the comptroller sends a team of auditors, paid for by your bank, to watch over day-to-day operations. Thirty nine per cent of your loans are classified as of this audit."

We didn't like the way the scoreboard was lighting up — at all.

A change had to be made, and it became my job to look for a new president. Before the search was over, I would have interviewed twenty six bank presidents.

"You know," I told friend Pat as we shared a drink one evening, "bank presidents are a lot more impressive when you're trying to borrow money than when you're trying to hire a chief executive."

There were plenty of prospects. We were not the only financial institution with problems. A lot of the big banks were in worse trouble. My search for a new president for Fidelity gave me an insight that few people had in those tumultuous times.

"We just wanted our customers to know before it's in the papers." The bank was one in which we kept a large deposit. "The board has just voted to write off seventy million dollars in bad loans."

That bank was so strong it survived the losses — brought about by the collapse in real estate in 1974. The severity of the problem in another major bank was revealed by what they paid each day in borrowing from other banks — while most banks were paying thirteen per cent for Fed Funds, they were having to pay seventeen because of their shaky condition. Hundreds of employees were let go and the value of the bank's stock was one tenth what it had been the previous year.

"What helped nail them," one of our directors said, "were the letters of credit they had issued. In order to get the accounts of national corporations, they extended the letters in amounts of over a million. They weren't called on until money got tight following the real estate debacle. Then, when everybody started scrambling for funds, the New York corporations borrowed the funds they were entitled to under the letters. The Atlanta bank was cleaned out. They couldn't make new loans to their regular customers."

It was the same kind of crunch that had caused my Dad to lose our home.

A friend from high school had made a life career at the bank. We had lunch.

"Clark," he told me, "when things were roaring along a few years ago, I took my profit sharing money and put it all in our bank's stock. I bought at $18. When the stock reached $32, I was rich. I had it made. Then things fell apart. The stock fell to $3 because of the losses. I'm not going to be able to retire. I won't have enough money to live on."

The principal villain was the REIT'S — the real estate investment trust idea that was presented to me during my final days as chairman.

They could grow larger — but there was no provision for them to retrench.

"I was president of the Great Dynasty Investment Trust," the former banker was working as a consultant to the Independent Bankers Association. "We had the biggest trust in this part of the country, financing several dozen major projects. We were showing a high rate of return, everybody wanted in on the easy real estate money, and we were growing like crazy. We had reached $500 million when things began to teeter. When we woke up one morning to find we had lost $50 million, I was asked to resign."

A former bank president, a graduate of Harvard, applied for the job of chief executive officer of our small bank — our total assets were just over $5 million at the time. His tale was even more bizarre.

"I left the bank in Atlanta," he told me, "to head up a bank in Alabama. Then, I was asked to take over a $500 million bank in Memphis. That bank was having troubles and I moved on to a bank in Florida."

The Florida bank was known as the Tiffany of Florida banks, in a wealthy part of the state, the bank had large deposits and a heavy amount of cash to invest.

"Total assets of the bank were 237 million," he said. By the time I got down there, the damage had already been done."

Along with other banks in the southeast, they were caught up in the real estate mania. What was so appealing was the high interest rate paid for construction loans. Not only was the rate high, but the loans were backed up by a takeout — permanent financing that paid off the construction loan. And the lender had a first mortgage on the property.

"The bank I joined in Florida had made their chief loan officer president of the REIT," he continued, "then the bank made loans to the REIT for the various projects. The former loan officer was paid according to the volume handled by the REIT and there was nobody on the bank's side to slow the process down."

As the bank made the loans, they sold participations to other cash heavy banks and the pace accelerated. It was going full blast when somebody missed a payment and everyone suddenly realized that more housing had been constructed than the market could absorb.

"When I arrived on the scene," the former president continued, "the bank's REIT had financed ninety condominium projects in Florida. Out of the ninety, ten were making interest only payments on the construction loans. The rest could make no payments at all."

I asked him why the takeouts didn't save the situation. He explained that they were based on sales being made or leases being signed — again, if nobody wanted the housing, the bank was stuck.

The bank was merged into another Florida bank, the stockholders lost their money, and lost the bank, and the president was out of a job. Now, conditions were such that he would have been happy to take the presidency of our little bank at a fraction of the salary he had commanded previously.

At the same time as the REIT explosion, another phenomenon was occurring in the metropolitan area. Because of the strong and continuing boom in real estate, land values had increased dramatically. Not only were they going up, but most investors had decided they would never go down. After all, prices had been on a one- way uphill climb for at least forty years. There seemed to be no down side risk in land speculation.

In the beginning, it was a matter of converting farm land to subdivisions with a dramatic increase in value. Then the pace quickened as the expressways moved office parks and regional centers farther and farther from the central core of the city, and the values for commercial land became even more astronomical.

Finally, the general population decided you couldn't lose in land and everybody wanted to wade in.

The REIT was conceived to give the small investor a share of the real estate development bonanza. Now, the land syndication was created to cut the small investor in on the boom in land values.

Land syndications were formed by either a realtor, attorney or accountant. A contract was signed for the purpose of purchasing a tract of land. Then shares were sold to investors who would take a pro rata share in making loan payments and a corresponding share in the profit from sale of the land at a later date.

In the beginning, it was a legitimate exercise, in that land could be bought by a syndication and held a short time until it was ready to be sold to a developer.

As more and more people got caught up in the land fever, more marginal land was purchased until, finally, the date at which the land would actually be developed had faded into the far distant future.

The idea only made sense when assuming the land would be sold before principal payments became due and before payments made had eaten up any profits to be realized. Interest payments were tax deductible which made it possible for the wealthy to come in for only a portion of the after tax cost of others.

"Jack was working for Union City," his lawyer told me, "then he sold some land his mother owned and realized a substantial profit for her. Then he got a real estate license, started to form syndications and to buy and sell land. It got so good he quit his job. The last three years, he has averaged 70 to 100 thousand dollars a year income just from land sales."

The syndicator usually took a five or ten per cent interest in the land for his work and had only a token amount or no money of his own at all in the syndication.

As time went on, the land deals became more and more speculative. Then the syndicators started setting up new syndications to buy from the old, with the lawyers or other syndicators taking a free ride.

The paper profits were impressive.

"The 'greater fool' theory keeps it going," a friend told me. "People will pay ridiculous prices assuming there is a greater fool out there somewhere who will pay him a profit. The system will work until we run out of fools or somebody misses a payment."

As happens with most fantasies involving the small investor, the end came suddenly — everybody woke up simultaneously and millions were lost.

When land stopped selling, the investors soon found they could not or did not want to continue making the interest payments. Most of the notes has an exculpatory clause that relieved them of the debt when the property was deeded back. The investor lost his substantial down payment plus whatever interest he had paid. If he had failed to have the exculpatory clause in the note and he was a professional man or otherwise had a substantial income, he was stuck. Or he could chose bankruptcy and lose most of what he had.

The group or individual who had sold the land was not much better off. Now he had to resume payments under his note for the land. He may have made a number of the deals and was in correspondingly hot water.

It turned out to be a rough game. The Bible says it is better to get rich slowly — the land syndicators were finding out why.

These things happened during the years I had planned to get rich from our new bank. In addition, the banking laws changed, allowing unlimited branching in our county by the large banks and destroying any advantage due to exlusiveness of our charter.

It was a triple whammy. I gave up any idea of getting rich and concentrated on just trying to hang on.

The lesson Dad had pounded into me with the sixty guitar lessons came into play at this late stage in my development.

I might not be any good at making money, but I was determined to hang in as long as I could.

And to pay back what I owed.

Along with the crowd, I had lost some money in a syndication. get their money out.

But the big blow for me personally came with my struggles to hold my bank stock.

To finance my five per cent of the bank's stock, I borrowed against the stock. Then, I borrowed against my land and put that cash in the bank to make payments on both loans.

I figured I could carry both loans in this way for about three years. By that time, my land would have increased in value and I could begin selling it and my bank stock would have tripled in value giving me even more strength.

Then came the OPEC oil embargo. And the collapse in land values around Atlanta that occurred shortly after we organized our bank.

Just before the bubble burst, I had shaken hands to sell my land for $3,000 an acre cash. This would have paid off everything I owed and would have given me a nice cash cushion as well. Then, by mutual agreement, the buyer and I decided not to conclude the deal.

A year after the bank opened, the bank stock was worth less than I had paid for it and I would have done well to sell my land for half what I had been offered the year I placed the big loan against it.

If I had given up at that point, the sale of the land would have just about paid off the $125,000 I had borrowed against it, and I would have still owed over a hundred thousand on the stock, with no way to pay off that loan without giving up the stock.

The good God has always sent my rescuer in unusual garb — first, it was the young boy who pulled me out of the line of fire of the sniper, then Frances married me and made the life I had been spared worth living. This time it was a special kind of problem — he sent Jessie.

Jessie is what she appears to be — a Presbyterian minister's wife. But there is more. She has sold more land under more adverse conditions than any agent in Rockdale or most other counties. And she doesn't know how to quit.

Raised on a plantation in south Georgia, Jessie can not only ride a horse, she knows how to walk land. And she has two sons she likes to favor.

The one hundred fifty acres Frances and I had bought with money we made selling off the back part of our first lot on Clairmont, had turned out to be one hundred seventy acres when we finally got it surveyed.

We gave ten per cent of the land to God, and He sent Jessie.

Now, Jessie came in and started selling five acre plots off my land. When Jessie goes out to sell something, she sells it.

"You have to make it easy for someone to do business with you," Jessie taught me. "That's why I never worry about getting a lot of earnest money. The main thing is to get the purchaser of a mind to buy the lot. Then he starts making plans in his own mind and you have a sale."

Jessie was selling my lots when other agents were hunkered around the office phone waiting for a call. She and her family had lived in College Park and knew a number of airline pilots who attended their church there. Now, she was in the process of moving the pilots to Rockdale.

Through her church, she knew everybody — and knew a lot about their plans.

When I had a payment deadline on a loan, Jessie would close the sale of a lot.

We had a couple of deadends we had to navigate during those years.

OPEC with its Arab oil embargo sent the price of oil soaring and killed the sale of lots like ours that were miles from where most people worked.

We held on for two years without making a sale.

Finally, things began to move again, I was able to cut a street into the property and Jessie resumed selling lots.

And I held on to my bank stock — and added some to what I original-ly had purchased as others dropped out.

It was a time to hang on. Fortunately, I had had some experience in doing that very thing. For the next twelve years, I would slog along, go-ing from bank to bank with my dog and pony show as I borrowed from Paul to pay Peter and vice versa. My land sold, a lot at a time, for just enough to keep me one jump ahead of my creditors and to make me an expert in juggling money.

At one time, I owed five banks in four cities. But I survived and our bank finally recovered, regrouped and surged ahead.

Our fourth president, Jim Miller, turned out to be as tough as the lion we were advertising and shared my ambition to have a large bank.

By the time my debt was paid, I was established as a developer, was chairman of a hundred million dollar bank with six offices, that was growing faster than ninety five per cent of the peer group banks in the U. S. I still owned my stock which finally was worth more than I paid for it.

I wasn't as rich as some people might have thought I was, but I had learned that with a little obedience to what the Bible says, it is possible to survive the storms that attack our houses. The years after I left politi-cal office were almost as exciting as being chairman — and a long way from the long, dull, gray of no future I had envisioned sitting in the hall-way that afternoon at Lawson.

When Jim Miller took over, we finally had a president who knew how to make Fidelity grow.

CHAPTER XLI

Under FAA regulations, pilots fall into two broad catagories. Those who fly by Visual Flight Rules and those who are allowed to fly in the clouds under Instrument Flight Rules. Securing a license to fly instrument flight rules is the most difficult rating offered by the FAA.

The VFR pilot maintains his correct alignment in the sky by looking at the horizon to keep his wings level.

Without instruments it is impossible to fly an airplane for very long without some visual reference to establish the attitude of the airplane. There is no 'seat of the pants' sensation or feeling that will tell the pilot whether he is right side up or upside down, climbing or diving, flying straight and level or banking in a turn.

It is hard for the non-flyer to believe, but it is true. The sensations the pilot has when he is surrounded by the soft whiteness of a cloud will make him believe he is in a position the opposite to the one he is actually in.

High performance planes, those with over 200 horsepower and retractable landing gear, are the most dangerous when in the hands of the unwary and untrained pilot.

And doctors and lawyers are the new pilots most likely to get into trouble. There are two reasons for this. They are among the few with the money to buy the high performance planes and they are in the habit of making critical decisions on partial information.

Pilots have a saying. There are old pilots and bold pilots, but there are no old, bold pilots. Surviving flying long enough to become a safe pilot requires a bigger dose of humility than some possess.

One of the Atlanta physicians took his high performance plane aloft one evening after dark. He had checked the weather by calling DeKalb-Peachtree and Hartsfield International — both reported unrestricted visibility.

The problem was, he took off from Stone Mountain, a small private airport not served by a tower — and there was cloud cover that was invisible at night.

When they examined the wreckage, which indicated the plane had hit the ground flying upside down at full throttle, the National Traffic Safety Board investigators theorized the following: apparently, after taking off and shortly thereafter losing his horizon as he entered the low lying cloud, the inexperienced pilot had rolled to an inverted position. Then, thinking he was climbing out of the clouds he had plowed into the ground.

There is a name for what happens when this kind of disorientation seizes the mind of the pilot. It's called vertigo, and it has something to do with the tiny hairs in the inner ear sending false signals to the brain. Without visual reference to override the false signals and without the discipline of instrument training, the results are often fatal. Once vertigo sets in, the pilot can look at his instruments and they are meaningless to him.

The novice pilot is taught, if he inadvertently flys into a cloud, to very carefully start a slow, banking one hundred eighty degree turn, so that he will break out of the clouds and be able to see the horizon at the earliest possible moment.

It happened to me one time and I couldn't believe how quickly the disorientation hits you. I got turned around and out of the clouds, but someway I lost a thousand feet in the process, and learned what it feels like to suddenly have less sense than a chicken.

The instrument pilot trainee learns to override the false sensations by spending many tiresome hours, in the simulator or in the airplane, his instructor by his side, a hood obstructing his view of the outside world, with total concentration on the instruments before him.

They call it scanning, but it means looking at three or more instruments virtually simultaneously. Eyes must dart from instrument to instrument and back in a constant sweep. Staring fixedly at one instrument for two or three seconds can start the plane into a spiraling dive.

There is a little airplane flying toward an artificial horizon that tells you your wings are level and whether the nose of the plane is pitched up or down. Then there is an air speed indicator, an altimeter that tells you how high up you are, provided it is set to the current barometric pressure. Another instrument tells whether you are diving or climbing and at what rate. A DG will tell you the direction you are flying, provided it is currently set to coincide with the magnetic compass. And another instrument will tell when you are banking at a standard rate so you can time your turns to end up on a desire heading.

Clint had given me enough hood work to meet the private pilot requirements and hopefully to keep me from killing myself.

As I flew on toward Batesville, the clouds were getting lower and closer together. They finally became a solid ceiling above me. I had dropped to 3,500 feet, which gave me 500 feet clearance below the clouds. With the haze that seemed to be thickening below me, I was experiencing some anxiety. As long as things didn't get worse, I'd be okay. And there were two small airports right on my flight path if I had to land.

Clint's words came back to me, 'A private pilot's license is a license to learn. All I can do is try to teach you enough so you won't kill yourself while you are learning.'

Life is hazardous. As in flying, there is not much problem when you are high in the air. It is coming in for a landing, descending to where the hills, valleys and telephone poles of the solid earth await your descent.

I was forty nine years old when I left the chairman's office.

Not only had I been waited on and catered to for four years to the point I had forgotten how to do for myself — I had another problem that was unique to the paraplegic.

Nobody knew what would happen to an old paraplegic — one who had been paralyzed for thirty years.

There weren't any other than us World War II pioneers.

I had read somewhere that a man should change jobs and objectives when he passed fifty. Go into something unrelated to his previous occupation.

A brain surgeon might elect to become a charter boat captain.

Or an accountant could go to Alaska and be a homesteader.

For my part, my dream was to do something where my survival would depend on my own skill and daring.

I was tired of delegating and negotiating. I wanted to do with my own hands.

It was a tall order for an old paraplegic.

While I was chairman, Frances and I had started renting a house for several weeks each summer on St. Simons Island, one of Georgia's Golden Isles.

The island is one of the most beautiful spots in the world. On one side is Sea Island and the famous Cloister that is visited by the wealthy from all over the world. Across the sound is Jekyll Island, at one time the winter haven of the Rockefellers and Goulds. Their large 'cottages', really mansions, still stand on the island which now belongs to the state and serves as one of its most popular recreation areas.

The small island of St. Simons is for the most part undeveloped, being held in large tracts, up until recent times. But there is an area along the coast with a small village of stores and churches and, until the last few years, modest frame cottages.

We rented a nice home on East Beach, a peninsula that extends out from the island with the sound on one side and Bloody Marsh on the other. Bloody Marsh gets its name from the last battle fought between the English and Spanish before the latter finally gave up their claim to this part of the new world.

We rented the house for six weeks in the summer. Frances and Bob would stay at the beach house and I would drive down for the weekends.

The most beautiful part of the Georgia coast are the unique live oaks found on the barrier islands like St. Simons. The trees branch out eight to ten feet above the ground and the limbs become as large as trees themselves. The growth is extemely slow, the annual rings being less than a quarter of an inch, and the wood is extremely heavy and dense. Old Ironsides, America's last wooden fighting ship, was built of timber from the St. Simons oaks and is still sea worthy today.

The wealthy come to adjoining Sea Island from all over the world and St. Simons is equally cosmopolitan. A large naval air station operated near there from World War II until recent times and many families of Navy personnel moved to the islands after retirement.

One of those families is headed by Mary and Joe Shelby.

Mary went to Ponce de Leon grammar school with me in Decatur. I had not seen her for many years. She and Frances became close friends during our summer visits.

After returning from my operation in Denver, we had decided to build a home on St. Simons. Frances found a beautiful lot. Only seventy by one hundred feet, it includes five of the old live oaks — each over two hundred years old — and a beautiful old cedar that leans at a 45 degree angle right in front of the house.

It's Frances' house. She found the lot, engaged the builder, had the house designed. It is beautiful. Framed by the ancient live oaks, with heavy Spanish moss hanging from its limbs, it is built like a Georgia swamp cabin. There is a long porch across the entire front of the house complete with rockers, flowers and hanging ferns. With a large screened porch on the side, it is built of cedar and the roof is shingled with thick cedar shakes that look as if they had been hacked out with an ax.

St. Simons is a friendly island. With a core of retired Navy people adept at making new friends quickly, there are a multitude of activities to bring people together. Soon we decided to enter Bob in school there and I continued to commute between the island and Decatur, being at St. Simons every weekend.

Mary's husband, Joe, is a retired chief petty officer. Standing six feet two, a former college football player, Joe is the kind of man who really runs the Navy. A master of the complex technology of naval aviation, Joe must have been an awe-inspiring sight in his chief petty officer's regalia.

Only slightly larger is Mary and Joe's son, Duncan. Coming through a door, Duncan leaves very little daylight to outline his massive dimensions. Duncan, at age 14, received the Carnegie medal for bravery. The powerful tide that sweeps between St. Simons and Jekyll on its way to Brunswick harbor was at full strength the day a woman visitor slipped and fell from the long old wooden pier that led out into the sound from St. Simons at the village. Without hesitation the 14 year old Duncan plunged after her, put his arm around her, and swam back against the heaving current to safety.

Being a Navy child, Duncan was raised near the ocean. Mary tells of him, at age 3, riding his tricycle back and forth on their family dock. The woman next door was excited and kept talking to Mary about how dangerous it was for a small child to be out there on a tricycle.

Finally, Duncan, a man of few words, had heard enough from the silly female. He backed up, got a running start, and pedaled the tricycle right off the end into the tidewater surrounding the dock.

Then, pulling the tricycle behind him, Duncan swam back to shore.

Because of Frances' and Mary's friendship, I soon came to know Joe and Duncan and they began to talk about taking me fishing. With the size of the two of them, we were soon making our way quite easily down the long ramp to the floating pier on the intercoastal waterway and from there to Duncan's 16 foot power boat. It would have been a major project, especially when the tide was low and the ramp back up was at a steep angle, but with the combined strength of Joe and Duncan I felt I wasn't really imposing on them.

After a few fishing trips, Joe and Duncan started talking about getting me into a canoe. The truth of the matter was that, while Duncan was a superb natural born fisherman, Joe was more interested in getting a workout and was really pretty bored sitting holding a pole.

I knew they couldn't be serious. When you say my legs are paralyzed, you're really not telling the whole story. My stomach muscles are also useless to me. Set me on a stool without anything to hold on to and I'd keel over. If I couldn't balance in a chair I knew I wouldn't do anything but roll over into the water if I got into something as unstable as a canoe.

But the talk persisted. I was told how beautiful the winding Satilla River is, slowly moving from the black Okefeenokee Swamp toward the ocean.

Joe had made up his mind he was going to have a paddle in his hand on our Saturday morning trips.

Finally, it was agreed that a canoe would be unstable for me. But that certainly a flat bottom boat would be satisfactory and Joe knew where he could borrow one. He was really just taking me on an adventure.

Not knowing what Joe was up to, I went along.

Bob and Joe Shelby on my first trip down the Satilla River. Before it was over, I was paddling and had transferred to a canoe.

Joe, a master of improvisation from his Navy days, next went to the local dump where he liberated a small, leatherette covered easy chair. Sawing off the legs, he and Duncan tied the red chair into the flat-bottomed boat and the great adventure was ready to begin.

Bob went along to paddle in front, Joe was paddling behind and I was sitting in the little red arm chair in the center.

The day we planned to go, it was raining. One of the things I was about to learn from Duncan and Joe was that you don't necessarily melt just because you get wet. Neither of them pay the slightest attention to walking around in the water, be it ocean, river, or heavy rain.

When we got to the creek bank, I noticed it went straight down about eight feet before the sandy beach next to the river leveled out. In my ignorance, I thought this would present a problem.

"Don't worry about it, Mr. Harrison," Duncan came around, opened the door, picked me up, walked down the near perpendicular bank and put me in the little, red easy chair.

The rain was falling gently, but steadily, as Joe poled the flat-bottom boat away from the shore, took his seat in the rear and began to paddle.

It was a new world for me. As soon as we left the car sitting on the bank, we were in the wilderness, the slowly winding river turned and twisted, giving us a moving panorama of forest, sand beaches and black water.

"How do you do that?" Duncan asked. He was in a canoe following as Joe paddled our flat-bottomed boat down the river. It was chilling to sit in the drizzling rain and I was getting colder by the minute.

"These are isometric exercises I take," I said through my clenched and chattering teeth.

"Gosh, how did you learn to do that, Mr. Harrison?" Duncan asked.

"From the dog, Duncan," I said shaking violently.

Joe looked around.

"What you need is a heater." He handed me a paddle.

It was a little awkward reaching over the arms of the chair. But Joe was right. Once I started paddling I was quite warm and comfortable.

I remembered Bob asking me when he was playing midget football as a young boy — it was bitterly cold — "Dad, how come it's warm out in the middle of the field and so cold on the side lines."

I didn't know it, but after thirty years of sitting on the side lines — as far as physical involvement in physical adventure — I was about to leave the cold and enter the heated middle of the field.

The water of the Satilla is black from the tannic acid of the cypress filled swamp and the river snakes between heavily wooded banks. Around every bend there is a beautiful white, sand beach and animal tracks reveal the near proximity of wild life.

"It's a lot easier in a canoe," Joe said, watching me reach out over the arms of the chair and the flat bottomed boat to take small bites of the water.

After several miles down the beautiful, black river, winding along under the low hanging branches of the virgin trees that lined each side of this wilderness, we pulled into a narrow creek and up to a narrow dock and slanting concrete boat ramp. Joe and Duncan picked me up and put me in the wheelchair on the dock.

I looked down at the narrow canoe, bobbing slightly from the waves we had created by disembarking.

"You win, Joe," I said. "Put me down in that thing."

I held on to the sides gingerly as Duncan slowly paddled our way back into the stream.

"Okay," I said, "let's go home." Beads of sweat had popped out on my forehead, but I had been converted. The canoe slid so easily and quietly in the water I was ready to explore with these two friends to see if a paralyzed man really could use one.

On our next trip, Joe had found a fibre glass cafeteria type chair, removed the legs and had it sitting on the bottom of the canoe. I got in and held tightly to the sides as Joe paddled us into the marsh that divides St. Simons from Sea Island. Every time Joe would take a long pull with his paddle, or a slight wave would rise from a passing power boat, I would hold on for dear life.

"We've got to attach the chair to the boat," Joe told me.

On our next trip, Duncan had clamped two long two by fours to the canoe, one on each side of my seat so I could get some side support and the chair wouldn't slide around as I moved. He had also brought along a small electric motor that, clamped to the side of the canoe, could move us in the water without paddling.

After making a couple of trips in the canoe with Joe, I decided I'd like to go out in the marsh alone.

Joe was non-communicative and non-participating as Duncan and I talked about the feasibility of my using the small motor to take a solo trip. Joe wanted no part of sending a high level paraplegic out alone in the marshes of Glynn.

Duncan felt it was a challenge.

"Mr. Harrison," he said, "I think I've got it figured out."

Duncan brought the blue pickup to my house early in the morning, loaded me in the front and we were off with the aluminum canoe protruding from the truck bed and the wheelchair standing in the back along side it.

Duncan clamped the two by fours to the canoe making the framework that would hold my seat and give me an arm rest. It looked a little strange but it was obvious my seat was not going to tip over the way it had on our honeymoon outing at Clearwater Lake, Minnesota.

"With this little motor," Duncan said proudly as he clamped the electric outboard to the side of the canoe, "you can go anywhere you want."

Cables led to the marine type battery between my legs. I looked at the setup dubiously. One thing was sure, I'd better be sure I didn't flip over into the salt water wired up like this.

With the little outboard churning away, I was soon around the bend from the boat ramp where Duncan stood, looking very thoughtful, as an inventor should, as I disappeared from sight.

Frankly, I was nervous. On our previous trips, I had left the navigation up to Joe and Duncan. Now, I was on my own and the marsh looked pretty much the same no matter where you were — light green grass hid any landmarks and dark green, lapping water formed a broad river with intersections leading farther into the tall grass as I plowed smoothly along.

I saw a row of posts that marked the remains of some kind of dock and tried to imprint that on my mind in relation to the turn off I'd take on my return trip to where Duncan stood on the boat ramp.

The only other land mark was the distant water tank just visible above the grass.

I took a right turn, recognized a spot where we had fished from the power boat and made another right into a narrow water way that wound between exposed mounds of oyster shells.

Looking around me, I no longer could see anything familiar — so I decided I'd had enough adventure and had better start looking for the way home. The wind was up, now, and had blown me back into a narrow passage of the grass land.

I got the canoe turned around and reved up the engine to start back.

My return route was against the wind and I was having my first of many experiences that placed me in opposition to that powerful natural force.

The canoe wouldn't budge out of the surrounding grass.

And I noticed the outboard motor slip slightly where it was clamped to the side of the boat.

Not being used, at that time, to being out among the elements alone, I could feel the panic begin to rise.

After all, I was paralyzed!

"That's all I need," I sweated, "let this outboard fall off the canoe and I'll never get out of here." And it would take a while to find me in a boat. There was a lot of marsh between St. Simons and Sea Island. Finally I thought, "To hell with it. Here goes nothing." I reached over and tightened the clamps as hard as desperation would get them. Then I put the little outboard on full power — and came planing out of the narrow passage.

In a couple of minutes, I recognized the oyster beds where we had fished and I started a left turn.

Right then, about fifty feet in front of me a big porpoise surfaced, then disappeared below the green water

"Man," I exulted, "this sure beats the hell out of staring at the wall."

Turning left into the main channel, I spotted the remains of the old dock and soon had entered the channel to the boat ramp.

Duncan was waiting at the ramp as I came plowing up the channel.

"How was it, Mr. Harrison?" Duncan asked as he lifted me back into the wheel chair. "Well, Duncan," I said with a grin, "I may never go alone again, but I'll tell you one thing. I'm a helluva navigator."

By the time we made our next trip, Joe devised a board that fits around the back of the seat and makes it a part of the canoe.

We were in business.

With the new seat arrangement and my paddle in my hands, I could balance without hanging onto the sides. And the fear was gone.

Early morning is the best time. Paddling down the broad tidal river through the marsh, the dark green water, light green marsh grass, black mud banks and the pink of dawn shining through the rising grey, marsh fog. Ninety-nine per cent of the visitors to the Golden Isles have never experienced the marshes of Glynn. They drive by in their automobiles and look out on a sea of green or brown grass. Or, they speed by in their high-powered speed boats along the inland waterway and see the same grass from the water side.

To see the marsh, you have to paddle your canoe or small flat bottomed boat slowly into the narrow serpentine water trails that disappear into the marsh grass. With civilization disappearing as quickly as you can round the first turn, you begin to become a part of the real marsh. Mullet jumping high out of the water as you approach, the small back object making a tiny wake that is the head of a swimming turtle, the birds, small and large, rising swiftly or slowly and majestically as you approach them, the huge porpoise surfacing a few feet from you in the larger waters, the small mink trailing along the muddy bank, the sucking holes in that mud as some creature burrows deeper, the hoards of fiddler crabs digging in or crawling out, the thousands of bulging eyed shrimp on the surface when there is a temperature inversion in the marsh water.

The most magnificent sight Joe and I experienced was the mating of male and female otters within ten feet of our canoe. They were magnificent animals, at least five feet long with heavy black fur and needle sharp flashing white teeth. After a moment of frozen action, they saw our silent canoe, disappeared, and a moment later surfaced a hundred yards down the waterway.

In the beginning, Joe would see things invisible to my unaccustomed eye, but more and more I began to see and experience the life of the marsh and it was a deep and moving experience.

There is so much beauty around us that we cannot see because of the blindness imposed by our particular mind set or worry distraction. Not just in the wilderness but in the city as well — our urban marsh of teeming life, where we shut out all but our own preoccupation.

My balance was improving to the point that I never had to grab the sides unless a passing speed boat sent a sudden wave that seemed about to upset us. With Joe's instruction, I soon was learning to turn into such waves and even they were no longer a problem.

Each time we made one of our weekend trips we became a little more daring as my skill increased. I needed help getting into and out of the boat, but once seated in the seat Joe and Duncan had devised, I could pull my own weight. And Joe and I had long hours to talk as we paddled slowly through the evolving marsh.

I was not afraid of the water. I had learned at the 'Y' that the water would support me and, with a proper breathing technique, I would survive in water for an indefinite period.

One of the best creeks in the marsh originates a few blocks from our house and twists down through Bloody Marsh to finally enter the sound at Gould's Inlet between the tips of East Beach and Sea Island. We could enter at the causeway to East Beach, paddle toward Gould's Inlet, then turn left up the broad waterway toward the Cloister, resort to the wealthy.

And we made that and other trips through various parts of the Intercoastal Waterway and the marsh at all times of the year, rain or shine. The worse the day, the better we liked it. On a bitter cold winter's day, we would paddle along, our jackets open, warm as toast and laugh to see a power boat streak by at thirty knots, the driver hunched and blue with cold in the driving wind.

Finally, we started entering the sound at Gould's Inlet, fighting the waves with the slapping paddles and waddling from side to side as we paralleled the beach. Then, we would turn and let the waves surf us in to a landing on the white beach as bathers stared at the sight we were creating by our porpoising arrival in the long aluminum hull.

On a calm day, Joe and I paddled across the broad sound from St. Simons Causeway to the beach at Jekyll, the adjoining island, watching thousands of jelly fish oscillating just below the water and the small triangular fin of baby sharks cutting the surface in the shallows.

In the canoe, we were just inches away from all this life.

The day we chose to turn over in the sound was a classic that none of us can explain to this day. Joe and Duncan had planned a trip down the Satilla that morning, but when I made a business appointment for later in the day, they changed and said we would enter off the causeway and paddle down the intercoastal waterway and back.

All the conditions were right for a disaster. Three men in a fifteen foot Gruman, three foot waves pounding in the sound, the water temperature 51 degrees and the outside temperature 45 with a chill factor in the blustering January wing well below freezing.

What bothers me most in winter is my hands. And they were blue now, as we paddled south on the waterway hugging the safety of the bank. The wind was whistling at a brisk pace when we turned and started back.

No other boats were to be seen. The rest of humanity was hunkered around family hearth or automobile heater when we decided for some reason we would cut across to the Sea Island Golf Course located on the west side of St. Simons. This meant we would be cutting across the edge of the open sound. As soon as we were out of the mouth of the channel, the first wave swamped us. There was no chance to ride over it. It simply folded up and over and filled our canoe with water. We went over and the three of us grabbed the canoe as it went bottom up.

The water was cold, but not as cold as the air had been. Temperature was not our immediate problem. From a craft that we could steer where we wanted to go, we were suddenly wallowing in the salt water, every wave crashing over our heads and going down our backs under our jackets and thermal underwear.

Instead of directing our course, we were at the mercy of the powerful channel tide that was, at that hour, leaving the port of Brunswick and rushing between the barrier islands toward the open sea.

"Let's get Clark back in the boat," Joe yelled over the noise crashing around us.

I maneuvered back to within the aluminum walls of the swamped craft, but the next wave flung me out, the canoe rolling over as I slid back into the open sea.

Then Joe and Duncan, exerting all their mighty strength tried to stand the canoe on its side.

"Make a sail of it," one yelled, "and maybe the wind will blow us toward the golf course."

The next wave brought the canoe crashing down on top of us and this time I lost my grip on it and went down under the water. I grabbed the canoe again as soon as I had surfaced.

It was becoming apparent that the mighty slate grey mass of rolling water had turned into an equalizer. Joe and Duncan could no more control the canoe than I could with my paralyzed legs trailing below the dark water.

There are two massive navigation towers in the sound that stand between where we had turned over and the golf course beach that was the closest land. Joe and Duncan thought we might reach them and be able to hold on there. But as we turned and twisted in the waves, it soon became apparent that the tide would sweep us right past that.

"Daddy," Duncan yelled above the sound of the crashing waves, "we're not going to make it. This tide is going to sweep us right past the pier, between the islands and out to the open sea."

We both knew what he was saying was true.

"I'm going to swim for it," Duncan shouted.

"No, son," Joe shouted, "you'll never make it. Hang on with us."

"I'm going," Duncan yelled and turned loose of the canoe.

It was a dark, cloudy day and visibility was restricted. We could just see Duncan's head from time to time as it would appear momentarily above the waves. It seemed impossible, with his heavy clothes, boots and the numbness of the cold that he could fight the powerful current and make it to the beach some two hundred yards away. Later, he said his strength was about gone when he finally touched ground below the clawing tidal power.

Against the dim sky, I finally saw Duncan's dark form in the distance as he rose and struggled up the beach to disappear from sight.

I was not worried about drowning. I knew that I could have stayed in the water indefinitely under normal conditions. I knew my enemy was not the water but was the cold that was slowly sapping my strength.

What I was trying with all my might to do was to keep my blood circulating against the numbing cold. I didn't feel the cold. My body heat was warming the water between my skin and the thermal underwear and only when a fresh wave would send cold water down my collar did I realize just how cold it was. It was just a matter of time until the cold would lower my body's temperature to the point where I would lose consciousness.

In the meantime, I was pulling myself up and down against the overturned canoe in an effort to keep the blood circulating.

Although my mind tried to reject the idea, I knew that Joe and I were going to die. With the island's population buttoned down on land against the January cold, with the tide sweeping us out to sea, it didn't matter that just a hundred yards away was the beach and safety. It seemed like a foolish way to die, so close to shore and safety, but it also seemed inevitable.

Seeing Duncan struggle to his feet on the beach gave me a great feeling of comfort. Joe and I had lived full lives, but Duncan, newly married, was just beginning his.

"Well, Lord," I thought, "this seems like a right pleasant way to go, and I can't think of a nicer fellow than Joe to go with."

I was losing consciousness when the big boat pulled along side us. I could barely see through the darkness that had become more dense as my mind began to drift and the cold caused my eyes to dim. I could hear faint voices that must have been near and I could still feel the canoe as it reared and plunged under my grasping arms.

A rope hit on top of my hands but slid away when I could not move to grasp it.

Then I lost consciousness. I remember a face close to mine and calling my name. I was on the ground, no longer tossing and swaying in the cold water. And I fainted away.

Next, I was in a brightly lit room, filled with voices. I was wrapped up tightly and a nurse was placing a fresh hot water bottle against the row of hot water bottles stacked against the covers.

"Your face looked like a purple, pinched monkey," Frances told me later. She had been at home when word came of the accident. By the time she got to the emergency room, I was regaining consciousness.

"You just about tore up the inside of our ambulance," the attendant told me, "you were grabbing for the oxygen equipment — anything you could get a hold of. They say they had to pry you loose from the canoe."

We were in intensive care now, my chest wired to a monitor that was recording my heart beat.

"Your temperature did not register when they got you here," the doctor said. "Our thermometer goes down only to ninety, so whatever your temperature was it was below ninety."

At eighty-eight degrees, the mind loses consciousness. At seventy-six degrees the heart begins fibrillation. After that comes heart failure and death.

We were alive because Duncan had made it to shore to alert people to the fact there was a canoe with two men hanging on in the stormy channel.

The big boat that came after us could not get to us — we were too far below their pounding craft.

Once again, for me, the good Lord had sent the least likely of rescuers to our aid.

Two teenage boys who have lived their lives in the house near St. Simons pier were home when Duncan came pounding on their door.

"We ran first to our motorboat," they said later. "But we couldn't get the motor started. Then we remembered our canoe. We ran, got it, and launched out just as you came down toward the pier."

There was a length of line that was tied to the front of our canoe, and the boy scouts grabbed that and towed us through the waves the few hundred feet to safety.

That afternoon, I felt fine, once I had warmed up. I had not swallowed a drop of water and the most serious matter, other than the hospital bill, was that I had lost my glasses. I had to have a pair sent down before I could drive back to Decatur.

"Doc," I said, "how about letting me go home. You've got a nice hospital, but you're really not set up to take care of a fellow like me."

"Well," he said, "you're probably right. Go on home."

Small black spots on the tips of two of my toes were the only reminders of how close to death from exposure we had come.

I got a big kick out of the headline in the Monday paper.

"Two local men rescued from sound."

I had finally made the paper with no mention of my political notoriety.

And, I thought, I really am a local man. I probably know that marsh better and I am definitely on more intimate terms with that cold, pounding sound than just about any native on the island.

CHAPTER XLII

Clawing its way through the denser air of the flat Delta country of Arkansas, the engine of the 140 kept a steady and deafening roar. The cloud layer ahead was definitely thickening and would soon constitute a solid overcast. Fortunately, the base was at four thousand feet and I would be able to stay comfortably below if the clouds remained at their current level.

The haze was thickening below me, however, and I was getting concerned about visibility as I came closer to the Mississippi River.

The little 140 is a great equalizer. Able to leap over tall buildings at a single bound — as well as other tall objects. And it can reduce the size of things. The mighty Mississippi looked like Georgia's Chattahoochee as I approached at thirty-five hundred feet. Then I spotted the tow boat pulling its long line of barges, also reduced to miniature size and the perspective was restored.

The curves and ox bow swirls of the river matched my chart to show I was still on course and had not lost my pilotage skill in the absence of a guiding VOR radio beam.

I was over the Mississippi Delta now, the fertile fields at rest in these September days. Now, I dropped to two thousand feet as I picked up Clarksdale to the right and the highway that leads past Marks to Dick Haltom's home town of Batesville — the place Dick had made famous in his descriptions of small town life as seen from the corner drug store. Dick did such a masterful job that Munson, our Lawson ward boy — future doctor — planned his trip home to California to include a stop at Batesville.

The world is a small place, and Dick proved that great men can come from and stay in small towns in Mississippi.

The more I experience, the less I believe in accidents and the more I believe in an overall guiding hand in the affairs of men and women willing to listen and to learn.

The year was 1974, shortly after we had finally opened our bank, in a small temporary building in Decatur. The board was waiting to start a meeting in my office when Clyde Shepherd came through the door.

"Clark," he said, "my nephew, James, has been injured. He's paralyzed."

The story was a strange one from the beginning.

The surf that pounds into the coast of Brazil at Rio de Janerio is spectacular, rising to ten feet or more before cresting and crashing toward the beach.

In this particular segment of the Brazilian coast, the land has been filled and built out to provide a highly expensive expansion for the bursting city. The result is a beach that drops precipitously as it enters the ocean causing the waves to collapse suddenly as they pound into the land.

The young man entering the ocean on this particular morning in 1974 was unusually talented and from a family who face the world and change the world's face.

On a round-the-world trip following his graduation from the University of Georgia, his particular interest at the moment was to find the biggest and best surf in the various parts of the globe.

Getting around the world was nothing new to the family. His grandfather, a general contractor who liked large challenges and large projects, was one of the men responsible for America's rapid deployment over the earth in World War II.

When the war ended, air fields had been built around the world by his company.

With the war over, those projects came to an abrupt end. And the company found itself overextended, with equipment and expense on a world wide scale and with financial obligations beyond the capacity of a privately owned company once the flow of money was cut off by the demobilizing government.

"When I was young, just getting into the business," the surfer's father told me later, "I had two ambitions. One was to make a million dollars, the other was to keep my dad from going bankrupt."

Today, the young man was going body surfing. Holding his body rigidly flat, without a surf board, he would catch the crest of a breaking wave and ride it into the beach.

What he was really about to do was to assume a new mission in life that would effect thousands of other young men and women in the years to come.

Throwing himself on the crest of a monster wave, he held himself rigid with a determination arising from generations of stubborn determined ancestors. Pounding toward the shore, the mighty wave suddenly, without warning, collapsed and was gone from beneath him.

If he had been relaxed and tumbling what happened next might have been avoided — but he was rigid and suddenly the whole leveraged weight of his body was concentrated as his most vulnerable spot.

His head hit the solid beach, and his neck snapped.

Rolling helplessly in the boiling sea, he swallowed the heavy salt water mixed with sand. Only the prompt action of his companion saved him from drowning.

James was taken to the Rio hospital and his parents arrived on the first available plane. The hospital worked hard to stabilize his condition but circumstances were far from ideal. Even the bed was too short for James lanky frame — his feet had to hang over the end.

Desperate efforts were made to get him back to the United States. His situation was so delicate that ordinary means of transporting him could have been fatal.

His throat opened by a tracheotomy to allow him to breathe, life was sustained through crisis after crisis as his lungs, damaged by the salt water and sand, struggled to get enough oxygen to his still body.

Finally, through the help of one of Georgia's senators, arrangements were made to fly James back to the U. S., at his family's expense, in the huge hospital airplane equipped to serve NASA in the recovery of the astronauts. Equipped with every device for life support, the plane safely returned James and his family to Atlanta.

Keeping up with his progress through Clyde, I was at Piedmont Hospital the Sunday morning after his return.

"We nearly lost him last night," I was in the reception room and Alana, James' mother was speaking. "His lungs absorbed so much salt water and sand they stay infected with pneumonia and pseudomonias."

They described taking turns sitting at James side to be sure he was able to breathe and to change his position on a regular basis to avoid the kind of bedsores that have plagued me.

On my second visit, I was able to visit his room. James is tall and his body looked like mine when I first returned from overseas. He was a skeleton covered with a light covering of flesh. At his throat was a hole, kept open by a tube that allowed him to breathe.

In the beginning, he had communicated by blinking his eyes. Now he was able to speak but I was unable to catch what he was saying sitting just a few feet away from him.

He was on a 'bed' not much wider than an ironing board suspended inside a large tubular steel circle. Called a "circle-lectric" bed the device was designed to shift his body weight as the bed revolved within the tubular frame. The idea was to avoid the pressure sores without having to disturb his position in the device.

I had told Alana and Harold about Craig Hospital in Denver. Here in Atlanta, James' condition remained precarious and the lung situation continued as a threat.

"Clyde," I had called the uncle after my latest Sunday morning visit, "they need to get James to Craig. Tell Harold to get on the plane and go out to look for himself. I know they can help James."

I knew the Shepherds would react to Craig's positive and optimistic methods of treatment. I also knew James would not be permanently paralyzed.

"He has feeling all over his body," Harold told me, "and he can move his right foot."

"He's not going to be paralyzed," I told Alana and Harold, "I've seen a lot of quads over the years and I've never heard of one who could move a foot."

Eight months after his injury, James walked out of Craig Hospital and returned to Atlanta.

Most families, having dodged the bullet, would have gotten as far from hospitals and paralyzed people as they could. Not the Shepherds.

"Clark," Harold said, "we've got to have a hospital like Craig in Atlanta."

We began to have organizational meetings and Harold, Alana and James made contact with Dr. Dave Apple, who shared the dream.

Dr. Apple, an orthopedic surgeon, had trained at a spinal cord center in California. An athlete himself, Dave serves as team doctor for the Atlanta pro basketball team, and understands the devastation spinal cord injury brings to the young and active person most likely to suffer this particular trauma.

With six beds, the pilot unit leased space at a general hospital in the area near the Shepherd's home. Bringing an occupational and a physical therapist from Craig, the program there was duplicated as a takeoff point for building an outstanding program.

"The center should be named Shepherd," I said at one of our early organizational meetings, "and James should be the president."

I had prayed for over two years for a Craig type treatment center in Atlanta. The answer that I now saw taking shape could not have been more dramatic.

Here was the one family in Atlanta, Georgia, with the intelligence, the skill, the dedication and the staying power to accomplish a task of this dimension. Such things in the past have been done by governments or large church groups. This would be done by a family with unique abilities, government and business contacts and a unique personal devotion.

The main business of the four Shepherd brothers who succeeded the globe straddling father, is building roads. A major portion of the expressways in Georgia are their product. Other large activities are carried on in various parts of the world and they are particularly involved in the push toward modernization of Saudi Arabia.

Reporting to work with the company shortly after his return from Craig, James shows a preference for being outside, directly involved in the projects — smelling the asphalt as it is poured.

But his first concern, and that of his mother, father, and wife Cathy — who was James therapist at Craig — has been the Shepherd Spinal Center. Alana is at the center every day and has organized and led the fund raising.

With the birth of James and Cathy's second child, Cathy's schedule at the clinic has been curtailed but her active involvement continues.

In the early days, I participated in a couple of shows we put on for prospective donors to the center. In my sweat pants and T-shirt, I showed how a fifty year old paraplegic can get down on a mat, exercise and then pull himself back up into the chair and then stand in a special rig to get weight on the legs. Being a retired politician, I made a speech while going through the program.

Mainly, my interest has been to visit the hospital and talk to the patients.

To a sixteen year old paraplegic.

"What do you like to do?"

"Well, before I got paralyzed I liked to go hunting and fishing."

"Then, you'd really enjoy canoeing."

He looked at me as if I'd taken leave of my senses.

"I couldn't get in a canoe," He said.

"Why not?"

"What would happen if I turned over?"

"Well," I said, "you would probably lose your pants. But I've found that if you wear suspenders that won't happen."

"But I can't swim."

"You mean you never learned to swim?"

"Well," he said, "of course, I was an excellent swimmer before I got hurt. But I'm paralyzed."

"You'll find out," I told him, "that you can swim about as well as you ever did."

He said a couple of his buddies had tried to take him swimming. Maybe he'd go do it.

What I had just told him had taken ten years for me to finally discover.

Patients now, including quadraplegics, are taken to a community pool and shown the techniques of swimming for the spinal cord injured. They find the water supports them while they move about with a freedom not experienced in any other environment.

Trips to the rifle range and wilderness canoe trips are included in the new recreational program as is active participation in basketball and track events.

Recently, a quadraplegic, a man not much younger than myself who had earned his living as a traveling salesman, took me to lunch. He was injured a little over a year ago and he is now driving his own van and planning to re-enter sales work. He was one of five quadraplegics who spent three nights in the north Georgia mountains.

"We went canoeing," he said. He had already told me he can swim quite comfortably.

"What kind of seat did they have in the canoe?" I asked.

He then described the arrangement Joe and Duncan originally had worked out for me and that I had passed on to the therapist.

I thought he would be using our seat, but I wanted to hear him describe the experience.

The average stay at Shepherd from injury to final discharge is about ninety days. In that Marine boot camp type experience, are compressed the knowledge hard earned by paraplegics and quadraplegics over a life time.

They are taught to raise up and to turn themselves in bed to avoid the bed sores the after effects of which still worry me today. They are taught to lift themselves from bed to chair to car. They are taught to swim and to drive and how to manage their personal care.

And, the depression is fought on an hourly and daily basis.

Young, active and strong attendants dress and act informally — no uniforms are allowed doctor or staff. Numerous expeditions to restaurants, shows and sporting events break the tedium. And many evenings there are parties.

Shepherd Spinal Center is to the newly spinal injured what Parris Island is to the Marine recruit.

Photo: Nick Arroyo/Shepherd Spinal Center

The future will see new activities and accomplishments not dreamed of now as the spinal cord injured learn and pass their lessons on to others.

Now, the center has its own building with eighty beds, connected by tunnel to the medical facilities of Piedmont Hospital, the place where I first visited James as he lay paralyzed from the neck down.

With over seventy foundations and hundreds of corporations supporting the work, the facility will never have a long term mortgage put on it — being debt free it will have the ability to serve its patients in ways not possible before.

It is the policy of the center to follow its alumni throughout the rest of their lives. The out patient clinic serves their medical needs and various seminars serve to exchange knowledge between patients and the center.

Having started its outdoor recreational program the next big move will be occupational guidance and assistance.

The first time Frances went in the new building, she had to get back outside away from the crowds. Her tears were flowing as she remembered the times she had waited for me outside operating rooms at Lawson, in Connecticut, in Minnesota, in Atlanta and finally in Denver.

"It's just like Craig," she said, looking at the broad halls, the large rooms and the big therapy spaces.

Christ was asked why the man was blind.

"So that God's glory might be revealed".

I do not know why James Shepherd was paralyzed.

But I do see the glory.

CHAPTER XLIII

It takes a while to see like a bird.

I never have really learned to think like a bird — except for the time I had vertigo and had the sense of a chicken — but I have gotten to where I can see pretty much like a bird.

When Clint first took me on a cross country flight we were following the VOR and looking for one of the nearby airports.

"Where would you say the airport is now," Clint asked me.

"I have no idea."

"Look down."

I looked out the left window. Right below us was the runway of the airport we were seeking.

It happened several times, and each time I was embarrassed, having had no inkling we were near our destination.

Once I learned the trick, I found out my passengers have the same problem I used to have. Usually, they don't see the runway until we are on short final.

It's a matter of training the eye where to look and what to look for and learning how things appear from various heights.

You learn to look in the direction you expect to find the object — then when the first glimmer appears you are ready and have it identified by the location of the glimmer.

Stone Mountain is an example. Depending on the condition of the haze, I have spotted it from as far away as Lake Jackson — some forty miles distant — but that's unusual.

Airports, the big ones, make a light colored slash in the distance — if they are sitting on high ground as Peachtree is — just point the plane at 319 degrees on the mag compass as you near Stone Mountain from the south and soon the airport will appear.

Smaller airports are spotted on the chart first, then the runway will appear to left or right.

Flying to St. Simons, I look for the gap between that island and Jekyll.

Going south, there is the big Georgia Power stack at Milledgeville on the left and the nuclear stacks at Macon on the right. Stay about half way between and you're on the route.

Just south of the line from Milledgeville to Macon you come upon the kaolin mines — jade green reservoirs of water and a large lime kiln.

Even when there are scattered clouds below, you will pick up the river that leads into Dublin, Georgia, at the proper moment and know you are right on course.

The airport at Dublin is a triangle — and then you are crossing I-16 — you cross the expressway following the big power line that runs on to Vidalia.

The airport at Vidalia is another triangle. Nine minutes later you cross the Altamaha River that leads to the coast right by the islands.

After a few dozen trips back and forth, it is possible to find your way as if on a familiar and well-beaten path.

Familiarity breeds confidence. Even the turn over in the January St. Simons sound was a confidence building experience as far as canoeing was concerned. For one thing, I found out I could survive for a long time in the water, without a life jacket, and that the only real danger was the cold that had almost drawn the last heat from my body.

After that experience, I decided I would like to try canoeing in the streams of north Georgia.

Barbara, who is one of God's children, was playing the part of a county recreation director at the time. She offered to be my teacher. Our first trip was one she had planned on the Chattahoochee to interest the politicians in preserving the river. It was mostly flat water but the beauty of the surrounding wilderness whetted my appetite.

Even where the river flows through the city, the banks are most likely to still be in a natural state and it is hard not to think you are in pristine wilderness.

On our second trip, we got into some white water. It was definitely different from the flat water in South Georgia. Less tiring because of the swift currents. More exciting because the danger is real.

"Now, Clark," Barbara told me, "you've got to learn to find the way the water flows around these rocks. Sometimes it looks like there is no way through, but if you study the situation a while there is usually one way to follow water deep enough to get through."

Looking down the broad river, we saw shores heavily treed on both sides, with fallen tree trunks extending out from the river banks, with lines of exposed rock, some large boulders, some runs where only the turbulence of the river indicated the rocks hidden below.

Then, we saw long stretches with no rock and an easy current flowing along.

On one of those stretches, paddling slowly down the broad stream, the excitement to come was first seen in the distance.

The tree line was uniform until a bend was passed, then, in the distance, we could see that the tops of the trees at the next curve were lower, as if the trees were short and stubby.

Next, we heard the noise.

A low rumble — increasing in volume as we neared the bend.

"Oh, oh," I thought as I visualized the roaring, tumbling water that was waiting just a few moments away now.

Rounding the bend we saw it. Rocks everywhere. Tongues of water along a boulder. Lines of rocks. Low hanging bows. Rushing water leaving the dam of the rocks amid tumbling spray leaping then falling to a level some five feet below.

The excitement was building as the canoe moved faster as it hit the white water. We both knew with one false move the canoe would flip over on its side, fill with water and become heavy as concrete in the swirling torrent.

"Do you see that tongue of water," Barbara was yelling now over the roaring waters, "right beside the boulder. Get the nose in there and I'll swing us into the trough. Pull right. Pull right. You got it, you got it. Hold that now. Push left. Push left. Here we go — oh — oh!!!"

Sliding, crashing, slamming, banging , shipping water as we round the boulder.

"Hey, I didn't like the way we did that." Barbara jumped in the water, grabbed the rope at the back of canoe, hauled us back upstream as she wadded through the icy water dragging the canoe and me behind her.

Next time, we did better. I was learning I could make the canoe go where I wanted it to — the front part anyway — by thrusting the paddle deep in the water and pulling it toward the canoe in a vertical position. Or, if there was room, I could bring the bow around by broad sweeps keeping the blade as far out from the boat as possible.

When we got in amongst the rocks, things happened in a hurry. It became possible to run straight at a big boulder, make a sharp right turn under the overhanging rock and escape injury — but you have to know what you are doing.

I didn't have a death wish. After the weeks, months and years lying in bed, staring at the wall, I did have a life wish and I couldn't get enough of canoeing.

Like the WAC at Lawson who was a trapeze artist, when I was charging down a swollen river, I felt really alive.

When we first opened Shepherd, I wanted to do something to help. I didn't have much money, and, no longer being King, very little influence with people with money.

On the other hand, I thought it a bit unusual a paraplegic would be doing white water in the North Georgia rivers. Maybe, I could raise some money and get some publicity for the center by use of my canoeing skill.

The idea was to lead to a full blown white water experience.

The small mountain community of Helen, Georgia, was having its second annual canoe race from the city limits of that town to Atlanta. The trip was some 100 miles down the rugged twisting mountain stream, through the full length of Lake Lanier and finally miles of the broad river at flood stage from the Buford dam into the city.

I say flood stage because by April the mountain streams have filled Lake Lanier and the cold waters are being heavily discharged under the dam.

In order to help raise money for the center, I announced I would make the trip in my canoe and the Shepherd Center would take pledges for my trip on a per mile basis.

I talked to a writer with the Journal Magazine, Phil Garner, and he was enthusiastic about the idea. He knew all the people in the little town of Helen would be also.

Helen had begun to build a reputation as an Alpine village, created in the north Georgia mountains, from the fertile imagination of a fellow named Pete Hodkinson and brought into reality by the labors of the local craftsmen. They had never been to Bavaria, but with Pete's urgings, they were rebuilding the store fronts in town and building hotels that looked like pictures they had seen of the Swiss Alps.

Pete, himself, was an unusual individual. He had come near dying in an auto collision that had left him with a piece of plastic where his forehead bone had been and with an attitude that in the limited time he had left he was going to have some fun in life and make his life count for something.

"Pete is a child," one of the attractive young women who worked with him told me, "we can be working hard, in the middle of a project, and Pete will suddenly say 'Let's have a picnic'. We'll drop everything, load up a basket with food and wine, pile in Pete's truck and head up the mountain."

Pete was fearless. When he decided to learn to fly an airplane, he bought a small Cessna and a book of instructions. The tale is that Pete taxied up and down the field checking the controls and reading about procedures, then, tossing the book out the window, he took off.

After mastering flying, Pete got the idea that the Alpine Village promotion would be helped by the use of a hot air balloon. Pete bought one, inflated it and got in the basket along with three other Helenians.

The rose quickly to about four thousand feet and were enjoying the view when suddenly the propane heater ran out of fuel. There was another fuel tank and they switched to that, but, somehow, the flint from the lighter that came with the outfit popped out over the side of the basket. Pete's next remark was classic.

"Does anybody have a match?"

The balloon was falling and picking up speed as the envelope began to collapse. The passengers frantically searched their pockets for a match.

"We finally found a match and got the fire started enough to partially inflate the balloon before we came crashing through the trees," Pete told me, "It inflated just enough to keep us from being killed."

Soon, Pete had made Helen a center for balloonists from all over the country by establishing an annual balloon race from Helen to the Atlantic Coast.

The canoe race came later and was in its second year when I heard of it.

I got some canoe and publicity specialists together for a meeting. About all that was agreed on was the fact that April was too cold for a mountain canoe trip. We set a date for another committee meeting and selected a July date for our attempt.

I told Phil Garner, the Journal Magazine reporter, about the committee meeting and that it had been decided to postpone my trip until July so that planning could be completed.

"Gosh," he said, "I'm sorry to hear that. Pete has got everything planned and is ready to release the publicity."

Next day I was in Helen.

Pete was in his office, surrounded by beautiful girl assistants, bearded mountaineers and displays showing Helen's evolution from North Georgia mountaineer town to a Bavarian Alps village. Across the floor were rail-road ties and rails for the proposed antique trolley that would haul tourists across the bottom land where the hotels and restaurants were being built.

"We've got the Atlanta papers covered," Pete was juggling three other projects along with my proposed canoe trip, "I've called Andy and WSB and they'll try to be here. Phil is going with you to write the magazine story. Dave knows the river and he's going to guide you down the first day. He can get you past Smith Island. Who's going with you in your canoe?"

"Barbara will go with me the first day," I said. "She still thinks we ought to wait for warmer weather."

"Be sure you wear your thermal underwear," Pete called as I was leaving. We had agreed that I would go April 1st — a couple of days before the scheduled race. Under the circumstances, I thought April Fools' Day would be appropriate. Pete figured we'd get some advance publicity for the race, which was to start that weekend.

I had never worried about turning over on my trips around the islands. In the first place, the water was calm, except for our trips in the sound, and I always had Joe with me and figured he could get me out of any situation that might arise. The only time I had turned over, we were in a rough sea. Now, I decided I'd better be sure I could get clear of the canoe under any circumstances if it flipped over. I was sure I could swim, but I was concerned my legs might get tangled with the canoe brace when I flipped over in the white water of the mountain river. And I wanted to be sure I could swim with my shoes and all my clothes on.

The YMCA had a canoe, so I arranged for several friends to help me get into the canoe in the Y swimming pool. I put on my thermal under-wear, clothes and shoes, paddled to the middle of the pool and rocked the canoe until it turned over.

To my delight, I found I slipped out of the canoe immediately when it flipped. And I seemed to be more buoyant with the extra clothing on.

The day Barbara and I drove to Helen for the start of the adventure was a beautiful mountain day with a bright sun shining. Dave and Ann run the canoe and back packing store at Helen and were expecting us.

Dave had been a builder, specializing in warehouses and commercial structures, and was one of the few who had been fortunate enough to get out of the business before the big collapse in real estate that occurred in 1974.

Both Ann and Dave love the mountains and what they are doing in their new life. Their small store was packed with the paraphernalia of outdoor mountain life and the yard was stacked with the rugged canoes built especially for white water mountain river running. I noticed Dave seemed a little distracted when I rolled in in my wheelchair.

After exchanging pleasantries, he said

"The river's pretty high. We've had a lot of rain this year."

I didn't say anything. Dave went out to take care of some chores. When he came back he said

"Well, if you want to try to go, I'd better drive down to the bridge and see what the water level guage shows."

I didn't say anything. Finally, Dave walked over, looked at me keenly and said

"Hell, you're going to go anyway, aren't you."

"Well," I said, "we did come up here to go down the river."

The newspaper publicity had resulted in a number of people pledging to the Shepherd Center an amount equal to their pledge times the number of miles I made it down the river. One company had pledged $15 a mile and with the smaller pledges the center would receive about three thousand dollars if I finished the hundred mile course.

Barbara and I start the 100 mile trip down the raging Chattahoochee River.
Photo: Floyd Jillson

Up until this time the river canoeing I had done had been under relatively mild conditions. As Barbara and I approached the river bank and looked at the water swirling and boiling beneath us, I knew we were going to travel fast if we traveled at all that day.

The canoe was up on the bank when I was helped in, then several men pushed it over the bank and into the swirling stream. I held a tree branch while Barbara carefully boarded behind me.

The moment Barbara gave the word and I turned loose of the branch we were flying down the river, dodging rocks and caroming under the bridge that leads into the business district of Helen.

"Stay left," Barbara shouted over the roar of the water, "between those rocks, pull right, pull right, that's it. Grab that branch."

We stopped the canoe after about two hundred yards to watch the canoe that had launched just ahead of us. They had tried the right side of the river and were already turned over. Phil, who was going to write the magazine story, was standing in the rushing waters. His canoe had filled when it capsized, becoming as heavy as concrete and had trapped his leg against a large rock. Fortunately, he extricated himself after a few minutes without breaking a bone.

With things sorted out, we took off again, shooting rapidly down a straight stretch of the river marked by crossing ripples that revealed the nature of rocks below. Nothing to slow us down, we had soon left civilization far behind.

Barbara and I would be the last ones to turn over.

The river was high and our progress was swift in the cool spring mountain air. The beauty of the budding trees, the boulders, eddies, pools that we wound around, between and over, the overhanging wilderness made a delightful and exciting trip.

At Smith Island, Dave, who was by himself leading us through the rocks and boulders, had us park on the side of the river.

"I'm going to cut across to the other side," Dave shouted.

The river divided at Smith Island and we had gone to the left where a portion of the river was dammed by rocks and the flow concentrated in a run between two boulders. With the river as high as it was, this made a huge torrent of roaring authority and power. Dave was paddling furiously, trying to get over to catch the main current that descended over a five foot drop into a large deep pool. Suddenly, the weight of the fast moving stream swung his canoe completely around. He thrust his paddle into the water to try to save himself but too late. The canoe capsized and

Dave and canoe were swept between the rocks down to a pool below where Dave was finally able to grab the canoe and fight his way to the river bank.

After portaging me and the canoe around the place that had been Dave's undoing, we set out again, gaining speed as the water volume increased with our descent down through the mountains.

Now, Barbara and I were the only two still dry. We were on a long run with no apparent obstacle in sight when we struck.

It was a submerged rock and it turned us over neatly and cleanly. I had no problem reaching the river bank but had to rescue my trousers and pull them back on. Fortunately, the long underwear preserved my modesty if not my dignity.

After being helped back in to the canoe, I was pretty cold. The sun could not reach us in the heavily wooded river bed and the cold mountain water had completely soaked our clothes. We had covered nineteen miles and the decision was made to get out at the next bridge.

When we got back to Helen, a party had been arranged in our honor. The liquor was flowing pretty well and it was nice to be warm and dry after our adventure.

"Well," Dave said, "it wouldn't have done any good to go look at that river gauge. The water had gotten so high and so rough the gauge was washed away."

One of those present at the party was a former commissioner of the county in which Helen is located.

"I've lived here all my life," Lanier told me, "and I've paddled this river since I was a kid. I tell you, I wouldn't have gotten in that river today."

Next day, Barbara had to go back to work and everybody agreed the river was too dangerous to re-enter in the mountains.

"We'll put you in just above Lake Lanier," Dave said, "then you can overlap to make up the mileage."

Sam, who works with me in the real estate business and two of his friends, Jim and Dozier agreed to go with me on the next lap. We made about fourteen miles from a point down in the lake to the Buford Dam.

It was flat water paddling — no current to speed us along — and it was tough going. The wind, as we paddled toward the distant dam, was directly in our faces and was whipping up waves that were about a foot high. We faced the sun and as it began to descend, that became a problem, blinding us with its glare.

At times, we were in the middle of the big lake, the waves slapping at the canoe and the wind increasing our work. By the time we reached the dam, dark was descending.

The following Monday, I had been called to testify at a trial concerning the crash of a Lear jet at DeKalb-Peachtree that had occurred right after I left office. While going into the courthouse, I met a friend who had been one of our most productive staff members and he agreed to go with me on the next leg of my river journey.

This time, we backtracked to the river just above the lake. My companion, who is one of the strongest Christians I know and one of the most interesting conversationalists, gave me the most delightful day of the adventure.

As we paddled, mile after mile through the big and very beautiful lake, we talked about our government and our faith. The wind was calm and the paddling was easy. The sun was going down and we had transversed almost the entire length of the lake, making up the river mileage I had missed. It was a beautiful day and I felt enriched by the opportunity for the undistrubed visit.

I didn't know it, but the next leg of the journey would be the most exciting and the most dangerous. For the first time, I would come to know the awesome power of the river.

Two of the officials of our bank had agreed to go with me. One, a big man of great physical power and a former college football player would go with me. The other would be in a rented canoe with his girl friend. I didn't know it, but the Lord was looking after me when he selected my canoe partner.

The lake, which supplies water and power to the Atlanta metropolitan area, extends for twenty miles into the North Georgia foothills, fanning out between the mountains along hundreds of miles of shoreline. The rain that year had been unusually heavy and the whole lake was about eight feet above normal.

The condition of the river below the Buford Dam depends on the level of discharge of water through the dam and that in turn is regulated by the Army Corps of Engineers. When water in the lake is low, the discharge rate is reduced and rocks that line the river bed are more exposed. The water held by the dam is released only to meet water requirements for the communities below the dam, creating power as a by product. At the foot of the dam, where the canoeists put in, is a sign warning of the discharge policy. A siren sounds when the sluice gates are about to be opened, giving the canoeist a few minutes to get in a safe situation before the flood starts.

In our ignorance, we blithely entered the river just below the dam. We didn't bother to read the warning sign.

The stream was broad, but seemed harmless enough. My companions had brought beer and sandwiches and we set off in a holiday mood, joking and calling to each other as we paddled along.

I noticed we were moving at a pretty good clip — it felt good and relaxing after the hours of flat water work — and there were no exposed rocks at all to impede our progress.

What we didn't know or appreciate was the fact that the water was being discharged continuously at a high volume sending the tons of weight with the careening power of molten steel. An irresistable force that swept all before it. I did notice as the water hit my hands it was extremely cold, having come from the bottom of the deep lake of mountain origin.

We were sweeping along, relaxing in the bright and warm sunshine and had even opened a can of beer that tasted good in the fresh air.

Suddenly, as we rounded a bend in the river, there before our startled eyes was a huge sand dredge, planted in the middle of the broad stream. We quickly diverted to go around it and thought we were clear when I looked down and saw a steel cable, stretched taunt and running from the dredge to the distant shore.

There was nothing we could do to avoid it. The river was moving us too rapidly and with too much force to slow down. The cable hit our boat half way between the water and the gunnel and flipped us.

Immediately, I was in the freezing water and was just able to grab the canoe before it slipped away. My companion, who was dressed in shorts and a tank top, grabbed the front of the canoe and began kicking with powerful strokes.

We were being rushed down a stream with vertical banks about six feet above the water line. The water was ice cold — much colder than the water had been in the St. Simons sound. I knew we had better get out of it quick.

Had my partner been any less powerful we might never have reached the bank. As it was, he was able to find a narrow ledge that ran along a short distance below the bank. He scrambled up on the ledge and with superhuman strength pulled the water filled canoe with me hanging on, to the water's edge.

I held on to a tree branch while he pulled the canoe up on the ledge, emptied it and righted it.

By some miracle we recovered our paddles and were soon ready to re-enter the river.

Our companions, who were behind us, were not as fortunate. They had been swept into the dredge and had just grabbed the superstructure before the canoe was pulled from beneath them to disappear under the big steel structure. Fortunately, they were both strong enough to pull themselves up on the dredge and to walk along the pipe that fed it back to the shore. They joined us on the river bank.

We had passed a couple in a rubber raft, traveling at a more leisurely pace because of the nature of their craft. The dredge was no problem to the rubber raft and now they spotted us on the bank and paddled over. They invited the canoeless couple to join them for the rest the down river journey. Apparently they had plenty of beer, so we left the four of them to follow us as we paddled back into the river.

This time, we treated the river with more respect. The volume, weight, and speed of its body seemed to increase as we paddled along and we were careful to stay clear of branches reaching out from the shore that might turn us over again.

A mile or more downriver, we saw an eerie sight.

Under the trees ahead of us, we saw just the tip of the other canoe protruding from the water. We paddled carefully toward it and grasping the branches of the tree that held it, we were able to stop without turning over. The canoe had been forced under by the weight of the river.

When the rubber raft caught up with us, the two men were able to force the canoe loose, right it and empty it. We had already recovered the paddles, and life jackets, and the cooler that held our beer. Soon we were reconstituted as a canoe party, waving to the rubber raft couple who were now able to regain their privacy.

We were thoroughly respectful of the river's power now, and we held to the center of the stream moving at an increasing rate of speed as we moved along.

The sun was descending below the dense, tall trees that lined the river bank. We had warmed up and dried out by now and were expecting to reach Atlanta before dark because of our fast rate of travel down the smooth wide river. All the boulders and stones were covered.

We were near the end of a long straight run when we looked back for our companions in the other canoe.

They weren't there.

We slowed and waited but still they didn't appear around the bend far back up the straight stretch of river.

"Something's happened," Bobby said.

"Yeah," I agreed, "we'd better stop and wait."

We headed toward the bank, carefully approaching the overhanging branches that were sweeping past in spite of our efforts to slow down. Finally, we both grabbed branches and swung the canoe toward an area sheltered from the full sweep of the river. We got the canoe lodged between two trees with the end pulled up on a narrow spit of sand still above the water's level.

"If the river doesn't rise anymore, I think you'll be safe here," Bobby said, "I'm going for help."

In the distance across a flat bottom land, we could see a cluster of long, low white buildings. Bobby set off at a run toward them.

He had been gone about half an hour, when the two life preservers and other debris from the other canoe floated past. Sitting alone at the river bank I knew now that the other canoe had capsized and my anxiety increased.

The group that was running toward me across the flat farmland were in the blue uniforms of a paramedic outfit. They were carrying a stretcher and they were excited.

"Where is the man who's paralyzed?" one of them shouted as they ran up to my canoe.

It took some fast talk on my part to keep them from loading me on the stretcher and running me back across the field.

"Look," I said, "I'm not the problem. All I'm worried about is the river rising. If you will just pull the canoe out of the river and out into this field, I'll wait here while you look for our friends."

Finally, they agreed to leave me until a jeep or helicopter came to get me and they set out at a run again.

Frog men and a power boat had been ordered by the time I rejoined the rescue effort assembled on the bridge we had last passed before discovering that the other couple was missing.

The couple on the rubber raft had gotten out at this bridge and had reported seeing nothing of the missing pair.

They had overturned, and, as we learned later had clung to the branches that overturned them and pulled themselves out of the river. They had walked to the road where a farmer in a truck picked them up and returned them to the dam where they had left their car. Fortunately, the farmer had seen the crowd when he was crossing the bridge later, had asked what the excitement was, and had brought the search to an end by his report. The police got us back to Duluth where I called home for somebody to pick us up.

"Alana," I had called her after I got back home, "I've got to finish the trip, but I've run out of paddlers."

"Let me think about it and I'll call you back," she said.

Alana and I are equally devoted to the Shepherd Center and we wanted to get all that three thousand that was pledged.

The young man, Fraser, who joined me next day at the Duluth bridge, is powerfully built. By that time, I was really apprehensive about getting back in the river and was glad I had somebody with me not as intimately acquainted with its power as I was.

The next morning, Fraser started out with a powerful stroke that caused the canoe to rock to the side each time he made his thrust. I grabbed for the gunnel of the boat.

"Fraser," I told him, "to be honest with you, I've been fighting this thing for four days now and I'm pretty tired. I'm just going to hang on and let you do the work."

Really, by this time the river was carrying us at a good clip, the water just as high as it had been the day before, and I didn't think he'd have to work too hard.

We went all the way to the end. So far in fact, that we had to double back when we got to the final dam — we couldn't pull the canoe over the mud flats at the dam — not with me in it. We turned around and headed back toward the last take out point we had passed. Two fishermen in a bass boat were hailed, and they were kind enough to tow us back up the river to where we could get out and reach a telephone.

I was exhausted but my friends and I had earned the three thousand, and the Shepherd Center was a reality.

We were starting with a paraplegic and a former quad having helped bring this unique facility into existence.

Since we were going to try to teach paras and quads to help themselves, that was a pretty good way to start.

CHAPTER XLIV

The Panola County Airport is easy to spot, even in thickening haze. It is just west of the large Sardia Lake dam and just east of the expressway connecting Batesville to Memphis.

The runway lies roughly east and west and now I have slowed the one forty's engine to 1800 rpm, have pulled on a notch of flaps and I swing right for a right base to land on runway 25.

"Panola County Traffic," I am talking on the frequency used for uncontrolled airports — 122.8. "This is Cherokee 8755 November entering right base landing runway 25."

As I turn final, I cut the rpm's to 1500, pull on two more notches of flaps and stabilize at seventy knots, cranking in full elevator trim to hold the nose up when I flare.

As I cross the numbers at the end of the runway, I'm just about ten feet above the ground, I cut the engine and hold the nose down to maintain air speed.

As I flare, I am just a foot above the surface, and I continue to pull back on the yoke pulling the nose up and letting the slowing of the plane ease the mains down upon the asphalt.

Turning the stubby winged plane on the runway, I taxi back toward the big hangar that is Panola county airport's one building.

Several single engine light planes are parked on the ramp and over to the left is a stained crop duster, its huge engine tilted up in front of the single Plexiglas enclosed cockpit. The oversized wings with their dusting pipes projecting from the trailing edge make the plane look something like a German Stuka dive bomber.

Inside the hangar, the local sky diving class is in session, the students counting the cadence one thousand one, one thousand two that is part of their death defying ritual.

I am known here now, having landed here ten days ago on the trip out.

"Well," Tommy Lou, who runs the place is standing at the office door hands on hips, "so, you finally made it. We've been wondering when you'd show up. The Haltoms just called."

Tommy Lou went inside to call and let the Haltoms know I had arrived. Sitting looking into the September sunshine, I thought about Dick and Nina and all the years we had shared.

Dick was one of the first to take advantage of the government's offer to pay half the cost of a house. His folks had given him a fifteen acre pecan grove and he and Nina built their ranch style house in the front corner of the land.

The first time Frances and I visited them, they had fenced in the grove and were raising cattle. Together the pecans and cattle constituted cash crops. They were raising their three sons in the comfortable place.

The two oldest boys, Bob and John, have their own families, and the youngest son, Crick, named for Dick's brother who died in a plane crash in the Pacific in World War II, is on his own now.

Dick Haltom and I at Batesville International Airport.
Photo: Rita Jean Murphree — The Panolian, Batesville, Miss.

The drug store has been modernized. Still in the same inside corner location on the Batesville Square, the pot bellied stove is gone and flourescent lights have taken the place of the big sky light.

Dick has had a partner now for several years. His dad has been gone for a long time, having continued to work in the store until his death in his nineties. Dick's mother suffered a stroke a while back and is confined to a wheelchair.

Looking at Mrs. Haltom, I realize again that we give the medals to the wrong heroes. Paralyzed on one side, she still insists on standing every day and on getting into a dining room chair for her own luncheon. Her eyes are bright and her mind continues the inquisitiveness that mark her as a former school teacher.

"Clark," she asks, "how was your trip? Did you have to climb very high to get over the Rockies?"

I tell her about going to 12,500 feet, about the problems of circling down around the mountains to land in Tucson, about the rugged peaks just off the California coast.

Dick told me that his mother had remarked on learning I was back in Batesville, "I didn't hear him come over the house."

Mrs. Haltom is the kind of woman who built America, who gave our men their fighting spirit, who equipped boys and girls with the tools for success and who endowed our people with an understanding of the meaning of dignity and freedom.

I think back to Miss Fidelle Miller, seventh grade, Winnona Park Grammar School. In one year, I learned the grammar and the computation skills that would get me through the schools and business that lay ahead. And, I learned the joy and confidence that comes from achieving tough goals.

Mrs. Haltom taught for ten years before marrying Mr. Haltom and raising her three sons.

When Dick first returned from the service, he lived with his folks in the big frame house using a long wooden ramp up to the side porch. The ramp is still there, looking pretty worn and weather beaten.

With one leg he can control, Dick began walking to and from the drug store, some four blocks away down a street shaded by large old trees. Then, while on the way to work one day, Dick's brace broke and he fell, breaking his good leg.

After that, Dick decided it wasn't worth it to risk another broken leg, so he took to the wheelchair permanently.

Dick's wheelchair, with his large personality and his swift way of moving, really is invisible and such a part of the scene around Batesville that nobody sees it at all anymore. Dick projects himself into the other person's problem. While he is helping them, all their attention is focused on the personal problem and away from any problem eye sight might tell them Dick has.

Dick did take one large move forward due to the broken leg. When he went back to Kennedy VA center for several weeks he met, dated and married Nina.

"They all hated Dick," Nina told me. "He came in and told all the other patients he wasn't a paraplegic, that he was just there because of the broken leg."

"Yeah," Dick said with a grin, "I told them I was sure glad I didn't have to put up with the wheelchair, the catheters and all the other paraphernalia of the paraplegic. 'What is that smell,' I'd say, 'how can you guys stand those smelly urinal bags?' They'd get raving mad at me."

Dick paid his expenses while courting Nina by becoming a dealer for Everest and Jennings, who make the metal wheelchairs that were standard for all patients in the early days. The government furnished the chairs but, as Dick explained, the patients had a lot of money and nothing to spend it on. They would order specially designed and built chairs with all kinds of optional equipment through Dick. Dick would load a couple of extra chairs in his car when he went to call on Nina and pay for his trip.

"I was out with one of the patients one day," Dick recalled, "and a stranger asked the paraplegic what he did. 'Do!' the patient shouted, 'Do! Why, man, it's a full time job just being a paraplegic!'"

Dick and I agreed he had a point. When I have to go to the bath and change my Mayo acquired appliance every other day, I have to get up at 5 a.m. in order to be at the office by 9 a.m. And when I add all the things I have to do to get the plane ready to fly, it becomes ridiculous. On the day I was to leave California heading home, Frances, forgetting the three hour time differential, woke me up at 4 a.m. to wish me a happy birthday — it was September 24 and I was 57. I went ahead and got up. When I finally took off at noon, having been busy since getting out of bed, I realized it had taken me eight hours to do all the things preparing myself to leave.

The weather turned bad after I arrived at Batesville so my visit was extended to several days. Far into the night and all day, Dick and I would talk about our days at the hospital and the men and women we had known.

"This has really been good for Dick," Nina told me, "he's taken off from the drug store for the first time in months."

We talked about about another couple who met at Kennedy and who married shortly after he left the hospital.

Jack and Helen adopted a little girl who is married herself, now. They have moved to Florida and live in a condominium. Jack, who was extremely active as a deacon in his Baptist church, had his own watch repair business, working out of his home for many years.

Jack still comes to Kennedy for his check up once a year, so Dick and Nina see them on those visits.

"Well," I said, "Jack has ended up with more money than the rest of us put together. He hangs on to it."

The last time I heard from Jack, I told Dick, he had bought something called a chariyacht — it has a small motor and is steered by a tiller. Jack described rolling his chair up a ramp into the back of the vehicle, pulling the ramp up to make the rear wall of the device and putting down the street or down the beach waving at the people.

Jack, with his strong religious faith, seemed to find more contentment than the rest of us. Jack did his watch repairing in his home. After lunch every day, he'd lie down and rest. Helen, a nurse before their marriage watched after his schedule and Jack never experienced the complications from bed sores and kidney infections that I did.

As they say, ninety per cent of the problems happen to ten per cent of the paraplegics.

Active in his church, Jack was a regular attendant to local football and baseball games and went fishing regularly in one of the nearby lakes.

"I'll never forget the night you O.D.ed," I said to Dick.

"Yeah," Dick said, "my pain was so intense that I started taking dope from the first and kept it up. I was in half dozen campaigns in the islands before I was wounded. One of my buddies was a medic. I was watching him put up supplies one day and asked him what was in some large capsule shaped packages. 'Single shot of morphine,' he said, 'just open the package, stick the needle in your arm and squeeze.'"

"I asked him for a couple," Dick continued, "and from then on I carried them in my combat jacket pocket. I used the first one the day I was wounded."

From then on, Dick used drugs daily to relieve the raging pain.

"I don't know what happened that day at Lawson," Dick told me, "I just must have had one too many and something snapped. I just was suddenly slipping away and couldn't find any way to get back."

Our beds were next to each other. The night he took the overdose, Dick would try to reach up and grab his 'monkey swing' — the rope suspended swing we used to turn from side to side. He would reach for it and miss it.

Our favorite nurse sat with Dick all night. At the time, I was spending my days and nights lying on my stomach to keep off the healing pressure sores. I'd wake up all during the night, raise up and look over at Dick. With the night light on, I could see the nurse leaning over him and, occasionally the doctor would come in for a few minutes.

"When I finally came around," Dick said, "I knew I'd never take heavy drugs again, and I never have. I decided I would have to take the pain — I couldn't go through another night like that."

I had a similar experience, and I'll never forget that. I've wondered if hell, being forever cast out and away from a loving God, might be like that. It was the most horrible experience of my life.

I was to have one of my pressure sores operated on. Looking back, it was totally unnecessary for me to have an anesthetic. I had no feeling in my hip. The operation was a complete failure and had to be repaired in a later operation. The surgeon was one none of us respected and he didn't last long on our ward. Apparently, he was totally incompetent — or at least we were convinced he was. In our direct way, the ward called him 'the butcher.'

The day he operated on me, I was brought into the operating room, and the attendant rolled an anesthetic machine right up to me, covered my mouth and nose with a mask and told me to breathe deeply.

Apparently it was pure ether. I felt like I was smothering. But the worst came after I lost consciousness.

Suddenly, I seemed to have become a thin red line in an infinity of total blackness. That thin red line was all that was left of my existence. The line was snaking up and down and seemed to be saying,

"Faster, faster, faster, faster."

I thought "It can't go any faster."

"Yes, I can, Yes I can, Yes I can, Yes I can," over and over, over and over, repeated into infinity.

I don't know how long it took me to recover consciousness, but that seemed an infinity also. I remember my mother sitting next to me. I would reach out toward her but I could never touch her and I kept slipping, slipping, slipping away.

It seemed like several days before I was able to grasp things normally and feel like I was a solid human being in a solid natural world.

"Do you remember how mad you would get about the nurses waking you in the morning?" I grinned at Dick.

"Yeah," he said, "I could never understand. I'd lie awake all night in pain. Then, just before daybreak, I'd finally fall asleep. Just about the time I did, they'd stick that damn thermometer in my mouth."

They wouldn't bother me. Dick would say, "Why don't you wake him up?"

"Clark likes to have his coffee before we take his temperature," the nurse would say.

"Well," I said, "I'd had a few screaming fits about that thermometer and they finally decided to leave me alone."

Maybe it had something to do with the fact I had four sisters while Dick was raised in a family of boys and didn't know there are a few techniques that work with women — sometimes.

Dick enjoyed his reputation as a curmudgeon of sorts. He liked to talk with a tone of commanding authority and to expound at length in the tone of an expert. Part of his image was to avoid any appearance of enjoying the finer, more artistic side of life.

For example, Dick hated flowers. "They make me feel like I just died," Dick had told me.

One morning, I was sitting in my big wooden wheelchair in the long hospital corridor outside our ward when a local lady, a volunteer for the Red Cross Grey Ladies, came by pushing a hospital litter loaded with flowers.

"Hello," I said, "those certainly are beautiful flowers."

She agreed and explained that they had been brought to the hospital by various volunteers to brighten the day for the wounded soldiers.

"I have a special request today," I told her. She was immediately attentive.

"My best friend, who is paralyzed, has just had a terrible thing happen," I said, assuming a worried expression. "He just got a letter from his girl friend back home. They have been going together since before he went in the Army, and now she has decided to marry another man."

We both agreed that was terrible and she wanted to know if there was anything she could do.

"Well," I said, "there is one thing. This friend of mine really loves flowers. He was telling me just the other day about his garden at home and how he looks forward to being back home where he can sit and enjoy his own flowers. I think it would help him if you have a few extra pots you could leave by his bed."

It was obvious that I would have her whole hearted cooperation and I followed as she pushed the litter into our ward.

I had left Dick asleep and found him still soundly under. I warned her to be quiet and soon most of her litter full of vases and pots were stacked around Dick's bed.

When the nurses saw what was happening, and having heard Dick carry on about how much he hated flowers, they pitched in to do their part. They went down the ward and got all the flowers the other patients had and soon a triple tier of flora rose on three sides of Dick's bed.

Dick really did feel he was in a mausoleum when he woke up.

"Oh, for goodness sakes and dear me" Dick moaned before he broke into a grin.

The flower episode was climaxed a week or so later when one of the Grey Ladies who was a close personal friend from Decatur came by.

"Clark," she said, "I've been bringing flowers from ladies all over Decatur to the hospital. They love sending them, but I know it would mean a great deal if I put an article in the paper telling how much you enjoy the flowers."

Dick was asleep in the bed next to mine.

"Mrs. Lee," I said, "the flowers are beautiful and mean a great deal to me. But, after all, I am a local boy and they would expect me to say so. I think it would mean more if one of the boys from another part of the country commented on them."

She agreed but was not sure who to ask for a quotation.

"Well," I said, "Dick there is asleep, but I know how he feels about the flowers because he has told me many times. Rather than wake him up, I'll just tell you what he said and you can put it in the paper."

Dick got such a kick out of the article quoting him about how much he enjoyed the beautiful flowers, that he sent the article to his mother in Batesville.

"Dick," Mrs. Haltom wrote, "you always told me you hated flowers."

There were about four of the assortment of WAC's, ward boys, nurses, doctors for each patient on the paraplegic ward, and there was generally something to watch.

Like the silly nurse who was always giggling. Jarbo, our big red-headed ward boy spanked her on the bottom one day and sent her crawling under the bed to safety — still giggling.

Generally there was horseplay, Rankin and Munson jitterbugging in the aisle, Marcus philosophizing, Hot Foot whining, the G. U. man pushing his cart of sterile water, emerson basins and catheters from bed to bed.

The WAC's did a good job and came from every walk of life. Some were diamonds in the rough of collectible quality and brilliance.

One complained of getting poison ivy on her fanny after a date that apparently ended among the pine straw on the forest floor.

Dick was especially fond of Alma, the tall, willowy girl who had seen much of life. She was a nurse, and officer, but unpretentious.

The one who threw her diamond ring into the bushes to confound her boy friend.

"As soon as he left," Alma was grinning, "I was down on my all fours in the bushes finding that diamond."

The WAC who did her part by kissing and hugging the patients behind the curtains that enclosed us at certain stages of the daily routine. After only a few months she was shipped home pregnant.

With all the activity, there were still times when things were slow and needed livening up.

One of Dick's special peeves was the occupational therapy offered to the patients. Dick said that, with his pain, trying to weave a basket or make something out of Plexiglas made him nervous.

On this particular day, an unsuspecting Gray Lady volunteer came by with a basket of leather materials for making billfolds.

"I know why you want me to make a billfold," Dick shouted at the poor lady. "It's to keep me from going crazy — well, I don't need a billfold, I've got a lot of billfolds."

At that, Dick pulled out a billfold and threw it on the floor, then another, then a third as the startled and dismayed Grey Lady beat a hasty retreat.

Dick had his pain but with parents like his and with a down to earth attitude there was never any doubt of Dick making it.

Some of the patients couldn't face the idea of being helpless for life.

"We had several who killed themselves in their new Oldsmobiles," Nina told me, "They would get those powerful cars up over ninety and run head on into a stone wall."

I recalled driving south from Memphis the time I revisitied Kennedy VA hospital. It was Sunday afternoon and a long line of traffic, bumper to bumper, was coming toward me as people returned to the city for the end of the weekend.

Suddenly, far down the line, a 98 Olds whipped out into my lane and came roaring at me at high speed. The line he was passing opened — and I slowed down — just enough for him to avoid hitting me.

"I figured it was one of the paraplegics," I told Dick, "Do you remember Davis?"

"Yeah," Dick said, "he starved himself to death. He just turned his face to the wall."

"And that black quad," I told Dick, "That made all of us sick. You remember he had pressure sores even on his shoulder blades. He choked to death at lunch one day."

There was another quad who didn't make it. He had been shot down over Europe, parachuted down and was in a POW camp for six months. He came home in good health. While on his terminal leave, he dove into the old swimming hole — he and his girlfriend were out alone that night skinny dipping — and he broke his neck. He was very high level and had trouble breathing. He got pneumonia and died within a couple of weeks.

"Did you know," I told Dick, "one of my friends who is a pathologist and who worked at the VA told me over five hundred quads were warehoused in a New York VA hospital at one time."

"Curly Williams had a lot of courage," I said. "You know when they operated on his kidney they could not give him an anesthetic because of a heart condition. And he had feeling. After it was over he told me 'Clark, you don't know what you'll endure to stay alive.'"

"What about Marcas?" Dick laughed. "One day a couple of the patients were moaning about their pains and miseries. One of them said 'Oh, I might as well be dead, hell couldn't be any worse than this.' Marcas raised up on his one good arm and yelled, 'Oh yeah, just strike a match and hold your finger over the flame.'"

"Dick, I said, "did you ever think about killing yourself?"

"Lord, no," Dick said, "I was hurting too bad."

"I never have either, Dick," I replied, "it must have something to do with the way we were raised. On the other hand, I don't believe I worry as much as some other people about dying."

"Of course," I said, "you and I had something some of them didn't. We both knew we had a family waiting for us. That no matter what shape we were in there would be no question about their wanting us. Some of those boys didn't have anything at home."

Dick had taken off from work during my visit and we talked continuously during my three day stay.

Sometimes, I wonder if it doesn't make sense — even from our human standpoint — to praise the Lord for the bad as well as the good that happens to us.

The hard times bind us together in friendships that become deeper and more meaningful as the years pass by.

CHAPTER XLV

As the 140 rose into the cool September air from Panola County Airport, or Batesville International as Dick Haltom called it, I rocked the wings to say goodbye to the man who had shared so much with me at Lawson General Hospital. Dick and I never tire of reliving those days and recalling the men and women we knew at the hospital.

The haze was still bad and, while I could see clearly looking straight down, slant vision was very limited. I took off my dark glasses and put on clear.

DeKalb-Peachtree was reported with a four hundred foot ceiling with fog, but the forecast was for VFR weather by the time I would get there.

Going over the things Dick and I had talked of, my mind dwelt again on those early days after my injury, and what these thirty seven years as a paraplegic have been.

Looking back, I realize my main vocation has been to be a paraplegic. Everything else had to be fitted around that.

As the paraplegic told Dick, "Do? Man, just being a paraplegic is a full time job."

Our problem in the early days was that we had no 'role' model, as the counselors say. We didn't think we had a future; and, looking around, we didn't see any old paraplegics or quads, much less any who had been able to accomplish or even to work.

Recently, I read a book about the experiments conducted by the Wright brothers that led to the first successful powered flight. They had the same problem that faced the early paraplegics. Nobody had ever flown and the idea of manned flight was considered impossible by all but a few dreamers. Not only did they not have a machine that would fly, they didn't really know the problems of three dimensional control, and they themselves did not comprehend the skills that would be required of the pilot.

Each step was a groping in the dark. They did not realize what a completely different world they were entering, how endless the learning process would be, and how costly in terms of human life and the expenditure of wealth as each step was taken.

I vividly remember two quadraplegics I visited with in those first days at Lawson General in 1943. Both were lieutenants from good family backgrounds, with the education and resources to face the future.

I can remember one had a unique sense of humor and an apparent light-hearted outlook on the future. He had spasms in his legs. He would arrange his feet so his legs would jump up and down in perfect time on the foot rests of his wheelchair. As he sat grinning at his audience.

I can remember a blind soldier who seemed always to be exuberant, talking loudly and laughing and joking.

And I knew they were wearing masks. They could see no future for themselves.

One of the passages in the Bible that hit me and that drew me to Christ was the part that talks of Him as the stone that was rejected and that became the head of the corner.

I felt that I had been rejected, and that the others I saw in the hospital with the so-called catastrophic injuries were rejected as well. But at the same time, I believed there would come a time when we could be the head of the corner.

Hitler planned an empire that would last a thousand years. In building his master race he set out to destroy the weak, the disabled, the dependent. The Third Reich lasted a little over ten years and Hitler died cursing the German people as weak and unworthy because they lost the war. To the last, he showed his great will power by simultaneously biting his cyanide pill and blowing his brains out with his German Luger.

It is a small thing, but one that made a deep impression on me. The airlines traditionally have suffered periodic and severe reverses. When I took my first trips by air, after the war, Delta Airlines in Atlanta always carried me on and off the plane; it was organized to do it, and did so as a matter of course and with courtesy. I thought all the airlines, did the same, until I took several trips that involved other airlines and found that Delta was the exception. Others required me to have an ambulance meet the plane and wanted me to have an attendant travel with me.

With a recent economic downturn, the airlines began to reduce payrolls by letting people go and by cutting salaries. The exception was Delta. I asked a friend who is a pilot for them if he had taken a pay cut.

"Oh, no," he said, "in fact, we just got a nice raise."

Not that those in wheelchairs were that important, but the character revealed by the action of Delta was. I believe God looks after the helpless, and those who help the helpless.

The thing that was so overwhelming in the early treatment of spinal cord injured was the magnitude of the problem. Paras and quads seemed as helpless as infants in the beginning. We required three or four attendants per patient, and months of hospitalization. We looked forward to a lifetime of dependence and uselessness. That was the picture, and only the vast resources of the triumphant American government seemed adequate to even try to attack the problem. A noble effort was begun for the wounded soldiers, but spending comparable resources for civilian injuries seemed beyond imagination. By prolonging life through the use of the so called wonder drugs, a problem that defied solution seemed the result.

Perhaps nature had known best in providing early death as the escape for the quad and the paraplegic.

Like the Wright brothers, we seemed to face the impossible without the means or method for success. But, like the Wright brothers, with the application of resources marshalled to fight the war, the effort was begun.

There were dedicated people willing to try the impossible.

And there were the patients themselves.

Scott, who wore blisters on his feet 'walking' in the one piece shoulder to foot brace. The quad who became a successful lawyer, insurance executive, real estate broker. The paraplegic mother who raised four children. And, finally, it was realized. The spinal cord injured are a new breed of people. With limited mobility, their imaginations can be fired to find the answers for themselves. Like the Wright brothers, they, themselves, could best learn how to operate in the new modum.

One of the things that makes flying so fascinating and so soul satisfying is the fact that, after all these years, after all these thousands who have learned to fly, each individual who starts out to master the skill is facing exactly the same challenge the Wright brothers faced — as far as the skill itself is concerned — and the dangers are identical and just as potentially deadly.

His equipment may be superior, he may have the benefit of the years of learning by others, he may have expert instruction, but, in the final analysis, it is up to the new student to master the same challenge the Wright brothers faced. His instructor and his equipment can take him to a point. From there, he is on his own.

The same is true of the spinal cord injured. The challenge is just as harsh, the labor as intense, the risks as grave as those that faced us in the beginning days. After the acute stage has passed and the spine is stabilized, after the drugs have been prescribed, after the admonitions given, the individual is on his own.

As Clint told me, "All I can do is teach you enough to keep you from killing yourself. You have to teach yourself how to fly."

Once the patient is discharged the hospital staff has to stand aside and see what the human mind and spirit can accomplish.

Where we spent a year and a half in the hospital, to emerge in worse shape than the day we entered, at Shepherd the average stay is ninety days.

And, when the patient leaves Shepherd, he starts his own struggle equipped with the skills that others who preceded him so laboriously learned.

Those skills can set his mind free to go the next step.

The rest is up to him.

And what does the man or woman who has traveled this lonely road have to offer?

For one thing, he is not easily frightened. When the worst has happened the daily trials of life seem less awesome.

He knows how to work through other people and how to understand their dreams and their frustrations.

He can face facts. One world leader said, "Facts are persistent things." The spinal cord injured faces the same persistent facts every day of his life; he learns to live with them and he ultimately reduces the impossible to manageable proportions.

He looks beyond tomorrow. The struggle is long, and the way is weary, so the ultimate goal must be kept in view.

He knows that basic principles must be followed, fundamental laws must be obeyed, for the long pull.

He respects other people, but not without recognizing their weaknesses. To the para or quad, all men are tall — seen from a sitting position — so height and physical size and strength are no factor in sizing up a man.

And a part of him is forever young.

My life stopped at age twenty, and I experienced those things my friends today fear about old age. I missed so much of the pleasures of youth that I have no desire to become old. I still have the thrill of looking forward to accomplishing things I thought for so long I would never be able to do.

And age is not the obstacle I once thought. I finally realized, I have the same day as my granddaughter Rachael — and as Teresa, the beautiful young woman who runs things in our office. The question is how we each use that day.

The severely disabled live a corporate life. We look at our peers and learn from them. We consider ouselves part of a moving body. We help each other. We rejoice at the victory of any one.

I think the most touching thing I've heard at Shepherd and the thing that illuminated the purpose of my life since 1944 was said by a young patient.

"What do you do, Mr. Harrison?" he asked me, "I know you are a member of the board here at Shepherd and that's important. But do you have a job?"

I knew exactly what he has saying. I had said the same thing to myself in the early years following my injury. What I really wanted to know was "What am I going to do. Will I ever be able to earn a living and to support a family?"

We know now it can be done and we know the future will be even brighter.

The young paraplegic, having himself earned his pilot's license, who sits at the head of the operating table at one of the nations's leading hospitals administering anesthesia.

The quad who has earned a national reputation as an artist.

The quads and paras now earning substantial livings as computer programmers.

No patient is turned away from Shepherd because of the severity of his injury. The hospital doesn't know how to turn away a patient for that reason — not with the chairman we have. Not after he spent weeks breathing through a hole in his neck.

No matter how high the level of injury, there is a place at the Shepherd Spinal Center. Requiring constant aid to breathe, one quad alumnus drives his own ten thousand dollar wheelchair, carrying his respirator as part of his mobile life style.

The secret that Shepherd discovered from Craig and that Craig learned from their patients is to put the load on the patient. Then the extra help can be dismissed and life can be lived without the inordinate expense or sacrifice by those interested in the individual.

Shepherd has refinded the process to a science. Shepherd is to the new para or quad what Paris Island is to the Marine recruit.

The para or quad is a new creature. He doesn't have the abilities he did have. But he does have abilities, and the task is to push him to develop those abilities to the maximum. And, again, the examples are there today for him to follow. In the future there will be more examples, more avenues opened, and no thought of committing suicide to avoid becoming a burden.

The results can be astounding.

One of the pioneers, and a member of the board at Shepherd, is a quad named Dave Webb. Well over six feet tall, Dave broke his neck diving through an inner tube at age fourteen. After his accident, he finished high school, college and law school.

Dave is a high level quad with very limited use of his hands. When it was considered impossible, Dave and his family decided that he would design some kind of vehicle he could drive.

"We first talked to some engineers at Lockheed Marietta," Dave's father said. "After showing great interest and referring us to various departments, nothing happened. We finally decided we'd have to do it ourselves."

Not only was the job impossible, but who would want to take the responsiblity of sending a man paralyzed from the neck down into freeway and downtown traffic?

"You mean you built it yourselves?" I asked.

"We subcontracted some parts of it," he replied, "but we designed it and we put it together."

Dave still drives the huge machine, over ten years later. Dave was too tall to fit into a standard van, so he bought an enclosed truck, mounted a lift on the back and attached a folding, mechanically operated ramp to the lift. Dave, in his electric wheelchair controls everything himself, mounting the lift, entering the truck and securing his chair behind the wheel. The controls are adapted to his limited use of hands and arms.

After vans began to be adapted for use by quads, Dave stuck to his big truck. Seeing it perform brings to mind Rube Goldberg — which is not surprising. Dave is a lawyer and his father an investment banker.

The truck has one big advantage. Dave can haul as many of his parlyzed friends as he wants. And he has hauled and inspired a large number.

Today, Dave is general counsel for one of the largest financial institutions in the southeast and his influence touches an ever growing circle of people and events.

Paras and quads are beginning to take a new pride in their accomplishments.

That pride is justified.

Don't think when you see a man or woman in a wheelchair that you are looking at an invalid. You may be looking at a superb athlete.

In addition to wheelchair basketball, swimming, canoeing, flying and the rest, there is the accomplishment of simple chores that make it possible to move about and to take part.

Moving from bed to chair, from chair to tub and back, into and out of an automobile — are balancing acts that are perfected by practice. Like football, being a good para or quad is a game of inches. We are constantly reaching to just beyond our finger tips, grasping with those fingertips, teetering on the edge, swinging and jumping to safety.

When the Wright brothers took their first glider to Kitty Hawk, hoping to add one more bit of knowledge to the accumulating attempts of man to fly, they had everything against them.

For centuries, man had dreamed of flight. The light weight materials finally used by the Wright brothers for their glider were available, but repeated efforts had convinced the best minds that such a thing was impossible.

Already, the deaths of early seekers for the secret of flight testified to that impossibility. Their first problem, that they did not know how to construct a machine that would conform to the unknown laws of flight was obvious.

Not so obvious was the fact that, even had they had the machine, they did not have the skill, the reflexes, the knowledge that would make flight possible.

By fortuitous accident, they designed their early gliders with an elevator extended out in front of the wing — not the best arrangement but one that kept them from killing themselves when the inevitable stalls occurred.

Inspiration, hard work, their scientific approach, led to final victory over a challenge that had confounded the ages.

In the same way, the future of the spinal cord injured seemed non-existent and the possiblity of a productive life apparently did not exist in the early days.

Penicillin saved our lives and the resources made available for war were so vast as to make a start toward solving the impossible riddle. When the early efforts finally began to open an avenue that looked promising, the spinal cord injured themselves, with nothing but time to think, to dream and to plan, entered the narrow opening breach and began to astound with their achievements.

Now that the examples are there, the future is unlimited. As we progress through this new age of automation and computers, the role of mind and will continues to expand and the key ingredient of any accomplishment becomes the ability to dream and to visualize.

I have lived many more years now than I would ever have believed possible in those early days after I was wounded — and I still am puzzled by the mystery and meaning of life.

One of the large problems the severely disabled faces is how to dignify the situation he finds himself in. For his part, he knows how difficult things are, how arduous, how heroic, really. And yet what he gets is not admiration, as a super athlete expending no more work or effort would. What he gets is pity and condescension. Unless he can rise above the contradiction of struggle and accomplishment being met by an attitude of those around him of pity and condescension, he will remain angry and confused.

And yet, it is possible to transcend that struggle.

The Catholic learns that our suffering and deprivation is our gift to Christ in return for all that he gave us.

For those who know Christ, that gives meaning enough.

A strange idea came to me from a source I cannot recall. That we, before coming to the world, are given a choice of the life we will live.

Obviously, the strongest in mind and spirit would be the only ones capable of taking on the bad assignments. And the life led in a deprived body assumes new dignity.

For myself, I only know that the faith in God I was taught as a child was my mainstay and my salvation when I faced the fear and danger of combat, the months of uselessness, the disappointments and the rejection.

I feel very close to Christ and to God. I pray constantly. I have been so dependent on Them and on the Holy Spirit that I cannot imagine my continued existence without that companionship.

Being given direct help is not a rare occurrance for me, it is a daily and almost hourly experience.

On several occasions, I have come close to death, either through physical accident or illness. Each time, I was saved, and I was helped, but more importantly, God's love and comfort surrounded me.

Like all humans, I am constantly in danger — my very life a fragile gift. I suppose I may differ from some in that I know the reality of my dependence.

It really makes little physical difference whether I am in my automobile, or high in the air in my plane, or going down a raging river in an instable canoe. If something should happen, and I didn't have the help God sends constantly, I would be just as helpless a block from my home in Decatur as I would be in some wilderness or some storm filled sky.

God's love is very real to me.

My sister, Brenda, was interviewed by the Gainesville newspaper while I was on one of my flights.

Brenda told the reporter she wasn't frightened when her brother decided to make the flight because, "he is a careful pilot".

Her brother is willing to take more chances than the average person, the article quoted her, because he "has no fear of death." Why should he fear death, she said, when he knows he will go to heaven when he dies. In the next life, she said, "Jesus will say, 'Now Clark, you can stand up and walk.'"

This book has really been as much or more about Frances than about me. And what she did so long ago is still a bright and shining thing for me and in my life.

I see her clearly now, her arms full of roses, the first time she visited me in the hospital.

I can never forget that she loved me and voluntarily assumed the burden that had been thrust upon me. It was her choice to marry a young boy, knowing he would never be whole, and to do it joyously.

Like Grandpa, I will never understand it.

But I can continue to enjoy and be supported by the nobility of her action.

Frances asked me to be honest with the people. I will try — and will fail, of course.

For one thing, she wants people to know that people in wheelchairs are still people. They can be just as mean, just as narrow and just as sinful.

And they usually are better off than a lot of people who get no sympathy at all.

Frances tried to tell her friends who expounded on my nobility. Knowing nothing about me, the fact that I came encased in a wheelchair imparted rare courage, fortitude and spirituality.

"I feel ashamed to complain when I see Clark," one would expound, "what are my little aches and pains compared to what he has suffered!"

"Listen," Frances tried to tell her, "I've got more pain in my little finger than he's got in his whole body."

Instead of laughing with her, her listeners were horrified, of course.

Some people have no sense of humor.

They looked mean at Frances and said no more.

"It's like being married to a national monument," she tried to explain, "really, he's no better than the rest of us."

No one would listen, of course.

Actually, I wasn't any worse than anybody else — until I got to be King. Then, I wasn't really any worse than most Kings.

But that is pretty bad.

Now that I am a has been, I am trying to go straight.

I hope all you readers will pray for me.

And I've still got my one forty — and money enough to buy gas so I can leap over tall buildings with a single bound.

As I fly over the low ridges of northern Alabama, my dream is of those first days. Of the shock of bone and nerve being smashed, of the helplessness of the army cot in the field hospital, of the thirteen years of infection and illness, of politics and of business. And of that runway that I am headed for now — where the hospital ship dropped its wing and finally settled, bringing me back to a home I didn't really want to see in my helpless condition.

I was headed back toward that runway now — but with a difference.

The plane was under my command now, the wings an extension of my own body, the engine a roaring enlargement of my own power, the chart a roadmap I read along with instruments to know where I am, what my altitude and airspeed are, and precisely when I will see our home airport again.

The air is an ocean — and with this new knowledge and skill, I can sail over every obstacle to whatever place I may desire.

No, I can't walk. But I can fly. And, as an old infantryman, I can tell you — flying beats the hell out of walking.

Entering the last leg of my trip, an Air Force fighter, on my level, crosses in front of me and in another moment I see McCullum Airport to my left, the massive Dobbins Airport, home of the Air Force and Navy fighters, to my right.

Kennesaw Mountain, where one of the last of the great battles on Sherman's road to Atlanta was fought, is down below me now.

Now, I am above the perimeter expressway that rings our city and that I helped plan. Perimeter Mall, with its hotels, office towers and shopping center built during our surging real estate boom is below me now, and I call DeKalb-Peachtree, the old Naval Air Station that had welcomed me home in 1945. The airport I had helped rename.

"Eight seven five five November, you can plan to enter a right base, land on runway two zero right. Report on base."

I am at twenty-five hundred feet. I ease down to slow cruise, twenty-one hundred revolutions per minute of the roaring engine as I search for and spot the parallel runways that are my destination.

"Peachtree Tower," I call the tower. "This is five five November, entering right base, landing runway two zero right."

"Roger, five five November," the tower reponds, "wind is two six zero at ten — gusts to seventeen — cleared to land."

Entering the base leg of the traffic pattern, I ease the engine down to eighteen hundred rpm and pull one notch of flaps. Then to fifteen hundred as I come opposite the big granary building. Another notch of flaps as I bank right and enter final, pulling the final notch of flaps and descending to five hundred feet as the air speed drops to seventy knots and I line up with the runway.

Rachael sees me off on one of my flights.

Photo: Ric Feld

Crab to the right, turning the nose of the plane into the crosswind. I am just above the asphalt as I pass over the big twenty painted in white on the end of the runway. Just before I touch down, I swing the nose back to the left by depressing the rudder bar and lower the right wing into the wind to counteract the right cross wind.

After all these years, it finally dawns on me.

That's why the hospital ship's wing had dipped just as we landed thirty seven years ago. He, too, was fighting a crosswind.

With the wing down, and the rudder holding the nose down the runway centerline, the right main touches, then the left, then the nose wheel.

I reach for the brake with my left hand while steering with my right hand on the rudder bar and turn right off the runway.

"Five five November," the tower calls, "give way to the Lear jet crossing your front. Call ground control on 121.7. Good day."

I stop the plane momentarily, let up the flaps, open the door and cut all electrical except for the rotating beacon and my radio to ground.

"Peachtree ground," I call, "this is Cherokee eight seven five five November, clear of the active, taxing to Epps."

"Five five November. Taxi to the ramp."

It has been a long flight.

But I am home.